DISCRETE
MATHEMATICAL
STRUCTURES WITH
APPLICATIONS
TO COMPUTER
SCIENCE

McGRAW-HILL COMPUTER SCIENCE SERIES

RICHARD W. HAMMING, Bell Telephone Laboratories

EDWARD A. FEIGENBAUM, Stanford University

**McGRAW-HILL
BOOK COMPANY**

New York
St. Louis
San Francisco
Auckland
Düsseldorf
Johannesburg
Kuala Lumpur
London
Mexico
Montreal
New Delhi
Panama
Paris
São Paulo
Singapore
Sydney
Tokyo
Toronto

**J. P. TREMBLAY
R. MANOHAR**

*Departments of Computational Science
and Mathematics
University of Saskatchewan, Saskatoon*

Discrete Mathematical Structures with Applications to Computer Science

This book was set in Modern 8A by Mono of Maryland.
The editors were Kenneth J. Bowman and Michael Gardner;
the production supervisor was Dennis J. Conroy.
The drawings were done by Eric G. Hieber Associates Inc.
Kingsport Press, Inc., was printer and binder.

Library of Congress Cataloging in Publication Data

Tremblay, Jean-Paul, date
    Discrete mathematical structures with applications to computer science.

    (McGraw-Hill computer science series)
    Includes bibliographies.
    1. Mathematics—1961–   2. Electronic data processing. 3. Machine theory. I.
Manohar, R., date joint author. II. Title.
QA39.2.T72   510'.2'40901   74-23954
ISBN 0-07-065142-6

**DISCRETE
MATHEMATICAL
STRUCTURES WITH
APPLICATIONS
TO COMPUTER
SCIENCE**

    7 8 9 10 KPKP   8321

CONTENTS

Several advanced books in computer science begin with a chapter consisting of a selection of mathematical topics that the reader is assumed to know. The exposition of such topics is usually brief, and the principal results that are summarized become prerequisites for the remainder of the text. It is not possible to learn these topics from such a brief treatment. Nor is it possible for undergraduate students in computer science to study all the topics they are required to know by attending courses dealing with each individual topic as given by mathematics departments. In general, the trend is to select several topics in mathematics that are essential to the study of many computer science areas and to expose the students to the mathematical prerequisites in some other way. A similar development has occurred in most engineering curricula. In the same spirit, this book discusses certain selected topics in mathematics which can be referred to as "discrete mathematics." No prerequisites except the mathematical maturity of a high school student are assumed. Although many students taking a course in discrete mathematics may have had a freshman course in calculus, such a course is by no means a prerequisite to the study of this book. However, any additional mathematical courses taken by students will aid in their development of mathematical maturity.

It is not our intention to cover all topics in discrete mathematics. The omission of counting techniques, permutations, and probability will be felt by some readers. We have assumed that many high school students will have had some exposure to these topics.

The selection of the topics was governed by our desire to introduce most of the basic terminology used in as many advanced courses in computer science as possible. In order to motivate the students properly, we feel that it is important to consider certain applications as the terminology is introduced. There are several advantages in using this approach. Students begin to see the relevance of abstract ideas and are therefore better motivated. Moreover, they gain confidence in applying these ideas to solve practical problems.

We wish to emphasize that concepts and terminology should be introduced well before they are used. Otherwise, students must invariably struggle both with the basic tools and with the subject matter to which the tools are applied. Most of the material in this book is properly a prerequisite to so many computer science courses that it should be taught no later than at the sophomore level. The book has been written with this objective in mind.

The mathematical topics to be discussed are logic, set theory, algebraic structures, Boolean algebra, graph theory, and basic computability theory. Although well-known and excellent books exist in these areas, we introduce these topics still keeping in mind that the reader will eventually use them in certain practical applications particularly related to computer science. We have strived to introduce the theoretical material in a reasonably mathematically precise manner whenever possible, while avoiding long philosophical discussions, questions of paradoxes, and any axiomatic approach to certain theories. The topics selected will also support the more advanced courses in computer science programs such as in the areas of automata, computability, artificial intelligence, formal languages and syntactical analysis, information organization and retrieval, switching theory, computer representation of discrete structures, and programming languages. It is hoped that a grasp of the theoretical material in this book will permit a student to understand most of the mathematical preliminaries which are briefly discussed at the beginning of many articles and books in the areas of computer science just mentioned.

Because the relation between the mathematics and how or where it could be applied may not be clear to the reader, the computer representation of certain mathematical structures is discussed. The need for discrete structures in computer science is motivated by the selection of certain applications from various areas in the field. Algorithms are developed for most applications, and computer programs are given for some of them. The computer representation and manipulation of discrete structures such as strings, trees, groups, and plexes are not discussed in great detail, but only to the extent which permits the formulation of a solution to a particular application.

Chapter 1 discusses mathematical logic. An elementary introduction to certain topics in logic is given to students in education, commerce, economics, and social sciences in courses usually entitled "Finite Mathematics." However, such discussions usually end with the construction of truth tables, and in certain instances a brief introduction to the inference theory of the statement calculus is included. In order for students to be able to read technical articles and books in computer science, it is necessary for them to know something about predicate calculus. Therefore, we have gone further in our discussion of logic than is usually done in books on finite mathematics. Yet we have avoided the philosophical discussions and intricate details that are found in the books on mathematical logic meant for mathematicians and philosophers. The chapter contains a brief introduction to the application of logic to two-state devices.

Chapter 2 deals with set theory. Some mathematical rigor is maintained in the discussions and proofs are sometimes given, but we do not raise the question of paradoxes and the axiomatic approach to set theory. Sets, relations, orderings, and recursive functions are discussed. The computer representation and manipulation of certain structures are introduced in this chapter. An example of the interrelationship of set theory and logic is given. The topic of recursion (and its implementation) is dealt with in some detail since many programming languages permit its use. Furthermore, the concept of recursion is important in its own right because computer scientists will encounter, throughout their careers, problems where recursion is unavoidable. The chapter concludes with an algorithm for proving theorems in the propositional calculus.

Chapter 3 discusses algebraic structures. Most books in modern algebra devote almost all their attention to group theory while little is said about semigroups and monoids. The latter are also emphasized in this chapter since it is semigroup and monoid theory which is very important in certain areas of computer science such as formal language theory, syntactic analysis, and automata. This chapter contains a number of applications dealing with topics such as the compilation of Polish expressions, languages and grammars, the theory of fast-adders, and error detecting and correcting codes.

Chapter 4 is concerned with Boolean algebra and its application to switching theory and sequential machines. An introduction to the minimization of Boolean functions and to its use in the logical design of digital computer systems is given. Sequential machines and their equivalence are also discussed.

Chapter 5 gives a brief introduction to graph theory. Elements of graph theory are indispensable in almost all computer science areas. Examples are given of its use in such areas as syntactic analysis, fault detection and diagnosis in computers, and minimal-path problems. The computer representation and manipulation of graphs are also discussed so that certain important algorithms can be included.

Finally, Chapter 6 gives a very brief introduction to computability theory. The equivalence of finite-state acceptors and regular grammars is shown. Finally, the concept of an effective procedure is introduced. It is shown that a Turing machine can evaluate any partial recursive function.

The exercises are of both a theoretical and a programming nature and are meant to further the understanding of the application of the concepts to various areas of computer science. The material in this book incorporates, in addition to logic, most of what the ACM Curriculum Committee on Computer Science recommends for the course "Introduction to Discrete Structures." [1]

---

[1] Course B3 in CACM 11, pp. 172–173, 1968.

We hope that this book will be of use to computer scientists, engineers, nonmathematics students who desire an intermediate coverage of topics in discrete mathematics, and mathematicians who want to familiarize themselves with the application of the theory to computer science. Students who have some previous background in modern logic and algebra will be able to master the material in one semester. For other students who have no previous knowledge of logic and algebra, this book can be used in a two-semester course. Certain topics can be selected to form a one-semester course. The omission of the applications discussed in the text will not result in any loss of continuity in the material. This book is based on the experience gained in teaching a course on discrete structures at the University of Saskatchewan at Saskatoon during the past four years.

A basic familiarity with either standard FORTRAN or PL/I is assumed. PL/I is useful in applications that involve recursion or list structures.

We owe a great deal to John A. Copeck and Richard F. Deutscher, who made many valuable criticisms and suggestions throughout the entire preparation and proofreading of the book. They also helped us in formulating and testing most of the algorithms. In particular, John Copeck assisted in the preparation of Chapter 1 and Sections 2-7, 4-4, 4-5, 5-2, 5-5, and 6-2. Also, Richard Deutscher assisted in the preparation of Chapter 2, Sections 4-4 and 5-1, and many of the figures.

We also thank Peter Hardie for his assistance in working out the details on fault diagnosis in Section 5-4 and Andrew Carson for his suggestions in Chapter 3. Robert Probert proofread Sections 5-1 and 6-2, Don McKillican and Allan Listol worked out the exercises, and Gail Galgan helped in proofreading and constructing the index. We owe a very special thanks to Alice Mae MacDonald who did such an excellent job of typing the manuscript, and to Helen Henderson and Dorothy Peake for providing typing support. This work would not have been possible without the support given by the University of Saskatchewan.

J. P. TREMBLAY
R. MANOHAR

**DISCRETE
MATHEMATICAL
STRUCTURES WITH
APPLICATIONS
TO COMPUTER
SCIENCE**

MATHEMATICAL LOGIC

INTRODUCTION

One of the main aims of logic is to provide rules by which one can determine whether any particular argument or reasoning is valid (correct).

Logic is concerned with all kinds of reasonings, whether they be legal arguments or mathematical proofs or conclusions in a scientific theory based upon a set of hypotheses. Because of the diversity of their application, these rules, called rules of inference, must be stated in general terms and must be independent of any particular argument or discipline involved. These rules should also be independent of any particular language used in the arguments. More precisely, in logic we are concerned with the forms of the arguments rather than with the arguments themselves. Like any other theory in science, the theory of inference is formulated in such a way that we should be able to decide about the validity of an argument by following the rules mechanically and independently of our own feelings about the argument. Of course, to proceed in this manner requires that the rules be stated unambiguously.

Any collection of rules or any theory needs a language in which these rules or theory can be stated. Natural languages are not always precise enough. They are also ambiguous and, as such, are not suitable for this purpose. It is therefore necessary first to develop a formal language called the *object language.* A formal language is one in which the syntax is well defined. In fact, every scientific discipline develops its own object language which consists of certain well-defined terms and well-specified uses of these terms. The only difference between logic and other disciplines is that in other disciplines we are concerned with the use of the object language while in logic we are as interested in analyzing our object language as we are in using it. In fact, in the first half of this chapter we shall be concerned with the development and analysis of an object language without considering its use in the theory of inference. This study has important applications in the design of computers and several other two-state devices, as is shown in Sec. 1-2.15. We emphasize this part of logic because the study of formal languages constitutes an important part in the development of means of communication with computing machines. This study is followed by the study of inference theory in Sec. 1-4. It soon becomes apparent that the object language developed thus far is very limited, and we cannot include some very simple argument forms in our inference theory. Therefore, in Sec. 1-5 we expand our object language to include predicates, and then in Sec. 1-6 we discuss the inference theory of predicate logic.

In order to avoid ambiguity, we use symbols which have been clearly defined in the object languages. An additional reason to use symbols is that they are easy to write and manipulate. Because of this use of symbols, the logic that we shall study is also called *symbolic logic.* Our study of the object language requires the use of another language. For this purpose we can choose any of the natural languages. In this case our choice is English, and so the statements about the object language will be made in English. This natural language (English) will then be called our *metalanguage.* Certain inherent difficulties in this procedure could be anticipated, because we wish to study a precise language while using another language which is not so precise.

1-1 STATEMENTS AND NOTATION

In this section we introduce certain basic units of our object language called primary (primitive, atomic) statements. We begin by assuming that the object language contains a set of declarative sentences which cannot be further broken down or analyzed into simpler sentences. These are the primary statements. Only those declarative sentences will be admitted in the object language which have one and only one of two possible values called "truth values." The two truth values are *true* and *false* and are denoted by the symbols T and F respectively. Occasionally they are also denoted by the symbols 1 and 0. The truth values have nothing to do with our feelings of the truth or falsity of these admissible sentences because these feelings are subjective and depend upon context. For our purpose, it is enough to assume that it is *possible* to assign one and only one of the two possible values to a declarative sentence. We are concerned in our study with the *effect* of assigning any particular truth value to declarative sentences rather than with the *actual* truth value of these sentences. Since we admit only two possible truth values, our logic is sometimes called a *two-valued logic.*

We develop a mechanism by which we can construct in our object language other declarative sentences having one of the two possible truth values. Note that we do not admit any other types of sentence, such as exclamatory, interrogative, etc., in the object language.

Declarative sentences in the object language are of two types. The first type includes those sentences which are considered to be primitive in the object language. These will be denoted by distinct symbols selected from the capital letters $A, B, C, \ldots, P, Q, \ldots$, while declarative sentences of the second type are obtained from the primitive ones by using certain symbols, called connectives, and certain punctuation marks, such as parentheses, to join primitive sentences. In any case, all the declarative sentences to which it is possible to assign one and only one of the two possible truth values are called *statements*. These statements which do not contain any of the connectives are called *atomic* (*primary, primitive*) *statements*.

We shall now give examples of sentences and show why some of them are not admissible in the object language and, hence, will not be symbolized.

1 Canada is a country.
2 Moscow is the capital of Spain.
3 This statement is false.
4 $1 + 101 = 110$.
5 Close the door.
6 Toronto is an old city.
7 Man will reach Mars by 1980.

Obviously Statements (1) and (2) have truth values *true* and *false* respectively. Statement (3) is not a statement according to our definition, because we cannot properly assign to it a definite truth value. If we assign the value *true*, then Sentence (3) says that Statement (3) is false. On the other hand, if we assign it the value *false*, then Sentence (3) implies that Statement (3) is true. This example illustrates a semantic paradox. In (4) we have a statement whose truth value depends upon the context; viz., if we are talking about numbers in the decimal system, then it is a false statement. On the other hand, for numbers in binary, it is a true statement. The truth value of a statement often depends upon its context, which is generally unstated but nonetheless understood. We shall soon see that we are not going to be preoccupied with the actual truth value of a statement. We shall be interested only in the fact that it *has* a truth value. In this sense (4), (6), and (7) are all statements. Note that Statement (6) is considered true in some parts of the world and false in certain other parts. The truth value of (7) could be determined only in the year 1980, or earlier if a man reaches Mars before that date. But this aspect is not of interest to us. Note that (5) is not a statement; it is a command.

Once we know those atomic statements which are admissible in the object language, we can use symbols to denote them. Methods of constructing and analyzing statements constructed from one or more atomic statements are discussed in Sec. 1-2, while the method of symbolizing atomic statements will be described here after we discuss some conventions regarding the use and mention of names in statements.

It is customary to use the *name* of an object, not the object itself, when making a statement about the object. As an example, consider the statement

8   This table is big.

The expression "this table" is used as a name of the object. The actual object, namely a particular table, is not used in the statement. It would be inconvenient to put the actual table in place of the expression "this table." Even for the case of small objects, where it may be possible to insert the actual object in place of its name, this practice would not permit us to make two simultaneous statements about the same object without using its name at one place or the other. For this reason it may be agreed that a statement about an object would contain never the object itself but only its name. In fact, we are so familiar with this convention that we take it for granted.

Consider, now, a situation in which we wish to discuss something about a *name*, so that the name is the object about which a statement is to be made. According to the rule just stated, we should use not the name itself in the statement but some name of that name. How does one give a name to a name? A usual method is to enclose the name in quotation marks and to treat it as a name for the name. For example, let us look at the following two statements.

9   Clara is smart.
10   "Clara" contains five letters.

In (9) something is said about a person whose name is Clara. But Statement (10) is not about a person but about a name. Thus "Clara" is used as a name of this name. By enclosing the name of a person in quotation marks it is made clear that the statement made in (10) is about a name and not about a person.

This convention can be explained alternatively by saying that we *use* a certain word in a sentence when that word serves as the name of an object under consideration. On the other hand, we *mention* a word in a sentence when that word is acting not as the name of an object but as the name of the word itself. To "mention" a word means that the word itself has been converted into an object of our consideration.

Throughout the text we shall be making statements not only about what we normally consider objects but also about other statements. Thus it would be necessary to name the statements under consideration. The same device used for naming names could also be used for naming statements. A statement enclosed in quotation marks will be used as the *name* of the statement. More generally, any expression enclosed in quotation marks will be used as the name of that expression. In other words, any expression that is mentioned is placed in quotation marks. The following statement illustrates the above discussion.

11   "Clara is smart" contains "Clara."

Statement (11) is a statement about Statement (9) and the word "Clara." Here Statement (9) was named first by enclosing it in quotation marks and then by using this name in (11) along with the name "Clara"!

In this discussion we have used certain other devices to name statements. One such device is to display a statement on a line separated from the main text. This method of display is assumed to have the same effect as that obtained by using quotation marks to delimit a statement within the text. Further, we have sometimes numbered these statements by inserting a number to the left of the statement. In a later reference this number is used as a name of the statement. This number is written within the text without quotation marks. Such a display and the numbering of statements permit some reduction in the number of quotation marks. Combinations of these different devices will be used throughout the text in naming statements. Thus the statement

12   "Clara is smart" is true.

could be written as "(9) is true," or equivalently,

12a   (9) is true.

A particular person or an object may have more than one name. It is an accepted principle that one may substitute for the name of an object in a given statement any other name of the same object without altering the meaning of the statement. This principle was used in Statements (12) and (12*a*).

We shall be using the name-forming devices just discussed to form the names of statements. Very often such distinctions are not made in mathematical writings, and generally the difference between the name and the object is assumed to be clear from the context. However, this practice sometimes leads to confusion.

A situation analogous to the name-object concept just discussed exists in many programming languages. In particular, the distinction between the name of a variable and its value is frequently required when a procedure (function or subroutine) is invoked (called). The arguments (also called actual parameters) in the statement which invokes the procedure are associated with the (formal) parameters of the procedure either by name or by value. If the association is made by value, then only the value of an argument is passed to its corresponding parameter. This procedure implies that we cannot change the value of the argument from within the function since it is not known where this argument is stored in the computer memory. On the other hand, a call-by-name association makes the name or address of the argument available to the procedure. Such an association allows the value of an argument to be changed by instructions in the procedure. We shall now discuss how call-by-name and call-by-value associations are made in a number of programming languages.

In certain versions of FORTRAN compilers (such as IBM's FORTRAN H and G) the name of an argument, not its value, is passed to a function or subroutine. This convention also applies to the case of an argument's being a constant. The address of a constant (stored in some symbol table of the compiler) is passed to the corresponding parameter of the function. This process could lead to catastrophic results. For example, consider the simple function FUN described by the following sequence of statements:

```
INTEGER FUNCTION FUN(I)
I = 5
FUN = I
RETURN
END
```

Suppose that the main program, which invokes FUN, consists of the trivial statements

$$K = 3$$
$$J = FUN(K) * 3$$
$$L = FUN(3) * 3$$
$$PRINT\ 10,\ J,\ L$$
$$10\ FORMAT(1H\ ,\ I3,\ I3)$$
$$STOP$$
$$END$$

This program yields values of 15 and 25 for variables J and L respectively. In the evaluation of J, the address of K is known within the function. K is changed in the function to a value of 5 by the statement I = 5. The functional value returned by the function is 5, and a value of 15 for J results. The computation of L, however, is quite different. The address of 3 is passed to the function. Since the corresponding parameter I is changed to 5, the value of 3 in the symbol table in the main program will also be changed to 5. Note that since all references to the symbol table entry for constant 3 were made at compile time, all such future references in the remainder of the main program still refer to that entry or location, but the value will now be 5, not 3. More specifically, the name 3 in the right operand of the multiplication of L has a value of 5.

In other versions of FORTRAN compilers, such results are prevented by creating a dummy variable for each argument that is a constant. These internal (dummy) variables are not accessible to the programmer. A change in parameter corresponding to a dummy variable changes the value of that variable, but it does not change the value of the original argument from which it was constructed.

WATFIV permits the passing of arguments by value by merely enclosing such arguments in slashes. For example, in the function call

$$TEST(I,/K/,5)$$

the value of K is passed to the function TEST.

In PL/I arguments can be passed by value or by name. An argument is passed by value if it is enclosed within parentheses; otherwise it is passed by name. In the function call

$$TEST(I,(K),5)$$

the arguments I and K are passed by name and by value respectively.

As mentioned earlier, we shall use the capital letters A, B, ..., P, Q, ... (with the exception of T and F) as well as subscripted capital letters to represent statements in symbolic logic. As an illustration, we write

13 P: It is raining today.

In Statement (13) we are including the information that "P" is a statement in symbolic logic which corresponds to the statement in English, "It is raining today." This situation is similar to the translation of the same statement into French as "Aujourd'hui il pleut." Thus "P" in (13)—"It is raining today"—and "Aujourd'hui il pleut" are the names of the same statement. Note that "P" and not P is used as the name of a statement.

1-2 CONNECTIVES

The notions of a statement and of its truth value have already been introduced. In the case of simple statements, their truth values are fairly obvious. However, it is possible to construct rather complicated statements from simpler statements by using certain connecting words or expressions known as "sentential connectives." Several such connectives are used in the English language. Because they are used with a variety of meanings, it is necessary to define a set of connectives with definite meanings. It is convenient to denote these new connectives by means of symbols. We define these connectives in this section and then develop methods to determine the truth values of statements that are formed by using them. Various properties of these statements and some relationships between them are also discussed. In addition, we show that the statements along with the connectives define an algebra that satisfies a set of properties. These properties enable us to do some calculations by using statements as objects. The algebra developed here has interesting and important applications in the field of switching theory and logical design of computers, as is shown in Sec. 1-2.15. Some of these results are also used in the theory of inference discussed in Sec. 1-4.

The statements that we consider initially are simple statements, called *atomic* or *primary statements*. As already indicated, new statements can be formed from atomic statements through the use of sentential connectives. The resulting statements are called *molecular* or *compound statements*. Thus the atomic statements are those which do not have any connectives.

In our everyday language we use connectives such as "and," "but," "or," etc., to combine two or more statements to form other statements. However, their use is not always precise and unambiguous. Therefore, we will not symbolize these connectives in our object language; however, we will define connectives which have some resemblance to the connectives in the English language.

The idea of using the capital letters $P, Q, \ldots, P_1, P_2, \ldots$ to denote statements was already introduced in Sec. 1-1. Now the same symbols, namely, the capital letters with or without subscripts, will also be used to denote arbitrary statements. In this sense, a statement "P" either denotes a particular statement or serves as a placeholder for any statement whatsoever. This dual use of the same symbol to denote either a definite statement, called a *constant*, or an arbitrary statement, called a *variable*, does not cause any confusion as its use will be clear from the context. The truth value of "P" is the truth value of the actual statement which it represents. It should be emphasized that when "P" is used as a statement variable, it has no truth value and as such does not represent a statement in symbolic logic. We understand that if it is to be replaced, then its replacement must be a statement. Then the truth value of P could be determined. It is convenient to call "P" in this case a "statement formula." We discuss the notion of "statement formula" in Sec. 1-2.4. However, in the sections that follow, we often abbreviate the term "statement formula" simply by "statement." This abbreviation keeps our discussion simple and emphasizes the meaning of the connectives introduced.

As an illustration, let

$$P: \text{It is raining today.}$$

$$Q: \text{It is snowing.}$$

and let R be a statement variable whose possible replacements are P and Q. If no replacement for R is specified, it remains a statement variable and has no truth value. On the other hand, the truth values of P and Q can be determined because they are statements.

1-2.1 Negation

The *negation* of a statement is generally formed by introducing the word "not" at a proper place in the statement or by prefixing the statement with the phrase "It is not the case that." If "P" denotes a statement, then the negation of "P" is written as "$\neg P$" and read as "not P." If the truth value of "P" is T, then the truth value of "$\neg P$" is F. Also if the truth value of "P" is F, then the truth value of "$\neg P$" is T. This definition of the negation is summarized by Table 1-2.1.

Notice that we have not used the quotation marks to denote the names of the statements in the table. This practice is in keeping with the one adopted earlier, when a statement was separated from the main text and written on a separate line. From now on we shall drop the quotation marks even within the text when we use symbolic names for the statements, except in the case where this practice may lead to confusion. We now illustrate the formation of the negation of a statement.

Consider the statement

$$P: \text{London is a city.}$$

Then $\neg P$ is the statement

$$\neg P: \text{It is not the case that London is a city.}$$

Normally $\neg P$ can be written as

$$\neg P: \text{London is not a city.}$$

Although the two statements "It is not the case that London is a city" and "London is not a city" are not identical, we have translated both of them by $\neg P$. The reason is that both these statements have the same meaning in English. A given statement in the object language is denoted by a symbol, and it may correspond to several statements in English. This multiplicity happens because in a natural language one can express oneself in a variety of ways.

As an illustration, if a statement is

$$P: \text{I went to my class yesterday.}$$

then $\neg P$ is any one of the following

    1   I did not go to my class yesterday.

Table 1-2.1 **TRUTH TABLE FOR NEGATION**

P	$\neg P$
T	F
F	T

2 I was absent from my class yesterday.

3 It is not the case that I went to my class yesterday.

The symbol "⌐" has been used here to denote the negation. Alternate symbols used in the literature are "∼," a bar, or "*NOT*," so that ⌐P is written as ∼P, $\bar{P}$, or *NOT P*. Note that a negation is called a connective although it only modifies a statement. In this sense, negation is a unary operation which operates on a single statement or a variable. The word "operation" will be explained in Chap. 2. For the present it is sufficient to note that an operation on statements generates other statements. We have chosen "⌐" to denote negation because this symbol is commonly used in the textbooks on logic and also in several programming languages, one of which will be used here.

1-2.2 Conjunction

The *conjunction* of two statements P and Q is the statement $P \wedge Q$ which is read as "P and Q." The statement $P \wedge Q$ has the truth value T whenever both P and Q have the truth value T; otherwise it has the truth value F. The conjunction is defined by Table 1-2.2.

EXAMPLE 1   Form the conjunction of

P: It is raining today.

Q: There are 20 tables in this room.

SOLUTION   It is raining today and there are 20 tables in this room.   ////

Normally, in our everyday language the conjunction "and" is used between two statements which have some kind of relation. Thus a statement "It is raining today and $2 + 2 = 4$" sounds odd, but in logic it is a perfectly acceptable statement formed from the statements "It is raining today" and "$2 + 2 = 4$."

EXAMPLE 2   Translate into symbolic form the statement

Jack and Jill went up the hill.

SOLUTION   In order to write it as a conjunction of two statements, it is necessary first to paraphrase the statement as

Jack went up the hill and Jill went up the hill.

Table 1-2.2   **TRUTH TABLE FOR CONJUNCTION**

P	Q	$P \wedge Q$
T	T	T
T	F	F
F	T	F
F	F	F

If we now write

P: Jack went up the hill.

Q: Jill went up the hill.

then the given statement can be written in symbolic form as $P \wedge Q$.   ////

So far we have seen that the symbol $\wedge$ is used as a translation of the connective "and" appearing in English. However, the connective "and" is sometimes used in a different sense, and in such cases it cannot be translated by the symbol $\wedge$ defined above. In order to see this difference, consider the statements:

1 Roses are red and violets are blue.
2 He opened the book and started to read.
3 Jack and Jill are cousins.

In Statement (1) the conjunction "and" is used in the same sense as the symbol $\wedge$. In (2) the word "and" is used in the sense of "and then," because the action described in "he started to read" occurs after the action described in "he opened the book." In (3) the word "and" is not a conjunction. Note that our definition of conjunction is symmetric as far as P and Q are concerned; that is to say, the truth values of $P \wedge Q$ and of $Q \wedge P$ are the same for specific values of P and Q. Obviously the truth value of (1) will not change if we write it as

Violets are blue and roses are red.

On the other hand, we cannot write (2) as

He started to read and opened the book.

These examples show that the symbol $\wedge$ has a specific meaning which corresponds to the connective "and" in general, although "and" may also be used with some other meanings. Some authors use the symbol &, or a dot, or "AND" to denote the conjunction. Note that the conjunction is a binary operation in the sense that it connects two statements to form a new statement.

1-2.3 Disjunction

The *disjunction* of two statements P and Q is the statement $P \vee Q$ which is read as "P or Q." The statement $P \vee Q$ has the truth value F only when both P and Q have the truth value F; otherwise it is *true*. The disjunction is defined by Table 1-2.3.

Table 1-2.3 TRUTH TABLE FOR DISJUNCTION

P	Q	$P \vee Q$
T	T	T
T	F	T
F	T	T
F	F	F

The connectives ⌐ and ∧ defined earlier have the same meaning as the words "not" and "and" in general. However, the connective ∨ is not always the same as the word "or" because of the fact that the word "or" in English is commonly used both as an "exclusive OR" and as an "inclusive OR." For example, consider the following statements:

1 I shall watch the game on television or go to the game.
2 There is something wrong with the bulb or with the wiring.
3 Twenty or thirty animals were killed in the fire today.

In Statement (1), the connective "or" is used in the exclusive sense; that is to say, one or the other possibility exists but not both. In (2) the intended meaning is clearly one or the other or both. The connective "or" used in (2) is the "inclusive OR." In (3) the "or" is used for indicating an approximate number of animals, and it is not used as a connective.

From the definition of disjunction it is clear that ∨ is "inclusive OR." The symbol ∨ comes from the Latin word "vel" which is the "inclusive OR." It is not necessary to introduce a new symbol for "exclusive OR," since there are other ways to express it in terms of the symbols already defined. We demonstrate this point in Sec. 1-2.14.

Normally in our everyday language, the disjunction "or" is used between two statements which have some kind of relationship between them. It is not necessary in logic that there be any relationship between them according to the definition of disjunction. The truth value of $P \vee Q$ depends only upon the truth values of P and Q. As before, it may be necessary to paraphrase given statements in English before they can be translated into symbolic form. Similarly, translations of statements from symbolic logic into statements in English may require paraphrasing in order to make them grammatically acceptable.

1-2.4 Statement Formulas and Truth Tables

We have defined the connectives ⌐, ∧, and ∨ so far. Other connectives will be defined subsequently. We shall occasionally distinguish between two types of statements in our symbolic language. Those statements which do not contain any connectives are called *atomic* or *primary* or *simple statements*. On the other hand, those statements which contain one or more primary statements and some connectives are called *molecular* or *composite* or *compound statements*. As an example, let P and Q be any two statements. Some of the compound statements formed by using P and Q are

$$\neg P \qquad P \vee Q \qquad (P \wedge Q) \vee (\neg P) \qquad P \wedge (\neg Q) \qquad (1)$$

The compound statements given above are statement formulas derived from the statement variables P and Q. Therefore, P and Q may be called the components of the statement formulas. Observe that in addition to the connectives we have also used parentheses in some cases in order to make the formula unambiguous. We discuss the rules of constructing statement formulas in Sec. 1-2.7.

Recall that a statement formula has no truth value. It is only when the statement variables in a formula are replaced by definite statements that we get a statement. This statement has a truth value which depends upon the truth values of the statements used in replacing the variables.

In the construction of formulas, the parentheses will be used in the same sense in which they are used in elementary arithmetic or algebra or sometimes in a computer programming language. This usage means that the expressions in the innermost parentheses are simplified first. With this convention in mind, $\neg(P \wedge Q)$ means the negation of $P \wedge Q$. Similarly $(P \wedge Q) \vee (Q \wedge R)$ means the disjunction of $P \wedge Q$ and $Q \wedge R$. $((P \wedge Q) \vee R) \wedge (\neg P)$ means the conjunction of $\neg P$ and $(P \wedge Q) \vee R$, while $(P \wedge Q) \vee R$ means the disjunction of $P \wedge Q$ and R.

In order to reduce the number of parentheses, we will assume that the negation affects as little as possible of what follows. Thus $\neg P \vee Q$ is written for $(\neg P) \vee Q$, and the negation means the negation of the statement immediately following the symbol $\neg$. On the other hand, according to our convention, $\neg(P \wedge Q) \vee R$ stands for the disjunction of $\neg(P \wedge Q)$ and R. The negation affects $P \wedge Q$ but not R.

Truth tables have already been introduced in the definitions of the connectives. Our basic concern is to determine the truth value of a statement formula for each possible combination of the truth values of the component statements. A table showing all such truth values is called the *truth table* of the formula. In Table 1-2.1 we constructed the truth table for $\neg P$. There is only one component or atomic statement, namely P, and so there are only two possible truth values to be considered. Thus Table 1-2.1 has only two rows. In Tables 1-2.2 and 1-2.3 we constructed truth tables for $P \wedge Q$ and $P \vee Q$ respectively. These statement formulas have two component statements, namely P and Q, and there are 2^2 possible combinations of truth values that must be considered. Thus each of the two tables has 2^2 rows. In general, if there are n distinct components in a statement formula, we need to consider 2^n possible combinations of truth values in order to obtain the truth table.

Two methods of constructing truth tables are shown in the following examples.

EXAMPLE 1   Construct the truth table for the statement formula $P \vee \neg Q$.

SOLUTION   It is necessary to consider all possible truth values of P and Q. These values are entered in the first two columns of Table 1-2.4 for both methods. In the table which is arrived at by method 1, the truth values of $\neg Q$ are entered

Table 1-2.4a

P	Q	$\neg Q$	$P \vee \neg Q$
T	T	F	T
T	F	T	T
F	T	F	F
F	F	T	T

Method 1

Table 1-2.4b

P	Q	P	$\vee$	$\neg$	Q
T	T	T	T	F	T
T	F	T	T	T	F
F	T	F	F	F	T
F	F	F	T	T	F
Step Number		1	3	2	1

Method 2

in the third column, and the truth values of $P \lor \neg Q$ are entered in the fourth column. In method 2, as given in Table 1-2.4b, a column is drawn for each statement as well as for the connectives that appear. The truth values are entered step by step. The step numbers at the bottom of the table show the sequence followed in arriving at the final step. ////

EXAMPLE 2 Construct the truth table for $P \land \neg P$.

SOLUTION See Table 1-2.5. Note that the truth value is F for every possible truth value of P. In this special case, the truth value of $P \land \neg P$ is independent of the truth value of P. ////

EXAMPLE 3 Construct the truth table for $(P \lor Q) \lor \neg P$.

SOLUTION See Table 1-2.6. In this case the truth value of the formula $(P \lor Q) \lor \neg P$ is independent of the truth values of P and Q. This independence is due to the special construction of the formula, as we shall see in Sec. 1-2.8. ////

Table 1-2.5

P	$\neg P$	$P \land \neg P$
T	F	F
F	T	F

Method 1

P	P	$\land$	$\neg$	P
T	T	F	F	T
F	F	F	T	F
Step Number	1	3	2	1

Method 2

Table 1-2.6

P	Q	$P \lor Q$	$\neg P$	$(P \lor Q) \lor \neg P$
T	T	T	F	T
T	F	T	F	T
F	T	T	T	T
F	F	F	T	T

Method 1

P	Q	$(P$	$\lor$	$Q)$	$\lor$	$\neg$	P
T	T	T	T	T	T	F	T
T	F	T	T	F	T	F	T
F	T	F	T	T	T	T	F
F	F	F	F	F	T	T	F
Step Number		1	2	1	3	2	1

Method 2

Observe that if the truth values of the component statements are known, then the truth value of the resulting statement can be readily determined from the truth table by reading along the row which corresponds to the correct truth values of the component statements.

EXERCISES 1-2.4

1 Using the statements

$$R: \text{Mark is rich.}$$

$$H: \text{Mark is happy.}$$

write the following statements in symbolic form:
(*a*) Mark is poor but happy.
(*b*) Mark is rich or unhappy.
(*c*) Mark is neither rich nor happy.
(*d*) Mark is poor or he is both rich and unhappy.

2 Construct the truth tables for the following formulas.
(*a*) $\neg(\neg P \vee \neg Q)$
(*b*) $\neg(\neg P \wedge \neg Q)$
(*c*) $P \wedge (P \vee Q)$
(*d*) $P \wedge (Q \wedge P)$
(*e*) $(\neg P \wedge (\neg Q \wedge R)) \vee (Q \wedge R) \vee (P \wedge R)$
(*f*) $(P \wedge Q) \vee (\neg P \wedge Q) \vee (P \wedge \neg Q) \vee (\neg P \wedge \neg Q)$

3 For what truth values will the following statement be true? "It is not the case that houses are cold or haunted and it is false that cottages are warm or houses ugly." (*Hint*: There are four atomic statements.)

4 Given the truth values of P and Q as T and those of R and S as F, find the truth values of the following:
(*a*) $P \vee (Q \wedge R)$
(*b*) $(P \wedge (Q \wedge R)) \vee \neg((P \vee Q) \wedge (R \vee S))$
(*c*) $(\neg(P \wedge Q) \vee \neg R) \vee (((\neg P \wedge Q) \vee \neg R) \wedge S)$

1-2.5 Logical Capabilities of Programming Languages

In this section we discuss the logical connectives available in certain programming languages and how these connectives can be used to generate a truth table for a statement formula. The logical connectives discussed thus far are available in most programming languages. In PL/I, the connectives $\wedge$, $\vee$, and $\neg$ are written as &, |, and $\neg$ respectively. The truth values T and F are written as '1'B and '0'B respectively. In ALGOL the connectives are represented as we have written them, while T and F are written as **true** and **false** respectively. FORTRAN also permits the use of logical variables and expressions, and it is these facilities which are to be discussed in this section.

In FORTRAN, the truth values T and F are denoted by the logical constants .TRUE. and .FALSE. respectively. Logical variables and expressions in the language assume only one of the logical values at any given time. All logical variables must be explicitly declared as in the statement

LOGICAL P, Q, R

which declares the three variables P, Q, and R.

The statement that a relation exists between arithmetic expressions is itself an expression that has a truth value; in FORTRAN, these expressions are formulated from the following *relational operators*:

.LT.($<$)   .LE.($\leq$)   .EQ.($=$)   .GE.($\geq$)   .GT.($>$)   .NE.($\neq$)

For example, if P has been declared LOGICAL, the statement

$$P = 5 * 2 .LT. 17$$

assigns a value of .TRUE. to P. Similarly, if Q has been appropriately declared, the statement

$$Q = A + 5 .GE. C + D$$

assigns the value .TRUE. to Q if A $+$ 5 is greater than or equal to C $+$ D when the statement is executed, and the value .FALSE. otherwise.

From the truth values arising, for example, from relations, more complex logical expressions can be obtained in FORTRAN by using one or more of the three logical connectives previously discussed. The logical operators .AND., .OR., and .NOT. correspond to the symbolic logical operators $\wedge$, $\vee$, and $\neg$ respectively. The statement

$$P \vee (\neg(Q \wedge R))$$

is equivalent to the FORTRAN statement

$$P .OR. (.NOT. (Q .AND. R))$$

Unnecessary parentheses are avoided in FORTRAN by using the following precedence scheme. The arithmetic operators, with their usual order of precedence, are the highest in rank and are consequently evaluated first. All relational operators have the same rank and are evaluated after the arithmetic operators. The logical operators are the last to be evaluated, and .NOT., .AND., and .OR. is their decreasing order of precedence. Of two or more binary operators having the same precedence value in an expression, the leftmost is evaluated first; for unary operators, it is the rightmost which is evaluated first. Thus, .NOT. P .AND. Q means (.NOT. P) .AND. Q; and A $+$ B $+$ 5.0 .LT. C $+$ D means ((A $+$ B) $+$ 5.0) .LT. (C $+$ D).

FORTRAN has a logical "IF statement" whose form is

$$\text{IF (logical expression) statement}$$

If the logical expression in the "IF statement" is true, then the statement following the expression is executed; otherwise, it is skipped. For example, when the statement

$$\text{IF (.NOT. P .OR. Q) GO TO 100}$$

is executed, it will not transfer control to statement 100 if P and Q have the values .TRUE. and .FALSE. respectively.

Arrays of logical variables can also be used in FORTRAN. The statement

$$\text{LOGICAL CASE(10)}$$

declares a one-dimensional array of type LOGICAL consisting of 10 elements. Elements of logical arrays are referenced in the same manner as any other subscripted variable.

Consider the problem of generating all possible assignments of truth values to the logical variables P, Q, and R, as shown in Table 1-2.7. There are $2^3 = 8$ possible assignments. Notice that the truth value of the variable P remains at the same value of T or F for each of four consecutive assignments of logical values. The values of variables Q and R remain at T or F for two assignments and one assignment of logical values respectively. The value of variable R changes more frequently than the value of variable Q, and that of Q more frequently than that of P. The number of times the kth logical variable remains at a constant truth value can be easily computed and is denoted by $BASE[k]$. In the case under discussion, we have three variables, and the values can be computed as

$$BASE[k] = 2^{(3-k)} \qquad k = 1, 2, 3$$

where we have associated $BASE[1]$, $BASE[2]$, and $BASE[3]$ with variables P, Q, and R respectively.

In addition to computing the $BASE$ elements, we also need to know the number of assignments which remain to be generated with a particular logical variable remaining at the same value. For example, if we had already generated the assignments TTT and TTF, then variable P would remain at its present value of T throughout the generation of the next two assignments. This information is stored in an element denoted by $LENGTH[k]$. For variable P, $LENGTH[1]$ would have a value of 2 after generation of TTT and TTF. The $LENGTH$ values associated with variables P, Q, and R are initially the same as their corresponding $BASE$ values. Therefore, initially

$$LENGTH[k] = BASE[k] \qquad k = 1, 2, 3$$

Every time an assignment is generated, each element of $LENGTH$ is decremented by 1. When the $LENGTH$ value associated with a variable becomes zero, then the truth value of that variable is negated, and the $LENGTH$ value is reset to the $BASE$ value. The algorithm for the generation of such assignments can now be precisely formulated.

Table 1-2.7

	P	Q	R
$BASE[1]$	T	T	T}——$BASE[3]$
	T	T	F
	T	F	T
	T	F	F
$BASE[2]$	F	T	T
	F	T	F
	F	F	T
	F	F	F

Algorithm *NEXT*   Given n logical variables having values stored in $CASE[1]$, $CASE[2]$, ..., $CASE[n]$ and two vectors *BASE* and *LENGTH* each having n elements, it is required to generate the next assignment of truth values for these variables.

1   [Initialize counter] Set $k \leftarrow 1$.
2   [Decrement $LENGTH[k]$] Set $LENGTH[k] \leftarrow LENGTH[k] - 1$.
3   [Negate variable and reset $LENGTH[k]$?] If $LENGTH[k] = 0$ then set $CASE[k] \leftarrow \neg CASE[k]$ and $LENGTH[k] \leftarrow BASE[k]$.
4   [Increment counter] Set $k \leftarrow k + 1$. If $k \leq n$ then go to step 2; otherwise Exit.   ////

A program for algorithm *NEXT* is given in Fig. 1-2.1. The subroutine has the four parameters CASE, N, BASE, and LENGTH. All parameters except N are arrays. The logical array CASE contains an assignment of truth values for the logical variables from which the subroutine is to generate a new assignment of values. For example, for the case of three logical variables, CASE(1), CASE(2), and CASE(3) could be associated with the variable names P, Q, and R respectively. The new assignment of truth values is returned to the main program via the logical array CASE.

Let us now consider the problem of constructing a truth table for a statement formula. The following straightforward algorithm uses the various logical arrays such as *CASE*, *BASE*, and *LENGTH* which were discussed in algorithm *NEXT*.

Algorithm *TRUTH*   Given a statement formula in n variables and subalgorithm *NEXT* which generates a new assignment of truth values, it is required to construct a truth table for the given statement formula.

1   [Initialize] Repeat for $k = 1, 2, ..., n$: Set $BASE[k] \leftarrow 2^{(n-k)}$, $LENGTH[k] \leftarrow BASE[k]$, and $CASE[k] \leftarrow F$. Set $i \leftarrow 1$ and print headings for the truth table.
2   [Evaluate statement] Substitute the logical values in array *CASE* into the statement formula. Print the values in array *CASE* and the value of the statement.
3   [Obtain next assignment for variables] Invoke subalgorithm *NEXT*.

```
        SUBROUTINE NEXT(CASE,N,BASE,LENGTH)
    C   GENERATE THE NEXT ASSIGNMENT OF LOGICAL VALUES.
        LOGICAL CASE(N)
        INTEGER BASE(N),LENGTH(N)
        DO 1 K = 1,N
        LENGTH(K) = LENGTH(K) - 1
        IF(LENGTH(K).NE.0) GO TO 1
        CASE(K) = .NOT.CASE(K)
        LENGTH(K) = BASE(K)
      1 CONTINUE
        END
```

FIGURE 1-2.1   Program for algorithm *NEXT*.

4 [Increment counter] Set $i \leftarrow i + 1$. If $i \leq 2^n$ then go to step 2; otherwise Exit.   ////

The FORTRAN program for the algorithm is given in Fig. 1-2.2. As an example, the formula

$$\neg(P \wedge Q) \vee (R \vee P)$$

was used in the program. The program consists of a main program, a subroutine, and a function. The subroutine NEXT, given in Fig. 1-2.1, generates an assignment each time it is invoked. The function LOGIC is very simple, and its purpose is to generate a single truth value for the statement formula each time the function is invoked. The number of logical variables in the given statement formula and their associated values are passed to the function LOGIC by using the integer variable N and the logical vector CASE respectively.

For our example, the variables P, Q, and R are denoted in the program by the subscripted variables CASE(1), CASE(2), and CASE(3) respectively.

Each time the main program needs a new assignment of truth values for the variables, it calls on procedure NEXT after which the function LOGIC is invoked to evaluate the statement formula for this new assignment of values. The main program computes the BASE and LENGTH vectors for subroutine NEXT.

Initially, all logical variables are set to false, which enables subroutine NEXT to obtain the next assignment. Note that all variables could have been set to true instead. This assignment, of course, would have produced a truth table with the same information as shown in the sample output but in a different order.

1-2.6 Conditional and Biconditional

If P and Q are any two statements, then the statement $P \rightarrow Q$ which is read as "If P, then Q" is called a *conditional* statement. The statement $P \rightarrow Q$ has a truth value F when Q has the truth value F and P the truth value T; otherwise it has the truth value T. The conditional is defined by Table 1-2.8.

The statement P is called the *antecedent* and Q the *consequent* in $P \rightarrow Q$. Again, according to the definition, it is not necessary that there be any kind of relation between P and Q in order to form $P \rightarrow Q$.

Table 1-2.8 TRUTH TABLE FOR CONDITIONAL

P	Q	$P \rightarrow Q$
T	T	T
T	F	F
F	T	T
F	F	T

```
C   MAINLINE
C   THIS PROGRAM EVALUATES A STATEMENT FORMULA
C   AND GENERATES ITS TRUTH TABLE.
C
C   VARIABLES
C   TITLE:    TITLE FOR THE STATEMENT FORMULA
C   NAME:     VARIABLE NAMES
C   VALUE:    LOGICAL VALUE OF STATEMENT FORMULA
C   NUMBER:   NUMBER OF ROWS IN THE TRUTH TABLE
C
C   DECLARATIONS AND TITLES
        INTEGER*2 NAME(3)/'P','Q','R'/
        REAL*8 TITLE(4)/'.NOT.(P.','AND.Q).O','R.(R.OR.','P)      '/
        LOGICAL CASE(10),LOGIC,VALUE
        INTEGER BASE(10),LENGTH(10)
C   INITIALIZE BASE, LENGTH, CASE, N, AND NUMBER.
        N = 3
        NUMBER = 2 ** N
        DO 1 K = 1,N
        BASE(K) = 2 ** (N - K)
        LENGTH(K) = BASE(K)
        CASE(K) = .FALSE.
      1 CONTINUE
C   OUTPUT HEADINGS
        WRITE(6,10) TITLE
     10 FORMAT('1',13X,'VARIABLES',13X,4A8)
        WRITE(6,20) NAME
     20 FORMAT(' ',8X,'CASE 1    2    3',/,' ',13X,3(A2,2X),21X,'VALUE',/)
C   FIND VALUE OF THE STATEMENT FORMULA, OUTPUT TRUTH VALUES,
C   AND GENERATE NEW TRUTH VALUES FOR THE LOGICAL VARIABLES.
        DO 2 I = 1,NUMBER
        VALUE = LOGIC(CASE,N)
        WRITE(6,30) (CASE(K),K = 1,N),VALUE
     30 FORMAT(' ',13X,3(L1,3X),23X,L1)
        CALL NEXT(CASE,N,BASE,LENGTH)
      2 CONTINUE
        STOP
        END


        LOGICAL FUNCTION LOGIC(CASE,N)
C   THIS FUNCTION DEFINES THE STATEMENT FORMULA TO BE EVALUATED.
        LOGICAL CASE(N)
        LOGIC = .NOT.(CASE(1).AND.CASE(2)).OR.(CASE(3).OR.CASE(1))
        RETURN
        END
```

	VARIABLES			.NOT.(P.AND.Q).OR.(R.OR.P)
CASE	1	2	3	
	P	Q	R	VALUE
	F	F	F	T
	F	F	T	T
	F	T	F	T
	F	T	T	T
	T	F	F	T
	T	F	T	T
	T	T	F	T
	T	T	T	T

FIGURE 1-2.2 Program for generating truth tables—mainline and function LOGIC.

EXAMPLE 1 Express in English the statement $P \rightarrow Q$ where

P: The sun is shining today.

Q: $2 + 7 > 4$.

SOLUTION If the sun is shining today, then $2 + 7 > 4$. ////

The conditional often appears very confusing to a beginner, particularly when one tries to translate a conditional in English into symbolic form. A variety of expressions are used in English which can be appropriately translated by the symbol $\rightarrow$. It is customary to represent any one of the following expressions by $P \rightarrow Q$:

1 Q is necessary for P.
2 P is sufficient for Q.
3 Q if P.
4 P only if Q.
5 P implies Q.

We shall avoid the translation "implies." Although, in mathematics, the statements "If P, then Q" and "P implies Q" are used interchangeably, we want to use the word "implies" in a different way.

In our everyday language, we use the conditional statements in a more restricted sense. It is customary to assume some kind of relationship or implication or feeling of cause and effect between the antecedent and the consequent in using the conditional. For example, the statement "If I get the book, then I shall read it tonight" sounds reasonable because the second statement "I shall read it (the book) tonight" refers to the book mentioned in the first part of the statement. On the other hand, a statement such as "If I get the book, then this room is red" does not make sense to us in our conventional language. However, according to our definition of the conditional, the last statement is perfectly acceptable and has a truth value which depends on the truth values of the two statements being connected.

The first two entries in Table 1-2.8 are similar to what we would expect in our everyday language. Thus, if P is true and Q is true, then $P \rightarrow Q$ is true. Similarly, if P is true and Q is false, then "If P, then Q" appears to be false. Consider, for example, the statement "If I get the money, then I shall buy the car." If I actually get the money and buy the car, then the statement appears to be correct or true. On the other hand, if I do not buy the car even though I get the money, then the statement is false. Normally, when a conditional statement is made, we assume that the antecedent is true. Because of this convention in English, the first two entries in the truth table do not appear strange. Referring to the above statement again, if I do not get the money and I still buy the car, it is not so clear whether the statement made earlier is true or false. Also, if I do not buy the car and I do not get the money, then it is not intuitively clear whether the statement made is true or false. It may be possible to justify entries in the last two rows of the truth table by considering special examples or even by emphasizing certain aspects of the statements given in the above examples. However, it is best to consider Table 1-2.8 as the definition of the conditional in which the entries in the last two rows are arbitrarily assigned in order to avoid any ambiguity. Any other choice for the last two entries would correspond to some other connective which has either been defined or will be defined. In general, the use of "If ..., then ..." in English has only partial resemblance to the use of the conditional → as defined here.

EXAMPLE 2 Write the following statement in symbolic form.

> If either Jerry takes Calculus or Ken takes Sociology, then Larry will take English.

SOLUTION Denoting the statements as

$$J: \text{ Jerry takes Calculus.}$$
$$K: \text{ Ken takes Sociology.}$$
$$L: \text{ Larry takes English.}$$

the above statement can be symbolized as

$$(J \vee K) \rightarrow L \qquad ////$$

EXAMPLE 3 Write in symbolic form the statement

> The crop will be destroyed if there is a flood.

SOLUTION Let the statements be denoted as

$$C: \text{ The crop will be destroyed.}$$
$$F: \text{ There is a flood.}$$

Note that the given statement uses "if" in the sense of "If ..., then ...." It is better to rewrite the given statement as "If there is a flood, then the crop will be destroyed." Now it is easy to symbolize it as

$$F \rightarrow C \qquad ////$$

EXAMPLE 4 Construct the truth table for $(P \rightarrow Q) \wedge (Q \rightarrow P)$.

SOLUTION See Table 1-2.9. Note that the given formula has the truth value T whenever both P and Q have identical truth values. ////

If P and Q are any two statements, then the statement $P \rightleftarrows Q$, which is read as "P if and only if Q" and abbreviated as "P iff Q," is called a *biconditional statement*. The statement $P \rightleftarrows Q$ has the truth value T whenever both P and

Table 1-2.9

P	Q	$P \rightarrow Q$	$Q \rightarrow P$	$(P \rightarrow Q) \wedge (Q \rightarrow P)$
T	T	T	T	T
T	F	F	T	F
F	T	T	F	F
F	F	T	T	T

Table 1-2.10 TRUTH TABLE FOR BICONDITIONAL

P	Q	$P \rightleftarrows Q$
T	T	T
T	F	F
F	T	F
F	F	T

Table 1-2.11

P	Q	$P \land Q$	$\neg(P \land Q)$	$\neg P$	$\neg Q$	$\neg P \lor \neg Q$	$\neg(P \land Q) \rightleftarrows (\neg P \lor \neg Q)$
T	T	T	F	F	F	F	T
T	F	F	T	F	T	T	T
F	T	F	T	T	F	T	T
F	F	F	T	T	T	T	T

Q have identical truth values. Table 1-2.10 defines the biconditional. The statement $P \rightleftarrows Q$ is also translated as "P is necessary and sufficient for Q." Note that the truth values of $(P \rightarrow Q) \land (Q \rightarrow P)$ given in Table 1-2.9 are identical to the truth values of $P \rightleftarrows Q$ defined here.

EXAMPLE 5   Construct the truth table for the formula

$$\neg(P \land Q) \rightleftarrows (\neg P \lor \neg Q)$$

SOLUTION   See Table 1-2.11. Note that the truth values of the given formula are T for all possible truth values of P and Q.   ////

EXERCISES 1-2.6

1 Show that the truth values of the following formulas are independent of their components.
  (a) $(P \land (P \rightarrow Q)) \rightarrow Q$
  (b) $(P \rightarrow Q) \rightleftarrows (\neg P \lor Q)$
  (c) $((P \rightarrow Q) \land (Q \rightarrow R)) \rightarrow (P \rightarrow R)$
  (d) $(P \rightleftarrows Q) \rightleftarrows ((P \land Q) \lor (\neg P \land \neg Q))$
2 Construct the truth tables of the following formulas.
  (a) $(Q \land (P \rightarrow Q)) \rightarrow P$
  (b) $\neg(P \lor (Q \land R)) \rightleftarrows ((P \lor Q) \land (P \lor R))$
3 A connective denoted by $\triangledown$ is defined by Table 1-2.12. Find a formula using P, Q, and the connectives $\land$, $\lor$, and $\neg$ whose truth values are identical to the truth values of $P \triangledown Q$.
4 Given the truth values of P and Q as T and those of R and S as F, find the truth values of the following:
  (a) $(\neg(P \land Q) \lor \neg R) \lor ((Q \rightleftarrows \neg P) \rightarrow (R \lor \neg S))$
  (b) $(P \rightleftarrows R) \land (\neg Q \rightarrow S)$
  (c) $(P \lor (Q \rightarrow (R \land \neg P))) \rightleftarrows (Q \lor \neg S)$

Table 1-2.12

P	Q	$P \,\underline{\vee}\, Q$
T	T	F
T	F	T
F	T	T
F	F	F

1-2.7 Well-formed Formulas

The notion of a statement formula has already been introduced. A statement formula is not a statement (although, for the sake of brevity, we have often called it a statement); however, a statement can be obtained from it by replacing the variables by statements. A *statement formula* is an expression which is a string consisting of variables (capital letters with or without subscripts), parentheses, and connective symbols. Not every string of these symbols is a formula. We shall now give a recursive definition of a statement formula, often called a well-formed formula (wff). A *well-formed formula* can be generated by the following rules:

1 A statement variable standing alone is a well-formed formula.

2 If A is a well-formed formula, then $\neg A$ is a well-formed formula.

3 If A and B are well-formed formulas, then $(A \wedge B)$, $(A \vee B)$, $(A \to B)$, and $(A \rightleftarrows B)$ are well-formed formulas.

4 A string of symbols containing the statement variables, connectives, and parentheses is a well-formed formula, iff it can be obtained by finitely many applications of the rules 1, 2, and 3.

According to this definition, the following are well-formed formulas:

$$\neg(P \wedge Q) \qquad \neg(P \vee Q) \qquad (P \to (P \vee Q)) \qquad (P \to (Q \to R))$$

$$(((P \to Q) \wedge (Q \to R)) \rightleftarrows (P \to R))$$

The following are not well-formed formulas.

1 $\neg P \wedge Q$. Obviously P and Q are well-formed formulas. A wff would be either $(\neg P \wedge Q)$ or $\neg(P \wedge Q)$.

2 $(P \to Q) \to (\wedge Q)$. This is not a wff because $\wedge Q$ is not.

3 $(P \to Q$. Note that $(P \to Q)$ is a wff.

4 $(P \wedge Q) \to Q)$. The reason for this not being a wff is that one of the parentheses in the beginning is missing. $((P \wedge Q) \to Q)$ is a wff, while $(P \wedge Q) \to Q$ is still not a wff.

It is possible to introduce some conventions so that the number of parentheses used can be reduced. In fact, there are conventions which, when followed, allow one to dispense with all the parentheses. We shall not discuss these conventions here. For the sake of convenience we shall omit the outer parentheses. Thus we write $P \wedge Q$ in place of $(P \wedge Q)$, $(P \wedge Q) \to Q$ in place of $((P \wedge Q) \to Q)$, and $((P \to Q) \wedge (Q \to R)) \rightleftarrows (P \to R)$ instead of $(((P \to Q) \wedge (Q \to R)) \rightleftarrows (P \to R))$. Since the only formulas we will encounter are well-formed formulas, we will refer to well-formed formulas as formulas.

1-2.8 Tautologies

Well-formed formulas have been defined. We also know how to construct the truth table of a given formula. Let us consider what a truth table represents. If definite statements are substituted for the variables in a formula, there results a statement. The truth value of this resulting statement depends upon the truth values of the statements substituted for the variables. Such a truth value appears as one of the entries in the final column of the truth table. Observe that this entry will not change even if any of the definite statements that replace particular variables are themselves replaced by other statements, as long as the truth values associated with all variables are unchanged. In other words, an entry in the final column depends only on the truth values of the statements assigned to the variables rather than on the statements themselves. Different rows correspond to different sets of truth value assignments. A truth table is therefore a summary of the truth values of the resulting statements for all possible assignments of values to the variables appearing in a formula. It must be emphasized that a statement formula does not have a truth value. In our discussion which follows we shall, for the sake of simplicity, use the expression "the truth value of a statement formula" to mean the entries in the final column of the truth table of the formula.

In general, the final column of a truth table of a given formula contains both T and F. There are some formulas whose truth values are always T or always F regardless of the truth value assignments to the variables. This situation occurs because of the special construction of these formulas. We have already seen some examples of such formulas.

Consider, for example, the statement formulas $P \vee \neg P$ and $P \wedge \neg P$ in Table 1-2.13. The truth values of $P \vee \neg P$ and $P \wedge \neg P$, which are T and F respectively, are independent of the statement by which the variable P may be replaced.

A statement formula which is true regardless of the truth values of the statements which replace the variables in it is called a *universally valid formula* or a *tautology* or a *logical truth*. A statement formula which is false regardless of the truth values of the statements which replace the variables in it is called a *contradiction*. Obviously, the negation of a contradiction is a tautology. We may say that a statement formula which is a tautology is *identically true* and a formula which is a contradiction is *identically false*.

A straightforward method to determine whether a given formula is a tautology is to construct its truth table. This process can always be used but often becomes tedious, particularly when the number of distinct variables is large or when the formula is complicated. Recall that the numbers of rows in a truth table is 2^n, where n is the number of distinct variables in the formula. Later,

Table 1-2.13

P	$\neg P$	$P \vee \neg P$	$P \wedge \neg P$
T	F	T	F
F	T	T	F

alternative methods will be developed that will be able to determine whether a statement formula is a tautology without having to construct its truth table.

A simple fact about tautologies is that the conjunction of two tautologies is also a tautology. Let us denote by A and B two statement formulas which are tautologies. If we assign any truth values to the variables of A and B, then the truth values of both A and B will be T. Thus the truth value of $A \wedge B$ will be T, so that $A \wedge B$ will be a tautology.

A formula A is called a *substitution instance* of another formula B if A can be obtained from B by substituting formulas for some variables of B, with the condition that the same formula is substituted for the same variable each time it occurs. We now illustrate this concept. Let

$$B: P \rightarrow (J \wedge P)$$

Substitute $R \rightleftarrows S$ for P in B, and we get

$$A: (R \rightleftarrows S) \rightarrow (J \wedge (R \rightleftarrows S))$$

Then A is a substitution instance of B. Note that

$$(R \rightleftarrows S) \rightarrow (J \wedge P)$$

is not a substitution instance of B because the variable P in $J \wedge P$ was not replaced by $R \rightleftarrows S$. It is possible to substitute more than one variable by other formulas, provided that all substitutions are considered to occur simultaneously. For example, substitution instances of $P \rightarrow \neg Q$ are

1. $(R \wedge \neg S) \rightarrow \neg (J \vee M)$
2. $(R \wedge \neg S) \rightarrow \neg (R \wedge \neg S)$
3. $(R \wedge \neg S) \rightarrow \neg P$
4. $Q \rightarrow \neg (P \wedge \neg Q)$

In (2) both P and Q have been replaced by $R \wedge \neg S$. In (4), P is replaced by Q and Q by $P \wedge \neg Q$.

Next, consider the following formulas which result from $P \rightarrow \neg Q$.

1. Substitute $P \vee Q$ for P and R for Q to get the substitution instance $(P \vee Q) \rightarrow \neg R$.
2. First substitute $P \vee Q$ for P to obtain the substitution instance $(P \vee Q) \rightarrow \neg Q$. Next, substitute R for Q in $(P \vee Q) \rightarrow \neg Q$, and we get $(P \vee R) \rightarrow \neg R$. This formula is a substitution instance of $(P \vee Q) \rightarrow \neg Q$, but it is not a substitution instance of $P \rightarrow \neg Q$ under the substitution $(P \vee Q)$ for P and R for Q. This statement is true because we did not substitute simultaneously as we did in (1).

It may be noted that in constructing substitution instances of a formula, substitutions are made for the atomic formula and never for the molecular formula. Thus $P \rightarrow Q$ is not a substitution instance of $P \rightarrow \neg R$, because it is R which must be replaced and not $\neg R$.

The importance of the above concept lies in the fact that any substitution instance of a tautology is a tautology. Consider the tautology $P \vee \neg P$. Regardless of what is substituted for P, the truth value of $P \vee \neg P$ is always T. Therefore, it we substitute any statement formula for P, the resulting formula will be a tautology. Hence the following substitution instances of $P \vee \neg P$ are tautologies.

$$(R \rightarrow S) \vee \neg(R \rightarrow S)$$

$$((P \vee S) \wedge R) \vee \neg((P \vee S) \wedge R)$$

$$(((P \vee \neg Q) \rightarrow R) \rightleftarrows S) \vee \neg(((P \vee \neg Q) \rightarrow R) \rightleftarrows S)$$

Thus, if it is possible to detect whether a given formula is a substitution instance of a tautology, then it is immediately known that the given formula is also a tautology. Similarly, one can start with a tautology and write a large number of formulas which are substitution instances of this tautology and hence are themselves tautologies.

EXERCISES 1-2.8

1 From the formulas given below select those which are well-formed according to the definition in Sec. 1-2.7, and indicate which ones are tautologies or contradictions.
  (a) $(P \rightarrow (P \vee Q))$
  (b) $((P \rightarrow (\neg P)) \rightarrow \neg P)$
  (c) $((\neg Q \wedge P) \wedge Q)$
  (d) $((P \rightarrow (Q \rightarrow R)) \rightarrow ((P \rightarrow Q) \rightarrow (P \rightarrow R)))$
  (e) $((\neg P \rightarrow Q) \rightarrow (Q \rightarrow P)))$
  (f) $((P \wedge Q) \rightleftarrows P)$
2 Produce the substitution instances of the following formulas for the given substitutions.
  (a) $(((P \rightarrow Q) \rightarrow P) \rightarrow P)$; substitute $(P \rightarrow Q)$ for P and $((P \wedge Q) \rightarrow R)$ for Q.
  (b) $((P \rightarrow Q) \rightarrow (Q \rightarrow P))$; substitute Q for P and $(P \wedge \neg P)$ for Q.
3 Determine the formulas which are substitution instances of other formulas in the list and give the substitutions.
  (a) $(P \rightarrow (Q \rightarrow P))$
  (b) $((((P \rightarrow Q) \wedge (R \rightarrow S)) \wedge (P \vee R)) \rightarrow (Q \vee S))$
  (c) $(Q \rightarrow ((P \rightarrow P) \rightarrow Q))$
  (d) $(P \rightarrow ((P \rightarrow (Q \rightarrow P)) \rightarrow P))$
  (e) $((((R \rightarrow S) \wedge (Q \rightarrow P)) \wedge (R \vee Q)) \rightarrow (S \vee P))$

1-2.9 Equivalence of Formulas

Let A and B be two statement formulas and let $P_1, P_2, \ldots, P_n$ denote all the variables occurring in both A and B. Consider an assignment of truth values to $P_1, P_2, \ldots, P_n$ and the resulting truth values of A and B. If the truth value of A is equal to the truth value of B for every one of the 2^n possible sets of truth values assigned to $P_1, P_2, \ldots, P_n$, then A and B are said to be *equivalent*. Assuming that the variables and the assignment of truth values to the variables appear in the same order in the truth tables of A and B, then the final columns in the truth tables for A and B are identical if A and B are equivalent.

Here are some examples of formulas which are equivalent. Verify their equivalence by truth tables.

1 $\neg \neg P$ is equivalent to P.
2 $P \vee P$ is equivalent to P.

3 $(P \wedge \neg P) \vee Q$ is equivalent to Q.
4 $P \vee \neg P$ is equivalent to $Q \vee \neg Q$.

In the definition of equivalence of two formulas, it is not necessary to assume that they both contain the same variables. This point is illustrated in the examples given in (3) and (4) above. It may, however, be noted that if two formulas are equivalent and a particular variable occurs in only one of them, then the truth value of this formula is independent of this variable. For example, in (3) the truth value of $(P \wedge \neg P) \vee Q$ is independent of the truth value of P. Similarly in (4), the truth values of $P \vee \neg P$ and $Q \vee \neg Q$ are each independent of P and Q.

Recalling the truth table (Table 1-2.10) in the definition of the biconditional, it is clear that $P \rightleftarrows Q$ is true whenever both P and Q have the same truth values. Therefore the statement formulas A and B are equivalent provided $A \rightleftarrows B$ is a tautology; and, conversely, if $A \rightleftarrows B$ is a tautology, then A and B are equivalent. We shall represent the equivalence of two formulas, say A and B, by writing "$A \Leftrightarrow B$," which is read as "A is equivalent to B." Note that the expression "$A \Leftrightarrow B$" which can also be displayed as

$$A \Leftrightarrow B$$

should be written as

$$\text{``}A\text{''} \Leftrightarrow \text{``}B\text{''}$$

according to the rules given earlier (in Sec. 1-1) regarding the use and mention of expressions. Observe that "$A \Leftrightarrow B$" is a statement in English (the metalanguage) and not in the object language. Also the symbol "$\Leftrightarrow$" is not a connective but a symbol in the metalanguage. Having noted this, we shall often drop the quotation marks because this will not lead to any ambiguity.

Equivalence is a symmetric relation; that is, "A is equivalent to B" is the same as "B is equivalent to A." Also if $A \Leftrightarrow B$ and $B \Leftrightarrow C$, then $A \Leftrightarrow C$. This relationship may also be expressed by saying that the equivalence of statement formulas is transitive.

As in the case of tautologies, one method to determine whether any two statement formulas are equivalent is to construct their truth tables. All combinations of truth values associated with the variables appearing in both formulas are presented in the table, and the final columns (for the two formulas) are compared.

EXAMPLE 1   Prove $(P \rightarrow Q) \Leftrightarrow (\neg P \vee Q)$.

SOLUTION   See Table 1-2.14. Note that the truth values in the columns for $P \rightarrow Q$ and $\neg P \vee Q$ are identical, and so the biconditional will have the truth value T. To compare columns, it is not necessary to form the biconditional; thus the last column could have been avoided.   ////

A list of some basic equivalent formulas which will be found useful is given in Table 1-2.15. In order to make the list complete, we use **T** and **F** as special variables in the sense that **T** can be replaced by only a tautology and **F** by only a contradiction.

Table 1-2.14

P	Q	$P \rightarrow Q$	$\neg P$	$\neg P \vee Q$	$(P \rightarrow Q) \rightleftarrows (\neg P \vee Q)$
T	T	T	F	T	T
T	F	F	F	F	T
F	T	T	T	T	T
F	F	T	T	T	T

In view of the associative laws, we can write $(P \vee Q) \vee R$ as $P \vee Q \vee R$, and $(P \wedge Q) \wedge R$ as $P \wedge Q \wedge R$.

In Table 1-2.15 we note that pairs of equivalent formulas are arranged two to a line such as

$$A_1 \Leftrightarrow B_1 \qquad A_2 \Leftrightarrow B_2$$

For each pair A_1, B_1 there is a corresponding pair A_2, B_2 in which $\vee$ is replaced by $\wedge$, $\wedge$ by $\vee$, **T** by **F**, and **F** by **T**. A_1 and A_2 are said to be duals of each other, and so are B_1 and B_2. Duality is discussed in Sec. 1-2.10.

In constructing substitution instances of a statement formula, we are allowed to substitute only for the variables appearing in the formula. Furthermore, the same formula is to be substituted for every occurrence of a particular variable. This rule ensures that substitution instances of a tautology are also tautologies. Consider now another process, called a *replacement process*, in which we replace any part of a statement formula which is itself a formula, be it atomic or molecular, by any other formula. For example, in the formula $(P \wedge Q) \rightarrow P$ we replace $(P \wedge Q)$ by $R \rightarrow (S \wedge \neg M)$ and the second P by $(P \wedge R) \rightarrow (\neg S \vee M)$ to obtain $(R \rightarrow (S \wedge \neg M)) \rightarrow ((P \wedge R) \rightarrow (\neg S \vee M))$. In general, a replacement yields a new formula, but it may not always be an interesting formula. However, if we impose the restriction that any part of a given formula that is to be replaced by another formula must be equivalent to that other formula, then the result is equivalent to the original formula. By this process one can obtain new formulas which are equivalent to the original formula. For example, we can replace P in $P \wedge Q$ by the formula $P \vee P$, since $P \vee P \Leftrightarrow P$, to get $(P \vee P) \wedge Q$ which is equivalent to $P \wedge Q$. Consequently, if we replace any part or parts of a tautology by formulas that are equivalent to these parts, we again get a tautology.

EXAMPLE 2 Show that $P \rightarrow (Q \rightarrow R) \Leftrightarrow P \rightarrow (\neg Q \vee R) \Leftrightarrow (P \wedge Q) \rightarrow R$.

SOLUTION Recall from Example 1 that $Q \rightarrow R \Leftrightarrow \neg Q \vee R$. Replacing $Q \rightarrow R$ by $\neg Q \vee R$, we get $P \rightarrow (\neg Q \vee R)$, which is equivalent to $\neg P \vee (\neg Q \vee R)$ by the same rule. Now

$$\neg P \vee (\neg Q \vee R) \Leftrightarrow (\neg P \vee \neg Q) \vee R \Leftrightarrow \neg (P \wedge Q) \vee R$$
$$\Leftrightarrow (P \wedge Q) \rightarrow R$$

using associativity of $\vee$, De Morgan's law, and the previously used rule. ////

Table 1-2.15   EQUIVALENT FORMULAS

$P \vee P \Leftrightarrow P$	$P \wedge P \Leftrightarrow P$	(Idempotent laws)	(1)
$(P \vee Q) \vee R \Leftrightarrow P \vee (Q \vee R)$	$(P \wedge Q) \wedge R \Leftrightarrow P \wedge (Q \wedge R)$	(Associative laws)	(2)
$P \vee Q \Leftrightarrow Q \vee P$	$P \wedge Q \Leftrightarrow Q \wedge P$	(Commutative laws)	(3)
$P \vee (Q \wedge R) \Leftrightarrow (P \vee Q) \wedge (P \vee R)$	$P \wedge (Q \vee R) \Leftrightarrow (P \wedge Q) \vee (P \wedge R)$	(Distributive laws)	(4)
$P \vee \mathbf{F} \Leftrightarrow P$	$P \wedge \mathbf{T} \Leftrightarrow P$		(5)
$P \vee \mathbf{T} \Leftrightarrow \mathbf{T}$	$P \wedge \mathbf{F} \Leftrightarrow \mathbf{F}$		(6)
$P \vee \neg P \Leftrightarrow \mathbf{T}$	$P \wedge \neg P \Leftrightarrow \mathbf{F}$		(7)
$P \vee (P \wedge Q) \Leftrightarrow P$	$P \wedge (P \vee Q) \Leftrightarrow P$	(Absorption laws)	(8)
$\neg (P \vee Q) \Leftrightarrow \neg P \wedge \neg Q$	$\neg (P \wedge Q) \Leftrightarrow \neg P \vee \neg Q$	(De Morgan's laws)	(9)

EXAMPLE 3 Show that $(\neg P \wedge (\neg Q \wedge R)) \vee (Q \wedge R) \vee (P \wedge R) \Leftrightarrow R$.

SOLUTION

$$(\neg P \wedge (\neg Q \wedge R)) \vee (Q \wedge R) \vee (P \wedge R)$$
$$\Leftrightarrow (\neg P \wedge (\neg Q \wedge R)) \vee ((Q \vee P) \wedge R) \qquad (4)$$
$$\Leftrightarrow ((\neg P \wedge \neg Q) \wedge R) \vee ((Q \vee P) \wedge R) \qquad (2)$$
$$\Leftrightarrow ((\neg P \wedge \neg Q) \vee (Q \vee P)) \wedge R \qquad (4)$$
$$\Leftrightarrow (\neg (P \vee Q) \vee (P \vee Q)) \wedge R \qquad (9), (3)$$
$$\Leftrightarrow \mathbf{T} \wedge R \qquad (7)$$
$$\Leftrightarrow R \qquad (5)$$

The basic equivalent statement formulas used are denoted by the numbers on the right-hand side which correspond to numbers in Table 1-2.15.   ////

EXAMPLE 4 Show that $((P \vee Q) \wedge \neg (\neg P \wedge (\neg Q \vee \neg R))) \vee (\neg P \wedge \neg Q) \vee (\neg P \wedge \neg R)$ is a tautology.

SOLUTION   Using De Morgan's laws, we obtain

$$\neg P \wedge \neg Q \Leftrightarrow \neg (P \vee Q) \qquad \neg P \wedge \neg R \Leftrightarrow \neg (P \vee R)$$
$$(\neg P \wedge \neg Q) \vee (\neg P \wedge \neg R) \Leftrightarrow \neg (P \vee Q) \vee \neg (P \vee R)$$
$$\Leftrightarrow \neg ((P \vee Q) \wedge (P \vee R))$$

Also

$$\neg (\neg P \wedge (\neg Q \vee \neg R) \Leftrightarrow \neg (\neg P \wedge \neg (Q \wedge R))$$
$$\Leftrightarrow P \vee (Q \wedge R) \Leftrightarrow (P \vee Q) \wedge (P \vee R)$$
$$(P \vee Q) \wedge ((P \vee Q) \wedge (P \vee R)) \Leftrightarrow (P \vee Q) \wedge (P \vee R)$$

Consequently, the given formula is equivalent to

$$((P \vee Q) \wedge (P \vee R)) \vee \neg ((P \vee Q) \wedge (P \vee R))$$

which is a substitution instance of $P \vee \neg P$.   ////

The equivalences given in Table 1-2.15 also describe the properties of the operators $\wedge$, $\vee$, and $\neg$ on the set of statements in symbolic logic. It is shown in Chap. 4 that the set of all statements under the operations $\wedge$, $\vee$, and $\neg$ is an algebra called the *statement algebra* which is a particular example of a Boolean algebra. A comparison of the statement algebra and the set algebra is given in Chap. 2.

1-2.10 Duality Law

In this section we shall consider formulas which contain the connectives $\wedge$, $\vee$, and $\neg$. There is no loss of generality in restricting our consideration to these connectives since we shall see later that any formula containing any other connective can be replaced by an equivalent formula containing only these three connectives.

Two formulas, A and A^*, are said to be *duals* of each other if either one can be obtained from the other by replacing $\wedge$ by $\vee$ and $\vee$ by $\wedge$. The connectives $\wedge$ and $\vee$ are also called *duals* of each other. If the formula A contains the special variables **T** or **F**, then A^*, its dual, is obtained by replacing **T** by **F** and **F** by **T** in addition to the above-mentioned interchanges.

EXAMPLE 1 Write the duals of (a) $(P \vee Q) \wedge R$; (b) $(P \wedge Q) \vee \mathbf{T}$; (c) $\neg(P \vee Q) \wedge (P \vee \neg(Q \wedge \neg S))$.

    SOLUTION The duals are (a) $(P \wedge Q) \vee R$, (b) $(P \vee Q) \wedge \mathbf{F}$, and (c) $\neg(P \wedge Q) \vee (P \wedge \neg(Q \vee \neg S))$.   ////

The following theorem shows the equivalence of a formula and one that is obtained from its dual.

Theorem 1-2.1 Let A and A^* be dual formulas and let $P_1, P_2, \ldots, P_n$ be all the atomic variables that occur in A and A^*. That is to say, we may write A as $A(P_1, P_2, \ldots, P_n)$ and A^* as $A^*(P_1, P_2, \ldots, P_n)$. Then through the use of De Morgan's laws

$$P \wedge Q \Leftrightarrow \neg(\neg P \vee \neg Q) \qquad P \vee Q \Leftrightarrow \neg(\neg P \wedge \neg Q)$$

we can show

$$\neg A(P_1, P_2, \ldots, P_n) \Leftrightarrow A^*(\neg P_1, \neg P_2, \ldots, \neg P_n) \tag{1}$$

Thus the negation of a formula is equivalent to its dual in which every variable is replaced by its negation. As a consequence of this fact, we also have

$$A(\neg P_1, \neg P_2, \ldots, \neg P_n) \Leftrightarrow \neg A^*(P_1, P_2, \ldots, P_n) \tag{2}$$

EXAMPLE 2 Verify equivalence (1) if $A(P, Q, R)$ is $\neg P \wedge \neg(Q \vee R)$.

    SOLUTION Now $A^*(P, Q, R)$ is $\neg P \vee \neg(Q \wedge R)$, and $A^*(\neg P, \neg Q, \neg R)$ is $\neg\neg P \vee \neg(\neg Q \wedge \neg R) \Leftrightarrow P \vee (Q \vee R)$. On the other hand, $\neg A(P, Q, R)$ is $\neg(\neg P \wedge \neg(Q \vee R)) \Leftrightarrow P \vee (Q \vee R)$.   ////

We shall now prove an interesting theorem which states that if any two formulas are equivalent, then their duals are also equivalent to each other. In other words, if $A \Leftrightarrow B$, then $A^* \Leftrightarrow B^*$.

Theorem 1-2.2 Let $P_1, P_2, \ldots, P_n$ be all the atomic variables appearing in the formulas A and B. Given that $A \Leftrightarrow B$ means "$A \rightleftarrows B$ is a tautology," then the following are also tautologies.

$$A(P_1, P_2, \ldots, P_n) \rightleftarrows B(P_1, P_2, \ldots, P_n)$$

$$A(\neg P_1, \neg P_2, \ldots, \neg P_n) \rightleftarrows B(\neg P_1, \neg P_2, \ldots, \neg P_n)$$

Using (2), we get

$$\neg A^*(P_1, P_2, \ldots, P_n) \rightleftarrows \neg B^*(P_1, P_2, \ldots, P_n)$$

Hence $A^* \Leftrightarrow B^*$.

This theorem explains why in Table 1-2.15 we have for every pair of equivalent formulas an equivalent pair of formulas consisting of duals of the first pair.

EXAMPLE 3 Show that

(a) $\neg(P \wedge Q) \rightarrow (\neg P \vee (\neg P \vee Q)) \Leftrightarrow (\neg P \vee Q)$

(b) $(P \vee Q) \wedge (\neg P \wedge (\neg P \wedge Q)) \Leftrightarrow (\neg P \wedge Q)$

SOLUTION

(a)
$$\neg(P \wedge Q) \rightarrow (\neg P \vee (\neg P \vee Q))$$
$$\Leftrightarrow (P \wedge Q) \vee (\neg P \vee (\neg P \vee Q)) \tag{3}$$
$$\Leftrightarrow (P \wedge Q) \vee (\neg P \vee Q)$$
$$\Leftrightarrow (P \wedge Q) \vee \neg P \vee Q$$
$$\Leftrightarrow ((P \vee \neg P) \wedge (Q \vee \neg P)) \vee Q$$
$$\Leftrightarrow (Q \vee \neg P) \vee Q \Leftrightarrow Q \vee \neg P \Leftrightarrow \neg P \vee Q$$

From (3) it follows that

$$(P \wedge Q) \vee (\neg P \vee (\neg P \vee Q)) \Leftrightarrow \neg P \vee Q$$

Writing the duals, we obtain by Theorem 1-2.2 that

$$(P \vee Q) \wedge (\neg P \wedge (\neg P \wedge Q)) \Leftrightarrow \neg P \wedge Q \qquad ////$$

1-2.11 Tautological Implications

Recall the definition of the conditional as given in Table 1-2.8. The connectives $\wedge$, $\vee$, and $\rightleftarrows$ are symmetric in the sense that $P \wedge Q \Leftrightarrow Q \wedge P$, $P \vee Q \Leftrightarrow Q \vee P$, and $P \rightleftarrows Q \Leftrightarrow Q \rightleftarrows P$. On the other hand, $P \rightarrow Q$ is not equivalent to $Q \rightarrow P$.

For any statement formula $P \rightarrow Q$, the statement formula $Q \rightarrow P$ is called its *converse*, $\neg P \rightarrow \neg Q$ is called its *inverse*, and $\neg Q \rightarrow \neg P$ is called its *contrapositive*.

From Table 1-2.16 it is clear that

$$P \rightarrow Q \Leftrightarrow \neg Q \rightarrow \neg P \qquad Q \rightarrow P \Leftrightarrow \neg P \rightarrow \neg Q$$

A statement A is said to *tautologically imply* a statement B if and only if $A \rightarrow B$ is a tautology. We shall denote this idea by $A \Rightarrow B$ which is read as "A implies B." Similar to the case with $\Leftrightarrow$, we note that $\Rightarrow$ is not a connective nor is $A \Rightarrow B$ a statement formula. Just as $A \Leftrightarrow B$ states that A and B are equiv-

Table 1-2.16

P	Q	$\neg P$	$\neg Q$	$P \rightarrow Q$	$\neg Q \rightarrow \neg P$
T	T	F	F	T	T
T	F	F	T	F	F
F	T	T	F	T	T
F	F	T	T	T	T

alent or that $A \rightleftarrows B$ is a tautology, in a similar manner $A \Rightarrow B$ states that $A \rightarrow B$ is a tautology or A tautologically implies B.

We have avoided using the expression "imply" to translate the conditional, so that we shall abbreviate "tautologically imply" simply as "imply." Obviously $A \Rightarrow B$ guarantees that B has the truth value T whenever A has the truth value T.

One can determine whether $A \Rightarrow B$ by constructing the truth tables of A and B in the same manner as was done in the determination of $A \Leftrightarrow B$.

The implications in Table 1-2.17 have important applications. All of them can be proved by truth table or by other methods.

In order to show any of the given implications, it is sufficient to show that an assignment of the truth value T to the antecedent of the corresponding conditional leads to the truth value T for the consequent. This procedure guarantees that the conditional becomes a tautology, thereby proving the implication. In (9), if we assume that $\neg Q \land (P \rightarrow Q)$ has the truth value T, then both $\neg Q$ and $P \rightarrow Q$ have the truth value T, which means that Q has the value F. $P \rightarrow Q$ has the truth value T, and hence P must have the value F. Therefore the consequent $\neg P$ must have the value T.

In (12), we assume that the antecedent is true. This assumption means that $P \lor Q$, $P \rightarrow R$, and $Q \rightarrow R$ are true. If P is true, then R must be true because $P \rightarrow R$ is true. If Q is true, then R must also be true. But at least one of P or Q is true by our assumption that $P \lor Q$ is true, and so R is true.

Another method to show $P \Rightarrow Q$ is to assume that the consequent Q has the value F and then show that this assumption leads to P's having the value F. Then $P \rightarrow Q$ must have the value T.

In (9) assume that $\neg P$ is false, so that P is true. Then $\neg Q \land (P \rightarrow Q)$ must be false. This statement holds because if Q is true, then $\neg Q$ is false, while if Q is false, then $P \rightarrow Q$ is false. Hence the implication in (9) is shown.

Example 4 in Sec. 1-2.6 shows the equivalence of the statements $P \rightleftarrows Q$ and $(P \rightarrow Q) \land (Q \rightarrow P)$; it is easy to verify that ($P \Rightarrow Q$ and $Q \Rightarrow P$) iff $P \Leftrightarrow Q$. This statement is an alternative definition of the equivalence of two formulas. If each of the two formulas A and B implies the other, then A and B are equivalent.

Table 1-2.17 IMPLICATIONS

$P \land Q \Rightarrow P$	(1)
$P \land Q \Rightarrow Q$	(2)
$P \Rightarrow P \lor Q$	(3)
$\neg P \Rightarrow P \rightarrow Q$	(4)
$Q \Rightarrow P \rightarrow Q$	(5)
$\neg(P \rightarrow Q) \Rightarrow P$	(6)
$\neg(P \rightarrow Q) \Rightarrow \neg Q$	(7)
$P \land (P \rightarrow Q) \Rightarrow Q$	(8)
$\neg Q \land (P \rightarrow Q) \Rightarrow \neg P$	(9)
$\neg P \land (P \lor Q) \Rightarrow Q$	(10)
$(P \rightarrow Q) \land (Q \rightarrow R) \Rightarrow P \rightarrow R$	(11)
$(P \lor Q) \land (P \rightarrow R) \land (Q \rightarrow R) \Rightarrow R$	(12)

There are several important facts about implication and equivalence that should be observed. If a formula is equivalent to a tautology, then it must be a tautology. Similarly, if a formula is implied by a tautology, then it is a tautology.

Both implication and equivalence are transitive. To say that equivalence is transitive means if $A \Leftrightarrow B$ and $B \Leftrightarrow C$, then $A \Leftrightarrow C$. This statement follows from the definition of equivalence. To show that the implication is also transitive, assume that $A \Rightarrow B$ and $B \Rightarrow C$. Then $A \rightarrow B$ and $B \rightarrow C$ are tautologies. Hence $(A \rightarrow B) \wedge (B \rightarrow C)$ is also a tautology. But from (11), $(A \rightarrow B) \wedge (B \rightarrow C) \Rightarrow (A \rightarrow C)$. Hence $A \rightarrow C$ is a tautology.

The transitivity of implications can also be applied in several stages. In order to show that $A \Rightarrow C$, it may be convenient to introduce a series of formulas $B_1, B_2, \ldots, B_m$ such that $A \Rightarrow B_1$, $B_1 \Rightarrow B_2$, $\ldots$, $B_{m-1} \Rightarrow B_m$, and $B_m \Rightarrow C$.

Another important property of implication is that if $A \Rightarrow B$ and $A \Rightarrow C$, then $A \Rightarrow (B \wedge C)$. By our assumption, if A is true, then B and C are both true. Thus $B \wedge C$ is true, and hence $A \rightarrow (B \wedge C)$ is true.

We can extend our notion of implication $P \Rightarrow Q$ to the case where several formulas, say $H_1, H_2, \ldots, H_m$, jointly imply a particular formula Q; that is, $H_1, H_2, \ldots, H_m \Rightarrow Q$ means $(H_1 \wedge H_2 \wedge \cdots \wedge H_m) \Rightarrow Q$.

An important theorem which is used in Sec. 1-4.1 follows.

Theorem 1-2.3 If $H_1, H_2, \ldots, H_m$ and P imply Q, then $H_1, H_2, \ldots, H_m$ imply $P \rightarrow Q$.

PROOF   From our assumption we have

$$(H_1 \wedge H_2 \wedge \cdots \wedge H_m \wedge P) \Rightarrow Q$$

This assumption means $(H_1 \wedge H_2 \wedge \cdots \wedge H_m \wedge P) \rightarrow Q$ is a tautology. Using the equivalence (see Example 2, Sec. 1-2.9)

$$P_1 \rightarrow (P_2 \rightarrow P_3) \Leftrightarrow (P_1 \wedge P_2) \rightarrow P_3$$

we can say that

$$(H_1 \wedge H_2 \wedge \cdots \wedge H_m) \rightarrow (P \rightarrow Q)$$

is a tautology. Hence the theorem.   ////

EXERCISES   1-2.11

1 Show the following implications.
   (a) $(P \wedge Q) \Rightarrow (P \rightarrow Q)$
   (b) $P \Rightarrow (Q \rightarrow P)$
   (c) $(P \rightarrow (Q \rightarrow R)) \Rightarrow (P \rightarrow Q) \rightarrow (P \rightarrow R)$
2 Show the following equivalences.
   (a) $P \rightarrow (Q \rightarrow P) \Leftrightarrow \neg P \rightarrow (P \rightarrow Q)$
   (b) $P \rightarrow (Q \vee R) \Leftrightarrow (P \rightarrow Q) \vee (P \rightarrow R)$
   (c) $(P \rightarrow Q) \wedge (R \rightarrow Q) \Leftrightarrow (P \vee R) \rightarrow Q$
   (d) $\neg(P \rightleftarrows Q) \Leftrightarrow (P \vee Q) \wedge \neg(P \wedge Q)$

3 Show the following implications without constructing the truth tables.

(*a*) $P \rightarrow Q \Rightarrow P \rightarrow (P \wedge Q)$

(*b*) $(P \rightarrow Q) \rightarrow Q \Rightarrow P \vee Q$

(*c*) $((P \vee \neg P) \rightarrow Q) \rightarrow ((P \vee \neg P) \rightarrow R) \Rightarrow (Q \rightarrow R)$ (see Sec. 1-6.3)

(*d*) $(Q \rightarrow (P \wedge \neg P)) \rightarrow (R \rightarrow (P \wedge \neg P)) \Rightarrow (R \rightarrow Q)$ (see Sec. 1-6.3)

4 Show that *P* is equivalent to the following formulas.

$$\neg \neg P \qquad P \wedge P \qquad P \vee P \qquad P \vee (P \wedge Q) \qquad P \wedge (P \vee Q)$$

$$(P \wedge Q) \vee (P \wedge \neg Q) \qquad (P \vee Q) \wedge (P \vee \neg Q)$$

5 Show the following equivalences.

(*a*) $\neg(P \wedge Q) \Leftrightarrow \neg P \vee \neg Q$

(*b*) $\neg(P \vee Q) \Leftrightarrow \neg P \wedge \neg Q$

(*c*) $\neg(P \rightarrow Q) \Leftrightarrow P \wedge \neg Q$

(*d*) $\neg(P \rightleftarrows Q) \Leftrightarrow (P \wedge \neg Q) \vee (\neg P \wedge Q)$

1-2.12 Formulas with Distinct Truth Tables

Using all the connectives defined so far and the rules for constructing well-formed formulas, it is possible to construct an unlimited number of statement formulas. We shall try to determine how many of these formulas have distinct truth tables.

Let us consider all possible truth tables that can be obtained when the formulas involve only one variable *P*. These possible truth tables are shown in Table 1-2.18.

Any formula involving only one variable will have one of these four truth tables. Obviously the simplest formulas corresponding to the entries under 1, 2, 3, and 4 are P, $\neg P$, $P \vee \neg P$, and $P \wedge \neg P$ respectively. Every other formula depending upon *P* alone would then be equivalent to one of these four formulas.

If we consider formulas obtained by using two variables *P* and *Q* and any of the connectives defined, we also obtain an unlimited number of formulas. The number of distinct truth tables for formulas involving two variables is given by $2^{2^2} = 2^4 = 16$. Since there are 2^2 rows in the truth table and since each row could have any of the two entries *T* or *F*, we have 2^{2^2} possible tables, as shown in Table 1-2.19.

Any formula involving only two variables will have one of these 16 truth tables. All those formulas which have one of these truth tables are equivalent to each other.

A statement formula containing *n* variables must have as its truth table one of the 2^{2^n} possible truth tables, each of them having 2^n rows. This fact suggests that there are many formulas which may look very different from one another but are equivalent.

Table 1-2.18

P	1	2	3	4
T	*T*	*F*	*T*	*F*
F	*F*	*T*	*T*	*F*

Table 1-2.19

P	Q	1	2	3	4	5	6	7	8	9	10	11	12	13	14	15	16
T	T	T	T	T	T	T	T	T	T	F	F	F	F	F	F	F	F
T	F	T	T	T	T	F	F	F	F	T	T	T	T	F	F	F	F
F	T	T	T	F	F	T	T	F	F	T	T	F	F	T	T	F	F
F	F	T	F	T	F	T	F	T	F	T	F	T	F	T	F	T	F

One method to determine whether two statement formulas A and B are equivalent is to construct their truth tables and compare them. This method is very tedious and difficult to implement even on a computer because the number of entries increases very rapidly as n increases (note that $2^{10} \simeq 1,000$). A better method would be to transform A and B to some standard forms A' and B' such that a simple comparison of A' and B' should establish whether $A \Leftrightarrow B$. This method is feasible; the standard forms are called canonical forms or normal forms and are discussed in Sec. 1-3.

1-2.13 Functionally Complete Sets of Connectives

So far we have defined the connectives $\land$, $\lor$, $\rceil$, $\rightarrow$, and $\rightleftarrows$. We introduce some other connectives in Sec. 1-2.14 because of their usefulness in certain applications. On the other hand, we show in this section that not all the connectives defined thus far are necessary. In fact, we can find certain proper subsets of these connectives which are sufficient to express any formula in an equivalent form. Any set of connectives in which every formula can be expressed in terms of an equivalent formula containing the connectives from this set is called a *functionally complete* set of connectives. It is assumed that such a functionally complete set does not contain any redundant connectives, i.e., a connective which can be expressed in terms of the other connectives.

In order to arrive at a functionally complete set, we first examine the following equivalence:

$$P \rightleftarrows Q \Leftrightarrow (P \rightarrow Q) \land (Q \rightarrow P)$$

This equivalence suggests that in any formula we can replace the part (here "part" means any part which is itself a formula) containing the biconditional by an equivalent formula not containing the biconditional. Thus all the biconditionals can be replaced in a formula.

EXAMPLE 1   Write an equivalent formula for $P \land (Q \rightleftarrows R) \lor (R \rightleftarrows P)$ which does not contain the biconditional.

SOLUTION

$$P \land (Q \rightleftarrows R) \lor (R \rightleftarrows P)$$
$$\Leftrightarrow P \land ((Q \rightarrow R) \land (R \rightarrow Q)) \lor ((R \rightarrow P) \land (P \rightarrow R))$$

Thus the equivalent formula is $P \land ((Q \rightarrow R) \land (R \rightarrow Q)) \lor ((R \rightarrow P) \land (P \rightarrow R))$.   ////

Next we now consider the equivalence $P \rightarrow Q \Leftrightarrow \rceil P \lor Q$. This equivalence suggests that the conditionals can also be eliminated by replacing those parts which contain conditionals by their equivalents.

EXAMPLE 2   Write an equivalent formula for $P \land (Q \rightleftarrows R)$ which contains neither the biconditional nor the conditional.

SOLUTION

$$P \wedge (Q \rightleftarrows R) \Leftrightarrow P \wedge ((Q \rightarrow R) \wedge (R \rightarrow Q))$$
$$\Leftrightarrow P \wedge ((\neg Q \vee R) \wedge (\neg R \vee Q))$$

Thus the required formula is $P \wedge (\neg Q \vee R) \wedge (\neg R \vee Q)$.   ////

Notice that from De Morgan's laws we have

$$P \wedge Q \Leftrightarrow \neg(\neg P \vee \neg Q) \qquad P \vee Q \Leftrightarrow \neg(\neg P \wedge \neg Q)$$

This first equivalence means that it is also possible to obtain a formula which is equivalent to a given formula in which conjunctions are eliminated. A similar procedure is possible for the elimination of disjunctions.

If we implement all the steps suggested above, we can first replace all biconditionals, then the conditionals, and finally all the conjunctions or all the disjunctions in any formula to obtain an equivalent formula which contains either the negation and disjunction only or the negation and conjunction only. This fact means that the sets of connectives $\{\wedge, \neg\}$ and $\{\vee, \neg\}$ are functionally complete.

One can show that $\{\neg\}$, $\{\wedge\}$, and $\{\vee\}$ are not functionally complete and neither is $\{\wedge, \vee\}$.

From the five connectives $\wedge, \vee, \neg, \rightarrow, \rightleftarrows$ we have obtained at least two sets of functionally complete connectives. A question arises whether there is any one connective which is functionally complete. The answer to such a question is no if only the above five connectives are considered. There are some connectives, which are defined in Sec. 1-2.14, that are functionally complete. The question of finding a functionally complete set with fewer connectives is not as theoretical as it may appear, because in physical two-state devices, which are described in Sec. 1-2.15, the connectives correspond to certain physical elements of the device. From the point of view of maintenance and economical production, it is sometimes necessary not to use a variety of different elements.

Note that if a given formula is replaced by an equivalent formula in which the number of different connectives is reduced, the resulting formula may become more complex. This is why we use a larger number of connectives than are needed. In Sec. 1-2.14 we define some more connectives which will be found useful.

EXERCISES 1-2.13

1 Write formulas which are equivalent to the formulas given below and which contain the connectives $\wedge$ and $\neg$ only.
   (*a*) $\neg(P \rightleftarrows (Q \rightarrow (R \vee P)))$
   (*b*) $((P \vee Q) \wedge R) \rightarrow (P \vee R)$
2 For each column in Table 1-2.19 write a formula, involving two variables P and Q, whose truth table corresponds to the truth values in the column chosen.
3 Show that $\{\wedge, \vee\}$, $\{\vee\}$, and $\{\neg\}$ are not functionally complete. (*Hint:* Write a formula which is a tautology.)

1-2.14 Other Connectives

It was shown earlier that not all connectives defined thus far are necessary for the description of the statement calculus. For any formula of the statement calculus, there exists an equivalent formula in which appear only those connectives belonging to one of the functionally complete sets. In spite of this fact, we did define other connectives because, by using them, some of the formulas become simpler. There are other connectives which serve similar purposes, and these will be defined in this section.

Let P and Q be any two formulas. Then the formula $P \bigtriangledown Q$, in which the connective $\bigtriangledown$ is called an *exclusive OR*, is true whenever either P or Q, but not both, is true. The exclusive OR is defined by Table 1-2.20. The exclusive OR is also called the *exclusive disjunction*. The following equivalences follow from its definition.

$$1 \quad P \bigtriangledown Q \Leftrightarrow Q \bigtriangledown P \qquad\qquad\qquad \text{(symmetric)}$$
$$2 \quad (P \bigtriangledown Q) \bigtriangledown R \Leftrightarrow P \vee (Q \bigtriangledown R) \qquad \text{(associative)}$$
$$3 \quad P \wedge (Q \bigtriangledown R) \Leftrightarrow (P \wedge Q) \bigtriangledown (P \wedge R) \qquad \text{(distributive)}$$
$$4 \quad (P \bigtriangledown Q) \Leftrightarrow (P \wedge \neg Q) \vee (\neg P \wedge Q)$$
$$5 \quad (P \bigtriangledown Q) \Leftrightarrow \neg (P \rightleftarrows Q)$$

One can also prove that if $P \bigtriangledown Q \Leftrightarrow R$, then $P \bigtriangledown R \Leftrightarrow Q$ and $Q \bigtriangledown R \Leftrightarrow P$, and $P \bigtriangledown Q \bigtriangledown R$ is a contradiction.

Given a formula in which $\bigtriangledown$ appears, it is possible to obtain an equivalent formula in which only the connectives $\wedge$, $\vee$, and $\neg$ appear by using the equivalence of the formulas in (4).

Other connectives which have useful applications in the design of computers are called *NAND* and *NOR*. The word "*NAND*" is a combination of "*NOT*" and "*AND*," where "*NOT*" stands for negation and "*AND*" for the conjunction. The connective *NAND* is denoted by the symbol $\uparrow$. For any two formulas P and Q

$$P \uparrow Q \Leftrightarrow \neg (P \wedge Q)$$

Another connective, useful in a similar context, is known as *NOR*, a combination of *NOT* and *OR*, where "*OR*" stands for the disjunction. The connective *NOR* is denoted by the symbol $\downarrow$. For any two formulas P and Q

$$P \downarrow Q \Leftrightarrow \neg (P \vee Q)$$

The connectives $\uparrow$ and $\downarrow$ have been defined in terms of the connectives $\wedge$, $\vee$, and $\neg$. Therefore, for any formula containing the connectives $\uparrow$ or $\downarrow$,

Table 1-2.20

P	Q	$P \bigtriangledown Q$
T	T	F
T	F	T
F	T	T
F	F	F

one can obtain an equivalent formula containing the connectives $\wedge$, $\vee$, and $\neg$ only. Note that $\uparrow$ and $\downarrow$ are duals of each other. Therefore, in order to obtain the dual of a formula which includes $\uparrow$ or $\downarrow$, we should interchange $\uparrow$ and $\downarrow$ in addition to making the other interchanges mentioned earlier.

We now show that each of the connectives $\uparrow$ and $\downarrow$ is functionally complete. In order to do this, it is sufficient to show that the sets of connectives $\{\wedge, \neg\}$ and $\{\vee, \neg\}$ can be expressed either in terms of $\uparrow$ alone or in terms of $\downarrow$ alone. The following equivalences express $\neg$, $\wedge$, and $\vee$ in terms of $\uparrow$ alone.

$$P \uparrow P \Leftrightarrow \neg(P \wedge P) \Leftrightarrow \neg P \vee \neg P \Leftrightarrow \neg P$$

$$(P \uparrow Q) \uparrow (P \uparrow Q) \Leftrightarrow \neg(P \uparrow Q) \Leftrightarrow P \wedge Q$$

$$(P \uparrow P) \uparrow (Q \uparrow Q) \Leftrightarrow \neg P \uparrow \neg Q \Leftrightarrow \neg(\neg P \wedge \neg Q) \Leftrightarrow P \vee Q$$

In a similar manner, the following equivalences express $\neg$, $\vee$, and $\wedge$ in terms of $\downarrow$ alone

$$P \downarrow P \Leftrightarrow \neg(P \vee P) \Leftrightarrow \neg P \wedge \neg P \Leftrightarrow \neg P$$

$$(P \downarrow Q) \downarrow (P \downarrow Q) \Leftrightarrow \neg(P \downarrow Q) \Leftrightarrow P \vee Q$$

$$(P \downarrow P) \downarrow (Q \downarrow Q) \Leftrightarrow \neg P \downarrow \neg Q \Leftrightarrow P \wedge Q$$

Because a single operator $NAND$ or NOR is functionally complete, we call each of the sets $\{\uparrow\}$ and $\{\downarrow\}$ a *minimal functionally complete set*, or, in short, a *minimal set*.

The idea of a minimal set of connectives is useful in the economics of the design of electronic circuits. It may be noted that although we can express any formula by an equivalent formula containing a single connective $\uparrow$ or $\downarrow$, we seldom do so because such formulas are often complicated. This fact explains why programming languages as well as our symbolic language have a number of connectives available.

We now list some of the basic properties of the connectives $NAND$ and NOR.

$$P \uparrow Q \Leftrightarrow Q \uparrow P \qquad P \downarrow Q \Leftrightarrow Q \downarrow P \qquad \text{(commutative)} \qquad (1)$$

$$P \uparrow (Q \uparrow R) \Leftrightarrow P \uparrow \neg(Q \wedge R) \Leftrightarrow \neg(P \wedge \neg(Q \wedge R))$$

$$\Leftrightarrow \neg P \vee (Q \wedge R) \qquad (2)$$

while

$$(P \uparrow Q) \uparrow R \Leftrightarrow (P \wedge Q) \vee \neg R$$

Thus the connective $\uparrow$ is not associative. Similarly

$$P \downarrow (Q \downarrow R) \Leftrightarrow \neg P \wedge (Q \vee R) \qquad (P \downarrow Q) \downarrow R \Leftrightarrow (P \vee Q) \wedge \neg R$$

It is possible to define $P \uparrow Q \uparrow R \Leftrightarrow \neg(P \wedge Q \wedge R)$. However, $P \uparrow Q \uparrow R$ is not equivalent to $P \uparrow (Q \uparrow R)$ or to $(P \uparrow Q) \uparrow R$ or to $Q \uparrow (P \uparrow R)$. This nonassociativity of the connectives $NAND$ and NOR creates some difficulty in using them.

$$P \uparrow Q \Leftrightarrow \neg(P \wedge Q) \Leftrightarrow \neg P \vee \neg Q \Leftrightarrow (\neg P \wedge Q)$$

$$\vee (P \wedge \neg Q) \vee (\neg P \wedge \neg Q) \qquad (3)$$

Similarly

$$P \downarrow Q \Leftrightarrow \neg(P \vee Q) \Leftrightarrow \neg P \wedge \neg Q \Leftrightarrow (\neg P \vee Q)$$
$$\wedge (P \vee \neg Q) \wedge (\neg P \vee \neg Q) \qquad (4)$$

EXERCISES 1-2.14

1 If $A(P, Q, R)$ is given by $P \uparrow (Q \wedge \neg(R \downarrow P))$, find its dual $A^*(P, Q, R)$. Also find formulas which are equivalent to A and A^*, but which contain the connectives $\wedge, \vee$, and $\neg$ only.

2 Express $P \rightarrow (\neg P \rightarrow Q)$ in terms of $\uparrow$ only. Express the same formula in terms of $\downarrow$ only.

3 Express $P \uparrow Q$ in terms of $\downarrow$ only.

1-2.15   Two-state Devices and Statement Logic

The statement logic that we have discussed so far is called *two-valued logic*, because we admit only those statements having a truth value of true or false. A similar situation exists in various electrical and mechanical devices which are assumed to be in one of two possible configurations; for this reason, they are called two-state devices. We first give several examples of such commonly known devices and then show their connection to two-valued logic.

An electric switch which is used for turning "on" and "off" an electric light is a two-state device. Normally, such a switch is operated manually; however, if it is operated automatically by electric power, we say the switch is relay-operated. A vacuum tube or a transistor is another two-state device in which the current is either passing (conducting) or not passing (nonconducting). A mechanical clutch can be engaged or disengaged. A small doughnut-shaped metal disc with a wire coil wrapped around it (called a magnetic core in computers) may be magnetized in one direction if the current is passed through the coil in one way and may be magnetized in the opposite direction if the current is reversed. Many other examples of two-state devices can be cited. A general discussion of such devices can be given by replacing the word "switch" by the word "gate" to mean a device which permits or stops the flow of not only electric current but any quantity that can go through the device, such as water, information, persons, etc.

Let us first consider the example of an electric lamp controlled by a mechanical switch. Such a circuit is displayed in Fig. 1-2.3. When the switch p is open, there is no current flowing in the circuit and the lamp s is "off." When p is closed, the lamp s is "on." The state of the switch and the lamp can be represented by the table of combinations in Fig. 1-2.3. Let us denote the statements as

P: The switch p is closed.

S: The lamp s is on.

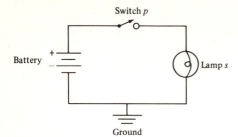

FIGURE 1-2.3 A switch as a two-state device.

State of switch p	State of light s
closed	on
open	off

Then we can rewrite the table of Fig. 1-2.3 as

$p(P)$	$s(S)$
1	1
0	0

Throughout this section we shall denote the truth values of statements $P, Q, \ldots$ by 1 and 0 in place of T and F respectively. At the same time, the input switches such as p or the output indicator such as the lamp s will be assigned the values 1 and 0 to correspond to the states when the current is flowing or not flowing. In such cases the table shown here can be understood to be either a truth table or a table that relates the input and the output values.

Next, consider an extension of the preceding circuit in which we have two switches p and q in series. The lamp s is turned on whenever both the switches p and q are closed. Such a circuit with its table of combinations is shown in Fig. 1-2.4. In the table, we have used the statements

$$P: \text{The switch } p \text{ is closed.}$$

$$Q: \text{The switch } q \text{ is closed.}$$

$$S: \text{The light } s \text{ is on.}$$

From the table it is clear that $P \wedge Q \Leftrightarrow S$.

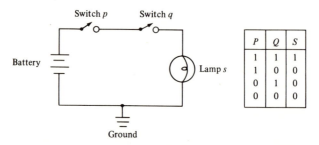

P	Q	S
1	1	1
1	0	0
0	1	0
0	0	0

FIGURE 1-2.4 A two-state device for AND logic.

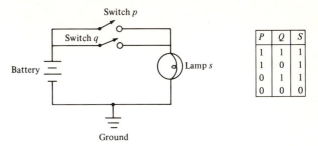

FIGURE 1-2.5 A two-state device for OR logic.

P	Q	S
1	1	1
1	0	1
0	1	1
0	0	0

Figure 1-2.5 contains a circuit and its associated table of combinations in which two switches are connected in parallel. From the table it is clear that $P \vee Q \Leftrightarrow S$.

We have just shown how the connectives $\wedge$ and $\vee$ correspond to switches connected in series and in parallel, respectively.

We now consider an example of a switch controlled by a relay. A simplified configuration and its associated table of combinations are given in Fig. 1-2.6. When the switch p is open (P is false, because we shall use P: The switch p is closed.), no current flows and the contact q which is normally closed remains closed and the contact r remains open. When p is closed, the current will flow from the battery through the coil which will cause the movement of a relay armature, which in turn causes the springs to move downward and the normally closed contact q to open while the normally open contact r closes. If p is opened, then the contact q closes and r opens because the spring moves upward to its original position. Thus with the statements P, Q, and R denoting the switches p, q, and r to be closed respectively, we can represent the operation of the device by the table of combinations in Fig. 1-2.6. In fact, the switches q and r are always in the opposite states, that is, $Q \Leftrightarrow \neg R$, $Q \Leftrightarrow \neg P$, and $R \Leftrightarrow P$. Note that the output Q is the negation of the input P.

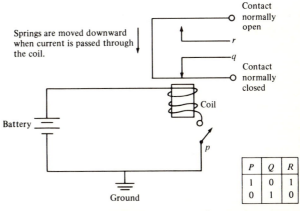

P	Q	R
1	0	1
0	1	0

FIGURE 1-2.6 A relay-switching device.

Instead of representing the logical connectives $\neg$, $\vee$, and $\wedge$ by the circuits just given or by some other equivalent circuits (consisting of semiconductor devices, for example), they are generally represented by block diagrams or *gates*. Each gate has one or more input wires and one output wire.

The logical connectives $\neg$, $\vee$, and $\wedge$ will be denoted by the symbols $^-$, $+$, and $\cdot$ respectively in the remainder of this section. This denotation is in keeping with the terminology used in switching theory.

The block-diagram symbol for an *OR* gate is shown in Fig. 1-2.7 along with the table of combinations relating the inputs and output of the gate. Any such gate is also called a *module*.

Figure 1-2.8 shows the block-diagram symbol for an *AND* gate as well as its associated table of combinations.

The negation operator can be represented by the block diagram in Fig. 1-2.9.

The block diagrams not only replace switches and relays but can also be used to represent "gates" in a more general sense. We may use p to denote voltage potential of an input which is "high" or "low" to allow a transistor to be in a conducting or nonconducting state. It is therefore convenient to use these modules and interpret the symbols according to the context. The number of inputs to *OR* gates and *AND* gates can be extended to more than 2.

The above modules, or gates, can be interconnected to realize various logical expressions. These systems of modules are known as logic or combinational networks. Figure 1-2.10a shows a logic network with three inputs a, b, and c and an output expression $(a + b) \cdot c$. Networks which form expressions $(a \cdot \bar{b}) + (\bar{a} \cdot b)$ and $(a + b) \cdot (\bar{a} + \bar{b})$ are given in Fig. 1-2.10b and c respectively.

Input		Output
p	q	$r(p + q)$
1	1	1
1	0	1
0	1	1
0	0	0

FIGURE 1-2.7   An *OR* gate.

Input		Output
p	q	$r(p \cdot q)$
1	1	1
1	0	0
0	1	0
0	0	0

FIGURE 1-2.8   An *AND* gate.

Input	Output
p	$r(\bar{p})$
1	0
0	1

FIGURE 1-2.9   A *NOT* gate.

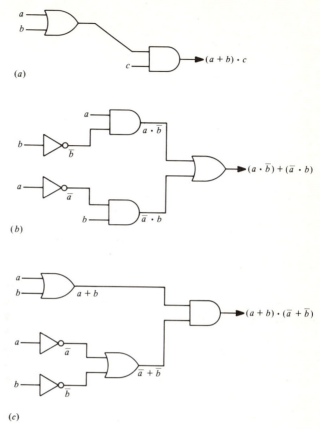

FIGURE 1-2.10 Logic networks. (a) Logic network for $(a + b) \cdot c$. (b) Logic network for $a \cdot \bar{b} + \bar{a} \cdot b$. (c) Logic network for $(a + b) \cdot (\bar{a} + \bar{b})$.

In the remainder of this section it is assumed that a variable and its negation are available without having to use an inverter. The mechanical relay was an example of a device which supplied both. There are other basic transistor devices which also supply both.

In order to simplify expressions by reducing the number of parentheses used, we specify that $\cdot$ has precedence over $+$. For example, $(a \cdot b) + (c \cdot d)$ will be written as $a \cdot b + c \cdot d$.

Consider the logical expression $a \cdot b + c \cdot d$, which consists of a disjunction of two conjunctions. A logic network to realize this expression can be a two-level network as shown in Fig. 1-2.11a. A *two-level network* is one in which the longest path through which information must pass from input to output is two gates. A two-level network consisting of AND gates at the input stage followed by OR gates at the output stage is sometimes called a *sum-of-products* (AND-to-OR) *network*.

Another possibility in a two-level network is to have OR gates at the input stage followed by AND gates at the output of the network. Such a configuration

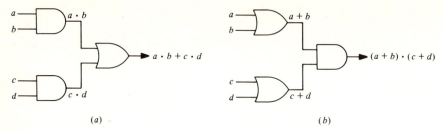

FIGURE 1-2.11 Two-level networks. (a) AND-to-OR logic network. (b) OR-to-AND logic network.

is shown for the expression $(a + b) \cdot (c + d)$ in Fig. 1-2.11b and is called a *product-of-sums* (OR-to-AND) *network*.

Other types of gates frequently used in computers are NOR gates and $NAND$ gates. Figure 1-2.12a represents a NOR gate and its associated table. Figure 1-2.12b is an equivalent representation of a NOR gate consisting of an OR gate followed by an inverter.

Figure 1-2.13a shows a $NAND$ gate with its table. The other part of the diagram is an equivalent $NAND$ gate representation consisting of an AND gate followed by an inverter.

In Sec. 1-2.14 it was shown that each of the connectives $NAND$ ($\uparrow$) and NOR ($\downarrow$) is functionally complete; either can be used to obtain the AND, OR, and NOT operations. The realizations of these operations in terms of $NAND$ gates and NOR gates only are given in Figs. 1-2.14 and 1-2.15 respectively. The

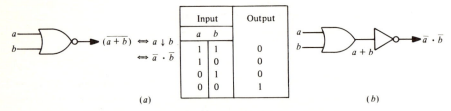

FIGURE 1-2.12 A NOR gate. (a) Block-diagram symbol and truth table for a NOR gate. (b) Equivalent NOR gate network.

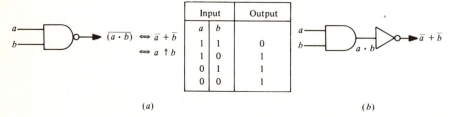

FIGURE 1-2.13 A $NAND$ gate. (a) Block-diagram symbol and truth table for a $NAND$ gate. (b) Equivalent $NAND$ gate network.

use of a single type of gate such as *NAND* or *NOR* is often preferred to a variety of gate types because it is cheaper to produce and maintain just one type of gate.

One method used to produce a circuit containing only *NAND* or only *NOR* gates is to replace the *AND*, *OR*, and *NOT* gates by NAND or NOR gates, according to Figs. 1-2.14 and 1-2.15. This replacement often results in a circuit which contains more *NAND* or *NOR* gates than necessary. There are other techniques to generate equivalent circuits containing fewer *NAND* or *NOR* gates. As an example, each of the circuits in Fig. 1-2.11, if substituted according to Figs. 1-2.14 and 1-2.15, would require nine gates. But Fig. 1-2.16 contains different realizations of the same expressions, using only three gates.

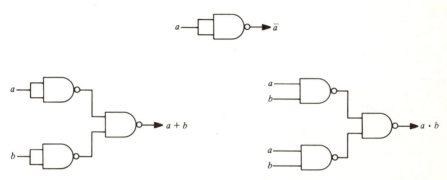

FIGURE 1-2.14. *NAND* gate generation of $+$, $\cdot$, and $^-$ operations.

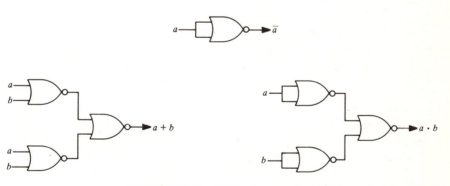

FIGURE 1-2.15. *NOR* gate generation of $+$, $\cdot$, and $^-$ operations.

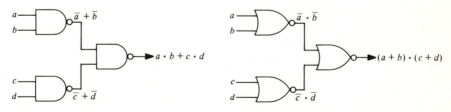

FIGURE 1-2.16. Two-level *NAND* and *NOR* gate networks.

So far we have discussed certain elements which correspond to some of the connectives of statement logic. Normally, if a formula containing these connectives is given, we can physically realize a circuit that corresponds to the formula by replacing the connectives by the appropriate gates and the variables by certain physical quantities such as voltage, current, etc. This method may, however, not yield the best design from the point of view of using a minimum number of gates, or the design it yields may not be a minimal design in some other sense. Sometimes even the formula may not be available and all we may have is its truth table. Even in this case, we may be required to physically realize the formula, not in any manner, but in some minimal way. The design procedure in both cases consists of the following steps:

1 Express the given information in terms of logical variables.
2 Get a formula for the required output in terms of the variables defined in step 1, using the logical connectives.
3 Obtain a formula which is logically equivalent to the one formed in step 2 and which will result in a least expensive (minimal) physical realization.
4 Replace the logical connectives in the formula in step 3 by proper logic blocks.

A discussion of step 3 is considered in some detail in Chap. 4. Steps 1 and 2 are explained by means of an example.

EXAMPLE 1   A certain government installation has an intruder alarm system which is to be operative only if a manual master switch situated at a security office is in the closed position. If this master switch is on (i.e., closed), an alarm will be sounded if a door to a restricted-access area within the installation is disturbed, or if the main gates to the installation are opened without the security officer first turning a special switch to the closed position. The restricted-access area door is equipped with a sensing device that causes a switch to set off the alarm if this door is disturbed in any way whenever the master switch is closed. However, the main gates are opened during daytime hours to allow the public to enter the installation grounds. Furthermore, at certain specified time intervals during a 24-hour period, the master switch is turned off to allow the authorized personnel to enter or leave the restricted-access area. During the period when the main gates are open and the master switch is turned off, it is required that some automatic recording instrument make an entry every time the door to the restricted-access area is opened.

SOLUTION   *Step 1*   Let us first designate each primary statement by a variable. This assignment will permit us to consider the assignment of all possible truth values to the variables. Thus let

A: The alarm will be given.

M: The manual master switch is closed.

G: The main gates to the installation are open.

R: The restricted-area door has been disturbed.

S: The special switch is closed.

E: The recording equipment is activated.

Step 2   The output variables are A and E. The conditions given in the problem require that

$$A \Leftrightarrow M \cdot (R + (G \cdot \bar{S}))$$
$$E \Leftrightarrow \bar{M} \cdot G \cdot R \qquad ////$$

EXERCISES   1-2.15

1   Construct a circuit diagram for a simple elevator control circuit which operates as follows. When a person pushes the button to summon the elevator to a floor, the elevator responds to this request unless it is already answering a previous call to another floor. In this latter case, the request is ignored. Assume that there are only three floors in the building.

2   For the formula $(P \wedge Q) \vee (\neg R \wedge \neg P)$, draw a corresponding circuit diagram using (*a*) *NOT, AND,* and *OR* gates; (*b*) *NAND* gates only.

EXERCISES   1-2

1   Show the equivalences (1) to (9) listed in Table 1-2.15 of Sec. 1-2.9.

2   Show the implications (1) to (12) listed in Table 1-2.17 of Sec. 1-2.11.

3   Show the following

$$\neg(P \uparrow Q) \Leftrightarrow \neg P \downarrow \neg Q \qquad \neg(P \downarrow Q) \Leftrightarrow \neg P \uparrow \neg Q$$

4   Write a formula which is equivalent to the formula

$$P \wedge (Q \rightleftarrows R)$$

and contains the connective *NAND* ($\uparrow$) only. Obtain an equivalent formula which contains the connective *NOR* ($\downarrow$) only.

5   Show that $P \wedge \neg P \wedge Q \Rightarrow R$ and $R \Rightarrow P \vee \neg P \vee Q$.

6   Show the equivalences (1) to (3) given in Sec. 1-2.14.

7   Show that the set $\{\neg, \rightarrow\}$ is functionally complete.

8   A connective denoted by $\dashrightarrow$ is defined by Table 1-2.21. Show that $\{\neg, \dashrightarrow\}$ is functionally complete.

9   Show the following equivalences.
   (*a*) $A \rightarrow (P \vee C) \Leftrightarrow (A \wedge \neg P) \rightarrow C$
   (*b*) $(P \rightarrow C) \wedge (Q \rightarrow C) \Leftrightarrow (P \vee Q) \rightarrow C$
   (*c*) $((Q \wedge A) \rightarrow C) \wedge (A \rightarrow (P \vee C)) \Leftrightarrow (A \wedge (P \rightarrow Q)) \rightarrow C$
   (*d*) $((P \wedge Q \wedge A) \rightarrow C) \wedge (A \rightarrow (P \vee Q \vee C)) \Leftrightarrow (A \wedge (P \rightleftarrows Q)) \rightarrow C$
   (See Sec. 1-4.4 for application of these equivalences.)

Table 1-2.21

P	Q	$P \dashrightarrow Q$
T	T	T
T	F	T
F	T	F
F	F	T

10 Obtain formulas having the simplest possible form which are equivalent to the formulas given here.

(a) $((P \rightarrow Q) \rightleftarrows (\neg Q \rightarrow \neg P)) \wedge R$
(b) $P \vee (\neg P \vee (Q \wedge \neg Q))$
(c) $(P \wedge (Q \wedge S)) \vee (\neg P \wedge (Q \wedge S))$

11 A chemical plant produces sulfuric acid with a pH value in the range 2.5 to 3.0. There is a main tank in which the acid is held while it is being diluted or heated (concentrated) to put it within this range. If an output valve which empties the tank is open, no heating or diluting can take place because the current batch is being moved out of the tank for final storage. Dilution will occur when the pH is less than 2.5 (as long as the tank is not full) and also whenever the level of the liquid remains below a specified level (the tank must be filled somehow after it has been emptied). Heating will take place when the pH is greater than 3.0 as long as the tank is not full. (A full tank would spill over during the agitation caused by vigorous heating.)

Express the control circuit as block diagrams for both the heating control and the dilution control.

1-3 NORMAL FORMS

Let $A(P_1, P_2, \ldots, P_n)$ be a statement formula where $P_1, P_2, \ldots, P_n$ are the atomic variables. If we consider all possible assignments of the truth values to $P_1, P_2, \ldots, P_n$ and obtain the resulting truth values of the formula A, then we get the truth table for A. Such a truth table contains 2^n rows. The formula may have the truth value T for all possible assignments of the truth values to the variables $P_1, P_2, \ldots, P_n$. In this case, A is said to be identically true, or a tautology. If A has the truth value F for all possible assignments of the truth values to $P_1, P_2, \ldots, P_n$, then A is said to be identically false, or a contradiction. Finally, if A has the truth value T for at least one combination of truth values assigned to $P_1, P_2, \ldots, P_n$, then A is said to be *satisfiable*.

The problem of determining, in a finite number of steps, whether a given statement formula is a tautology or a contradiction or at least satisfiable is known as a *decision problem*. Obviously, the construction of truth tables involves a finite number of steps, and, as such, a decision problem in the statement calculus always has a solution. Similarly, decision problems can be posed for other logical systems, particularly for the predicate calculus. However, in the latter case, the solution of the decision problem may not be simple.

As was mentioned earlier, the construction of truth tables may not be practical, even with the aid of a computer. We therefore consider other procedures known as reduction to normal forms.

1-3.1 Disjunctive Normal Forms

It will be convenient to use the word "product" in place of "conjunction" and "sum" in place of "disjunction" in our current discussion.

A product of the variables and their negations in a formula is called an *elementary product*. Similarly, a sum of the variables and their negations is called an *elementary sum*.

Let P and Q be any two atomic variables. Then P, $\neg P \wedge Q$, $\neg Q \wedge P \wedge$

$\neg P$, $P \wedge \neg P$, and $Q \wedge \neg P$ are some examples of elementary products. On the other hand, P, $\neg P \vee Q$, $\neg Q \vee P \vee \neg P$, $P \vee \neg P$, and $Q \vee \neg P$ are examples of elementary sums of the two variables. Any part of an elementary sum or product which is itself an elementary sum or product is called a *factor* of the original elementary sum or product. Thus $\neg Q$, $P \wedge \neg P$, and $\neg Q \wedge P$ are some of the factors of $\neg Q \wedge P \wedge \neg P$. The following statements hold for elementary sums and products.

> A necessary and sufficient condition for an elementary product to be identically false is that it contain at least one pair of factors in which one is the negation of the other.

> A necessary and sufficient condition for an elementary sum to be identically true is that it contain at least one pair of factors in which one is the negation of the other.

We shall now prove the first of these two statements. The proof of the second will follow along the same lines.

We know that for any variable P, $P \wedge \neg P$ is identically false. Hence if $P \wedge \neg P$ appears in the elementary product, then the product is identically false. On the other hand, if an elementary product is identically false and does not contain at least one factor of this type, then we can assign truth values T and F to variables and negated variables, respectively, that appear in the product. This assignment would mean that the elementary product has the truth value T. But that statement is contrary to our assumption. Hence the statement follows.

A formula which is equivalent to a given formula and which consists of a sum of elementary products is called a *disjunctive normal form* of the given formula.

We shall first discuss a procedure by which one can obtain a disjunctive normal form of a given formula. It has already been shown that if the connectives $\rightarrow$ and $\rightleftarrows$ appear in the given formula, then an equivalent formula can be obtained in which "$\rightarrow$" and "$\rightleftarrows$" are replaced by $\wedge$, $\vee$, and $\neg$. This statement would be true of any other connective yet undefined. The truth of this statement will become apparent after our discussion of principal disjunctive normal forms. Therefore, there is no loss of generality in assuming that the given formula contains the connectives $\wedge$, $\vee$, and $\neg$ only.

If the negation is applied to the formula or to a part of the formula and not to the variables appearing in it, then by using De Morgan's laws an equivalent formula can be obtained in which the negation is applied to the variables only. After this step, the formula obtained may still fail to be in disjunctive normal form because there may be some parts of it which are products of sums. By repeated application of the distributive laws we obtain the required normal form.

EXAMPLE 1   Obtain disjunctive normal forms of (a) $P \wedge (P \rightarrow Q)$; (b) $\neg(P \vee Q) \rightleftarrows (P \wedge Q)$.

SOLUTION

(a) $P \wedge (P \rightarrow Q) \Leftrightarrow P \wedge (\neg P \vee Q) \Leftrightarrow (P \wedge \neg P) \vee (P \wedge Q)$
(b) $\neg(P \vee Q) \rightleftarrows (P \wedge Q)$

$$\Leftrightarrow (\neg(P \vee Q) \wedge (P \wedge Q)) \vee ((P \vee Q) \wedge \neg(P \wedge Q))$$

[using $R \rightleftarrows S \Leftrightarrow (R \wedge S) \vee (\neg R \wedge \neg S)$]

$$\Leftrightarrow (\neg P \wedge \neg Q \wedge P \wedge Q) \vee ((P \vee Q) \wedge (\neg P \vee \neg Q))$$

$$\Leftrightarrow (\neg P \wedge \neg Q \wedge P \wedge Q) \vee ((P \vee Q) \wedge \neg P)$$

$$\vee ((P \vee Q) \wedge \neg Q)$$

$$\Leftrightarrow (\neg P \wedge \neg Q \wedge P \wedge Q) \vee (P \wedge \neg P) \vee (Q \wedge \neg P)$$

$$\vee (P \wedge \neg Q) \vee (Q \wedge \neg Q)$$

which is the required disjunctive normal form.   ////

The disjunctive normal form of a given formula is not unique. In fact, different disjunctive normal forms can be obtained for a given formula if the distributive laws are applied in different ways. Apart from this fact, the factors in each elementary product, as well as the factors in the sum, can be commuted. However, we shall not consider as distinct the various disjunctive normal forms obtained by reordering the factors either in the elementary products or in the sums.

Consider the formula $P \vee (Q \wedge R)$. Here the formula is already in the disjunctive normal form. However, we may write

$$P \vee (Q \wedge R) \Leftrightarrow (P \vee Q) \wedge (P \vee R) \Leftrightarrow (P \wedge P)$$

$$\vee (P \wedge Q) \vee (P \wedge R) \vee (Q \wedge R)$$

the last equivalent formula being another equivalent disjunctive normal form. Of course, different disjunctive normal forms of the same formula are equivalent. In order to arrive at a unique normal form of a given formula, we introduce the principal disjunctive normal form in Sec. 1-3.3.

Finally, we remark that a given formula is identically false if every elementary product appearing in its disjunctive normal form is identically false. For the assumption to be true, every elementary product would have to have at least two factors, of which one is the negation of the other.

1-3.2 Conjunctive Normal Forms

A formula which is equivalent to a given formula and which consists of a product of elementary sums is called a *conjunctive normal form* of the given formula.

The method for obtaining a conjunctive normal form of a given formula is similar to the one given for disjunctive normal forms and will be demonstrated by examples. Again, the conjunctive normal form is not unique. Furthermore, a given formula is identically true if every elementary sum in its conjunctive normal form is identically true. This would be the case if every elementary sum appearing in the formula had at least two factors, of which one is the negation of the other.

EXAMPLE 1   Obtain a conjunctive normal form of each of the formulas given in Example 1 of Sec. 1-3.1.

SOLUTION

(a) $P \wedge (P \rightarrow Q) \Leftrightarrow P \wedge (\neg P \vee Q)$. Hence $P \wedge (\neg P \vee Q)$ is a required form.

(b) $\neg(P \vee Q) \rightleftarrows (P \wedge Q) \Leftrightarrow (\neg(P \vee Q) \rightarrow (P \wedge Q)) \wedge ((P \wedge Q)$

$$\rightarrow \neg(P \vee Q))$$

$$[\text{using } R \rightleftarrows S \Leftrightarrow (R \rightarrow S) \wedge (S \rightarrow R)]$$

$$\Leftrightarrow ((P \vee Q) \vee (P \wedge Q)) \wedge (\neg(P \wedge Q)$$
$$\vee (\neg P \wedge \neg Q))$$

$$\Leftrightarrow ((P \vee Q \vee P) \wedge (P \vee Q \vee Q))$$
$$\wedge ((\neg P \vee \neg Q) \vee (\neg P \wedge \neg Q))$$

$$\Leftrightarrow (P \vee Q \vee P) \wedge (P \vee Q \vee Q)$$
$$\wedge (\neg P \vee \neg Q \vee \neg P) \wedge (\neg P \vee \neg Q \vee \neg Q)$$

////

EXAMPLE 2 Show that the formula $Q \vee (P \wedge \neg Q) \vee (\neg P \wedge \neg Q)$ is a tautology.

SOLUTION First we obtain a conjunctive normal form of the given formula.

$$Q \vee (P \wedge \neg Q) \vee (\neg P \wedge \neg Q) \Leftrightarrow Q \vee ((P \vee \neg P) \wedge \neg Q)$$

$$\Leftrightarrow (Q \vee (P \vee \neg P)) \wedge (Q \vee \neg Q)$$

$$\Leftrightarrow (Q \vee P \vee \neg P) \wedge (Q \vee \neg Q)$$

Since each of the elementary sums is a tautology, the given formula is a tautology. ////

1-3.3 Principal Disjunctive Normal Forms

Let P and Q be two statement variables. Let us construct all possible formulas which consist of conjunctions of P or its negation and conjunctions of Q or its negation. None of the formulas should contain both a variable and its negation. Furthermore, any formula which is obtained by commuting the formulas in the conjunction is not included in the list because such a formula will be equivalent to one included in the list. For example, either $P \wedge Q$ or $Q \wedge P$ is included, but not both. For two variables P and Q, there are 2^2 such formulas given by

$$P \wedge Q \qquad P \wedge \neg Q \qquad \neg P \wedge Q \qquad \text{and} \qquad \neg P \wedge \neg Q$$

These formulas are called *minterms* or Boolean conjunctions of P and Q. From the truth tables of these minterms, it is clear that no two minterms are equivalent. Each minterm has the truth value T for exactly one combination of the truth values of the variables P and Q. This fact is shown in Table 1-3.1.

We assert that if the truth table of any formula containing only the variables P and Q is known, then one can easily obtain an equivalent formula which consists of a disjunction of some of the minterms. This statement is demonstrated as follows.

For every truth value T in the truth table of the given formula, select the

Table 1-3.1

P	Q	$P \wedge Q$	$P \wedge \neg Q$	$\neg P \wedge Q$	$\neg P \wedge \neg Q$
T	T	T	F	F	F
T	F	F	T	F	F
F	T	F	F	T	F
F	F	F	F	F	T

minterm which also has the value T for the same combination of the truth values of P and Q. The disjunction of these minterms will then be equivalent to the given formula.

This discussion provides the basis for a proof that a formula containing any connective is equivalent to a formula containing $\wedge$, $\vee$, and $\neg$.

For a given formula, an equivalent formula consisting of disjunctions of minterms only is known as its *principal disjunctive normal form*. Such a normal form is also called the *sum-of-products canonical form*.

EXAMPLE 1 The truth tables for $P \to Q$, $P \vee Q$, and $\neg(P \wedge Q)$ are given in Table 1-3.2. Obtain the principal disjunctive normal forms of these formulas.

SOLUTION

$$P \to Q \Leftrightarrow (P \wedge Q) \vee (\neg P \wedge Q) \vee (\neg P \wedge \neg Q)$$

$$P \vee Q \Leftrightarrow (P \wedge Q) \vee (P \wedge \neg Q) \vee (\neg P \wedge Q)$$

$$\neg(P \wedge Q) \Leftrightarrow (P \wedge \neg Q) \vee (\neg P \wedge Q) \vee (\neg P \wedge \neg Q) \qquad ////$$

Note that the number of minterms appearing in the normal form is the same as the number of entries with the truth value T in the truth table of the given formula. Thus every formula which is not a contradiction has an equivalent principal disjunctive normal form. Further, such a normal form is unique, except for the rearrangements of the factors in the disjunctions as well as in each of the minterms. One can get a unique normal form by imposing a certain order in which the variables appear in the minterms as well as a definite order in which the minterms appear in the disjunction. In that case, if two given formulas are equivalent, then both of them must have identical principal disjunctive normal forms. Therefore, if we can devise a method other than the construction of truth tables to obtain the principal disjunctive normal form of a given formula, then

Table 1-3.2

P	Q	$P \to Q$	$P \vee Q$	$\neg(P \wedge Q)$
T	T	T	T	F
T	F	F	T	T
F	T	T	T	T
F	F	T	F	T

the same method can be used to determine whether two given formulas are equivalent.

Although our discussion of the principal disjunctive normal form was restricted to formulas containing only two variables, it is possible to define the minterms for three or more variables. Minterms for the three variables P, Q, and R are

$$P \wedge Q \wedge R \qquad P \wedge Q \wedge \neg R \qquad P \wedge \neg Q \wedge R \qquad P \wedge \neg Q \wedge \neg R$$
$$\neg P \wedge Q \wedge R \qquad \neg P \wedge Q \wedge \neg R \qquad \neg P \wedge \neg Q \wedge R \qquad \neg P \wedge \neg Q \wedge \neg R$$

These minterms satisfy properties similar to those given for two variables. An equivalent principal disjunctive normal form of any formula which depends upon the variables P, Q, and R can be obtained. Note that there are 2^3 minterms for three variables or, more generally, 2^n minterms for n variables. For any formula containing n variables which are denoted by P_1, P_2, ..., P_n, an equivalent disjunctive normal form can be obtained by selecting appropriate minterms out of the set of 2^n possible minterms.

If a formula is a tautology, then obviously all the minterms appear in its principal disjunctive normal form; it is also possible to determine whether a given formula is a tautology by obtaining its principal disjunctive normal form.

In order to obtain the principal disjunctive normal form of a given formula without constructing its truth table, one may first replace the conditionals and biconditionals by their equivalent formulas containing only $\wedge$, $\vee$, and $\neg$. Next, the negations are applied to the variables by using De Morgan's laws followed by the application of distributive laws, as was done earlier in obtaining the disjunctive or conjunctive normal forms. Any elementary product which is a contradiction is dropped. Minterms are obtained in the disjunctions by introducing the missing factors. Identical minterms appearing in the disjunctions are deleted. This procedure is demonstrated by means of examples.

EXAMPLE 2   Obtain the principal disjunctive normal forms of (a) $\neg P \vee Q$; (b) $(P \wedge Q) \vee (\neg P \wedge R) \vee (Q \wedge R)$.

SOLUTION

(a) $\neg P \vee Q \Leftrightarrow (\neg P \wedge (Q \vee \neg Q)) \vee (Q \wedge (P \vee \neg P))$

$$(A \wedge \mathbf{T} \Leftrightarrow A)$$

$\Leftrightarrow (\neg P \wedge Q) \vee (\neg P \wedge \neg Q) \vee (Q \wedge P) \vee (Q \wedge \neg P)$

(distributive laws)

$\Leftrightarrow (\neg P \wedge Q) \vee (\neg P \wedge \neg Q) \vee (P \wedge Q)$

(commutative law and $P \vee P \Leftrightarrow P$)

(See Example 1.)

(b) $(P \wedge Q) \vee (\neg P \wedge R) \vee (Q \wedge R)$

$\Leftrightarrow (P \wedge Q \wedge (R \vee \neg R)) \vee (\neg P \wedge R \wedge (Q \vee \neg Q))$
$\vee (Q \wedge R \wedge (P \vee \neg P))$

$\Leftrightarrow (P \wedge Q \wedge R) \vee (P \wedge Q \wedge \neg R) \vee (\neg P \wedge Q \wedge R)$
$\vee (\neg P \wedge \neg Q \wedge R)$ ////

EXAMPLE 3 Show that the following are equivalent formulas.

(a) $P \lor (P \land Q) \Leftrightarrow P$
(b) $P \lor (\neg P \land Q) \Leftrightarrow P \lor Q$

SOLUTION We write the principal disjunctive normal form of each formula and compare these normal forms.

(a) $P \lor (P \land Q) \Leftrightarrow (P \land (Q \lor \neg Q)) \lor (P \land Q) \Leftrightarrow (P \land Q) \lor (P \land \neg Q)$

$$P \Leftrightarrow P \land (Q \lor \neg Q) \Leftrightarrow (P \land Q) \lor (P \land \neg Q)$$

(b) $P \lor (\neg P \land Q) \Leftrightarrow (P \land (Q \lor \neg Q)) \lor (\neg P \land Q)$

$$\Leftrightarrow (P \land Q) \lor (P \land \neg Q) \lor (\neg P \land Q)$$

$$P \lor Q \Leftrightarrow (P \land (Q \lor \neg Q)) \lor (Q \land (P \lor \neg P))$$

$$\Leftrightarrow (P \land Q) \lor (P \land \neg Q) \lor (\neg P \land Q) \qquad ////$$

EXAMPLE 4 Obtain the principal disjunctive normal form of

$$P \to ((P \to Q) \land \neg(\neg Q \lor \neg P))$$

SOLUTION Using $P \to Q \Leftrightarrow \neg P \lor Q$ and De Morgan's law, we obtain

$$P \to ((P \to Q) \land \neg(\neg Q \lor \neg P))$$

$$\Leftrightarrow \neg P \lor ((\neg P \lor Q) \land (Q \land P))$$

$$\Leftrightarrow \neg P \lor (\neg P \land (Q \land P)) \lor (Q \land (Q \land P))$$

$$\Leftrightarrow \neg P \lor (Q \land P)$$

$$\Leftrightarrow (\neg P \land (Q \lor \neg Q)) \lor (Q \land P)$$

$$\Leftrightarrow (\neg P \land Q) \lor (\neg P \land \neg Q) \lor (P \land Q) \qquad ////$$

The procedure described above becomes tedious if the given formula is complicated and contains more than two or three variables. When the number of variables is large, even a comparison of two principal disjunctive normal forms becomes cumbersome. In Sec. 1-3.5, we describe an ordering procedure for the variables and a notation which make such a comparison easy. We also discuss in Chap. 2 a computer program to obtain the sum-of-products canonical form for a given formula.

1-3.4 Principal Conjunctive Normal Forms

In order to define the principal conjunctive normal form, we first define formulas which are called maxterms. For a given number of variables, the *maxterm* consists of disjunctions in which each variable or its negation, but not both, appears only once. Thus the maxterms are the duals of minterms. Either from the duality principle or directly from the truth tables, it can be ascertained that each of the maxterms has the truth value F for exactly one combination of the truth values of the variables. Also different maxterms have the truth value F for different combinations of the truth values of the variables.

For a given formula, an equivalent formula consisting of conjunctions of the maxterms only is known as its *principal conjunctive normal form*. This normal form is also called the *product-of-sums canonical form*. Every formula which is not a tautology has an equivalent principal conjunctive normal form which is unique except for the rearrangement of the factors in the maxterms as well as in their conjunctions. The method for obtaining the principal conjunctive normal form for a given formula is similar to the one described previously for the principal disjunctive normal form. In fact, all the assertions made for the principal disjunctive normal forms can also be made for the principal conjunctive normal forms by the duality principle.

If the principal disjunctive (conjunctive) normal form of a given formula A containing n variables is known, then the principal disjunctive (conjunctive) normal form of $\neg A$ will consist of the disjunction (conjunction) of the remaining minterms (maxterms) which do not appear in the principal disjunctive (conjunctive) normal form of A. From $A \Leftrightarrow \neg\neg A$ one can obtain the principal conjunctive (disjunctive) normal form of A by repeated applications of De Morgan's laws to the principal disjunctive (conjunctive) normal form of $\neg A$. This procedure will be illustrated by an example.

In order to determine whether two given formulas A and B are equivalent, one can obtain any of the principal normal forms of the two formulas and compare them. It is not necessary to assume that both formulas have the same variables. In fact, each formula can be assumed to depend upon all the variables that appear in both formulas, by introducing the missing variables and then reducing them to their principal normal forms.

EXAMPLE 1   Obtain the principal conjunctive normal form of the formula S given by $(\neg P \to R) \wedge (Q \rightleftarrows P)$.

SOLUTION

$$(\neg P \to R) \wedge (Q \rightleftarrows P)$$
$$\Leftrightarrow (P \vee R) \wedge ((Q \to P) \wedge (P \to Q))$$
$$\Leftrightarrow (P \vee R) \wedge (\neg Q \vee P) \wedge (\neg P \vee Q)$$
$$\Leftrightarrow (P \vee R \vee (Q \wedge \neg Q)) \wedge (\neg Q \vee P \vee (R \wedge \neg R))$$
$$\quad \wedge (\neg P \vee Q \vee (R \wedge \neg R))$$
$$\Leftrightarrow (P \vee Q \vee R) \wedge (P \vee \neg Q \vee R) \wedge (P \vee \neg Q \vee \neg R)$$
$$\quad \wedge (\neg P \vee Q \vee R) \wedge (\neg P \vee Q \vee \neg R)$$

Now the conjunctive normal form of $\neg S$ can easily be obtained by writing the conjunction of the remaining maxterms; thus, $\neg S$ has the principal conjunctive normal form

$$(P \vee Q \vee \neg R) \wedge (\neg P \vee \neg Q \vee R) \wedge (\neg P \vee \neg Q \vee \neg R)$$

By considering $\neg\neg S$, we obtain

$$\neg (P \vee Q \vee \neg R) \vee \neg(\neg P \vee \neg Q \vee R) \vee \neg(\neg P \vee \neg Q \vee \neg R)$$
$$\Leftrightarrow (\neg P \wedge \neg Q \wedge R) \vee (P \wedge Q \wedge \neg R) \vee (P \wedge Q \wedge R)$$

which is the principal disjunctive normal form of S. ////

EXAMPLE 2   The truth table for a formula A is given in Table 1-3.3. Determine its disjunctive and conjunctive normal forms.

SOLUTION   By choosing the minterms corresponding to each T value of A, we obtain

$$A \Leftrightarrow (P \wedge \neg Q \wedge R) \vee (\neg P \wedge Q \wedge R) \vee (\neg P \wedge Q \wedge \neg R)$$
$$\vee (\neg P \wedge \neg Q \wedge \neg R)$$

Similarly

$$A \Leftrightarrow (\neg P \vee \neg Q \vee \neg R) \wedge (\neg P \vee \neg Q \vee R) \wedge (\neg P \vee Q \vee R)$$
$$\wedge (P \vee Q \vee \neg R)$$

Here the maxterms appearing in the normal form correspond to the F values of A. The maxterms are written down by including the variable if its truth value is F and its negation if the value is T.   ////

1-3.5   Ordering and Uniqueness of Normal Forms

Given any n statement variables, let us first arrange them in some fixed order. If capital letters are used to denote the variables, then they may be arranged in alphabetical order. If subscripted letters are also used, then the following is an illustration of the order that may be used:

$$A, B, \ldots, Z, A_1, B_1, \ldots, Z_1, A_2, B_2, \ldots$$

As an example, if the variables are P_1, Q, R_3, S_1, T_2, and Q_3, then they may be arranged as

$$Q, P_1, S_1, T_2, Q_3, R_3$$

Once the variables have been arranged in a particular order, it is possible to designate them as the first variable, second variable, and so on.

Let us assume that n variables are given and are arranged in a particular order. The 2^n minterms corresponding to the n variables can be designated by $m_0, m_1, \ldots, m_{2^n-1}$. If we write the subscript of any particular minterm in binary and add an appropriate number of zeros on the left (if necessary) so that the number of digits in the subscript is exactly n, then we can obtain the corresponding minterm in the following manner. If in the ith location from the left there

Table 1-3.3

P	Q	R	A
T	T	T	F
T	T	F	F
T	F	T	T
T	F	F	F
F	T	T	T
F	T	F	T
F	F	T	F
F	F	F	T

appears 1, then the ith variable appears in the conjunction. If 0 appears in the ith location from the left, then the negation of the ith variable appears in the conjunction forming the minterm. Thus each of $m_0, m_1, \ldots, m_{2^n-1}$ corresponds to a unique minterm, which can be determined from the binary representation of the subscript. Conversely, given any minterm, one can find which of m_0, $m_1, \ldots, m_{2^n-1}$ designates it.

Let P, Q, and R be three variables arranged in that order. The corresponding minterms are denoted by $m_0, m_1, \ldots, m_7$. We can write the subscript 5 in binary as 101, and the minterm m_5 is $P \wedge \neg Q \wedge R$. Similarly m_0 corresponds to $\neg P \wedge \neg Q \wedge \neg R$. To obtain the minterm m_3, we write 3 as 11 and append a zero on the left to get 011, and m_3 is $\neg P \wedge Q \wedge R$.

If we have six variables $P_1, P_2, \ldots, P_6$, then there are $2^6 = 64$ minterms denoted by $m_0, m_1, \ldots, m_{63}$. To get a minterm, m_{38} say, we write 38 in binary as 100110; then the minterm m_{38} is $P_1 \wedge \neg P_2 \wedge \neg P_3 \wedge P_4 \wedge P_5 \wedge \neg P_6$.

Having developed a notation for the representation of the minterms, which can be further simplified by writing only the subscripts of $m_0, m_1, \ldots, m_{2^n-1}$, we designate the disjunction (sum) of minterms by the compact notation $\sum$. Using such a notation, the sum-of-products canonical form representing the disjunction of m_i, m_j, and m_k can be written down as $\sum i,j,k$. As an example, it is known that

$$(P \wedge Q) \vee (\neg P \wedge R) \vee (Q \wedge R) \Leftrightarrow (\neg P \wedge \neg Q \wedge R)$$
$$\vee (\neg P \wedge Q \wedge R) \vee (P \wedge Q \wedge \neg R) \vee (P \wedge Q \wedge R)$$

Thus we denote the principal disjunctive normal form of

$$(P \wedge Q) \vee (\neg P \wedge R) \vee (Q \wedge R)$$

as $\sum 1,3,6,7$. With this type of representation and simplification of notation, it is easy to compare two principal disjunctive normal forms.

We now proceed to obtain a similar representation for the product-of-sums (principal conjunctive normal) forms. We denote the maxterms of n variables by $M_0, M_1, \ldots, M_{2^n}-1$. Again, the maxterm corresponding to M_j, say, is obtained by writing j in binary and appending the required number of zeros to the left in order to get n digits. If 0 appears in the ith location from the left of this binary number, then the ith variable appears in the disjunction, while if 1 appears in the ith location, then the negation of the ith variable appears. Thus the binary representation of the subscript uniquely determines the maxterm, and, conversely, every binary representation of numbers between 0 and $2^n - 1$ determines a maxterm. Note that the convention regarding 1 and 0 here is the opposite of what was used for minterms. This convention is adopted with a view to connect the two principal normal forms of any given formula.

The maxterms, $M_0, M_1, \ldots, M_7$, corresponding to three variables P, Q, and R, are

$$P \vee Q \vee R \qquad P \vee Q \vee \neg R \qquad P \vee \neg Q \vee R \qquad P \vee \neg Q \vee \neg R$$
$$\neg P \vee Q \vee R \qquad \neg P \vee Q \vee \neg R \qquad \neg P \vee \neg Q \vee R \qquad \neg P \vee \neg Q \vee \neg R$$

As before, further simplification is introduced by using $\prod$ to denote the conjunction (product) of maxterms. Thus $\prod i,j,k$ represents the conjunction of maxterms M_i, M_j, M_k.

To illustrate this discussion, we consider $(P \wedge Q) \vee (\neg P \wedge R)$. We obtain its principal conjunctive normal form as follows.

$(P \wedge Q) \vee (\neg P \wedge R)$

$\Leftrightarrow ((P \wedge Q) \vee \neg P) \wedge ((P \wedge Q) \vee R)$

$\Leftrightarrow (P \vee \neg P) \wedge (Q \vee \neg P) \wedge (P \vee R) \wedge (Q \vee R)$

$\Leftrightarrow (Q \vee \neg P \vee (R \wedge \neg R)) \wedge (P \vee R \vee (Q \wedge \neg Q))$

$\qquad \wedge (Q \vee R \vee (P \wedge \neg P))$

$\Leftrightarrow (Q \vee \neg P \vee R) \wedge (Q \vee \neg P \vee \neg R) \wedge (P \vee R \vee Q)$

$\qquad \wedge (P \vee R \vee \neg Q) \wedge (Q \vee R \vee P) \wedge (Q \vee R \vee \neg P)$

$\Leftrightarrow (\neg P \vee Q \vee R) \wedge (\neg P \vee Q \vee \neg R) \wedge (P \vee Q \vee R)$

$\qquad \wedge (P \vee \neg Q \vee R)$

Thus the product-of-sums canonical form of $(P \wedge Q) \vee (\neg P \wedge R)$ can be represented as $\prod 0,2,4,5$. Note that its disjunctive normal form is

$$(P \wedge Q \wedge R) \vee (P \wedge Q \wedge \neg R) \vee (\neg P \wedge Q \wedge R)$$

$$\vee (\neg P \wedge \neg Q \wedge R) \Leftrightarrow \sum 1,3,6,7$$

More generally, given any formula containing n variables and using the above notations to represent the equivalent principal disjunctive and conjunctive normal forms, we see clearly that all numbers lying between 0 and $2^n - 1$ which do not appear in one normal form will appear in the other. This statement follows from the principle of duality and the discussion given earlier regarding the relation between these two principal normal forms.

EXERCISES   1-3.5

1   Write equivalent forms for the following formulas in which negations are applied to the variables only.
   (a) $\neg(P \vee Q)$ (d) $\neg(P \rightleftarrows Q)$
   (b) $\neg(P \wedge Q)$ (e) $\neg(P \uparrow Q)$
   (c) $\neg(P \rightarrow Q)$ (f) $\neg(P \downarrow Q)$
   Obtain the principal conjunctive normal forms of (a), (c), and (d).

2   Obtain the product-of-sums canonical forms of the following formulas.
   (a) $(P \wedge Q \wedge R) \vee (\neg P \wedge R \wedge Q) \vee (\neg P \wedge \neg Q \wedge \neg R)$
   (b) $(\neg S \wedge \neg P \wedge R \wedge Q) \vee (S \wedge P \wedge \neg R \wedge \neg Q) \vee (\neg S \wedge P \wedge R \wedge \neg Q) \vee$
       $(Q \wedge \neg P \wedge \neg R \wedge S) \vee (P \wedge \neg S \wedge \neg R \wedge Q)$
   (c) $(P \wedge Q) \vee (\neg P \wedge Q) \vee (P \wedge \neg Q)$
   (d) $(P \wedge Q) \vee (\neg P \wedge Q \wedge R)$

3   Obtain the principal disjunctive and conjunctive normal forms of the following formulas.
   (a) $(\neg P \vee \neg Q) \rightarrow (P \rightleftarrows \neg Q)$ (d) $(P \rightarrow (Q \wedge R)) \wedge (\neg P \rightarrow (\neg Q \wedge \neg R))$
   (b) $Q \wedge (P \vee \neg Q)$ (e) $P \rightarrow (P \wedge (Q \rightarrow P))$
   (c) $P \vee (\neg P \rightarrow (Q \vee (\neg Q \rightarrow R)))$ (f) $(Q \rightarrow P) \wedge (\neg P \wedge Q)$
   Which of the above formulas are tautologies?

1-3.6 Completely Parenthesized Infix Notation and Polish Notation

In this section we discuss the problem of translating a given logical expression or a statement formula into some target language such as machine language or assembly language. Also, from a given statement formula we wish to determine mechanically its truth value for various assignments of truth values to its variables. In order to do such an evaluation, it is first necessary for us to examine our notations, symbols, and rules for writing a well-formed formula.

In writing a statement formula, parentheses have been used whenever necessary. In fact, our definition of well-formed formulas as given in Sec. 1-2.7 imposes upon us the condition that a certain number of parentheses must be used. In order that the number of parentheses not become excessively large, we developed certain conventions. The first such convention developed and incorporated in the definition of the well-formed formula stated that if A is a well-formed formula, then $\neg A$ is a well-formed formula. No parentheses were used with A. This means $\neg$ has the highest precedence and applies to any well-formed formula following it. In this way, $\neg P \vee Q$ is understood to mean $(\neg P) \vee Q$, not $\neg(P \vee Q)$. Also $\neg(P \vee Q) \wedge R$ stands for $(\neg(P \vee Q) \wedge R)$. The next convention suggested was that the outermost parentheses of an expression be dropped, so that $(P \wedge Q) \vee R$ was taken to be a well-formed formula instead of $((P \wedge Q) \vee R)$ as required by the original definition. Nested parentheses have also been used. It is understood that the proper subexpression to be considered first is obtained by scanning from left to right up to the first right parenthesis encountered and then scanning left until a left parenthesis is detected. If an evaluation of such an expression is to be done mechanically, the number of parentheses should be reduced by adopting certain conventions so that an excessive number of scannings of the expression is avoided.

One method of reducing the number of parentheses further is to prescribe an order of precedence for the connectives. Once this order is prescribed, further reductions can be made by requiring that for any two binary connectives appearing in a formula which have the same precedence, the left one is evaluated first. The same requirement can be stated by saying that the binary connectives are *left-associative*, while $\neg$ is *right-associative*. Such a convention is commonly used in arithmetic; for example, $4 + 6 \times 3 - 7$ stands for $[4 + (6 \times 3)] - 7$.

Let us restrict ourselves to formulas containing the connectives $\neg$, $\wedge$, and $\vee$ and assume this order of precedence: $\neg$, then $\wedge$, and then $\vee$. First we consider an expression which does not contain any parentheses, such as

$$P \vee \underbrace{Q \wedge R} \vee \underbrace{S \wedge T}$$
$$\underbrace{}_{1} \quad \underbrace{}_{2}$$
$$\underbrace{}_{3}$$
$$\underbrace{}_{4}$$

According to our convention, the above expression stands for $(P \vee (Q \wedge R)) \vee (S \wedge T)$. For the evaluation of this expression we must scan from left to right repeatedly. The numbers below the subexpressions indicate the steps of such an evaluation. This process of evaluation is inefficient because of the repeated scanning that must be done.

If there are parentheses in an expression, then the order of precedence is altered by the parentheses. For example, in $(P \lor Q) \land R$ we evaluate first $P \lor Q$ and then $(P \lor Q) \land R$. In fact, it is possible to write expressions which make the order of evaluation of subexpressions independent of the precedence of the connectives. This task is accomplished by parenthesizing subexpressions in such a way that corresponding to each connective there is a pair of parentheses. This pair encloses the operator (connective) and its operands. We now define the *parenthetical level* of an operator as the total number of pairs of parentheses that surround it. A pair of parentheses has the same parenthetical level as that of the operator to which it corresponds, i.e., of the operator which is immediately enclosed by this pair. Such an expression is called a *fully parenthesized expression*. For example, in the fully parenthesized expression

$$(P \lor ((Q \land R) \land (\neg S)))$$
$$1 3 2 3$$

the integers below the operators specify the parenthetical level of each operator. When such an expression is evaluated, the subexpression containing the operator with the highest parenthetical level is evaluated first. In the case where more than one operator has the highest parenthetical level (as in the above example), we evaluate them one after the other from left to right. Once the subexpressions containing operators at the highest parenthetical level have been evaluated, the subexpressions containing the operators at the next highest level are evaluated in the same way. Thus, in the above example the subexpressions are evaluated in the following order

$$(Q \land R) \qquad (\neg S) \qquad ((Q \land R) \land (\neg S)) \qquad (P \lor ((Q \land R) \land (\neg S)))$$

As mentioned earlier, for a fully parenthesized expression no convention regarding the order of precedence of an operator is needed.

In the one case when the order of precedence of the operators is prescribed and the expressions are partly parenthesized, or in the other case when the expressions are fully parenthesized, a repeated scanning from left to right is still needed in order to evaluate an expression. The reason is that the operators appear along with the operands inside the expression. The notation used so far was to write the operator (at least the binary) between the operands, for example, $P \land Q$. Such a notation is called an *infix notation*. Repeated scanning is avoided if the infix expression is converted first to an equivalent parenthesis-free *suffix* or *prefix* expression in which the subexpressions have the form

operand   operand   operator

or

operator   operand   operand

in place of an infix form where we have

operand   operator   operand

This type of notation is known as *Łukasiewiczian notation* (due to the Polish logician Jan Łukasiewicz) or "reverse Polish" or "Polish" notation. For example, the expressions given in each row of Table 1-3.4 are equivalent.

Table 1-3.4

Infix	Suffix	Prefix
A	A	A
$A \lor B$	$AB \lor$	$\lor AB$
$A \lor B \lor C$	$AB \lor C \lor$	$\lor \lor ABC$
$A \lor (B \lor C)$	$ABC \lor \lor$	$\lor A \lor BC$
$A \lor B \land C$	$ABC \land \lor$	$\lor A \land BC$
$A \land (B \lor C)$	$ABC \lor \land$	$\land A \lor BC$
$A \land B \land C$	$AB \land C \land$	$\land \land ABC$
$A \land \neg B$	$AB \neg \land$	$\land A \neg B$
$A \land (B \lor \neg C)$	$ABC \neg \lor \land$	$\land A \lor B \neg C$

Note that in both the suffix and prefix equivalents of an infix expression the variables are in the same relative position. The only differences are that the expressions in suffix or prefix form are parenthesis-free and that the operators are rearranged according to the rules of precedence for the operators and to the overruling of the precedence rules by the use of parentheses.

A fully parenthesized infix expression can be directly translated to prefix notation by beginning with the conversion of the inner parenthesized subexpression and then proceeding toward the outside of the expression. In the case of the fully parenthesized expression

$$(A \lor ((B \land C) \land D))$$
$$1 \qquad 3 \qquad 2$$

the innermost parenthesized subexpression of level 3 is

$$(B \land C)$$

and it is converted to $\land BC$. This prefix subexpression becomes the first operand of the operator $\land$ at level 2. Therefore the subexpression $\land BC \land D$ of level 2 is converted to the prefix equivalent of $\land \land BCD$, and finally at level 1 the term $A \lor \land \land BCD$ is converted to the final prefix form of $\lor A \land \land BCD$.

Programmers, of course, do not program expressions in fully parenthesized form. Certain FORTRAN and other compilers initially convert partially parenthesized expressions to a fully parenthesized form before conversion to a suffix form is performed. (Suffix form seems to be more convenient for some compilers.)

Let us consider the problem of mechanically converting a *parenthesis-free* expression (containing $\lor$, $\land$, and $\neg$) into prefix form. As was mentioned previously, only the operators are rearranged in order to obtain the prefix Polish equivalent. In scanning right to left, the rightmost operator having the highest precedence will be the first operator to be encountered in the prefix string. The next highest precedence operator will be the second operator to be encountered in the expression. Note that for infix expressions if we do not specify that a leftmost (or rightmost in the case of the negation operator) operator has precedence over other operators of equal precedence, then the prefix equivalent is not unique. For example, the expression $A \lor B \lor C$ would be converted to $\lor A \lor BC$ or $\lor \lor ABC$ if no mention was made that the leftmost operator $\lor$ in the infix string has precedence over the remaining operator. From this fact it is clear that when we scan a prefix expression from right to left, we encounter the operators in the same order in which we would have evaluated them by following the precedence convention for operators in the infix expression. For example, the prefix equivalent of $A \vee B \wedge C$, $\vee A \wedge BC$, where the operator $\wedge$ is encountered before $\vee$ in a right-to-left scan, indicates that the conjunction is to be evaluated before the disjunction.

In practice it is often necessary to evaluate expressions, i.e., to determine their truth value for a given set of truth values assigned to their variables. This evaluation can be done more easily by using a prefix (suffix) representation of the expression, because scanning of the expression is required in only one direction, viz., from right to left (left to right) and only once, whereas for the infix expression the scanning has to be done several times and in both directions. For example, to evaluate the prefix expression $\vee A \wedge BC$, we scan this string from right to left until we encounter $\wedge$. The two operands, viz., B and C, which appear immediately to the right of this operator are its operands, and the expression $\wedge BC$ is replaced by its truth value. Let us assume that this value is denoted by T_1. Note that T_1 is either T or F. This fact reduces the original prefix string to $\vee A T_1$. Continuing the scanning beyond T_1, the next operator we encounter is $\vee$ whose operands are A and T_1, and the evaluation results in a value which we will denote by T_2.

This method of evaluating prefix expressions can be summarized by the following four rules which are repeatedly applied until all operators have been processed.

1   Find the rightmost operator in the expression.
2   Select the two operands immediately to the right of the operator found.
3   Perform the indicated operation.
4   Replace the operator and operands with the result.

As a further example, the prefix expression $\vee A \wedge \wedge BCD$ which corresponds to the infix expression $A \vee (B \wedge C) \wedge D$ is evaluated here for values of $A = F$, $B = T$, $C = T$, and $D = T$.

Prefix form	Current operator	Current operands	Computed value
$\vee A \wedge \wedge BCD$	$\wedge$	B, C	$T_1 = T$
$\vee A \wedge T_1 D$	$\wedge$	T_1, D	$T_2 = T$
$\vee A T_2$	$\vee$	A, T_2	$T_3 = T$
T_3	—	—	

We will return to this topic in Sec. 3-4.

Note that the preceding discussion applies equally well to suffix expressions. All that is needed is to change prefix to suffix, left to right, and right to left.

EXERCISES   1-3.6

1   Write the following formulas in prefix and suffix form. The following precedence is assumed: $\rightleftarrows, \rightarrow, \vee, \wedge, \neg$ ($\neg$ having the highest precedence).

$(a)\ \ P \rightarrow Q \lor R \lor S$
$(b)\ \ Q \land \neg(R \rightleftarrows P \lor Q)$
$(c)\ \ P \land \neg R \rightarrow Q \rightleftarrows P \land Q$
$(d)\ \ \neg\neg P \lor Q \land R \lor \neg Q$

2 Convert the following prefix and suffix formulas into completely parenthesized form. Also write them in an infix form, using the above order of precedence to minimize the number of parentheses.

$(a)\ \ \rightarrow \neg P \lor Q \rightleftarrows R \neg S$
$(b)\ \ \rightarrow \rightarrow PQ \rightarrow \rightarrow QR \rightarrow PR$
$(c)\ \ P \neg P \rightarrow P \rightarrow P \rightarrow$
$(d)\ \ PQ \rightarrow RQ \rightarrow \land PR \lor \land Q \rightarrow$

1-4 THE THEORY OF INFERENCE FOR STATEMENT CALCULUS

The main function of logic is to provide rules of inference, or principles of reasoning. The theory associated with such rules is known as inference theory because it is concerned with the inferring of a conclusion from certain premises. When a conclusion is derived from a set of premises by using the accepted rules of reasoning, then such a process of derivation is called a *deduction* or a *formal proof*. In a formal proof, every rule of inference that is used at any stage in the derivation is acknowledged. In mathematical literature, the proofs given are generally *informal* in the sense that many steps in the derivation are either omitted or considered to be understood.

An important difference between the reasoning used in any general discussion and that used in mathematics is that the premises used are believed to be true either from experience or from faith, and if proper rules are followed, then one expects the conclusion to be true. In mathematics, one is solely concerned with the conclusion which is obtained by following the rules of logic. This conclusion, called a theorem, can be inferred from a set of premises, called the axioms of the theory. The truth value plays no part in the theory.

Now we come to the questions of what we mean by the rules and theory of inference. The rules of inference are criteria for determining the validity of an argument. These rules are stated in terms of the forms of the statements (premises and conclusions) involved rather than in terms of the actual statements or their truth values. Therefore, the rules will be given in terms of statement formulas rather than in terms of any specific statements. These rules are not arbitrary in the sense that they allow us to indicate as valid at least those arguments which we would normally expect to be valid. In addition, neither do they characterize as valid those arguments which we would normally consider as invalid.

In any argument, a conclusion is admitted to be true provided that the premises (assumptions, axioms, hypotheses) are accepted as true and the reasoning used in deriving the conclusion from the premises follows certain accepted rules of logical inference. Such an argument is called *sound*. In any argument, we are always concerned with its soundness. In logic the situation is slightly different, and we concentrate our attention on the study of the rules of inference by which conclusions are derived from premises. Any conclusion which is arrived at by following these rules is called a *valid conclusion*, and the argument is called a *valid argument*. The actual truth values of the premises do not play any part in the determination of the validity of the argument. In short, in logic we are concerned with the validity but not necessarily with the soundness of an argument.

1-4.1 Validity Using Truth Tables

Let A and B be two statement formulas. We say that "B *logically follows from* A" or "B is a *valid conclusion* (*consequence*) of the premise A" iff $A \to B$ is a tautology, that is, $A \Rightarrow B$.

Just as the definition of implication was extended to include a set of formulas rather than a single formula, we say that from a set of premises $\{H_1, H_2, \ldots, H_m\}$ a conclusion C follows logically iff

$$H_1 \wedge H_2 \wedge \cdots \wedge H_m \Rightarrow C \qquad (1)$$

Given a set of premises and a conclusion, it is possible to determine whether the conclusion logically follows (we shall simply say "follows") from the given premises by constructing truth tables as follows.

Let $P_1, P_2, \ldots, P_n$ be all the atomic variables appearing in the premises $H_1, H_2, \ldots, H_m$ and the conclusion C. If all possible combinations of truth values are assigned to $P_1, P_2, \ldots, P_n$ and if the truth values of $H_1, H_2, \ldots, H_m$ and C are entered in a table, then it is easy to see from such a table whether (1) is true. We look for the rows in which all $H_1, H_2, \ldots, H_m$ have the value T. If, for every such row, C also has the value T, then (1) holds. Alternatively, we may look for the rows in which C has the value F. If, in every such row, at least one of the values of $H_1, H_2, \ldots, H_m$ is F, then (1) also holds. We call such a method a "truth table technique" for the determination of the validity of a conclusion and demonstrate this technique by examples.

EXAMPLE 1 Determine whether the conclusion C follows logically from the premises H_1 and H_2.

(a) $H_1: P \to Q$ $H_2: P$ $C: Q$

(b) $H_1: P \to Q$ $H_2: \neg P$ $C: Q$

(c) $H_1: P \to Q$ $H_2: \neg(P \wedge Q)$ $C: \neg P$

(d) $H_1: \neg P$ $H_2: P \rightleftarrows Q$ $C: \neg(P \wedge Q)$

(e) $H_1: P \to Q$ $H_2: Q$ $C: P$

SOLUTION   We first construct the appropriate truth table, as shown in Table 1.4.1. For (a) we observe that the first row is the only row in which both

Table 1-4.1

P	Q	$P \to Q$	$\neg P$	$\neg Q$	$\neg(P \wedge Q)$	$P \rightleftarrows Q$
T	T	T	F	F	F	T
T	F	F	F	T	T	F
F	T	T	T	F	T	F
F	F	T	T	T	T	T

the premises have the value T. The conclusion also has the value T in that row. Hence it is valid. In (b) observe the third and fourth rows. The conclusion Q is true only in the third row, but not in the fourth, and hence the conclusion is not valid. Similarly, we can show that the conclusions are valid in (c) and (d) but not in (e).

The conclusion P in (e) does not follow logically from the premises $P \rightarrow Q$ and Q, no matter which statements in English are translated as P and Q or what the truth value of the conclusion P may be. As a particular case, consider the argument

H_1: If Canada is a country, then New York is a city.: $(P \rightarrow Q)$
H_2: New York is a city.: (Q)
Conclusion C: Canada is a country.: (P)

Note that both the premises and the conclusion have the truth value T. However, the conclusion does not follow logically from the premises. This example is chosen to emphasize the fact that we are not so much concerned with the conclusion's being true or false as we are with determining whether the conclusion follows from the premises, i.e., whether the argument is valid or invalid.   ////

Theoretically, it is possible to determine in a finite number of steps whether a conclusion follows from a given set of premises by constructing the appropriate truth table. However, this method becomes tedious when the number of atomic variables present in all the formulas representing the premises and conclusion is large. This disadvantage, coupled with the fact that the inference theory is applicable in more general situations where the truth table technique is no longer available, suggests that we should investigate other possible methods. This investigating will be done in the following sections.

EXERCISES 1-4.1

1 Show that the conclusion C follows from the premises $H_1, H_2, \ldots$ in the following cases.
  (a) H_1: $P \rightarrow Q$ C: $P \rightarrow (P \wedge Q)$
  (b) H_1: $\neg P \vee Q$ H_2: $\neg(Q \wedge \neg R)$ H_3: $\neg R$ C: $\neg P$
  (c) H_1: $\neg P$ H_2: $P \vee Q$ C: Q
  (d) H_1: $\neg Q$ H_2: $P \rightarrow Q$ C: $\neg P$
  (e) H_1: $P \rightarrow Q$ H_2: $Q \rightarrow R$ C: $P \rightarrow R$
  (f) H_1: R H_2: $P \vee \neg P$ C: R
2 Determine whether the conclusion C is valid in the following, when $H_1, H_2, \ldots$ are the premises.
  (a) H_1: $P \rightarrow Q$ H_2: $\neg Q$ C: P
  (b) H_1: $P \vee Q$ H_2: $P \rightarrow R$ H_3: $Q \rightarrow R$ C: R
  (c) H_1: $P \rightarrow (Q \rightarrow R)$ H_2: $P \wedge Q$ C: R
  (d) H_1: $P \rightarrow (Q \rightarrow R)$ H_2: R C: P
  (e) H_1: $\neg P$ H_2: $P \vee Q$ C: $P \wedge Q$
3 Without constructing a truth table, show that $A \wedge E$ is not a valid consequence of

$$A \rightleftarrows B \qquad B \rightleftarrows (C \wedge D) \qquad C \rightleftarrows (A \vee E) \qquad A \vee E$$

Also show that $A \vee C$ is not a valid consequence of

$$A \rightleftarrows (B \rightarrow C) \qquad B \rightleftarrows (\neg A \vee \neg C) \qquad C \rightleftarrows (A \vee \neg B) \qquad B$$

4 Show that $L \lor M$ follows from

$$P \land Q \land R \qquad (Q \rightleftarrows R) \rightarrow (L \lor M)$$

5 Show without constructing truth tables that the following statements cannot all be true simultaneously.

(a) $P \rightleftarrows Q \qquad Q \rightarrow R \qquad \neg R \lor S \qquad \neg P \rightarrow S \qquad \neg S$

(b) $R \lor M \qquad \neg R \lor S \qquad \neg M \qquad \neg S$

1-4.2 Rules of Inference

We now describe the process of derivation by which one demonstrates that a particular formula is a valid consequence of a given set of premises. Before we do this, we give two rules of inference which are called rules **P** and **T**.

Rule **P**: A premise may be introduced at any point in the derivation.

Rule **T**: A formula S may be introduced in a derivation if S is tautologically implied by any one or more of the preceding formulas in the derivation.

Before we proceed with the actual process of derivation, we list some important implications and equivalences that will be referred to frequently.

Not all the implications and equivalences listed in Tables 1-4.2 and 1-4.3 respectively are independent of one another. One could start with only a minimum number of them and derive the others by using the above rules of inference. Such an axiomatic approach will not be followed. We list here most of the important implications and equivalences and show how some of them are used in a derivation. Those which are used more often than the others are given special names because of their importance.

EXAMPLE 1 Demonstrate that R is a valid inference from the premises $P \rightarrow Q, Q \rightarrow R$, and P.

SOLUTION

{1}	(1)	$P \rightarrow Q$	Rule **P**
{2}	(2)	P	Rule **P**
{1, 2}	(3)	Q	Rule **T**, (1), (2), and I_{11} (modus ponens)
{4}	(4)	$Q \rightarrow R$	Rule **P**
{1, 2, 4}	(5)	R	Rule **T**, (3), (4), and I_{11}

The second column of numbers designates the formula as well as the line of derivation in which it occurs. The set of numbers in braces (the first column) for each line shows the premises on which the formula in the line depends. On the right, **P** or **T** represents the rule of inference, followed by a comment showing from which formulas and tautology that particular formula has been obtained. For example, if we follow this notation, the third line shows that the formula in this line is numbered (3) and has been obtained from premises in (1) and (2). The comment on the right says that the formula Q has been introduced using rule **T** and also indicates the details of the application of rule **T**.   ////

Table 1-4.2 IMPLICATIONS

I_1	$P \wedge Q \Rightarrow P$	(simplification)
I_2	$P \wedge Q \Rightarrow Q$	
I_3	$P \Rightarrow P \vee Q$	(addition)
I_4	$Q \Rightarrow P \vee Q$	
I_5	$\neg P \Rightarrow P \rightarrow Q$	
I_6	$Q \Rightarrow P \rightarrow Q$	
I_7	$\neg(P \rightarrow Q) \Rightarrow P$	
I_8	$\neg(P \rightarrow Q) \Rightarrow \neg Q$	
I_9	$P, Q \Rightarrow P \wedge Q$	
I_{10}	$\neg P, P \vee Q \Rightarrow Q$	(disjunctive syllogism)
I_{11}	$P, P \rightarrow Q \Rightarrow Q$	(modus ponens)
I_{12}	$\neg Q, P \rightarrow Q \Rightarrow \neg P$	(modus tollens)
I_{13}	$P \rightarrow Q, Q \rightarrow R \Rightarrow P \rightarrow R$	(hypothetical syllogism)
I_{14}	$P \vee Q, P \rightarrow R, Q \rightarrow R \Rightarrow R$	(dilemma)

Table 1-4.3 EQUIVALENCES

E_1	$\neg\neg P \Leftrightarrow P$	(double negation)
E_2	$P \wedge Q \Leftrightarrow Q \wedge P$	(commutative laws)
E_3	$P \vee Q \Leftrightarrow Q \vee P$	
E_4	$(P \wedge Q) \wedge R \Leftrightarrow P \wedge (Q \wedge R)$	(associative laws)
E_5	$(P \vee Q) \vee R \Leftrightarrow P \vee (Q \vee R)$	
E_6	$P \wedge (Q \vee R) \Leftrightarrow (P \wedge Q) \vee (P \wedge R)$	(distributive laws)
E_7	$P \vee (Q \wedge R) \Leftrightarrow (P \vee Q) \wedge (P \vee R)$	
E_8	$\neg(P \wedge Q) \Leftrightarrow \neg P \vee \neg Q$	(De Morgan's laws)
E_9	$\neg(P \vee Q) \Leftrightarrow \neg P \wedge \neg Q$	
E_{10}	$P \vee P \Leftrightarrow P$	
E_{11}	$P \wedge P \Leftrightarrow P$	
E_{12}	$R \vee (P \wedge \neg P) \Leftrightarrow R$	
E_{13}	$R \wedge (P \vee \neg P) \Leftrightarrow R$	
E_{14}	$R \vee (P \vee \neg P) \Leftrightarrow \mathbf{T}$	
E_{15}	$R \wedge (P \wedge \neg P) \Leftrightarrow \mathbf{F}$	
E_{16}	$P \rightarrow Q \Leftrightarrow \neg P \vee Q$	
E_{17}	$\neg(P \rightarrow Q) \Leftrightarrow P \wedge \neg Q$	
E_{18}	$P \rightarrow Q \Leftrightarrow \neg Q \rightarrow \neg P$	
E_{19}	$P \rightarrow (Q \rightarrow R) \Leftrightarrow (P \wedge Q) \rightarrow R$	
E_{20}	$\neg(P \rightleftarrows Q) \Leftrightarrow P \rightleftarrows \neg Q$	
E_{21}	$P \rightleftarrows Q \Leftrightarrow (P \rightarrow Q) \wedge (Q \rightarrow P)$	
E_{22}	$(P \rightleftarrows Q) \Leftrightarrow (P \wedge Q) \vee (\neg P \wedge \neg Q)$	

EXAMPLE 2 Show that $R \vee S$ follows logically from the premises $C \vee D$, $(C \vee D) \rightarrow \neg H$, $\neg H \rightarrow (A \wedge \neg B)$, and $(A \wedge \neg B) \rightarrow (R \vee S)$.

SOLUTION

$\{1\}$	(1)	$(C \vee D) \rightarrow \neg H$	**P**
$\{2\}$	(2)	$\neg H \rightarrow (A \wedge \neg B)$	**P**
$\{1, 2\}$	(3)	$(C \vee D) \rightarrow (A \wedge \neg B)$	**T**, (1), (2), and I_{13}
$\{4\}$	(4)	$(A \wedge \neg B) \rightarrow (R \vee S)$	**P**
$\{1, 2, 4\}$	(5)	$(C \vee D) \rightarrow (R \vee S)$	**T**, (3), (4), and I_{13}
$\{6\}$	(6)	$C \vee D$	**P**
$\{1, 2, 4, 6\}$	(7)	$R \vee S$	**T**, (5), (6), and I_{11}

The two tautologies frequently used in the above derivations are I_{13}, known as hypothetical syllogism, and I_{11}, known as modus ponens. ////

EXAMPLE 3   Show that $S \lor R$ is tautologically implied by $(P \lor Q) \land (P \to R) \land (Q \to S)$.

SOLUTION

{1}	(1)	$P \lor Q$	**P**
{1}	(2)	$\neg P \to Q$	**T**, (1), E_1, and E_{16}
{3}	(3)	$Q \to S$	**P**
{1, 3}	(4)	$\neg P \to S$	**T**, (2), (3), and I_{13}
{1, 3}	(5)	$\neg S \to P$	**T**, (4), E_{18}, and E_1
{6}	(6)	$P \to R$	**P**
{1, 3, 6}	(7)	$\neg S \to R$	**T**, (5), (6), and I_{13}
{1, 3, 6}	(8)	$S \lor R$	**T**, (7), E_{16}, and E_1 ////

EXAMPLE 4   Show that $R \land (P \lor Q)$ is a valid conclusion from the premises $P \lor Q, Q \to R, P \to M$, and $\neg M$.

SOLUTION

{1}	(1)	$P \to M$	**P**
{2}	(2)	$\neg M$	**P**
{1, 2}	(3)	$\neg P$	**T**, (1), (2), and I_{12}
{4}	(4)	$P \lor Q$	**P**
{1, 2, 4}	(5)	Q	**T**, (3), (4), and I_{10}
{6}	(6)	$Q \to R$	**P**
{1, 2, 4, 6}	(7)	R	**T**, (5), (6), and I_{11}
{1, 2, 4, 6}	(8)	$R \land (P \lor Q)$	**T**, (4), (7), and I_9 ////

EXAMPLE 5   Show I_{12}: $\neg Q, P \to Q \Rightarrow \neg P$.

SOLUTION

{1}	(1)	$P \to Q$	**P**
{1}	(2)	$\neg Q \to \neg P$	**T**, (1), and E_{18}
{3}	(3)	$\neg Q$	**P**
{1, 3}	(4)	$\neg P$	**T**, (2), (3), and I_{11} ////

We shall now introduce a third inference rule, known as rule **CP** or rule of conditional proof.

Rule **CP**   If we can derive S from R and a set of premises, then we can derive $R \to S$ from the set of premises alone.

Rule **CP** is not new for our purpose here because it follows from the equivalence E_{19} which states that

$$(P \wedge R) \rightarrow S \Leftrightarrow P \rightarrow (R \rightarrow S)$$

Let P denote the conjunction of the set of premises and let R be any formula. The above equivalence states that if R is included as an additional premise and S is derived from $P \wedge R$, then $R \rightarrow S$ can be derived from the premises P alone.

Rule **CP** is also called the *deduction theorem* and is generally used if the conclusion is of the form $R \rightarrow S$. In such cases, R is taken as an additional premise and S is derived from the given premises and R.

EXAMPLE 6 Show that $R \rightarrow S$ can be derived from the premises $P \rightarrow (Q \rightarrow S)$, $\neg R \vee P$, and Q.

SOLUTION Instead of deriving $R \rightarrow S$, we shall include R as an additional premise and show S first.

{1}	(1)	$\neg R \vee P$	**P**
{2}	(2)	R	**P** (assumed premise)
{1, 2}	(3)	P	**T**, (1), (2), and I_{10}
{4}	(4)	$P \rightarrow (Q \rightarrow S)$	**P**
{1, 2, 4}	(5)	$Q \rightarrow S$	**T**, (3), (4), and I_{11}
{6}	(6)	Q	**P**
{1, 2, 4, 6}	(7)	S	**T**, (5), (6), and I_{11}
{1, 4, 6}	(8)	$R \rightarrow S$	**CP** ////

These examples show that a derivation consists of a sequence of formulas, each formula in the sequence being either a premise or tautologically implied by formulas appearing before.

In Sec. 1-3.1 we discussed the decision problem in terms of determining whether a given formula is a tautology. We can extend this notion to the determination of validity of arguments. Accordingly, if one can determine in a finite number of steps whether an argument is valid, then the decision problem for validity is solvable.

One solution to the decision problem for validity is provided by the truth table method. Use of this method is often not practical. The method of derivation just discussed provides only a partial solution to the decision problem, because if an argument is valid, then it is possible to show by this method that the argument is valid. On the other hand, if an argument is not valid, then it is very difficult to decide, after a finite number of steps, that this is the case. There are other methods of derivation which do allow one to determine, after a finite number of steps, whether an argument is or is not valid. One such method is described in Sec. 1-4.4, and its computer implementation is given later in Sec. 2-7.

We shall now give some examples of derivation involving statements in

English. We first symbolize the given statements and then use the method of derivation just discussed.

EXAMPLE 7   "If there was a ball game, then traveling was difficult. If they arrived on time, then traveling was not difficult. They arrived on time. Therefore, there was no ball game." Show that these statements constitute a valid argument.

   SOLUTION   Let

$$P: \text{There was a ball game.}$$

$$Q: \text{Traveling was difficult.}$$

$$R: \text{They arrived on time.}$$

We are required to show that from the premises $P \to Q$, $R \to \neg Q$, and R the conclusion $\neg P$ follows. (Complete the rest of the derivation.)   ////

EXAMPLE 8   If A works hard, then either B or C will enjoy themselves. If B enjoys himself, then A will not work hard. If D enjoys himself, then C will not. Therefore, if A works hard, D will not enjoy himself.

   SOLUTION   Let A: A works hard; B: B will enjoy himself; C: C will enjoy himself; D: D will enjoy himself. Show that $A \to \neg D$ follows from $A \to B \lor C$, $B \to \neg A$, and $D \to \neg C$. Since the conclusion is given in the form of a condition $A \to \neg D$, include A as an additional premise and show that $\neg D$ follows logically from all the premises including A. Finally, use rule **CP** to obtain the result.   ////

1-4.3   Consistency of Premises and Indirect Method of Proof

A set of formulas $H_1, H_2, \ldots, H_m$ is said to be consistent if their conjunction has the truth value T for some assignment of the truth values to the atomic variables appearing in $H_1, H_2, \ldots, H_m$. If, for every assignment of the truth values to the atomic variables, at least one of the formulas $H_1, H_2, \ldots, H_m$ is false, so that their conjunction is identically false, then the formulas $H_1, H_2, \ldots, H_m$ are called *inconsistent*.

Alternatively, a set of formulas $H_1, H_2, \ldots, H_m$ is inconsistent if their conjunction implies a contradiction, that is,

$$H_1 \land H_2 \land \cdots \land H_m \Rightarrow R \land \neg R$$

where R is any formula. Note that $R \land \neg R$ is a contradiction, and it is necessary and sufficient for the implication that $H_1 \land H_2 \land \cdots \land H_m$ be a contradiction.

The notion of inconsistency is used in a procedure called *proof by contradiction* or *reductio ad absurdum* or *indirect method of proof*. In order to show that a conclusion C follows logically from the premises $H_1, H_2, \ldots, H_m$, we assume that C is false and consider $\neg C$ as an additional premise. If the new set of premises is inconsistent, so that they imply a contradiction, then the assumption that $\neg C$ is true does not hold simultaneously with $H_1 \land H_2 \land \cdots \land H_m$ being true. Therefore, C is true whenever $H_1 \land H_2 \land \cdots \land H_m$ is true. Thus, C follows logically from the premises $H_1, H_2, \ldots, H_m$.

EXAMPLE 1 Show that $\neg(P \wedge Q)$ follows from $\neg P \wedge \neg Q$.

SOLUTION We introduce $\neg\neg(P \wedge Q)$ as an additional premise and show that this additional premise leads to a contradiction.

{1}	(1)	$\neg\neg(P \wedge Q)$	**P** (assumed)	
{1}	(2)	$P \wedge Q$	**T**, (1), and E_1	
{1}	(3)	P	**T**, (2), and I_1	
{4}	(4)	$\neg P \wedge \neg Q$	**P**	
{4}	(5)	$\neg P$	**T**, (4), I_1	
{1, 4}	(6)	$P \wedge \neg P$	**T**, (3), (5), I_9	////

EXAMPLE 2 Show that the following premises are inconsistent.

1 If Jack misses many classes through illness, then he fails high school.
2 If Jack fails high school, then he is uneducated.
3 If Jack reads a lot of books, then he is not uneducated.
4 Jack misses many classes through illness and reads a lot of books.

SOLUTION

E: Jack misses many classes.

S: Jack fails high school.

A: Jack reads a lot of books.

H: Jack is uneducated.

The premises are $E \to S$, $S \to H$, $A \to \neg H$, and $E \wedge A$.

{1}	(1)	$E \to S$	**P**	
{2}	(2)	$S \to H$	**P**	
{1, 2}	(3)	$E \to H$	**T**, (1), (2), and I_{13}	
{4}	(4)	$A \to \neg H$	**P**	
{4}	(5)	$H \to \neg A$	**T**, (4), E_{18}	
{1, 2, 4}	(6)	$E \to \neg A$	**T**, (3), (5), I_{13}	
{1, 2, 4}	(7)	$\neg E \vee \neg A$	**T**, (6), E_{16}	
{1, 2, 4}	(8)	$\neg(E \wedge A)$	**T**, (7), E_8	
{9}	(9)	$E \wedge A$	**P**	
{1, 2, 4, 9}	(10)	$(E \wedge A) \wedge \neg(E \wedge A)$	**T**, (8), (9), I_9	////

Proof by contradiction is sometimes convenient. However, it can always be eliminated and replaced by a conditional proof (**CP**). Observe that

$$P \to (Q \wedge \neg Q) \Rightarrow \neg P \qquad (1)$$

In the proof by contradiction we show

$$H_1, H_2, \ldots, H_m \Rightarrow C$$

by showing

$$H_1, H_2, \ldots, H_m, \neg C \Rightarrow R \wedge \neg R \qquad (2)$$

Now (2) can be converted to the following by using rule **CP**

$$H_1, H_2, \ldots, H_m \Rightarrow \neg C \rightarrow (R \wedge \neg R) \qquad (3)$$

From (3) and (1) and E_1, we can show

$$H_1, H_2, \ldots, H_m \Rightarrow C$$

which is the required derivation.

1-4.4 Automatic Theorem Proving

In this section we reformulate the rules of inference theory for statement calculus and describe a procedure of derivation which can be conducted mechanically. The formulation given earlier could not be used for this purpose because the construction of a derivation depends heavily upon the skill, experience, and ingenuity of the person to make the right decision at every step.

Let us first examine the shortcomings of procedures used in any derivation of Sec. 1-4.2. Rule **P** permits the introduction of a premise at any point in the derivation, but does not suggest either the premise or the step at which it should be introduced. Rule **T** allows us to introduce any formula which follows from the previous steps. However, there is no definite choice of such a formula, nor is there any guidance for the use of any particular equivalence. Similarly, rule **CP** does not tell anything about the stages at which an antecedent is to be introduced as an assumed premise, nor does it indicate the stage at which it is again incorporated into the conditional. At every step, such decisions are taken from a large number of alternatives, with the ultimate aim of reaching the conclusion. Such a procedure is far from mechanical.

We shall now describe a set of rules and a procedure which allow one to construct each step of derivation in a specified manner without recourse to any ingenuity and finally to arrive at a last step which clearly indicates whether a given conclusion follows from the premises. In this sense, not only is our procedure here mechanical, but it also becomes a full decision process for validity.

The formulation described here is essentially based upon the work of Hao Wang.[1] Our system consisting of 10 rules, an axiom schema, and rules of well-formed sequents and formulas will now be described.

1 Variables: The capital letters A, B, C, $\ldots$, P, Q, R, $\ldots$ are used as statement variables. They are also used as statement formulas; however, in such cases the context will clearly indicate this usage.

2 Connectives: The connectives $\neg$, $\wedge$, $\vee$, $\rightarrow$, and $\rightleftarrows$ appear in the formulas with the order of precedence as given; viz., $\neg$ has the highest precedence, followed by $\wedge$, and so on. The concept of well-formed formula is the same as

---

[1] Hao Wang, Towards Mechanical Mathematics, *IBM J. Res. Devel.*, **4(1):** 2–22 (1960).

given in Sec. 1-2.7 with the additional assumption of the precedence and associativity of the connectives needed in order to reduce the number of parentheses
appearing in a formula.

   3 String of Formulas: A *string of formulas* is defined as follows.

(a) Any formula is a string of formulas.
(b) If α and β are strings of formulas, then α, β and β, α are strings of formulas.
(c) Only those strings which are obtained by steps (a) and (b) are strings of
     formulas, with the exception of the empty string which is also a string of
     formulas.

For our purpose here, the order in which the formulas appear in any string is not
important, and so the strings A, B, C; B, C, A; A, C, B; etc., are the same.

   4 Sequents: If α and β are strings of formulas, then $\alpha \xrightarrow{s} \beta$ is called
a *sequent* in which α is denoted the antecedent and β the consequent of the
sequent.

   A sequent $\alpha \xrightarrow{s} \beta$ is true iff either at least one of the formulas of the antecedent is false or at least one of the formulas of the consequent is true. Thus
$A, B, C \xrightarrow{s} D, E, F$ is true iff $A \wedge B \wedge C \to D \vee E \vee F$ is true. In this sense, the
symbol "$\xrightarrow{s}$" is a generalization of the connective $\to$ to strings of formulas.

   In the same manner, we shall use the symbol "$\xRightarrow{s}$," applied to strings of
formulas, as a generalization of the symbol "$\Rightarrow$." Thus $A \Rightarrow B$ means "A implies
B" or "$A \to B$ is a tautology," while $\alpha \xRightarrow{s} \beta$ means that $\alpha \xrightarrow{s} \beta$ is true. For example, $P, Q, R \xRightarrow{s} P, N$.

   Occasionally we have sequents which have empty strings of formulas as
antecedent or as consequent. The empty antecedent is interpreted as the logical
constant *"true"* or **T**, and the empty consequent is interpreted as the logical constant *"false"* or **F**.

   5 Axiom Schema: If α and β are strings of formulas such that every for-
mula in both α and β is a variable only, then the sequent $\alpha \xrightarrow{s} \beta$ is an *axiom* iff α
and β have at least one variable in common. As an example, $A, B, C \xrightarrow{s} P, B, R$,
where A, B, C, P, and R are variables, is an axiom.

   Note that if $\alpha \xrightarrow{s} \beta$ is an axiom, then $\alpha \xRightarrow{s} \beta$.

   6 Theorem: The following sequents are theorems of our system.

(a) Every axiom is a theorem.
(b) If a sequent α is a theorem and a sequent β results from α through the use
     of one of the 10 rules of the system which are given below, then β is a theo-
     rem.
(c) Sequents obtained by (a) and (b) are the only theorems.

Note that we have used α and β temporarily to denote sequents for the purpose
of the above description.

   7 Rules: The following rules are used to combine formulas within strings
by introducing connectives. Corresponding to each of the connectives there are
two rules, one for the introduction of the connective in the antecedent and the
other for its introduction in the consequent. In the description of these rules,
α, β, γ, ... are strings of formulas while X and Y are formulas to which the connectives are applied.

Antecedent Rules

Rule $\daleth \Rightarrow$: If $\alpha, \beta \overset{s}{\Rightarrow} X, \gamma$, then $\alpha, \daleth X, \beta \overset{s}{\Rightarrow} \gamma$.

Rule $\wedge \Rightarrow$: If $X, Y, \alpha, \beta \overset{s}{\Rightarrow} \gamma$, then $\alpha, X \wedge Y, \beta \overset{s}{\Rightarrow} \gamma$.

Rule $\vee \Rightarrow$: If $X, \alpha, \beta \overset{s}{\Rightarrow} \gamma$ and $Y, \alpha, \beta \overset{s}{\Rightarrow} \gamma$, then $\alpha, X \vee Y, \beta \overset{s}{\Rightarrow} \gamma$.

Rule $\rightarrow \Rightarrow$: If $Y, \alpha, \beta \overset{s}{\Rightarrow} \gamma$ and $\alpha, \beta \overset{s}{\Rightarrow} X, \gamma$, then $\alpha, X \rightarrow Y, \beta \overset{s}{\Rightarrow} \gamma$.

Rule $\rightleftarrows \Rightarrow$: If $X, Y, \alpha, \beta \overset{s}{\Rightarrow} \gamma$ and $\alpha, \beta \overset{s}{\Rightarrow} X, Y, \gamma$, then $\alpha, X \rightleftarrows Y, \beta \overset{s}{\Rightarrow} \gamma$.

Consequent Rules

Rule $\Rightarrow \daleth$: If $X, \alpha \overset{s}{\Rightarrow} \beta, \gamma$, then $\alpha \overset{s}{\Rightarrow} \beta, \daleth X, \gamma$.

Rule $\Rightarrow \wedge$: If $\alpha \overset{s}{\Rightarrow} X, \beta, \gamma$ and $\alpha \overset{s}{\Rightarrow} Y, \beta, \gamma$, then $\alpha \overset{s}{\Rightarrow} \beta, X \wedge Y, \gamma$.

Rule $\Rightarrow \vee$: If $\alpha \overset{s}{\Rightarrow} X, Y, \beta, \gamma$, then $\alpha \overset{s}{\Rightarrow} \beta, X \vee Y, \gamma$.

Rule $\Rightarrow \rightarrow$: If $X, \alpha \overset{s}{\Rightarrow} Y, \beta, \gamma$, then $\alpha \overset{s}{\Rightarrow} \beta, X \rightarrow Y, \gamma$.

Rule $\Rightarrow \rightleftarrows$: If $X, \alpha \overset{s}{\Rightarrow} Y, \beta, \gamma$ and $Y, \alpha \overset{s}{\Rightarrow} X, \beta, \gamma$, then $\alpha \overset{s}{\Rightarrow} \beta, X \rightleftarrows Y, \gamma$.

Note that the order in which the formulas and strings of formulas appear in a string in any of the above rules is unimportant. However, some kind of ordering is necessary in writing down the strings of formulas when an algorithm is written for computer implementation of the procedure described here. We have used a certain order in writing these rules with this point in mind. A computer algorithm is given in Sec. 2-7.

The system described here is equivalent to the one described earlier except that the procedures and techniques of derivation are different. This difference does not affect the validity of an argument. Some of the rules just given correspond to certain equivalences given earlier (see Problem 9 in Exercises 1-2).

The description of our system is complete. We shall now describe the procedure used in practice.

In the method of derivation given in Sec. 1–4, we showed that a conclusion C follows from the premises $H_1, H_2, \ldots, H_m$ by constructing a derivation whose last step was C, and $H_1, H_2, \ldots, H_m$ were introduced at various stages by using rule **P**. This method essentially means showing

$$H_1, H_2, \ldots, H_m \Rightarrow C \qquad (1)$$

Another way of stating (1) is

$$H_1 \rightarrow (H_2 \rightarrow (H_3 \cdots (H_m \rightarrow C) \cdots)) \qquad (2)$$

is a tautology (see Sec. 1-2.11).

Our new formulation is premise-free, so that in order to show that C follows from $H_1, H_2, \ldots, H_m$, we establish that

$$\overset{s}{\rightarrow} H_1 \rightarrow (H_2 \rightarrow (H_3 \cdots (H_m \rightarrow C) \cdots)) \qquad (3)$$

is a theorem. We must show that

$$\overset{s}{\Rightarrow} H_1 \rightarrow (H_2 \rightarrow (H_3 \cdots (H_m \rightarrow C) \cdots)) \qquad (4)$$

Our procedure involves showing (3) to be a theorem. For this purpose, we first assume (4) and then show that this assumption is or is not justified. This task is accomplished by working backward from (4), using the rules, and showing that (4) holds if some simpler sequent is a theorem. (By a simpler sequent we mean a sequent in which some connective is eliminated in one of the formulas appearing in the antecedent or the consequent.) We continue working backward until we arrive at the simplest possible sequents, i.e., those which do not have any connectives. If these sequents are axioms, then we have justified our assumption of (4). If at least one of the simplest sequents is not an axiom, then the assumption of (4) is not justified and C does not follow from $H_1, H_2, \ldots, H_m$. In the case when C follows from $H_1, H_2, \ldots, H_m$, the derivation of (4) is easily constructed by simply working through the same steps, starting from the axioms obtained. We now demonstrate this procedure by means of examples.

EXAMPLE 1   Show that $P \vee Q$ follows from P.

SOLUTION   We need to show that

$$(1) \quad \overset{s}{\Rightarrow} P \to (P \vee Q)$$

$$(1) \quad \text{if } (2)\ P \overset{s}{\Rightarrow} P \vee Q \qquad (\Rightarrow\to)$$

$$(2) \quad \text{if } (3)\ P \overset{s}{\Rightarrow} P, Q \qquad (\Rightarrow\vee)$$

We first eliminate the connective $\to$ in (1). Using the rule $\Rightarrow\to$ we have "if $P \overset{s}{\Rightarrow} P \vee Q$ then $\overset{s}{\Rightarrow} P \to (P \vee Q)$." Here we have named $P \overset{s}{\Rightarrow} P \vee Q$ by (2). Each line of derivation thus introduces the name as well as gives a rule. Note also that "(1) if (2)" means "if (2) then (1)." The chain of arguments is then given by (1) holds if (2), and (2) holds if (3). Finally (3) is a theorem, because it is an axiom. The actual derivation is simply a reversal of these steps in which (3) is an axiom that leads to $\overset{s}{\Rightarrow} P \to (P \vee Q)$ as shown.

$$(a) \quad P \overset{s}{\Rightarrow} P, Q \qquad \text{Axiom}$$

$$(b) \quad P \overset{s}{\Rightarrow} P \vee Q \qquad \text{Rule } (\Rightarrow\vee),\ (a)$$

$$(c) \quad \overset{s}{\Rightarrow} P \to (P \vee Q) \qquad \text{Rule } (\Rightarrow\to),\ (b) \qquad ////$$

EXAMPLE 2   Show that $\overset{s}{\Rightarrow} (\neg Q \wedge (P \to Q)) \to \neg P$.

SOLUTION

$$(1) \quad \overset{s}{\Rightarrow} (\neg Q \wedge (P \to Q)) \to \neg P$$

$$(1) \quad \text{if } (2)\ \neg Q \wedge (P \to Q) \overset{s}{\Rightarrow} \neg P \qquad (\Rightarrow\to)$$

$$(2) \quad \text{if } (3)\ \neg Q, P \to Q \overset{s}{\Rightarrow} \neg P \qquad (\wedge\Rightarrow)$$

$$(3) \quad \text{if } (4)\ P \to Q \overset{s}{\Rightarrow} \neg P, Q \qquad (\neg\Rightarrow)$$

$$(4) \quad \text{if } (5)\ Q \overset{s}{\Rightarrow} \neg P, Q \text{ and } (6) \overset{s}{\Rightarrow} P, \neg P, Q \qquad (\to\Rightarrow)$$

$$(5) \quad \text{if } (7)\ P, Q \overset{s}{\Rightarrow} Q \qquad (\Rightarrow\neg)$$

$$(6) \quad \text{if } (8)\ P \overset{s}{\Rightarrow} P, Q \qquad (\Rightarrow\neg)$$

Now (7) and (8) are axioms, hence the theorem (1) follows. We omit the derivation, which is easily obtained by starting with the axioms (7) and (8) and retracing the steps. $\qquad ////$

Note that in the solution of Example 2 in the second step we have two alternatives available, viz., to eliminate either $\wedge$ in the antecedent of (2) or $\rceil$ in the consequent. It is immaterial which elimination is carried out first. When the process is carried out on a computer, we shall adopt the convention that for any number of possible connectives that are available for elimination at a stage, the one on the left is eliminated first. This procedure was actually followed in the solution. We shall not follow this convention when the solution is obtained by hand.

EXAMPLE 3   Does P follow from $P \vee Q$?

SOLUTION   We investigate whether $\overset{s}{\rightarrow} (P \vee Q) \rightarrow P$ is a theorem. Assume (1) $\overset{s}{\Rightarrow} (P \vee Q) \rightarrow P$.

(1)   if (2) $P \vee Q \overset{s}{\Rightarrow} P$ $\qquad\qquad\qquad$ $(\Rightarrow\rightarrow)$

(2)   if (3) $P \overset{s}{\Rightarrow} P$ and (4) $Q \overset{s}{\Rightarrow} P$ $\quad$ $(\vee\Rightarrow)$

Note that (3) is an axiom, but (4) is not. Hence P does not follow from $P \vee Q$.

$////$

In some cases the derivation is longer if this procedure is used. The reason is that for every connective appearing there is at least one step introduced. In some steps a branching appears, and then we have to pursue two steps. We shall now consider an example for which the derivation was given earlier in Sec. 1-4.1.

EXAMPLE 4   Show that $S \vee R$ is tautologically implied by $(P \vee Q) \wedge (P \rightarrow R) \wedge (Q \rightarrow S)$ (see Example 3, Sec. 1-4.1).

SOLUTION   To show

(1) $\overset{s}{\Rightarrow} ((P \vee Q) \wedge (P \rightarrow R) \wedge (Q \rightarrow S)) \rightarrow (S \vee R)$

(1)   if (2) $(P \vee Q) \wedge (P \rightarrow R) \wedge (Q \rightarrow S) \overset{s}{\Rightarrow} (S \vee R)$ $\qquad$ $(\Rightarrow\rightarrow)$

(2)   if (3) $(P \vee Q) \wedge (P \rightarrow R) \wedge (Q \rightarrow S) \overset{s}{\Rightarrow} S, R$ $\qquad$ $(\Rightarrow\vee)$

(3)   if (4) $(P \vee Q), (P \rightarrow R), (Q \rightarrow S) \overset{s}{\Rightarrow} S, R$ $\qquad$ $(\wedge\Rightarrow \text{twice})$

(4)   if (5) $P, P \rightarrow R, Q \rightarrow S \overset{s}{\Rightarrow} S, R$

$\qquad$ and (6) $Q, P \rightarrow R, Q \rightarrow S \overset{s}{\Rightarrow} S, R$ $\qquad$ $(\vee\Rightarrow)$

(5)   if (7) $P, R, Q \rightarrow S \overset{s}{\Rightarrow} S, R$ and (8) $P, Q \rightarrow S \overset{s}{\Rightarrow} P, S, R$ $\quad$ $(\rightarrow\Rightarrow)$

(7)   if (9) $P, R, S \overset{s}{\Rightarrow} S, R$ and (10) $P, R \overset{s}{\Rightarrow} S, R, Q$ $\qquad$ $(\rightarrow\Rightarrow)$

(8)   if (11) $P, S \overset{s}{\Rightarrow} P, S, R$ and (12) $P \overset{s}{\Rightarrow} P, S, R, Q$ $\qquad$ $(\rightarrow\Rightarrow)$

(6)   if (13) $Q, R, Q \rightarrow S \overset{s}{\Rightarrow} S, R$ and (14) $Q, Q \rightarrow S \overset{s}{\Rightarrow} S, R, P$ $\quad$ $(\rightarrow\Rightarrow)$

(13)   if (15) $Q, R, S \overset{s}{\Rightarrow} S, R$ and (16) $Q, R \overset{s}{\Rightarrow} S, R, Q$ $\qquad$ $(\rightarrow\Rightarrow)$

(14)   if (17) $Q, S \overset{s}{\Rightarrow} S, R, P$ and (18) $Q \overset{s}{\Rightarrow} S, R, P, Q$ $\qquad$ $(\rightarrow\Rightarrow)$

Now, (9) to (12) and (15) to (18) are all axioms; therefore the result follows. The nesting of steps shows how the branching occurs. $\qquad\qquad\qquad$ $////$

EXERCISES 1-4

1 Show the validity of the following arguments, for which the premises are given on the left and the conclusion on the right.

   (*a*) $\neg(P \wedge \neg Q), \neg Q \vee R, \neg R$ $\neg P$

   (*b*) $(A \rightarrow B) \wedge (A \rightarrow C), \neg(B \wedge C), D \vee A$ D

   (*c*) $\neg J \rightarrow (M \vee N), (H \vee G) \rightarrow \neg J, H \vee G$ $M \vee N$

   (*d*) $P \rightarrow Q, (\neg Q \vee R) \wedge \neg R, \neg(\neg P \wedge S)$ $\neg S$

   (*e*) $(P \wedge Q) \rightarrow R, \neg R \vee S, \neg S$ $\neg P \vee \neg Q$

   (*f*) $P \rightarrow Q, Q \rightarrow \neg R, R, P \vee (J \wedge S)$ $J \wedge S$

   (*g*) $B \wedge C, (B \rightleftarrows C) \rightarrow (H \vee G)$ $G \vee H$

   (*h*) $(P \rightarrow Q) \rightarrow R, P \wedge S, Q \wedge \mathbf{T}$ R

2 Derive the following, using rule **CP** if necessary.

   (*a*) $\neg P \vee Q, \neg Q \vee R, R \rightarrow S \Rightarrow P \rightarrow S$

   (*b*) $P, P \rightarrow (Q \rightarrow (R \wedge S)) \Rightarrow Q \rightarrow S$

   (*c*) $P \rightarrow Q \Rightarrow P \rightarrow (P \wedge Q)$

   (*d*) $(P \vee Q) \rightarrow R \Rightarrow (P \wedge Q) \rightarrow R$

   (*e*) $P \rightarrow (Q \rightarrow R), Q \rightarrow (R \rightarrow S) \Rightarrow P \rightarrow (Q \rightarrow S)$

3 Prove $\neg P \wedge (P \vee Q) \Rightarrow Q$, using E_{12}, E_6, E_3, and I_2 only.

4 Show that the following sets of premises are inconsistent.

   (*a*) $P \rightarrow Q, P \rightarrow R, Q \rightarrow \neg R, P$

   (*b*) $A \rightarrow (B \rightarrow C), D \rightarrow (B \wedge \neg C), A \wedge D$

   Hence show that $P \rightarrow Q, P \rightarrow R, Q \rightarrow \neg R, P \Rightarrow M$, and

$$A \rightarrow (B \rightarrow C), D \rightarrow (B \wedge \neg C), A \wedge D \Rightarrow P$$

5 Show the following (use indirect method if needed).

   (*a*) $(R \rightarrow \neg Q), R \vee S, S \rightarrow \neg Q, P \rightarrow Q \Rightarrow \neg P$

   (*b*) $S \rightarrow \neg Q, S \vee R, \neg R, \neg R \rightleftarrows Q \Rightarrow \neg P$

   (*c*) $\neg(P \rightarrow Q) \rightarrow \neg(R \vee S), ((Q \rightarrow P) \vee \neg R), R \Rightarrow P \rightleftarrows Q$

6 Show the following, using the system given in Sec. 1-4.4.

   (*a*) $P \Rightarrow (\neg P \rightarrow Q)$

   (*b*) $P \wedge \neg P \wedge Q \Rightarrow R$

   (*c*) $R \Rightarrow P \vee \neg P \vee Q$

   (*d*) $P, \neg P \vee (P \wedge Q) \Rightarrow Q$

   (*e*) $\neg(P \wedge Q) \Rightarrow \neg P \vee \neg Q$

1-5 THE PREDICATE CALCULUS

So far our discussion of symbolic logic has been limited to the consideration of statements and statement formulas. The inference theory was also restricted in the sense that the premises and conclusions were all statements. The symbols $P, Q, R, \ldots, P_1, Q_1, \ldots$ were used for statements or statement variables. The statements were taken as basic units of statement calculus, and no analysis of any atomic statement was admitted. Only compound formulas were analyzed, and this analysis was done by studying the forms of the compound formulas, i.e., the connections between the constituent atomic statements. It was not possible to express the fact that any two atomic statements have some features in common. In order to investigate questions of this nature, we introduce the concept of a predicate in an atomic statement. The logic based upon the analysis of predicates in any statement is called *predicate logic*.

1-5.1 Predicates

Let us first consider the two statements

John is a bachelor.

Smith is a bachelor.

Obviously, if we express these statements by symbols, we require two different symbols to denote them. Such symbols do not reveal the common features of these two statements; viz., both are statements about two different individuals who are bachelors. If we introduce some symbol to denote "is a bachelor" and a method to join it with symbols denoting the names of individuals, then we will have a symbolism to denote statements about any individual's being a bachelor. The part "is a bachelor" is called a *predicate*. Another consideration which leads to some similar device for the representation of statements is suggested by the following argument.

All human beings are mortal.

John is a human being.

Therefore, John is a mortal.

Such a conclusion seems intuitively true. However, it does not follow from the inference theory of the statement calculus developed earlier. The reason for this deficiency is the fact that the statement "All human beings are mortal" cannot be analyzed to say anything about an individual. If we could separate the part "are mortal" from the part "All human beings," then it might be possible to consider any particular human being.

We shall symbolize a predicate by a capital letter and the names of individuals or objects in general by small letters. We shall soon see that using capital letters to symbolize statements as well as predicates will not lead to any confusion. Every predicate describes something about one or more objects (the word "object" is being used in a very general sense to include individuals as well). Therefore, a statement could be written symbolically in terms of the predicate letter followed by the name or names of the objects to which the predicate is applied.

We again consider the statements

1 John is a bachelor.
2 Smith is a bachelor.

Denote the predicate "is a bachelor" symbolically by the predicate letter B, "John" by j, and "Smith" by s. Then Statements (1) and (2) can be written as $B(j)$ and $B(s)$ respectively. In general, any statement of the type "p is Q" where Q is a predicate and p is the subject can be denoted by $Q(p)$.

A statement which is expressed by using a predicate letter must have at least one name of an object associated with the predicate. When an appropriate number of names are associated with a predicate, then we get a statement. Using a capital letter to denote a predicate may not indicate the appropriate number of names associated with it. Normally, this number is clear from the context or from the notation being used. This numbering can also be accomplished by attaching a superscript to a predicate letter, indicating the number of names that are to be appended to the letter. A predicate requiring m $(m > 0)$ names is called an m-place predicate. For example, B in (1) and (2) is a 1-place predicate. Another example is that "L: is less than" is a 2-place predicate. In order to extend our definition to $m = 0$, we shall call a statement a 0-place predicate because no names are associated with a statement.

Let R denote the predicate "is red" and let p denote "This painting." Then the statement

3   This painting is red.

can be symbolized by $R(p)$. Further, the connectives described earlier can now be used to form compound statements such as "John is a bachelor, and this painting is red," which can be written as $B(j) \wedge R(p)$. Other connectives can also be used to form statements such as

$$B(j) \rightarrow R(p) \qquad \neg R(p) \qquad B(j) \vee R(p) \qquad \text{etc.}$$

Consider, now, statements involving the names of two objects, such as

4   Jack is taller than Jill.
5   Canada is to the north of the United States.

The predicates "is taller than" and "is to the north of" are 2-place predicates because names of two objects are needed to complete a statement involving these predicates. If the letter G symbolizes "is taller than," j_1 denotes "Jack," and j_2 denotes "Jill," then Statement (4) can be translated as $G(j_1, j_2)$. Note that the order in which the names appear in the statement as well as in the predicate is important. Similarly, if N denotes the predicate "is to the north of," c: Canada, and s: United States, then (5) is symbolized as $N(c, s)$. Obviously, $N(s, c)$ is the statement "The United States is to the north of Canada."

Examples of 3-place predicates and 4-place predicates are:

6   Susan sits between Ralph and Bill.
7   Green and Miller played bridge against Johnston and Smith.

In general, an n-place predicate requires n names of objects to be inserted in fixed positions in order to obtain a statement. The position of these names is important. If S is an n-place predicate letter and $a_1, a_2, \ldots, a_n$ are the names of objects, then $S(a_1, a_2, \ldots, a_n)$ is a statement. If we use this convention, every predicate symbol is followed by an appropriate number of letters, which are the names of objects, enclosed in parentheses and separated by commas. Occasionally, the parentheses and the commas are dropped. The definition does not require that the names be chosen from any fixed set. For example, if B denotes the predicate "is a bachelor" and t denotes "This table," then $B(t)$ symbolizes "This table is a bachelor." In our everyday language, the only admissible name in this context would be that of an individual. However, such restrictions are not necessary according to the rules given above. We show a method of imposing such restrictions in Sec. 1-5.5.

1-5.2   The Statement Function, Variables, and Quantifiers

Let H be the predicate "is a mortal," b the name "Mr. Brown," c "Canada," and s "A shirt." Then $H(b)$, $H(c)$, and $H(s)$ all denote statements. In fact, these statements have a common form. If we write $H(x)$ for "x is mortal," then $H(b)$, $H(c)$, $H(s)$, and others having the same form can be obtained from $H(x)$ by replacing x by an appropriate name. Note that $H(x)$ is not a statement, but it results in a statement when x is replaced by the name of an object. The letter x used here is a placeholder. From now on we shall use small letters as individual or object variables as well as names of objects.

A *simple statement function* of one variable is defined to be an expression consisting of a predicate symbol and an individual variable. Such a statement function becomes a statement when the variable is replaced by the name of any object. The statement resulting from a replacement is called a *substitution instance* of the statement function and is a formula of statement calculus.

The word "simple" in the above definition distinguishes the simple statement function from those statement functions which are obtained from combining one or more simple statement functions and the logical connectives. For example, if we let $M(x)$ be "x is a man" and $H(x)$ be "x is a mortal," then we can form *compound statement functions* such as

$$M(x) \wedge H(x) \qquad M(x) \rightarrow H(x) \qquad \neg H(x) \qquad M(x) \vee \neg H(x) \qquad \text{etc.}$$

An extension of this idea to the statement functions of two or more variables is straightforward. Consider, for example, the statement function of two variables:

> 1 $G(x, y)$: x is taller than y.

If both x and y are replaced by the names of objects, we get a statement. If m represents Mr. Miller and f Mr. Fox, then we have

$$G(m, f): \text{Mr. Miller is taller than Mr. Fox.}$$

and

$$G(f, m): \text{Mr. Fox is taller than Mr. Miller.}$$

It is possible to form statement functions of two variables by using statement functions of one variable. For example, given

$$M(x): x \text{ is a man.}$$
$$H(y): y \text{ is a mortal.}$$

then we may write

$$M(x) \wedge H(y): x \text{ is a man and } y \text{ is a mortal.}$$

It is not possible, however, to write every statement function of two variables using statement functions of one variable.

One way of obtaining statements from any statement function is to replace the variables by the names of objects. There is another way in which statements can be obtained. In order to understand this alternative method, we first consider some familiar equations in elementary algebra.

$\quad$ *2* $\quad x + 2 = 5$
$\quad$ *3* $\quad x^2 + 1 = 0$
$\quad$ *4* $\quad (x - 1) * (x - \frac{1}{2}) = 0$
$\quad$ *5* $\quad x^2 - 1 = (x - 1) * (x + 1)$

In algebra, it is conventional to assume that the variable x is to be replaced by numbers (real, complex, rational, integer, etc.). In the above equations, we would not normally consider substituting for x the name of a person or object instead of numbers. We may state this idea by saying that the *universe* of the variable x is the set of real numbers or complex numbers or integers, etc. The restriction depends upon the problem under consideration. For example, we may be interested in only the real solution or the positive solution in a particular case. In Statement (2), if x is replaced by a real number, we get a statement. The resulting statement is true when 3 is substituted for x, while, for every other substitution, the resulting statement is false. In (3) there is no real number which, when substituted for x, gives a true statement. If, however, the universe of x includes complex numbers as well, then we find that there are two substitution instances which give true statements. In (4), if the universe of x is assumed to be integers, then there is only one number which produces a true statement when substituted. The situation is slightly different in (5) in the sense that if any number is substituted for x, then the resulting statement is true. Therefore, we may say that

$\quad$ *6* $\quad$ For any number x, $x^2 - 1 = (x - 1) * (x + 1)$.

Note that (6) is a statement and not a statement function even though a variable x appears in it. In fact, the addition of the phrase "For any number x," has changed the situation. The letter x, as used in (6), is different from the variable x used in Statements (2) to (5). In (6) the variable x need not be replaced by any name to obtain a statement. In mathematics this distinction is often not made. Occasionally when a statement involves an equality, a distinction is made by using the symbol $\equiv$ instead of the equality sign to show that it is a statement. In this case, (6) would be written as $x^2 - 1 \equiv (x - 1) * (x + 1)$. A similar situation occurs when a statement function does not involve an equality, and a distinction is necessary in logic between these two different uses of the variables.

$\quad$ Let us first consider the following statements. Each one is a statement about all individuals or objects belonging to a certain set.

$\quad$ *7* $\quad$ All men are mortal.
$\quad$ *8* $\quad$ Every apple is red.
$\quad$ *9* $\quad$ Any integer is either positive or negative.

Let us paraphrase these in the following manner.

$\quad$ *7a* $\quad$ For all x, if x is a man, then x is a mortal.
$\quad$ *8a* $\quad$ For all x, if x is an apple, then x is red.
$\quad$ *9a* $\quad$ For all x, if x is a integer, then x is either positive or negative.

$\quad$ We have already shown how statement functions such as "x is a man," "x is an apple," or "x is red" can be written by using predicate symbols. If we introduce a symbol to denote the phrase "For all x," then it would be possible to symbolize Statements (7a), (8a), and (9a).

We symbolize "For all x" by the symbol "$(\forall x)$" or by "(x)" with an understanding that this symbol be placed before the statement function to which this phrase is applied. Using

$M(x)$: x is man. $H(x)$: x is a mortal.

$A(x)$: x is an apple. $R(x)$: x is red.

$N(x)$: x is an integer. $P(x)$: x is either positive or negative.

we write $(7a)$, $(8a)$, and $(9a)$ as

7b $(x)(M(x) \rightarrow H(x))$
8b $(x)(A(x) \rightarrow R(x))$
9b $(x)(N(x) \rightarrow P(x))$

Sometimes $(x)(M(x) \rightarrow H(x))$ is also written as $(\forall x)(M(x) \rightarrow H(x))$. The symbols (x) or $(\forall x)$ are called *universal quantifiers*. Strictly speaking, the quantification symbol is "$(\ )$" or "$(\forall\ )$," and it contains the variable which is to be quantified. It is now possible for us to quantify any statement function of one variable to obtain a statement. Thus $(x)M(x)$ is a statement which can be translated as

10   For all x, x is a man.
10a For every x, x is a man.
10b Everything is a man.

In order to determine the truth values of any one of these statements involving a universal quantifier, one may be tempted to consider the truth values of the statement function which is quantified. This method is not possible for two reasons. First, statement functions do not have truth values. When the variables are replaced by the names of objects, we get statements which have a truth value. Second, in most cases there is an infinite number of statements that can be produced by such substitutions.

Note that the particular variable appearing in the statements involving a quantifier is not important because the statements remain unchanged if x is replaced by y throughout. Thus the statements $(x)(M(x) \rightarrow H(x))$ and $(y)(M(y) \rightarrow H(y))$ are equivalent.

Sometimes it is necessary to use more than one universal quantifier in a statement. For example consider

$$G(x, y): x \text{ is taller than } y.$$

We can state that "For any x and any y, if x is taller than y, then y is not taller than x" or "For any x and y, if x is taller than y, then it is not true that y is taller than x." This statement can now be symbolized as

$$(x)(y)(G(x, y) \rightarrow \neg G(y, x))$$

The universal quantifier was used to translate expressions such as "for all," "every," and "for any." Another quantifier will now be introduced to symbolize expressions such as "for some," "there is at least one," or "there exists some" (note that "some" is used in the sense of "at least one").

Consider the following statements:

11   There exists a man.
12   Some men are clever.
13   Some real numbers are rational.

The first statement can be expressed in various ways, two such ways being

11a   There exists an x such that x is a man.
11b   There is at least one x such that x is a man.

Similarly, (12) can be written as

12a   There exists an x such that x is a man and x is clever.
12b   There exists at least one x such that x is a man and x is clever.

Such a rephrasing allows us to introduce the symbol "$(\exists x)$," called the *existential quantifier*, which symbolizes expressions such as "there is at least one x such that" or "there exists an x such that" or "for some x." Writing

$$M(x): x \text{ is a man.}$$

$$C(x): \ x \text{ is clever.}$$

$$R_1(x): x \text{ is a real number.}$$

$$R_2(x): x \text{ is rational.}$$

and using the existential quantifier, we can write the Statements (11) to (13) as

11c $(\exists x)(M(x))$
12c $(\exists x)(M(x) \land C(x))$
13c $(\exists x)(R_1(x) \land R_2(x))$

It may be noted that a conjunction has been used in writing the statements of the form "Some A are B," while a conditional was used in writing statements of the form "All A are B." To a beginner this usage may appear confusing. We show in Sec. 1-5.5 why these connectives are the right ones to be used in these cases.

1-5.3   Predicate Formulas

Recall that capital letters were first used to denote some definite statements. Subsequently they were used as placeholders for the statements, and, in this sense, they were called statement variables. These statement variables were also considered as special cases of statement formulas.

In Secs. 1-5.1 and 1-5.2 the capital letters were introduced as definite predicates. It was suggested that a superscript n be used along with the capital letters in order to indicate that the capital letter is used as an n-place predicate. However, this notation was not necessary because an n-place predicate symbol must be followed by n object variables. Such variables are called *object* or *individual variables* and are denoted by lowercase letters. When used as an n-place predicate, the capital letter is followed by n individual variables which are enclosed in parentheses and separated by commas. For example, $P(x_1, x_2, \ldots, x_n)$ denotes an n-place predicate formula in which the letter P is an n-place predicate and

$x_1, x_2, \ldots, x_n$ are individual variables. In general, $P(x_1, x_2, \ldots, x_n)$ will be called an *atomic formula* of predicate calculus. It may be noted that our symbolism includes the atomic formulas of the statement calculus as special cases ($n = 0$). The following are some examples of atomic formulas.

$$R \qquad Q(x) \qquad P(x, y) \qquad A(x, y, z) \qquad P(a, y) \qquad \text{and} \qquad A(x, a, z)$$

A well-formed formula of predicate calculus is obtained by using the following rules.

    1   An atomic formula is a well-formed formula.

    2   If A is a well-formed formula, then $\neg A$ is a well-formed formula.

    3   If A and B are well-formed formulas, then $(A \wedge B)$, $(A \vee B)$, $(A \rightarrow B)$, and $(A \rightleftarrows B)$ are also well-formed formulas.

    4   If A is a well-formed formula and x is any variable, then $(x)A$ and $(\exists x)A$ are well-formed formulas.

    5   Only those formulas obtained by using rules (1) to (4) are well-formed formulas.

    Since we will be concerned with only well-formed formulas, we shall use the term "formula" for "well-formed formula." We shall follow the same conventions regarding the use of parentheses as was done in the case of statement formulas.

1-5.4 Free and Bound Variables

Given a formula containing a part of the form $(x)P(x)$ or $(\exists x)P(x)$, such a part is called an *x*-bound part of the formula. Any occurrence of x in an *x*-bound part of a formula is called a *bound occurrence* of x, while any occurrence of x or of any variable that is not a bound occurrence is called a *free occurrence*. Further, the formula $P(x)$ either in $(x)P(x)$ or in $(\exists x)P(x)$ is described as the *scope* of the quantifier. In other words, the scope of a quantifier is the formula immediately following the quantifier. If the scope is an atomic formula, then no parentheses are used to enclose the formula; otherwise parentheses are needed. As illustrations, consider the following formulas:

$$(x)P(x, y) \qquad\qquad\qquad (1)$$

$$(x)(P(x) \rightarrow Q(x)) \qquad\qquad\qquad (2)$$

$$(x)(P(x) \rightarrow (\exists y)R(x, y)) \qquad\qquad\qquad (3)$$

$$(x)(P(x) \rightarrow R(x)) \vee (x)(P(x) \rightarrow Q(x)) \qquad\qquad\qquad (4)$$

$$(\exists x)(P(x) \wedge Q(x)) \qquad\qquad\qquad (5)$$

$$(\exists x)P(x) \wedge Q(x) \qquad\qquad\qquad (6)$$

    In (1), $P(x, y)$ is the scope of the quantifier, and both occurrences of x are bound occurrences, while the occurrence of y is a free occurrence. In (2), the scope of the universal quantifier is $P(x) \rightarrow Q(x)$, and all occurrences of x are bound. In (3), the scope of (x) is $P(x) \rightarrow (\exists y)R(x, y)$, while the scope of $(\exists y)$ is $R(x, y)$. All occurrences of both x and y are bound occurrences. In (4), the scope of the first quantifier is $P(x) \rightarrow R(x)$, and the scope of the second is

$P(x) \rightarrow Q(x)$. All occurrences of x are bound occurrences. In (5), the scope of $(\exists x)$ is $P(x) \wedge Q(x)$. However, in (6) the scope of $(\exists x)$ is $P(x)$, and the last occurrence of x in $Q(x)$ is free.

It is useful to note that in the bound occurrence of a variable, the letter which is used to represent the variable is not important. In fact, any other letter can be used as a variable without affecting the formula, provided that the new letter is not used elsewhere in the formula. Thus the formulas

$$(x)P(x, y) \qquad \text{and} \qquad (z)P(z, y)$$

are the same. Further, the bound occurrence of a variable cannot be substituted by a constant; only a free occurrence of a variable can be. For example, $(x)P(x) \wedge Q(a)$ is a substitution instance of $(x)P(x) \wedge Q(y)$. In fact, $(x)P(x) \wedge Q(a)$ can be expressed in English as "Every x has the property P, and a has the property Q." A change of variables in the bound occurrence is not a substitution instance. Sometimes it is useful to change the variables in order to avoid confusion. In (6), it is better to write $(y)P(y) \wedge Q(x)$ instead of $(x)P(x) \wedge Q(x)$, so as to separate the free and bound occurrences of variables. Occasionally, one may come across a formula of the type $(x)P(y)$ in which the occurrence of y is free and the scope of (x) does not contain an x; in such a case, we have a vacuous use of (x). Finally, it may be mentioned that in a statement every occurrence of a variable must be bound, and no variable should have a free occurrence. In the case where a free variable occurs in a formula, then we have a statement function.

EXAMPLE 1   Let

$$P(x): x \text{ is a person.}$$

$$F(x, y): x \text{ is the father of } y.$$

$$M(x, y): x \text{ is the mother of } y.$$

Write the predicate "x is the father of the mother of y."

SOLUTION   In order to symbolize the predicate, we name a person called z as the mother of y. Obviously we want to say that x is the father of z and z the mother of y. It is assumed that such a person z exists. We symbolize the predicate as

$$(\exists z)(P(z) \wedge F(x, z) \wedge M(z, y)) \qquad ////$$

EXAMPLE 2   Symbolize the expression "All the world loves a lover."

SOLUTION   First note that the quotation really means that everybody loves a lover. Now let

$$P(x): x \text{ is a person.}$$

$$L(x): x \text{ is a lover.}$$

$$R(x, y): x \text{ loves } y.$$

The required expression is

$$(x)(P(x) \rightarrow (y)(P(y) \wedge L(y) \rightarrow R(x, y))) \qquad ////$$

1-5.5 The Universe of Discourse

Example 2 in Sec. 1-5.4 shows that the process of symbolizing a statement in predicate calculus can be quite complicated. However, some simplification can be introduced by limiting the class of individuals or objects under consideration. This limitation means that the variables which are quantified stand for only those objects which are members of a particular set or class. Such a restricted class is called the *universe of discourse* or the *domain* of individuals or simply the *universe*. If the discussion refers to human beings only, then the universe of discourse is the class of human beings. In elementary algebra or number theory, the universe of discourse could be numbers (real, complex, rational, etc.).

EXAMPLE 1   Symbolize the statement "All men are giants."

SOLUTION   Using

$$G(x): x \text{ is a giant.}$$

$$M(x): x \text{ is a man.}$$

the given statement can be symbolized as $(x)(M(x) \rightarrow G(x))$. However, if we restrict the variable x to the universe which is the class of men, then the statement is

$$(x)G(x) \qquad ////$$

EXAMPLE 2   Consider the statement "Given any positive integer, there is a greater positive integer." Symbolize this statement with and without using the set of positive integers as the universe of discourse.

SOLUTION   Let the variables x and y be restricted to the set of positive integers. Then the above statement can be paraphrased as follows: For all x, there exists a y such that y is greater than x. If $G(x, y)$ is "x is greater than y," then the given statement is $(x)(\exists y)G(y, x)$. If we do not impose the restriction on the universe of discourse and if we write $P(x)$ for "x is a positive integer," then we can symbolize the given statement as $(x)(P(x) \rightarrow (\exists y)(P(y) \wedge G(y, x)))$.

$$////$$

The universe of discourse, if any, must be explicitly stated, because the truth value of a statement depends upon it. For instance, consider the predicate

$$Q(x): x \text{ is less than } 5.$$

and the statements $(x)Q(x)$ and $(\exists x)Q(x)$. If the universe of discourse is given by the sets

1 $\{-1, 0, 1, 2, 4\}$
2 $\{3, -2, 7, 8, -2\}$
3 $\{15, 20, 24\}$

then $(x)Q(x)$ is true for the universe of discourse (1) and false for (2) and (3). The statement $(\exists x)Q(x)$ is true for both (1) and (2), but false for (3).

It may be noted that there are two ways of obtaining a 0-place predicate from an n-place predicate. The first way is to substitute names of objects from the universe of discourse for the variables; the second method is to quantify in such a way that all occurrences of individual variables are bound. In both cases no further substitution of individual variables is possible. Obviously, the 0-place predicates are statements in statement calculus.

At the end of Sec. 1-5.2 it was mentioned that in symbolizing expressions of the type "All A are B" the correct connective that should be used is the conditional. On the other hand, for symbolizing expressions of the type "Some A are B," the correct connective is the conjunction. Using particular examples, we now show how the meaning changes if the correct connectives are not used.

Consider the statement

1   All cats are animals.

which is true for any universe of discourse. In particular, let the universe of discourse E be {Cuddle, Ginger, 0, 1}, where the first two elements are the names of cats. Obviously Statement (1) is true over E. Now consider the statements $(x)(C(x) \rightarrow A(x))$ and $(x)(C(x) \wedge A(x))$, where $C(x): x$ is a cat, and $A(x): x$ is an animal. In $C(x) \rightarrow A(x)$, if x is replaced by any of the elements of E, then we get a true statement; hence $(x)(C(x) \rightarrow A(x))$ is true over E. On the other hand, $(x)(C(x) \wedge A(x))$ is false over E because $C(x) \wedge A(x)$ assumes the value false when x is replaced by 0 or 1. This means that Statement (1) cannot be symbolized as $(x)(C(x) \wedge A(x))$.

Now consider the statement

2   Some cats are black.

Let E be as above with the understanding that both Cuddle and Ginger are white cats, and let $B(x): x$ is black. In this case there is no black cat in the universe E, and (2) is false. The statement $(\exists x)(C(x) \wedge B(x))$ is also false over E because there is no black cat in E. On the other hand, $(\exists x)(C(x) \rightarrow B(x))$ is true because $C(x) \rightarrow B(x)$ is true when x is replaced by 0 or 1. Thus we have demonstrated that the conditional is not the correct connective to use in this case.

EXERCISES   1-5

1   Which of the following are statements?
  (*a*) $(x)(P(x) \vee Q(x)) \wedge R$
  (*b*) $(x)(P(x) \wedge Q(x)) \wedge (\exists x) S(x)$
  (*c*) $(x)(P(x) \wedge Q(x)) \wedge S(x)$

2   Indicate the variables that are free and bound. Also show the scope of the quantifiers.
  (*a*) $(x)(P(x) \wedge R(x)) \rightarrow (\ x) P(x) \wedge Q(x)$
  (*b*) $(x)(P(x) \wedge (\exists x) Q(x)) \vee ((x) P(x) \rightarrow Q(x))$
  (*c*) $(x)(P(x) \rightleftarrows Q(x) \wedge (\exists x) R(x)) \wedge S(x)$

3   If the universe of discourse is the set {a, b, c}, eliminate the quantifiers in the following formulas.
  (*a*) $(x) P(x)$
  (*b*) $(x) R(x) \wedge (x) S(x)$
  (*c*) $(\ x) R(x) \wedge (\exists x) S(x)$
  (*d*) $(x)(P(x) \rightarrow Q(x))$
  (*e*) $(x) \neg P(x) \vee (x) P(x)$

4 Find the truth values of
   (a) $(x)(P(x) \lor Q(x))$, where $P(x): x = 1$, $Q(x): x = 2$, and the universe of discourse is $\{1, 2\}$.
   (b) $(x)(P \rightarrow Q(x)) \lor R(a)$, where $P: 2 > 1$, $Q(x): x \leq 3$, $R(x): x > 5$, and $a: 5$, with the universe being $\{-2, 3, 6\}$.
   (c) $(\exists x)(P(x) \rightarrow Q(x)) \land \mathbf{T}$, where $P(x): x > 2$, $Q(x): x = 0$, and $\mathbf{T}$ is any tautology, with the universe of discourse as $\{1\}$.
5 Show that $(\exists z)(Q(z) \land R(z))$ is not implied by the formulas $(\exists x)(P(x) \land Q(x))$ and $(\exists y)(P(y) \land R(y))$, by assuming a universe of discourse which has two elements.

1-6 INFERENCE THEORY OF THE PREDICATE CALCULUS

In this section we first generalize the concepts of equivalence and implication to formulas of the predicate calculus. We shall use the same terminology and symbolism as that used for the statement calculus. In fact, our discussion will include statement calculus as a special case. After defining the concept of validity involving predicate formulas, we derive several valid formulas which will be useful in the inference theory of predicate logic.

1-6.1 Valid Formulas and Equivalences

The formulas of the predicate calculus are assumed to contain statement variables, predicates, and object variables. The object variables are assumed to belong to a set called the universe of discourse or the domain of the object variable. Such a universe may be finite or infinite. The term "variable" includes constants as a special case. In a predicate formula, when all the object variables are replaced by definite names of objects and the statement variables by statements, we obtain a statement which has a truth value T or F.

Notice that the formulas of predicate calculus as given here do not contain predicate variables. They contain predicates; i.e., every predicate letter is intended to be a definite predicate, and hence is not available for substitution. However, we will use formulas without specifying the definite predicate used. In such cases, predicate letters are interpreted as definite predicates.

Let A and B be any two predicate formulas defined over a common universe denoted by the symbol E. If, for every assignment of object names from the universe of discourse E to each of the variables appearing in A and B, the resulting statements have the same truth values, then the predicate formulas A and B are said to be *equivalent to each other over E*. This idea is symbolized by writing $A \Leftrightarrow B$ over E. If E is arbitrary, then we say that A and B are equivalent, that is, $A \Leftrightarrow B$. The definition of implication can be extended in the same way. It is assumed that the same object names are assigned to the same variables throughout both A and B. Similarly, a formula A is said to be valid in E written $\vdash A$ in E if, for every assignment of object names from E to the corresponding variables in A and for every assignment of statements to statement variables, the resulting statements have the truth value T. As before, if a formula is valid for an arbitrary E, then it is written as $\vdash A$.

Note that $A \Leftrightarrow B$ requires that the equivalence of A and B be examined over all universes, and the same is true for $\vdash A$, since these statements are made for any arbitrary universe.

It is possible to determine by truth table methods whether a formula is valid in E, where E is a finite universe of discourse. Even this method may not be practical when the number of elements in E is large. It is impossible when the number of elements in E is infinite. The determination of validity of a formula by truth tables would involve examination for all possible universes, which is impossible. Of course, methods of derivation are still available in all such cases, and these are discussed in Sec. 1-6.4. Similar remarks apply for the determination of equivalence of two formulas. Sometimes a negative approach is possible in the sense that if any particular assignment of values to the variables in a formula results in a statement that is false, then the formula cannot be valid. A similar remark can be made about the equivalence of two formulas.

Formulas of the predicate calculus that involve quantifiers and no free variables are also formulas of the statement calculus. Therefore, substitution instances of all the tautologies by these formulas yield any number of special tautologies. For example, consider the tautologies of the statement calculus given by

$$P \vee \neg P \qquad P \rightarrow Q \rightleftarrows \neg P \vee Q$$

and substitute the formulas $(x)R(x)$ and $(\exists x)S(x)$ for P and Q respectively. It is assumed that $(x)R(x)$ and $(\exists x)S(x)$ do not contain any free variables. The following tautologies are obtained.

$$((x)R(x)) \vee \neg((x)R(x))$$

$$((x)R(x)) \rightarrow ((\exists x)S(x)) \rightleftarrows \neg((x)R(x)) \vee ((\exists x)S(x))$$

These tautologies form only a very special class of valid formulas of the predicate calculus. Another class of valid formulas that follow from the tautologies of the statement calculus will now be discussed.

Recall that any substitution instance of a tautology is also a tautology in the statement calculus. A *substitution instance* is one in which any variable in a formula is consistently replaced by any other formula throughout. A similar situation exists for predicate formulas. We shall call a predicate formula a *prime (atomic, simple) formula* if no sentential connectives appear in it. In general, a tautology of the statement calculus remains a valid formula of the predicate calculus when prime formulas are substituted for statement variables throughout the formula. Thus all the implications and equivalences of the statement calculus given in Sec. 1-4.2 can be considered as implications and equivalences of the predicate calculus in which the statement variables are replaced by prime predicate formulas. As an illustration, let $A(x)$, $B(x)$, and $C(x, y)$ denote any prime formulas of the predicate calculus. Then the following are valid formulas of the predicate calculus.

$$\neg\neg A(x) \rightleftarrows A(x) \qquad\qquad E_1$$

$$C(x, y) \wedge B(x) \rightleftarrows B(x) \wedge C(x, y) \qquad E_2$$

$$A(x) \rightarrow B(x) \rightleftarrows \neg A(x) \vee B(x) \qquad E_{16}$$

In fact, Tables 1-4.2 and 1-4.3 can be considered as implications and equivalences of the predicate calculus with the understanding that the atomic variables there stand for prime predicate formulas.

The valid formulas obtained in this manner do not exhaust all possible valid formulas. There are several other valid formulas, particularly those involving quantifiers, which are useful. Such valid formulas are obtained in Sec. 1-6.4 by using the inference theory of predicate logic.

1-6.2 Some Valid Formulas over Finite Universes

In this and in the following section we denote predicate formulas by capital letters such as A, B, C, $\cdots$ followed by object variables x, y, $\cdots$. Thus $A(x)$, $A(x, y)$, $B(y)$, and $C(x, y, z)$ are examples of predicate formulas. Some clarification is necessary at this stage. In the formula $A(x)$, we wish to say that A is a predicate formula in which x is one of the free variables. This variable x is of interest to us, and we want to emphasize the dependence of A on it. For example, we may write $B(x)$ for $(y)P(y) \vee Q(x)$.

If in a formula $A(x)$ we replace each free occurrence of the variable x by another variable y, then we say that y is *substituted* for x in the formula, and the resulting formula is denoted by $A(y)$. For such a substitution, the formula $A(x)$ must be free for y. A formula $A(x)$ is said to be *free for y* if no free occurrence of x is in the scope of the quantifiers (y) or $(\exists y)$. If $A(x)$ is not free for y, then it is necessary to change the variable y, appearing as a bound variable, to another variable before substituting y for x. If y is to be substituted, then it is usually a good idea to make all the bound variables different from y. The following examples show what $A(y)$ is for a given $A(x)$.

$A(x)$	$A(y)$
$P(x,y) \wedge (\exists y)Q(y)$	$P(y,y) \wedge (\exists y)Q(y)$ or $P(y,y) \wedge (\exists z)Q(z)$
$(S(x) \wedge S(y)) \vee (x)R(x)$	$(S(y) \wedge S(y)) \vee (x)R(x)$ or $(S(y) \wedge S(y)) \vee (z)R(z)$

The following formulas are not free for y.

$$P(x, y) \wedge (y)Q(x, y) \qquad (y)(S(y) \rightarrow S(x))$$

In order to substitute y in place of the variable x in these formulas, it is necessary to first make them free for y as follows:

$A(x)$	$A(y)$
$P(x,y) \wedge (z)Q(x,z)$	$P(y,y) \wedge (z)Q(y,z)$
$(z)(S(z) \rightarrow S(x))$	$(z)(S(z) \rightarrow S(y))$

If the universe of discourse is a finite set, then all possible substitutions of the object variables can be enumerated. However, it is not possible to enumerate all possible substitutions if the universe of discourse is infinite. We shall now give some equivalences which hold for a finite universe. Later we show that these equivalences also hold for an arbitrary universe.

Let the universe of discourse be denoted by a finite set S given by

$$S = \{a_1, a_2, \cdots, a_n\}$$

From the meaning of the quantifiers and by simple enumeration of all the objects in S, it is easy to see that

$$(x)A(x) \Leftrightarrow A(a_1) \wedge A(a_2) \wedge \cdots \wedge A(a_n) \tag{1}$$

$$(\exists x)A(x) \Leftrightarrow A(a_1) \vee A(a_2) \vee \cdots \vee A(a_n) \tag{2}$$

Equivalences (1) and (2) over S show that the quantifiers can be dispensed with if the universe of discourse is finite.

Two equivalences that can be proved easily with the help of (1), (2), and De Morgan's laws are

$$\neg((x)A(x)) \Leftrightarrow (\exists x) \neg A(x) \tag{3}$$

$$\neg((\exists x)A(x)) \Leftrightarrow (x) \neg A(x) \tag{4}$$

We present a proof of (3).

$$\neg((x)A(x)) \Leftrightarrow \neg(A(a_1) \wedge A(a_2) \wedge \cdots \wedge A(a_n))$$

$$\Leftrightarrow \neg A(a_1) \vee \neg A(a_2) \vee \cdots \vee \neg A(a_n)$$

$$\Leftrightarrow (\exists x) \neg A(x)$$

The proof of (4) is similar.

If we assume that the negation appearing before a quantifier negates not the quantifier but the whole quantified statement, then we can eliminate certain parentheses used in (3) and (4) and rewrite the equivalences as

$$\neg(x)A(x) \Leftrightarrow (\exists x) \neg A(x)$$

$$\neg(\exists x)A(x) \Leftrightarrow (x) \neg A(x)$$

If the universal and existential quantifiers are called *duals* of each other, then the above equivalences can be summarized by saying that the negation of a quantified formula is equivalent to a formula in which the quantifier is replaced by its dual and the scope of the quantifier by its negation.

EXAMPLE 1   Negate the following statements.

> (a) Ottawa is a small town.
> (b) Every city in Canada is clean.

SOLUTION   Some possible negations are as follows:

> (a) It is not the case that Ottawa is a small town.
>   Ottawa is *not* a small town.
> (b) It is not the case that every city in Canada is clean.
>   Not every city in Canada is clean.
>   *Some* city in Canada is *not* clean.   ////

Note the difference between the negations of quantified and nonquantified statements. It is incorrect to negate (b) as "Every city in Canada is not clean."

The proof by enumeration of the equivalences (3) and (4) over S cannot be extended to the case when the universe of discourse is infinite. There are many such equivalences which can easily be shown to hold for a finite universe but which also hold for an arbitrary universe. These are discussed in the next section.

1-6.3 Special Valid Formulas Involving Quantifiers

In this section we do not put any restriction on the universe of discourse, and we assume it to be arbitrary. As a special case, it may be finite or infinite. To start, we give four implications. These will be used in the theory of inference of the predicate calculus and will permit us to either remove or add quantifiers during the course of a derivation.

Let $A(x)$ be a predicate formula where x is a particular object variable of interest. Then

$$(x)A(x) \Rightarrow A(y) \qquad (1)$$

where y is substituted for x in $A(x)$ to obtain $A(y)$, as explained in Sec. 1-6.2.

In order to show (1), we assume that $(x)A(x)$ is true. Obviously, $A(y)$ must also be true. Hence the implication (1) holds. In case $(x)A(x)$ is false, nothing need be proved. This implication can be written in a more convenient form as

$$(x)A(x) \Rightarrow A(x) \qquad (2)$$

Implication (2) will be called the rule of *universal specification* (or *instantiation*) and will be denoted by **US** in the theory of inference. It states that from a universally valid premise $(x)A(x)$, we can conclude a specific case $A(x)$, so that one can drop the quantifier in the derivation.

For the next implication, let x be any object variable, B be any formula not containing any free occurrence of x, and $A(x)$ be any formula. Then

$$(B \rightarrow A(x)) \Rightarrow (B \rightarrow (x)A(x)) \qquad (3)$$

Implication (3) states that if $A(x)$ follows logically from B, then we can conclude $(x)A(x)$ from B.

For the truth of (3), note that if $B \rightarrow A(x)$ is assumed to be true for any variable x, then changing x does not change the truth value of B. Thus $B \rightarrow (x)A(x)$ must also be true. It is important to note that the variable x in $A(x)$ is arbitrary in the sense that nothing that appears in B affects the arbitrariness of x. Certain restrictions are discussed in Sec. 1-6.4 which guarantee this statement.

As a special case of (3), let us replace B by $P \vee \neg P$, where P is any statement variable. Since $P \vee \neg P$ is a tautology, from

$$(P \vee \neg P) \rightarrow A(x) \Rightarrow (P \vee \neg P) \rightarrow (x)A(x)$$

we get the implication (see problem 3 in Exercises 1-2.11)

$$A(x) \Rightarrow (x)A(x) \qquad (4)$$

Implication (4) permits us to conclude $(x)A(x)$ from $A(x)$; i.e., it permits us to add the universal quantifier in the conclusion during the course of derivation. This rule is therefore called the rule of *universal generalization* and will be denoted by **UG**.

Corresponding to the rules cited in (2) and (4) which permit the universal quantifier to be removed or added during the course of a derivation, we also have two more rules which will permit us to remove or add the existential quantifier during the course of a derivation.

The following implications, derivable under assumptions similar to those used for (2) and (4), establish such rules:

$$(\exists x) A(x) \Rightarrow A(y) \tag{5}$$

$$A(y) \Rightarrow (\exists x) A(x) \tag{6}$$

Implication (5) is known as *existential specification*, abbreviated here as **ES**, while (6) is known as *existential generalization*, or **EG**. That some care is necessary in the interpretation of these rules will be discussed in the next section.

Some other important implications and equivalences involving the quantifiers are listed in Tables 1-6.1 and 1-6.2. These can be proved by using the definitions of the quantifiers and arguments similar to the one given above. In certain other cases it is more convenient to prove them by using the method of derivation given in the next section. If a formula A does not depend upon the variable x, then $(x)A \Leftrightarrow A$ and $(\exists x) A(x) \Leftrightarrow A$, and the implications I_{15} and I_{16} become E_{27} and E_{28}. Using E_{23}, we can easily prove

$$(\exists x) (A(x) \to B(x)) \Leftrightarrow (x) A(x) \to (\exists x) B(x) \qquad E_{33}$$

Similarly, from I_{15} and I_{16} we can prove

$$(\exists x) A(x) \to (x) B(x) \Leftrightarrow (x) (A(x) \to B(x)) \qquad E_{34}$$

We shall frequently use some of the equivalences and implications given in Tables 1-4.2, 1-4.3, 1-6.1, and 1-6.2 for the derivation of a conclusion from a set of premises.

Table 1-6.1

$(\exists x)(A(x) \lor B(x)) \Leftrightarrow (\exists x)A(x) \lor (\exists x)B(x)$	E_{23}
$(x)(A(x) \land B(x)) \Leftrightarrow (x)A(x) \land (x)B(x)$	E_{24}
$\neg(\exists x)A(x) \Leftrightarrow (x)\neg A(x)$	E_{25}
$\neg(x)A(x) \Leftrightarrow (\exists x)\neg A(x)$	E_{26}
$(x)A(x) \lor (x)B(x) \Rightarrow (x)(A(x) \lor B(x))$	I_{15}
$(\exists x)(A(x) \land B(x)) \Rightarrow (\exists x)A(x) \land (\exists x)B(x)$	I_{16}

Table 1-6.2

$(x)(A \lor B(x)) \Leftrightarrow A \lor (x)B(x)$	E_{27}
$(\exists x)(A \land B(x)) \Leftrightarrow A \land (\exists x)B(x)$	E_{28}
$(x)A(x) \to B \Leftrightarrow (\exists x)(A(x) \to B)$	E_{29}
$(\exists x)A(x) \to B \Leftrightarrow (x)(A(x) \to B)$	E_{30}
$A \to (x)B(x) \Leftrightarrow (x)(A \to B(x))$	E_{31}
$A \to (\exists x)B(x) \Leftrightarrow (\exists x)(A \to B(x))$	E_{32}

1-6.4 Theory of Inference for The Predicate Calculus

The method of derivation involving predicate formulas uses the rules of inference given for the statement calculus and also certain additional rules which are required to deal with the formulas involving quantifiers. The rules **P** and **T**, regarding the introduction of a premise at any stage of derivation and the introduction of any formula which follows logically from the formulas already introduced, remain the same. If the conclusion is given in the form of a conditional, we shall also use the rule of conditional proof called **CP**. Occasionally, we may use the indirect method of proof in introducing the negation of the conclusion as an additional premise in order to arrive at a contradiction.

The equivalences and implications of the statement calculus can be used in the process of derivation as before, except that the formulas involved are generalized to predicates. But these formulas do not have any quantifiers in them, while some of the premises or the conclusion may be quantified. In order to use the equivalences and implications, we need some rules on how to eliminate quantifiers during the course of derivation. This elimination is done by *rules of specification* called rules **US** and **ES**. Once the quantifiers are eliminated, the derivation proceeds as in the case of the statement calculus, and the conclusion is reached. It may happen that the desired conclusion is quantified. In this case, we need *rules of generalization* called rules **UG** and **EG**, which can be used to attach a quantifier.

The rules of generalization and specification follow. Here $A(x)$ is used to denote a formula with a free occurrence of x. $A(y)$ denotes a formula obtained by the substitution of y for x in $A(x)$. Recall that for such a substitution $A(x)$ must be free for y.

Rule **US** (Universal Specification) From $(x)A(x)$ one can conclude $A(y)$.

Rule **ES** (Existential Specification) From $(\exists x)A(x)$ one can conclude $A(y)$ provided that y is not free in any given premise and also not free in any prior step of the derivation. These requirements can easily be met by choosing a new variable each time **ES** is used. (The conditions of **ES** are more restrictive than ordinarily required, but they do not affect the possibility of deriving any conclusion.)

Rule **EG** (Existential Generalization) From $A(x)$ one can conclude $(\exists y)A(y)$.

Rule **UG** (Universal Generalization) From $A(x)$ one can conclude $(y)A(y)$ provided that x is not free in any of the given premises and provided that if x is free in a prior step which resulted from use of **ES**, then no variables introduced by that use of **ES** appear free in $A(x)$.

We shall now show, by means of an example, how an invalid conclusion could be arrived at if the second restriction on rule **UG** were not imposed. The other restrictions on **ES** and **UG** are easy to understand.

Let $D(u, v)$: u is divisible by v. Assume that the universe of discourse is $\{5, 7, 10, 11\}$, so that the statement $(\exists u)D(u, 5)$ is true because both $D(5, 5)$

and $D(10, 5)$ are true. On the other hand, $(y)D(y, 5)$ is false because $D(7, 5)$ and $D(11, 5)$ are false. Consider now the following derivation.

$\{1\}$	(1)	$(\exists u)D(u, 5)$	**P**
$\{1\}$	(2)	$D(x, 5)$	**ES**, (1)
$\{1\}$	(3)	$(y)D(y, 5)$	**UG**, (2) (neglecting second restriction)

In step 3 we have obtained from $D(x, 5)$ the conclusion $(y)D(y, 5)$. Obviously x is not free in the premise, and so the first restriction is satisfied. But x is free in step 2 which resulted by use of **ES**, and that x has been introduced by use of **ES** and appears free in $D(x, 5)$; hence it cannot be generalized. This is the reason why we obtained a false conclusion from a true premise.

We now give several examples with comments to explain the method of derivation. In the first two examples we use the principles **UG** and **US**, but not **EG** and **ES**.

EXAMPLE 1 Show that $(x)(H(x) \rightarrow M(x)) \wedge H(s) \Rightarrow M(s)$. Note that this problem is a symbolic translation of a well-known argument known as the "Socrates argument" which is given by:

> All men are mortal.
>
> Socrates is a man.
>
> Therefore Socrates is a mortal.

If we denote $H(x): x$ is a man, $M(x): x$ is a mortal, and s: Socrates, we can put the argument in the above form.

SOLUTION

$\{1\}$	(1)	$(x)(H(x) \rightarrow M(x))$	**P**
$\{1\}$	(2)	$H(s) \rightarrow M(s)$	**US**, (1)
$\{3\}$	(3)	$H(s)$	**P**
$\{1, 3\}$	(4)	$M(s)$	**T**, (2), (3), I_{11}

Note that in step 2 first we remove the universal quantifier.   ////

EXAMPLE 2 Show that

$$(x)(P(x) \rightarrow Q(x)) \wedge (x)(Q(x) \rightarrow R(x)) \Rightarrow (x)(P(x) \rightarrow R(x))$$

SOLUTION

$\{1\}$	(1)	$(x)(P(x) \rightarrow Q(x))$	**P**
$\{1\}$	(2)	$P(y) \rightarrow Q(y)$	**US**, (1)
$\{3\}$	(3)	$(x)(Q(x) \rightarrow R(x))$	**P**
$\{3\}$	(4)	$Q(y) \rightarrow R(y)$	**US**, (3)
$\{1, 3\}$	(5)	$P(y) \rightarrow R(y)$	**T**, (2), (4), I_{13}
$\{1, 3\}$	(6)	$(x)(P(x) \rightarrow R(x))$	**UG**, (5) ////

EXAMPLE 3 Show that $(\exists x)M(x)$ follows logically from the premises

$$(x)(H(x) \rightarrow M(x)) \qquad \text{and} \qquad (\exists x)H(x)$$

SOLUTION

{1}	(1)	$(\exists x)H(x)$	**P**
{1}	(2)	$H(y)$	**ES**, (1)
{3}	(3)	$(x)(H(x) \rightarrow M(x))$	**P**
{3}	(4)	$H(y) \rightarrow M(y)$	**US**, (3)
{1, 3}	(5)	$M(y)$	**T**, (2), (4), I_{11}
{1, 3}	(6)	$(\exists x)M(x)$	**EG**, (5)

Note that in step 2 the variable y is introduced by **ES**. Therefore a conclusion such as $(x)M(x)$ could not follow from step 5 because it would violate the rules given for **UG**. ////

EXAMPLE 4 Prove that

$$(\exists x)(P(x) \wedge Q(x)) \Rightarrow (\exists x)P(x) \wedge (\exists x)Q(x)$$

SOLUTION

{1}	(1)	$(\exists x)(P(x) \wedge Q(x))$	**P**
{1}	(2)	$P(y) \wedge Q(y)$	**ES**, (1), y fixed
{1}	(3)	$P(y)$	**T**, (2), I_1
{1}	(4)	$Q(y)$	**T**, (2), I_2
{1}	(5)	$(\exists x)P(x)$	**EG**, (3)
{1}	(6)	$(\exists x)Q(x)$	**EG**, (4)
{1}	(7)	$(\exists x)P(x) \wedge (\exists x)Q(x)$	**T**, (4), (5), I_9	////

It is instructive to try to prove the converse which does not hold. The derivation is

(1)	$(\exists x)P(x) \wedge (\exists x)Q(x)$	**P**
(2)	$(\exists x)P(x)$	**T**, (1), I_1
(3)	$(\exists x)Q(x)$	**T**, (1), I_2
(4)	$P(y)$	**ES**, (2)
(5)	$Q(z)$	**ES**, (3)

Note that in step 4, y is fixed, and it is no longer possible to use that variable again in step 5.

EXAMPLE 5 Show that from

(a) $(\exists x)(F(x) \wedge S(x)) \rightarrow (y)(M(y) \rightarrow W(y))$
(b) $(\exists y)(M(y) \wedge \neg W(y))$

the conclusion $(x)(F(x) \rightarrow \neg S(x))$ follows.

SOLUTION

{1}	(1)	$(\exists y)(M(y) \wedge \neg W(y))$	**P**
{1}	(2)	$M(z) \wedge \neg W(z)$	**ES**, (1)
{1}	(3)	$\neg(M(z) \to W(z))$	**T**, (2), E_{17}
{1}	(4)	$(\exists y)\neg(M(y) \to W(y))$	**EG**, (3)
{1}	(5)	$\neg(y)(M(y) \to W(y))$	E_{26}, (4)
{6}	(6)	$(\exists x)(F(x) \wedge S(x)) \to (y)(M(y) \to W(y))$	**P**
{1, 6}	(7)	$\neg(\exists x)(F(x) \wedge S(x))$	**T**, (5), (6), I_{12}
{1, 6}	(8)	$(x)\neg(F(x) \wedge S(x))$	**T**, (7), E_{25}
{1, 6}	(9)	$\neg(F(x) \wedge S(x))$	**US**, (8)
{1, 6}	(10)	$F(x) \to \neg S(x)$	**T**, (9), E_9, E_{16}, E_{17}
{1, 6}	(11)	$(x)(F(x) \to \neg S(x))$	**UG**, (10)

EXAMPLE 6 Show that

$$(x)(P(x) \vee Q(x)) \Rightarrow (x)P(x) \vee (\exists x)Q(x)$$

SOLUTION We shall use the indirect method of proof by assuming $\neg((x)P(x) \vee (\exists x)Q(x))$ as an additional premise.

{1}	(1)	$\neg((x)P(x) \vee (\exists x)Q(x))$	**P** (assumed)
{1}	(2)	$\neg(x)P(x) \wedge \neg(\exists x)Q(x)$	**T**, (1), E_9
{1}	(3)	$\neg(x)P(x)$	**T**, (2), I_1
{1}	(4)	$(\exists x)\neg P(x)$	**T**, (3), E_{26}
{1}	(5)	$\neg(\exists x)Q(x)$	**T**, (2), I_2
{1}	(6)	$(x)\neg Q(x)$	**T**, (5), E_{25}
{1}	(7)	$\neg P(y)$	**ES**, (4)
{1}	(8)	$\neg Q(y)$	**US**, (6)
{1}	(9)	$\neg P(y) \wedge \neg Q(y)$	**T**, (7), (8), I_9
{1}	(10)	$\neg(P(y) \vee Q(y))$	**T**, (9), E_9
{11}	(11)	$(x)(P(x) \vee Q(x))$	**P**
{11}	(12)	$P(y) \vee Q(y)$	**US**, (11)
{1, 11}	(13)	$\neg(P(y) \vee Q(y)) \wedge (P(y) \vee Q(y))$	**T**, (10), (12), I_9 contradiction

$////$

1-6.5 Formulas Involving More Than One Quantifier

So far we have considered only those formulas in which the universal and existential quantifiers appear singly. We shall now consider cases in which the quantifiers occur in combinations. These combinations are possible even in the case of 1-place predicates, and they become particularly important in the case of n-place predicates $(n \geq 2)$. For example, if $P(x, y)$ is a 2-place predicate formula, then the following possibilities exist:

$$(x)(y)P(x, y) \qquad (x)(\exists y)P(x, y) \qquad (\exists x)(y)P(x, y)$$
$$(\exists x)(\exists y)P(x, y) \qquad (y)(x)P(x, y) \qquad (\exists y)(x)P(x, y)$$
$$(y)(\exists x)P(x, y) \qquad (\exists y)(\exists x)P(x, y)$$

It is understood that $(x)(y)P(x, y)$ stands for $(x)((y)P(x, y))$ and $(\exists x)(y)P(x, y)$ for $(\exists x)((y)P(x, y))$. The brackets are not used because even without them there is no possibility of misunderstanding the meaning. From the meaning of the quantifiers, the following formulas can be obtained.

$$(x)(y)P(x, y) \Leftrightarrow (y)(x)P(x, y) \tag{1}$$
$$(x)(y)P(x, y) \Rightarrow (\exists y)(x)P(x, y) \tag{2}$$
$$(y)(x)P(x, y) \Rightarrow (\exists x)(y)P(x, y) \tag{3}$$
$$(\exists y)(x)P(x, y) \Rightarrow (x)(\exists y)P(x, y) \tag{4}$$
$$(\exists x)(y)P(x, y) \Rightarrow (y)(\exists x)P(x, y) \tag{5}$$
$$(x)(\exists y)P(x, y) \Rightarrow (\exists y)(\exists x)P(x, y) \tag{6}$$
$$(y)(\exists x)P(x, y) \Rightarrow (\exists x)(\exists y)P(x, y) \tag{7}$$
$$(\exists x)(\exists y)P(x, y) \Leftrightarrow (\exists y)(\exists x)P(x, y) \tag{8}$$

Figure 1-6.1 shows implications (2) to (7) and equivalences (1) and (8). One can also prove these implications and equivalences using the method of derivation given in the previous section.

The negation of any of the above formulas can be obtained by repeated applications of the equivalences E_{25} and E_{26} of Sec. 1-6.3. For example,

$$\neg(\exists y)(x)P(x, y) \Leftrightarrow (y)(\neg(x)P(x, y)) \Leftrightarrow (y)(\exists x)\neg P(x, y)$$

The negations of other formulas of this type are obtained in a similar manner.

The inference rules and the method of derivation as given in Sec. 1-6.4 also apply to n-place predicate formulas. Obviously, some special care would

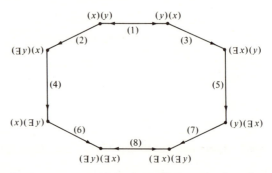

FIGURE 1-6.1 Graphical representation of relationships among formulas involving two quantifiers.

now be needed in the use of the rules **UG**, **EG**, **US**, and **ES**. In the case of **US** and **ES**, the specific variable should be chosen in such a way that it is different from the bound variable used elsewhere. To illustrate this discussion, we consider the formula $(x)(\exists y)P(x, y)$. Using **US**, we can write any of the formulas

$$(\exists y)P(x, y) \qquad (\exists y)P(z, y)$$

but we should not write $(\exists y)P(y, y)$ because the variable y is used as a bound variable; that is, $(\exists y)P(x, y)$ is not free for y. Similarly, in using **EG**, one should be careful. For example, from $(x)P(x, y)$ we can generalize

$$(\exists y)(x)P(x, y) \qquad \text{or} \qquad (\exists z)(x)P(x, z)$$

but not $(\exists x)(x)P(x, x)$. Similar care is required in the use of **UG** and **ES**.

EXAMPLE 1   Show that $\neg P(a, b)$ follows logically from $(x)(y)(P(x, y) \rightarrow W(x, y))$ and $\neg W(a, b)$.

    SOLUTION

{1}	(1)	$(x)(y)(P(x, y) \rightarrow W(x, y))$	**P**
{1}	(2)	$(y)(P(a, y) \rightarrow W(a, y))$	**US**, (1)
{1}	(3)	$P(a, b) \rightarrow W(a, b)$	**US**, (2)
{1}	(4)	$\neg W(a, b)$	**P**
{1, 4}	(5)	$\neg P(a, b)$	**T**, (3), (4), I_{12} ////

EXERCISES   1-6

1 Show that $P(x) \wedge (x)Q(x) \Rightarrow (\exists x)(P(x) \wedge Q(x))$.

2 Explain why the following steps in the derivations are not correct.
    (a) (1) $(x)P(x) \rightarrow Q(x)$
        (2) $P(x) \rightarrow Q(x)$ (1), **US**
    (b) (1) $(x)P(x) \rightarrow Q(x)$
        (2) $P(y) \rightarrow Q(x)$ (1), **US**
    (c) (1) $(x)(P(x) \vee Q(x))$
        (2) $P(a) \vee Q(b)$ (1), **US**
    (d) (1) $(x)(P(x) \vee (\exists x)(Q(x) \wedge R(x)))$
        (2) $P(a) \vee (\exists x)(Q(x) \wedge R(a))$ (1), **US**

3 What is wrong in the following steps of derivation?
    (a) (1) $P(x) \rightarrow Q(x)$ **P**
        (2) $(\exists x)P(x) \rightarrow Q(x)$ (1), **EG**
    (b) (1) $P(a) \rightarrow Q(b)$ **P**
        (2) $(\exists x)(P(x) \rightarrow Q(x))$ (1), **EG**
    (c) (1) $P(a) \wedge (\exists x)(P(a) \wedge Q(x))$ **P**
        (2) $(\exists x)(P(x) \wedge (\exists x)(P(x) \wedge Q(x)))$ (1), **EG**

4 Demonstrate the following implications.
    (a) $\neg((\exists x)P(x) \wedge Q(a)) \Rightarrow (\exists x)P(x) \rightarrow \neg Q(a)$
    (b) $(x)(\neg P(x) \rightarrow Q(x)), (x)\neg Q(x) \Rightarrow P(a)$
    (c) $(x)(P(x) \rightarrow Q(x)), (x)(Q(x) \rightarrow R(x)) \Rightarrow P(x) \rightarrow R(x)$
    (d) $(x)(P(x) \vee Q(x)), (x)\neg P(x) \Rightarrow (\exists x)Q(x)$

(e) $(x)(P(x) \lor Q(x))$, $(x)\neg P(x) \Rightarrow (x)Q(x)$

(f) $\neg(x)(P(x) \land Q(x))$, $(x)P(x) \Rightarrow \neg(x)Q(x)$

5 There is a mistake in the following derivation. Find it. Is the conclusion valid? If so, obtain a correct derivation.

$\{1\}$	(1)	$(x)(P(x) \to Q(x))$	**P**
$\{1\}$	(2)	$P(y) \to Q(y)$	**US**, (1)
$\{3\}$	(3)	$(\exists x)P(x)$	**P**
$\{3\}$	(4)	$P(y)$	**ES**, (3)
$\{1,3\}$	(5)	$Q(y)$	**T**, (2), (4), I_{11}
$\{1,3\}$	(6)	$(\exists x)Q(x)$	**EG**, (5)

6 Given the premise $(x)(\exists y)P(x,y)$, find the mistake in the following derivation.

$\{1\}$	(1)	$(x)(\exists y)P(x,y)$	**P**
$\{1\}$	(2)	$(\exists y)P(z,y)$	**US**, (1)
$\{1\}$	(3)	$P(z,w)$	**ES**, (2)
$\{1\}$	(4)	$(x)P(x,w)$	**UG**, (3)
$\{1\}$	(5)	$(\exists y)(x)P(x,y)$	**EG**, (4)

7 Are the following conclusions validly derivable from the premises given?

(a) $(x)(P(x) \to Q(x))$, $(\exists y)P(y)$ $C: (\exists z)Q(z)$

(b) $(\exists x)(P(x) \land Q(x))$ $C: (x)P(x)$

(c) $(\exists x)P(x)$, $(\exists x)Q(x)$ $C: (\exists x)(P(x) \land Q(x))$

(d) $(x)(P(x) \to Q(x))$, $\neg Q(a)$ $C: (x)\neg P(x)$

8 Using **CP** or otherwise, show the following implications.

(a) $(\exists x)P(x) \to (x)Q(x) \Rightarrow (x)(P(x) \to Q(x))$

(b) $(x)(P(x) \to Q(x))$, $(x)(R(x) \to \neg Q(x)) \Rightarrow (x)(R(x) \to \neg P(x))$

(c) $(x)(P(x) \to Q(x)) \Rightarrow (x)P(x) \to (x)Q(x)$

9 Construct the derivation of the following equivalences.

(a) $(\exists x)P(x) \to (x)Q(x) \Leftrightarrow (x)(P(x) \to Q(x))$—without using E_{34}

(b) $P \to (\exists x)Q(x) \Leftrightarrow (\exists x)(P \to Q(x))$—without using E_{32}

10 Show the following by constructing derivations.

(a) $(\exists x)P(x) \to (x)((P(x) \lor Q(x)) \to R(x))$, $(\exists x)P(x)$, $(\exists x)Q(x) \Rightarrow (\exists x)(\exists y)(R(x) \land R(y))$

(b) $(x)(P(x) \to (Q(y) \land R(x)))$, $(\exists x)P(x) \Rightarrow Q(y) \land (\exists x)(P(x) \land R(x))$

(c) $(x)(H(x) \to A(x)) \Rightarrow (x)((\exists y)(H(y) \land N(x,y)) \to (\exists y)(A(y) \land N(x,y)))$

BIBLIOGRAPHY

BARTEE, THOMAS: "Digital Computer Fundamentals," 3d ed., McGraw-Hill Book Company, New York, 1962.

DIETMEYER, DONALD L.: "Logic Design of Digital Systems," Allyn and Bacon, Inc., Boston, 1971.

DINKINES, FLORA: "Introduction to Mathematical Logic," Appleton-Century-Crofts, Inc., New York, 1964.

EXNER, ROBERT M., and MYRON F. ROSSKOPF: "Logic in Elementary Mathematics," McGraw-Hill Book Company, New York, 1950.

HILBERT, D., and W. ACKERMANN: "Principles of Mathematical Logic," Chelsea Publishing Company, New York, 1950.

KOHAVI, ZVI: "Switching and Finite Automata Theory," McGraw-Hill Book Company, New York, 1970.

NOVIKOV, P. S.: "Elements of Mathematical Logic," translated by Leo F. Boron, Addison-

Wesley Publishing Company, Inc., Reading, Mass., 1964.

POLLOCK, JOHN L.: "An Introduction to Symbolic Logic," Holt, Rinehart and Winston, Inc., New York, 1969.

ROSSER, J. BARKLEY: "Logic for Mathematicians," McGraw-Hill Book Company, New York, 1953.

SŁUPECKI, J., and L. BORKOWSKI: "Elements of Mathematical Logic and Set Theory," translated by O. Wojtasiewiez, Pergamon Press, Oxford, 1967.

STOLL, ROBERT R.: "Set Theory and Logic," W. H. Freeman and Company, Publishers, San Francisco, 1963.

SUPPES, PATRICK: "Introduction to Logic," D. Van Nostrand Company, Inc., Princeton, N.J., (1957), reprinted 1960.

——— and SHIRLEY HILL: "First Course in Mathematical Logic," Blaisdell Publishing Company, Waltham, Mass., 1964.

2

SET THEORY

INTRODUCTION

The concept of a set is used in various disciplines and particularly often in mathematics. In this chapter, we introduce elementary set theory. An axiomatic approach to the discussion and questions of a philosophical nature will be avoided. Although our presentation remains informal, we try to indicate formal proofs which use the notation and the rules of inference given in Chap. 1. As we proceed, an analogy will be drawn between the statement calculus and the set operations leading to a set algebra which is similar to the statement algebra given earlier. Initially, the notation of set theory is introduced and certain operations are defined. Then follows an introduction to the representation of discrete structures. The concepts of relations, orderings, and functions are presented after a discussion of the algebra of sets. A particular type of function known as a binary operation prepares us for a discussion of algebraic structures, which form the subject matter of Chap. 3. A special function known as a hashing function, which maps a name into an integer and permits us to handle nonnumeric data, is discussed. The natural numbers are introduced, and the principle of mathematical induction is given. A discussion of recursive functions then follows. Certain applications meant to motivate the reader and relate the key theoretical concepts to practical situations are given throughout the chapter. Some of these are presented as algorithms which can easily be implemented on a computer. An algorithm based on the discussion of automatic theorem proving in the statement calculus (Sec. 1-4.4) is also given.

2-1 BASIC CONCEPTS OF SET THEORY

In this section first we introduce the notation used for specifying sets. The concepts of membership and inclusion are given. Certain special sets such as the universal set, empty set, and the power set of a given set are introduced. Next, various set operations are defined. Finally, some of the basic identities of set algebra are derived.

2-1.1 Notation

Rather than defining the term "set," here we give only an intuitive idea of what a set is. By a *set* we mean a collection of objects of any sort. The word "object" is used here in a very broad sense to include even abstract objects. The following examples will illustrate the concept of a set.

The *set* of all Canadians

A *pair* of shoes

A *bouquet* of flowers

The *set* of all ideas contained in a book

A *flock* of sheep

A *collection* of rocks

Note that we encounter many words which convey the same idea as that of a set. Some of these words, however, are used in a more restricted sense than the term "set," while the others are synonyms. We shall use the words "class," "aggregate," and "collection" as synonyms of the word "set," particularly to avoid using the same word repeatedly in a given sentence. For example, a set of sets may be called a collection of sets.

Generally speaking, we think of a set as a collection of objects which share some common property. For example, in mathematics it is common to consider a set of lines, a set of triangles, a set of real numbers, etc. However, this restriction is not necessary, and a set consisting of a horse, the letter A, a jacket, and Mr. Smith is an acceptable example of a set, although it may be uninteresting and not important.

A fundamental concept of set theory is that of membership or belonging to a set. Any object belonging to a set is called a *member* or an *element* of that set. A set is said to be *well defined* if it is possible to determine, by means of certain rules, whether any given object is a member of the set.

Capital letters, with or without subscripts, will be used throughout to denote sets, and lowercase letters will be used to denote the elements. Some exceptions to these rules will be made in order to conform to standard practice.

If an element p belongs to a set A, then we write

$$p \in A$$

which is read as "p is an element of the set A" or "p belongs to the set A," or "p is in A." If there exists an object q which does not belong to the set A, then we express this fact as

$$q \notin A$$

which is equivalent to the negation of the statement "q is in A," that is,

$$\neg(q \in A) \Leftrightarrow q \notin A$$

There are several ways in which a set can be specified. For example, a set consisting of the elements 1, 3, and a is generally written as

$$\{1, 3, a\}$$

The names of the elements are enclosed in braces and separated by commas. If we wish to denote this set as S, then we write

$$S = \{1, 3, a\}$$

where the equality sign is understood to mean that S is the set $\{1, 3, a\}$. Obviously,

$$1 \in S \qquad 3 \in S \qquad a \in S \qquad \text{and} \qquad 2 \notin S$$

This method of specifying a set is not convenient, and it is not always possible to use it. In general, a set can be defined or characterized by a predicate. Examples of such sets are

$$S_1 = \{x \mid x \text{ is an odd positive integer}\}$$
$$S_2 = \{x \mid x \text{ is a province of Canada}\}$$
$$S_3 = \{x \mid x \text{ is a river}\}$$
$$S_4 = \{x \mid x = a \text{ or } x = b\}$$

If we let $P(x)$ denote any predicate, then $\{x \mid P(x)\}$ defines a set. An element b belongs to this set if $P(b)$ is true; otherwise b does not belong to the set. This statement would be written symbolically as

$$(y)(P(y) \Leftrightarrow y \in \{x \mid P(x)\})$$

If we denote the set $\{x \mid P(x)\}$ by A, then $A = \{x \mid P(x)\}$ and

$$(y)(y \in A \Leftrightarrow y \in \{x \mid x \in A\})$$

Other sets which are specified by listing the elements can also be characterized by means of predicates. For example, the set $\{1, 3, a\}$ could be defined as

$$\{x \mid (x = 1) \lor (x = 3) \lor (x = a)\}$$

Although it is possible to characterize any set by a predicate, it is sometimes convenient to specify sets by yet another method, such as

$$S_5 = \{1, 3, 5, \ldots\}$$
$$S_6 = \{2, 4, 6, \ldots, 18\}$$
$$S_7 = \{a, a^2, a^3, \ldots\}$$

In this representation the missing elements can be determined from the elements present and from the context.

The number of distinct elements present in a set may be finite or infinite. We shall call a set *finite* if it contains a finite number of distinguishable elements; otherwise, a set is *infinite*. Precise definitions of a finite and an infinite set are given in Sec. 2-5.2.

Note that no restriction has been placed on the objects that can be members of a set. It is not unusual to have sets whose members are themselves sets, such as

$$S = \{a, \{1, 2\}, p, \{q\}\}$$

However, it is important to distinguish between the set $\{q\}$, which is an element of S, and the element q, which is a member of $\{q\}$ but not a member of S.

2-1.2 Inclusion and Equality of Sets

In Sec. 2-1.1, we discussed the notion of membership of an element in a set. Another basic concept in set theory is that of inclusion.

Definition 2-1.1 Let A and B be any two sets. If every element of A is an element of B, then A is called a *subset* of B, or A is said to be *included* in B, or B *includes* A. Symbolically, this relation is denoted by $A \subseteq B$, or equivalently by $B \supseteq A$. Alternatively,

$$A \subseteq B \Leftrightarrow (x)(x \in A \rightarrow x \in B) \Leftrightarrow B \supseteq A$$

It is important at this stage to distinguish between membership and inclusion. We illustrate the difference between these two. Let

$$A = \{1, 2, 3\} \qquad B = \{1, 2\} \qquad C = \{1, 3\} \qquad \text{and} \qquad D = \{3\}$$

then
$$B \subseteq A \qquad C \subseteq A \qquad \text{and} \qquad D \subseteq A$$

or
$$\{1, 2\} \subseteq \{1, 2, 3\} \qquad \{1, 3\} \subseteq \{1, 2, 3\} \qquad \{3\} \subseteq \{1, 2, 3\}$$

On the other hand, $1 \in \{1, 2, 3\}$, and 1 is not included in $\{1, 2, 3\}$, though $\{1\} \subseteq \{1, 2, 3\}$. Only a set can be included in or can be a subset of another set, while only elements can be members of a set. Of course, a set may sometimes have other sets as elements. For example, if $A = \{\{1\}, 2, 3\}$, then

$$\{1\} \in A \qquad \{\{1\}, 2\} \subseteq A \qquad \{\{1\}\} \subseteq A \qquad 2 \in A \qquad \{2, 3\} \subseteq A$$

The following are some of the important properties of set inclusion. For any sets A, B, and C

$$A \subseteq A \qquad \text{(reflexive)} \qquad (1)$$

$$(A \subseteq B) \wedge (B \subseteq C) \Rightarrow (A \subseteq C) \qquad \text{(transitive)} \qquad (2)$$

It is enough to note at this stage that set inclusion is reflexive and transitive. These terms are explained in Sec. 2-3.2. The proof of Statement (1) is obvious, while Statement (2) can be proved by using the implication

$$(x)\,(x \in A \to x \in B) \land (x)\,(x \in B \to x \in C) \Rightarrow (x)\,(x \in A \to x \in C)$$

(see Example 2, Sec. 1-6.4). For two sets A and B, note that $A \subseteq B$ does not necessarily imply $B \subseteq A$ except for the following case.

Definition 2-1.2 Two sets A and B are said to be *equal* (extensionally equal) iff $A \subseteq B$ and $B \subseteq A$, or symbolically,

$$A = B \Leftrightarrow (A \subseteq B \land B \subseteq A)$$

From the equivalence

$$(x)\,((P(x) \to Q(x)) \land (Q(x) \to P(x))) \Leftrightarrow (x)\,(P(x) \rightleftarrows Q(x))$$

we can alternatively define the equality of two sets as

$$A = B \Leftrightarrow (x)\,(x \in A \rightleftarrows x \in B)$$

We now give some examples of sets that are equal and sets that are not equal.

$\{1, 2, 4\} = \{1, 2, 2, 4\}$.

$\{1, 4, 2\} = \{1, 2, 4\}$.

If $P = \{\{1, 2\}, 4\}$ and $Q = \{1, 2, 4\}$, then $P \neq Q$.

$\{\{1\}\} \neq \{1\}$ because $\{1\} \in \{\{1\}\}$ while $1 \in \{1\}$.

If $A = \{x \mid x(x - 1) = 0\}$ and $B = \{0, 1\}$, then $A = B$.

$\{1, 3, 5, \ldots\} = \{x \mid x \text{ is an odd positive integer}\}$.

From the definition of equality of sets it is clear that

$$A = B \Leftrightarrow B = A$$

The equality of sets is reflexive, symmetric, and transitive.

Definition 2-1.3 A set A is called a *proper subset* of a set B if $A \subseteq B$ and $A \neq B$. Symbolically it is written as $A \subset B$, so that

$$A \subset B \Leftrightarrow (A \subseteq B \land A \neq B)$$

$A \subset B$ is also called a proper inclusion.

A proper inclusion is not reflexive; however, it is transitive, i.e.,

$$(A \subset B) \land (B \subset C) \Rightarrow (A \subset C)$$

We shall now introduce two special sets, of which one includes every set under discussion while the other is included in every set under discussion.

Definition 2-1.4 A set is called a *universal set* if it includes every set under discussion. A universal set will be denoted by E.

It follows from the definition that for any set A, we have $A \subseteq E$. Thus every element $x \in E$, that is, $(x)(x \in E)$ is identically true. One could specify E in a variety of ways, e.g.,

$$E = \{x \mid P(x) \vee \neg P(x)\}$$

where $P(x)$ is any predicate. It is easy to show that all such sets are equal to the set E. The introduction of the universal set makes the notion of $b \notin A$ more definite in the sense that b is assumed to be in E. The universal set is the same as the universe of discourse given in Sec. 1-5.5.

Definition 2-1.5 A set which does not contain any element is called an *empty set* or a *null set*. An empty set will be denoted by $\varnothing$.

It follows from the definition that for an empty set $\varnothing$ and any $x, x \in \varnothing$ is a contradiction, that is, $(x)(x \in \varnothing)$ is a contradiction. Thus for any set A, $\varnothing \subseteq A$, because $(x)(x \in \varnothing \Rightarrow x \in A)$. One could specify $\varnothing$ in a variety of ways, e.g.,

$$\varnothing = \{x \mid P(x) \wedge \neg P(x)\}$$

where $P(x)$ is any predicate. It is easy to show that all such sets are identical to the set $\varnothing$.

2-1.3 The Power Set

Given any set A, we know that the null set $\varnothing$ and the set A are both subsets of A. Also for any element $a \in A$, the set $\{a\}$ is a subset of A. Similarly, we can consider other subsets of A. Rather than finding individual subsets of A, we would like to say something about the set of all subsets of A.

Definition 2-1.6 For a set A, a collection or family of all subsets of A is called the *power set* of A. The power set of A is denoted by $\rho(A)$ or 2^A, so that

$$\rho(A) = 2^A = \{x \mid x \subseteq A\}$$

Let us consider some finite sets and their power sets. The power set of the null set $\varnothing$ has only the element $\varnothing$; hence $\rho(\varnothing) = \{\varnothing\}$. For a set $S_1 = \{a\}$, the power set $\rho(S_1) = \{\varnothing, \{a\}\} = \{\varnothing, S_1\}$. For $S_2 = \{a, b\}$, $\rho(S_2) = \{\varnothing, \{a\}, \{b\}, S_2\}$, and for $S_3 = \{a, b, c\}$, $\rho(S_3) = \{\varnothing, \{a\}, \{b\}, \{c\}, \{a, b\}, \{b, c\}, \{a, c\}, S_3\}$.

We now introduce a notation by which one can designate every subset of a finite set in a unique manner. Before we describe this notation, it would be useful to assume that the elements of the given set are ordered in some way, so that a particular element may be called the first element, the next element the second, and so on. No such ordering of the elements of a set is implied in the definition of a set. However, for the purpose of representing a set on a computer it is generally necessary to prescribe some arbitrary order; i.e., to each element is attached a label which describes the position of the element with respect to other elements of the set. As an example, let us assume that in the set S_2 given earlier we let a be the first element and b be the second element. Now, in any subset of a given set, some elements of the set are present while the remaining ones are absent. We shall use this idea, together with the ordering prescribed on the elements of a given set, to designate the subsets. For example, the subsets of S_2 may be designated as

$$\varnothing = B_{00} \qquad \{a\} = B_{10} \qquad \{b\} = B_{01} \qquad \text{and} \qquad \{a, b\} = B_{11}$$

where the subscripts of B contain 1 or 0 in the first position on the left depending on whether the first element, viz., a, is present (or not). Similarly, the subscript has 1 or 0 in the second position from the left depending on whether b, the second member, is present (or not). As there are only two elements in S_2, we need only the subscripts 00, 01, 10, and 11. Conversely, given any one of these $2^2 = 4$ subscripts, we can determine the elements of the corresponding subset. For example, $B_{01} = \{b\}$. Note that it is only the subscript that determines the elements of the subset. The use of the letter B in naming the subsets is incidental. A similar technique has been used earlier in assigning names to maxterms and minterms. This method will also be used in the representation of data on a computer.

Consider the set $J = \{00, 01, 10, 11\}$ or $J = \{i \mid i$ is a binary integer, $00 \le i \le 11\}$; then $\rho(S_2) = \{B_i \mid i \in J\}$. Similarly,

$$\rho(S_3) = \{B_i \mid i \in J\}$$

where $J = \{i \mid i$ is a binary integer, $000 \le i \le 111\}$. From $S_3 = \{a, b, c\}$ we have $B_{001} = \{c\}$, $B_{101} = \{a, c\}$, and $B_{011} = \{b, c\}$.

The above notation can be generalized to designate the subsets of a set having n distinct elements. Obviously, there are 2^n such subsets. The subscripts designating the subsets range over the binary representations of the decimal integers 0 to $2^n - 1$. Care must be taken to insert as many zeros on the left of this binary integer as necessary in order to have exactly n digits in all. One can use decimal integers from 0 to $2^n - 1$ and convert them only at the time when the elements of the corresponding subsets are to be determined. As an illustration, let $S_6 = \{a_1, a_2, \ldots, a_6\}$. Obviously, there are 2^6 subsets of S_6, which we shall designate by $B_0, B_1, \ldots B_{2^6-1}$. The following examples illustrate the method to determine the elements of any subset.

$$B_7 = B_{111} = B_{000111} = \{a_4, a_5, a_6\}$$

$$B_{12} = B_{1100} = B_{001100} = \{a_3, a_4\}$$

The method of employing subscripts to designate the elements of a family of sets is used very often. Here we have used it to designate the members of a power set. It is convenient to introduce the concept of an indexed set at this stage.

Definition 2-1.7 Let $J = \{s_1, s_2, s_3, \ldots\}$ and A be a family of sets $A = \{A_{s_1}, A_{s_2}, A_{s_3}, \ldots\}$ such that for any $s_i \in J$ there corresponds a set $A_{s_i} \in A$, and also $A_{s_i} = A_{s_j}$ iff $s_i = s_j$, then A is called an *indexed set*, J the *index set*, and any subscript such as s_i in A_{s_i} is called an *index*.

An indexed family of sets can also be written as

$$A = \{A_i\}_{i \in J}$$

In particular, if $J = \mathbf{I} = \{1, 2, 3, \ldots\}$, then $A = \{A_1, A_2, A_3, \ldots\}$. Also, if $J = \mathbf{I}_n = \{1, 2, \ldots, n\}$, then $A = \{A_1, A_2, \ldots, A_n\} = \{A_i\}_{i \in I_n}$. For a set S containing n elements, the power set $\rho(S)$ is written as the indexed set

$$\rho(S) = \{B_i\}_{i \in J} \qquad J = \{0, 1, 2, \ldots, 2^n - 1\}$$

EXERCISES 2-1.3

1 Give another description of the following sets and indicate those which are infinite sets.
   (a) $\{x \mid x$ is an integer and $5 \leq x \leq 12\}$.
   (b) $\{2, 4, 8, \ldots\}$.
   (c) All the countries of the world.

2 Given $S = \{2, a, \{3\}, 4\}$ and $R = \{\{a\}, 3, 4, 1\}$, indicate whether the following are true or false.
   (a) $\{a\} \in S$
   (b) $\{a\} \in R$
   (c) $\{a, 4, \{3\}\} \subseteq S$
   (d) $\{\{a\}, 1, 3, 4\} \subset R$
   (e) $R = S$
   (f) $\{a\} \subseteq S$
   (g) $\{a\} \subseteq R$
   (h) $\varnothing \subset R$
   (i) $\varnothing \subseteq \{\{a\}\} \subseteq R \subseteq E$
   (j) $\{\varnothing\} \subseteq S$
   (k) $\varnothing \in R$
   (l) $\varnothing \subseteq \{\{3\}, 4\}$

3 Show that

$$(R \subseteq S) \wedge (S \subset Q) \Rightarrow R \subset Q$$

Is it correct to replace $R \subset Q$ by $R \subseteq Q$? Explain your answer.

4 Give the power sets of the following.
   (a) $\{a, \{b\}\}$
   (b) $\{1, \varnothing\}$
   (c) $\{X, Y, Z\}$

5 Given $S = \{a_1, a_2, \ldots, a_8\}$, what subsets are represented by B_{17} and B_{31}? Also, how will you designate the subsets $\{a_2, a_6, a_7\}$ and $\{a_1, a_8\}$?

2-1.4 Some Operations on Sets

In this section we introduce certain basic operations on sets. Using these operations, one can construct new sets by combining the elements of given sets. While the term "operation" and its properties are discussed in Sec. 2-4.4, it suffices to say here that operations on one or more sets produce other sets according to certain rules.

Definition 2-1.8 The *intersection* of any two sets A and B, written as $A \cap B$, is the set consisting of all the elements which belong to both A and B. Symbolically,

$$A \cap B = \{x \mid (x \in A) \wedge (x \in B)\}$$

From the definition of intersection it follows that for any sets A and B,

$$A \cap B = B \cap A \qquad A \cap A = A \qquad \text{and } A \cap \emptyset = \emptyset \qquad (1)$$

The first of these equalities shows that the intersection is commutative. The importance of the other two will be discussed later. The commutativity of intersection can be proved in the following manner. For any x,

$$
\begin{aligned}
x \in A \cap B &\Leftrightarrow x \in \{x \mid (x \in A) \wedge (x \in B)\} \\
&\Leftrightarrow (x \in A) \wedge (x \in B) \\
&\Leftrightarrow (x \in B) \wedge (x \in A) \\
&\Leftrightarrow x \in \{x \mid (x \in B) \wedge (x \in A)\} \\
&\Leftrightarrow x \in B \cap A
\end{aligned}
$$

The other two equalities in Eq. (1) can be proved in a similar manner.

Since $A \cap B$ is a set, we can consider its intersection with another set C, so that

$$(A \cap B) \cap C = \{x \mid x \in A \cap B \wedge x \in C\}$$

Using $(x \in A \wedge x \in B) \wedge x \in C \Leftrightarrow x \in A \wedge (x \in B \wedge x \in C)$, we can easily show that

$$(A \cap B) \cap C = A \cap (B \cap C) \qquad \text{(associative)} \qquad (2)$$

In view of Eq. (2), we can write $(A \cap B) \cap C$ as $A \cap B \cap C$.

For an indexed set $A = \{A_1, A_2, \ldots, A_n\} = \{A_i\}_{i \in I_n}$ where $I_n = \{1, 2, \ldots, n\}$, we write

$$A_1 \cap A_2 \cap \cdots \cap A_n = \bigcap_{i=1}^{n} A_i = \bigcap_{i \in I_n} A_i$$

In general, for any index set J,

$$\bigcap_{i \in J} A_i = \{x \mid x \in A_i \text{ for all } i \in J\}$$

Definition 2-1.9 Two sets A and B are called *disjoint* iff $A \cap B = \emptyset$, that is, A and B have no element in common.

Definition 2-1.10 A collection of sets is called a *disjoint collection* if, for every pair of sets in the collection, the two sets are disjoint. The elements of a disjoint collection are said to be *mutually disjoint*.

Let A be an indexed set $A = \{A_i\}_{i \in J}$. The set A is a disjoint collection iff $A_i \cap A_j = \emptyset$ for all $i, j \in J$, $i \neq j$.

EXAMPLE 1 If $A_1 = \{\{1, 2\}, \{3\}\}$, $A_2 = \{\{1\}, \{2, 3\}\}$, and $A_3 = \{\{1, 2, 3\}\}$, then show that A_1, A_2, and A_3 are mutually disjoint.

SOLUTION Note that $A_1 \cap A_2 = \emptyset$, $A_1 \cap A_3 = \emptyset$ and $A_2 \cap A_3 = \emptyset$. ////

EXAMPLE 2 Show that $A \subseteq B \Leftrightarrow A \cap B = A$.

SOLUTION Note that for any x,

$$x \in A \to x \in B \Leftrightarrow (x \in A \wedge x \in B) \rightleftarrows x \in A$$

which follows from $P \to Q \Leftrightarrow ((P \wedge Q) \rightleftarrows P)$. Now

$$A \subseteq B \Leftrightarrow (x)(x \in A \to x \in B)$$

while

$$A \cap B = A \Leftrightarrow (x)(x \in A \wedge x \in B \rightleftarrows x \in A) \qquad ////$$

Definition 2-1.11 For any two sets A and B, the *union* of A and B, written as $A \cup B$, is the set of all elements which are members of the set A or the set B or both. Symbolically, it is written as

$$A \cup B = \{x \mid x \in A \vee x \in B\}$$

From the definition, it follows that

$$A \cup B = B \cup A \quad \text{(commutative)} \quad A \cup \emptyset = A \quad A \cup A = A$$

$$(A \cup B) \cup C = A \cup (B \cup C) \quad \text{(associative)} \qquad (3)$$

The last equality in Eq. (3) suggests that we can write $(A \cup B) \cup C$ as $A \cup B \cup C$. Note that

$$A \cup B \cup C = \{x \mid x \in A \vee x \in B \vee x \in C\}$$

We shall now prove one of the equalities in Eq. (3), viz., $A \cup A = A$. The proofs of the other equalities are similar. For any x,

$$x \in A \cup A \Leftrightarrow x \in \{x \mid x \in A \vee x \in A\}$$
$$\Leftrightarrow x \in A \vee x \in A$$
$$\Leftrightarrow x \in A$$
$$\Leftrightarrow x \in \{x \mid x \in A\}$$
$$\Leftrightarrow x \in A$$

For any indexed set $A = \{A_i\}_{i \in J}$,

$$\bigcup_{i \in J} A_i = \{x \mid x \in A_i \text{ for at least one } i \in J\}$$

For $J = \mathbf{I}_n = \{1, 2, \ldots, n\}$, we may write

$$\bigcup_{i=1}^{n} A_i = A_1 \cup A_2 \cup \cdots \cup A_n$$

EXAMPLE 3 What are $S \cup Q$ and $S \cap Q$ if $S = \{a, b, p, q\}$ and $Q = \{a, p, t\}$?

SOLUTION

$$S \cup Q = \{a, b, p, q, t\} \qquad S \cap Q = \{a, p\} \qquad ////$$

EXAMPLE 4 If $A_1 = \{1, 2\}$, $A_2 = \{2, 3\}$, and $A_3 = \{1, 2, 3, 6\}$, what are

$\bigcup\limits_{i=1}^{3} A_i$ and $\bigcap\limits_{i=1}^{3} A_i$?

SOLUTION

$$\bigcup\limits_{i=1}^{3} A_i = \{1, 2, 3, 6\} \qquad \bigcap\limits_{i=1}^{3} A_i = \{2\} \qquad ////$$

Definition 2-1.12 Let A and B be any two sets. The *relative complement* of B in A (or of B with respect to A), written as $A - B$, is the set consisting of all elements of A which are not elements of B, that is,

$$A - B = \{x \mid x \in A \wedge x \notin B\} = \{x \mid x \in A \wedge \neg(x \in B)\}$$

The relative complement of B in A is also called the *difference* of A and B.

Definition 2-1.13 Let E be the universal set. For any set A, the relative complement of A with respect to E, that is, $E - A$, is called the *absolute complement* of A. The absolute complement of a set A is often called the *complement* of A and is denoted by $\sim A$. Symbolically,

$$\sim A = E - A = \{x \mid x \in E \wedge x \notin A\} = \{x \mid x \notin A\} = \{x \mid \neg(x \in A)\}$$

The following equalities follow from the definition of the complement.

$$\sim(\sim A) = \sim\sim A = A \quad \sim\varnothing = E \quad \sim E = \varnothing \quad A \cup \sim A = E \quad A \cap \sim A = \varnothing \tag{4}$$

We now prove one of these equalities, viz., that $A \cup \sim A = E$:

$$(A \cup \sim A) = \{x \mid x \in A \vee x \notin A\} = E$$

EXAMPLE 5 Given $A = \{2, 5, 6\}$, $B = \{3, 4, 2\}$, $C = \{1, 3, 4\}$, find $A - B$ and $B - A$. Show that $A - B \neq B - A$ and $A - C = A$.

SOLUTION $A - B = \{5, 6\}$, $B - A = \{3, 4\}$, and $A - C = \{2, 5, 6\}$

$////$

EXAMPLE 6 Show that (a) $A - B = A \cap \sim B$ and (b) $A \subseteq B \Leftrightarrow \sim B \subseteq \sim A$.

SOLUTION

(a) For any x,

$$x \in A - B \Leftrightarrow x \in \{x \mid x \in A \wedge x \notin B\}$$
$$\Leftrightarrow x \in (A \cap \sim B)$$

(b)
$$A \subseteq B \Leftrightarrow (x)(x \in A \to x \in B)$$
$$\Leftrightarrow (x)(\neg(x \in B) \to \neg(x \in A))$$
$$\Leftrightarrow (x)(x \notin B) \to x \notin A)$$
$$\Leftrightarrow \sim B \subseteq \sim A \qquad\qquad ////$$

EXAMPLE 7 Show that for any two sets A and B
$$A - (A \cap B) = A - B$$

SOLUTION For any x,
$$x \in A - (A \cap B) \Leftrightarrow x \in \{x \mid x \in A \land x \notin (A \cap B)\}$$
$$\Leftrightarrow x \in A \land \sim(x \in A \land x \in B)$$
$$\Leftrightarrow x \in A \land (x \notin A \lor x \notin B)$$
$$\Leftrightarrow (x \in A \land x \notin A) \lor (x \in A \land x \notin B)$$
$$\Leftrightarrow x \in A \land x \notin B$$
$$\Leftrightarrow x \in \{x \mid x \in A \land x \notin B\}$$

Definition 2-1.14 Let A and B be any two sets. The *symmetric difference* (or *Boolean sum*) of A and B is the set $A + B$ defined by
$$A + B = (A - B) \cup (B - A) \text{ or } x \in A + B \Leftrightarrow x \in \{x \mid x \in A \ \overline{\lor} \ x \in B\}$$
where $\overline{\lor}$ is the exclusive disjunction.

The following equalities are interesting and easy to prove.
$$A + B = B + A \qquad (A + B) + C = A + (B + C) \qquad A + \varnothing = A$$
$$A + A = \varnothing \qquad \text{and} \qquad A + B = (A \cap \sim B) \cup (B \cap \sim A) \qquad (5)$$

We shall now prove one of these, viz., $A + \varnothing = A$. For any x,
$$x \in A + \varnothing \Leftrightarrow x \in \{x \mid (x \in A \land x \notin \varnothing) \lor (x \in \varnothing \land x \notin A)\}$$
$$\Leftrightarrow (x \in A \land x \notin \varnothing) \lor (x \in \varnothing \land x \notin A)$$
$$\Leftrightarrow (x \in A) \lor \mathbf{F}$$
$$\Leftrightarrow x \in A$$
$$\Leftrightarrow x \in \{x \mid x \in A\}$$
$$\Leftrightarrow x \in A$$

The programming of these set operations is discussed in Sec. 2-2.

EXERCISES 2-1.4

1 Prove the equalities in Eqs. (1).
2 Given $A = \{x \mid x$ is an integer and $1 \leq x \leq 5\}$, $B = \{3, 4, 5, 17\}$, and $C = \{1, 2, 3, \ldots\}$, find $A \cap B$, $A \cap C$, $A \cup B$, and $A \cup C$.
3 Show that $A \subseteq A \cup B$ and $A \cap B \subseteq A$.

4 Show that $A \subseteq B \Leftrightarrow A \cup B = B$.

5 If $S = \{a, b, c\}$, find nonempty disjoint sets A_1 and A_2 such that $A_1 \cup A_2 = S$. Find other solutions to this problem.

6 Prove the equalities in Eqs. (4) and (5).

7 Given $A = \{2, 3, 4\}$, $B = \{1, 2\}$, and $C = \{4, 5, 6\}$, find $A + B$, $B + C$, $A + B + C$, and $(A + B) + (B + C)$.

2-1.5 Venn Diagrams

Introduction of the universal set permits the use of a pictorial device to study the connection between the subsets of a universal set and their intersection, union, difference, and other operations. The diagrams used are called Venn diagrams. A *Venn diagram* is a schematic representation of a set by a set of points. The universal set E is represented by a set of points in a rectangle (or any other figure), and a subset, say A, of E is represented by the interior of a circle or some other simple closed curve inside the rectangle. In Fig. 2-1.1 the shaded areas represent the sets indicated below each figure. The Venn diagram for $A \subseteq B$ and $A \cap B = \varnothing$ are also given. From some of the Venn diagrams it is

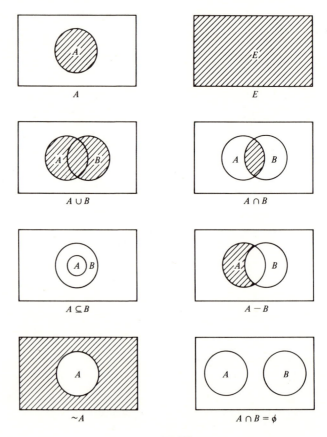

FIGURE 2-1.1 Venn diagrams.

easy to see that the following hold:

$$A \cup B = B \cup A \qquad A \cap B = B \cap A \qquad \sim(\sim A) = A$$

Furthermore, if $A \subseteq B$, then

$$A - B = \varnothing \qquad A \cap B = A \qquad \text{and} \qquad A \cup B = B$$

It should be emphasized that the above relations between the subsets are only suggested by the Venn diagram. Venn diagrams do not provide proofs that such relations are true in general for all subsets of E. We shall demonstrate this point by a particular example.

Consider the Venn diagrams given in Fig. 2-1.2. From the first two Venn diagrams it appears that

$$A \cup B = (A \cap \sim B) \cup (B \cap \sim A) \cup (A \cap B) \tag{1}$$

From the third Venn diagram it appears that

$$A \cup B = (A \cap \sim B) \cup (B \cap \sim A)$$

This equality is not true in general, although it happens to be true for the two disjoint sets A and B.

A formal proof of Eq. (1) will now be outlined. For any x,

$$x \in A \cup B \Leftrightarrow x \in \{x \mid x \in A \lor x \in B\}$$

$x \in (A \cap \sim B) \cup (B \cap \sim A) \cup (A \cap B)$

$\Leftrightarrow x \in \{x \mid x \in (A \cap \sim B) \lor x \in (B \cap \sim A) \lor x \in (A \cap B)\}$

$\Leftrightarrow x \in (A \cap \sim B) \lor x \in (B \cap \sim A) \lor x \in (A \cap B)$

$\Leftrightarrow (x \in A \land x \in \sim B) \lor (x \in B \land x \in \sim A) \lor (x \in A \land x \in B)$

$\Leftrightarrow (x \in A \land (x \in \sim B \lor x \in B)) \lor (x \in B \land x \in \sim A)$

$\Leftrightarrow (x \in A \lor x \in B) \land (x \in A \lor x \in \sim A)$

$\Leftrightarrow (x \in A \lor x \in B)$

$\Leftrightarrow x \in \{x \mid x \in A \lor x \in B\}$

$\Leftrightarrow x \in A \cup B$

Consider the Venn diagrams in Fig. 2-1.3. From the third and fifth Venn diagrams it appears that

$$A \cap (B \cup C) = (A \cap B) \cup (A \cap C) \tag{2}$$

Similarly, one can show that for any three sets A, B, and C,

$$A \cup (B \cap C) = (A \cup B) \cap (A \cup C) \tag{3}$$

Equations (2) and (3) are known as the *distributive laws of union and intersection*.

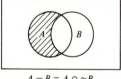

$$A - B = A \cap \sim B$$

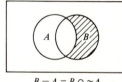

$$B - A = B \cap \sim A$$

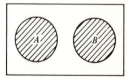

$$A \cup B$$

FIGURE 2-1.2

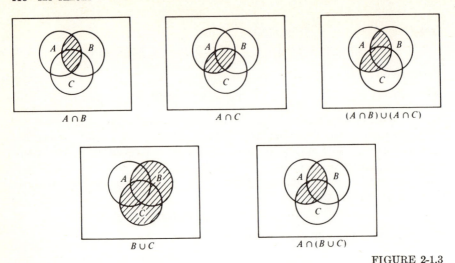

FIGURE 2-1.3

We shall now prove Eq. (3). For any x,

$$x \in A \cup (B \cap C) \Leftrightarrow x \in \{x \mid x \in A \vee x \in (B \cap C)\}$$
$$\Leftrightarrow x \in \{x \mid x \in A \vee (x \in B \wedge x \in C)\}$$
$$\Leftrightarrow x \in \{x \mid (x \in A \vee x \in B) \wedge (x \in A \vee x \in C)\}$$
$$\Leftrightarrow x \in (A \cup B) \cap (A \cup C)$$

EXERCISES   2-1.5

1   Prove Eq. (2).
2   Draw a Venn diagram to illustrate Eq. (3).

2-1.6   Some Basic Set Identities

Set operations such as union, intersection, complementation, etc., have been defined. With the help of these operations one can construct new sets from given sets. Capital letters have been used to denote definite sets. These letters have also been used as set variables. This practice is similar to the one employed in the statement calculus. Capital letters such as A, B, C, ... are used as set variables; they are not exactly sets, but *set formulas*. The operations on sets can also be extended to set formulas, so that $A \cup B$, $A \cap B$, $\sim A$, etc., are all set formulas. Any well-formed string involving set variables, the operations $\cap$, $\cup$, $\sim$, and parentheses is a set formula which will also be called a set for the sake of brevity.

In fact, one obtains a set from a set formula by replacing the variables by definite sets. Two set formulas are said to be equal if they are equal as sets whenever the set variables appearing in both the formulas are replaced by any sets. It is assumed that any particular variable is replaced by the same set throughout both formulas. Since the equality of set formulas does not depend upon the sets which replace the variables, these equalities are called set *identities*. Some of the basic identities describe certain properties of the operations involved and are given special names. These properties describe an algebra called set algebra. We shall see in Chap. 4 that both the statement algebra and the set algebra are particular cases of an abstract algebra called a Boolean algebra. This fact also explains why one could see similarities between the operators in the statement calculus and the operations of set theory. For all the identities listed in this section, we have also listed the corresponding equivalences from the statement calculus. Similar equivalences hold for the predicate calculus.

Not all the identities listed here are independent. Some of the identities can be proved by assuming certain other identities. However, we have listed these identities in order to include all those identities which exhibit some basic and useful properties. Most of these identities have been proved earlier in this section, and the others can be proved either by using the same technique or by using the identities already known to be true.

In our discussion here we assume that all the sets involved are subsets of a universal set E. Although such an assumption is not necessary for many of the identities, there is no loss of generality. Furthermore, some of the identities do require such an assumption, particularly those involving complementation.

Set Algebra	Statement Algebra	
	Idempotent laws	
$A \cup A = A$	$P \vee P \Leftrightarrow P$	(1)
$A \cap A = A$	$P \wedge P \Leftrightarrow P$	
	Associative laws	
$(A \cup B) \cup C = A \cup (B \cup C)$	$(P \vee Q) \vee R \Leftrightarrow P \vee (Q \vee R)$	(2)
$(A \cap B) \cap C = A \cap (B \cap C)$	$(P \wedge Q) \wedge R \Leftrightarrow P \wedge (Q \wedge R)$	
	Commutative laws	
$A \cup B = B \cup A$	$P \vee Q \Leftrightarrow Q \vee P$	(3)
$A \cap B = B \cap A$	$P \wedge Q \Leftrightarrow Q \wedge P$	
	Distributive laws	
$A \cup (B \cap C) = (A \cup B) \cap (A \cup C)$	$P \vee (Q \wedge R) \Leftrightarrow (P \vee Q) \wedge (Q \vee R)$	(4)
$A \cap (B \cup C) = (A \cap B) \cup (A \cap C)$	$P \wedge (Q \vee R) \Leftrightarrow (P \wedge Q) \vee (P \wedge R)$	
$A \cup \varnothing = A$	$P \vee \mathbf{F} \Leftrightarrow P$	(5)
$A \cap E = A$	$P \wedge \mathbf{T} \Leftrightarrow P$	
$A \cup E = E$	$P \vee \mathbf{T} \Leftrightarrow \mathbf{T}$	(6)
$A \cap \varnothing = \varnothing$	$P \wedge \mathbf{F} \Leftrightarrow \mathbf{F}$	
$A \cup {\sim}A = E$	$P \vee \neg P \Leftrightarrow \mathbf{T}$	(7)
$A \cap {\sim}A = \varnothing$	$P \wedge \neg P \Leftrightarrow \mathbf{F}$	
	Absorption laws	
$A \cup (A \cap B) = A$	$P \vee (P \wedge Q) \Leftrightarrow P$	(8)
$A \cap (A \cup B) = A$	$P \wedge (P \vee Q) \Leftrightarrow P$	
	De Morgan's laws	
${\sim}(A \cup B) = {\sim}A \cap {\sim}B$	$\neg(P \vee Q) \Leftrightarrow \neg P \wedge \neg Q$	(9)
${\sim}(A \cap B) = {\sim}A \cup {\sim}B$	$\neg(P \wedge Q) \Leftrightarrow \neg P \vee \neg Q$	
${\sim}\varnothing = E$	$\neg \mathbf{F} \Leftrightarrow \mathbf{T}$	(10)
${\sim}E = \varnothing$	$\neg \mathbf{T} \Leftrightarrow \mathbf{F}$	
${\sim}({\sim}A) = A$	$\neg \neg P \Leftrightarrow P$	(11)

All the identities just given are presented in pairs except for the identity (11). This pairing is done because a principle of duality similar to the one given for statement algebra (see Sec. 1-2.10) also holds in the case of set algebra. In fact, the principle of duality holds for any Boolean algebra. At present it is sufficient to note that given any identity of the set algebra, one can obtain another identity by interchanging $\cup$ with $\cap$ and E with $\varnothing$.

Assuming identities (4) to (6), we shall prove the absorption laws. First note that

$$A \cup (A \cap B) = (A \cup A) \cap (A \cup B) = A \cap (A \cup B)$$

from the distributive and idempotent laws. Now

$$
\begin{aligned}
A \cup (A \cap B) &= (A \cap E) \cup (A \cap B) &&\text{from (5)} \\
&= A \cap (E \cup B) &&\text{from (4)} \\
&= A \cap E &&\text{from (6)} \\
&= A &&\text{from (5)}
\end{aligned}
$$

Alternatively one can prove it as follows. For any x,

$$
\begin{aligned}
x \in A \cup (A \cap B) &\Leftrightarrow x \in \{x \mid (x \in A) \vee ((x \in A) \wedge (x \in B))\} \\
&\Leftrightarrow x \in \{x \mid x \in A\} \\
&\Leftrightarrow x \in A
\end{aligned}
$$

using the absorption laws of predicate calculus.

In order to complete our discussion, we list some implications and certain set inclusions

$$(A \cup B \neq \varnothing) \Rightarrow (A \neq \varnothing) \vee (B \neq \varnothing) \qquad (12)$$

$$(A \cap B \neq \varnothing) \Rightarrow (A \neq \varnothing) \wedge (B \neq \varnothing) \qquad (13)$$

To prove the implication (12), let us assume that $A \neq \varnothing \vee B \neq \varnothing$ is *false*. This requires that $A \neq \varnothing$ is *false* and also that $B \neq \varnothing$ is *false*, that is, $A = B = \varnothing$. But then $A \cup B = \varnothing$, so that $A \cup B \neq \varnothing$ is also *false*. Hence the implication is proved. One could also have proved (12) by assuming that $A \cup B \neq \varnothing$ is *true* and showing that this assumption requires $A \neq \varnothing \vee B \neq \varnothing$ to be *true*. Implication (13) can be proved in a similar manner.

The following inclusions follow from the definition and have been proved earlier in this section.

$$A \cap B \subseteq A \qquad A \cap B \subseteq B \qquad A \subseteq A \cup B \qquad A - B \subseteq A \qquad (14)$$

Let A be a family of indexed sets over an index set $\mathbf{I}$ such that $A = \{A_1, A_2, \ldots\} = \{A_i\}_{i \in \mathbf{I}}$. Then

$$\bigcup_{i \in \mathbf{I}} A_i = \{x \mid x \in A_i \text{ for some } i \in \mathbf{I}\} \qquad (15)$$

$$\bigcap_{i \in \mathbf{I}} A_i = \{x \mid x \in A_i \text{ for every } i \in \mathbf{I}\} \qquad (16)$$

The associative laws and the distributive laws can be generalized in the following manner.

$$B \cup \left(\bigcap_{i \in I} A_i \right) = \bigcap_{i \in I} (B \cup A_i) \tag{17}$$

$$B \cap \left(\bigcup_{i \in I} A_i \right) = \bigcup_{i \in I} (B \cap A_i)$$

The identities (17) can be proved using mathematical induction discussed later in Sec. 2-5.1. We now give some examples illustrating the above operations.

EXAMPLE 1   Verify the identities (17) for

$$A_1 = \{1, 5\} \qquad A_2 = \{1, 2, 4, 6\} \qquad A_3 = \{3, 4, 7\}$$

$$B = \{2, 4\} \qquad \text{and} \qquad I = \{1, 2, 3\}$$

SOLUTION

$$\bigcup_{i \in I} A_i = \{1, 2, 3, 4, 5, 6, 7\}$$

$$\bigcap_{i \in I} A_i = \varnothing$$

$$B \cup \left(\bigcap_{i \in I} A_i \right) = \{2, 4\}$$

$$\bigcap_{i \in I} (B \cup A_i) = \{1, 2, 4, 5\} \cap \{1, 2, 4, 6\} \cap \{2, 3, 4, 7\} = \{2, 4\}$$

$$B \cap \left(\bigcup_{i \in I} A_i \right) = \{2, 4\}$$

$$\bigcup_{i \in I} (B \cap A_i) = \varnothing \cup \{2, 4\} \cup \{4\} = \{2, 4\} \qquad\qquad ////$$

2-1.7   The Principle of Specification

The idea of a set was discussed in the beginning of this chapter, although we had used the notion earlier in Chap. 1 while discussing the universe of discourse or the domain of the object variable (see Sec. 1-5.5). The universe of discourse was defined as the set of all objects under consideration, and this set is the same as the universal set defined in Sec. 2-1.2.

A set is usually defined by means of a predicate. The connection between a predicate and a set defined by it is known as the *principle of specification*, which states that every predicate specifies a set which is a subset of a universal set. The subset specified by a predicate is called an *extension* of the predicate in the universal set. This method has been used extensively in defining sets. For example, if $P(x)$ is a predicate, then a set A is called an extension of $P(x)$ if

$$A = \{x \mid P(x)\}$$

A predicate can be considered as a condition, and any object of the universal set satisfying the condition is then an element of the set which is an extension of the predicate. Obviously, if two predicates are equivalent, then they have the same extension, and the two sets specified by equivalent predicates are equal. In other words, if $P(x) \Leftrightarrow Q(x)$, then $A = B$ where A and B are the extensions of $P(x)$ and $Q(x)$, respectively. We now have an analogy between the equality of sets and the equivalence of predicates. A similar analogy exists between set inclusion and implication. If $P(x) \Rightarrow Q(x)$, then $A \subseteq B$ where, again, A and B are extensions of $P(x)$ and $Q(x)$ respectively.

If $P(x)$ is identically *true* for all x in E, then the extension of $P(x)$ in the universal set is the universal set itself. Similarly, if $P(x)$ is identically *false* for all x in E, then the extension of $P(x)$ in E is the null set. Recall that the universal set and the null set were defined as extensions of $P(x) \vee \neg P(x)$ and $P(x) \wedge \neg P(x)$ respectively. However, any other identically *true* (valid) and *false* predicates could have been used to define them.

If A and B are extensions of the predicates $P(x)$ and $Q(x)$, respectively, in a universal set E, then it is easy to see that $A \cup B$ and $A \cap B$ are the extensions of $P(x) \vee Q(x)$ and $P(x) \wedge Q(x)$ respectively. Similarly $\sim A$ is the extension of $\neg P(x)$. The extension of $P(x) \to Q(x)$ is the set $\sim A \cup B$, and that of $P(x) \rightleftarrows Q(x)$ is the set $(\sim A \cup B) \cap (A \cup \sim B)$. Thus the new sets formed from the sets A and B can be interpreted in terms of extensions of formulas containing $P(x)$ and $Q(x)$.

From the above discussion it is clear that all the identities of set theory given in the previous section should follow from the corresponding equivalence of predicate formulas. Similarly, the inclusions of sets should follow from the corresponding implications of predicates. If we replace the predicates by their extensions—$\wedge$ by $\cap$, $\vee$ by $\cup$, and $\neg$ by $\sim$—in any predicate formula, then we obtain the corresponding formula of set theory. Also, the equivalences and implications are replaced by equality and inclusions of sets. In fact, this technique has often been used in proving the identities and other relations of set theory so far. For example, let us consider

$$\neg(P(x) \vee Q(x)) \Leftrightarrow \neg P(x) \wedge \neg Q(x)$$

If A and B denote the extensions of $P(x)$ and $Q(x)$ respectively, then we can write

$$\sim(A \cup B) = \sim A \cap \sim B$$

Similarly, from

$$P(x) \vee (Q(x) \wedge R(x)) \Leftrightarrow (P(x) \vee Q(x)) \wedge (P(x) \vee R(x))$$

we get

$$A \cup (B \cap C) = (A \cup B) \cap (A \cup C) \qquad [C \text{ is the extension of } R(x)]$$

2-1.8 Ordered Pairs and n-tuples

So far we have been solely concerned with sets, their equality, and operations on sets to form new sets. We now introduce the notion of an ordered pair. Although it is possible to define ordered pairs rigorously, we shall give an intuitive definition.

An *ordered pair* consists of two objects in a given fixed order. Note that an ordered pair is not a set consisting of two elements. The ordering of the two objects is important. The two objects need not be distinct. We shall denote an ordered pair by $\langle x, y \rangle$. A familiar example of an ordered pair is the representation of a point in a two-dimensional plane in cartesian coordinates. Accordingly, the ordered pairs $\langle 1, 3 \rangle$, $\langle 2, 4 \rangle$, $\langle 1, 2 \rangle$, and $\langle 2, 1 \rangle$ represent different points in a plane.

The *equality* of two ordered pairs $\langle x, y \rangle$ and $\langle u, v \rangle$ is defined by

$$\langle x, y \rangle = \langle u, v \rangle \Leftrightarrow ((x = u) \wedge (y = v)) \tag{1}$$

so that $\langle 1, 2 \rangle \neq \langle 2, 1 \rangle$ and $\langle 1, 1 \rangle \neq \langle 2, 2 \rangle$. A distinction between ordered pairs and sets containing two elements will be clear from the following examples:

$$\{a, b\} = \{b, a\} = \{a, a, b\} \qquad \{a, a\} = \{a\} \qquad \langle a, b \rangle \neq \langle b, a \rangle \qquad \langle a, a \rangle \neq \{a\}$$

The idea of an ordered pair can be extended to define an ordered triple, and, more generally, an n-tuple.

An *ordered triple* is an ordered pair whose first member is itself an ordered pair. Thus an ordered triple can be written as $\langle \langle x, y \rangle, z \rangle$. From the definition of the equality of an ordered pair, we can arrive at the equality of ordered triples $\langle \langle x, y \rangle, z \rangle$ and $\langle \langle u, v \rangle, w \rangle$:

$$\langle \langle x, y \rangle, z \rangle = \langle \langle u, v \rangle, w \rangle \qquad \text{iff} \qquad \langle x, y \rangle = \langle u, v \rangle \wedge z = w$$

But, $\langle x, y \rangle = \langle u, v \rangle$ if $(x = u \wedge y = v)$. Therefore

$$\langle \langle x, y \rangle, z \rangle = \langle \langle u, v \rangle, w \rangle \Leftrightarrow ((x = u) \wedge (y = v) \wedge (z = w)) \tag{2}$$

From the above definition of equality of an ordered triple, we may write an ordered triple as $\langle x, y, z \rangle$ with an understanding that $\langle x, y, z \rangle$ stands for $\langle \langle x, y \rangle, z \rangle$. Note that

$$\langle x, y, z \rangle \neq \langle y, x, z \rangle \neq \langle x, z, y \rangle$$

An ordered quadruple can be defined as an ordered pair whose first member is an ordered triple. Thus, an ordered quadruple is written as $\langle \langle x, y, z \rangle, u \rangle$ which is actually $\langle \langle \langle x, y \rangle, z \rangle, u \rangle$. It is easy to show that two ordered quadruples $\langle \langle x, y, z \rangle, u \rangle$ and $\langle \langle p, q, r \rangle, s \rangle$ are equal provided that

$$(x = p) \wedge (y = q) \wedge (z = r) \wedge (u = s) \tag{3}$$

In view of this fact, we shall write an ordered quadruple as $\langle x, y, z, u \rangle$.

Continuing this process, an ordered n-tuple is defined to be an ordered pair whose first member is an ordered $(n - 1)$-tuple. We write an ordered n-tuple as $\langle \langle x_1, x_2, \ldots, x_{n-1} \rangle, x_n \rangle$. Further, given two ordered n-tuples $\langle \langle x_1, x_2, \ldots, x_{n-1} \rangle, x_n \rangle$ and $\langle \langle u_1, u_2, \ldots, u_{n-1} \rangle, u_n \rangle$, we have

$$\langle \langle x_1, x_2, \ldots, x_{n-1} \rangle, x_n \rangle = \langle \langle u_1, u_2, \ldots, u_{n-1} \rangle, u_n \rangle$$
$$\Leftrightarrow ((x_1 = u_1) \wedge (x_2 = u_2) \wedge \cdots \wedge (x_n = u_n))$$

Therefore, an ordered n-tuple will be written as $\langle x_1, x_2, \ldots, x_n \rangle$.

2-1.9 Cartesian Products

Definition 2-1.15 Let A and B be any two sets. The set of all ordered pairs such that the first member of the ordered pair is an element of A and the second member is an element of B is called the *cartesian product* of A

and B and is written as $A \times B$. Accordingly,

$$A \times B = \{\langle x, y \rangle \mid (x \in A) \wedge (y \in B)\}$$

EXAMPLE 1   If $A = \{\alpha, \beta\}$ and $B = \{1, 2, 3\}$, what are $A \times B$, $B \times A$, $A \times A$, $B \times B$, and $(A \times B) \cap (B \times A)$?

SOLUTION

$$A \times B = \{\langle \alpha, 1 \rangle, \langle \alpha, 2 \rangle, \langle \alpha, 3 \rangle, \langle \beta, 1 \rangle, \langle \beta, 2 \rangle, \langle \beta, 3 \rangle\}$$
$$B \times A = \{\langle 1, \alpha \rangle, \langle 2, \alpha \rangle, \langle 3, \alpha \rangle, \langle 1, \beta \rangle, \langle 2, \beta \rangle, \langle 3, \beta \rangle\}$$
$$A \times A = \{\langle \alpha, \alpha \rangle, \langle \alpha, \beta \rangle, \langle \beta, \alpha \rangle, \langle \beta, \beta \rangle\}$$
$$B \times B = \{\langle 1, 1 \rangle, \langle 1, 2 \rangle, \langle 1, 3 \rangle, \langle 2, 1 \rangle, \langle 2, 2 \rangle, \langle 2, 3 \rangle, \langle 3, 1 \rangle,$$
$$\langle 3, 2 \rangle, \langle 3. 3 \rangle\}$$

$(A \times B) \cap (B \times A) = \varnothing$ ////

EXAMPLE 2   If $A = \varnothing$ and $B = \{1, 2, 3\}$ what are $A \times B$ and $B \times A$?

SOLUTION

$$A \times B = \varnothing = B \times A \qquad ////$$

Before we consider the cartesian product of more than two sets let us consider the expressions $(A \times B) \times C$ and $A \times (B \times C)$. From the definition it follows that

$$(A \times B) \times C = \{\langle \langle a, b \rangle, c \rangle \mid (\langle a, b \rangle \in A \times B) \wedge (c \in C)\}$$
$$= \{\langle a, b, c \rangle \mid (a \in A) \wedge (b \in B) \wedge (c \in C)\} \qquad (1)$$

The last step follows from our definition of the ordered triple given in Sec. 2-1.8. Next,

$$A \times (B \times C) = \{\langle a, \langle b, c \rangle \rangle \mid (a \in A) \wedge (\langle b, c \rangle \in B \times C)\}$$

Here $\langle a, \langle b, c \rangle \rangle$ is not an ordered triple. If we consider $(A \times B) \times C$ as an ordered pair, then the first member is an ordered pair and the second member is an element of C. On the other hand, $A \times (B \times C)$ is an ordered pair in which the first member is an element of A while the second member is an ordered pair. This fact shows that

$$(A \times B) \times C \neq A \times (B \times C)$$

Before defining the cartesian product of any finite number of sets, we shall show that the cartesian product satisfies the following distributive properties. For any three sets A, B, and C

$$A \times (B \cup C) = (A \times B) \cup (A \times C)$$
$$A \times (B \cap C) = (A \times B) \cap (A \times C) \qquad (2)$$

We now prove the first of these two identities.

$$A \times (B \cup C) = \{\langle x \; y\rangle \mid (x \in A) \wedge (y \in B \cup C)\}$$
$$= \{\langle x, y\rangle \mid (x \in A) \wedge ((y \in B) \vee (y \in C))\}$$
$$= \{\langle x, y\rangle \mid ((x \in A) \wedge (y \in B)) \vee ((x \in A) \wedge (y \in C))\}$$
$$= (A \times B) \cup (A \times C)$$

The second equality in Eq. (2) can be proved in a similar manner.

Let $A = \{A_i\}_{i \in \mathbf{I}_n}$ be an indexed set and $\mathbf{I}_n = \{1, 2, \ldots, n\}$. We denote the cartesian product of the sets $A_1, A_2, \ldots, A_n$ by

$$\underset{i \in \mathbf{I}_n}{\times} A_i = A_1 \times A_2 \times \cdots \times A_n$$

which is defined by

$$\underset{i \in \mathbf{I}_1}{\times} A_i = A_1 \quad \text{and} \quad \underset{i \in \mathbf{I}_m}{\times} A_i = (\underset{i \in \mathbf{I}_{m-1}}{\times} A_i) \times A_m \quad \text{for } m = 2, 3, \ldots, n$$

According to the above definition,

$$A_1 \times A_2 \times A_3 = (A_1 \times A_2) \times A_3$$

and

$$A_1 \times A_2 \times A_3 \times A_4 = (A_1 \times A_2 \times A_3) \times A_4$$
$$= ((A_1 \times A_2) \times A_3) \times A_4$$

Our definition of cartesian product of n sets is related to the definition of n-tuples in the sense that

$$A_1 \times A_2 \times \ldots \times A_n = \{\langle x_1, x_2, \ldots, x_n\rangle \mid (x_1 \in A_1)$$
$$\wedge (x_2 \in A_2) \wedge \cdots \wedge (x_n \in A_n)\}$$

The cartesian product $A \times A$ is also written as A^2, and similarly $A \times A \times A$ as A^3, and so on.

EXERCISES 2-1

1 Give examples of sets A, B, C such that $A \cup B = A \cup C$, but $B \neq C$.

2 Write the sets

$$\varnothing \cap \{\varnothing\} \qquad \{\varnothing\} \cap \{\varnothing\} \qquad \{\varnothing, \{\varnothing\}\} - \varnothing$$

3 Write the members of $\{a, b\} \times \{1, 2, 3\}$.

4 Write $A \times B \times C$, B^2, A^3, $B^2 \times A$, and $A \times B$ where $A = \{1\}$, $B = \{a, b\}$, and $C = \{2, 3\}$.

5 Show by means of an example that $A \times B \neq B \times A$ and $(A \times B) \times C \neq A \times (B \times C)$.

6 Show that for any two sets A and B

$$\rho(A) \cup \rho(B) \subseteq \rho(A \cup B)$$
$$\rho(A) \cap \rho(B) = \rho(A \cap B)$$

Show by means of an example that

$$\rho(A) \cup \rho(B) \neq \rho(A \cup B)$$

7 Prove the identities

$$A \cap A = A \qquad A \cap \varnothing = \varnothing \qquad A \cap E = A \qquad \text{and } A \cup E = E$$

8 Show that $A \times (B \cap C) = (A \times B) \cap (A \times C)$.

9 Prove that

$$(A \cap B) \cup (A \cap \sim B) = A$$

and

$$A \cap (\sim A \cup B) = A \cap B$$

10 Show that $A \times B = B \times A \Leftrightarrow (A = \varnothing) \vee (B = \varnothing) \vee (A = B)$.

11 Show that $(A \cap B) \cup C = A \cap (B \cup C)$ iff $C \subseteq A$.

12 Draw Venn diagrams showing

$$A \cup B \subset A \cup C \qquad \text{but} \qquad B \not\subset C$$
$$A \cap B \subset A \cap C \qquad \text{but} \qquad B \not\subset C$$
$$A \cup B = A \cup C \qquad \text{but} \qquad B \neq C$$
$$A \cap B = A \cap C \qquad \text{but} \qquad B \neq C$$

13 Draw Venn diagrams and show the sets

$$\sim B \qquad \sim(A \cup B) \qquad B - (\sim A) \qquad \sim A \cup B \qquad \sim A \cap B$$

where $A \cap B \neq \varnothing$.

14 Show that $(A + B) + C = A + (B + C)$.

15 Prove that $A + A = \varnothing$ and $A + \varnothing = A$.

16 Show that $(A - B) - C = (A - C) - (B - C)$.

17 Prove that $(A \cap B) \times (C \cap D) = (A \times C) \cap (B \times D)$.

2-2 REPRESENTATION OF DISCRETE STRUCTURES

A number of applications involving discrete mathematical structures will be discussed throughout this book. Under discrete mathematical structures we include sets, ordered sets, and other structures such as trees and graphs which will be discussed in Chap. 5. These applications require that discrete structures be represented in some suitable manner. This will be the topic of the present section.

2-2.1 Data Structures

If the representation for a discrete structure does not exist in the programming language being used, then the program for a particular algorithm may be quite complex. For example, in a payroll (data processing) application a treelike representation of information for an employee such as in Fig. 2-2.1 may be required. This structure does not exist in certain programming languages, such as FORTRAN. It does not mean that we cannot program a payroll application in FORTRAN. It could be done by writing programs to construct and manipulate trees, but the programs would be complex. It would be more suitable to use a data processing language such as COBOL in this case. Ideally, the programming language chosen for the implementation of an algorithm should possess the particular representations chosen for the discrete structures in the problem being

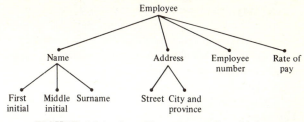

FIGURE 2-2.1   A treelike representation of information.

solved. In practice, the choice of a language may be dictated by what is available at a particular computing center, what language is preferred by some key personnel, etc.

The task of writing a computer program for a problem is made simpler if the problem can be analyzed in terms of subproblems. This structuring process in problem solving is usually reflected in the program. The program tends to be modular or consists of a number of small parts, an approach to problem solving and organization that has had a profound impact on the design of many programming languages. Processes, or modules, concerned with operations performed on data structures are frequently represented by subroutines or functions, and for the program implementation of any significant problem the organization of a program into suitable modules or subroutines is indispensible. Indeed, the simplest way to write programs is to organize them in such a modular fashion.

In organizing the solution to a problem, one is concerned with two classes of concepts. The first class deals with particular *data structures*, which are the result of an individual's interpretation of a problem, expressed by the preparation and recording of data which must be manipulated in some way according to certain processes. The second class of concepts deals with the operations that must be performed on such data structures. The terms "data structure" and "discrete structure" are considered to be equivalent in our discussions.

The class of concepts dealing with data structures has become increasingly important in recent years. Initially, computers were used to solve primarily numerical scientific problems, but this situation has changed drastically with the emerging interest in many nonnumerical problems. Associated with the solution of numerical problems were rather primitive data structures such as variables, vectors, and arrays. These structures were, for most cases, adequate for the solution of numerical problems. However, in the solution of nonnumerical problems these primitive data structures were clearly not sufficiently powerful to specify the more complex structural relationships in the data.

Data in a particular problem consist of a set of elementary items or atoms of data. An atom usually consists of single elements such as integers, bits, characters, or a set of such items. A person solving a particular problem is concerned with establishing certain paths of accessibility between atoms of data. The choice of atoms of data is a necessary and key step in defining and, therefore, solving a problem. The possible ways in which the data items or atoms are structured define different *data structures*. By choosing a particular structure for the data items, certain items become immediate neighbors while others are related in a weaker way. The interpretation of two items being immediate neighbors is that of adjacency relative to the ordering relation that may be imposed by the structure. Ordering relations are discussed in Sec. 2-3.9.

Let us now consider a general classification of data structures. In so doing, we will introduce well-known data structures and a number of associated operations which are used to manipulate them.

A frequently used data structure operation is one which *creates* a structure. This creation is usually accomplished in a computer program by using a declaration statement. Data structures can be *destroyed* or *erased*. Many programming languages do not permit the destruction of data structures once they have been created since all creations are performed at compile time. Another operation used in conjunction with data structures is one which changes data in the structure. This operation is called *updating* and can change, add, or delete an element in a structure.

Data can be classified as *batches*, *vectors*, and *plexes*. A *batch* is an unordered set of objects which can be of fixed or variable size. The *size* of a structure here is defined to be its number of data items. Batches are very frequently used in the solution of data processing problems. A *vector* is an ordered set which consists of a fixed number of objects. No deletion or addition operations are performed on vectors. At best, certain elements are changed to some value which we have previously decided to use as representing an element to be ignored. The setting of an element in an array to zero to "delete" it is an example. A *plex*, on the other hand, is an ordered set consisting of a variable number of elements to which additions and deletions can be made.

A plex which displays the relationship of adjacency between elements is said to be *linear*. Any other plex is said to be *nonlinear*. The term "list" is also used in the literature to refer to what we have called a plex, and the term "linear list" is used instead of linear plex. We shall concern ourselves with linear plexes in the remainder of this section.

Operations performed on plexes include those which are performed on vectors. However, there is one important difference in that the size of a plex may be changed by updating. Indeed, updating may add or delete elements as well as change existing elements. The addition and deletion of elements in a plex are specified by position, so that we may want to delete the ith element of a plex or add a new element before or after the ith existing element. Frequently, it may be required to add or delete an element whose position in a plex is based on the value of some element (as in sorting). It may be required to add or delete a given element to or from a plex respectively preceding or following an element that has a specified value or satisfies a particular relationship.

Certain plexes permit the deletion of any of its elements and the addition of an element in any position. An important subclass of plexes permits the addition or deletion of an element to occur only at one end. A plex belonging to this subclass is called a *stack*. The addition operation is referred to as "push," the deletion operation as "pop." The most and least accessible elements in a stack are known as the *top* and *bottom* of the stack respectively. Since addition and deletion operations are performed at the same end of a stack, the elements can be removed only in the opposite order from that in which they were added to the stack. This phenomenon is observed in conjunction with recursive functions in

Sec. 2-6.2, and such a plex is frequently referred to as a LIFO (last in, first out) plex.

A common example of a stack phenomenon, which permits the selection of only its end element, is a pile of trays in a cafeteria. These are supported by some kind of spring action in such a manner that a person desiring a tray finds that only one is available at a time at the surface of the tray counter. The removal of the top tray causes the load on the spring to be lighter, and the next tray to appear at the surface of the counter. A tray which is placed on the pile causes the entire pile to be pushed down and that tray to appear above the tray counter.

Another important subclass of plexes permits deletions to be performed at one end of a plex and additions at the other. The information in such a plex is processed in the same order that it was received, that is, on a first in, first out (FIFO) basis. This type of plex is frequently referred to as a *queue*. The updater may be restricted to the examination of elements at only one end in the case of a queue. If no such restriction is made, any element in a plex can be selected. A familiar example of a queue is a checkout line at a supermarket cash register. The first person in line is (usually) the first to be checked out.

A similar type of restriction may be specified for changing elements in a plex. It may be required to examine the top element in a stack or the front element of a queue with a view to altering (not adding or deleting) it. This operation is sometimes extended to other elements of the structure (besides the top or front elements of a stack or queue respectively).

We shall deal with examples of nonlinear plexes in subsequent chapters. The following section is concerned with the representation of data structures in the memory of a computer.

2-2.2 Storage Structures

It is very important in solving a problem to distinguish explicitly between data structures, on the one hand, and the ways by which these structures are represented in the memory of a particular computer dictated by a specific hardware and software system, on the other hand. The way in which a particular data structure is represented in the memory of a computer is known as a *storage structure*. The distinction between a data structure and its corresponding storage structure is often confused. This leads to a loss of efficiency, and prevents the problem solver from making optimal use of available tools and resources. There are many possible memory configurations or storage structures corresponding to a particular data structure. For example, there are a number of possible storage structures for a data structure such as an array. It is also possible for two data structures to be represented by the same storage structure. In many instances, almost exclusive attention is directed toward the storage structures for certain given data, and little attention is given to the data structure per se. In essence, there is significant confusion between the properties that belong to the interpretation and meaning of the data on the one hand and the storage structures that can be selected to represent them in a programming system on the other.

In discussing storage structures we will be primarily concerned with the core memory of the conventional digital computer. The main memory of such a computer is organized into an ordered sequence of words. Each word contains from 8 to 64 bits, and its contents can be referenced by using an address. For efficiency reasons, it is desirable to arrange data in such a manner that a particular element of the data can be referenced by computing its address rather than by searching for it. It is therefore preferable to have a memory organization which can be addressed by location.

There are two possible ways that can be used to obtain an address of an element.

The first method of obtaining an address is by using the description of the data being sought. This type of address is known as a *computed address*. This method of obtaining an address is used very extensively in programming languages to compute the address of an element of an array and in the acquisition of the next instruction to be executed in the object program.

The second method of obtaining an address is to store it somewhere in the memory of the computer. This type of address is referred to as a *link* or *pointer address*. In programming languages the addresses of the actual arguments of a procedure are stored in the computer memory. The return address which is used by a procedure to return to the calling program is also stored, not computed. Certain structures require a combination of computed and link addresses.

2-2.3 Sequential Allocation

Integers, real numbers, and character strings are considered to be primitive data structures because the instruction repertoire of a computer has instructions which will manipulate these primitive structures. We can perform the common arithmetic operations on numbers. A word which contains a character string can be modified by using a number of machine language instructions.

We now turn to the representation in storage of more complex data structures. Actually a complex (nonprimitive) data structure can be considered to consist of a structured set of primitive data structures. A vector may consist of an ordered set of integers, or a plex may consist of a set of elements, each element (node) consisting of two basic fields such as an integer and a real number.

The most straightforward way of representing a vector or a plex in the memory of a computer is to store their elements or nodes one after the other. A vector will have its elements adjacent to one another in memory. This method of allocating memory to a structure is called *sequential allocation*.

One of the simplest data structures which makes use of computed addresses to locate its elements is the vector. Normally a sequence of (contiguous) memory locations are sequentially allocated to the vector. Assuming that each element requires one word of memory, an n-element vector will occupy n consecutive words in memory. The size of a vector is fixed and therefore requires a fixed number of memory locations. In general, a vector A can be represented as in Fig. 2-2.2 where L_0 is the address of the first word allocated to the first element of A and where m represents the number of words allocated to each element.

In certain programming languages, memory allocation is performed at compile time where the size of the vector obtained in the dimensioning statement is saved along with the starting address L_0.

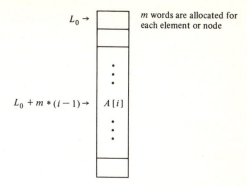

$L_0 \rightarrow$

m words are allocated for
each element or node

$L_0 + m * (i-1) \rightarrow$ $A[i]$

FIGURE 2-2.2   Representation of a
vector.

A multidimensional array can be represented by an equivalent one-dimensional array. For example, a two-dimensional array consisting of three rows and columns could be stored sequentially by columns as

$$A[1, 1]A[2, 1]A[3, 1]A[1, 2]A[2, 2]A[3, 2]A[1, 3]A[2, 3]A[3\ 3]$$
$$\uparrow \qquad\qquad\qquad\qquad\qquad\qquad \uparrow$$
$$L_0$$

The address of element $A[i, j]$ can be obtained by evaluating the expression

$$L_0 + (j - 1) * 3 + i - 1$$

For element $A[2, 3]$, the address is given as $L_0 + 7$. In general, for a two-dimensional array consisting of n rows and m columns, which is stored by *columns*, the address of element $A[i, j]$ is given by the linear expression

$$L_0 + (j - 1) * n + (i - 1)$$

In many programming languages a two-dimensional array will be stored row by row (sometimes referred to as row major order) instead of column by column (column major order). An array consisting of n rows and m columns will be stored sequentially as

$$A[1, 1]A[1, 2]\cdots A[1, m]A[2, 1]A[2, 2]\cdots A[2, m]\cdots A[n, 1]A[n, 2]\cdots A[n, m]$$

The address of matrix element $A[i, j]$ is given by the expression

$$L_0 + (i - 1) * m + (j - 1)$$

In discussions of sequential allocation, arrays are one of the first data structures that come to mind. The adjacency of primitive elements, however, may be described at the lowest possible level of machine organization. Sequences of bits, or bit strings, are often allocated storage sequentially. For example, in a computer with a word size of 32 bits and 8-bit bytes, if a bit string is to represent n bits, then $\lceil n/8 \rceil$ (the least integer greater than or equal to $n/8$) consecutive bytes are allocated as its storage structure. Not only are these bytes adjacent, but we also describe the bits as being arranged in a sequential manner. An important application of bit strings to set theory is the subject of Sec. 2-2.5.

2-2.4 Pointers and Linked Allocation

The previous section discussed at some length how the address of an element in a data structure could be obtained by direct computation. The data structures discussed were linearly ordered, and this ordering relation was specified in the corresponding storage structures by using sequential allocation. There was no need for an element to specify where the next element would be found.

Consider a list consisting of elements which individually vary in size. The task of directly computing the address of a particular element becomes much more difficult. An obvious method of obtaining the address of a node (element) is to store it in the computer memory. This address was previously defined as a link or pointer address. If the list in question has n nodes, we can store the address of each node in a vector consisting of n elements. The first element of the vector will contain the address of the first node of the list, the second element the address of the second node, and so on.

There are many applications which, by their very nature, have data which are continually being updated (additions, deletions, etc.). Each time a change occurs, significant manipulation of the data is required. The representation of the data by sequentially allocated lists in some of these cases results in an inefficient use of memory and wasted computational time, and, indeed, for certain problems this method of allocation is totally unacceptable.

The interpretation of a pointer as an address is a natural one. Most computers use addresses to find the next instruction to be executed and its operand(s). In many hardware configurations special registers are used to store such addresses.

A pointer can be regarded as a general type of structure because when a pointer to a data structure is given, then its contents become accessible. Pointers are always of the same length (usually no longer than a half-word), and this property enables the manipulation of pointers to be performed in a uniform manner by using simple allocation techniques regardless of the configurations of the structures they may point to.

In the sequential-allocation method one is able to compute an address of an element provided that the storage structure is organized in some uniform manner. Pointers permit the referencing of structures in a uniform way regardless of the organization of the structure being referenced. Pointers are capable of representing a much more complex relationship between elements of a structure than a linear order.

The use of pointers or links to refer to elements of a data structure (which is linearly ordered) implies that elements which are adjacent because of the linear ordering need not be physically adjacent in memory. This type of allocation scheme is called *linked allocation*. We now turn to the problem of representing structures by this type of allocation.

A plex has been defined to consist of an ordered set of elements which may vary in number. The previous subsection was concerned with representation of the relationship of adjacency between elements in a plex. There are many other structures that can be represented by a plex where the relationships that exist between elements are much more complex than that of adjacency.

The simplest form that can be used to represent a linear plex is to expand each node to contain a link or pointer to the next node. This representation will be called a *one-way chain* or *singly linked linear list*, which can be displayed as in Fig. 2-2.3*a* in which the variable *FIRST* contains an address or pointer which gives the location of the first node of the list. Each node is divided into two parts. The first part represents the original information contents of the element, and the second part contains the address of the next node. The last node does not have a successor, and, consequently, no actual address is stored in the pointer field. In such a case, a null value is stored as the address. The "arrow" emanating from the link field of a particular node indicates its successor node in the structure. For example, the linked list in Fig. 2-2.3*b* represents a five-node list whose elements are located in memory locations 1000, 1002, 1010, 1007, and 1005 respectively. We again emphasize that the only purpose of the links is to specify which node is next in the linear ordering. The link address of *NULL* (indicated by the slash) in the last node signals the end of the list. *NULL* is not an address of any possible node, but is a special value which cannot be mistaken for an address. For this reason, *NULL* is used as a special list delimiter. It is possible for a list to have no nodes at all. Such a list is called an empty list and is denoted by assigning a value of *NULL* to *FIRST* in our example.

Let us compare the operations commonly performed on sequentially allocated and linked lists. Consider the operations of insertion and deletion in the case of a sequentially allocated list. If we have a five-element list and it is required to insert a new element between the first and second elements, then the last four elements of the list must be moved so as to make room for the new element. For a list that contains many nodes, this way of performing an insertion is rather inefficient especially if many insertions are to be performed. The principle applies in the case of a deletion where all elements after the element being deleted must be moved up so as to take up the vacant space caused by the element removed from the list.

In the case of linked allocation, an addition is performed in a straightfor-

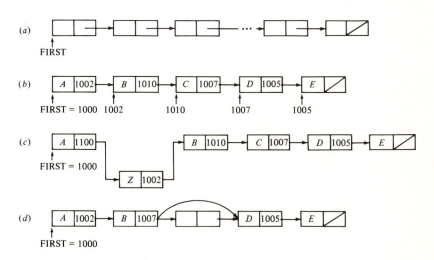

FIGURE 2-2.3   Linked lists.

ward manner. If a new element is to be inserted following the first element, in the preceding five-element linked list this insertion can be accomplished by merely interchanging pointers, as shown in Fig. 2-2.3c. The deletion of the third element from the original list can be performed in a similar fashion, as shown in Fig. 2-2.3d. It is clear that the insertion and deletion operations are more efficient when performed on linked lists than when performed on sequentially allocated lists.

If a particular node in a linked list is required, one has to follow the links from the first node onward until it is found. This method is clearly inferior to the computed-address technique associated with sequential allocation.

If, in a particular application, it is required to examine every node in the list, then it is only slightly more time-consuming to go through a linked list than a sequential list.

It is easier to join or split two linked lists than it is in the case of sequential allocation. This task can be accomplished merely by interchanging pointers and does not require the movement of nodes.

The pointers or links consume additional memory, but if only part of a memory word is being used, then a pointer can be stored in the remaining part. It is possible to group nodes so as to require only one link per several nodes. The cost of storing pointers may not be too expensive in many cases.

Since the memory address number in the link field has been used for illustration purposes in the present discussion and is of no concern (and indeed unknown) to the programmer in practice, the arrow symbol will be used exclusively to denote a successor node.

We mentioned the use of pointers in this section only to specify the linear ordering (adjacency) among elements, but pointers can be used to specify more complex relations between nodes such as that of a tree or a directed graph. This relation is difficult and indeed for certain graphs impossible to specify by using sequential allocation. These more complex structures can be specified by placing in the nodes a number of pointers. It is possible for a particular node to belong to several lists with this technique. A further discussion of this topic is given in Chap. 5.

From this discussion and some of the applications which follow, it will become clear that for certain operations linked allocation is more efficient than sequential allocation, and yet for other operations the opposite holds. In a typical application, both types of allocations are used.

Consider the familiar symbol manipulation problem of performing various operations on polynomials such as addition, subtraction, multiplication, division, differentiation, etc. Let us direct our attention, in particular, to the manipulation of polynomials in two variables. It may be required, for example, to write a program which subtracts polynomial $x^2 + 3xy + y^2 + y - x$ from polynomial $2x^2 + 5xy + y^2$ to give a result of $x^2 + 2xy - y + x$. We are interested in finding a suitable representation for polynomials so that the operations just mentioned can be performed in a reasonably efficient manner. If we are to manipulate polynomials, it is clear that individual terms must be selected. In particular, we must distinguish between variables, coefficients, and exponents within each term.

It is possible to represent a polynomial as a character string and solve the problem by searching for the various parts of a term. This approach tends to be complex, especially if one tries to program in a language with only primitive string processing capabilities.

A two-dimensional array can be used to represent a polynomial in two variables. In a programming language that permits subscripts to have zero values, the coefficients of the term $x^i y^j$ would be stored in the element identified by row i and column j of the array (assuming the existence of a zeroth row and zeroth column). If we restrict the size of an array to a maximum of 5 rows and 5 columns, then the powers of x and y in any term of the polynomial must not exceed a value of 4. The array representing the polynomial $2x^2 + 5xy + y^2$ is given as

$$
\begin{array}{ccccc}
0 & 0 & 1 & 0 & 0 \\
0 & 5 & 0 & 0 & 0 \\
2 & 0 & 0 & 0 & 0 \\
0 & 0 & 0 & 0 & 0 \\
0 & 0 & 0 & 0 & 0
\end{array}
$$

and the array for $x^2 + 3xy + y^2 + y - x$ is

$$
\begin{array}{ccccc}
0 & 1 & 1 & 0 & 0 \\
-1 & 3 & 0 & 0 & 0 \\
1 & 0 & 0 & 0 & 0 \\
0 & 0 & 0 & 0 & 0 \\
0 & 0 & 0 & 0 & 0
\end{array}
$$

Once we have an algorithm for converting the input data to an array representing a polynomial and another for converting an array to an appropriate output form, then addition and subtraction of polynomials reduce to the adding and subtracting of corresponding elements in the two arrays respectively. This problem is left as an exercise. A number of disadvantages are evident in using this representation. In the first case, the array tends to be sparsely filled with nonzero elements. Second, the powers of the polynomials are restricted. Furthermore, the memory requirements associated with certain operations were not always predictable, as in the case of polynomial division, and so one was faced with the situation of not knowing how much memory to reserve for the polynomial generated by such an operation. This reason is why linked allocation should be used in this case. Before describing how it can be used, we will consider the different classes of operations we can perform on linear linked lists.

Data in any type of application are required to be manipulated according to certain operations. If this processing is to be performed by the use of a computer, the first task to be accomplished is the adequate representation of the data in the computer memory. The difficulty and complexity of this task depend to a large extent on the particular programming language that is used to program the algorithms associated with an application. Certain languages have been specifically designed for manipulating linked lists. One such prominent language is LISP 1.5. In other cases, common procedures or functions to be performed on linked lists have been written as subprograms in a simple "host" language. An example of such a case is the list processing language SLIP which consists of a number of subprograms which are written in the FORTRAN language. We will make use of the PL/I language to represent certain common operations performed on lists.

There are a number of classes of operations which are associated with linked lists. The first class of such operations is independent of the data contained in the nodes of a list. These operations include the insertion, deletion, and selection of nodes. Programming languages which possess list processing capabilities usually have these operations built in.

Another class of operations associated with list structures is the operation which converts the raw data from a human-readable form to a corresponding machine form. The inverse operation of converting an internal structure to a suitable human-readable form is also required. These operations are clearly data-dependent, and attention must be given to the interpretation that is associated with the structures. List processing languages will have some standard basic routines for such operations, but any additional routines must be programmed.

Finally, there are operations that must be programmed to manipulate the data according to what is required in a particular application at hand. In the case of polynomial manipulation, for example, such operations would include the addition, subtraction, multiplication, division, differentiation, and integration of polynomials. Once a programmer has access to all the routines for the three classes mentioned above, the task of programming an algorithm is much simpler.

Let us consider the problem of describing singly linked linear list representations and operations in an algorithmic notation and also in the PL/I language. A node consists of a number of fields, each of which can represent an integer, a real number, etc., except for one field (usually the last for purposes of illustration), called a pointer, which contains the location of the next node in the list. This location is specified as a computer memory address.

Consider the example of representing a term of a polynomial in the variables x and y. A typical node will be represented as

XEXP	YEXP	COEF	LINK

which consists of four sequentially allocated fields that we will collectively refer to as *TERM*. The first two fields represent the power of the variables x and y respectively. The third and fourth fields represent the coefficient of the term in the polynomial and the address of the next term in the polynomial, respectively. For example, the term $3xy^2$ would be represented as

The selection of a particular field within a node for the example of our polynomial is an easy matter. Our algorithmic notation will allow the referencing of any field of a node, given the pointer P to that node. $COEF(P)$ denotes the coefficient field of a node pointed to by P. Similarly, the exponents of x and y are given by $XEXP(P)$ and $YEXP(P)$ respectively, and the pointer to the next node is given by $LINK(P)$.

Consider as an example the representation of the polynomial

$$x^2 + 3xy + y^2$$

as a linked list. Assume that the nodes in the list are to be stored so that a term pointed to by P will precede another term indicated by Q if $XEXP(P)$ is greater than $XEXP(Q)$; or, if they are equal, then $YEXP(P)$ must be greater than $YEXP(Q)$. For our example the list can be represented as

$FIRST$

Let us now consider the more difficult problem of inserting a node into a linked list. There are a number of steps necessary to accomplish this task. First, the values for the various fields of the new node must be obtained either from an input operation or as the result of a computation. Second, we must somehow obtain a node from available storage. Finally, the values of the fields obtained in the first step are copied in the appropriate field positions of the new node, which is then placed in the linked list. The linking of the new node to its successor in the existing list is accomplished by setting the pointer field of the former to a value that gives the location of the latter.

In our algorithms we will assume that we have an available area of storage and that we can request a node from this area. In our polynomial example, the assignment statement

$$P \leftarrow TERM$$

creates a new node consisting of the four fields previously described, with the location of the first field being copied in the pointer variable P. At this point, the fields $XEXP(P)$, $YEXP(P)$, $COEF(P)$, and $LINK(P)$ have undefined values. When a node is no longer required, we can return it to available storage. This return will be specified simply by stating, for example,

Restore node P to the availability area.

After this action is taken, the node is assumed to be inaccessible, and P is undefined.

We can now formulate an algorithm which will insert a term of a polynomial into a linked list.

Algorithm $INSERT$ Given the definition of the node structure $TERM$ and an availability area from which we can obtain such nodes, it is required to insert in the linked list a node which will immediately precede the node whose address is designated by the pointer $FIRST$. The fields of the new term have exponents for x and y and a coefficient value represented by the variables NX, NY, and $NCOEF$ respectively. P is an auxiliary pointer variable.

    1   [Obtain a node from available storage.] $P \leftarrow TERM$.
    2   [Initialize numeric fields.] Set $XEXP(P) \leftarrow NX$, $YEXP(P) \leftarrow NY$, and $COEF(P) \leftarrow NCOEF$.

3 [Set link to the list.] Set $LINK(P) \leftarrow FIRST$, $INSERT \leftarrow P$, and Exit.

Algorithm *INSERT* performs all its insertions at one end of the linked list. In general, it is also possible to perform insertions at the other end or in the middle of the list. The zero polynomial (polynomial with no terms) is represented by the null pointer. Before any term of a polynomial is added to a list, its first node pointer, which we will call *POLY*, has a value of *NULL*. It is quite possible in adding and subtracting polynomials to get a cancellation of terms, which will result in a zero polynomial.

The algorithm will be invoked as a function whose name is *INSERT*. The address of the created node is assigned to *INSERT* immediately prior to the exit, and it is this value that will replace the function call.   ////

In algorithm *INSERT* we assume the existence of the required structure, *TERM*. In PL/I programs, however, we must define any such datatype. We now turn to the programming aspects of how this is accomplished. For linked list processing applications it is necessary to use a structure declared to be of the BASED storage class. The declaration statement

> DECLARE
> 1 TERM BASED(P),
>   2 XEXP BINARY FIXED,
>   2 YEXP BINARY FIXED,
>   2 COEF BINARY FLOAT,
>   2 LINK POINTER;

defines the structure of a polynomial term. The node TERM, at level 1, collectively represents the four fields at level 2. The fields XEXP, YEXP, and COEF are capable of containing the required numeric data. LINK is given the POINTER attribute which specifies that the value of LINK will usually denote the address of a BASED datatype such as TERM. The variable P, following BASED, is implicitly defined as a pointer variable, and its purpose will be discussed shortly.

This declaration merely defines the structure TERM; it does not create any nodes. The programmer has complete control over obtaining required nodes from an available area of memory. The execution of the statement

> ALLOCATE TERM;

creates a node and automatically assigns the address of the new node to P. Note that many TERM nodes may be in use at one time, but each one must be generated by the execution of an ALLOCATE statement.

The referencing of a node or a particular field is accomplished by using pointer qualification. For example, P−>TERM would denote the node generated by the preceding ALLOCATE statement. Each field could also be referenced as Q−>XEXP, Q−>YEXP, Q−>COEF, or Q−>LINK. The imitation arrow is a minus sign followed immediately by a "greater than" sign. As an example, we can add the coefficients of two polynomial terms, indicated by P and Q, using the statement

> X = Q−>COEF + P−>COEF;

PL/I not only allows the allocation of based structures, but also permits the freeing of such datatypes to available storage. All this is accomplished by the statement

$$\text{FREE P->TERM;}$$

when the node indicated by pointer P is to be restored to the availability area.

It was mentioned that pointer variables usually specify an address. An exception is that they may be assigned the value returned by PL/I's built-in NULL function. This value cannot be related to any address and therefore cannot be interpreted as a pointer to a node. NULL returns the same value on each invocation, and therefore it can be used as an end delimiter. The comparisons "equal" and "not equal" can be made between NULL and a pointer variable as well as between two pointer variables.

These PL/I programming concepts should provide an adequate background for the list processing programs in this and other sections. A program for algorithm *INSERT* is given in Fig. 2-2.4. In procedure INSERT and also the subprogram of Fig. 2-2.7 (DELETE), the structure TERM is not declared. It is assumed that these procedures are nested within an invoking routine in which the necessary declarations are made.

Now that it is possible to invoke the procedure INSERT, the construction of a linked list for a polynomial is achieved by having a zero polynomial initially and repeatedly invoking the insertion function until all terms of the polynomial are processed. For the polynomial $x^2 + 3xy + y^2$, this process must be done 3 times. Since we want the first element of the list to be x^2, we start by inserting the term y^2 followed by the insertion of $3xy$, etc. (we actually have a linked list here).

If the pointer to the first node of the list is POLY, then the program in Fig. 2-2.5 will construct the above polynomial. A trace of this invoking procedure is given in Fig. 2-2.6.

Let us examine another equally important algorithm, that of deleting a node from a linked list.

Algorithm *DELETE*   Given a variable *FIRST* whose value denotes the address of the first node in the linked list, it is required to delete the node whose address

```
INSERT:
        PROCEDURE(NX,NY,NCOEF,FIRST) RETURNS(POINTER);
/*INSERT A NODE IN THE LINKED LIST WHICH WILL IMMEDIATELY PRECEDE THE
   NODE WHOSE ADDRESS IS DESIGNATED BY THE POINTER FIRST.  INITIALIZE
   THE NODE'S FIELDS TO NX, NY, AND NCOEF.  RETURN THE POINTER TO THE
   NEW NODE.                                                        */
        DECLARE
             (NX,NY) BINARY FIXED,
             NCOEF BINARY FLOAT,
             FIRST POINTER;
        ALLOCATE TERM;
        P->XEXP = NX;
        P->YEXP = NY;
        P->COEF = NCOEF;
        P->LINK = FIRST;
        RETURN(P);
END INSERT;
```

FIGURE 2-2.4   PL/I procedure for algorithm *INSERT*.

```
POLYST:
    PROCEDURE OPTIONS(MAIN);
/*CONSTRUCT A LINKED LIST REPRESENTATION OF A POLYNOMIAL USING
    THE INSERT PROCEDURE. */
    DECLARE
        1 TERM BASED(P),
            2 XEXP BINARY FIXED,
            2 YEXP BINARY FIXED,
            2 COEF BINARY FLOAT,
            2 LINK POINTER,
        Q POINTER,
        POLY POINTER,
        INSERT ENTRY(BIN FIXED,BIN FIXED,BIN FLOAT,PTR) RETURNS(PTR);

    POLY = NULL; /* INITIALIZE */

    POLY = INSERT(0,2,1,POLY); /* INSERT LAST TERM OF POLYNOMIAL */

    POLY = INSERT(1,1,3,POLY); /* INSERT SECOND TERM OF POLYNOMIAL */

    POLY = INSERT(2,0,1,POLY); /* INSERT FIRST TERM OF POLYNOMIAL */

END POLYST;
```

FIGURE 2-2.5   Construction of the polynomial $x^2 + 3xy + y^2$.

is given by variable X. Auxiliary pointer variables $NEXT$ and $PRED$ are used
The list is composed of nodes with structure previously described as $TERM$.

1   [Empty list?] If $FIRST = NULL$ then write 'underflow' and Exit.
2   [Delete first node?] If $X = FIRST$ then set $FIRST \leftarrow LINK(FIRST)$
and go to step 8.
3   [Initiate search for predecessor of X.] Set $NEXT \leftarrow FIRST$.
4   [Update pointers.] Set $PRED \leftarrow NEXT$ and $NEXT \leftarrow LINK(NEXT)$.
5   [End of list?] If $NEXT = NULL$ then write 'node not found' and
Exit.
6   [Is this node X?] If $NEXT \neq X$ then go to step 4.
7   [Delete X.] Set $LINK(PRED) \leftarrow LINK(X)$.
8   [Return node X.] Restore node X to the availability area and Exit.

The first step in the algorithm checks for an underflow. The second step
determines whether the node to be deleted is the first node of the list, and if it
is, then the second node of the list becomes the new first node. In the case of a list
containing a single node, the pointer variable $FIRST$ will assume the null value
as a result of the deletion.

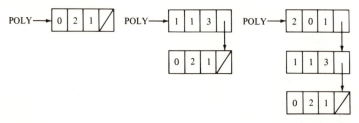

FIGURE 2-2.6   Trace of the construction of a linked list for polynomial
$x^2 + 3xy + y^2$.

If X is not the first node in the list, then a search to find the immediate predecessor of X (*PRED* in the algorithm) is launched. This search is accomplished by chaining through the list and storing the address of the next node in variable *NEXT* until X is found. A value of *"NULL"* for *NEXT* indicates that the node to be deleted has not been found in the list and that an error has been made. When variables *NEXT* and X contain the same value, we are now in a position to change the link field of the predecessor node of X to point to its successor node ($LINK(X)$). This change is accomplished in step 7 of the algorithm, and finally the deleted node is returned to the availability list.   ////

A PL/I procedure for the algorithm is given in Fig. 2-2.7.

2-2.5   An Application of Bit Represented Sets

For any representation of a set, it will be necessary to assign an arbitrary ordering to the elements of the set. Such an ordering will be assumed throughout this discussion.

Let us consider the problem of determining whether two sets are equal. Intuitively, the basic operation required for checking the equality of sets is the comparison of their elements. This requirement implies that each individual element of a set must at some time be selected for comparison. We can do this by

```
DELETE:
        PROCEDURE(X,FIRST);
/*FIND AND DELETE NODE X FROM THE
  POLYNOMIAL LIST POINTED TO BY FIRST. */
        DECLARE
            (X,FIRST,NEXT,PRED) POINTER;
        IF FIRST = NULL
        THEN
            DO;/* INDICATE THAT LIST IS EMPTY */
                PUT SKIP LIST('LIST UNDERFLOW');
                RETURN;
            END;
        IF X = FIRST
        THEN
            DO; /* DELETE THE FIRST NODE */
                FIRST = FIRST->LINK;
                GO TO FREE_NODE;
            END;
        NEXT = FIRST; /*INITIATE SEARCH */
LOOP:   PRED = NEXT; /* UPDATE NEXT AND PRED */
        NEXT = NEXT->LINK;
        IF NEXT = NULL
        THEN
            DO; /*INDICATE NODE WAS NOT FOUND */
                PUT SKIP LIST('NODE NOT FOUND');
                RETURN;
            END;
        IF NEXT ¬= X
        THEN GO TO LOOP;
        PRED->LINK = X->LINK; /* DELETE X */
FREE_NODE: FREE X->TERM; /*RESTORE NODE X TO THE AVAILABILITY AREA */
        RETURN;
END DELETE;
```

FIGURE 2-2.7   PL/I procedure for algorithm *DELETE*.

using a vector (of integers or strings) to represent a set, since each element could then be selected by appending a subscript to the set name. If vectors are chosen as representations of sets, then the algorithms for testing set equality or performing set operations tend to be complex and inefficient. For these reasons we will not discuss the vector representation any further, but pursue a different approach.

Recall that in Sec. 2-1.3 each subset of a given set was referenced by a letter with a binary subscript. For example, given the set $S_3 = \{a, b, c\}$, the subset $\{a, c\}$ was denoted B_{101}. The 1 bits in 101 indicate that the first and third elements of S_3 are in the subset. Similarly, assume that a universal set, say E, has n elements, each element being distinguishable as first, second, or third, and so on (E is ordered in the sense of Sec. 2-1.8). We will need a sequence of n bits to represent a subset A of this universal set. When we number the bit positions from left to right as 1 to n, each bit corresponds to a particular element in set E. If A contains the ith element of E, then the ith bit of the representative bit sequence will be a 1; otherwise it will be a 0.

Along with this convenient and compact representation of sets, we can achieve simplicity and speed in performing set operations and comparing sets. Obviously, two sets are equal if bit sequences representing them are equal. Using the logical operations AND, NOT, and OR available on most computers and in certain programming languages, we can perform the set operations of intersection, complementation, and union respectively. As an example, consider the two subsets $\{a, c\}$ and $\{c, e\}$ of $\{a, b, c, d, e\}$. They are represented by the bit sequences 10100 and 00101 respectively. To find the intersection of the sets, we perform the operation

$$10100 \land 00101 \qquad (AND \text{ corresponding bits})$$

giving the bit sequence 00100, representing $\{c\}$. Similarly,

$$10100 \lor 00101 \qquad (OR \text{ corresponding bits})$$

will give 10101, denoting the union $\{a, c, e\}$ of $\{a, c\}$ and $\{c, e\}$, and

$$\neg 10100 \qquad (\text{negate each bit})$$

will give the sequence 01011, denoting $\{b, d, e\}$, the absolute complement of $\{a, c\}$. Bit strings and operations on them will prove useful in the following discussion of the retrieval of information from a file.

Predicate logic and set theory play a very important role in the area of information organization and retrieval. A literature search of a certain topic area in a library system or the number of graduate students who are married and in the College of Engineering in a student record application may be required. This type of application occurs in so many different situations that a special class of languages known as question-answering languages has been created. A typical statement in such languages specifies a predicate whose extension set is required.

We first give a number of definitions which are used in dealing with information, and then proceed to consider as a concrete example a simple student record application.

A collection of information concerning a particular item or individual is called a *record*. Each portion of this record which gives one specific attribute of the item or individual is a *field*. A set of records is a *file*. If a file contains information on a complete set, for example, all books in a library or all employees working for a corporation, then the file is a *master file*. A subset of a file is a *subfile*. In information retrieval, records having specified values in particular fields must be searched for. A *query* is used to formally describe the subfile of records being requested.

Consider a file of student records which have four fields, one each for student number, sex, college, and marital status. If a request is made for information pertaining to students in the College of Engineering, then every record must be scanned to determine which are required. Even greater difficulty would be encountered in searching for information on married students in engineering, as both the college and marital status fields must be considered. Is there an easier way to find the records containing this data?

If we assume that the master file is ordered, that is, we can identify a first record, second record, and so on, then we can specify beforehand a number of subsets in the file. This can be done compactly by using bit represented sets. Obviously many bit strings would be required to directly specify all possible subfiles which may be requested. To resolve this problem, only one bit string should be established for each specific value a field may have. Most information requests will be satisfied by the specified subsets or by logical operations performed on their bit string representations, as previously described.

The purpose of this approach is to avoid the complex and lengthy search often necessary for the retrieval of information. Bit string represented subsets sacrifice a minimum of storage space in order to decrease search time. Note, however, that they should not be used to specify records having a certain value in a field which has many possible values. For example, a student number field will have a different value for each record, and it is therefore not practical to allocate a bit string for each student number. When used in conjunction with a field such as marital status, only several bit strings are necessary to specify each possible status subset. For example, the bit string 10010110... could be used to indicate that the first, fourth, sixth, etc. records pertain to married students.

We will give a PL/I program to demonstrate the construction and use of bit string represented subsets of a master student file. An array of structures denoted by STUDENT is used for the master file. Each element of this array is subdivided into the fields NUMBER, SEX, COLLEGE, and MARTIAL_ STATUS, thus representing one record. Information is coded for the latter three fields, as shown in the program comments of Fig. 2-2.8. A bit string array is allocated for each of these fields. One bit string is used for each code a field may contain, and it is simply referenced by that code. This means, for example, that SEX_FILE(1) and SEX_FILE(2) will indicate the subfiles or subsets of records referring to male and female students respectively. SEX_FILE(1) therefore indicates the extension set of the predicate

x is a male student.

Similarly, COLLEGE_FILE(2) is a bit string indicating the extension set of the predicate

$$x \text{ is a commerce student.}$$

We can find the extension set of the predicate

$$x \text{ is a male commerce student.}$$

by finding the intersection of the two preceding extension sets. This is done by performing the logical operation

$$\text{SEX\_FILE}(1)\&\text{COLLEGE\_FILE}(2)$$

```
BITSETS:
    PROCEDURE OPTIONS(MAIN);
/*THIS PROGRAM INPUTS CODED INFORMATION ABOUT STUDENTS, CREATING A
  MASTER FILE AND THREE BIT STRING ARRAYS. THE MASTER FILE CONSISTS OF
  AN ARRAY OF STRUCTURES NAMED STUDENT. EACH ELEMENT OF THIS ARRAY
  HAS FOUR FIELDS NAMED AND CONTAINING CODES AS FOLLOWS:
          NUMBER          - A SIX DIGIT STUDENT NUMBER
          SEX             - 1 - MALE
                          - 2 - FEMALE
          COLLEGE         - 1 - ARTS AND SCIENCE
                          - 2 - COMMERCE
                          - 3 - ENGINEERING
                          - 4 - GRADUATE STUDIES
                          - 5 - HOME ECONOMICS
                          - 6 - AGRICULTURE
          MARITAL_STATUS  - 1 - SINGLE
                          - 2 - MARRIED
                          - 3 - OTHER
  FOR THE FIELDS SEX, COLLEGE, AND MARITAL_STATUS, THE ARRAYS SEX_FILE,
  COLLEGE_FILE, AND STATUS_FILE ARE ESTABLISHED AS REPRESENTATIONS OF
  MUTUALLY EXCLUSIVE SUBSETS OF THE MASTER FILE. THE ELEMENTS OF THESE
  ARRAYS ARE BIT STRINGS HAVING A LENGTH EQUAL TO THE NUMBER OF RECORDS
  IN THE MASTER FILE. THERE ARE A TOTAL OF 11 BIT STRINGS, ONE FOR
  EACH OF THE ABOVE CODES. EACH STRING INITIALLY CONSISTS ENTIRELY OF
  '0' BITS.
  THE FIRST PART OF THE MAIN PROGRAM INPUTS THE STUDENT FILE AND
  CONSTRUCTS THE BIT REPRESENTED SETS AS FOLLOWS: FOR THE ITH RECORD,
  IF THE CODES J, K, AND M ARE IN THE FIELDS SEX, COLLEGE, AND MARITAL_
  STATUS RESPECTIVELY, THEN THE ITH BIT OF BIT STRINGS SEX_FILE(J),
  COLLEGE_FILE(K), AND STATUS_FILE(M) ARE SET TO '1'B.
  BEGINNING AT THE LABEL QUERY, A NUMBER OF EXTENSION SETS OF CERTAIN
  PREDICATES ARE PRINTED USING PROCEDURE OUTPUT. THE FIRST INVOCATION
  PRINTS EVERY RECORD AND THE NEXT FIVE PRINT CERTAIN SUBSETS OF THE
  MASTER FILE. THE USE OF LOGICAL CONNECTIVES IN FINDING
  INTERSECTIONS, UNIONS, OR COMPLEMENTATIONS OF EXTENSION SETS IS
  DEMONSTRATED.                                                    */
    GET LIST(N);
BEGIN; /* AUTOMATIC STORAGE ALLOCATION */
    DECLARE
        1 STUDENT(N),
            2 NUMBER FIXED(6),
            2 SEX FIXED(1),
            2 COLLEGE FIXED(1),
            2 MARITAL_STATUS FIXED(1),
        (SEX_FILE(2),COLLEGE_FILE(6),STATUS_FILE(3)) BIT(N)
            INITIAL((11)(1)'0'B),
        SEX_WORD(2) CHAR(10) INITIAL('MALE','FEMALE'),
        COLLEGE_WORD(6) CHAR(20) INITIAL('ARTS AND SCIENCE','COMMERCE',
            'ENGINEERING','GRADUATE STUDIES','HOME ECONOMICS',
            'AGRICULTURE'),
        STATUS_WORD(3) CHAR(7) INITIAL('SINGLE','MARRIED','OTHER'),
        I BINARY FIXED,
        HEADINGS CHAR(54) INITIAL
            ('NUMBER     SEX        COLLEGE               MARITAL STATUS');
```

FIGURE 2-2.8 PL/I program applying bit represented sets.

```
      DO I = 1 TO N; /*INPUT A RECORD AND PUT '1' BITS IN BIT STRINGS.*/
        GET LIST(STUDENT(I));
        SUBSTR(SEX_FILE(SEX(I)),I,1) = '1'B;
        SUBSTR(COLLEGE_FILE(COLLEGE(I)),I,1) = '1'B;
        SUBSTR(STATUS_FILE(MARITAL_STATUS(I)),I,1) = '1'B;
      END;
QUERY:
      CALL OUTPUT('ALL STUDENTS',SEX_FILE(1)|SEX_FILE(2));
      CALL OUTPUT('FEMALE STUDENTS',(SEX_FILE(2)));
      CALL OUTPUT('ARTS STUDENTS',(COLLEGE_FILE(1)));
      CALL OUTPUT('UNMARRIED STUDENTS IN ARTS',COLLEGE_FILE(1)&
        ¬STATUS_FILE(2));
      CALL OUTPUT('MALE STUDENTS IN COMMERCE, ARTS, OR ENGINEERING',
        (COLLEGE_FILE(1)|COLLEGE_FILE(2)|COLLEGE_FILE(3))&SEX_FILE(1));
      CALL OUTPUT('STUDENTS WHO ARE FEMALE AND SINGLE OR IN HOME '||
        'ECONOMICS',(SEX_FILE(2)&STATUS_FILE(1))|COLLEGE_FILE(5));

OUTPUT:
      PROCEDURE (TITLE,STRING);

  /*        O U T P U T

TITLE: DESCRIBES RECORDS TO BE OUTPUT.
STRING: BIT STRING INDICATING WHICH RECORDS SHOULD BE OUTPUT.
HEADINGS: FOR THE OUTPUT FIELDS.
I: INDEX TO '1' BITS IN STRING.
ALL OTHER VARIABLES ARE DECLARED IN THE MAIN PROCEDURE.
  SCAN STRING AND OUTPUT THE RECORDS IN THE STUDENT FILE CORRESPONDING
  TO THE '1' BITS.  EACH '1' BIT IS CHANGED TO A '0' BIT AFTER IT IS
  SCANNED.  THIS PROCEDURE DOES NOT PRESERVE STRING SO THE
  CORRESPONDING ARGUMENT MUST BE PASSED BY VALUE.          */
      DECLARE
        TITLE CHAR(60) VARYING,
        STRING BIT(*),
        I BINARY FIXED;
      PUT SKIP(2) LIST(TITLE);
      PUT SKIP EDIT(HEADINGS)(A(54));
      DO WHILE('1'B); /* SCAN STRING FOR '1' BITS */
        I = INDEX(STRING,'1'B);
        IF I = 0 /* ALL REQUIRED RECORDS HAVE BEEN PRINTED */
        THEN RETURN;
        SUBSTR(STRING,I,1)='0'B;
        PUT SKIP EDIT(NUMBER(I),SEX_WORD(SEX(I)),
          COLLEGE_WORD(COLLEGE(I)),STATUS_WORD(MARITAL_STATUS(I)))
          (F(6),X(4),A(10),A(20),A(7));
      END;
END OUTPUT;

END; /* OF BEGIN BLOCK */

END BITSETS;
```

FIGURE 2-2.8 (Continued)

in PL/I. This operation is the required formal query. Similarly, unions and complementations of extension sets can be obtained using the "|" (OR) and "¬" (NOT) operators.

The PL/I program in Fig. 2-2.8 demonstrates the use of these concepts. Notice the built-in functions SUBSTR and INDEX. For example, the statement

$$\text{SUBSTR(STRING, I, 1)} = \text{'0'B;}$$

replaces the Ith bit in STRING by '0'B. The statement

$$\text{I} = \text{INDEX(STRING, '1'B)};$$

assigns to I an integer value which indicates the position in STRING of the leftmost occurrence of '1'B. If there is no such occurrence, zero is assigned to 1.

```
ALL STUDENTS
NUMBER     SEX        COLLEGE             MARITAL STATUS
596426     MALE       COMMERCE            MARRIED
600868     MALE       GRADUATE STUDIES    MARRIED
621656     MALE       ENGINEERING         MARRIED
640621     MALE       ARTS AND SCIENCE    MARRIED
552079     FEMALE     ARTS AND SCIENCE    MARRIED
572281     MALE       ARTS AND SCIENCE    OTHER
572915     MALE       ENGINEERING         OTHER
672919     FEMALE     COMMERCE            SINGLE
581242     MALE       ENGINEERING         SINGLE
581614     FEMALE     HOME ECONOMICS      SINGLE
683369     FEMALE     ARTS AND SCIENCE    OTHER
690528     FEMALE     HOME ECONOMICS      MARRIED
702136     FEMALE     HOME ECONOMICS      SINGLE
703062     MALE       AGRICULTURE         SINGLE
720153     MALE       ARTS AND SCIENCE    SINGLE

FEMALE STUDENTS
NUMBER     SEX        COLLEGE             MARITAL STATUS
652079     FEMALE     ARTS AND SCIENCE    MARRIED
572919     FEMALE     COMMERCE            SINGLE
581614     FEMALE     HOME ECONOMICS      SINGLE
683369     FEMALE     ARTS AND SCIENCE    OTHER
690528     FEMALE     HOME ECONOMICS      MARRIED
702136     FEMALE     HOME ECONOMICS      SINGLE

ARTS STUDENTS
NUMBER     SEX        COLLEGE             MARITAL STATUS
640621     MALE       ARTS AND SCIENCE    MARRIED
652079     FEMALE     ARTS AND SCIENCE    MARRIED
572281     MALE       ARTS AND SCIENCE    OTHER
683369     FEMALE     ARTS AND SCIENCE    OTHER
720153     MALE       ARTS AND SCIENCE    SINGLE

UNMARRIED STUDENTS IN ARTS
NUMBER     SEX        COLLEGE             MARITAL STATUS
572281     MALE       ARTS AND SCIENCE    OTHER
683369     FEMALE     ARTS AND SCIENCE    OTHER
720153     MALE       ARTS AND SCIENCE    SINGLE

MALE STUDENTS IN COMMERCE, ARTS, OR ENGINEERING
NUMBER     SEX        COLLEGE             MARITAL STATUS
596426     MALE       COMMERCE            MARRIED
621656     MALE       ENGINEERING         MARRIED
640621     MALE       ARTS AND SCIENCE    MARRIED
672281     MALE       ARTS AND SCIENCE    OTHER
572915     MALE       ENGINEERING         OTHER
581242     MALE       ENGINEERING         SINGLE
720153     MALE       ARTS AND SCIENCE    SINGLE

STUDENTS WHO ARE FEMALE AND SINGLE OR IN HOME ECONOMICS
NUMBER     SEX        COLLEGE             MARITAL STATUS
572919     FEMALE     COMMERCE            SINGLE
581614     FEMALE     HOME ECONOMICS      SINGLE
690528     FEMALE     HOME ECONOMICS      MARRIED
702136     FEMALE     HOME ECONOMICS      SINGLE
```

FIGURE 2-2.8   (Continued)

Note that the records were manually sorted by student number. This assumption is not necessary for the proper functioning of the program.

Special care must be taken in the use of procedure OUTPUT. It prints the records indicated by the value of STRING. TITLE is a character description of the records printed. Note that the value, not the name, of STRING's corresponding argument is passed. This passing of value is necessary because OUTPUT replaces each detected '1'B by '0'B, thus destroying the original string passed.

EXERCISES 2-2

1 Consider a two-dimensional array A whose subscript limits are

$$-3 \leq i \leq 6 \qquad 3 \leq j \leq 10$$

Give the addressing function for the element $A[i, j]$ where the storage representation is in row major order.

2 Consider a two-dimensional array A whose subscript limits are

$$-2 \leq i \leq 5 \qquad 2 \leq j \leq 7$$

Give the addressing function for the element $A[i, j]$ where the storage representation is in column major order.

3 Based on the discussion in the text of representing polynomials in two variables by the use of matrices, formulate an input algorithm to convert a polynomial to its matrix representation and a converse output algorithm. Assume that each polynomial in variables x and y is given on *one* card and has the form for polynomial

$$2x^2 + 5xy + y^2$$

of

$$2x2+5xy+y2$$

with *no* blanks used for spacing the terms. If a variable is present but its exponent is omitted, it is assumed to have a value of 1. If the coefficient of a polynomial term is omitted, its value is also assumed to be 1. The coefficients are assumed to be real numbers.

4 Using the algorithms developed in Problem 3, write an algorithm which will add two polynomials.

5 Using the algorithms developed in Problem 3, devise an algorithm which will multiply two polynomials. Note that the resulting polynomial will, in general, have higher-order terms than the polynomials being multiplied and therefore an appropriate size matrix must be declared.

6 Formulate an algorithm which appends (concatenates) a list to another list.

7 Assume that one is given an ordered linked linear list whose typical node consists of an information field and a link field as shown below:

$$\boxed{INFO \mid LINK}$$

The list is ordered on the field $INFO$ in the sense that node P precedes node Q in the list if and only if $INFO(P) < INFO(Q)$. It is required to devise an algorithm which inserts a new node whose information field is denoted by X, such that the updated list will remain ordered. Write a program corresponding to the algorthim devised.

8 Given a simple linked list whose first node is denoted by the pointer variable $FIRST$, it is required to deconcatenate (or split) this list into two simple linked lists. The node denoted by the pointer variable $SPLIT$ is to be the first element in the second linked list. Formulate a step-by-step algorithm to perform this task.

9 Given a simple linked list whose typical node is represented by

$$\boxed{INFO \mid LINK}$$

and whose first node is denoted by the pointer variable $FIRST$, it is required to devise an algorithm that will copy this list. The new list has nodes of the form

$$\boxed{FIELD \mid PTR}$$

and the pointer variable $BEGIN$ is to denote the first node. The variables $INFO$ and $FIELD$ represent the information content of a node, while $LINK$ and PTR are variables containing the address of the next node. Give the name $COPY$ to the algorithm.

10 Suppose that you are given a simple linked list whose first node is denoted by the pointer variable $FIRST$ and whose typical node is represented by

$$\boxed{KEY \mid LINK}$$

where the variables KEY and $LINK$ represent the information and link fields of the node, respectively. The list is ordered on the field KEY such that the first and last nodes contain the smallest and largest values of the field. It is desired to delete a number of consecutive nodes whose KEY values are greater than or equal to $KMIN$ and less than $KMAX$. For example, an initial list with $KMIN$ and $KMAX$ having values of 25 and 40, respectively, could look like this:

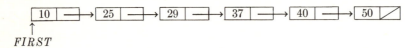

$FIRST$

After deleting the designated nodes, the updated list would reduce to the following:

$$\boxed{10 \mid \longrightarrow} \boxed{40 \mid \longrightarrow} \boxed{50 \mid}$$

$FIRST$

In this example, we dropped the nodes whose KEY field values are 25, 29, and 37. Formulate an algorithm and write a program which will accomplish the deletion operation for an arbitrary linked list.

2-3 RELATIONS AND ORDERING

The concept of a relation is a basic concept in everyday life as well as in mathematics. We have already used various relations. Associated with a relation is the act of comparing objects which are related to one another. The ability of a computer to perform different tasks based upon the result of a comparison is one of its most important attributes which is used several times during the execution of a typical program. In this section we first formalize the concept of a relation and then discuss methods of representing a relation by using a matrix or its graph. The relation matrix is useful in determining the properties of a relation and also in representing a relation on a computer. Various basic properties of relations are given, and certain important classes of relations are introduced. Among these, the compatibility relation and the equivalence relation have useful applications in the design of digital computers and other sequential machines. Partial ordering and its associated terminology are introduced next. The material in Chap. 4 is based upon these notions. Several relations given as examples in this section are used throughout the book. Algorithms to determine certain properties of relations are also given.

2-3.1   Relations

The word "relation" suggests some familiar examples of relations such as the relation of father to son, mother to son, brother to sister, etc. Familiar examples in arithmetic are relations such as "greater than," "less than," or that of equality between two real numbers. We also know the relation between the area of a circle and its radius and between the area of a square and its side. These examples suggest relationships between two objects. The relation between parents and child, the coincidence of three lines, and that of a point lying between two points are examples of relations among three objects. Similar examples exist for relations among four or more objects.

Here, we shall only consider relations, called binary relations, between a pair of objects. Before we give a set-theoretic definition of a relation, we note that a relation between two objects can be defined by listing the two objects as an ordered pair. A set of all such ordered pairs, in each of which the first member has some definite relationship to the second, describes a particular relationship. Of course, we have been motivated by relationships which are familiar and could be given a name. However, this is an undue restriction which will not appear in our definition of a relation.

Definition 2-3.1   Any set of ordered pairs defines a *binary relation*.

We shall call a binary relation simply a relation. It is sometimes convenient to express the fact that a particular ordered pair, say $\langle x, y \rangle \in R$, where R is a relation, by writing $x \, R \, y$ which may be read as "x is in relation R to y."

In mathematics, relations are often denoted by special symbols rather than by capital letters. A familiar example is the relation "greater than" for real numbers. This relation is denoted by $>$. In fact, $>$ should be considered as the name of a set whose elements are ordered pairs. Each member of any of the ordered pairs in the set is a real number, and if a and b are two real numbers such that $a > b$, then we say that $\langle a, b \rangle \in >$, or $a > b$. More precisely the relation $>$ is

$$> = \{ \langle x, y \rangle \mid x, y \text{ are real numbers and } x > y \} \qquad (1)$$

The relation of father to his child can be described by a set, say F, of ordered pairs in which the first member is the name of the father and the second the name of his child. That is,

$$F = \{ \langle x, y \rangle \mid x \text{ is the father of } y \} \qquad (2)$$

The definition of relation permits any set of ordered pairs to define a relation. For example, the set S given by

$$S = \{ \langle 2, 4 \rangle, \langle 1, 3 \rangle, \langle \lambda, 6 \rangle, \langle \text{Joan}, \mu \rangle \} \qquad (3)$$

can be considered as a relation. Of course, such a relation may not be familiar or interesting.

Let **R** denote the set of real numbers. Then

$$Q = \{ \langle x^2, x \rangle \mid x \in \mathbf{R} \} \qquad (4)$$

defines the relation of the square of a real number.

Definition 2-3.2   Let S be a binary relation. The set $D(S)$ of all objects x such that for some y, $\langle x, y \rangle \in S$ is called the *domain* of S, that is,

$$D(S) = \{ x \mid (\exists y)(\langle x, y \rangle \in S) \}$$

Similarly, the set $R(S)$ of all objects y such that for some x, $\langle x, y \rangle \in S$ is called the *range* of S, that is,

$$R(S) = \{ y \mid (\exists x)(\langle x, y \rangle \in S) \}$$

For the relation S described in Eq. (3) we have

$$D(S) = \{2, 1, \lambda, \text{Joan}\} \qquad \text{and} \qquad R(S) = \{4, 3, 6, \mu\}$$

Let X and Y be any two sets. A subset of the cartesian product $X \times Y$ defines a relation, say C. For any such relation C, we have $D(C) \subseteq X$ and $R(C) \subseteq Y$, and the relation C is said to be from X to Y. If $Y = X$, then C is said to be a relation from X to X. In such a case, C is called a relation in X. Thus any relation in X is a subset of $X \times X$. The set $X \times X$ itself defines a relation in X and is called a *universal relation* in X, while the empty set which is also a subset of $X \times X$ is called a *void relation* in X.

The relations given in Eqs. (1) and (4) are in the set **R** of real numbers. The relation in Eq. (2) is in the set of all human beings. It could also be considered as a relation from the set of all males to the set of human beings. The relation S in Eq. (3) can be considered from a set X to a set Y where $\{2, 1, \lambda,$ Joan$\} \subseteq X$ and $\{4, 3, 6, \mu\} \subseteq Y$. In fact any relation from a set X to a set Y can also be considered as a relation in $X \cup Y$.

If **R** is the set of real numbers, then the elements of $\mathbf{R} \times \mathbf{R}$ can be represented by points in a plane, as shown in Sec. 2-1.8. Some of the subsets of $\mathbf{R} \times \mathbf{R}$ define familiar relations which can be shown graphically. For example, consider the relations in which $x * y$ means xy

$$R_1 = \{ \langle x, y \rangle \mid \langle x, y \rangle \in \mathbf{R} \times \mathbf{R} \wedge x * y \geq 1 \}$$
$$R_2 = \{ \langle x, y \rangle \mid \langle x, y \rangle \in \mathbf{R} \times \mathbf{R} \wedge x^2 + y^2 \leq 9 \} \qquad (5)$$
$$R_3 = \{ \langle x, y \rangle \mid \langle x, y \rangle \in \mathbf{R} \times \mathbf{R} \wedge y^2 < x \}$$

R_1 can be represented by points on one side of a hyperbola, R_2 by points inside or on a circle of radius 3, and R_3 by points on one side of a parabola. These relations are displayed in Fig. 2-3.1.

A relation has been defined as a set of ordered pairs. It is therefore possible to apply the usual operations of sets to relations as well. The resulting sets will also be ordered pairs and will define some relation. If R and S denote two relations, then $R \cap S$ defines a relation such that

$$x \, (R \cap S) \, y \Leftrightarrow x \, R \, y \wedge x \, S \, y$$

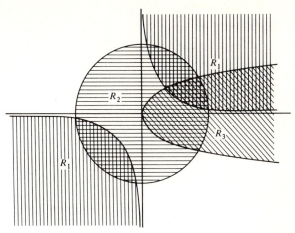

FIGURE 2-3.1

Similarly, $R \cup S$ is a relation such that

$$x \ (R \cup S) \ y \Leftrightarrow x \ R \ y \lor x \ S \ y$$

Also

$$x \ (R - S) \ y \Leftrightarrow x \ R \ y \land x \not S \ y$$

and

$$x \ (\sim R) \ y \Leftrightarrow x \not R \ y$$

EXAMPLE 1   (a) Let $X = \{1, 2, 3, 4\}$. If

$R = \{\langle x, y \rangle \mid x \in X \land y \in X \land ((x - y) \text{ is an integral nonzero multiple of 2})\}$
$\ \ = \{\langle 1, 3 \rangle, \langle 3, 1 \rangle, \langle 2, 4 \rangle, \langle 4, 2 \rangle\}$

$S = \{\langle x, y \rangle \mid x \in X \land y \in X \land ((x - y) \text{ is an integral nonzero multiple of 3})\}$
$\ \ = \{\langle 1, 4 \rangle, \langle 4, 1 \rangle\}$

Find $R \cup S$ and $R \cap S$.

(b) If $X = \{1, 2, 3, \ldots\}$, what is $R \cap S$ for R and S as defined in (a)?

SOLUTION

(a) $R \cup S = \{\langle 1, 3 \rangle, \langle 3, 1 \rangle, \langle 2, 4 \rangle, \langle 4, 2 \rangle, \langle 1, 4 \rangle, \langle 4, 1 \rangle\}$ and $R \cap S = \varnothing$.
(b) $R \cap S = \{\langle x, y \rangle \mid x \in X \land y \in X \land ((x - y) \text{ is a nonzero multiple of 6})\}$.

////

Let us return to the relations R_1, R_2, R_3 given in Eq. (5). The predicates P_1, P_2, and P_3 defined by

$$P_1 : x * y \geq 1 \qquad P_2 : x^2 + y^2 \leq 9 \qquad P_3 : y^2 < x$$

describe the relations R_1, R_2, and R_3 respectively. Recall from Sec. 2-1.7 that associated with each predicate is an extension set. A more complex predicate such as $P_1 \land P_2 \land P_3$ having an extension set $R_1 \cap R_2 \cap R_3$ can be written. Given the coordinates of a point $\langle x, y \rangle$, it is instructive to determine whether $\langle x, y \rangle$ is a member of each of the following sets:

$$R_4 = R_1 \cap R_2 \cap R_3$$
$$= \{\langle x, y\rangle \mid \langle x, y\rangle \in \mathbf{R} \times \mathbf{R} \wedge x * y \geq 1 \wedge x^2 + y^2 \leq 9 \wedge y^2 < x\}$$
$$R_5 = R_2 \cap (R_1 \cup R_3) \cap \sim(R_1 \cap R_3)$$
$$= \{\langle x, y\rangle \mid \langle x, y\rangle \in \mathbf{R} \times \mathbf{R} \wedge x^2 + y^2 \leq 9 \wedge (x * y \geq 1 \vee y^2 < x)$$
$$\wedge \sim(x * y \geq 1 \wedge y^2 < x)\}$$
$$R_6 = R_1 \cap \sim R_2 \cap R_3$$
$$= \{\langle x, y\rangle \mid \langle x, y\rangle \in \mathbf{R} \times \mathbf{R} \wedge x * y \geq 1 \wedge \sim(x^2 + y^2 \leq 9) \wedge y^2 < x\}$$
$$R_7 = \sim(R_1 \cup R_3) \cap R_2$$
$$= \{\langle x, y\rangle \mid \langle x, y\rangle \in \mathbf{R} \times \mathbf{R} \wedge \sim(x * y \geq 1 \vee y^2 < x) \wedge x^2 + y^2 \leq 9\}$$

R_4 includes all points lying within the circle and the parabola and above the hyperbola of the first quadrant. R_5 includes all points within the circle which lie either within the parabola or above the hyperbola of the first quadrant, but not both, and all points within the circle and below the hyperbola in the third quadrant. R_6 includes all points lying above the hyperbola and within the parabola in the first quadrant. R_7 includes all points lying within the circle and between the hyperbolic curves but not within the parabola.

These newly defined sets can pictorially be represented as shown in Fig. 2-3.2. The program given in Fig. 2-3.3 reads a number of coordinate points and determines whether these points lie in the sets R_4 to R_7. Note that the relations R_4 to R_7 are written as predicates P_4 to P_7 in the program.

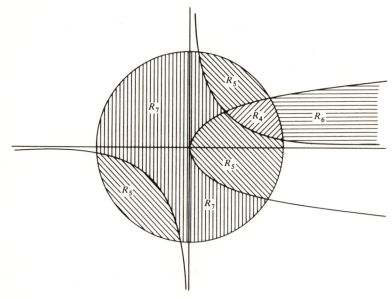

FIGURE 2-3.2

```
C   THIS PROGRAM READS PAIRS OF NUMBERS, X AND Y, AND DETERMINES THE
C   TRUTH VALUES OF THE PREDICATES P(1), P(2), AND P(3).
C   IF THE TRUTH VALUE OF A PREDICATE IS TRUE THEN THE POINT (X,Y) IS
C   AN ELEMENT OF THE RELATION WHICH IS AN EXTENSION SET OF THE
C   PREDICATE, OTHERWISE IT IS NOT.
C   IN ADDITION, THE TRUTH VALUES OF PREDICATES P(4), P(5), P(6), AND
C   P(7) ARE FOUND.  THESE PREDICATES DEFINE RELATIONS WHICH ARE OBTAINED
C   BY PERFORMING THE OPERATIONS OF UNION, INTERSECTION, AND
C   COMPLEMENTATION ON THE EXTENSION SETS OF P(1), P(2) AND P(3).
C
C   P MUST BE A LOGICAL ARRAY
      LOGICAL P(7)
C
C   PRINT HEADINGS
      WRITE(6,10)
   10 FORMAT('1',5X,'(X,Y) POINTS',22X,'PREDICATES',//,' ',5X,'X',9X,
     1'Y',9X,'P1    P2    P3    P4    P5    P6    P7')
C
C   READ X AND Y COORDINATES
    1 READ(5,15,END=2)X,Y
   15 FORMAT(F5.2,2X,F5.2)
C
C   EVALUATE PREDICATES P(1), P(2), AND P(3)
      P(1) = X * Y .GE. 1.
      P(2) = X ** 2 + Y ** 2 .LE. 9
      P(3) = Y ** 2 .LT. X
C
C   EVALUATE THE PREDICATES WHICH DEFINE SETS OBTAINED THROUGH
C   OPERATIONS ON THE EXTENSION SETS OF P(1), P(2) AND P(3).
      P(4) = P(1) .AND. P(2) .AND. P(3)
      P(5) = P(2) .AND. (P(1) .OR. P(3)) .AND. .NOT.(P(1) .AND .P(3))
      P(6) = P(1) .AND. .NOT.P(2) .AND. P(3)
      P(7) = .NOT.(P(1) .OR. P(3)) .AND. P(2)
C
C   OUTPUT X, Y AND THE TRUTH VALUES OF THE PREDICATES.
      WRITE(6,20)X,Y,(P(I),I = 1,7)
   20 FORMAT('0',3X,F5.2,5X,F5.2,3X,7(L6))
      GO TO 1
    2 STOP
      END
```

(X,Y) POINTS		PREDICATES						
X	Y	P1	P2	P3	P4	P5	P6	P7
-0.60	0.70	F	T	F	F	F	F	T
1.11	0.50	F	T	T	F	T	F	F
2.20	1.30	T	T	T	T	F	F	F
4.80	1.90	T	F	T	F	F	T	F
-5.00	-1.00	T	F	F	F	F	F	F
1.00	2.30	T	T	F	F	T	F	F
5.00	0.15	F	F	T	F	F	F	F

FIGURE 2-3.3 FORTRAN program for testing membership of coordinates in relations.

EXERCISES 2-3.1

1 Let

$$P = \{\langle 1, 2\rangle, \langle 2, 4\rangle, \langle 3, 3\rangle\} \quad \text{and} \quad Q = \{\langle 1, 3\rangle, \langle 2, 4\rangle, \langle 4, 2\rangle\}$$

Find $P \cup Q$, $P \cap Q$, $D(P)$, $D(Q)$, $D(P \cup Q)$, $R(P)$, $R(Q)$, and $R(P \cap Q)$. Show that

$$D(P \cup Q) = D(P) \cup D(Q)$$

and

$$R(P \cap Q) \subseteq R(P) \cap R(Q)$$

2   What are the ranges of the relations

$$S = \{\langle x, x^2 \rangle \mid x \in \mathbf{N}\} \qquad \text{and} \qquad T = \{\langle x, 2x \rangle \mid x \in \mathbf{N}\}$$

where $\mathbf{N} = \{0, 1, 2, \ldots\}$? Find $R \cup S$ and $R \cap S$.

3   Let L denote the relation "less than or equal to" and D denote the relation "divides," where $x \, D \, y$ means "x divides y." Both L and D are defined on the set $\{1, 2, 3, 6\}$. Write L and D as sets, and find $L \cap D$.

2-3.2   Properties of Binary Relations in a Set

Definition 2-3.3   A binary relation R in a set X is *reflexive* if, for every $x \in X$, $x \, R \, x$, that is, $\langle x, x \rangle \in R$, or

$$R \text{ is reflexive in } X \Leftrightarrow (x)(x \in X \to x \, R \, x)$$

The relation $\leq$ is reflexive in the set of real numbers since, for any x, we have $x \leq x$. Similarly, the relation of inclusion is reflexive in the family of all subsets of a universal set. The relation of equality of sets is also reflexive. However, the relation $<$ is not reflexive in the set of real numbers, and the relation of proper inclusion is not reflexive in the family of subsets of a universal set.

Definition 2-3.4   A relation R in a set X is *symmetric* if, for every x and y in X, whenever $x \, R \, y$, then $y \, R \, x$. That is,

$$R \text{ is symmetric in } X \Leftrightarrow (x)(y)(x \in X \wedge y \in X \wedge x \, R \, y \to y \, R \, x)$$

The relations $\leq$ and $<$ are not symmetric in the set of real numbers, while the relation of equality is. The relation of similarity in the set of triangles in a plane is both reflexive and symmetric. The relation of being a brother is not symmetric in the set of all people. However, in the set of all males it is symmetric.

Definition 2-3.5   A relation R in a set X is *transitive* if, for every x, y, and z in X, whenever $x \, R \, y$ and $y \, R \, z$, then $x \, R \, z$. That is,

$$R \text{ is transitive in } X \Leftrightarrow (x)(y)(z)(x \in X \wedge y \in X \wedge z \in X$$
$$\wedge \, x \, R \, y \wedge y \, R \, z \to x \, R \, z)$$

The relations $\leq$, $<$, and $=$ are transitive in the set of real numbers. The relations $\subseteq$, $\subset$, and equality are also transitive in the family of subsets of a universal set. The relation of similarity of triangles in a plane is transitive, while the relation of being a mother is not.

Definition 2-3.6   A relation R in a set X is *irreflexive* if, for every $x \in X$, $\langle x, x \rangle \notin R$.

Note that any relation which is not reflexive is not necessarily irreflexive, and vice versa. The relation $<$ in the set of real numbers is irreflexive because for no x do we have $x < x$. Similarly, the relation of proper inclusion in the set of all nonempty subsets of a universal set is irreflexive. The following is a simple example of a relation in $\{1, 2, 3\}$ which is not reflexive and not irreflexive:

$$S = \{\langle 1, 1 \rangle, \langle 1, 2 \rangle, \langle 3, 2 \rangle, \langle 2, 3 \rangle, \langle 3, 3 \rangle\}$$

Definition 2-3.7 A relation R in a set X is *antisymmetric* if, for every x and y in X, whenever $x R y$ and $y R x$, then $x = y$. Symbolically, R is antisymmetric in x iff

$$(x)(y)(x \in X \wedge y \in X \wedge x R y \wedge y R x \rightarrow x = y)$$

Note that it is possible to have a relation which is both symmetric and antisymmetric. This is obviously the case when each element is either related to itself or not related to any element.

Some known relations and their properties are now given.

Let **R** be the set of real numbers. The relations $>$ (greater than) and $<$ (less than) in **R** are both irreflexive and transitive. Also the relation $=$ (equality) in **R** is reflexive, symmetric, and transitive.

Let X be the set of all courses offered at a university, and for $x \in X$ and $y \in X$, $x R y$ if x is a prerequisite for y. The relation of being a prerequisite is irreflexive and transitive.

Let X be the set of all male Canadians and let $x R y$, where $x \in X$ and $y \in X$, denote the relation "x is a brother of y." The relation R is irreflexive and symmetric but not transitive. In general, any relation which is irreflexive and symmetric cannot be transitive because $x R y \wedge y R x \Rightarrow x R x$, which is not true.

Let X be the collection of the subsets of a universal set. The relation of inclusion in X is reflexive, antisymmetric, and transitive. Also, the relation of proper inclusion in X is irreflexive, antisymmetric, and transitive.

Several important classes of relations having one or more of the properties given here will be discussed later in this section.

EXERCISES 2-3.2

1 Give an example of a relation which is neither reflexive nor irreflexive.

2 Give an example of a relation which is both symmetric and antisymmetric.

3 If relations R and S are both reflexive, show that $R \cup S$ and $R \cap S$ are also reflexive.

4 If relations R and S are reflexive, symmetric, and transitive, show that $R \cap S$ is also reflexive, symmetric, and transitive.

5 Show whether the following relations are transitive:

$$R_1 = \{\langle 1, 1 \rangle\} \qquad R_2 = \{\langle 1, 2 \rangle, \langle 2, 2 \rangle\}$$
$$R_3 = \{\langle 1, 2 \rangle, \langle 2, 3 \rangle, \langle 1, 3 \rangle, \langle 2, 1 \rangle\}$$

6 Given $S = \{1, 2, 3, 4\}$ and a relation R on S defined by

$$R = \{\langle 1, 2 \rangle, \langle 4, 3 \rangle, \langle 2, 2 \rangle, \langle 2, 1 \rangle, \langle 3, 1 \rangle\}$$

show that R is not transitive. Find a relation $R_1 \supseteq R$ such that R_1 is transitive. Can you find another relation $R_2 \supseteq R$ which is also transitive?

7 Given $S = \{1, 2, \ldots, 10\}$ and a relation R on S where

$$R = \{\langle x, y \rangle \mid x + y = 10\}$$

what are the properties of the relation R?

8 Let R be a relation on the set of positive real numbers so that its graphical representation consists of points in the first quadrant of the cartesian plane. What can we expect if R is (a) reflexive, (b) symmetric, and (c) transitive?

9 Show that the relations L and D given in Problem 3 of Exercises 2-3.1 are both reflexive, antisymmetric, and transitive. Give another example of such a relation. Draw the graphs of these relations as defined in Sec. 2-3.3.

2-3.3 Relation Matrix and the Graph of a Relation

A relation R from a finite set X to a finite set Y can also be represented by a matrix called the *relation matrix* of R.

Let $X = \{x_1, x_2, \ldots, x_m\}$, $Y = \{y_1, y_2, \ldots, y_n\}$, and R be a relation from X to Y. The relation matrix of R can be obtained by first constructing a table whose columns are preceded by a column consisting of successive elements of X and whose rows are headed by a row consisting of the successive elements of Y. If $x_i \, R \, y_j$, then we enter a 1 in the ith row and jth column. If $x_k \, \not{R} \, x_l$, then we enter a zero in the kth row and lth column. As a special case, consider $m = 3$, $n = 2$, and R given by

$$R = \{\langle x_1, y_1 \rangle, \langle x_2, y_1 \rangle, \langle x_3, y_2 \rangle, \langle x_2, y_2 \rangle\} \tag{1}$$

The required table for R is Table 2-3.1.

If we assume that the elements of X and Y appear in a certain order, then the relation R can be represented by a matrix whose elements are 1s and 0s. This matrix can be written down from the table constructed or can be defined in the following manner.

$$r_{ij} = \begin{cases} 1 & \text{if } x_i \, R \, y_j \\ 0 & \text{if } x_i \, \not{R} \, y_j \end{cases}$$

where r_{ij} is the element in the ith row and jth column. The matrix obtained in this way is called the relation matrix. If X has m elements and Y has n elements, then the relation matrix is an $m \times n$ matrix. For the relation R given in Eq. (1), the relation matrix is

$$\begin{bmatrix} 1 & 0 \\ 1 & 1 \\ 0 & 1 \end{bmatrix}$$

Table 2-3.1

	y_1	y_2
x_1	1	0
x_2	1	1
x_3	0	1

One can not only write a relation matrix when a relation R is given but also obtain the relation if the relation matrix is given.

Throughout the remainder of this subsection we shall assume that the relations are defined in a set, say X. A relation matrix reflects some of the properties of a relation in a set. If a relation is reflexive, then all the diagonal entries must be 1. If a relation is symmetric, then the relation matrix is symmetric. If a relation is antisymmetric, then its matrix is such that if $r_{ij} = 1$, then $r_{ji} = 0$ for $i \neq j$.

A relation can also be represented pictorially by drawing its *graph*. Although we shall introduce some of the concepts of graph theory which are discussed in Chap. 5, here we shall use graphs only as a tool to represent relations. Let R be a relation in a set $X = \{x_1, \ldots, x_m\}$. The elements of X are represented by points or circles called *nodes*. The nodes corresponding to x_i and x_j are labeled x_i and x_j respectively. These nodes may also be called vertices. If $x_i R x_j$, that is, if $\langle x_i, x_j \rangle \in R$, then we connect nodes x_i and x_j by means of an arc and put an arrow on the arc in the direction from x_i to x_j. When all the nodes corresponding to the ordered pairs in R are connected by arcs with proper arrows, we get a graph (directed graph) of the relation R. If $x_i R x_j$ and $x_j R x_i$, then we draw two arcs between x_i and x_j. For the sake of simplicity, we may replace the two arcs by one arc with arrows pointing in both directions. If $x_i R x_i$, we get an arc which starts from node x_i and returns to node x_i. Such an arc is called a *loop*. In Fig. 2-3.4 we show some arcs.

From the graph of a relation it is possible to observe some of its properties. If a relation is reflexive, then there must be a loop at each node. On the other hand, if the relation is irreflexive, then there is no loop at any node. If a relation is symmetric and if one node is connected to another, then there must be a return arc from the second node to the first. For antisymmetric relations no such direct return path should exist (see Fig. 2-3.5). If a relation is transitive, the situation is not so simple. In any case, its graph must have loops of the type shown in Fig. 2-3.6.

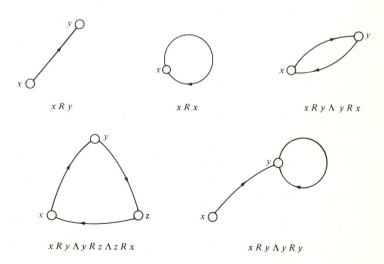

$x R y$

$x R x$

$x R y \wedge y R x$

$x R y \wedge y R z \wedge z R x$

$x R y \wedge y R y$

FIGURE 2-3.4 Graphs of relations.

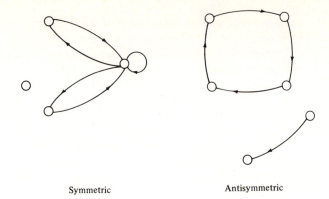

Symmetric   Antisymmetric

FIGURE 2-3.5   Symmetric and antisymmetric relations.

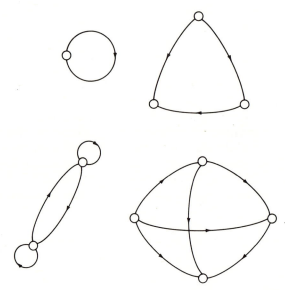

FIGURE 2-3.6   Transitive relations.

EXAMPLE 1   Let $X = \{1, 2, 3, 4\}$ and $R = \{\langle x, y \rangle \mid x > y\}$. Draw the graph of R and also give its matrix.

SOLUTION   The graph and the corresponding relation matrix for the relation $R = \{\langle 4, 1 \rangle, \langle 4, 2 \rangle, \langle 4, 3 \rangle, \langle 3, 1 \rangle, \langle 3, 2 \rangle, \langle 2, 1 \rangle\}$ is given in Fig. 2-3.7.   ////

EXAMPLE 2   Let $A = \{a, b, c\}$ and denote the subsets of A by $B_0, \ldots, B_7$ according to the convention given in Sec. 2-1.3. Thus $B_0 = \varnothing$, $B_1 = \{c\}$, $B_2 = \{b\}$, $B_3 = \{b, c\}$, $B_4 = \{a\}$, $B_5 = \{a, c\}$, $B_6 = \{a, b\}$, and $B_7 = \{a, b, c\}$. If R is the relation of *proper inclusion* on the subsets $B_0, \ldots, B_7$, then give the matrix of the relation.

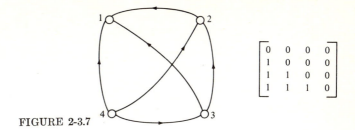

FIGURE 2-3.7

SOLUTION

$$\begin{bmatrix} 0 & 1 & 1 & 1 & 1 & 1 & 1 & 1 \\ 0 & 0 & 0 & 1 & 0 & 1 & 0 & 1 \\ 0 & 0 & 0 & 1 & 0 & 0 & 1 & 1 \\ 0 & 0 & 0 & 0 & 0 & 0 & 0 & 1 \\ 0 & 0 & 0 & 0 & 0 & 1 & 1 & 1 \\ 0 & 0 & 0 & 0 & 0 & 0 & 0 & 1 \\ 0 & 0 & 0 & 0 & 0 & 0 & 0 & 1 \\ 0 & 0 & 0 & 0 & 0 & 0 & 0 & 0 \end{bmatrix}$$

The relations given in Examples 1 and 2 are both transitive, antisymmetric, and irreflexive. This class of relations will be discussed in Sec. 2-3.8.

EXAMPLE 3   Determine the properties of the relations given by the graphs shown in Fig. 2-3.8, and also write the corresponding relation matrices.

SOLUTION   The relation given by the graph in (a) is antisymmetric, in (b) is reflexive, in (c) it is reflexive and symmetric, while in (d) it is transitive. The required matrices are

(a) $\begin{bmatrix} 0 & 1 & 1 & 0 & 0 \\ 0 & 0 & 0 & 0 & 0 \\ 0 & 0 & 0 & 1 & 1 \\ 0 & 0 & 0 & 0 & 0 \\ 0 & 0 & 0 & 0 & 0 \end{bmatrix}$ (b) $\begin{bmatrix} 1 & 0 & 0 \\ 0 & 1 & 0 \\ 0 & 0 & 1 \end{bmatrix}$ (c) $\begin{bmatrix} 1 & 1 & 0 & 1 \\ 1 & 1 & 1 & 0 \\ 0 & 1 & 1 & 0 \\ 1 & 0 & 0 & 1 \end{bmatrix}$ (d) $\begin{bmatrix} 0 & 0 & 1 & 1 \\ 1 & 0 & 1 & 1 \\ 0 & 0 & 0 & 1 \\ 0 & 0 & 0 & 0 \end{bmatrix}$

////

When the number of elements in a set X over which a relation R is defined is large (say greater than or equal to 5 or 6), both the graphical and the matrix

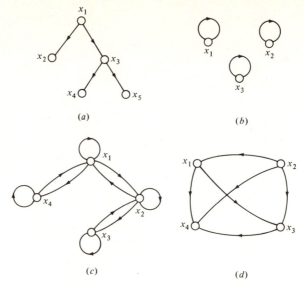

FIGURE 2-3.8

representations of the relation become unwieldy. In these cases, however, the matrix representation can be easily represented on a computer. When a relation matrix is available, it is easy to determine whether a given relation is reflexive or symmetric. It is not always easy to determine from the matrix whether the relation is transitive. We now present two algorithms. The first determines from a relation matrix whether the relation is reflexive and symmetric. The second algorithm then determines whether the relation is also transitive. Relations which are reflexive, symmetric, and transitive are called *equivalence relations*. Equivalence relations are discussed in Sec. 2-3.5.

The entries of the relation matrix are denoted by T and F instead of 1 and 0 in order to conserve storage. Note that in FORTRAN only 1 byte is needed for each logical entry, but at least 2 bytes are required for an integer entry.

Algorithm *REFSYM* Given a relation matrix R representing a relation in the set of positive integers from 1 to n inclusive, it is required to determine if the relation represented by R is symmetric and reflexive. If it is, the variable *FLAG* which is initially *false* is given the truth value *true*; otherwise *FLAG* remains *false*.

1 [Scan each row.] Repeat steps 2 and 3 for $i = 1, 2, \ldots, n$.
2 [Reflexive?] If $R[i, i] = F$ then Exit.
3 [Symmetric?] Repeat for $j = i + 1, i + 2, \ldots, n$:
   If $R[i\ j] \rightleftarrows R[j, i] = F$ then Exit.
4 [Successful test.] Set $FLAG \leftarrow T$ and Exit.

This algorithm scans each row of the matrix from the diagonal element to the right. If a diagonal element has the truth value F, then the algorithm is terminated in step 2 with *FLAG* remaining *false*. Step 3 scans each row in the upper triangle of the matrix. If an entry has a truth value which differs from the truth value of its reflection, then the algorithm is terminated with *FLAG* remaining *false*.

If the algorithm completely scans all the rows, then *FLAG* is set to T, indicating that the relation represented by the relation matrix R is symmetric and reflexive. A subprogram REFSYM is given in Fig. 2-3.9. An example will be given in Sec. 2-3.5. ////

We now give an algorithm to determine whether a given relation which is both reflexive and symmetric is also transitive. The test for transitivity is simplified when a relation is symmetric because ordinarily $i\,R\,j$ and $j\,R\,k$ imply $i\,R\,k$, but in the case of a symmetric relation $i\,R\,j$ and $i\,R\,k$ imply $j\,R\,k$. Algorithm *TRANS* determines whether a given symmetric relation is transitive.

Algorithm *TRANS* Given a relation matrix R which represents a symmetric and reflexive relation, it is required to determine if this relation is transitive. The relation is in the set $\{1, 2, \ldots, n\}$. If it is transitive, then FLAG, which is initially *false*, is set to *true*.

  1 [Scan each row.] Repeat steps 2 and 3 for $i = 1, 2, \ldots, n - 2$.
  2 [Scan to right of diagonal.] Repeat step 3 for $j = i + 1, i + 2, \ldots, n - 1$.
  3 [Transitive?] If $R[i, j] = T$ then repeat for $k = j + 1, j + 2, \ldots, n$: If $R[i, k] = T$ and $R[j, k] = F$ then Exit.
  4 [Successful test.] Set $FLAG \leftarrow T$ and Exit.

This algorithm scans only the rows in the upper triangular part of the matrix. The first element to the right of the diagonal which has the truth value T is found. This element is $R[i, j]$. All the following *true* elements are found,

```
      SUBROUTINE REFSYM(A,N,FLAG)
C  THIS SUBROUTINE RECEIVES A LOGICAL ARRAY A WHICH REPRESENTS THE
C  RELATION MATRIX OF A RELATION ON THE SET OF POSITIVE INTEGERS FROM
C  ONE TO N INCLUSIVE.  IF THE RELATION REPRESENTED BY A IS REFLEXIVE
C  AND SYMMETRIC, FLAG, WHICH IS INITIALLY FALSE IS SET TO TRUE.
C  OTHERWISE FLAG IS STILL FALSE WHEN RETURNED TO THE MAINLINE.
C
      LOGICAL*1 A(N,N),FLAG
C
C  I IS THE ROW COUNTER.
      DO 10 I = 1,N
C
C  REFLEXIVE?
      IF(.NOT.A(I,I)) RETURN
      IF(I .EQ. N) GO TO 20
C
C  J IS THE COLUMN COUNTER AND RANGES FROM I+1 TO N.
      K = I + 1
      DO 10 J = K,N
C
C  SYMMETRIC? A(I,J) IFF A(J,I).
      IF(.NOT.((.NOT.A(I,J).OR.A(J,I)).AND.(.NOT.A(J,I).OR.A(I,J))))
     1RETURN
   10 CONTINUE
   20 FLAG = .TRUE.
      RETURN
      END
```

FIGURE 2-3.9 FORTRAN subroutine for algorithm *REFSYM*.

and for each such $R[i, k]$, if $R[j, k]$ is *false*, then the relation is not transitive and the algorithm is finished; otherwise transitivity can be tested further. This test must be performed for all *true* $R[i, j]$ such that $i < j < n$.

Each row, excepting the last, is scanned in this manner. After row $n - 2$ is completed, *FLAG* is set to *true*, indicating that the relation is transitive. A FORTRAN subroutine for this algorithm is given in Fig. 2-3.10. ////

A program which first puts a relation given as a set of ordered pairs into a relation matrix and then determines whether the relation is reflexive, symmetric, and transitive is given in Sec. 2-3.5 along with a further subprogram which obtains equivalence classes.

2-3.4 Partition and Covering of a Set

Definition 2-3.8 Let S be a given set and $A = \{A_1, A_2, \ldots, A_m\}$ where each A_i, $i = 1, \ldots, m$, is a subset of S and

$$\bigcup_{i=1}^{m} A_i = S$$

```
      SUBROUTINE TRANS(A,N,FLAG)
C     THIS SUBROUTINE IS INVOKED AFTER THE RELATION MATRIX A HAS BEEN
C     PROVED TO REPRESENT A REFLEXIVE AND SYMMETRIC RELATION.  IF THE
C     RELATION IS TRANSITIVE, THEN FLAG, WHICH WAS RESET TO FALSE IS SET TO
C     TRUE, INDICATING THAT THE RELATION IS AN EQUIVALENCE RELATION.
C     OTHERWISE, FLAG REMAINS FALSE ON RETURN.
C
      LOGICAL*1 A(N,N),FLAG
C
C     CHECK FOR TRIVIAL CASE:  N = 1 OR N = 2
      IF(N.EQ.1.OR.N.EQ.2) GO TO 20
C
C     I IS THE ROW COUNTER.
      NMIN2 = N - 2
      DO 10 I = 1,NMIN2
C
C     J IS A COLUMN COUNTER RANGING FROM I+1 TO N-1.
      L = I + 1
      NMIN1 = N - 1
      DO 10 J = L,NMIN1
C
C     FIND A PAIR (I,J) FOR WHICH I AND J ARE RELATED.
      IF(.NOT.A(I,J)) GO TO 10
C     K SCANS FROM COLUMN J+1 TO N.
      M = J + 1
      DO 5 K = M,N
C
C     FIND THE FOLLOWING RELATED PAIRS IN ROW I.
      IF(.NOT.A(I,K)) GO TO 5
C
C     TRANSITIVE?  A(I,J) AND A(I,K) IMPLIES A(K,J).
      IF(.NOT.A(K,J)) RETURN
    5 CONTINUE
   10 CONTINUE
C
C     THE RELATION IS AN EQUIVALENCE RELATION.
   20 FLAG = .TRUE.
      RETURN
      END
```

FIGURE 2-3.10 FORTRAN subroutine for algorithm *TRANS*.

Then the set A is called a *covering* of S, and the sets A_1, A_2, ..., A_m are said to *cover* S. If, in addition, the elements of A, which are subsets of S, are mutually disjoint, then A is called a *partition* of S, and the sets A_1, A_2, ..., A_m are called the *blocks* of the partition.

For example, let $S = \{a, b, c\}$ and consider the following collections of subsets of S.

$$A = \{\{a, b\}, \{b, c\}\} \qquad B = \{\{a\}, \{a, c\}\} \qquad C = \{\{a\}, \{b, c\}\}$$
$$D = \{\{a, b, c\}\} \qquad E = \{\{a\}, \{b\}, \{c\}\} \qquad F = \{\{a\}, \{a, b\}, \{a, c\}\}$$

The sets A and F are coverings of S while C, D, and E are partitions of S. Of course, every partition is also a covering. The set B is neither a partition nor a covering of S. The partition D has only one block while E has three. In the case of the given set S, we cannot have more than three blocks in any partition. In fact, for any finite set, the smallest partition consists of the set itself as a block while the largest partition consists of blocks containing only single elements.

Two partitions are said to be equal if they are equal as sets. For a finite set, every partition is a finite partition, i.e., every partition contains only a finite number of blocks.

It will be shown in Sec. 2-3.5 that an equivalence relation on a set partitions the set. Another relation on a set known as a compatibility relation as described in Sec. 2-3.6 defines certain coverings of the set.

Now we discuss some partitions of the universal set E which are generated by the subsets of E. Let us first consider a subset A of E. The subsets A and $\sim A$ generate a partition of E (see Fig. 2-3.11a) since

$$E = A \cup \sim A$$

Next let A and B be any two subsets of E, and consider the sets

$$I_0 = \sim A \cap \sim B \qquad I_1 = \sim A \cap B \qquad I_2 = A \cap \sim B \qquad \text{and} \qquad I_3 = A \cap B$$

The sets I_0, I_1, I_2, and I_3 are called the complete intersections or the *minterms* generated by the subsets A and B. It is easy to see that I_0, I_1, I_2, and I_3 are mutually disjoint and

$$E = I_0 \cup I_1 \cup I_2 \cup I_3 = \bigcup_{j=0}^{3} I_j$$

The complete intersections or the minterms are the blocks of a partition of E generated by A and B (see Fig. 2-3.11b).

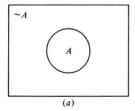

(a)

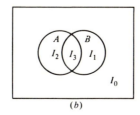

(b)

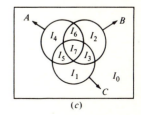

(c)

FIGURE 2-3.11   Complete intersections.

Let A, B, and C be three subsets of E and let the 2^3 minterms, denoted by I_0, I_1, ..., I_7 (see Fig. 2-3.11c), be as follows:

$$I_0 = \sim A \cap \sim B \cap \sim C \qquad I_1 = \sim A \cap \sim B \cap C$$
$$I_2 = \sim A \cap B \cap \sim C \qquad I_3 = \sim A \cap B \cap C$$
$$I_4 = A \cap \sim B \cap \sim C \qquad I_5 = A \cap \sim B \cap C$$
$$I_6 = A \cap B \cap \sim C \qquad I_7 = A \cap B \cap C$$

The subscript of I shows indirectly the minterm under consideration. In order to obtain the minterm, first we write the subscript as a binary integer containing three digits (since there are three subsets under consideration). The appearance of 1 or 0 in the first position on the left indicates the presence of A or $\sim A$, respectively. This relation also holds for the second and third positions. The notation is similar to the one used in Secs. 1-3.5 and 2-1.3. For example, $I_5 = A \cap \sim B \cap C$ since 5 written as a binary integer is 101.

In general, if A_1, A_2, ..., A_n are any n subsets of the universal set E, then the complete intersections or minterms generated by these n subsets are denoted by I_0, I_1, ..., I_{2^n-1} (see Sec. 2-1.3). These are mutually disjoint and are such that

$$E = \bigcup_{j=0}^{2^n-1} I_j$$

One can recognize a similarity between the minterms defined here and those given in the statement calculus. We shall return to a general discussion of this in Chap. 4.

EXERCISES 2-3.4

1 Define a well-formed formula of set theory in the same manner as in the definition given in Sec. 1-2.7, using the operators $\cap$, $\cup$, and $\sim$ only.
2 Show that for any formula in set theory involving set variables A and B and the operations $\cap$, $\cup$, and $\sim$, one can obtain another formula which is equal to the given formula and which contains the union of minterms only.
3 Show that the set of operations $\{\cup, \sim\}$ is functionally complete for formulas in set theory (*Hint:* Follow the same procedure used in Sec. 1-2.13).
4 Write the duals of minterms and discuss some of their important properties.

2-3.5 Equivalence Relations

Definition 2-3.9 A relation R in a set X is called an *equivalence relation* if it is reflexive, symmetric, and transitive.

If R is an equivalence relation in a set X, then $D(R)$, the domain of R, is X itself. Therefore R will be called a relation on X. The following are some examples of equivalence relations.

1 Equality of numbers on a set of real numbers
2 Equality of subsets of a universal set

3 Similarity of triangles on the set of triangles

4 Relation of lines being parallel on a set of lines in a plane

5 Relation of living in the same town on the set of persons living in Canada

6 Relation of statements being equivalent in the set of statements

EXAMPLE 1   Let $X = \{1, 2, 3, 4\}$ and

$$R = \{\langle 1, 1 \rangle, \langle 1, 4 \rangle, \langle 4, 1 \rangle, \langle 4, 4 \rangle, \langle 2, 2 \rangle, \langle 2, 3 \rangle, \langle 3, 2 \rangle, \langle 3, 3 \rangle\}$$

Write the matrix of R and sketch its graph.

SOLUTION   The matrix and the graph of R are given in Fig. 2-3.12. It is clear that R is an equivalence relation.   ////

EXAMPLE 2   Let $X = \{1, 2, \ldots, 7\}$ and

$$R = \{\langle x, y \rangle \mid x - y \text{ is divisible by } 3\}$$

Show that R is an equivalence relation. Draw the graph of R.

SOLUTION   See Fig. 2-3.13. One can see from the figure that R is an equivalence relation. It is possible to prove this statement without using the graph of the relation in the following manner:

1   For any $a \in X$, $a - a$ is divisible by 3; hence $a \, R \, a$, or R is reflexive.

2   For any $a, b \in X$, if $a - b$ is divisible by 3, then $b - a$ is also divisible by 3; that is, $a \, R \, b \Rightarrow b \, R \, a$. Thus R is symmetric.

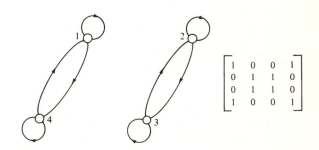

$$\begin{bmatrix} 1 & 0 & 0 & 1 \\ 0 & 1 & 1 & 0 \\ 0 & 1 & 1 & 0 \\ 1 & 0 & 0 & 1 \end{bmatrix}$$

FIGURE 2-3.12   An equivalence relation

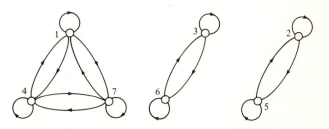

FIGURE 2-3.13

3   For $a, b, c \in X$, if $a \, R \, b$ and $b \, R \, c$, then both $a - b$ and $b - c$ are divisible by 3, so that $a - c = (a - b) + (b - c)$ is also divisible by 3, and hence $a \, R \, c$. Thus R is transitive.   ////

Example 2 is a special case of a more general relation of equality in the modular number system. Let I denote the set of all positive integers, and let m be a positive integer. For $x \in I$ and $y \in I$, define R as

$$R = \{\langle x, y \rangle \mid x - y \text{ is divisible by } m\}$$

Note that "$x - y$ is divisible by m" is equivalent to the statement that both x and y have the same remainder when each is divided by m. It is customary to denote R by $\equiv$ and to write $x \, R \, y$ as $x \equiv y \ (m)$ or $x \equiv y \pmod{m}$, which is read as "x equals y modulo m." The relation $\equiv$ is also called a *congruence relation*. We define congruence relations in Sec. 3-1.2.

Definition 2-3.10   Let R be an equivalence relation on a set X. For any $x \in X$, the set $[x]_R \subseteq X$ given by

$$[x]_R = \{y \mid y \in X \wedge x \, R \, y\}$$

is called an *R-equivalence class* generated by $x \in X$.

Accordingly, the set $[x]_R$ consists of all the R-relatives of x in the set X. Sometimes $[x]_R$ is also written as x/R. We shall now study some properties of the equivalence classes generated by the elements of X.

1   For any element $x \in X$, we have $x \, R \, x$ because R is reflexive; therefore $x \in [x]_R$.

2   Let $y \in X$ be any other element such that $x \, R \, y$, so that $y \in [x]_R$. Because of the symmetry of R, $y \, R \, x$ and $x \in [y]_R$. Now, if there is an element $z \in [y]_R$, then z must be in $[x]_R$ because $y \, R \, z$, along with $x \, R \, y$, implies $x \, R \, z$. Thus $[y]_R \subseteq [x]_R$. By symmetry we must also have $[x]_R \subseteq [y]_R$. Finally, from $[y]_R \subseteq [x]_R$ and $[x]_R \subseteq [y]_R$, we have $[x]_R = [y]_R$.

3   In step 2 it is shown that if $x \, R \, y$, then $[x]_R = [y]_R$. We now show that if $x \not{R} y$, then $[x]_R$ and $[y]_R$ must be disjoint. This demonstration can be done by assuming that there is at least one element $z \in [x]_R$ and also $z \in [y]_R$; that is, $x \, R \, z$ and $y \, R \, z$, but this would imply $z \, R \, y$, and then from transitivity, $x \, R \, y$, which is a contradiction.

The above result shows that the R-equivalence class generated by any element $y \in X$ is equal to the R-equivalence class generated by $x \in X$ provided that $y \in [x]_R$. Otherwise the R-equivalence classes generated by x and y are disjoint. Further, each element of X generates an R-equivalence class which is nonempty. Therefore the R-equivalence classes generated by the elements of X cover X, that is, their union is the set X. Since the R-equivalence classes generated by any two elements are either equal or disjoint, we can say that the family of R-equivalence classes generated by the elements of X defines a partition of X. Such a partition is unique because an R-equivalence class of any element of X is unique. We now formulate this idea as a theorem.

Theorem 2-3.1 Every equivalence relation on a set generates a unique partition of the set. The blocks of this partition correspond to the R-equivalence classes.

As we have denoted the R-equivalence class generated by an element $x \in X$ by $[x]_R$, or x/R, we shall denote the family of equivalence classes by X/R, which is also written as X modulo R, or in short as X mod R. X/R is called the *quotient set* of X by R. Note that the elements of X/R are the equivalence classes which are themselves sets. They are, in fact, subsets of X or elements of the power set $\rho(X)$.

We consider now two special equivalence relations on a set X. The first such relation is $R_1 = X \times X$, and every element of X is in R_1-relation to all the elements of X. In this case the quotient set of X by R_1 is the set $\{X\}$. The other relation R_2 is such that every element of X is related to itself and to no other element. Such a relation is called an *identity relation*. An identity relation is an equivalence relation, and the quotient set of X by R_2 consists of sets which each contain a single element. Thus R_2 generates the largest partition of X.

EXAMPLE 3   Let $\mathbf{Z}$ be the set of integers and let R be the relation called "congruence modulo 3" defined by

$$R = \{\langle x, y \rangle \mid x \in \mathbf{Z} \wedge y \in \mathbf{Z} \wedge (x - y) \text{ is divisible by } 3\}$$

Determine the equivalence classes generated by the elements of $\mathbf{Z}$.

SOLUTION   The equivalence classes are

$$[0]_R = \{\ldots, -6, -3, 0, 3, 6, \ldots\}$$
$$[1]_R = \{\ldots, -5, -2, 1, 4, 7, \ldots\}$$
$$[2]_R = \{\ldots, -4, -1, 2, 5, 8 \ldots\}$$
$$\mathbf{Z}/R = \{[0]_R, [1]_R, [2]_R\} \qquad ////$$

In a similar manner one can find the equivalence classes generated by a relation "congruence modulo m" for any integer m.

EXAMPLE 4   Let S be the set of all statement functions in n variables and let R be the relation given by

$$R = \{\langle x \ y \rangle \mid x \in S \wedge y \in S \wedge x \Leftrightarrow y\}$$

Discuss the equivalence classes generated by the elements of S.

SOLUTION   The number of possible distinct truth tables for statement functions which depend upon n statement variables is 2^{2^n} (see Sec. 1-2.12). Thus there are 2^{2^n} R-equivalence classes generated by the elements of S. $\qquad ////$

So far we have considered the partition of a set generated by an equivalence relation. Now we shall show that the converse of Theorem 2-3.1 also holds, i.e., if we start with a definite partition, say C, of a given set X, then we can define an equivalence relation which corresponds to this partition. For any $x \in X$, there is a set $C_1 \in C$ such that $x \in C_1$; also x does not belong to any other element of C. We now take all the elements of $C_1 \times C_1$ as members of a relation R. Thus every element of X that is in C_1 is an R-relative of every other member of C_1. Furthermore, no other member of X which is not in C_1 is related to the elements of C_1. Similarly, for every other member of the partition C, we form members of the relation R. If $C = \{C_1, C_2, C_3, \ldots, C_m\}$, then $R = (C_1 \times C_1) \cup (C_2 \times C_2) \cup \cdots \cup (C_m \times C_m)$. It is easy to see that R is an equivalence relation. Thus for every partition C we can define an equivalence relation.

EXAMPLE 5 Let $X = \{a, b, c, d, e\}$ and let $C = \{\{a, b\}, \{c\}, \{d, e\}\}$. Show that the partition C defines an equivalence relation on X.

SOLUTION

$$R = \{\langle a, a \rangle, \langle b, b \rangle, \langle a, b \rangle, \langle b, a \rangle, \langle c, c \rangle, \langle d, d \rangle, \langle e, e \rangle, \langle d, e \rangle, \langle e, d \rangle\} \qquad ////$$

It has been shown that an equivalence relation on a set generates a partition of the set, and conversely. It may happen that two relations, which may have been defined in different ways, generate the same partition. Since a relation is a set, any two relations consisting of equal sets are indistinguishable for our purpose. This statement will be true of every partition of the set as well. The following serves as an illustration.

Let $X = \{1, 2, \ldots, 9\}$ and $R_1 = \{\langle x, y \rangle \mid x \in X \wedge y \in X \wedge (x - y)$ is divisible by 3$\}$. Further, let

$R_2 = \{\langle x, y \rangle \mid x \in X \wedge y \in X$ and x, y are in same column of matrix A$\}$

where

$$A = \begin{bmatrix} 1 & 2 & 3 \\ 4 & 5 & 6 \\ 7 & 8 & 9 \end{bmatrix}$$

Although R_1 and R_2 have been defined differently, $R_1 = R_2$.

In Sec. 2-3.3 we have already given algorithms to determine whether a given relation R on a set is an equivalence relation. Once it is determined, our next task is to obtain the equivalence classes. Before giving an algorithm for this purpose, let us discuss the technique that will be used for the representation of the equivalence classes in the algorithm.

Given a set $\{1, 2, \ldots, n\}$ and an equivalence relation R on it, the equivalence classes can be represented by means of two vectors, each having n elements. These vectors are called $FIRST$ and $MEMBER$. The ith component of $FIRST$ for $1 \leq i \leq n$ contains the number which is the first element in the equivalence class to which i belongs. The ith component of $MEMBER$ contains the number which follows i in the equivalence class, unless i is the last element, in which case $MEMBER[i]$ is equal to zero.

As an example, let the set be $\{1, 2, 3, 4, 5, 6\}$ and the equivalence classes be $\{1, 3, 6\}$, $\{2\}$, and $\{4, 5\}$. The vectors $FIRST$ and $MEMBER$ representing these equivalence classes are shown in Fig. 2-3.14.

	FIRST			MEMBER
	1	1		3
	2	2		0
	1	3		6
	4	4		5
	4	5		0
	1	6		0

FIGURE 2-3.14   Vector representation of equivalence classes.

Note that the vector structure employed here is useful in several ways. For example, if we wish to know whether 1 and 3 are in the same class, then the answer is yes because $FIRST[1]$ is equal to $FIRST[3]$. Also, to obtain the number of equivalence classes, we simply count the zero elements in $MEMBER$.

The following algorithm will set up vectors $FIRST$ and $MEMBER$.

Algorithm $CLASS$ Given a relation matrix R representing an equivalence relation in a set of integers $\{1, 2, \ldots, n\}$, it is required to set up the $FIRST$ and $MEMBER$ vectors as described. All elements of vector $FIRST$ are initially zero. The vector $OUTPUT$ will be used to print the members of an equivalence class.

1 [Initialize row counter.] Set $i \leftarrow 0$ (i is an index to the rows of R and the vector $FIRST$).

2 [Scan next row.] Set $i \leftarrow i + 1$. If $i > n$ then Exit.

3 [Is i in a previous class?] If $FIRST[i] \neq 0$ then go to step 2; otherwise set $k \leftarrow i$ and $m \leftarrow 0$ (k is the previous element found which belongs to an equivalence class, and m is the index to the $OUTPUT$ vector).

4 [Scan row starting at diagonal.] Repeat steps 5 and 6 for $j = i$, $i + 1, \ldots, n$.

5 [All members found?] If $j > n$ then $MEMBER[k] \leftarrow 0$, print class members from $OUTPUT$, and go to step 2.

6 [Is i related to j?] If $R[i, j] = T$ then $MEMBER[k] \leftarrow j$, $FIRST[j] \leftarrow i$, $k \leftarrow j$, $m \leftarrow m + 1$, and $OUTPUT[m] \leftarrow j$.

In this algorithm, the vector $FIRST$ is scanned for zero elements. When one is found, the corresponding ith row of the relation matrix is scanned, starting with the ith column, for entries with truth value T. For each such entry in the jth column, $FIRST[j]$ is set to i, j is put in the $OUTPUT$ vector, and $MEMBER[k]$ is set to j. Here k indicates the column subscript of the preceding true entry. In the case when $j = i$, k also equal to i, and therefore a discrepancy arises. That is, $MEMBER[k] \leftarrow j$ means $MEMBER[i] \leftarrow i$, but this problem is resolved when the next j is found since k remains equal to i in the assignment $k \leftarrow j$. When all columns have been scanned, the members of an equivalence class are obtained as output, and $MEMBER[k]$ is set to zero, indicating k is the last element in the equivalence class.   ////

```
      SUBROUTINE CLASS(A,N,FIRST,MEMBER)
C  THIS SUBROUTINE RECEIVES A RELATION MATRIX A WHICH REPRESENTS AN
C  EQUIVALENCE RELATION.  THE ARRAYS FIRST AND MEMBER ARE SET UP TO
C  REPRESENT THE EQUIVALENCE CLASSES.  ARRAY FIRST INITIALLY CONTAINS
C  ZEROS.  THE EQUIVALENCE CLASSES ARE PRINTED WITH THE AID OF ARRAY
C  OUTPUT.
C
      LOGICAL*1 A(N,N)
      INTEGER*2 FIRST(N),MEMBER(N),OUTPUT(10)
C
C  PRINT HEADING.
      WRITE(6,98)
   98 FORMAT('-',20X,'EQUIVALENCE CLASSES')
C
C  I IS THE ROW COUNTER.
      DO 20 I = 1,N
C
C  IF I IS ALREADY IN AN EQUIVALENCE CLASS, SKIP THE ITH ROW.
      IF(FIRST(I) .NE. 0) GO TO 20
C
C  K IS THE LAST NUMBER FOUND IN THE EQUIVALENCE CLASS.
C  J IS THE COLUMN COUNTER.
C  M COUNTS THE ELEMENTS OF THE EQUIVALENCE CLASS.
      K = I
      M = 0
      DO 10 J = I,N
C
C  FIND A J WHICH IS RELATED TO I.
      IF(.NOT.A(I,J)) GO TO 10
C
C  I IS THE FIRST NUMBER IN THE EQUIVALENCE CLASS TO WHICH J BELONGS.
C  J IS THE NEXT MEMBER OF THE CLASS TO WHICH K BELONGS.
      FIRST(J) = I
      MEMBER(K) = J
      K = J
      M = M + 1
      OUTPUT(M) = J
   10 CONTINUE
C
C  AT THIS POINT, ALL MEMBERS OF AN EQUIVALENCE CLASS HAVE BEEN FOUND.
C  PRINT THESE MEMBERS.
      MEMBER(K) = 0
      WRITE(6,99)(OUTPUT(L),L = 1,M)
   99 FORMAT('0',20X,10(I4))
   20 CONTINUE
      RETURN
      END
```

FIGURE 2-3.15   FORTRAN subroutine for algorithm *CLASS*.

A FORTRAN subroutine for *CLASS* is given in Fig. 2-3.15.

We now give a mainline program in Fig. 2-3.16a which first reads each ordered pair of a relation from one data card. The end of the data is signaled by the first element of an ordered pair having a value zero. The remainder of the mainline program uses the subprograms REFSYM, TRANS, and CLASS given here and in Sec. 2-3.3.

Given a relation R on the set $\{1, 2, \ldots, 10\}$ defined by

$$1\,R\,1, 2\,R\,2, 3\,R\,3, 4\,R\,4, 5\,R\,5, 6\,R\,6, 7\,R\,7, 8\,R\,8, 9\,R\,9, 10\,R\,10,$$

$$1\,R\,2, 1\,R\,8, 2\,R\,1, 2\,R\,8, 4\,R\,6, 6\,R\,4, 6\,R\,7, 7\,R\,6, 7\,R\,4, 4\,R\,7,$$

$$8\,R\,1, 8\,R\,2$$

the output obtained is shown in Fig. 2-3.16b.

2-3.6   Compatibility Relations

Definition 2-3.11   A relation R in X is said to be a *compatibility relation* if it is reflexive and symmetric.

Obviously all equivalence relations are compatibility relations. We shall, however, be concerned with those compatibility relations which are not equivalence relations. The following is an example of a compatibility relation.

Let $X = \{$ball, bed, dog, let, egg$\}$, and let the relation R be given by

$$R = \{\langle x, y \rangle \mid x, y \in X \wedge x\,R\,y \text{ if } x \text{ and } y \text{ contain some common letter}\}$$

```
C     MAINLINE
C     THIS PROGRAM READS ORDERED PAIRS OF NUMBERS AND PUTS THEM INTO A
C     RELATION MATRIX REPRESENTED BY THE LOGICAL ARRAY,A.  IT IS THEN
C     DETERMINED IF THE RELATION REPRESENTED BY A IS AN EQUIVALENCE
C     RELATION USING SUBROUTINES REFSYM AND TRANS WHICH TEST FOR THE
C     REFLEXIVE, SYMMETRIC, AND TRANSITIVE PROPERTIES.  IF IT IS AN
C     EQUIVALENCE RELATION, THE EQUIVALENCE CLASSES ARE PRINTED AND PUT
C     INTO A STRUCTURE CONSISTING OF ARRAYS FIRST AND MEMBER.
C     THE RELATION IS ON THE SET OF INTEGERS BETWEEN 1 AND 10 SO ALL ARRAY
C     DIMENSIONS WILL BE 10.
C
      LOGICAL*1 A(10,10)/100*.FALSE./,FLAG/.FALSE./
      INTEGER*2 FIRST(10)/10*0/,MEMBER(10)
C
C     READ THE ORDERED PAIRS AND REPRESENT THEM IN THE MATRIX.
   10 READ(5,98,END=20)I,J
   98 FORMAT(2I2)
      A(I,J) = .TRUE.
      GO TO 10
   20 N = 10
C
C     PRINT RELATION MATRIX.
      WRITE(6,97)(K,K = 1,N),(I,(A(I,J),J = 1,N),I = 1,N)
   97 FORMAT('-',31X,'RELATION MATRIX',/,'0',17X,10(I4),10(/,'0',15X,I2,
     1 10(L4)))
C
C     REFLEXIVE AND SYMMETRIC TEST.
      CALL REFSYM(A,N,FLAG)
C     IF FLAG IS STILL FALSE PRINT MESSAGE AND TERMINATE, OTHERWISE
C     TEST TRANSITIVITY.
      IF(.NOT.FLAG) GO TO 30
      FLAG = .FALSE.
      CALL TRANS(A,N,FLAG)
C
C     IF FLAG IS STILL FALSE TERMINATE.
      IF(.NOT.FLAG) GO TO 30
      WRITE(6,96)
   96 FORMAT('-',20X,'THE RELATION IS AN EQUIVALENCE RELATION.')
C
C     FIND THE EQUIVALENCE CLASSES.
      CALL CLASS(A,N,FIRST,MEMBER)
      WRITE(6,95)(FIRST(I),I = 1,10)
      WRITE(6,94)(MEMBER(I),I = 1,10)
   95 FORMAT('0',20X,'FIRST    ',10(I4))
   94 FORMAT('0',20X,'MEMBER   ',10(I4))
      STOP
C
C     THE RELATION IS NOT AN EQUIVALENCE RELATION.
   30 WRITE(6,93)
   93 FORMAT('-',20X,'THE RELATION IS NOT AN EQUIVALENCE RELATION.')
      STOP
      END
```

FIGURE 2-3.16a   Main program and output for equivalence class program.

RELATION MATRIX

	1	2	3	4	5	6	7	8	9	10
1	T	T	F	F	F	F	F	T	F	F
2	T	T	F	F	F	F	F	T	F	F
3	F	F	T	F	F	F	F	F	F	F
4	F	F	F	T	F	T	T	F	F	F
5	F	F	F	F	T	F	F	F	F	F
6	F	F	F	T	F	T	T	F	F	F
7	F	F	F	T	F	T	T	F	F	F
8	T	T	F	F	F	F	F	T	F	F
9	F	F	F	F	F	F	F	F	T	F
10	F	F	F	F	F	F	F	F	F	T

THE RELATION IS AN EQUIVALENCE RELATION.

EQUIVALENCE CLASSES

1	2	8
3		
4	6	7
5		
9		
10		

FIRST	1	1	3	4	5	4	4	1	9	10
MEMBER	2	8	0	6	0	7	0	0	0	0

FIGURE 2-3.16b.

Then R is a compatibility relation, and x, y are called compatible if $x\,R\,y$. A compatibility relation is sometimes denoted by $\approx$. Note that ball $\approx$ bed, bed $\approx$ egg, but ball $\not\approx$ egg. Thus $\approx$ is not transitive. Denoting "ball" by x_1, "bed" by x_2, "dog" by x_3, "let" by x_4, and "egg" by x_5, the graph of $\approx$ is given in Fig. 2-3.17a.

Since $\approx$ is a compatibility relation, it is not necessary to draw the loops at each element nor is it necessary to draw both $x\,R\,y$ and $y\,R\,x$. Thus we can simplify the graph of $\approx$, as shown in Fig. 2-3.17b. Note that the elements in each of the sets $\{x_1, x_2, x_4\}$ and $\{x_2, x_3, x_5\}$ are related to each other, i.e., the elements are mutually compatible. Further, these two sets define a covering of X. The set $\{x_2, x_4, x_5\}$ also has elements compatible to each other.

The relation matrix of a compatibility relation is symmetric and has its diagonal elements unity. It is, therefore, sufficient to give only the elements of the lower triangular part of the relation matrix in such a case. For the compatibility relation we have been discussing, the relation matrix can be obtained from Table 2-3.2.

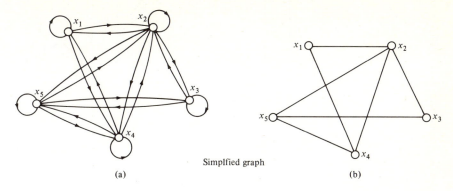

Simplified graph

(a)   (b)

FIGURE 2-3.17   Graphs of compatibility relation $\approx$.

Although an equivalence relation on a set defines a partition of the set into equivalence classes, a compatibility relation does not necessarily define a partition. However, a compatibility relation does define a covering of the set.

Definition 2-3.12   Let X be a set and $\approx$ a compatibility relation on X. A subset $A \subseteq X$ is called a *maximal compatibility block* if any element of A is compatible to every other element of A and no element of $X - A$ is compatible to all the elements of A.

It is clear from Fig. 2-3.17b that the subset $\{x_1, x_2, x_4\}$ is a maximal compatibility block; so, too, are the subsets $\{x_2, x_3, x_5\}$ and $\{x_2, x_4, x_5\}$. These sets are not mutually disjoint, and therefore they only define a covering of X.

To find the maximal compatibility blocks corresponding to a compatibility relation on a set X, first we draw a simplified graph of the compatibility relation and pick from this graph the largest complete polygons. By a "largest complete polygon" we mean a polygon in which any vertex is connected to every other vertex. For example, a triangle is always a complete polygon, but for a quadrilateral to be a complete polygon we must have the two diagonals present. In addition to these examples, any element of the set which is related only to itself forms a maximal compatibility block. Similarly, any two elements which are compatible to one another but to no other elements also form a maximal compatibility block. We now give some graphs of compatibility relations, the corresponding relation matrices, and the maximal compatibility blocks.

The maximal compatibility blocks of the relations shown in Figs. 2-3.18

Table 2-3.2

x_2	1			
x_3	0	1		
x_4	1	1	0	
x_5	0	1	1	1
	x_1	x_2	x_3	x_4

2	0			
3	1	1		
4	1	0	1	
5	0	1	0	1
	1	2	3	4

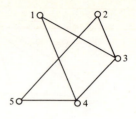

FIGURE 2-3.18

2	1				
3	1	1			
4	1	1	1		
5	0	1	0	0	
6	0	0	1	0	1
	1	2	3	4	5

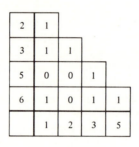
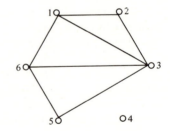

FIGURE 2-3.19

2	1			
3	1	1		
5	0	0	1	
6	1	0	1	1
	1	2	3	5

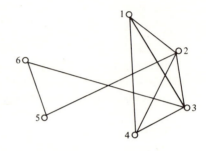

FIGURE 2-3.20

to 2-3.20 are given by

$$\{1, 3, 4\} \qquad \{2, 3\} \qquad \{4, 5\} \qquad \{2, 5\}$$
$$\{1, 2, 3, 4\} \qquad \{2, 5\} \qquad \{3, 6\} \qquad \{5, 6\}$$

and

$$\{1, 2, 3\} \qquad \{1, 3, 6\} \qquad \{3, 5, 6\} \qquad \{4\}$$

respectively. For the compatibility relation of the example discussed earlier and given in Fig. 2-3.17, the maximal compatibility blocks are $\{x_1, x_2, x_4\}$, $\{x_2, x_3, x_5\}$, and $\{x_2, x_4, x_5\}$.

Another procedure for finding the maximal compatibility blocks from the table of the relation matrix can be described in the following manner. It is assumed that first a simplified table is obtained in which those elements which are only compatible to themselves are deleted, because they are in a maximal compatibility block by themselves and are in no other compatibility block. Such blocks are included in the list at the end (see Fig. 2-3.20).

1 Start in the rightmost column of the table and proceed to the left until a column containing at least one nonzero entry is encountered. List all the compatible pairs represented by the entries in that column.

2 Proceed left to the next column that contains at least one nonzero entry. If any element is compatible to all the members of some previously defined compatibility class, then add this element to that class. If a member is compatible to only some members of a previously defined class, then form a new class which includes all the members that are compatible. Next, list all the compatible pairs not included in any previously defined class.

3 Repeat step 2 until all the columns are considered.

The final sets of compatibility classes including those which are isolated elements constitute the maximal compatibility classes.

Compatibility relations are useful in solving certain minimization problems of switching theory, particularly for incompletely specified minimization problems.

EXERCISES 2-3.6

1 Let R denote a relation on the set of ordered pairs of positive integers such that $\langle x, y \rangle R \langle u, v \rangle$ iff $xv = yu$. Show that R is an equivalence relation.

2 Given a set $S = \{1, 2, 3, 4, 5\}$, find the equivalence relation on S which generates the partition $\{\overline{1, 2}, \overline{3}, \overline{4, 5}\}$. Draw the graph of the relation.

3 Prove that the relation "congruence modulo m" given by

$$\equiv \, = \{\langle x, y \rangle \mid x - y \text{ is divisible by } m\}$$

over the set of positive integers is an equivalence relation. Show also that if $x_1 \equiv y_1$ and $x_2 \equiv y_2$, then $(x_1 + x_2) \equiv (y_1 + y_2)$.

4 Given a covering of the set $S = \{A_1, A_2, \ldots, A_n\}$, show how we can write a compatibility relation which defines this covering.

5 Let the compatibility relation on a set $\{x_1, x_2, \ldots, x_6\}$ be given by the matrix

x_2	1				
x_3	1	1			
x_4	0	0	1		
x_5	0	0	1	1	
x_6	1	0	1	0	1
	x_1	x_2	x_3	x_4	x_5

Draw the graph and find the maximal compatibility blocks of the relation.

2-3.7   Composition of Binary Relations

Since a binary relation is a set of ordered pairs, the usual operations such as union, intersection, etc., on these sets produce other relations. This topic was discussed in Sec. 2-3.1. We shall now consider another operation on relations—relations which are formed in two or more stages. Familiar examples of such relations are the relation of being a nephew or a brother's or sister's son, the relation of an uncle or a father's or mother's brother, and the relation of being a grandfather which is a father's or mother's father. These relations can be produced in the following manner.

> **Definition 2-3.13**   Let R be a relation from X to Y and S be a relation from Y to Z. Then a relation written as $R \circ S$ is called a *composite relation* of R and S where
>
> $$R \circ S = \{ \langle x, z \rangle \mid x \in X \land z \in Z \land (\exists y)(y \in Y \land \langle x, y \rangle \in R \land \langle y, z \rangle \in S \}$$
>
> The operation of obtaining $R \circ S$ from R and S is called *composition* of relations.

Note that $R \circ S$ is empty if the intersection of the range of R and the domain of S is empty. $R \circ S$ is nonempty if there is at least one ordered pair $\langle x, y \rangle \in R$ such that the second member $y \in Y$ of the ordered pair is a first member in an ordered pair in S. For the relation $R \circ S$, the domain is a subset of X and the range is a subset of Z. In fact, the domain is a subset of the domain of R, and its range is a subset of the range of S. From the graphs of R and S one can easily construct the graph of $R \circ S$. As an example, see Fig. 2-3.21.

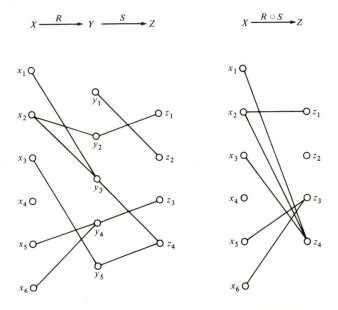

FIGURE 2-3.21   Relations R, S, and $R \circ S$.

The operation of composition is a binary operation on relations, and it produces a relation from two relations. The same operations can be applied again to produce other relations. For example, let R be a relation from X to Y, S a relation from Y to Z, and P a relation from Z to W. Then $R \circ S$ is a relation from X to Z. We can form $(R \circ S) \circ P$, which is a relation from X to W. Similarly, we can also form $R \circ (S \circ P)$, which again is a relation from X to W.

Let us assume that $(R \circ S) \circ P$ is nonempty, and let $\langle x, y \rangle \in R$, $\langle y, z \rangle \in S$, and $\langle z, w \rangle \in P$. This assumption means $\langle x, z \rangle \in R \circ S$ and $\langle x, w \rangle \in (R \circ S) \circ P$. Of course, $\langle y, w \rangle \in S \circ P$ and $\langle x, w \rangle \in R \circ (S \circ P)$, which shows that

$$(R \circ S) \circ P = R \circ (S \circ P)$$

This result can be stated by saying that the operation of composition on relations is associative. We may delete the parentheses in writing $(R \circ S) \circ P$, so that

$$(R \circ S) \circ P = R \circ (S \circ P) = R \circ S \circ P$$

The same result follows from the partial graph given in Fig. 2-3.22.

EXAMPLE 1 Let $R = \{\langle 1, 2 \rangle, \langle 3, 4 \rangle, \langle 2, 2 \rangle\}$ and $S = \{\langle 4, 2 \rangle, \langle 2, 5 \rangle, \langle 3, 1 \rangle, \langle 1, 3 \rangle\}$. Find $R \circ S$, $S \circ R$, $R \circ (S \circ R)$, $(R \circ S) \circ R$, $R \circ R$, $S \circ S$, and $R \circ R \circ R$.

SOLUTION

$$R \circ S = \{\langle 1, 5 \rangle, \langle 3, 2 \rangle, \langle 2, 5 \rangle\}$$
$$S \circ R = \{\langle 4, 2 \rangle, \langle 3, 2 \rangle, \langle 1, 4 \rangle\} \neq R \circ S$$
$$(R \circ S) \circ R = \{\langle 3, 2 \rangle\}$$
$$R \circ (S \circ R) = \{\langle 3, 2 \rangle\} = (R \circ S) \circ R$$
$$R \circ R = \{\langle 1, 2 \rangle, \langle 2, 2 \rangle\}$$
$$S \circ S = \{\langle 4, 5 \rangle, \langle 3, 3 \rangle, \langle 1, 1 \rangle\}$$
$$R \circ R \circ R = \{\langle 1, 2 \rangle, \langle 2, 2 \rangle\} \qquad ////$$

EXAMPLE 2 Let R and S be two relations on a set of positive integers $\mathbf{I}$:

$$R = \{\langle x, 2x \rangle \mid x \in \mathbf{I}\} \qquad S = \{\langle x, 7x \rangle \mid x \in \mathbf{I}\}$$

Find $R \circ S$, $R \circ R$, $R \circ R \circ R$, and $R \circ S \circ R$.

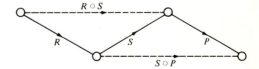

FIGURE 2-3.22 Associativity of composition.

SOLUTION

$$R \circ S = \{\langle x, 14x \rangle \mid x \in \mathbf{I}\} = S \circ R$$

$$R \circ R = \{\langle x, 4x \rangle \mid x \in \mathbf{I}\}$$

$$R \circ R \circ R = \{\langle x, 8x \rangle \mid x \in \mathbf{I}\}$$

$$R \circ S \circ R = \{\langle x, 28x \rangle \mid x \in \mathbf{I}\} \qquad ////$$

We know that the relation matrix of a relation R from a set $X = \{x_1, x_2, \ldots, x_m\}$ to a set $Y = \{y_1, y_2, \ldots, y_n\}$ is given by a matrix having m rows and n columns. We shall denote the relation matrix of R by M_R. M_R has entries which are 1s and 0s. Similarly the relation matrix M_S of a relation S from the set Y to a set $Z = \{z_1, z_2, \ldots, z_p\}$ is an $n \times p$ matrix. The relation matrix of $R \circ S$ can be obtained from the matrices M_R and M_S in the following manner.

From the definition it is clear that $\langle x_i, z_k \rangle \in R \circ S$ if there is at least one element of Y, say y_j, such that $\langle x_i, y_j \rangle \in R$ and $\langle y_j, z_k \rangle \in S$. There may be more than one element of Y which has properties similar to those of y_j; for example, $\langle x_i, y_r \rangle \in R$ and $\langle y_r, z_k \rangle \in S$. In all such cases, $\langle x_i, z_k \rangle \in R \circ S$. Thus when we scan the ith row of M_R and kth column of M_S and we come across at least one j, such that the entries in the jth location of the row as well as the column under consideration are 1s, then the entry in the ith row and kth column of $M_{R \circ S}$ is also 1; otherwise it is 0. Scanning a row of M_R along with every column of M_S gives one row of $M_{R \circ S}$. Similarly, we can obtain all the other rows.

EXAMPLE 3 For the relations R and S given in Example 1 over the set $\{1, 2, \ldots, 5\}$, obtain the relation matrices for $R \circ S$ and $S \circ R$.

SOLUTION

$$
\begin{bmatrix}
0 & 1 & 0 & 0 & 0 \\
0 & 1 & 0 & 0 & 0 \\
0 & 0 & 0 & 1 & 0 \\
0 & 0 & 0 & 0 & 0 \\
0 & 0 & 0 & 0 & 0
\end{bmatrix}
\circ
\begin{bmatrix}
0 & 0 & 1 & 0 & 0 \\
0 & 0 & 0 & 0 & 1 \\
1 & 0 & 0 & 0 & 0 \\
0 & 1 & 0 & 0 & 0 \\
0 & 0 & 0 & 0 & 0
\end{bmatrix}
=
\begin{bmatrix}
0 & 0 & 0 & 0 & 1 \\
0 & 0 & 0 & 0 & 1 \\
0 & 1 & 0 & 0 & 0 \\
0 & 0 & 0 & 0 & 0 \\
0 & 0 & 0 & 0 & 0
\end{bmatrix}
$$

$$\qquad M_R \qquad\qquad M_S \qquad\qquad M_{R \circ S}$$

$$
\begin{bmatrix}
0 & 0 & 1 & 0 & 0 \\
0 & 0 & 0 & 0 & 1 \\
1 & 0 & 0 & 0 & 0 \\
0 & 1 & 0 & 0 & 0 \\
0 & 0 & 0 & 0 & 0
\end{bmatrix}
\circ
\begin{bmatrix}
0 & 1 & 0 & 0 & 0 \\
0 & 1 & 0 & 0 & 0 \\
0 & 0 & 0 & 1 & 0 \\
0 & 0 & 0 & 0 & 0 \\
0 & 0 & 0 & 0 & 0
\end{bmatrix}
=
\begin{bmatrix}
0 & 0 & 0 & 1 & 0 \\
0 & 0 & 0 & 0 & 0 \\
0 & 1 & 0 & 0 & 0 \\
0 & 1 & 0 & 0 & 0 \\
0 & 0 & 0 & 0 & 0
\end{bmatrix}
$$

$$\qquad M_S \qquad\qquad M_R \qquad\qquad M_{S \circ R}$$

In general, let the relations A and B be represented by $n \times m$ and $m \times r$ matrices respectively. Then the composition $A \circ B$ which we denote by the relation matrix C is expressed as

$$c_{ij} = \bigvee_{k=1}^{m} a_{ik} \wedge b_{kj} \qquad i = 1, 2, \ldots, n; j = 1, 2, \ldots, r$$

where $a_{ik} \wedge b_{kj}$ and $\bigvee_{k=1}^{m}$ indicate bit-ANDing and bit-ORing respectively

(see Sec. 2-2.5).

Definition 2-3.14 Given a relation R from X to Y, a relation $\tilde{R}$ from Y to X is called the *converse* of R, where the ordered pairs of $\tilde{R}$ are obtained by interchanging the members in each of the ordered pairs of R. This means, for $x \in X$ and $y \in Y$, that $x\,R\,y \Leftrightarrow y\,\tilde{R}\,x$.

From the definition of $\tilde{R}$ it follows that $\tilde{\tilde{R}} = R$. The relation matrix $M_{\tilde{R}}$ of $\tilde{R}$ can be obtained by simply interchanging the rows and columns of M_R. Such a matrix is called the *transpose* of M_R. Therefore

$$M_{\tilde{R}} = \text{transpose of } M_R$$

The graph of $\tilde{R}$ is also obtained from that of R by simply reversing the arrows on each arc.

We shall now consider the converse of a composite relation. For this purpose, let R be a relation from X to Y and S be a relation from Y to Z. Obviously, $\tilde{R}$ is a relation from Y to X, $\tilde{S}$ from Z to Y; $R \circ S$ is a relation from X to Z, and $R \overset{\sim}{} S$ is a relation from Z to X. Also the relation $\tilde{S} \circ \tilde{R}$ is from Z to X. We now show that

$$R \overset{\sim}{} S = \tilde{S} \circ \tilde{R}$$

If $x\,R\,y$ and $y\,S\,z$, then $x\,(R \circ S)\,z$ and $z\,(R \overset{\sim}{} S)\,x$. But $z\,\tilde{S}\,y$ and $y\,\tilde{R}\,x$, so that $z\,(\tilde{S} \circ \tilde{R})\,x$. This is true for any $x \in X$ and $z \in Z$; hence the required result.

The same rule can be expressed in terms of the relation matrices by saying that the transpose of $M_{R \circ S}$ is the same as the matrix $M_{\tilde{S} \circ \tilde{R}}$. The matrix $M_{\tilde{S} \circ \tilde{R}}$ can be obtained from the matrices $M_{\tilde{S}}$ and $M_{\tilde{R}}$, which in turn can be obtained from the matrices M_S and M_R.

EXAMPLE 4 Given the relation matrices M_R and M_S, find $M_{R \circ S}$, $M_{\tilde{R}}$, $M_{\tilde{S}}$, $M_{R \overset{\sim}{} S}$, and show that $M_{R \overset{\sim}{} S} = M_{\tilde{S} \circ \tilde{R}}$.

$$M_R = \begin{bmatrix} 1 & 0 & 1 \\ 1 & 1 & 0 \\ 1 & 1 & 1 \end{bmatrix} \qquad M_S = \begin{bmatrix} 1 & 0 & 0 & 1 & 0 \\ 1 & 0 & 1 & 0 & 1 \\ 0 & 1 & 0 & 1 & 0 \end{bmatrix}$$

SOLUTION

$$M_{\tilde{R}} = \begin{bmatrix} 1 & 1 & 1 \\ 0 & 1 & 1 \\ 1 & 0 & 1 \end{bmatrix} = \text{transpose of } M_R$$

$$M_{\tilde{S}} = \begin{bmatrix} 1 & 1 & 0 \\ 0 & 0 & 1 \\ 0 & 1 & 0 \\ 1 & 0 & 1 \\ 0 & 1 & 0 \end{bmatrix} = \text{transpose of } M_S$$

$$M_{R \circ S} = \begin{bmatrix} 1 & 1 & 0 & 1 & 0 \\ 1 & 0 & 1 & 1 & 1 \\ 1 & 1 & 1 & 1 & 1 \end{bmatrix} \qquad M_{\widetilde{R \circ S}} = \begin{bmatrix} 1 & 1 & 1 \\ 1 & 0 & 1 \\ 0 & 1 & 1 \\ 1 & 1 & 1 \\ 0 & 1 & 1 \end{bmatrix}$$

$$M_{\tilde{S} \circ \tilde{R}} = \begin{bmatrix} 1 & 1 & 1 \\ 1 & 0 & 1 \\ 0 & 1 & 1 \\ 1 & 1 & 1 \\ 0 & 1 & 1 \end{bmatrix} = M_{\widetilde{R \circ S}} \qquad ////$$

The following hold for any relations R and S.

1 $\tilde{\tilde{R}} = R$
2 $R = S \Leftrightarrow \tilde{R} = \tilde{S}$
3 $R \subseteq S \Leftrightarrow \tilde{R} \subseteq \tilde{S}$
4 $R \,\tilde{\cup}\, S = \tilde{R} \cup \tilde{S}$
5 $R \,\tilde{\cap}\, S = \tilde{R} \cap \tilde{S}$

We shall leave the proofs as exercises.

Let us now consider some distinct relations R_1, R_2, R_3, R_4 in a set

$X = \{a, b, c\}$ given by

$$R_1 = \{\langle a, b \rangle, \langle a, c \rangle, \langle c, b \rangle\}$$
$$R_2 = \{\langle a, b \rangle, \langle b, c \rangle, \langle c, a \rangle\}$$
$$R_3 = \{\langle a, b \rangle, \langle b, c \rangle, \langle c, c \rangle\}$$
$$R_4 = \{\langle a, b \rangle, \langle b, a \rangle, \langle c, c \rangle\}$$

Denoting the composition of a relation by itself as

$$R \circ R = R^2 \qquad R \circ R \circ R = R \circ R^2 = R^3 \qquad \cdots \qquad R \circ R^{m-1} = R^m \qquad \cdots$$

let us write the powers of the given relations. Clearly

$$R_1{}^2 = \{\langle a, b \rangle\} \qquad R_1{}^3 = \varnothing \qquad R_1{}^4 = \varnothing \qquad \cdots$$
$$R_2{}^2 = \{\langle a, c \rangle, \langle b, a \rangle, \langle c, b \rangle\} \qquad R_2{}^3 = \{\langle a, a \rangle, \langle b, b \rangle, \langle c, c \rangle\}$$
$$R_2{}^4 = R_2 \qquad R_2{}^5 = R_2{}^2 \qquad R_2{}^6 = R_2{}^3 \qquad \cdots$$
$$R_3{}^2 = \{\langle a, c \rangle, \langle b, c \rangle, \langle c, c \rangle\} = R_3{}^3 = R_3{}^4 = R_3{}^5 \cdots$$
$$R_4{}^2 = \{\langle a, a \rangle, \langle b, b \rangle, \langle c, c \rangle\} \qquad R_4{}^3 = R_4 \qquad R_4{}^5 = R_4{}^2 \qquad \cdots$$

Given a finite set X, containing n elements, and a relation R in X, we can interpret R^m $(m = 1, 2, \ldots)$ in terms of its graph. This interpretation is done for a number of applications in Chap. 5. With the help of such an interpretation or from the examples given here, it is possible to say that there are at most n distinct powers of R, for R^m, $m > n$, can be expressed in terms of $R, R^2, \ldots, R^n$. Our next step is to construct the relation in X given by

$$R^+ = R \cup R^2 \cup R^3 \cup \cdots$$

Naturally, this construction will require only a finite number of powers of R to be calculated, and these calculations can easily be performed by using the matrix representation of the relation R and the Boolean multiplication of these matrices. Let us now see what the corresponding relations $R_1{}^+$, $R_2{}^+$, $R_3{}^+$, and $R_4{}^+$ are

$$R_1{}^+ = R_1 \cup R_1{}^2 \cup R_1{}^3 \cdots = R_1$$
$$R_2{}^+ = R_2 \cup R_2{}^2 \cup R_2{}^3 \cdots = R_2 \cup R_2{}^2 \cup R_2{}^3$$
$$= \{\langle a, b \rangle, \langle b, c \rangle, \langle c, a \rangle, \langle a, c \rangle, \langle b, a \rangle, \langle c, b \rangle, \langle a, a \rangle, \langle b, b \rangle, \langle c, c \rangle\}$$
$$R_3{}^+ = \{\langle a, b \rangle, \langle b, c \rangle, \langle c, c \rangle, \langle a, c \rangle\}$$
$$R_4{}^+ = \{\langle a, b \rangle, \langle b, a \rangle, \langle c, c \rangle, \langle a, a \rangle, \langle b, b \rangle\}$$

Observe that the relations $R_1{}^+, R_2{}^+, \ldots, R_4{}^+$ are all transitive and that $R_1 \subseteq R_1{}^+$, $R_2 \subseteq R_2{}^+, \ldots, R_4 \subseteq R_4{}^+$. From the graphs of these relations one can easily see that $R_i{}^+$ is obtained from R_i $(i = 1, 2, 3, 4)$ by adding only those ordered pairs to R_i such that $R_i{}^+$ is transitive. We now define R^+ in general.

Definition 2-3.15 Let X be any finite set and R be a relation in X. The relation $R^+ = R \cup R^2 \cup R^3 \cup \cdots$ in X is called the *transitive closure* of R in X.

Theorem 2-3.2 The transitive closure R^+ of a relation R in a finite set X is transitive. Also for any other transitive relation P in X such that $R \subseteq P$, we have $R^+ \subseteq P$. In this sense, R^+ is the smallest transitive relation containing R.

PROOF First, to show that R^+ is transitive, let us assume that $a \, R^+ \, b$ and $b \, R^+ \, c$ for some a, b, $c \in X$. Since $a \, R^+ \, b$, we must have a sequence of elements $d_1, d_2, \ldots, d_k \in X$ such that $d_1 = a$, $d_k = b$, and $d_1 \, R \, d_2$, $d_2 \, R \, d_3$, $\ldots$, $d_{k-1} \, R \, d_k$. Here we have assumed that $a \, R^k \, b$ for some k. Similarly, since $b \, R^+ \, c$, we must have a sequence of elements, say $e_1, e_2, \ldots, e_j$, such that $e_1 = b$, $e_j = c$, and $e_1 \, R \, e_2$, $e_2 \, R \, e_3$, $\ldots$, $e_{j-1} \, R \, e_j$. Here we have assumed that $b \, R^j \, c$ for some j. It follows from these assumptions that $a \, R^{k+j} \, c$, implying that $a \, R^+ \, c$. Hence R^+ must be transitive.

Let us now assume that $a \, R^+ \, b$ for some a, $b \in X$, so that there exists a sequence of elements $c_1, c_2, \ldots, c_m \in X$ such that $a = c_1$, $b = c_m$, and $c_i \, R \, c_{i+1}$ for $i = 1, 2, \ldots, m - 1$. If there is a transitive relation P in X such that $R \subseteq P$, then $c_i \, P \, c_{i+1}$ for $i = 1, 2, \ldots, m - 1$, so that $c_1 \, P \, c_m$, that is, $a \, P \, b$. Since $\langle a, b \rangle$ is an arbitrary element of R^+, we see by the same argument that $R^+ \subseteq P$. Hence R^+ is the smallest transitive relation which includes R. ////

Transitive closures of relations have important applications in certain areas such as networks, syntactic analysis, fault detection and diagnosis in switching circuits, etc. A number of these applications are discussed in Chap. 5.

EXERCISES 2-3.7

1 Prove the equivalences and equalities (1) to (5) given at the end of the section (following Example 4).
2 Show that if a relation R is reflexive, then $\tilde{R}$ is also reflexive. Show also that similar remarks hold if R is transitive, irreflexive, symmetric, or antisymmetric.
3 What nonzero entries are there in the relation matrix of $R \cap \tilde{R}$ if R is an antisymmetric relation?
4 Let E be the identity relation on a set X and R be any relation in X; show that $E \cup R \cup \tilde{R}$ is a compatibility relation.
5 Given the relation matrix M_R of a relation R on the set $\{a, b, c\}$, find the relation matrices of $\tilde{R}$, $R^2 = R \circ R$, $R^3 = R \circ R \circ R$, and $R \circ \tilde{R}$.

$$M_R = \begin{bmatrix} 1 & 0 & 1 \\ 1 & 1 & 0 \\ 1 & 1 & 1 \end{bmatrix}$$

6 Two equivalence relations R and S are given by their relation matrices M_R and M_S. Show that $R \circ S$ is not an equivalence relation.

$$M_R = \begin{bmatrix} 1 & 1 & 0 \\ 1 & 1 & 0 \\ 0 & 0 & 1 \end{bmatrix} \qquad M_S = \begin{bmatrix} 1 & 1 & 0 \\ 1 & 1 & 1 \\ 0 & 1 & 1 \end{bmatrix}$$

Obtain equivalence relations R_1 and R_2 on $\{1, 2, 3\}$ such that $R_1 \circ R_2$ is also an equivalence relation.

2-3.8 Partial Ordering

Definition 2-3.16 A binary relation R in a set P is called a *partial order relation* or a *partial ordering* in P iff R is reflexive, antisymmetric, and transitive.

It is conventional to denote a partial ordering by the symbol $\leq$. This symbol does not necessarily mean "less than or equal to" as is used for real numbers. Since the relation of partial ordering is reflexive, we shall henceforth call it a relation on a set, say P. If $\leq$ is a partial ordering on P, then the ordered pair $\langle P, \leq \rangle$ is called a *partially ordered set* or a *poset*.

Definition 2-3.17 Let $\langle P, \leq \rangle$ be a partially ordered set. If for every $x, y \in P$ we have either $x \leq y \vee y \leq x$, then $\leq$ is called a *simple ordering* or *linear ordering* on P, and $\langle P, \leq \rangle$ is called a *totally ordered* or *simply ordered set* or a *chain*.

Note that it is not necessary to have $x \leq y$ or $y \leq x$ for every x and y in a partially ordered set P. In fact, x may not be related to y, in which case we say that x and y are *incomparable*.

If R is a partial ordering on P, then it is easy to see that the converse of R, namely $\tilde{R}$, is also a partial ordering on P. If R is denoted by $\leq$, then $\tilde{R}$ is denoted by $\geq$. This means that if $\langle P, \leq \rangle$ is a partially ordered set, then $\langle P, \geq \rangle$ is also a partially ordered set. $\langle P, \geq \rangle$ is called the dual of $\langle P, \leq \rangle$.

We now define another relationship which is associated with every partial ordering $\leq$ on P and which is denoted by $<$. This relation $<$ is defined, for every $x, y \in P$, as

$$x < y \Leftrightarrow x \leq y \wedge x \neq y$$

Similarly, corresponding to the converse partial ordering $\geq$, there is a relation $>$ such that

$$x > y \Leftrightarrow x \geq y \wedge x \neq y$$

Note that the relations $<$ and $>$ are antisymmetric and transitive. In addition, these relations are irreflexive. We now give some partial order relations which are frequently used.

1 Less Than or Equal to, Greater Than or Equal to: Let R be the set of real numbers. The relation "*less than or equal to*," or $\leq$, is a partial ordering on R. The converse of this relation, "*greater than or equal to*," or $\geq$, is also a partial ordering on R. Associated relations are "*less than*," or $<$, and "*greater than*," or $>$, respectively.

2 Inclusion: Let $\rho(A) = 2^A = X$ be the power set of A, that is, X is the set of subsets of A. The relation of inclusion ($\subseteq$) on X is a partial ordering. Associated with the relation $\subseteq$ is a relation called proper inclusion ($\subset$) which is irreflexive, antisymmetric, and transitive.

As a special case, we let $A = \{a, b, c\}$. Then

$$X = \rho(A) = \{\varnothing, \{a\}, \{b\}, \{c\}, \{a, b\}, \{a, c\}, \{b, c\}, A\}$$

It is easy to write the elements of the relation $\subseteq$. Note that $\{a\}$ and $\{b, c\}$, $\{a, b\}$ and $\{a, c\}$, etc., are incomparable.

3 Divides and Integral Multiple: If a and b are positive integers, then we say "a divides b," written $a \mid b$, iff there is an integer c such that $ac = b$. Alternatively, we say that "b is an *integral multiple of a*." The relation "*divides*" is a partial order relation. Let X be the set of positive integers. The relations "divides" and "integral multiple of" are partial orderings on X, and each is the converse of the other.

As a special case, let $X = \{2, 3, 6, 8\}$ and let $\leq$ be the relation "divides" on X. Then

$$\leq = \{\langle 2, 2\rangle, \langle 3, 3\rangle, \langle 6, 6\rangle, \langle 8, 8\rangle, \langle 2, 8\rangle, \langle 2, 6\rangle, \langle 3, 6\rangle\}$$

The relation "integral multiple of," written as $\geq$, is given by

$$\geq = \{\langle 2, 2\rangle, \langle 3, 3\rangle, \langle 6, 6\rangle, \langle 8, 8\rangle, \langle 8, 2\rangle, \langle 6, 2\rangle, \langle 6, 3\rangle\}$$

4 Lexicographic Ordering: A useful example of simple or total ordering is the lexicographic ordering. We shall define it for certain ordered pairs first and then generalize it.

Let R be the set of real numbers and let $P = R \times R$. The relation $\geq$ on R is assumed to be the usual relation of "greater than or equal to." For any two ordered pairs $\langle x_1, y_1\rangle$ and $\langle x_2, y_2\rangle$ in P, we define the total ordering relation S as follows:

$$\langle x_1, y_1\rangle \, S \, \langle x_2, y_2\rangle \Leftrightarrow (x_1 > x_2) \vee ((x_1 = x_2) \wedge (y_1 \geq y_2))$$

It is clear that if $\langle x_1, y_1\rangle \not{S} \langle x_2, y_2\rangle$, then we must have $\langle x_2, y_2\rangle \, S \, \langle x_1, y_1\rangle$, so that S is a total ordering on P. The partial ordering S is called the *lexicographic ordering*. The significance of the terminology will become clear after we generalize the above ordering relation. The following are some of the ordered pairs of P which are S-related:

$$\langle 2, 2\rangle \, S \, \langle 2, 1\rangle$$
$$\langle 3, 1\rangle \, S \, \langle 1, 5\rangle$$
$$\langle 2, 2\rangle \, S \, \langle 2, 2\rangle$$
$$\langle 3, 2\rangle \, S \, \langle 1, 1\rangle$$

We now generalize this concept. For this purpose, let R be a total ordering relation on a set X and let

$$P = X \cup X^2 \cup X^3 \cup \cdots \cup X^n = \bigcup_i X^i \qquad (n = 1, 2, 3, \ldots)$$

This equation means that the set P consists of strings of elements of X of length less than or equal to n. We may assume some fixed value of n. A string of length p may be considered as an ordered p-tuple. We now define a total ordering S on P called lexicographic ordering. For this purpose, let $\langle u_1, u_2, \ldots, u_p\rangle$ and $\langle v_1, v_2, \ldots, v_q\rangle$, with $p \leq q$, be any two elements of P. Note that before starting, to compare two strings to determine the ordering in P, the strings are interchanged if necessary so that $p \leq q$. Now

$$\langle u_1, u_2, \ldots, u_p\rangle \, S \, \langle v_1, v_2, \ldots, v_q\rangle$$

if any one of the following holds:

1   $\langle u_1, u_2, \ldots, u_p \rangle = \langle v_1, v_2, \ldots, v_p \rangle$

2   $u_1 \neq v_1$ and $u_1 \, R \, v_1$ in X

3   $u_i = v_i$, $i = 1, 2, \ldots, k$ $(k < p)$, and $u_{k+1} \neq v_{k+1}$ and $u_{k+1} \, R \, v_{k+1}$ in X

If none of these conditions is satisfied, then

$$\langle v_1, v_2, \ldots, v_q \rangle \, S \, \langle u_1, u_2, \ldots, u_p \rangle$$

As a special case of lexicographic ordering, let $X = \{a, b, c, \ldots, z\}$ and let R be a simple ordering on X denoted by $\leq$ where $a \leq b \leq c \leq \cdots \leq z$ and $P = X \cup X^2 \cup X^3$. Thus, P consists of all "words" or strings of 3 or fewer than 3 letters from X. Let S denote the lexicographic ordering on P described earlier. We will have

me S met	by condition 1
bet S met	by condition 2
beg S bet	by condition 3
get S go	by the last rule

since "go" and "get" are compared and the conditions 1, 2, and 3 are not satisfied.

The order in which the words in an English dictionary appear is a familiar example of lexicographic ordering. Instead of using S to denote the lexicographic ordering, it is customary to use names such as "lexically less than or equal to" or "lexically greater than."

We shall now describe how the lexicographic ordering is used in sorting character data on a computer. For this purpose, let X denote the set of characters available on a particular computer. It is necessary first to define a simple ordering on the elements of X (frequently called the collating sequence). One method is to compare the numeric values of the coded representation of each character in the computer by using the relation "less than or equal to." This ordering may vary from one computer to another. An example of a code which has such an ordering is the Extended Binary Coded Decimal Interchange Code (EBCDIC). In any case, we have a totally ordered set $\langle X, \leq \rangle$, and character strings are formed from the elements of X. Since blanks are also permitted to appear in such strings, a blank is treated as a character, i.e., an element of X. It is convenient to assume that a blank is less than all other elements of X. Not only do blanks appear inside a string, but sometimes it will be convenient to add blanks at the end of a string. It will be assumed that such additions do not alter the relative ordering of a string.

Now we consider how two given strings of equal length are compared for the purpose of ordering them lexicographically. If one string is shorter than the other, we simply assume that it is padded at the right end (because we shall assume the scanning is done from left to right) with the number of blanks sufficient that both strings to be compared are of equal length. In some cases, it may be necessary to distinguish between a given string and the one to which some blanks are added. This distinction can be made by comparing the strings for lexical equality and then comparing them according to their lengths.

The primitive algorithm $SORT$ which follows is based on lexicographic comparisons.

Algorithm $SORT$ Given a vector $NAME$ which contains m character strings, it is required to sort these strings into the proper lexicographic order. To assist in this process, the character string variable $TEMP$, the logical variable $FLAG$, and parameters i and j are used.

    1 [Repeat for $m - 1$ passes] Repeat steps 2 to 4 inclusive for $i = 1$, $2, \ldots, m - 1$ and then Exit.
    2 [Scan to element $m - i$] Set $FLAG \leftarrow T$. Repeat step 3 for $j = 1, 2, \ldots$, $m - i$.
    3 [Exchange required?] If $NAME[j] > NAME[j + 1]$ then set $TEMP \leftarrow NAME[j]$, $NAME[j] \leftarrow NAME[j + 1]$, $NAME[j + 1] \leftarrow TEMP$ and $FLAG \leftarrow F$.
    4 [Pass without exchange?] If $FLAG$ then Exit.

The purpose of this algorithm is to sort the m character sequences in $NAME$ into an ascending lexicographic order; that is, $NAME[j]$ must not be lexically greater than $NAME[j + 1]$ for $j = 1, 2, \ldots, m - 1$. When i is equal to 1, all adjacent elements are compared and those which are out of order are exchanged. When this comparison is done for elements j and $j + 1$, with j ranging from 1 to $m - i$, in this specific case we are assured that element m will contain the lexically greatest string. When i is equal to 2, the pass will be completed with the second greatest string in position $m - 1$ of $NAME$. A maximum of $m - 1$ such passes are performed, and on the ith pass, $m - i$ comparisons must be made. Of course, on completion of a pass without any exchanges, all elements are in the proper order and the algorithm is complete, as indicated by $FLAG$.

$$////$$

2-3.9 Partially Ordered Set: Representation and Associated Terminology

In a partially ordered set $\langle P, \leq \rangle$, an element $y \in P$ is said to *cover* an element $x \in P$ if $x < y$ and if there does not exist any element $z \in P$ such that $x \leq z$ and $z \leq y$; that is,

$$y \text{ covers } x \Leftrightarrow (x < y \wedge (x \leq z \leq y \Rightarrow x = z \vee z = y))$$

Sometimes the term "immediate predecessor" is also used. Note that "cover" as used here should not be confused with the "cover" of a set defined in Sec. 2-3.4.
    A partial ordering $\leq$ on a set P can be represented by means of a diagram known as a Hasse diagram or a partially ordered set diagram of $\langle P, \leq \rangle$. In such a diagram, each element is represented by a small circle or a dot. The circle for $x \in P$ is drawn below the circle for $y \in P$ if $x < y$, and a line is drawn between x and y if y covers x. If $x < y$ but y does not cover x, then x and y are not connected directly by a single line. However, they are connected through one or more elements of P. It is possible to obtain the set of ordered pairs in $\leq$ from

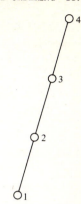

FIGURE 2-3.23   Hasse diagram.

such a diagram. Several examples of partially ordered sets and their Hasse diagrams follow.

For a totally ordered set $\langle P, \leq \rangle$, the Hasse diagram consists of circles, one below the other, as in Fig. 2-3.23. Thus a totally ordered set is called a chain. If we let $P = \{1, 2, 3, 4\}$ and $\leq$ be the relation "less than or equal to," then the Hasse diagram is as shown in Fig. 2-3.23.

Consider the set $P = \{\varnothing, \{a\}, \{a, b\}, \{a, b, c\}\}$ and the relation of inclusion $\subseteq$ on P. The Hasse diagram of $\langle P, \subseteq \rangle$ is similar to that given in Fig. 2-3.23 except that the nodes are relabeled.

The two relations defined above are not equal, but they have the same Hasse diagram. Such situations will be shown to occur frequently, and the reason for these occurrences is explained in Chap. 4 in the discussion of the order isomorphism of two partially ordered sets.

EXAMPLE 1   Let $X = \{2, 3, 6, 12, 24, 36\}$ and the relation $\leq$ be such that $x \leq y$ if x divides y. Draw the Hasse diagram of $\langle X, \leq \rangle$.

SOLUTION   The Hasse diagram is given in Fig. 2-3.24.   ////

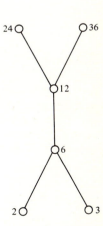

FIGURE 2-3.24   Hasse diagram of divides relation.

EXAMPLE 2   Let A be a given finite set and $\rho(A)$ its power set. Let $\subseteq$ be the inclusion relation on the elements of $\rho(A)$. Draw Hasse diagrams of $\langle \rho(A), \subseteq \rangle$ for (a) $A = \{a\}$; (b) $A = \{a, b\}$; (c) $A = \{a, b, c\}$; (d) $A = \{a, b, c, d\}$.

SOLUTION   The required Hasse diagrams are given in Fig. 2-3.25a to d.

$////$

The following points may be noted about Hasse diagrams in general. For a given partially ordered set, a Hasse diagram is not unique, as can be seen from Fig. 2-3.25b. From a Hasse diagram of $\langle P, \leq \rangle$, the Hasse diagram of $\langle P, \geq \rangle$, which is the dual of $\langle P, \leq \rangle$, can be obtained by rotating the diagram through 180° so that the points at the top become the points at the bottom. Some Hasse diagrams have a unique point which is above all the other points, and similarly some Hasse diagrams have a unique point which is below all other points. Such was the case for all the Hasse diagrams given in Example 2, while the Hasse diagram given in Example 1 does not possess this property. The Hasse diagrams become more complicated when the number of elements in the partially ordered set is large.

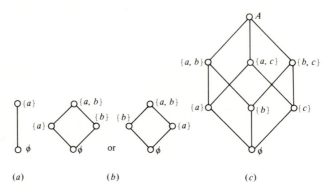

(a)   (b)   (c)

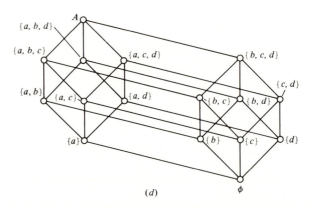

(d)

FIGURE 2-3.25   Hasse diagrams of $\langle \rho(A), \subseteq \rangle$.

EXAMPLE 3   Let A be the set of factors of a particular positive integer m and let $\leq$ be the relation divides, i.e.,

$$\leq \ = \ \{\, \langle x, y \rangle \mid x \in A \wedge y \in A \wedge (x \text{ divides } y)\,\}$$

Draw Hasse diagrams for (a) $m = 2$; (b) $m = 6$; (c) $m = 30$; (d) $m = 210$; (e) $m = 12$; and (f) $m = 45$.

SOLUTION   The required Hasse diagrams for (a) to (d) are the same as given in Fig. 2-3.25a to d. Hasse diagrams of (e) and (f) are given in Fig. 2-3.26.

$////$

In Examples 2 and 3 we saw that the Hasse diagrams (a) to (d) are identical. However, Hasse diagrams (e) and (f) of Example 3 cannot be given by the Hasse diagram of any power set of a set, because a power set has 2^n elements, while in (e) and (f) we only have 6 elements in each of the partially ordered sets. Of course, in all the cases given in Example 3 we again have a single element at the top and a single element at the bottom because if p is any divisor of m, we have $1 \leq p \leq m$.

Hasse diagrams can also be drawn for any relation which is antisymmetric and transitive but not necessarily reflexive. Examples of such relations are proper inclusion and any relation $<$ associated with the partial ordering relation $\leq$. Any family tree or organization chart of the military or of any establishment is a Hasse diagram in this sense. We shall, however, assume that a Hasse diagram represents a partial ordering unless otherwise stated. Some Hasse diagrams are given in Fig. 2-3.27.

We shall now introduce terminology for partially ordered sets which will be found useful in Chap. 4. To this end, let $\langle P, \leq \rangle$ denote a partially ordered set.

If there exists an element $y \in P$ such that $y \leq x$ for all $x \in P$, then y is called the *least member* in P relative to the partial ordering $\leq$. Similarly, if there exists an element $y \in P$ such that $x \leq y$ for all $x \in P$, then y is called the *greatest*

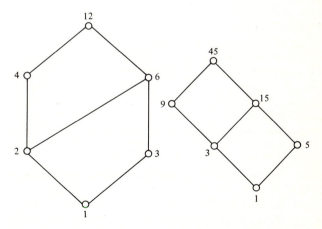

FIGURE 2-3.26

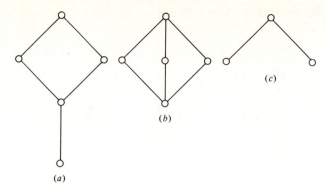

FIGURE 2-3.27

member in P relative to $\leq$. From the definition it is clear that the least member, if it exists, is unique; so also is the greatest member. It may happen that the least or the greatest member does not exist. The least member is usually denoted by 0 and the greatest by 1.

If the Hasse diagram of a partially ordered set is available, then it is easy to see whether the least or the greatest member exists. From Fig. 2-3.23 it is clear that the least member is 1 and the greatest is 4. In Example 1 there is no least or greatest member, while in Example 2 the least member is $\varnothing$ and the greatest member is A in all cases. In every simple ordering or chain, the least and the greatest members always exist. The Hasse diagram of Fig. 2-3.27c shows that the greatest member exists but there is no least member.

An element $y \in P$ is called a *minimal member* of P relative to a partial ordering $\leq$ if for no $x \in P$ is $x < y$. A minimal member need not be unique. All those members which appear at the lowest level of a Hasse diagram of a partially ordered set are minimal members. Similarly, an element $y \in P$ is called a *maximal member* of P relative to a partial ordering $\leq$ if for no $x \in P$ is $y < x$. In the Hasse diagram of Fig. 2-3.27c, there are two minimal members and one maximal member. Distinct minimal members are incomparable, and distinct maximal members are also incomparable.

It is not always necessary to draw the Hasse diagram of a partially ordered set in order to determine the least, greatest, maximal, and minimal members. However, their determination becomes simple when such a diagram is available.

We now extend these ideas to the subsets of a partially ordered set.

Definition 2-3.18 Let $\langle P, \leq \rangle$ be a partially ordered set and let $A \subseteq P$. Any element $x \in P$ is an *upper bound* for A if for all $a \in A$, $a \leq x$. Similarly, any element $x \in P$ is a *lower bound* for A if for all $a \in A$, $x \leq a$.

Let us consider the partially ordered set $\langle \rho(A), \subseteq \rangle$ in Example 2c. We choose a subset B of $\rho(A)$ given by $\{\{b, c\}, \{b\}, \{c\}\}$. Then $\{b, c\}$ and A are upper bounds for B, while $\varnothing$ is its lower bound. For the subset $C = \{\{a, c\}, \{c\}\}$, the upper bounds are $\{a, c\}$ and A while the lower bounds are $\{c\}$ and $\varnothing$. In Example 1, if $A = \{2, 3, 6\}$, then 6, 12, 24, and 36 are upper bounds for A, and there is no lower bound.

Note that upper and lower bounds of a subset are not necessarily unique. We therefore define the following terms.

Definition 2-3.19   Let $\langle P, \leq \rangle$ be a partially ordered set and let $A \subseteq P$. An element $x \in P$ is a *least upper bound*, or *supremum*, for A if x is an upper bound for A and $x \leq y$ where y is any upper bound for A. Similarly, the *greatest lower bound*, or *infimum*, for A is an element $x \in P$ such that x is a lower bound and $y \leq x$ for all lower bounds y.

A least upper bound, if it exists, is unique, and the same is true for a greatest lower bound. The least upper bound is abbreviated as "LUB" or "sup," and the greatest lower bound is abbreviated as "GLB" or "inf."

For a simply ordered set or a chain, every subset has a supremum and an infimum. Similarly, the partially ordered sets given in Examples 2 and 3 are such that every subset has a supremum and an infimum. This, however, is not generally the case, as can be seen from Example 1 in which the set $A = \{2, 3, 6\}$ has the LUB $A = 6$, while the GLB A does not exist. Similarly, for the subset $\{2, 3\}$, the supremum is again 6, but there is no infimum. For the subset $\{12, 6\}$, the supremum is 12 and the infimum is 6. The partially ordered sets which are such that every subset has a supremum and an infimum form an important subclass of partially ordered sets. Such sets are discussed in Chap. 4.

For a partially ordered set $\langle P, \leq \rangle$, we know that its dual $\langle P, \geq \rangle$ is also a partially ordered set. The least member of P relative to the ordering $\leq$ is the greatest member in P relative to the ordering $\geq$, and vice versa. Similarly, the maximal and minimal elements are interchanged. For any subset $A \subseteq P$, the GLB A in $\langle P, \leq \rangle$ is the same as the LUB A in $\langle P, \geq \rangle$.

We shall end this section by defining a property which has important applications in the use of the principle of transfinite induction.

Definition 2-3.20   A partially ordered set is called *well-ordered* if every nonempty subset of it has a least member.

As a consequence of this definition, it follows that every well-ordered set is totally ordered, because for any subset, say $\{x, y\}$, we must have either x or y as its least member. Of course, every totally ordered set need not be well-ordered. A finite totally ordered set is also well-ordered.

A simple example of a well-ordered set is the set $\mathbf{I}_n = \{1, 2, \ldots, n\}$ or the set $\mathbf{I} = \{1, 2, \ldots\}$. Similarly the sets $\mathbf{I}_n \times \mathbf{I}_n$ or $\mathbf{I} \times \mathbf{I}$ are well-ordered under the natural ordering of "less than or equal." It is possible, however, to define a certain partial ordering on $\mathbf{I} \times \mathbf{I}$ such that it is no longer a well-ordered set.

EXERCISES 2-3.9

1   Draw the Hasse diagrams of the following sets under the partial ordering relation "divides," and indicate those which are totally ordered.

$\{2, 6, 24\}$ $\{3, 5, 15\}$ $\{1, 2, 3, 6, 12\}$ $\{2, 4, 8, 16\}$ $\{3, 9, 27, 54\}$

2   If R is a partial ordering relation on a set X and $A \subseteq X$, show that $R \cap (A \times A)$ is a partial ordering relation on A.

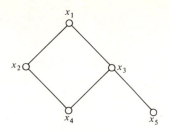

FIGURE 2-3.28

3   Give an example of a set X such that $\langle \rho(X), \subseteq \rangle$ is a totally ordered set.

4   Give a relation which is both a partial ordering relation and an equivalence relation on a set.

5   Let S denote the set of all the partial ordering relations on a set P. Define a partial ordering relation on S and interpret this relation in terms of the elements of P.

6   Figure 2-3.28 gives the Hasse diagram of a partially ordered set $\langle P, R \rangle$, where $P = \{x_1, x_2, \ldots, x_5\}$. Find which of the following are true: $x_1 \, R \, x_2, \, x_4 \, R \, x_1, \, x_3 \, R \, x_5, \, x_2 \, R \, x_5, \, x_1 \, R \, x_1, \, x_2 \, R \, x_3,$ and $x_4 \, R \, x_5$. Find the least and greatest members in P if they exist. Also find the maximal and minimal elements of P. Find the upper and lower bounds of $\{x_2, x_3, x_4\}, \{x_3, x_4, x_5\},$ and $\{x_1, x_2, x_3\}$. Also indicate the LUB and GLB of these subsets if they exist.

7   Show that there are only five distinct Hasse diagrams for partially ordered sets that contain three elements.

2-4   FUNCTIONS

In this section we study a particular class of relations called functions. We are primarily concerned with discrete functions which transform a finite set into another finite set. There are several such transformations involved in the computer implementation of any program. Computer output can be considered as a function of the input. A compiler transforms a program into a set of machine language instructions (the object program). After introducing the concept of function in general, we discuss unary and binary operations which form a class of functions. Such operations have important applications in the study of algebraic structures in Chaps. 3 and 4. Also discussed is a special class of functions known as hashing functions that are used in organizing files on a computer, along with other techniques associated with such organizations. A PL/I program for the construction of a symbol table is also given.

2-4.1   Definition and Introduction

Definition 2-4.1   Let X and Y be any two sets. A relation f from X to Y is called a *function* if for every $x \in X$ there is a unique $y \in Y$ such that $\langle x, y \rangle \in f$.

Note that the definition of function requires that a relation must satisfy two additional conditions in order to qualify as a function. The first condition is that every $x \in X$ must be related to some $y \in Y$, that is, the domain of f must be X and not merely a subset of X. The second requirement of uniqueness can be expressed as

$$\langle x, y \rangle \in f \wedge \langle x, z \rangle \in f \Rightarrow y = z$$

Terms such as "transformation," "map" (or "mapping"), "correspondence," and "operation" are used as synonyms for "function." The notations $f: X \to Y$ or $X \xrightarrow{f} Y$ are used to express f as a function from X to Y. Pictorially, a function is generally shown as in Fig. 2-4.1.

For a function $f: X \to Y$, if $\langle x, y \rangle \in f$, then x is called an *argument* and the corresponding y is called the *image* of x under f. Instead of writing $\langle x, y \rangle \in f$, it is customary to write $y = f(x)$ and to call y the *value of the function f at x*. Other ways of expressing $y = f(x)$ are $f: x \to y$, $x \xrightarrow{f} y$, and, of course, $\langle x, y \rangle \in f$. As an extension of this notation to the whole set X, we sometimes denote the range of f, viz., R_f, by $f(X)$. The range of f is defined as

$$\{y \mid \exists x \in X \wedge y = f(x)\}$$

It was mentioned that the domain of f is X, that is, $D_f = X$. The range of f is denoted by R_f and $R_f \subseteq Y$. The set Y is called the *codomain* of f. Some authors permit $D_f \subseteq X$, but according to our definition $D_f = X$.

Since a function is a relation, we can use a relation matrix or a graph to represent it in some cases. Note that from the definition of a function it follows that every row of its relation matrix must have only one entry which is 1 while all other entries in this row are 0s. Therefore, one can replace the relation matrix by a single column, i.e., a vector consisting of entries which are images of the arguments. Thus the column consists of entries which show a correspondence between the argument and the image of the function under the argument. In certain other cases, this correspondence can be expressed more easily by a rule. For example, $f(x) = x^2$ for $x \in \mathbf{R}$ represents the function $\{\langle x, x^2 \rangle \mid x \in \mathbf{R}\}$ where $\mathbf{R}$ is the set of real numbers and $f: \mathbf{R} \to \mathbf{R}$. Graphs of some functions are shown in Fig. 2-4.2.

Note that more than one element $x \in X$ may have the same function value; for example, $g(x_1) = g(x_2) = y_3$ for the function g whose graph is given in Fig. 2-4.2.

The following are some illustrations of functions.

1   Let $X = \{1, 5, P, \text{Jack}\}$, $Y = \{2, 5, 7, q, \text{Jill}\}$, and $f = \{\langle 1, 2 \rangle, \langle 5, 7 \rangle, \langle P, q \rangle, \langle \text{Jack}, q \rangle\}$. Obviously $D_f = X$, $R_f = \{2, 7, q\}$, and $f(1) = 2$, $f(5) = 7$, $f(P) = q$, $f(\text{Jack}) = q$.

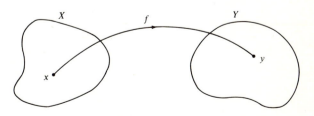

FIGURE 2-4.1   Representation of a function.

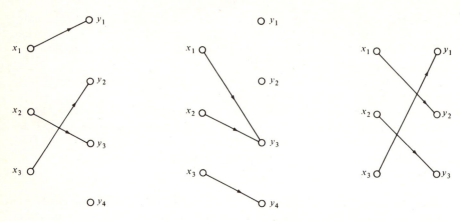

FIGURE 2-4.2   Graphs of functions.

2   Let $X = Y = \mathbf{R}$ and $f(x) = x^2 + 2$. $D_f = \mathbf{R}$ and $R_f \subseteq \mathbf{R}$. The values of f for different values of $x \in \mathbf{R}$ all lie on a parabola, as shown in Fig. 2-4.3.

3   Let $X = Y = \mathbf{R}$ and let

$$f = \{\langle x, x^2 \rangle \mid x \in \mathbf{R}\}$$

$$g = \{\langle x^2, x \rangle \mid x \in \mathbf{R}\}$$

Clearly f is a function from X to Y. However, g is not a function because the uniqueness condition is violated, as can be seen by noting that for any real number a, $\langle a^2, a \rangle$ and $\langle a^2, -a \rangle$ are both in g.

4   Let E be the universal set and $\rho(E)$ be its power set. For any two sets $A, B \in \rho(E)$, the operations of union and intersection are mappings from

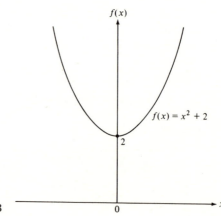

FIGURE 2-4.3

$\rho(E) \times \rho(E)$ to $\rho(E)$. Similarly, complementation is a mapping from $\rho(E)$ to $\rho(E)$.

5 Let P be the set of all positive integers and $\sigma: P \to P$ be such that $\sigma(n) = n + 1$ where $n \in P$. Obviously $\sigma(1) = 2$, $\sigma(2) = 3$, ... The function σ is called *Peano's successor function* and is used in the description of integers in Sec. 2-5.1.

6 Let X be the set of all statements in logic and let Y denote the set $\{T, F\}$, where T and F denote the truth values. The assignment of truth values to statements can be considered as a mapping from X to Y.

7 Let functions f and g be defined by

$$f = \{\langle x, \lfloor x \rfloor \rangle \mid x \in \mathbf{R} \wedge \lfloor x \rfloor = \text{the greatest integer less than or equal to } x\}$$

$$g = \{\langle x, \lceil x \rceil \rangle \mid x \in \mathbf{R} \wedge \lceil x \rceil = \text{the least integer greater than or equal to } x\}$$

The function $f(x) = \lfloor x \rfloor$ is frequently called the *floor* of x, and similarly, the function $g(x) = \lceil x \rceil$ is called the *ceiling* of x. As examples, study the following:

$$f(3.75) = \lfloor 3.75 \rfloor = 3 \qquad \lfloor 4 \rfloor = 4 \qquad \lfloor -3.75 \rfloor = -4$$

$$g(3.33) = \lceil 3.33 \rceil = 4 \qquad \lceil 4 \rceil = 4 \qquad \lceil -3.33 \rceil = -3$$

8 A program written in a high-level language is transformed (or mapped) into a machine language by a compiler. Similarly, the output from a computer is a function of its input.

Definition 2-4.2 If $f: X \to Y$ and $A \subseteq X$, then $f \cap (A \times Y)$ is a function from $A \to Y$ called the *restriction* of f to A and is sometimes written as f/A. If g is a restriction of f, then f is called the *extension* of g.

Note that $(f/A): A \to Y$ is such that for any $a \in A$, $(f/A)(a) = f(a)$. The domain of f/A is A, while that of f is X. Obviously, if g is a restriction of f, then $D_g \subseteq D_f$ and $g(x) = f(x)$ for $x \in D_g$ and $g \subseteq f$. As illustrations of these concepts, consider the following:

9 Let $f: \mathbf{R} \to \mathbf{R}$ be given by $f(x) = x^2$ as in (3). If $\mathbf{N}$ is the set of natural numbers, $\{0, 1, 2, \ldots\}$, then $\mathbf{N} \subseteq \mathbf{R}$ and

$$f/\mathbf{N} = \{\langle 0, 0 \rangle, \langle 1, 1 \rangle, \langle 2, 4 \rangle, \langle 3, 9 \rangle, \ldots\}$$

10 Let $f: \mathbf{R} \to \mathbf{R}$ be given by $f(x) = |x|$, where $|x|$ denotes the absolute value of x. Let $\mathbf{R}_+$ be the set of positive real numbers and $g: \mathbf{R}_+ \to \mathbf{R}$ be given by $g(x) = x$; then g is a restriction of f, that is, $g = f/\mathbf{R}_+$ and f is the extension of g in $\mathbf{R}$.

Equality of functions can be defined in terms of the equality of sets since functions are sets of ordered pairs. This definition also requires that equal functions have the same domain and the same range.

We know that not all possible subsets of $X \times Y$ are functions from X to Y. The collection of all those subsets of $X \times Y$ which define a function is denoted by Y^X. The reason for using this notation will be clear from the following illustration.

11   Let $X = \{a, b, c\}$ and $Y = \{0, 1\}$. Then

$$X \times Y = \{\langle a, 0 \rangle, \langle b, 0 \rangle, \langle c, 0 \rangle, \langle a, 1 \rangle, \langle b, 1 \rangle, \langle c, 1 \rangle\}$$

and there are 2^6 possible subsets of $X \times Y$. Of these, only the following 2^3 subsets define functions from X to Y.

$$f_0 = \{\langle a, 0 \rangle, \langle b, 0 \rangle, \langle c, 0 \rangle\} \qquad f_4 = \{\langle a, 1 \rangle, \langle b, 0 \rangle, \langle c, 0 \rangle\}$$

$$f_1 = \{\langle a, 0 \rangle, \langle b, 0 \rangle, \langle c, 1 \rangle\} \qquad f_5 = \{\langle a, 1 \rangle, \langle b, 0 \rangle, \langle c, 1 \rangle\}$$

$$f_2 = \{\langle a, 0 \rangle, \langle b, 1 \rangle, \langle c, 0 \rangle\} \qquad f_6 = \{\langle a, 1 \rangle, \langle b, 1 \rangle, \langle c, 0 \rangle\}$$

$$f_3 = \{\langle a, 0 \rangle, \langle b, 1 \rangle, \langle c, 1 \rangle\} \qquad f_7 = \{\langle a, 1 \rangle, \langle b, 1 \rangle, \langle c, 1 \rangle\}$$

In order to determine the number of functions from X to Y when both X and Y are finite, let us assume that X and Y have m and n distinct elements respectively. Since the domain of any function from X to Y is X, there are exactly m ordered pairs in each of the functions. Further, any element $x \in X$ can have any one of the n elements of Y as its image; therefore there are n^m possible functions which are distinct. In illustration (11), $m = 3$ and $n = 2$ and there are $2^3 = 8$ functions. The number n^m also explains why the notation Y^X was used to represent the set of all functions from X to Y. The same notation is used even when X or Y are infinite sets. It must be emphasized that the number of functions depends upon the number of elements in the sets X and Y and not on the sets. Therefore, in illustration (11) if Y is any set having 2 elements, the number of functions from X to Y will still be 8.

In the construction of truth tables of a statement function of n variables, we had 2^n rows because each row defined a distinct function from the set of n variables to the set $\{T, F\}$ of truth values.

Definition 2-4.3   A mapping of $f: X \rightarrow Y$ is called *onto* (*surjective*, a *surjection*) if the range $R_f = Y$; otherwise it is called *into*.

In Fig. 2-4.2 the function h is an onto mapping, while the others are into mappings. Illustrations (1), (2), (3), and (5) are into mappings while (4) and (6) are onto.

Definition 2-4.4   A mapping $f: X \rightarrow Y$ is called *one-to-one* (*injective*, or *1-1*) if distinct elements of X are mapped into distinct elements of Y. In other words, f is one-to-one if

$$x_1 \neq x_2 \Rightarrow f(x_1) \neq f(x_2)$$

or equivalently

$$f(x_1) = f(x_2) \Rightarrow x_1 = x_2$$

In Fig. 2-4.2, f and h are both one-to-one. Also the mapping in illustration

(5) is one-to-one, and so is $f/\mathbf{N}$ in (9). Although f in (10) is not one-to-one, its restriction g is.

It is easy to see that when X and Y are finite sets, a mapping $f\colon X \to Y$ can be one-to-one only if the number of elements in X is less than or equal to the number of elements in Y.

Definition 2-4.5 A mapping $f\colon X \to Y$ is called *one-to-one onto* (*bijective*) if it is both one-to-one and onto. Such a mapping is also called a one-to-one correspondence between X and Y.

For $f\colon X \to Y$ to be bijective when X and Y are finite requires that the number of elements in X be the same as the number of elements in Y. The function h whose graph is shown in Fig. 2-4.2 is bijective. Similarly, $f(x) = 2x + 1$ and $g(x) = x$ for $x \in \mathbf{R}$ are also bijective mappings from $\mathbf{R}$ to $\mathbf{R}$. We shall be interested in bijective mappings in the next section where it is shown that such functions have inverses.

EXERCISES 2-4–1

1 Let $\mathbf{N}$ be the set of natural numbers including zero. Determine which of the following functions are one-to-one, which are onto, and which are one-to-one onto.

(a) $f\colon \mathbf{N} \to \mathbf{N}$ $f(j) = j^2 + 2$

(b) $f\colon \mathbf{N} \to \mathbf{N}$ $f(j) = j \pmod 3$

(c) $f\colon \mathbf{N} \to \mathbf{N}$ $f(j) = \begin{cases} 1 & j \text{ is odd} \\ 0 & j \text{ is even} \end{cases}$

(d) $f\colon \mathbf{N} \to \{0, 1\}$ $f(j) = \begin{cases} 0 & j \text{ is odd} \\ 1 & j \text{ is even} \end{cases}$

2 Let $\mathbf{I}$ be the set of integers, $\mathbf{I}_+$ the set of positive integers, and $\mathbf{I}_p = \{0, 1, 2, \ldots, p-1\}$. Determine which of the following functions are one-to-one, which are onto, and which are one-to-one onto.

(a) $f\colon \mathbf{I} \to \mathbf{I}$ $f(j) = \begin{cases} j/2 & j \text{ is even} \\ (j-1)/2 & j \text{ is odd} \end{cases}$

(b) $f\colon \mathbf{I}_+ \to \mathbf{I}_+$ $f(x) = $ greatest integer $\le \sqrt{x}$

(c) $f\colon \mathbf{I}_7 \to \mathbf{I}_7$ $f(x) = 3x \pmod 7$

(d) $f\colon \mathbf{I}_4 \to \mathbf{I}_4$ $f(x) = 3x \pmod 4$

3 If X and Y are finite sets, find a necessary condition for the existence of one-to-one mappings from X to Y.

4 Do the following sets define functions? If so, give their domain and range in each case.

(a) $\{\langle 1, \langle 2, 3\rangle\rangle, \langle 2, \langle 3, 4\rangle\rangle, \langle 3, \langle 1, 4\rangle\rangle, \langle 4, \langle 1, 4\rangle\rangle\}$

(b) $\{\langle 1, \langle 2, 3\rangle\rangle, \langle 2, \langle 3, 4\rangle\rangle, \langle 3, \langle 3, 2\rangle\rangle\}$

(c) $\{\langle 1, \langle 2, 3\rangle\rangle, \langle 2, \langle 3, 4\rangle\rangle, \langle 1, \langle 2, 4\rangle\rangle\}$

(d) $\{\langle 1, \langle 2, 3\rangle\rangle, \langle 2, \langle 2, 3\rangle\rangle, \langle 3, \langle 2, 3\rangle\rangle\}$

5 List all possible functions from $X = \{a, b, c\}$ to $Y = \{0, 1\}$ and indicate in each case whether the function is one-to-one, is onto, and is one-to-one onto.

6 If $A = \{1, 2, \ldots, n\}$, show that any function from A to A which is one-to-one must also be onto, and conversely.

7 Show that the functions f and g which both are from $\mathbf{N} \times \mathbf{N}$ to $\mathbf{N}$ given by $f \langle x, y \rangle = x + y$ and $g \langle x, y \rangle = xy$ are onto but not one-to-one.

2-4.2 Composition of Functions

The operation of composition of relations can be extended to functions in the following manner.

Definition 2-4.6 Let $f: X \to Y$ and $g: Y \to Z$ be two functions. The *composite relation* $g \circ f$ such that

$$g \circ f = \{ \langle x, z \rangle \mid (x \in X) \wedge (z \in Z) \wedge (\exists y)(y \in Y$$
$$\wedge \; y = f(x) \wedge z = g(y)) \}$$

is called the *composition* of functions or *relative product* of functions f and g. More precisely, $g \circ f$ is called the *left composition* of g with f.

Note that in the above definition it is assumed that the range R_f of f is a subset of the domain of g, which is Y, that is $R_f \subseteq D_g$; otherwise, $g \circ f$ is empty. Assuming that $g \circ f$ is not empty, we now show that $g \circ f$ is a function from X to Z. For this purpose, let us assume that $\langle x, z_1 \rangle$ and $\langle x, z_2 \rangle$ are both in $g \circ f$. This assumption requires that there is a $y \in Y$ such that $y = f(x)$ and $z_1 = g(y)$; also $z_2 = g(y)$. Since g is a function, we cannot have $z_1 = g(y)$ and $z_2 = g(y)$; hence $g \circ f$ is a function. Any function g for which $g \circ f$ can be formed is said to be *left-composable* with the function f. In such a case, $(g \circ f)(x) = g(f(x))$, where x is in the domain of $g \circ f$. The composition of functions is shown in Fig. 2-4.4.

Given $f: X \to Y$ and $g: Y \to Z$, we have the composite function $g \circ f$. However, the composite function $f \circ g$ may or may not exist. For the existence of $f \circ g$, it is necessary that $R_g \subseteq D_f$. For functions $f: X \to X$ and $g: X \to X$, the composite functions such as $f \circ g, g \circ f, f \circ f, g \circ g$, etc., can be formed. This point will be demonstrated by means of examples.

Consider three functions $f: X \to Y$, $g: Y \to Z$, and $h: Z \to W$. The composite functions $(g \circ f): X \to Z$ and $(h \circ g): Y \to W$ can be formed. Other composite functions such as $h \circ (g \circ f)$ and $(h \circ g) \circ f$ can also be formed. Both of these functions are from X to W. Assuming $y = f(x)$, $z = g(y)$, and $w = h(z)$, we have $\langle x, y \rangle \in f$, $\langle y, z \rangle \in g$, $\langle z, w \rangle \in h$ and $\langle x, z \rangle \in g \circ f$. $\langle y, w \rangle \in h \circ g$. Continuing the same argument, $\langle x, w \rangle \in h \circ (g \circ f)$. Similarly $\langle x, w \rangle \in (h \circ g) \circ f$. This fact being true for any x and corresponding w, we have (see also Fig. 2-4.5)

$$h \circ (g \circ f) = (h \circ g) \circ f \tag{1}$$

Thus the composition of functions is associative, and we may drop the parentheses in writing the functions in (1), so that $h \circ g \circ f = h \circ (g \circ f) = (h \circ g) \circ f$.

The composition of functions is also shown in Fig. 2-4.6.

EXAMPLE 1   Let $X = \{1, 2, 3\}$, $Y = \{p, q\}$, and $Z = \{a, b\}$. Also let $f: X \to Y$ be $f = \{ \langle 1, p \rangle, \langle 2, p \rangle, \langle 3, q \rangle \}$ and $g: Y \to Z$ be given by $g = \{ \langle p, b \rangle, \langle q, b \rangle \}$. Find $g \circ f$.

SOLUTION $g \circ f = \{ \langle 1, b \rangle, \langle 2, b \rangle, \langle 3, b \rangle \}$.   ////

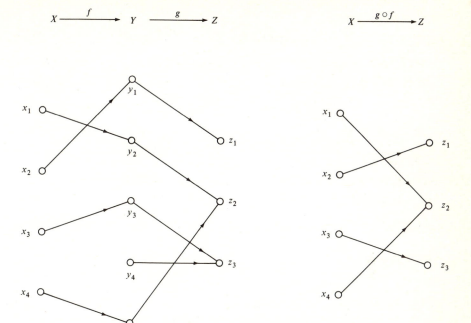

FIGURE 2-4.4 Composition of functions

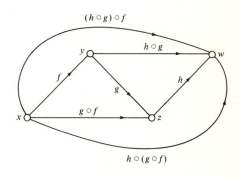

FIGURE 2-4.5

EXAMPLE 2 Let $X = \{1, 2, 3\}$ and $f, g, h,$ and s be functions from X to X given by

$$f = \{\langle 1, 2 \rangle, \langle 2, 3 \rangle, \langle 3, 1 \rangle\} \qquad g = \{\langle 1, 2 \rangle, \langle 2, 1 \rangle, \langle 3, 3 \rangle\}$$
$$h = \{\langle 1, 1 \rangle, \langle 2, 2 \rangle, \langle 3, 1 \rangle\} \qquad s = \{\langle 1, 1 \rangle, \langle 2, 2 \rangle, \langle 3, 3 \rangle\}$$

Find $f \circ g; g \circ f; f \circ h \circ g; s \circ g; g \circ s; s \circ s;$ and $f \circ s.$

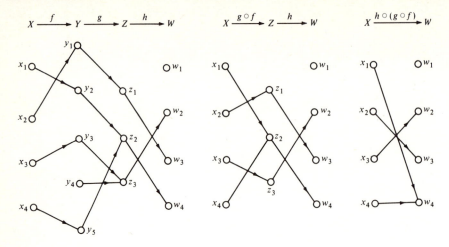

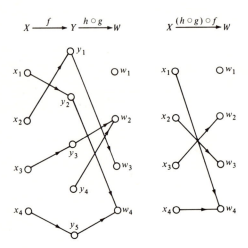

FIGURE 2-4.6

SOLUTION

$$f \circ g = \{\langle 1, 3 \rangle, \langle 2, 2 \rangle, \langle 3, 1 \rangle\}$$

$$g \circ f = \{\langle 1, 1 \rangle, \langle 2, 3 \rangle, \langle 3, 2 \rangle\} \neq f \circ g$$

$$f \circ h \circ g = \{\langle 1, 3 \rangle, \langle 2, 2 \rangle, \langle 3, 2 \rangle\}$$

$$s \circ g = \{\langle 1, 2 \rangle, \langle 2, 1 \rangle, \langle 3, 3 \rangle\} = g = g \circ s$$

$$s \circ s = \{\langle 1, 1 \rangle, \langle 2, 2 \rangle, \langle 3, 3 \rangle\} = s$$

$$f \circ s = \{\langle 1, 2 \rangle, \langle 2, 3 \rangle, \langle 3, 1 \rangle\} = f$$

Observe that $s \circ s = s$; $f \circ s = s \circ f = f$; $g \circ s = s \circ g = g$; and $h \circ s = s \circ h = h$.

////

EXAMPLE 3 Let $f(x) = x + 2$, $g(x) = x - 2$, and $h(x) = 3x$ for $x \in \mathbf{R}$, where $\mathbf{R}$ is the set of real numbers. Find $g \circ f; f \circ g; f \circ f; g \circ g; f \circ h; h \circ g; h \circ f;$ and $f \circ h \circ g$.

SOLUTION

$$g \circ f = \{\langle x, x \rangle \mid x \in \mathbf{R}\}$$
$$f \circ g = \{\langle x, x \rangle \mid x \in \mathbf{R}\} = g \circ f$$
$$f \circ f = \{\langle x, x + 4 \rangle \mid x \in \mathbf{R}\}$$
$$g \circ g = \{\langle x, x - 4 \rangle \mid x \in \mathbf{R}\}$$
$$f \circ h = \{\langle x, 3x + 2 \rangle \mid x \in \mathbf{R}\}$$
$$h \circ g = \{\langle x, 3x - 6 \rangle \mid x \in \mathbf{R}\}$$
$$h \circ f = \{\langle x, 3x + 6 \rangle \mid x \in \mathbf{R}\}$$
$$(f \circ h) \circ g = \{\langle x, 3x - 4 \rangle \mid x \in \mathbf{R}\} = f \circ (h \circ g) = f \circ h \circ g \qquad ////$$

EXAMPLE 4 Let $f: \mathbf{R} \to \mathbf{R}$ be given by $f(x) = -x^2$ and $g: \mathbf{R}_+ \to \mathbf{R}_+$ be given by $g(x) = \sqrt{x}$ where $\mathbf{R}_+$ is the set of nonnegative real numbers and $\mathbf{R}$ is the set of real numbers. Find $f \circ g$. Is $g \circ f$ defined?

SOLUTION $(f \circ g)(x) = -x$ for all $x \in \mathbf{R}_+$. The function $f \circ g: \mathbf{R}_+ \to \mathbf{R}$ is defined because the range of g is $\mathbf{R}_+ \subseteq \mathbf{R}$ and $\mathbf{R}$ is the domain of f. On the other hand, the range of f is not included in the domain of g; therefore $g \circ f$ is not defined. The only element common to R_f and D_g is 0. $////$

2-4.3 Inverse Functions

The converse of a relation R from X to Y was defined in Sec. 2-3.7 to be a relation $\tilde{R}$ from Y to X such that $\langle y, x \rangle \in \tilde{R} \Leftrightarrow \langle x, y \rangle \in R$; that is, the ordered pairs of $\tilde{R}$ are obtained from those of R by simply interchanging the members. The situation is not quite the same for functions. Let $\tilde{f}$ denote the converse of f, where f is considered as a relation from $X \to Y$. Naturally $\tilde{f}$ may not be a function, first, because the domain of $\tilde{f}$ may not be Y but only a subset of Y, and second, $\tilde{f}$ may not be a function from D_f to X because it may not satisfy the uniqueness condition. For example, $\langle x_1, y \rangle$ and $\langle x_2, y \rangle$ may be in f, so that $\langle y, x_1 \rangle$ and $\langle y, x_2 \rangle$ will be in $\tilde{f}$. In certain special cases, $\tilde{f}$ may be a function from a subset of Y to X or even from Y to X. The following examples illustrate the situation.

1 Let $X = \{1, 2, 3\}$, $Y = \{p, q, r\}$, and $f: X \to Y$ be given by $f = \{\langle 1, p \rangle, \langle 2, q \rangle, \langle 3, q \rangle\}$. Then $\tilde{f} = \{\langle p, 1 \rangle, \langle q, 2 \rangle, \langle q, 3 \rangle\}$ and $\tilde{f}$ is not a function.

2 Let $\mathbf{R}$ be the set of real numbers and let $f: \mathbf{R} \to \mathbf{R}$ be given by

$$f = \{\langle x, x^2 \rangle \mid x \in \mathbf{R}\}$$

Then $\tilde{f} = \{\langle x^2, x \rangle \mid x \in \mathbf{R}\}$ is not a function.

3 Let $\mathbf{R}$ be the set of real numbers and let $f: \mathbf{R} \to \mathbf{R}$ be given by

$$f = \{\langle x, x + 2 \rangle \mid x \in \mathbf{R}\}$$

Then $\tilde{f} = \{\langle x + 2, x \rangle \mid x \in \mathbf{R}\}$ is a function from $\mathbf{R}$ to $\mathbf{R}$.

4 Let $X = \{0, 1\}$, $Y = \{p, q, r, s\}$, and $f = \{\langle 0, p \rangle, \langle 1, r \rangle\}$. Then $\breve{f} = \{\langle p, 0 \rangle, \langle r, 1 \rangle\}$ is a function from a subset of Y to X, that is, $\breve{f}: \{p, r\} \rightarrow \{0, 1\}$.

It is easy to see that for a given $f: X \rightarrow Y$, $\breve{f}$ is a function only if f is one-to-one. But this condition does not guarantee that $\breve{f}$ is a function from Y to X. However, if f is one-to-one and onto, i.e., if f is bijective, then $\breve{f}$ is a function from Y to X. In such cases, $\breve{f}$ is written as f^{-1} so that $f^{-1}: Y \rightarrow X$ and f^{-1} is called the *inverse* of the function f. If f^{-1} exists, then f is called *invertible*. Obviously f^{-1} is also one-to-one and onto.

Definition 2-4.7 A mapping $I_x: X \rightarrow X$ is called an *identity map* if $I_x = \{\langle x, x \rangle \mid x \in X\}$.

Observe that for any function $g: X \rightarrow X$ the functions $I_x \circ g$ and $g \circ I_x$ are both equal to g. Also for any function $f: X \rightarrow Y$, we have $f \circ I_x = f$. These properties of the identity function can be used in stating the following theorems about the inverse of a function.

Theorem 2-4.1 If $f: X \rightarrow Y$ is invertible, then

$$f^{-1} \circ f = I_x \qquad \text{and} \qquad f \circ f^{-1} = I_y \qquad (1)$$

Theorem 2-4.2 Let $f: X \rightarrow Y$ and $g: Y \rightarrow X$. The function g is equal to f^{-1} only if

$$g \circ f = I_x \qquad \text{and} \qquad f \circ g = I_y \qquad (2)$$

Both the conditions given in (2) are necessary, as can be seen from the graphs of f and g shown in Fig. 2-4.7 where $g \circ f = I_x$ but $f \circ g \neq I_y$ and $g \neq f^{-1}$.

PROOF For a proof of Theorem 2-4.2, first we show that if there is any other function $h: Y \rightarrow X$ such that

$$h \circ f = I_x \qquad \text{and} \qquad f \circ h = I_y \qquad (3)$$

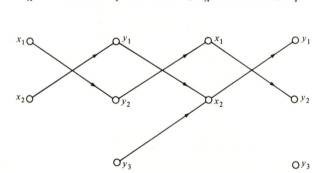

FIGURE 2-4.7

then $h = g$. Once this is proved, then $g = f^{-1}$ follows from Eq. (1). From Eqs. (2) and (3)

$$(h \circ f) \circ g = h \circ (f \circ g) = h \circ I_y = h = I_x \circ g = g$$

Let $f: X \to Y$ and $g: Y \to Z$ be such that $g \circ f: X \to Z$ can be constructed. If f and g are both one-to-one and onto, then $g \circ f$ will also be one-to-one and onto, and the inverses f^{-1}, g^{-1}, and $(g \circ f)^{-1}$ exist and are one-to-one and onto. Since $f^{-1}: Y \to X$ and $g^{-1}: Z \to Y$, we can form $f^{-1} \circ g^{-1}$. Both $(g \circ f)^{-1}$ and $f^{-1} \circ g^{-1}$ are functions from Z to X. Consider now any $x \in X$, and let $y = f(x)$ and $z = g(y)$. Thus, $\langle x, z \rangle \in g \circ f$ and $\langle z, x \rangle \in (g \circ f)^{-1}$. On the other hand, $x = f^{-1}(y)$ and $y = g^{-1}(z)$, so that $\langle z, x \rangle \in f^{-1} \circ g^{-1}$. This is true for any x, y, and z which satisfy $y = f(x)$ and $z = g(y)$; hence

$$(g \circ f)^{-1} = f^{-1} \circ g^{-1}$$

i.e., the inverse of a composite function can be expressed in terms of the composition of the inverses in the reverse order. ////

In the remaining part of this section, we consider mappings which are bijective and from a set X onto itself. For this purpose, let F_x denote the collection of all bijective functions from X onto X, so that the elements of F_x are all invertible functions. The following properties hold.

1 For any $f, g \in F_x, f \circ g$, and $g \circ f$ are also in F_x. This is called the closure property of the operation of composition, which is discussed in Sec. 2-4.4.

2 For any $f, g, h \in F_x$,

$$(f \circ g) \circ h = f \circ (g \circ h)$$

i.e., composition is associative.

3 There exists a function $I_x \in F_x$ called the *identity map* such that for any $f \in F_x$

$$I_x \circ f = f \circ I_x = f$$

4 For every $f \in F_x$, there exists an inverse function $f^{-1} \in F_x$ such that

$$f \circ f^{-1} = f^{-1} \circ f = I_x$$

In fact, (1) and (2) hold for all the elements of X^X, that is, for all the functions from X to X and not only for the elements of F_x.

EXAMPLE 1 Show that the functions $f(x) = x^3$ and $g(x) = x^{1/3}$ for $x \in \mathbf{R}$ are inverses of one another.

    SOLUTION Since $(f \circ g)(x) = f(x^{1/3}) = x = I_x$ and $(g \circ f)(x) = g(x^3) = x = I_x$, then $f = g^{-1}$ or $g = f^{-1}$. ////

EXAMPLE 2 Let F_x be the set of all one-to-one onto mappings from X onto X, where $X = \{1, 2, 3\}$. Find all the elements of F_x and find the inverse of each element.

    SOLUTION The graphs of functions shown in Fig. 2-4.8 represent the elements of $F_x = \{ f_1, f_2, f_3, f_4, f_5, f_6 \}$, where $f_1^{-1} = f_1, f_2^{-1} = f_2, f_3^{-1} = f_3, f_4^{-1} = f_4,$

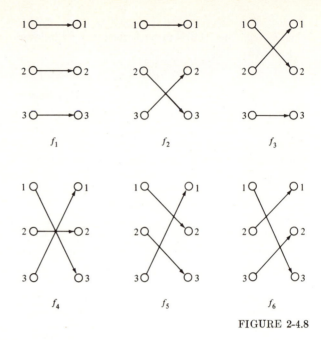

FIGURE 2-4.8

Table 2-4.1

$\circ$	f_1	f_2	f_3	f_4	f_5	f_6
f_1	f_1	f_2	f_3	f_4	f_5	f_6
f_2	f_2	f_1	f_6	f_5	f_4	f_3
f_3	f_3	f_5	f_1	f_6	f_2	f_4
f_4	f_4	f_6	f_5	f_1	f_3	f_2
f_5	f_5	f_3	f_4	f_2	f_6	f_1
f_6	f_6	f_4	f_2	f_3	f_1	f_5

and $f_5^{-1} = f_6$. Other compositions of the elements of F_x are given in Table 2-4.1, in which $f_i \circ f_j$ is entered at the intersection of the ith row and jth column.   ////

The functions defined in Example 2 show the permutations of the elements of the set X. There are $3! = 6$ such permutations of 3 elements, and hence there are 6 functions from X to X which are bijective. If a set X has n elements, then there are $n!$ functions from X to X which are bijective.

EXERCISES 2-4.3

1 Let $f: \mathbf{R} \to \mathbf{R}$ and $g: \mathbf{R} \to \mathbf{R}$, where $\mathbf{R}$ is the set of real numbers. Find $f \circ g$ and $g \circ f$, where $f(x) = x^2 - 2$ and $g(x) = x + 4$. State whether these functions are injective, surjective, and bijective.
2 If $f: X \to Y$ and $g: Y \to Z$ and both f and g are onto, show that $g \circ f$ is also onto. Is $g \circ f$ one-to-one if both g and f are one-to-one?

3   Let $f: \mathbf{R} \rightarrow \mathbf{R}$ be given by $f(x) = x^3 - 2$. Find f^{-1}.

4   How many functions are there from X to Y for the sets given below? Find also the number of functions which are one-to-one, onto, and one-to-one onto.

(*a*) $X = \{1, 2, 3\}$ $Y = \{1, 2, 3\}$
(*b*) $X = \{1, 2, 3, 4\}$ $Y = \{1, 2, 3\}$
(*c*) $X = \{1, 2, 3\}$ $Y = \{1, 2, 3, 4\}$

5   Show that there exists a one-to-one mapping from $A \times B$ to $B \times A$. Is it also onto?

6   Let $X = \{1, 2, 3, 4\}$. Define a function $f: X \rightarrow X$ such that $f \neq I_x$ and is one-to-one. Find $f \circ f = f^2$, $f^3 = f \circ f^2$, f^{-1}, and $f \circ f^{-1}$. Can you find another one-to-one function $g: X \rightarrow X$ such that $g \neq I_x$ but $g \circ g = I_x$?

2-4.4   Binary and *n*-ary Operations

In Sec. 2-4.1 we discussed functions from a set X to a set Y. Now we restrict our discussion to functions from a set $X \times X$ to X, or more generally to functions from X^n to X, where $n = 1, 2, \ldots$. Such a mapping prescribes a unique value in X to every ordered pair or n-tuple whose members are also in X.

> **Definition 2-4.8**   Let X be a set and f be a mapping $f: X \times X \rightarrow X$. Then f is called a *binary operation* on X. In general, a mapping $f: X^n \rightarrow X$ is called an *n-ary operation* and n is called the *order* of the operation. For $n = 1$, $f: X \rightarrow X$ is called a *unary* operation.

If an operation (or a mapping) on the members of a set produces images which are also members of the same set, then the set is said to be *closed* under that operation, and this property is called the *closure* property. The definition of binary or n-ary operations implies that the sets on which such operations are defined are closed under these operations. This property distinguishes the binary or n-ary operations from other functions.

The operations of addition, multiplication, and subtraction are binary operations on the set of integers and also on the set of real numbers. The operation of division is not a binary operation on these sets. Operations of set union and intersection are binary operations on the set of subsets of a universal set. They are also binary operations on the power set of any set. The operation of complementation (absolute or relative) is a unary operation on such sets. The operations of conjunction and disjunction are binary operations on the set of statements as well as on the set of statement formulas in statement logic. The operation of negation is a unary operation on such sets. Another example of a binary operation is the composition of bijective functions from a set X to X.

Sometimes a binary operation can be conveniently specified by a table called the composition table. Such a table was given in Example 2 of the previous subsection. The composition tables for the binary operations of union and intersection over the power set $\rho(A) = \{B_0, B_1, B_2, B_3\}$, where $A = \{a, b\}$, are given in Table 2-4.2 where $B_0 = \varnothing$, $B_1 = \{b\}$, $B_2 = \{a\}$, and $B_3 = \{a, b\} = A$.

It is customary to denote a binary operation by a symbol such as $+$, $-$, $\circ$, $*$, $\triangle$, $\cup$, $\cap$, $\vee$, $\wedge$, etc., and the value of the operation (or function) by placing the operator between the two operands. For example, $f \langle x, y \rangle$ may be written as $x f y$ or $x * y$. A similar notation is used in arithmetic where we write the

Table 2-4.2

∪	B_0	B_1	B_2	B_3		∩	B_0	B_1	B_2	B_3
B_0	B_0	B_1	B_2	B_3		B_0	B_0	B_0	B_0	B_0
B_1	B_1	B_1	B_3	B_3		B_1	B_0	B_1	B_0	B_1
B_2	B_2	B_3	B_2	B_3		B_2	B_0	B_0	B_2	B_2
B_3	B_3	B_3	B_3	B_3		B_3	B_0	B_1	B_2	B_3

sum of two real numbers x and y as $x + y$. Also in set theory the union of two sets A and B is written as $A \cup B$.

Now we discuss some general properties of binary operations. For this purpose we shall consider X to be any set.

Definition 2-4.9 A binary operation $f: X \times X \to X$ is said to be *commutative* if for every $x, y \in X$,

$$f \langle x, y \rangle = f \langle y, x \rangle$$

Definition 2-4.10 A binary operation $f: X \times X \to X$ is said to be *associative* if for every $x, y, z \in X$,

$$f \langle f \langle x, y \rangle, z \rangle = f \langle x, f \langle y, z \rangle \rangle$$

Definitions 2-4.9 and 2-4.10 can be rewritten using $*$ to denote the binary relation on X. That is, $*$ is commutative if for any $x, y \in X$, $x * y = y * x$. Similarly $*$ is associative on X if for any $x, y, z \in X$,

$$(x * y) * z = x * (y * z)$$

Definition 2-4.11 A binary operation $f: X \times X \to X$ is said to be *distributive* over the operation $g: X \times X \to X$ if for every $x, y, z \in X$

$$f \langle x, g \langle y, z \rangle \rangle = g \langle f \langle x, y \rangle, f \langle x, z \rangle \rangle$$

If we denote f by $*$ and g by $\circ$ we say $*$ is distributive over $\circ$ if for any $x, y, z \in X$

$$x * (y \circ z) = (x * y) \circ (x * z)$$

The operations of addition and multiplication over the set of real numbers are commutative and associative. Union and intersection over the power set of any set are other examples of commutative and associative operations. The operation of subtraction over the set of real numbers is not commutative. It was also shown that the composition of bijective functions from a set X to X is not commutative. The operation of multiplication is distributive over that of addition. Both union and intersection of sets distribute over each other.

Given a binary operation $*$ on a set X, we now define certain distinguished elements of X which are associated with the operation. Such elements may or may not exist.

Definition 2-4.12 Let $*$ be a binary operation on X. If there exists an element $e_l \in X$ such that $e_l * x = x$ for every $x \in X$, then e_l is called a *left identity* with respect to $*$. Similarly, if there exists an element $e_r \in X$ such that $x * e_r = x$ for every $x \in X$, then e_r is called a *right identity* with respect to $*$.

We now give a theorem which relates left and right identities if both of them exist.

Theorem 2-4.3 Let $*$ be a binary operation, and let e_l and e_r be left and right identities with respect to $*$. Then $e_l = e_r = e$ (say), such that $e * x = x * e = x$ for every $x \in X$, and in such a case $e \in X$ is unique and is called the *identity* with respect to $*$.

PROOF Since e_l and e_r are left and right identities,

$$e_l * e_r = e_l = e_r$$

Next, let us assume e_1 and e_2 are two distinct identities. Then

$$e_1 * e_2 = e_1 = e_2$$

which is a contradiction; hence an identity, if it exists, is unique.   ////

For a commutative binary operation, a left identity is also a right identity, and hence any left or right identity is the identity.

The element 0 is the identity for addition, and 1 is the identity for multiplication over a set of real numbers. Similarly the empty set $\varnothing$ is the identity for the operation of union, and the universal set E is the identity for the operation of intersection over the subsets of a universal set. The identity mapping defined in Sec. 2-4.3 is the identity with respect to composition of bijective functions from a set X to X. A contradiction, i.e., an identically false statement, is an identity for disjunction, while a tautology is an identity for conjunction of statements.

Definition 2-4.13 Let $*$ be a binary operation on X. If there exists an element $0_l \in X$ such that $0_l * x = 0_l$ for every $x \in X$, then 0_l is called a *left zero* with respect to $*$. Similarly, if there exists an element $0_r \in X$ such that $x * 0_r = 0_r$ for every $x \in X$, then 0_r is called a *right zero* with respect to $*$.

A theorem similar to Theorem 2-4.3 can now be given.

Theorem 2-4.4 Let $*$ be a binary operation, and 0_l and 0_r be left and right zeros with respect to $*$. Then $0_l = 0_r = 0$ such that

$$0 * x = x * 0 = 0 \qquad \text{for all } x \in X$$

$0 \in X$ is unique and is called the *zero* with respect to $*$.

The element 0 is the zero for multiplication on a set of real numbers. The empty set $\varnothing$ is the zero for intersection, and the universal set E is the zero for the union of subsets of a universal set.

Definition 2-4.14 Let $*$ be a binary operation on X. An element $a \in X$ is called *idempotent* with respect to $*$ if $a * a = a$.

The identity and zero elements with respect to a binary operation are idempotent. There may be other idempotent elements besides the identity and zero elements. For example, every set is idempotent with respect to the operations of union and intersection.

Definition 2-4.15 Let $*$ be a binary operation on X with the identity e. An element $a \in X$ is said to be *left-invertible* if there exists an element $x_l \in X$ such that $x_l * a = e$. x_l is called a *left inverse* of a. Similarly, $a \in X$ is said to be *right-invertible* if there exists an element $x_r \in X$ such that $a * x_r = e$. x_r is called a *right inverse* of a. If an element $a \in X$ is both left-invertible and right-invertible, then a is called *invertible*.

Obviously, if a binary operation $*$ on X with the identity e is commutative, then any element that is left- or right-invertible is invertible. For operations which are associative, we can prove the following theorem.

Theorem 2-4.5 Let $*$ be a binary operation on X which is associative and which has the identity $e \in X$. If an element $a \in X$ is invertible, then both its left and right inverses are equal. Such an element is called the inverse of a because it is unique.

PROOF Let x_l and x_r be any left and right inverses of a respectively. We show that $x_l = x_r$ as follows.

$$x_l * a = a * x_r = e$$

hence

$$x_l * a * x_r = (x_l * a) * x_r = x_l * (a * x_r) = e * x_r = x_r = x_l * e = x_l$$

Here we have used the associativity of the operation $*$.

To show uniqueness, let us assume that x and y are two distinct inverses of a. Thus

$$y = y * e = y * (a * x) = (y * a) * x = e * x = x$$

which is a contradiction. ////

The unique inverse of an element $a \in X$, if it exists, is denoted by a^{-1}, so that

$$a^{-1} * a = a * a^{-1} = e$$

From symmetry it follows that $(a^{-1})^{-1} = a$.

In any binary operation the identity element, if it exists, is invertible. Since it is also idempotent, the identity is its own inverse. Other invertible elements may or may not exist. For example, every real number $a \in \mathbf{R}$ has an inverse $-a \in \mathbf{R}$ for the operation of addition. Similarly, for the operation of multiplication, the inverse of every nonzero real number $a \in \mathbf{R}$ is $1/a \in \mathbf{R}$. For a set A which is a subset of a universal set, the set A is idempotent for the operations of union as well as intersection. In Example 2 of Sec. 2-4.3, all the functions are invertible for the operation of composition. It may be noted that a zero element with respect to an operation cannot be invertible.

Definition 2-4.16 An element $a \in X$ is called *cancellable* with respect to a binary operation $*$ on X, if for every $x, y \in X$,

$$(a * x = a * y) \lor (x * a = y * a) \Rightarrow (x = y)$$

If the operation $*$ is associative and the element $a \in X$ is invertible, then a is cancellable. However, there are cases where an element is cancellable but not necessarily invertible. For example, in the set of integers any nonzero integer is cancellable with respect to the operation of multiplication, although the only integer which is invertible is the identity, that is, 1.

The properties of binary operations given here are used in Chaps. 3 and 4. We have not discussed n-ary operations in general because we will be most concerned with unary and binary operations.

Given a set X and a binary operation $*$ on X, we have represented the value of the binary operation $*$ on any two elements $x, y \in X$ by writing $x * y$. Since $x * y \in X$, we may again apply the same or any other binary operation, say $+$, on $x * y$ and an element of X, say z. Obviously the following possibilities exist:

$$(x * y) * z \qquad z * (x * y) \qquad (x * y) + z \qquad z + (x * y)$$

The parentheses have been used in the usual sense to indicate that in all these cases $x * y$ is obtained first. If the operation $*$ is associative, then $(x * y) * z = x * (y * z)$, and we may drop the parentheses. In other words, the order in which the two binary operations are carried out is not important. Sometimes the parentheses are dropped even though the operation is not associative. In such cases, a convention is adopted regarding the order in which the operations are performed. For example, in a computer program using FORTRAN, A + B + C is understood to be (A + B) + C. Note that (A + B) + C may not be equal to A + (B + C) due to rounding-off operations on a computer. In any case, we say that the operation $+$ is assumed to be left-associative. In the case of the assignment A ← B, we understand A ← (B ← C), that is, the operation is right-associative. Similarly for a logical expression $\neg\neg P$, it is assumed that we have $\neg(\neg P)$, where $\neg P$ is formed first. Since subtraction is not associative, we write (A − B) − C as distinct from A − (B − C). However, in FORTRAN A − B − C is understood to mean (A − B) − C, and so subtraction is left-associative. It is very important to know whether an operation is understood to be left- or right-associative. This need to know is greater in the case of programming languages than in mathematics where parentheses are always used except when an operation is associative.

EXERCISES   2-4.4

1   Let $g: \mathbf{I} \times \mathbf{I} \to \mathbf{I}$ where $\mathbf{I}$ is the set of integers and

$$g \langle x, y \rangle = x * y = x + y - xy$$

Show that the binary operation $*$ is commutative and associative. Find the identity element and indicate the inverse of each element.

2   Let $*$ denote a binary operation on the set of natural numbers given by $x * y = x$. Show that $*$ is not commutative, but is associative. Which elements are idempotent? Are there any left or right identities?

3   Let $x * y =$ lowest common multiple of x and y, where $*$ is a binary operation on the set of positive integers. Show that $*$ is commutative and associative. Find the identity element and also state which elements are idempotent.

4   Let $\mathbf{I}_p = \{0, 1, 2, \ldots, p - 1\}$. The operations $+_p$ and $*_p$ are given by $x +_p y = (x + y) \pmod p$ and $x *_p y = xy \pmod p$. Give composition tables for these operations for $p = 3$ and 4. Indicate the identity and zero elements. Does the operation $*_p$ distribute over $+_p$?

5   Show that $x * y = x - y$ is not a binary operation over the set of natural numbers, but that it is a binary operation on the set of integers. Is it commutative or associative?

6   Show that $x * y = x^y$ is a binary operation on the set of positive integers. Determine whether $*$ is commutative or associative.

7   How many distinct binary operations are there on the set $\{0, 1\}$? Give their composition tables and indicate which ones are commutative or associative. Can you determine the number of distinct binary operations on any finite set?

2-4.5   Characteristic Function of a Set

In this section we shall discuss functions from the universal set E to the set $\{0, 1\}$. These functions are associated with sets in the same way as the principle of specification given in Sec. 2-1.7. A one-to-one correspondence is established between these functions and the sets. With the use of these functions, statements about sets and their operations can be represented on a computer in terms of binary numbers; hence their manipulation becomes easier.

Definition 2-4.17   Let E be a universal set and A be a subset of E. The function $\psi_A: E \to \{0, 1\}$ defined by

$$\psi_A(x) = \begin{cases} 1 & \text{if } x \in A \\ 0 & \text{if } x \notin A \end{cases}$$

is called the *characteristic function* of the set A.

As an example, let E be the set of all persons living in Toronto and let F be the set of all females in Toronto. Then ψ_F associates the number 1 with each female and 0 with each male in Toronto.

The following properties suggest how one can use the characteristic functions of sets to determine set relations.

Let A and B be any two subsets of a universal set E. Then the following hold for all $x \in E$.

$$\psi_A(x) = 0 \Leftrightarrow A = \varnothing \tag{1}$$

$$\psi_A(x) = 1 \Leftrightarrow A = E \tag{2}$$

$$\psi_A(x) \leq \psi_B(x) \Leftrightarrow A \subseteq B \tag{3}$$

$$\psi_A(x) = \psi_B(x) \Leftrightarrow A = B \tag{4}$$

$$\psi_{A \cap B}(x) = \psi_A(x) * \psi_B(x) \tag{5}$$

$$\psi_{A \cup B}(x) = \psi_A(x) + \psi_B(x) - \psi_{A \cap B}(x) \tag{6}$$

$$\psi_{\sim A}(x) = 1 - \psi_A(x) \tag{7}$$

$$\psi_{A-B}(x) = \psi_{A \cap \sim B}(x) = \psi_A(x) - \psi_{A \cap B}(x) \tag{8}$$

Note that the operations $\leq$, $=$, $+$, $*$, and $-$ used with the characteristic functions are the usual arithmetic operations because the values of the characteristic functions are always either 1 or 0. On the other hand, the equality used for sets is the usual set equality. Other set operations used above are $\cup$, $\cap$, $\sim$, and $-$. The above properties can easily be proved using the definition of characteristic functions. For example, (5) can be proved as follows:

$x \in A \cap B \Leftrightarrow x \in A \wedge x \in B$, so that $\psi_A(x) = 1$ and $\psi_B(x) = 1$ and $\psi_{A \cap B}(x) = 1 * 1 = 1$. If $x \notin A \cap B$, then $\psi_{A \cap B}(x) = 0$ and $\psi_A(x) = 0$ or $\psi_B(x) = 0$. Consequently $\psi_A(x) * \psi_B(x) = 0$.

Many set identities and other relations can be proved by using characteristic functions and the usual arithmetic operations and relations.

EXAMPLE 1 Show that $A \cap (B \cup C) = (A \cap B) \cup (A \cap C)$.

SOLUTION

$$
\begin{aligned}
\psi_{A \cap (B \cup C)}(x) &= \psi_A(x) * \psi_{B \cup C}(x) && \text{(using 5)} \\
&= \psi_A(x)(\psi_B(x) + \psi_C(x) - \psi_{B \cap C}(x)) && \text{(using 6)} \\
&= \psi_A(x) * \psi_B(x) + \psi_A(x) * \psi_C(x) \\
&\quad - \psi_A(x) * \psi_{B \cap C}(x) \\
&= \psi_{A \cap B}(x) + \psi_{A \cap C}(x) - \psi_{A \cap (B \cap C)}(x) && \text{(using 5)} \\
&= \psi_{A \cap B}(x) + \psi_{A \cap C}(x) - \psi_{A \cap B \cap C}(x) \\
&= \psi_{A \cap B}(x) + \psi_{A \cap C}(x) - \psi_{(A \cap B) \cap (A \cap C)}(x) \\
&= \psi_{(A \cap B) \cup (A \cap C)}(x) && \text{(using 6)} \qquad ////
\end{aligned}
$$

EXAMPLE 2 Show that $\sim\sim A = A$.

SOLUTION

$$
\begin{aligned}
\psi_{\sim\sim A}(x) &= 1 - \psi_{\sim A}(x) \\
&= 1 - (1 - \psi_A(x)) && \text{(using 7)} \\
&= \psi_A(x) && \qquad ////
\end{aligned}
$$

The notation used for naming the subsets of a finite set introduced earlier in Sec. 2-1.3 can now be explained by using the characteristic function. Consider $E = \{a, b, c\}$. The subsets of E are $\varnothing$, $\{a\}$, $\{b\}$, $\{c\}$, $\{a, b\}$, $\{a, c\}$, $\{b, c\}$, and $\{a, b, c\}$. The values of the characteristic functions of these subsets are given in Table 2-4.3. The values of the characteristic function of any of the subsets of E consist of three binary digits or binary triples. If we let

$$B = \{000, 001, 010, 011, 100, 101, 110, 111\}$$

then Table 2-4.3 can be considered as a mapping from the power set of E to B. This mapping is one-to-one and onto and hence describes a one-to-one correspondence between the sets $\rho(E)$ and B. The elements of B were used to denote the corresponding subsets.

Consider a universal set E and a mapping f from the set E to a finite set $\{a_1, a_2, \ldots, a_n\}$ where $a_1, a_2, \ldots, a_n$ are all distinct. Let A_1 be the set of elements of E such that $f(x) = a_1$ for $x \in A_1$. Similarly define the subsets $A_2, A_3, \ldots, A_n$ of E. Obviously, $A_1, A_2, \ldots, A_n$ are all disjoint; in addition, $A_1 \cup A_2 \cup \cdots \cup A_n = E$, that is, $A_1, A_2, \ldots, A_n$ are the blocks of a partition of E. It is possible to write

$$f(x) = \sum_{i=1}^{n} a_i * \psi_{A_i}(x)$$

A function $f(x)$ which has a finite set of possible values is called a *simple function*. Obviously the range of a simple function is a finite set. It is possible to extend the above description to functions which have countably infinite distinct values.

Finally, we consider the characteristic functions of certain sets which were called minterms, or complete intersections in Sec. 2-3.4. It was noted that the minterms generated by a finite number of sets define a partition of the universal set. Let $X_1, X_2, \ldots, X_n$ be any n subsets of a universal set E and let $I_0, I_1, \ldots, I_{2^n-1}$ be the minterms or complete intersections of $X_1, X_2, \ldots, X_n$. Any element $x \in E$ is a member of only one of the minterms. If $x \in I_j$, then $\psi_{I_j}(x) = 1$ and $\psi_{I_m}(x) = 0$ for $m \neq j$. This statement holds for any $x \in I_j$. Now let us form a new set, say F, from the sets $X_1, \ldots, X_n$ by using the operations of union, intersection, and complementation. Then the characteristic function of F will remain constant over the sets of minterms.

2-4.6 Hashing Functions

In Sec. 2-2.5 we introduced terms such as "file," "record," "field," etc., which are used frequently in connection with the storage of information on a computer. An example of a file is the symbol table of a compiler or an assembler which con-

Table 2-4.3

x	$\varnothing$	$\{a\}$	$\{b\}$	$\{c\}$	$\{a, b\}$	$\{a, c\}$	$\{b, c\}$	$\{a, b, c\}$
a	0	1	0	0	1	1	0	1
b	0	0	1	0	1	0	1	1
c	0	0	0	1	0	1	1	1

tains variable names, labels, and literals, together with any associated values (addresses and values of variables or literals). Each entry in a symbol table can be considered as a record. In this section we discuss some aspects of file organization that require the insertion, deletion, and searching of records in a file. Hashing functions are introduced during the course of this discussion. A familiarity with the characteristics of magnetic tape and also with direct-access storage devices such as magnetic drum, disk, etc., is assumed.

In the case of a magnetic tape, we know that binary-encoded information can be read from or written on a tape as the tape moves past a stationary read/write head. Records are stored consecutively on a tape and are accessed by skip-forward, skip-backward, or rewind operations. Although computer tape units read and write at high speeds, there are certain disadvantages associated with their use. For example, the process of locating a particular record is time-consuming. On the other hand, for direct- (or random-) access storage devices, a particular location where data are stored has a unique address and hence can be accessed rapidly.

In the files that we consider here and more generally, each record contains a field which is designated as a *key* to that record. The key has a value that identifies a record and thus is an indication of where a record is stored or found in computer storage. For example, in a student history file, a field which represents a student number in each student record could be treated as a key. Such a key could also be used to specify an ordering on the student records.

Let us first consider sequential files in which the records are stored in successive physical locations of memory or a storage device. In fact, this restriction is necessary for files stored on magnetic tape or punched cards. Such a file may be unsorted or sorted. Here "sorting" means ordering the records in some way by using the key values. If a file is unsorted, then a record can be inserted very easily at one end, but deleting a record is not as simple. If it is desired to access a particular record according to its key, then the file must be searched sequentially from its beginning until that record is found. The average time to complete such a search is proportional to $n/2$ where n is the number of records in the file. This process is very time-consuming, and an alternative procedure known as *binary search* could be used to reduce the search time.

In order to use the binary search procedure, it is necessary that the records in a sequential file be stored according to an alphabetically or numerically increasing order of the keys. We shall assume that such is the case. Now, given a key value of a particular record to be searched, first the middle record of the file is located, and then the value of its key is compared with that of the record under consideration. If the value of the key is the same as that of the middle record, then the search is complete. If the value of the key is less than that of the middle record, then the first half of the file is examined by repeatedly using the same procedure until the record is located. On the other hand, if the value of the key is greater than that of the middle record, the second half of the file is searched in the same way. The average time for a binary search is proportional to $\log_2 n$, which is a considerable improvement over the time required for a linear search on an unordered file. This improvement is significant when n is large. For small n, the work involved in ordering and the complexity of programming may not justify a binary search. Further, a binary search is not suitable when a file is stored on magnetic tape, because the time taken to skip forward and backward to the midpoint several times during the search would be considerable.

Although a record insertion in an unordered file is an easy task, it becomes complicated in the case of an ordered sequential file. Deletions from a sequential file are time-consuming both in an ordered and in an unordered file.

From this discussion it appears that sequential files are not suitable from the point of view of organization because, of three operations—deletion, insertion, and search—only one can be performed efficiently on either an ordered or an unordered file. However, there are many data processing applications which require sequential processing of records in a file. As an example, consider the case in which a master file of records is updated from a transaction file, which has been ordered in the same way as the master file. In such cases, magnetic tape and punched card storage are quite efficient.

An alternative to sequential processing is random processing, in which the records in a file are processed in any order. Direct organization of files can be used in this type of processing. In direct organization, the address of a record is obtained by performing some reproducible arithmetic or logical operation on the internal bit representation of its key. Any transformation which maps the internal bit representation of the set of keys to a set of addresses is called a *hashing function*. Various hashing functions are available. Two commonly used hashing functions are obtained by what are known as the division method and the mid-square method.

Before we describe the hashing function obtained by the division method, note that every key has a binary representation, which may be treated as a binary number. Let this numerical value of a key be denoted by k, and let n be a fixed integer (preferably prime) which is suitably chosen. Then the hashing function h defined by the division method is

$$h(k) = k \ (\text{mod } n)$$

that is, $h(k)$ is the remainder of dividing k by n and is therefore an element of $\{0, 1, \ldots, n - 1\}$. Thus the hashing function maps the set of keys to the set of n addresses, viz., the set $\{0, 1, \ldots, n - 1\}$, which may be called the address set. The choice of n depends upon the fact that a good hashing function should uniformly distribute the records over the elements of the address set.

A hashing function quite often maps different keys to the same element of the address set. Thus the set of records is partitioned into n equivalence classes. Those records which are mapped to the same address are in the same equivalence class. It is therefore necessary to provide storage space for and also a method of finding the "colliding" or "overflow" records when more than one record has the same address. There are many techniques, called *collision resolution techniques*, for this purpose. One method, called *open addressing*, probes possible addresses in some reproducible order and inserts the colliding record at the first empty location found. The data structure used in this case would be a vector, each element of which is capable of holding a record. There are many variations of this basic concept. Another method known as *chaining* uses a linear linked list to represent each equivalence class in memory. In other words, a one-to-one correspondence is established between the equivalence classes and linked lists.

An algorithm for inserting a record in a directly organized file which uses chaining would proceed as follows. First the key of the record is mapped into an address using a hashing function. In this sense, the record belongs to an equivalence class. Corresponding to the equivalence class there is a linked list of that class. If the record is not already in the linked list of that class, then it is added to the end of the list. The search for or the deletion of a record can be performed in a similar manner.

We can achieve greater efficiency (in terms of speed, not required storage) with direct organization of files than with sequentially organized files if we make proper choices of hashing functions and collision resolution techniques. The importance of a suitable hashing function cannot be overemphasized. Ideally, it would be desirable to have a function which results in all equivalence classes having an equal number of records. The worst possible case is the one where all key values would be mapped into the same number (one equivalence class), thereby causing the insertion and fetching algorithms to be no more efficient than those in a linear search method. It is a nontrivial matter to obtain the "proper" hashing function, since the size of the equivalence classes which it induces depends on the key values being used (i.e., on the domain of the function). The functions used should not be too complex since the time taken to evaluate the function for a particular argument must be added to the insertion and fetch times. It is usually possible to live within this constraint because of the computer's great speed in doing arithmetic computations.

Another important factor in attaining reasonable efficiency is keeping the size of each equivalence class relatively small, but at the same time keeping the memory requirements to a minimum. For example, if it is known that, on an average, a file will have 125 entries at any given time, then one would ideally want approximately 125 equivalence classes. In such a case, the average number of comparisons necessary for accessing an entry would be no more than 2.

As mentioned earlier in this subsection, a symbol table is an example of a file. We shall now discuss by means of an example how variable names and labels can be inserted into a symbol table. Due to the random nature of insertions, the direct organization of files may best be applied. The division hashing function will be used together with the chaining method previously described. To simplify the discussion, the values associated with the entries in the symbol table will be omitted.

As an example, assume that the hashing function gives the following results:

The names AB12, LL, F, and LLLL are all mapped into the number 0.

The names A1 and DDCC are all mapped into the number 2.

The names B2 and AA are all mapped into the number 4.

The names VV and B are all mapped into the number 6.

The name C is mapped into the number 7.

Let us use a one-dimensional array called *EQUIV* consisting of 100 elements. Each element of *EQUIV* contains the address of the first node of the linked list representing a particular equivalence class. If there are no names in a certain

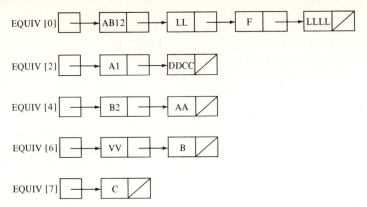

FIGURE 2-4.9

```
HASHING:
     PROCEDURE OPTIONS(MAIN);
/*THIS PROGRAM BUILDS A DICTIONARY OF NAMES CONSISTING OF 1 TO 12
  ALPHANUMERIC CHARACTERS.  EACH NAME IS HASHED INTO AN INTEGER
  WHICH IS BETWEEN 0 AND N-1 INCLUSIVE AND DENOTES TO WHICH OF N
  POSSIBLE EQUIVALENCE CLASSES NAME BELONGS.  PROCEDURE ENTER PUTS
  NAME IN THE SYMBOL FIELD OF A NODE WHICH IS PLACED AT THE END OF
  ONE OF THE LISTS POINTED TO BY AN ELEMENT OF THE POINTER ARRAY
  EQUIV.                                                        */
     DECLARE
          1 RECORD BASED(NEW),
               2 SYMBOL CHARACTER(12),
               2 LINK POINTER,
            NAME CHARACTER(12) VARYING,
            (I,N) BINARY FIXED,
            PTR POINTER;
     GET LIST(N); /* READ NUMBER OF EQUIVALENCE CLASSES */
BEGIN; /* AUTOMATIC STORAGE ALLOCATION */
     DECLARE
          HASH RETURNS(BINARY FIXED),
          EQUIV(0:N - 1) POINTER;
     ON ENDFILE(SYSIN) GO TO OUTPUT;
     DO I = 0 TO N - 1;
          EQUIV(I) = NULL;
     END;
     PUT EDIT('NAME','HASHED INTO')(X(30),A(20),A(11));
READ:  /* GET NEXT NAME FOR DICTIONARY*/
     GET LIST(NAME);
     CALL ENTER; /* INSERT NAME IN DICTIONARY*/
     GO TO READ;
OUTPUT: /* OUTPUT CONTENTS OF EACH EQUIVALENCE CLASS */
     DO I = 0 TO N - 1;
          PUT SKIP(2) EDIT('EQUIVALENCE CLASS NUMBER ',I)(X(30),A(25),
                                                          F(2));
          PTR = EQUIV(I); /* SCAN LIST */
          DO WHILE (PTR ¬= NULL);
               PUT SKIP EDIT(PTR->SYMBOL)(X(41),A(12));
               PTR = PTR->LINK;
          END;
     END;
```

FIGURE 2-4.10 PL/I program demonstrating a hashing function.

equivalence class, then the corresponding element in the array *EQUIV* has a value of *NULL*. For the equivalence class consisting of the names AB12, LL, F, and LLLL which are mapped into zero, the diagram in Fig. 2-4.9 gives the structures. The other classes are also given.

We now turn to the formulation of an insertion algorithm for the symbol-table system.

```
ENTER:
        PROCEDURE;
/*EACH ELEMENT OF ARRAY EQUIV IS A POINTER TO A LIST OF NAMES WHICH
 HAVE BEEN MAPPED INTO THE EQUIVALENCE CLASS REFERENCED BY THE
 SUBSCRIPT OF THE ELEMENT.  THIS PROCEDURE PUTS NAME IN A NODE AT THE
 END OF THE LIST WHICH BELONGS TO THE EQUIVALENCE CLASS DENOTED
 BY THE INTEGER RANDOM.*/
        DECLARE
            POINTER POINTER,
        RANDOM BINARY FIXED;
        RANDOM = HASH(NAME); /*COMPUTE THE HASH NUMBER*/
        PUT SKIP EDIT(NAME,RANDOM)(X(30),A(25),F(2));
        IF EQUIV(RANDOM) = NULL
        THEN /* EQUIVALENCE CLASS IS EMPTY */
            DO;
                ALLOCATE RECORD;
                EQUIV(RANDOM) = NEW;
                NEW->SYMBOL = NAME;
                NEW->LINK = NULL;
                RETURN;
            END;
        POINTER = EQUIV(RANDOM); /* INITIATE SEARCH FOR NAME */
SEARCH: /* OF LIST FOR AN OCCURRENCE OF NAME */
        IF POINTER->SYMBOL = NAME THEN RETURN;
        IF POINTER->LINK = NULL
        THEN /* INSERT A NEW NODE */
            DO;
                ALLOCATE RECORD;
                NEW->SYMBOL = NAME;
                POINTER->LINK = NEW;
                NEW->LINK = NULL;
                RETURN;
            END;
        POINTER = POINTER->LINK; /* CONTINUE SEARCH */
        GO TO SEARCH;
END ENTER;

HASH: /* MAP NAME TO A NUMBER BETWEEN 0 AND N-1 */
        PROCEDURE(NAME) RETURNS(BINARY FIXED);
        DECLARE
            NAME CHARACTER(12) VARYING,
            BITNAME BIT(96) VARYING,
            NUMBER BINARY FIXED(31);
        BITNAME=UNSPEC(NAME); /* OBTAIN BIT REPRESENTATION OF NAME */
        IF LENGTH(BITNAME) > 24
        THEN NUMBER = SUBSTR(BITNAME,2,32);
        ELSE NUMBER = BITNAME;
        RETURN(MOD(NUMBER,N));
END HASH;

END; /* OF BEGIN BLOCK */

END HASHING;
```

FIGURE 2-4.10   (Continued)

Algorithm *ENTER* (Enters a new name in a symbol table) Given a one-dimensional reference array *EQUIV*, each element of which contains a pointer to an equivalence class, and a hashing function *HASH*, which maps a name into an integer, it is required to append the entry denoted by *NAME* to the end of the appropriate equivalence class (if it is not already there). The typical node in the list representing an equivalence class consists of an information field and a link field denoted by *SYMBOL* and *LINK* respectively. This node structure is referred to as *RECORD*.

    1 [Compute the hash number] Set $RANDOM \leftarrow HASH(NAME)$.

    2 [Is the equivalence class empty?] If $EQUIV[RANDOM] \neq NULL$ then go to step 4.

    3 [Enter *NAME* in empty class] Set $NEW \leftarrow RECORD,\ EQUIV$

$[RANDOM] \leftarrow NEW, SYMBOL(NEW) \leftarrow NAME, LINK(NEW) \leftarrow NULL$, and Exit.

    4   [Initiate search for $NAME$] Set $POINTER \leftarrow EQUIV[RANDOM]$.

    5   [Begin search] If $SYMBOL(POINTER) = NAME$ then Exit.

    6   [End of equivalence class?] If $LINK(POINTER) = NULL$ then set $NEW \leftarrow RECORD, SYMBOL(NEW) \leftarrow NAME, LINK(POINTER) \leftarrow NEW, LINK(NEW) \leftarrow NULL$, and Exit; otherwise set $POINTER \leftarrow LINK(POINTER)$ and go to step 5.   ////

NAME	HASHED INTO
ABSOLUTE	5
C	8
DEFINED	5
ENTER	7
POINTER	4
NEW	10
SYMBOL	4
LINK	5
HASHING	7
RANDOM	3
MOD	7
NAME	3
END	1
ENTER	7
EQUIVALENCE	9
POINTER	4
X	0
Y	1
Z	2

```
EQUIVALENCE CLASS NUMBER  0
              X

EQUIVALENCE CLASS NUMBER  1
              END
              Y

EQUIVALENCE CLASS NUMBER  2
              Z

EQUIVALENCE CLASS NUMBER  3
              RANDOM
              NAME

EQUIVALENCE CLASS NUMBER  4
              POINTER
              SYMBOL

EQUIVALENCE CLASS NUMBER  5
              ABSOLUTE
              DEFINED
              LINK

EQUIVALENCE CLASS NUMBER  6

EQUIVALENCE CLASS NUMBER  7
              ENTER
              HASHING
              MOD

EQUIVALENCE CLASS NUMBER  8
              C

EQUIVALENCE CLASS NUMBER  9
              EQUIVALENCE

EQUIVALENCE CLASS NUMBER  10
              NEW
```

FIGURE 2-4.10 (Continued)

The previous algorithm is reasonably simple and requires no further comment.

The PL/I program in Fig. 2-4.10 constructs a symbol table. It consists of a hashing function, a procedure based on the preceding algorithm, and a mainline program. The hashing function finds the remainder on dividing the bit representation (obtained by using UNSPEC) of NAME by N. If NAME contains more than three characters, then only the first three are used in the process. The MOD function is used to find the remainder when NUMBER is divided by N.

The main program is written so that up to 25 equivalence classes can be handled in the symbol table. Each name to be inserted is on one input card. On an end-of-file, control transfers to the statement labeled OUTPUT. At this point, each simple linked list representing an equivalence class is scanned, and each name in it is printed.

EXERCISES 2-4.6

1 The midsquare hashing method follows:
  (*a*) Square part of the key, or the whole key if possible.
  (*b*) Either (1) extract n digits from the middle of the result to give $h(\text{key}) \in \{0, 1, \ldots, 10^n - 1\}$, or (2) extract n bits from the middle of the result to give $h(\text{key}) \in \{0, 1, \ldots, 2^n - 1\}$.
  Write a program which uses this procedure to hash a set of variable names. The midsquare method frequently gives satisfactory results, but in many cases the keys are unevenly distributed over the required range.

2 A hashing method often implemented, called *folding*, is performed by dividing the key into several parts and adding the parts to form a number in the required range. For example, if we have 8-digit keys and wish to obtain a 3-digit address, we may do the following:

$$h(97434658) = 974 + 346 + 58 = 378$$
$$h(31269857) = 312 + 698 + 57 = 67$$

Note that the final carry is ignored.
  Implement this method in a computer program.

3 Compare the results of applying the division, midsquare, and folding hashing functions to a fixed set of keys. Make sure the range is the same or almost the same in each case. Which method distributes the keys most evenly over the elements of the range?

EXERCISES 2-4

1 Show that

$$f(A \cup B) = f(A) \cup f(B)$$
$$f(A \cap B) \subseteq f(A) \cap f(B)$$

Construct an example to show that in general it is not possible to replace $\subseteq$ by $=$ in the second relation. Under what condition will $f(A \cap B) = f(A) \cap f(B)$?

2 Show that $f: X \rightarrow Y$ is one-to-one iff any proper subsets of X are mapped into proper subsets of Y; that is, if $A \subset B \subseteq X$, then $f(A) \subset f(B) \subseteq Y$.

3 Let $\mathbf{I}_p = \{0, 1, \ldots, p - 1\}$ and $f_r: \mathbf{I}_p \rightarrow \mathbf{I}_p$ be given by

$$f_r(x) = rx \;(\mathrm{mod}\; p)$$

where $r = 0, 1, \ldots, p - 1$. Show that f is not bijective for any r unless p is prime.

4 Determine the set of all bijective mappings on the set $\{1, 2\}$. Determine the identity element and inverses of each element under the composition of functions on this set.

5 Let $f: \mathbf{R} \rightarrow \mathbf{R}$ be given by $f(x) = x^2$ and $g: \mathbf{R} - \{2\} \rightarrow \mathbf{R}$ be given by $g(x) = x/(x - 2)$. Find $f \circ g$. Is $g \circ f$ defined?

6 Let X be a set and $\rho(X)$ its power set. Show that the operations of union and intersection on $\rho(X)$ are both associative and commutative. Also every element of $\rho(X)$ is idempotent under these operations. Determine the zeroes, and show that the operations distribute over each other.

7 Show that the operation of symmetric difference $\triangle$ defined by

$$A \triangle B = (A \cup B) - (A \cap B)$$

is commutative and associative and has an identity element. Show that the inverse of A is A itself. Show that the operation of intersection, but not that of union, distributes over $\triangle$.

8 Consider the set $\mathbf{I}_+$ of positive integers and let $\mathbf{N}$ be the set of natural numbers (including zero). Observe that for any $x \in \mathbf{I}_+$ we have

$$x = 2^r(2s + 1)$$

for some r, s $\mathbf{N}$. This means that we can define a mapping $f: \mathbf{I}_+ \rightarrow \mathbf{N} \times \mathbf{N}$ such $f(x) = \langle r, s \rangle$, as indicated above. Show that f is one-to-one onto.

2-5   NATURAL NUMBERS

We are all familiar with the set of natural numbers and many of their properties. In this section we examine the set of natural numbers and introduce a method of generating such a set by starting with the null set and a function called the successor function. We then study some important properties (axioms) of the set of natural numbers. One of the axioms leads us to formulate the principle of mathematical induction. The use of natural numbers for counting enables us to define the notion of similarity, or equipotence, of two sets and the cardinal number of a set. The concepts of finite and infinite sets are introduced. These concepts have important applications in the theory of automata. Later in Chap. 3 we list the operations of addition and multiplication as well as the ordering relation on the set of natural numbers.

2-5.1   Peano Axioms and Mathematical Induction

The set $\mathbf{N} = \{0, 1, 2, 3, \ldots\}$ of natural numbers (including zero) can be generated by starting with a null set $\varnothing$ and the notion of a successor set. A *successor set* of a set A is denoted by A^+ and defined to be the set $A^+ = A \cup \{A\}$.

Let $\varnothing$ be the empty set, and obtain the successor sets $\varnothing^+$, $(\varnothing^+)^+$, $((\varnothing^+)^+)^+$, ... These sets are

$$\varnothing \qquad \varnothing \cup \{\varnothing\} \qquad \varnothing \cup \{\varnothing\} \cup \{\varnothing \cup \{\varnothing\}\} \qquad \varnothing \cup \{\varnothing\} \cup \{\varnothing \cup \{\varnothing\}\}$$
$$\cup \{\varnothing \cup \{\varnothing\} \cup \{\varnothing \cup \{\varnothing\}\}\} \qquad \cdots$$

These sets can be simplified to

$$\varnothing \qquad \{\varnothing\} \qquad \{\varnothing, \{\varnothing\}\} \qquad \{\varnothing, \{\varnothing\}, \{\varnothing, \{\varnothing\}\}\} \qquad \cdots$$

If we rename the set $\varnothing$ as 0, then $\varnothing^+ = 0^+ = \{\varnothing\} = 1$, $1^+ = \{\varnothing, \{\varnothing\}\} = \{0, 1\} = 2$, and $2^+ = \{\varnothing, \{\varnothing\}, \{\varnothing, \{\varnothing\}\}\} = 3, \ldots$, and we get the set $\{0, 1, 2, 3, \ldots\}$ in which each element is a successor set of the previous element except for the element 0 which is assumed to be present. This discussion can be summarized by saying that the set of natural numbers can be obtained from the following axioms, known as Peano axioms.

1 $0 \in \mathbf{N}$ (where $0 = \varnothing$).
2   If $n \in \mathbf{N}$, then $n^+ \in \mathbf{N}$ where $n^+ = n \cup \{n\}$.
3   If a subset $S \subseteq \mathbf{N}$ possesses the properties
     (a) $0 \in S$, and
     (b) if $n \in S$, then $n^+ \in S$
     then $S = \mathbf{N}$.

Property 3 is known as the *minimality property* and asserts the fact that a minimal set satisfying *(a)* and *(b)* is the set of natural numbers. It is convenient to write n^+ as $n + 1$, although we need not necessarily consider $+$ as an operation on $\mathbf{N}$.

Property 3 is also the basis of the *principle of mathematical induction*, which is frequently employed in proofs. We shall put axiom 3 in an equivalent form.

3'   If $P(n)$ is any property (or predicate) defined over the set of natural numbers and *(a)* If $P(0)$ is *true*, *(b)* If $P(m) \Rightarrow P(m^+)$ for any $m \in \mathbf{N}$, then $P(n)$ holds for all $n \in \mathbf{N}$.

It is easy to see the equivalence of 3 and 3' by choosing S in axiom 3 as $S = \{m \in \mathbf{N} \mid P(m)\}$.

The principle of mathematical induction is used in proving a collection of statements which can be put in one-to-one correspondence with the set of natural numbers. It was shown earlier in the theory of inference that a finite set of statements can be proved one after the other by showing $S_1 \Rightarrow S_2$, $S_2 \Rightarrow S_3$, $S_3 \Rightarrow S_4$, and so on. But such a method cannot be justified for an infinite number of statements.

In the formulation of the principle of mathematical induction as given in axiom 3', we began with the element 0. However, this is not necessary as we can start with any natural number n_0. In this case, the conclusion is *true* for all $n \geq n_0$.

We shall give here several examples to illustrate the application of the principle of mathematical induction.

EXAMPLE 1   Show that $n < 2^n$.

     SOLUTION   Let $P(n): n < 2^n$.
(a) For $n = 0$, $P(0): 0 < 2^0 = 1$, so that $P(0)$ is *true*.
(b) For some arbitrary choice of $m \in \mathbf{N}$, assume that $P(m)$ holds, that is, $P(m):$

$m < 2^m$. From this, by adding 1 to both sides, we get

$$m + 1 < 2^m + 1 < 2^m + 2^m = 2^m * 2 = 2^{m+1}$$

which is exactly $P(m + 1)$. So $P(m) \Rightarrow P(m + 1)$. Hence from the principle of mathematical induction, $P(n)$ is *true* for all $n \in \mathbf{N}$. ////

EXAMPLE 2 Show that $2^n < n!$ for $n \geq 4$.

SOLUTION Let $P(n): 2^n < n!$. Obviously $P(1)$, $P(2)$, $P(3)$ are not *true*. We also do not need them to be *true*. Now $P(4): 2^4 = 16 < 4! = 24$, so that $P(4)$ holds. Assume that $P(m)$ holds for any $m > 4$, and so

$$2^m < m!$$

Multiply both sides by 2 to get

$$2 * 2^m = 2^{m+1} < 2(m!) < (m + 1) * (m!) = (m + 1)!$$

This equation means that $P(m + 1)$ holds. Hence $P(n)$ holds for all $n \in \mathbf{N}$ and $n \geq 4$. ////

EXAMPLE 3 Show that

$$B \cup \left(\bigcap_{i=1}^{n} A_i \right) = \bigcap_{i=1}^{n} (B \cup A_i)$$

SOLUTION Let $P(n): B \cup \left(\bigcap_{i=1}^{n} A_i \right) = \bigcap_{i=1}^{n} (B \cup A_i)$

For $n = 2$, $\qquad B \cup (A_1 \cap A_2) = (B \cup A_1) \cap (B \cup A_2)$

which follows from the distributive law of union and intersection. Note that here we are trying to prove that the distributive law holds over the intersection of any number of sets. Assume now that $P(m)$ holds for any m, so that

$$B \cup \left(\bigcap_{i=1}^{m} A_i \right) = \bigcap_{i=1}^{m} (B \cup A_i)$$

Now

$$B \cup \left(\bigcap_{i=1}^{m+1} A_i \right) = B \cup \left(\bigcap_{i=1}^{m} A_i \cap A_{m+1} \right)$$

$$= \left(B \cup \left(\bigcap_{i=1}^{m} A_i \right) \right) \cap (B \cup A_{m+1})$$

using $P(2)$ for sets $\bigcap_{i=1}^{m} A_i$ and A_{m+1}

$$= \left(\bigcap_{i=1}^{m} (B \cup A_i) \right) \cap (B \cup A_{m+1})$$

$$= \bigcap_{i=1}^{m+1} (B \cup A_i)$$

Here we have used the fact that $P(2)$ and $P(m)$ hold, and we have shown that $P(m + 1)$ holds. Hence $P(n)$ is *true* for all n. ////

EXAMPLE 4 Show that $n^3 + 2n$ is divisible by 3.

SOLUTION Let $P(n): n^3 + 2n$ is divisible by 3. Now $P(0): 0$ is divisible by 3, so that $P(0)$ is *true*. Let us assume for any m, $P(m)$ is *true*, that is, $m^3 + 2m$ is divisible by 3.

Now
$$(m + 1)^3 + 2(m + 1) = m^3 + 3m^2 + 3m + 1 + 2m + 2$$
$$= m^3 + 3m^2 + 5m + 3$$
$$= m^3 + 2m + 3(m^2 + m + 1)$$

Since $m^3 + 2m$ is assumed to be divisible by 3 and $3(m^2 + m + 1)$ is also divisible by 3, $(m + 1)^3 + 2(m + 1)$ is divisible by 3; that is, $P(m + 1)$ is true. Hence $P(n)$ is *true* for all $n \in \mathbf{N}$. ////

The definition of well-formed formula given in Sec. 1-2.7 and the definition of cartesian product of n sets in Sec. 2-1.9 were inductive definitions. In general, an inductive definition of a property or set P is given in the following manner.

1 Given a finite set A whose elements have the property P.
2 The elements of a set B, all of which are constructed from A, satisfy the property P.
3 The elements constructed as in (1) and (2) are the only elements satisfying the property P.

In fact, the set of natural numbers is defined in a similar manner. We shall make use of the inductive definition in defining a class of functions known as recursive functions in Sec. 2-6.1.

In general, an inductive definition of a property, or more precisely a set P, consists of three main steps. The first step consists of naming the elements of a set, say A, to be the *basic* elements of P. The next step consists of a set of rules which define how other elements of P can be obtained from the elements of A by means of some n-ary operations. This step is called the *inductive step*. Finally, the last step, which is often omitted, states that P consists of only those elements which are obtained according to steps 1 and 2. It is assumed that all objects in the definition are the elements of a universal set.

The definition of the set $\mathbf{N}$ of natural numbers given here was of this form. Also the definition of well-formed formulas was of this form, in which the inductive step contained the unary operation $\rceil$ and the binary operations $\wedge$, $\vee$, $\rightarrow$, and $\rightleftarrows$.

EXAMPLE 5 Find the set given by the following definition:

1 $3 \in P$.
2 For $x, y \in P$, $x + y \in P$.
3 Only those elements obtained from steps (1) and (2) are in P.

SOLUTION The set P consists of positive integers which are multiples of 3. ////

EXAMPLE 6   Give an inductive definition of the set

$$P = \{2, 3, 4, \ldots\} = \mathbf{N} - \{0, 1\}$$

SOLUTION

1   $2 \in P$ and $3 \in P$.
2   If $x, y \in P$, then $x + y \in P$.
3   Only those elements obtained from steps 1 and 2 are in P.   ////

EXAMPLE 7   Show that all the functions of the form $f(x) = x + a$ for $a \in \mathbf{N}$ are defined by the following. It is assumed that the universal set is $\mathbf{N}$.

1   $I(x) = x$ and $S(x) = x + 1$ are in P.
2   For $f, g \in P$, $f \circ g$ is also in P.
3   Only those functions obtained from steps (1) and (2) are in P.

SOLUTION   It is easy to see by induction that $f(x) = x + a$ is in P, because $I(x) = x + 0$ is in P and if $f_k(x) = x + k$, $k \in \mathbf{N}$, is in P, then $(S \circ f_k)(x) = S(x + k) = (x + k) + 1$ or $f_{k+1}(x)$ is also in P. Hence $f(x) = x + a$ is in P. Now if $f(x) = x + a$ and $g(x) = x + b$, then

$$(f \circ g)(x) = f(x + b) = x + a + b = x + (a + b)$$

which is also of the form $x + a$. This guarantees that step 2 generates only the functions which are required.   ////

EXAMPLE 8   Give an inductive definition of the well-formed formulas of set theory involving the operations $\cap$, $\cup$, and $\sim$.

SOLUTION

1   The symbols $A, B, C, \ldots$ are wff's.
2   (a) If X is a wff, so is $\sim X$.
      (b) If X and Y are wff's, so are $(X \cup Y)$ and $(X \cap Y)$.
3   The only wff's are those obtained by using steps 1 and 2.   ////

2-5.2   Cardinality

In the previous section we were concerned with the generation of the set of natural numbers. We are all familiar with a useful application of the set of natural numbers in counting. This property of natural numbers is used in measuring the "size" of a set and in comparing the "sizes" of any two sets.

The first question that we should examine is how do we count, say the number of people in a room, the number of books on a shelf, or the number of elements in a set. What we do is establish a one-to-one correspondence between the objects to be counted and the set of integers $\{1, 2, 3, \ldots, n\}$. From this correspondence we say that the number of objects is n. We now generalize this concept.

Definition 2-5.1   Two sets A and B are said to be *equipotent* (or *equivalent* or to have the same *cardinality*, or to be *similar*) and written as $A \sim B$ if and only if there is one-to-one correspondence between the elements of A and those of B.

Note that one-to-one correspondence can be established by showing a mapping $f: A \rightarrow B$ which is one-to-one and onto.

EXAMPLE 1   Let $\mathbf{N} = \{0, 1, 2, \ldots\}$ and $\mathbf{N}_2 = \{0, 2, 4, \ldots\}$. Show that $\mathbf{N} \sim \mathbf{N}_2$.

SOLUTION   Let $f: \mathbf{N} \rightarrow \mathbf{N}_2$ be defined by $f(n) = 2n$, $n \in \mathbf{N}$. The function f establishes a one-to-one correspondence between $\mathbf{N}$ and $\mathbf{N}_2$. Hence $\mathbf{N} \sim \mathbf{N}_2$. Note that $\mathbf{N}_2 \subset \mathbf{N}$.   ////

EXAMPLE 2   Let P be the set of all positive real numbers and S be the subset of P given by $S = \{x \mid x \in P \wedge 0 < x < 1\}$. Show that $S \sim P$.

SOLUTION   Let $f: P \rightarrow S$ be defined by $f(x) = x/(1 + x)$ for $x \in P$. Obviously the range of f is in S. Further, for any $y \in S$, we have $x = y/(1 - y)$, so that f is one-to-one and onto.   ////

The one-to-one correspondence established in showing that any two sets are equipotent is not unique. However, any one-to-one correspondence is enough to show that the two sets are equipotent.

It is easy to see that equipotence is an equivalence relation on a family of sets and hence partitions the family of sets into equivalence classes.

Definition 2-5.2   Let F be a family of sets and let $\sim$ denote the relation of equipotence on F. The equivalence classes of F under the relation $\sim$ are called *cardinal numbers*. For any set $A \in F$, the equivalence class to which A belongs is denoted by $[A]$ or $\bar{\bar{A}}$ or Card A and is called the *cardinal number of A*. For $A, B \in F$

$$\bar{\bar{A}} = \bar{\bar{B}} \Leftrightarrow A \sim B$$

We shall now show how the cardinal numbers of some sets can be represented by means of natural numbers. Recall that the natural numbers have been defined as sets, starting from the null set and then constructing the successor sets. The cardinal numbers are also defined as sets. We shall first start with the empty set and denote its cardinal number by 0. For our present discussion, we shall denote the cardinal number of a set A by $k(A)$, so that $k(\varnothing) = 0$. If an element $p \notin A$, where A is some set with the cardinal number $k(A)$, then the cardinal number of the set $A \cup \{p\}$, that is, $k(A \cup \{p\})$, can be written as $[k(A)]^+$ or $k(A) + 1$. This notation is justified by observing that if $A \sim B$, so that $k(A) = k(B)$, and if $p \notin A$ and $q \notin B$, then $k(A \cup \{p\}) = k(B \cup \{q\})$. The last equality follows from the fact that a one-to-one correspondence can be established between the sets $A \cup \{p\}$ and $B \cup \{q\}$. By following this convention, we can build sets starting from the null set and building successive unions such that the cardinalities of these sets can be represented by the natural numbers. For example, let $A_1 = \{a\}$, $A_2 = \{a, b\}$, $A_3 = \{a, b, c\}$, ... We then have

$$A_1 = \{a\} \cup \varnothing \qquad \qquad \text{hence } k(A_1) = 0^+ = 1$$

$$A_2 = \{a, b\} = A_1 \cup \{b\} \qquad \text{hence } k(A_2) = 1^+ = 2$$

$$A_3 = \{a, b, c\} = A_2 \cup \{c\} \qquad \text{hence } k(A_3) = 2^+ = 3$$

and so on. Accordingly, the cardinal number of a set containing n elements can be denoted by the natural number n.

It is not possible to represent the cardinality of every set by means of natural numbers because there are sets which cannot be built up by successive unions, as was done above. In any case, we now have a definition of a finite set as follows.

Definition 2-5.3 Any set whose cardinal number is a natural number is a *finite set*. Also any set which is not finite is called an *infinite set*.

Definition 2-5.4 Any set which is equipotent to the set of natural numbers is called *denumerable*.

The cardinality of a denumerable set is denoted by the symbol $\aleph_0$ called aleph null. We shall restrict the use of $k(A)$ to denote only the cardinality of a finite set A.

Definition 2-5.5 A set is called *countable* if it is finite or denumerable, and a set is called *nondenumerable* if it is infinite and not denumerable.

An important difference between a finite and an infinite set is that no proper subset of a finite set can be equipotent to the set itself, because a one-to-one correspondence between the elements of such sets is impossible. However, for infinite sets this is not necessarily the case, as can be seen from some of the examples given here. Some authors take these as definitions of finite and infinite sets. We shall now prove a theorem about infinite sets which are denumerable.

Theorem 2-5.1 An infinite subset of a denumerable set is also denumerable.

PROOF Let S be an infinite subset of a given denumerable set A. Obviously $A \sim \mathbf{N}$, and there exists a one-to-one correspondence between the elements of A and the set $\mathbf{N}$ of natural numbers. Consequently, we have a function $f: \mathbf{N} \to A$ given by $f(n) = x$ for $x \in A$, which is one-to-one and onto. Thus the elements of A can be arranged as $f(1), f(2), \ldots$. Now, delete from this list those elements which are not present in S. The number of the remaining elements is still infinite because S is infinite. Let us denote these elements by $f(i_1), f(i_2), \ldots$. Define a function $g: \mathbf{N} \to S$ such that $g(n) = f(i_n)$; then g is one-to-one and onto S, so that S is also denumerable. ////

EXAMPLE 3 Show that the set of integers, positive, negative, and zero is denumerable.

SOLUTION Let $\mathbf{I} = \{\ldots, -2, -1, 0, 1, 2, \ldots\}$. If we enumerate the elements of $\mathbf{I}$, we can establish the following one-to-one correspondence between $\mathbf{I}$ and $\mathbf{N}$.

0	1	2	3	4	5	...
$\updownarrow$	$\updownarrow$	$\updownarrow$	$\updownarrow$	$\updownarrow$	$\updownarrow$	...
0	-1	1	-2	2	-3	...

This correspondence shows that $\mathbf{I} \sim \mathbf{N}$. Alternatively, we can define a function $f\colon \mathbf{N} \to \mathbf{I}$ where

$$f(n) = \begin{cases} \dfrac{n}{2} & \text{if } n \text{ is even} \\[2ex] -\dfrac{n+1}{2} & \text{if } n \text{ is odd} \end{cases}$$

This mapping is one-to-one and onto, hence $\mathbf{I} \sim \mathbf{N}$. ////

A sequence which is used to establish a one-to-one correspondence with the elements of a set is called an *enumeration*. In Example 3 we used the sequence 0, -1, 1, -2, ... as an enumeration of the integers.

EXAMPLE 4 Show that the set $\mathbf{N} \times \mathbf{N}$ is denumerable. Hence the set of positive rational numbers, as well as the set of rational numbers, is also denumerable.

SOLUTION Write the elements of $\mathbf{N} \times \mathbf{N}$ as shown in Table 2-5.1. We now arrange the elements of $\mathbf{N} \times \mathbf{N}$ in the order shown by the arrows, viz,

$$\langle 0,0 \rangle \quad \langle 0,1 \rangle \quad \langle 1,0 \rangle \quad \langle 0,2 \rangle \quad \langle 1,1 \rangle \quad \langle 2,0 \rangle \quad \langle 0,3 \rangle \quad \langle 1,2 \rangle \quad \langle 2,1 \rangle \quad \langle 3,0 \rangle \quad \ldots$$

and establish a one-to-one correspondence between these elements and the elements of $\mathbf{N}$. The one-to-one correspondence can be expressed by $f\colon \mathbf{N} \times \mathbf{N} \to \mathbf{N}$

$$f(m, n) = \tfrac{1}{2}(m + n + 1)(m + n) + m$$

which shows that $\mathbf{N} \times \mathbf{N}$ is denumerable.

Let us now obtain a subset S of $\mathbf{N} \times \mathbf{N}$ by deleting all pairs (m, n) in which m and n are not relatively prime (that is, m and n have a common factor which is an integer greater than 1). Obviously S contains at least the elements $\langle 1, 1 \rangle$,

Table 2-5.1

$\langle 2, 1 \rangle$, $\langle 3, 1 \rangle$, ..., so that S is infinite. Since $\mathbf{N} \times \mathbf{N}$ is infinite and denumerable and S is an infinite subset of $\mathbf{N} \times \mathbf{N}$, S is denumerable. The set S is equipotent to the set of positive rational numbers $\mathbf{Q}^+$ by observing the correspondence $\langle m, n \rangle \leftrightarrow m/n$. Therefore $\mathbf{Q}^+$ is denumerable.   ////

From this example, it may appear that all the infinite sets are denumerable, but such is not the case. For example, we shall show that the set of real numbers is not denumerable. Our proof is based upon Cantor's diagonal argument and the indirect method. We first assume that the set $\mathbf{R}$ is denumerable and then show that a member of the set different from all those enumerated exists, showing that the enumeration is not exhaustive, and hence arriving at a contradiction. The argument is called "diagonal" because to obtain this particular member, we move along the diagonal of an array. The diagonal argument is employed frequently in the theory of automata and other logical investigations. This method of proof can be used for showing the nondenumerability of other sets as well.

Theorem 2-5.2   Show that the set $\mathbf{R}$ of real numbers is not denumerable.

PROOF

(a) It is sufficient to show that the set S given by

$$S = \{x \mid (x \in \mathbf{R}) \wedge (0 < x < 1)\}$$

is nondenumerable because $S \sim \mathbf{R}$ follows from the mapping $f: S \to \mathbf{R}$ given by (see also Example 2)

$$f(x) = \begin{cases} \dfrac{1}{2x} - 1 & 0 < x \leq \frac{1}{2} \\[3mm] \dfrac{1}{2(x-1)} + 1 & \frac{1}{2} \leq x < 1 \end{cases}$$

which is one-to-one and onto and

$$f^{-1}(x) = \begin{cases} \dfrac{1}{2(x+1)} & x \geq 0 \\[3mm] \dfrac{1}{2(x-1)} + 1 & x \leq 0 \end{cases}$$

(b) Let us assume that S is denumerable, so that we can arrange the elements of S in an infinite sequence $s_1, s_2, \ldots, s_n, \ldots$. Now we know that any positive number less than 1 can be expressed as

$$s = 0.y_1y_2y_3\ldots$$

where $y_i \in \{0, 1, 2, \ldots, 9\}$ and $\{y_1, y_2, \ldots\}$ has an infinite number of nonzero elements. This statement is true because numbers such as 0.2 and 0.123 can be written as $0.1999\ldots$ and $0.122999\ldots$ respectively. In view of this fact, we express the elements $s_1, s_2, \ldots$ as

$$s_1 = 0.a_{11}a_{12}a_{13}\ldots a_{1n}\ldots$$

$$s_2 = 0.a_{21}a_{22}a_{23}\ldots a_{2n}\ldots$$

$$s_3 = 0.a_{31}a_{32}a_{33}\ldots a_{3n}\ldots$$

$$\ldots\ldots\ldots\ldots\ldots\ldots\ldots\ldots$$

Next, let us construct a real number

$$r = 0.b_1b_2b_3\ldots b_n\ldots$$

by choosing $b_j = 1$ if $a_{jj} \neq 1$ and $b_j = 2$ if $a_{jj} = 1$, for $j = 1, 2, 3, \ldots$. Obviously r is different from all the numbers $s_1, s_2, s_3, \ldots$ because it differs from s_1 in position 1, from s_2 in position 2, and so on. This shows that $r \notin S$, which is a contradiction. Hence S is nondenumerable. $\qquad ////$

This result is true for the set of real numbers lying in any interval (a, b) where $b > a$. The cardinality of all these sets which are equipotent is denoted by $\mathbf{c}$ and is called the *power of continuum*. The sets $\mathbf{R}^2$, $\mathbf{R}^3$, $\ldots$ also have the cardinality $\mathbf{c}$.

So far, we have seen examples of infinite sets which are denumerable and have cardinality $\aleph_0$. On the other hand, we have also seen examples of infinite sets which are nondenumerable and have cardinality $\mathbf{c}$. There are several questions which can be asked at this stage. Are there other infinite sets whose cardinal numbers are different from $\aleph_0$ and $\mathbf{c}$? Can we compare the cardinal numbers and arrange them in some order? Before we answer some of these questions, we introduce an ordering relation on the family of subsets of the universal set and a corresponding ordering on the set of cardinal numbers.

Definition 2-5.6 If A and B are sets such that A is equipotent to a subset of B, then we say that A is *dominated* by B or A *precedes* B and write $A \preceq B$. If α and β denote the cardinal numbers of the sets A and B, respectively, and if $A \preceq B$, then we say that α is *less than or equal to* β. Symbolically,

$$A \preceq B \Leftrightarrow \alpha \leq \beta$$

The choice of the term "less than or equal to" to express the relation on the set of cardinal numbers is based on the fact that for finite sets, $A \preceq B$ implies that the natural number representing $k(A)$ is less than or equal to the natural number representing $k(B)$.

From the definition, it is clear that the relations $\preceq$ and $\leq$ are both reflexive and transitive. These relations are also antisymmetric. This fact follows from a theorem known as the Schröder-Bernstein theorem, which we do not prove here. In any case, these two relations are partial ordering relations. It can also be shown that they are total orderings on the respective sets. Thus for any two sets A and B, we have either $A \preceq B$ or $B \preceq A$. Associated with the ordering relations $\preceq$ and $\leq$ we also have the relations $\prec$ and $<$ given by

$$A \prec B \Leftrightarrow A \preceq B \quad \text{and} \quad A \nsim B$$

$$\alpha < \beta \Leftrightarrow \alpha \leq \beta \quad \text{and} \quad \alpha \neq \beta$$

Since the set of natural numbers is a proper subset of the real numbers, we have $\mathbf{N} \prec \mathbf{R}$ and $\aleph_0 < \mathbf{c}$. Now we return to the question of whether for a given set we can find another set whose cardinality is greater than that of the given set. For finite sets, such a construction is easy and was given earlier. For infinite sets, a theorem due to Cantor shows the existence of such sets.

Theorem 2-5.3 For any set A, $A \prec 2^A$ where 2^A is the power set of A. If α is the cardinality of A and 2^α denotes the cardinality of 2^A, then $\alpha < 2^\alpha$.

PROOF Let $f: A \to 2^A$ be defined by $f(a) = \{a\}$ for every $a \in A$. Obviously f is one-to-one, and hence $A \leq 2^A$. To show that $A \not\sim 2^A$, we shall use the indirect method of proof. Assume that a function $g: A \to 2^A$ exists which is one-to-one and onto. If $a \in g(a)$, we call a an "interior member" of A. Similarly, if $a \notin g(a)$, then we call a an "exterior member" of A. Now let a set B be the set of exterior members of A, that is,

$$B = \{x \mid (x \in A) \land (x \notin g(x))\}$$

Obviously $B \subseteq A$ and hence $B \in 2^A$. Since g is onto, there must be an element $b \in A$ such that $g(b) = B$. Now two cases exist: either $b \in B$, so that $g(b) = B$ and b is an interior member, which is a contradiction; or $b \notin B$ and hence $b \in g(b) = B$, which is again a contradiction. Hence $g: A \to 2^A$ is not one-to-one and onto. Therefore $A \not\sim 2^A$ and $A \prec 2^A$. ////

Although we do not prove it here, note that for the set $\mathbf{N}$ of natural numbers the cardinality of the power set 2^N is $\mathbf{c}$, and hence 2^N is also nondenumerable. There are many interesting theorems regarding infinite sets, but we shall not discuss them here.

The concepts discussed in this section are used extensively in computer science. In particular, the proof technique of diagonalization is used extensively in computability theory. In the areas of formal languages and automata we will be concerned with domains other than the natural numbers. A one-to-one correspondence between elements in a nonarithmetic system and the natural numbers can be made. This type of numbering (called Gödel numbering) permits statements about elements in the nonnumeric system to be transformed into corresponding statements about natural numbers. Since much is known about the natural numbers, we can indirectly prove assertions made in a nonnumeric system by proving the corresponding assertions in the natural number system.

Gödel numbering is one technique used for establishing a one-to-one correspondence between nonnumeric elements and a subset of the natural numbers. This method is based on the existence of a unique representation of any natural number as a product of successive prime numbers raised to certain powers. There are other methods available that provide a one-to-one mapping of nonnumeric items onto the natural numbers, methods which may well be simpler than Gödel numbering.

One such method makes use of n-adic number systems. An n-adic number system, for $n > 0$, is a positional number system in which a number is written as a sequence of digits, each selected from the set $\{1, 2, \cdots, n\}$, and the weight value associated with each digit position is n raised to some nonnegative power.

The n-adic number $d_m d_{m-1} \cdots d_2 d_1$ represents the value $\sum_{i=1}^{m} d_i n^{i-1}$. For $n = 2$, these numbers are called *dyadic numbers*, and an m-digit dyadic number has the value $d_1 + 2d_2 + 4d_3 + \cdots + 2^{m-1} d_m$. Thus, the dyadic number 12221 represents the value 45 (because $45 = 1 + 2 \cdot 2 + 4 \cdot 2 + 8 \cdot 2 + 16 \cdot 1$). Note that for $n = 1$, we have a monadic number system in which the value of the monadic number is given by the number of digits used to represent it. Such a system is commonly called a *tally system*.

Clearly, the set of n-adic numbers, for any $n > 0$, can be put in one-to-one correspondence with the positive integers. The number zero, however, cannot be represented in an n-adic system as we have defined it. But we can extend an n-adic number system to include "0" as an n-adic number symbol representing the value zero, though we do not permit "0" to be a digit. The n-adic numbers, thus augmented by "0," can now be mapped onto the natural numbers.

Any nonnumeric item can be considered a finite sequence of symbols, each selected from a finite set of symbols $\{s_1, s_2, \ldots, s_n\}$. To each symbol s_i we assign the number i. The set $\{1, 2, \ldots, n\}$ can then be considered the set of digits of an n-adic number system, and each nonnumeric item can be translated into an n-adic number by replacing each symbol s_i in the sequence by its assigned digit i. (A sequence of length zero is translated into the n-adic number 0.) Because the n-adic numbers are one-to-one with the natural numbers, we now have a one-to-one mapping of the nonnumeric items onto the natural numbers. We shall make use of this translation technique in Sec. 6-2.

EXERCISES 2-5

1 Show that $S(n) = 1 + 2 + \cdots + n = n(n+1)/2$.

2 Prove that

$$\frac{1}{1 \cdot 2} + \frac{1}{2 \cdot 3} + \cdots + \frac{1}{n(n+1)} = \frac{n}{n+1}$$

3 Show that

$$2 + 2^2 + 2^3 + \cdots + 2^n = 2^{n+1} - 2$$

4 Show that the set of ordered pairs $\mathbf{N} \times \mathbf{N}$ is countable. (*Hint*: Use the result of Problem 8 in Exercises 2-4.)

5 Show that the following intervals have the power of the continuum: $[a, b]$, $[a, b)$, (a, b), $(a, b]$.

6 If two sets A_1 and A_2 are both denumerable and disjoint, show that $A_1 \cup A_2$ is also denumerable. Using mathematical induction, show also that the union of a finite number of sets which are denumerable is also denumerable. (*Hint*: Map A_1 on $\mathbf{N} \times \{0\}$ and A_2 on $\mathbf{N} \times \{1\}$.)

7 If two sets A_1 and A_2 are both denumerable, then show that $A_1 \times A_2$ is also denumerable.

8 Show that $\mathbf{R} \times \mathbf{R}$ has the power of the continuum.

9 It is known that every real number x, $0 \le x \le 1$, has a p-adic expansion $\sum_{i=1}^{\infty} n_i p^{-i}$, where $p > 1$, $p \in \mathbf{N}$, and $0 \le n_i \le p - 1$. In particular, if $p = 2$, the expansion is called a *dyadic expansion*. Such an expansion is unique, unless x is a nonzero number of the form $\sum_{i=1}^{M} n_i p^{-i}$. In such case, there are two possible expansions: one of which is finite as shown, and the other is infinite. If we agree to use the infinite expansion in the latter case, show that the set $C = \{x \in \mathbf{R} \mid 0 \leq x \leq 1\}$ is such that $C \subseteq 2^{\mathbf{N}}$. Also show that the cardinality of $2^{\mathbf{N}}$ is C.

10 Given the set of symbols $\{a, b, c\}$ and the correspondence $f(a) = 1, f(b) = 2, f(c) = 3$, write the triadic numbers and natural numbers associated with the items cab, $bbca$, cba.

11 Given the symbols $\{P, L, E, K, H\}$ and the correspondence $f(E) = 1, f(H) = 2, f(K) = 3, f(L) = 4, f(P) = 5$, along with the pentadic (5-adic) number system, what is the nonnumeric string associated with the natural number 300?

12 Prove that the set of natural numbers is in one-to-one correspondence with the set of symbols of the form $'c_1 c_2 \ldots c_n'$, $n = 1, 2, \ldots, \in \{a, b\}$.

2-6 RECURSION

We have already seen a procedure in Sec. 1-4 by which one can prove the validity of a conclusion in a mechanical way, i.e., by following a set of rules. Such mechanical procedures are needed if an end result is to be obtained by using a machine. In fact, automata theory is concerned with the study of mathematical models of computing devices (or machines) and the types of problems that can be solved by such machines. Given a particular problem, the standard procedure for determining whether it is mechanically "solvable" is to reduce the problem (by Gödel numbering, say) to an equivalent one consisting of a function on the natural numbers and then to decide whether such a function can be evaluated by mechanical means. Functions that can be evaluated by mechanical means are said to be "effectively computable" or "simply computable." We discuss computable functions at some length in Chap. 6. In this section we first define a class of functions inductively and show that any such function can be evaluated in a purely mechanical manner. The notions of recursive sets and predicates are also introduced. The more general concept of the decision problem associated with a set is briefly discussed. Finally, a discussion of recursion in computer programming is given.

2-6.1 Recursive Functions, Sets, and Predicates

In this section we study an important class of functions called recursive functions. We shall restrict ourselves to only those functions whose arguments and values are natural numbers. Such functions are called *number-theoretic*. In general, we shall consider number-theoretic functions of n variables which will be denoted as $f \langle x_1, x_2, \ldots, x_n \rangle$. From now on, we shall not mention the fact—although it is assumed throughout—that all functions are number-theoretic. Any function $f: \mathbf{N}^n \to \mathbf{N}$ is called *total* because it is defined for every n-tuple in $\mathbf{N}^n$. On the other hand, if $f: D \to \mathbf{N}$ where $D \subseteq \mathbf{N}^n$, then f is called *partial*. Examples of such functions are

  1 $f \langle x, y \rangle = x + y$, which is defined for all $x, y \in \mathbf{N}$ and hence is a total function.

  2 $g \langle x, y \rangle = x - y$, which is defined for only those $x, y \in \mathbf{N}$ which satisfy $x \geq y$. Hence $g \langle x, y \rangle$ is partial.

Every total function of n variables is also an n-ary operation on $\mathbf{N}$ according to our definition.

We now give a set of three functions called the *initial functions*, which are used in defining other functions by induction.

$$Z\colon Z(x) = 0 \qquad\qquad\qquad \textit{zero function}$$

$$S\colon S(x) = x + 1 \qquad\qquad \textit{successor function}$$

$$U_i{}^n\colon U_i{}^n \langle x_1, x_2, \ldots, x_n \rangle = x_i \qquad \textit{projection function}$$

The projection function is also called the *generalized identity function*. As examples, we have $U_1{}^2 \langle x, y \rangle = x$, $U_2{}^3 \langle 2, 4, 6 \rangle = 4$, etc.

The operation of composition will be used to generate other functions. Composition of functions was defined in Sec. 2-4.2 for functions of one variable. The same idea can be extended to functions of more than one variable. For example, let $f_1 \langle x, y \rangle$, $f_2 \langle x, y \rangle$, and $g \langle x, y \rangle$ be any three functions. The composition of g with f_1 and f_2 is a function h given by

$$h \langle x, y \rangle = g \langle f_1 \langle x, y \rangle, f_2 \langle x, y \rangle \rangle$$

Naturally, for h to be nonempty, it is necessary that the domain of g include $R_{f_1} \times R_{f_2}$ where R_{f_1} and R_{f_2} are the ranges of f_1 and f_2, respectively. Also the domain of h is $D_{f_1} \cap D_{f_2}$, where D_{f_1} and D_{f_2} are the domains of f_1 and f_2 respectively. If f_1, f_2, and g are total, then h is also total. In general, let $f_1, f_2, \ldots, f_n$ each be partial functions of m variables, and let g be a partial function of n variables. Then the composition of g with $f_1, f_2, \ldots, f_n$ produces a partial function h given by

$$h \langle x_1, \ldots, x_m \rangle = g \langle f_1 \langle x_1, \ldots, x_m \rangle, \ldots, f_n \langle x_1, \ldots, x_m \rangle \rangle$$

It is assumed that the domain of g includes the n-tuples $\times_{i \in \mathbf{I}_n} R_{f_i}$, $\mathbf{I}_n = \{1, 2, \ldots, n\}$ and R_{f_i} denotes the range of f_i. Also the domain of h is given by $\cap_{i \in \mathbf{I}_n} D_{f_i}$ where D_{f_i} is the domain of f_i. The function h is total iff $f_1, f_2, \ldots, f_n$ and g are total.

As an example, let

$$f_1 \langle x, y \rangle = x + y \qquad f_2 \langle x, y \rangle = xy + y^2 \qquad g \langle x, y \rangle = xy$$

Then

$$h \langle x, y \rangle = g \langle f_1 \langle x, y \rangle, f_2 \langle x, y \rangle \rangle$$
$$= g \langle x + y, xy + y^2 \rangle$$
$$= (x + y)(xy + y^2)$$

Here h is total, because f_1, f_2, and g are all total.

Given a function $f \langle x_1, x_2, \ldots, x_n \rangle$ of n variables, it may be convenient to consider $n - 1$ of the variables as fixed and vary only the remaining variable over the set of natural numbers or over a subset of it. For example, we may treat x as fixed and vary y in $f \langle x, y \rangle$ to obtain $f \langle x, 0 \rangle$, $f \langle x, 1 \rangle$, $f \langle x, 2 \rangle$, $\ldots$. In a mechanical process of computing the value of a function, this procedure can be used conveniently although it appears too cumbersome for hand computation. Thus, to determine $f \langle 2, 3 \rangle$, where $f \langle x, y \rangle = x + y$, we assume that $f \langle 2, 0 \rangle = 2$ is given and then proceed to evaluate $f \langle 2, 1 \rangle$, $f \langle 2, 2 \rangle$, and finally $f \langle 2, 3 \rangle$. Each functional value (except $f \langle 2, 0 \rangle$) is computed by adding 1 to the previous value until the desired result is obtained. The computation for $f \langle 2, 3 \rangle$ is

$$f \langle 2, 3 \rangle = [(f \langle 2, 0 \rangle + 1) + 1] + 1$$

$$= [(2 + 1) + 1] + 1 = (3 + 1) + 1 = 4 + 1 = 5$$

It is assumed that we have a mechanism by which we can determine the value of the function when an argument is zero and also its value for the argument $n + 1$ from the value of the function when the argument is n. Such a procedure will now be described. The arguments which are considered to be fixed are called *parameters*, while the one which is assumed to vary is considered a variable for that discussion.

The following operation which defines a function $f \langle x_1, x_2, \ldots, x_n, y \rangle$ of $n + 1$ variables by using two other functions $g \langle x_1, x_2, \ldots, x_n \rangle$ and $h \langle x_1, x_2, \ldots, x_n, y, z \rangle$ of n and $n + 2$ variables, respectively, is called *recursion*.

$$f \langle x_1, x_2, \ldots, x_n, 0 \rangle = g \langle x_1, x_2, \ldots, x_n \rangle$$

$$f \langle x_1, x_2, \ldots, x_n, y + 1 \rangle = h \langle x_1, x_2, \ldots, x_n, y, f \langle x_1, x_2, \ldots x_n, y \rangle \rangle$$

In this definition, the variable y is assumed to be the inductive variable in the sense that the value of f at $y + 1$ is expressed in terms of the value of f at y. The variables $x_1, x_2, \ldots, x_n$ are treated as parameters and are assumed to remain fixed throughout the definition. Also it is assumed that both the functions g and h are known. We shall now impose restrictions on g and h which will guarantee that the function f which is defined recursively, as above, can actually be computed and is total. The operation of recursion will be used frequently in this section.

Definition 2-6.1   A function f is called *primitive recursive* iff it can be obtained from the initial functions by a finite number of operations of composition and recursion.

From this definition it follows that it is not always necessary to use only the initial functions in the construction of a particular primitive recursive function. For example, if we already have a set of functions $f_1, f_2, \ldots, f_k$ which are primitive recursive, then we could use any of these functions along with the initial functions to obtain another primitive recursive function, provided we restrict ourselves to the operations of composition and recursion only. In the examples given here, first we construct some primitive recursive functions by using the initial functions alone, and then we gradually use these functions wherever required in order to construct other primitive recursive functions. Of course, all primitive recursive functions are total.

EXAMPLE 1   Show that the function $f \langle x, y \rangle = x + y$ is primitive recursive·

SOLUTION   Notice that $x + (y + 1) = (x + y) + 1$, so that

$$f \langle x, y + 1 \rangle = f \langle x, y \rangle + 1 = S(f \langle x, y \rangle)$$

also

$$f \langle x, 0 \rangle = x$$

We can now formally define $f \langle x, y \rangle$ as

$$f \langle x, 0 \rangle = x = U_1^1 \langle x \rangle$$
$$f \langle x, y + 1 \rangle = S(U_3^3 \langle x, y, f \langle x, y \rangle))$$

Here the base function is $g(x) = U_1^1(x)$, and the inductive-step function is $h \langle x, y, z \rangle = S(U_3^3 \langle x, y, z \rangle)$. In order to see how we can use the above definition to actually compute the value of $f \langle 2, 4 \rangle$, for example, we have

$$f \langle 2, 0 \rangle = 2$$
$$f \langle 2, 4 \rangle = S(f \langle 2, 3 \rangle) = S(S(f \langle 2, 2 \rangle))$$
$$= S(S(S(f \langle 2, 1 \rangle))) = S(S(S(S(f \langle 2, 0 \rangle))))$$
$$= S(S(S(S(2)))) = S(S(S(3))) = S(S(4))$$
$$= S(5) = 6 \qquad \qquad ////$$

EXAMPLE 2 Using recursion, define the multiplication function $*$ given by

$$g \langle x, y \rangle = x * y$$

SOLUTION   Since $g \langle x, 0 \rangle = 0$ and $g \langle x, y + 1 \rangle = g \langle x, y \rangle + x$, we write

$$g \langle x, 0 \rangle = Z(x)$$
$$g \langle x, y + 1 \rangle = f \langle U_3^3 \langle x, y, g \langle x, y \rangle \rangle, U_1^3 \langle x, y, g \langle x, y \rangle \rangle \rangle$$

where f is the addition function given in Example 1. $////$

The following are some of the primitive recursive functions which are used frequently. In some cases we give only an informal definition, although a formal definition using the initial functions and other primitive recursive functions can be given easily.

1   *Sign function or nonzero test function, sg:*

$$sg(0) = 0 \qquad sg(y + 1) = 1$$

or

$$sg(0) = Z(0) \qquad sg(y + 1) = S(Z(U_2^2 \langle y, sg(y) \rangle))$$

2   *Zero test function, $\overline{sg}$*

$$\overline{sg}(0) = 1 \qquad \overline{sg}(y + 1) = 0$$

3   *Predecessor function, P:*

$$P(0) = 0 \qquad P(y + 1) = y = U_1^2(y, P(y))$$

Note that

$$P(0) = 0 \qquad P(1) = 0 \qquad P(2) = 1 \qquad P(3) = 2 \quad \cdots$$

4   *Odd and even parity function, Pr:*

$$Pr(0) = 0 \qquad Pr(y + 1) = \overline{sg}(U_2^2(y, Pr(y)))$$

$$Pr(0) = 0 \qquad Pr(1) = 1 \qquad Pr(2) = 0 \qquad Pr(3) = 1 \quad \cdots$$

5 *Proper subtraction function,* $\div$:

$$x \div 0 = x \qquad x \div (y + 1) = P(x \div y)$$

Note that $x \div y = 0$ for $x < y$ and $x \div y = x - y$ for $x \geq y$.

6 *Absolute value function,* $|\ |$:

$$|x - y| = (x \div y) + (y \div x)$$

7 $\min \langle x, y \rangle$ = minimum of x and y

$$\min \langle x, y \rangle = x \div (x \div y)$$

Similarly, $\max \langle x, y \rangle$ = maximum of x and y

$$\max \langle x, y \rangle = y + (x \div y)$$

8 *The square function,* $f(y) = y^2$:

$$f(y) = y^2 = U_1{}^1(y) * U_1{}^1(y)$$

EXAMPLE 3   Show that $f \langle x, y \rangle = x^y$ is a primitive recursive function.

SOLUTION   Note that $x^0 = 1$ for $x \neq 0$, and we put $x^0 = 0$ for $x = 0$. Also $x^{y+1} = x^y * x$; hence $f \langle x, y \rangle = x^y$ is defined as

$f \langle x, 0 \rangle = sg(x)$

$f \langle x, y + 1 \rangle = x * f \langle x, y \rangle = U_1{}^3 \langle x, y, f \langle x, y \rangle \rangle * U_3{}^3 \langle x, y, f \langle x, y \rangle \rangle$ ////

EXAMPLE 4   Show that if $f \langle x, y \rangle$ defines the remainder upon division of y by x, then it is a primitive recursive function.

SOLUTION   For $y = 0$, $f \langle x, 0 \rangle = 0$. Also the value of $f \langle x, y \rangle$ increases by 1 when y is increased by 1, until the value becomes equal to x, in which case it is put equal to 0 and the process continues. We therefore build a function which increases by 1 each time y increases by 1, that is, $S(f \langle x, y \rangle)$. Now, we multiply this function by another primitive recursive function which becomes 0 whenever $S(f \langle x, y \rangle) = x$. Also this other function must be 1 whenever $S(f \langle x, y \rangle) \neq x$, but $S(f \langle x, y \rangle)$ is always $\leq x$ and hence such a function is $sg(x \div S(f \langle x, y \rangle))$. Thus the required definition of $f \langle x, y \rangle$ is

$$f \langle x, 0 \rangle = 0$$
$$f \langle x, y + 1 \rangle = S(f \langle x, y \rangle) * sg(x \div S(f \langle x, y \rangle)) \qquad ////$$

EXAMPLE 5   Show that the function $[x/2]$ which is equal to the greatest integer which is $\leq x/2$ is primitive recursive.

SOLUTION   Now $[0/2] = 0, [1/2] = 0, [2/2] = 1, [3/2] = 1$, etc., so that $[x/2] = x/2$ when x is even and $[x/2] = (x - 1)/2$ when x is odd. In order to distinguish between even and odd functions, we have already defined the parity function which is primitive recursive.

$$[0/2] = 0 \qquad [(y + 1)/2] = [y/2] + Pr(y)$$

where $Pr(y)$ denotes the parity function which is 1 when y is odd and which is 0 when y is even. ////

Recall that a set of ordered pairs defines a binary relation. Similarly, a set of n-tuples defines an n-ary relation. If the n-tuples are defined over the set of natural numbers only, then such an n-ary relation is called *number-theoretic*. Thus any set $R \subseteq \mathbf{N}^n$ defines a number-theoretic n-ary relation. As in the case of functions, in this section we restrict ourselves to only number-theoretic relations. Any such relation can also be described by an n-ary predicate. The characteristic function of a relation R can now be defined as

$$\psi_R \langle x_1, x_2, \ldots, x_n \rangle = \begin{cases} 1 & \text{if } \langle x_1, x_2, \ldots, x_n \rangle \in R \\ 0 & \text{if } \langle x_1, x_2, \ldots, x_n \rangle \notin R \end{cases}$$

Here $R \subseteq \mathbf{N}^n$ and $\langle x_1, x_2, \ldots, x_n \rangle \in \mathbf{N}^n$.

Definition 2-6.2 A relation R is said to be *primitive recursive* if its characteristic function is primitive recursive. The corresponding predicate is also called primitive recursive.

EXAMPLE 6 Show that $\{ \langle x, x \rangle \mid x \in \mathbf{N} \}$ which defines the relation of equality is primitive recursive.

SOLUTION Obviously $f \langle x, y \rangle = \overline{sg}(\mid x - y \mid)$ defines a primitive recursive function such that $f \langle x, y \rangle = 1$ for $x = y$ and otherwise $f \langle x, y \rangle = 0$. Thus, $f \langle x, y \rangle$ is the required characteristic function which is primitive recursive.   ////

EXAMPLE 7 Show that for any fixed k the relation given by $\{ \langle k, y \rangle \mid y > k \}$ is primitive recursive.

SOLUTION $sg(y \dotminus k)$ is the characteristic function of the required relation.   ////

EXAMPLE 8 Show that the function $f \langle x_1, x_2, y \rangle$ defined as

$$f \langle x_1, x_2, y \rangle = \begin{cases} x_2 & x_1 > y \\ (x_1 * y) + x_2 & x_1 \leq y \end{cases}$$

is primitive recursive.

SOLUTION The required function can be expressed as

$$x_2 + (x_1 * y) * \overline{sg}(x_1 \dotminus y) \qquad ////$$

We shall now introduce an operation which will be used to generate a larger class of functions that includes the class of primitive recursive functions.

Definition 2-6.3 Let $g \langle x_1, x_2, \ldots, x_n, y \rangle$ be a total function. If there exists at least one value of y, say $\bar{y} \in \mathbf{N}$, such that the function $g \langle x_1, x_2, \ldots, x_n, \bar{y} \rangle = 0$ for all n-tuples $\langle x_1, x_2, \ldots, x_n \rangle \in \mathbf{N}^n$, then g is called a *regular* function.

Not all total functions are regular, as can be seen from $g \langle x, y \rangle = \mid y^2 - x \mid$. Obviously $g \langle x, y \rangle$ is total, but $\mid y^2 - x \mid = 0$ for only those values of x which are perfect squares and not for all values of x. This fact shows that there is no value of $y \in \mathbf{N}$ such that $| y^2 - x | = 0$ for all x. On the other hand, the function $y \mathbin{\dot{-}} x$ is regular because for $y = 0$, $y \mathbin{\dot{-}} x$ is zero for all x.

Definition 2-6.4 A function $f \langle x_1, x_2, \ldots, x_n \rangle$ is said to be defined from a total function $g \langle x_1, x_2, \ldots, x_n, y \rangle$ by *minimization (minimalization)* or μ *operation* if

$$f \langle x_1, x_2, \ldots, x_n \rangle = \begin{cases} \mu_y(g \langle x_1, x_2, \ldots, x_n, y \rangle = 0) & \text{if there is such a } y \\ \text{undefined} & \text{otherwise} \end{cases}$$

where μ_y means the least y greater than or equal to zero.

From the definition it follows that $f \langle x_1, x_2, \ldots, x_n \rangle$ is well-defined and total if g is regular. If g is not regular, then the operation of minimization may produce a partial function.

Definition 2-6.5 A function is said to be *recursive* iff it can be obtained from the initial functions by a finite number of applications of the operations of composition, recursion, and minimization over regular functions.

It is clear from the definition that the set of recursive functions properly includes the set of primitive recursive functions. Also the set of recursive functions is closed under the operations of composition, recursion, and minimization over regular functions. If we remove the restriction for the operation of minimization, so that it can be performed over any total function and not necessarily over just regular ones, we get a still larger class of functions defined as partial recursive functions.

Definition 2-6.6 A function is said to be *partial recursive* iff it can be obtained from the initial functions by a finite number of applications of the operations of composition, recursion, and minimization.

As was done in the case of primitive recursive functions, it is not necessary to start always from the initial functions in order to construct other functions in the class. In fact, if a set of recursive functions is known, they can be used along with the admissible operations to generate other recursive functions.

EXAMPLE 9 Show that the function $f(x) = x/2$ is a partial recursive function.

SOLUTION Let $g \langle x, y \rangle = | 2y - x |$. The function g is not regular because $| 2y - x | = 0$ only for even values of x. Define

$$f(x) = \mu_y(| 2y - x | = 0)$$

Then $f(x) = x/2$ for x even.   ////

EXAMPLE 10 Let $\lfloor \sqrt{x} \rfloor$ be the greatest integer $\leq \sqrt{x}$. Show that $\lfloor \sqrt{x} \rfloor$ is primitive recursive.

SOLUTION Observe that $(y + 1)^2 \doteq x$ is zero for $(y + 1)^2 \leq x$ and non-zero for $(y + 1)^2 > x$. Therefore, $\overline{sg}((y + 1)^2 \doteq x)$ is 1 if $(y + 1)^2 \leq x$ and cannot be equal to 0. The smallest value of y for which $(y + 1)^2 > x$ is the required number $\lfloor \sqrt{x} \rfloor$; hence

$$\lfloor \sqrt{x} \rfloor = \mu_y(\overline{sg}((y + 1)^2 \doteq x) = 0$$

Note that $\lfloor \sqrt{x} \rfloor$ is defined for all x and hence is a recursive function.   ////

Any n-ary relation $R \subseteq \mathbf{N}^n$ was defined to be primitive recursive if its characteristic function ψ_R of R is primitive recursive. In a similar manner, we can extend this definition to recursive and partial recursive relations. In general, any set A is called recursive (partial recursive) if its characteristic function ψ_A is recursive (partial recursive). It is assumed that we are considering only sets whose elements are natural numbers or sets of n-tuples over the natural numbers or those sets whose elements can be mapped into $\mathbf{N}$.

In Sec. 2-4.5 it was shown that for any set A whose characteristic function is ψ_A, the characteristic function of $\sim A$ is given by $1 - \psi_A$. Similarly, for any two sets A and B with characteristic functions ψ_A and ψ_B, the characteristic functions of $A \cup B$ and $A \cap B$ can also be obtained easily. These ideas can now be extended to recursive sets. If a set A is recursive, that is, ψ_A is recursive, then $\sim A$ is also recursive because

$$\psi_{\sim A} = 1 \doteq \psi_A = \overline{sg}(\psi_A)$$

Also, if the sets A and B are recursive, then $A \cap B$ and $A \cup B$ are recursive because

$$\psi_{A \cap B} = \psi_A * \psi_B$$
$$\psi_{A \cup B} = (\psi_A + \psi_B) \doteq \psi_{A \cap B}$$

These results show that the class of recursive sets (relations) is closed under the set operations $\sim$, $\cap$, and $\cup$, and consequently it is closed under any other set operation.

EXAMPLE 11 Show that the sets of even and odd natural numbers are both recursive.

SOLUTION Recall that the parity function is the required characteristic function for the set E of even natural numbers. Hence E is primitive recursive. Also, the set of odd natural numbers is $\sim E$; hence $\sim E$ is also primitive recursive.   ////

EXAMPLE 12 Show that the set of divisors of a positive integer n is recursive.

SOLUTION A number $x \leq n$ is a divisor of n iff $| x * i - n |$ is equal to zero for one fixed value of i, $1 \leq i \leq n$. This means that $| x * i - n |$ is nonzero for all $1 \leq i \leq n$, if x is not a divisor. Therefore, the characteristic function of the required set is

$$\psi_B(x) = \sum_{i=1}^{n} \overline{sg} \, | x * i - n |$$

where B denotes the set of divisors of n.   ////

The concept of the extension of a predicate was introduced in Sec. 2-1.7. A predicate whose extension is a set of integers is said to be a *number-theoretic* predicate. All the predicates in this section are assumed to be number-theoretic. Such a predicate is primitive recursive (recursive) iff its extension is primitive recursive (recursive). The characteristic function of a predicate is the characteristic function of its extension. If A is the extension of predicate P and ψ_P denotes the characteristic function of the predicate P, then

$$\psi_P = \psi_A$$

For example, the predicates "is even" and "is a divisor of n" are recursive because their extensions are recursive sets.

If A and B are the extensions of predicates P and Q respectively, then, by definition,

$$\psi_{P \neg Q} = \psi_{A \cup B} \qquad \psi_{P \wedge Q} = \psi_{A \cap B} \qquad \psi_{\neg P} = \psi_{\sim A}$$

It directly follows that if P and Q are recursive, then so are predicates $P \vee Q$, $P \wedge Q$, and $\neg P$.

EXAMPLE 13   Let $D(x)$ denote "number of divisors of x." Show that $D(x)$ is primitive recursive.

SOLUTION   It was shown in Example 4 that the function which defines the remainder upon division of y by x is primitive recursive. We shall denote such a function by $rm \langle x, y \rangle$. If a number x divides y, then the remainder is 0 and $\overline{sg}(rm \langle x, y \rangle) = 1$. Therefore, the number of divisors of y is given by

$$D(y) = \sum_{x=1}^{y} \overline{sg}(rm \langle x, y \rangle)$$

This shows that $D(y)$ is primitive recursive.   ////

EXAMPLE 14   Show that the predicate "x is prime" is primitive recursive.

SOLUTION   A number x is a prime iff it has only two divisors 1 and x, also if it is not 1 or 0. Therefore, the characteristic function of the extension of "x is not a prime" is

$$\psi_{\sim Pr}(x) = sg(D(x) \dot{-} 2) + \overline{sg}(|x - 1|) + \overline{sg}(|x - 0|)$$

Hence $\psi_{Pr}(x)$ is also primitive recursive and is given by $1 \dot{-} \psi_{\sim Pr}(x)$.   ////

In our discussion thus far we considered only one induction variable in the definition of recursion. It is possible to consider two or more induction variables. Note that in the definition of $f \langle x_1, x_2, \ldots, x_n, y \rangle$ using recursion, $x_1, x_2, \ldots, x_n$ were treated as parameters and only y was treated as the induction variable. Now we define a function in which we have two induction variables and no parameters. This function will be used in the next section and is known as Ackermann's function. The function $A \langle x, y \rangle$ is defined by

$$A \langle 0, y \rangle = y + 1$$
$$A \langle x + 1, 0 \rangle = A \langle x, 1 \rangle$$
$$A \langle x + 1, y + 1 \rangle = A \langle x, A \langle x + 1, y \rangle \rangle$$

Observe that one can construct the value of $A \langle x, y \rangle$ for fixed values of x and y by using the above definition. Therefore, $A \langle x, y \rangle$ is well defined and total. It is known that $A \langle x, y \rangle$ is not primitive recursive, but recursive. We now demonstrate how the above definitions can be used in finding the value of $A \langle 2, 2 \rangle$.

$$A \langle 2, 2 \rangle = A \langle 1, A \langle 2, 1 \rangle \rangle$$
$$A \langle 2, 1 \rangle = A \langle 1, A \langle 2, 0 \rangle \rangle$$
$$= A \langle 1, A \langle 1, 1 \rangle \rangle$$

$$A \langle 1, 1 \rangle = A \langle 0, A \langle 1, 0 \rangle \rangle$$
$$= A \langle 0, A \langle 0, 1 \rangle \rangle$$
$$= A \langle 0, 2 \rangle$$
$$= 3$$

$$A \langle 2, 1 \rangle = A \langle 1, 3 \rangle$$
$$= A \langle 0, A \langle 1, 2 \rangle \rangle$$
$$A \langle 1, 2 \rangle = A \langle 0, A \langle 1, 1 \rangle \rangle$$
$$= A \langle 0, 3 \rangle$$
$$= 4$$

$$A \langle 2, 1 \rangle = A \langle 0, 4 \rangle$$
$$= 5$$
$$A \langle 2, 2 \rangle = A \langle 1, 5 \rangle$$
$$= A \langle 0, A \langle 1, 4 \rangle \rangle$$
$$A \langle 1, 4 \rangle = A \langle 0, A \langle 1, 3 \rangle \rangle$$
$$A \langle 1, 3 \rangle = A \langle 0, A \langle 1, 2 \rangle \rangle$$
$$= A \langle 0, 4 \rangle$$
$$= 5$$

$$A \langle 1, 4 \rangle = A \langle 0, 5 \rangle$$
$$= 6$$
$$A \langle 2, 2 \rangle = A \langle 0, 6 \rangle$$
$$= 7$$

It was shown earlier that a set is recursive iff the characteristic function is recursive. A characteristic function of a set determines whether a particular element x is or is not a member of the set. This determining process is called a *decision problem* associated with the set. It is desirable that such a decision problem be solved mechanically. This solution can be accomplished if the characteristic function of the set is recursive.

Therefore the decision problem for a set of integers can be reformulated as whether the characteristic function of a set, or equivalently its defining predicate, is recursive. If the answer is yes, then the decision problem is said to be *recursively solvable*; otherwise it is recursively unsolvable. By "solvable" we mean mechanically solvable (in the sense of induction). There are problems which are solvable, but this fact cannot be shown by purely mechanical means.

Suppose that we are interested in generating or enumerating elements of a set whose members are integers. We can consider the enumeration process as the generation of elements by a function. A set is said to be *recursively enumerable* if it is the range of a recursive function. Given an element z which is in the set, in a finite number of computations of the recursive function z will be generated. If we start with successive argument values from zero for the function, then at some point an argument x will be reached for which the functional value is z. If, however, z does not belong to the set, then z's not being generated in a finite number of steps is no guarantee that z does not belong to the set.

We have introduced the notion of a *semidecision* problem associated with a set. If an element belongs to a set, then we can say yes, but if it does not, we cannot say no. The following examples distinguish a fully decidable procedure from a semidecidable one.

Algorithm prime Given an integer i greater than 1, this algorithm will determine whether the integer is a prime number. Remember that the only divisors of a prime number are 1 and the number itself.

1 [Initialize] Set $j \leftarrow 2$.
2 [Finished?] If $j \geq i$ then output $"i$ is prime$"$ and Exit.
3 [Does j divide i?] If $j \mid i$ then output $"i$ is not prime$"$ and Exit.
4 [Increment counter] Set $j \leftarrow j + 1$, go to step 2.   ////

For any value of i the algorithm will answer yes or no. The algorithm could have been made more efficient by noting that if a number is not a prime, then a divisor must be less than or equal to the square root of the number.

Algorithm perfect This algorithm decides whether there exists a perfect number greater than some integer i. Consider the set of all divisors of a number except the number itself. A perfect number is one whose sum of all such divisors equals the number. The number 6 is a perfect number since $1 + 2 + 3 = 6$.

1 [Initialize k] Set $k \leftarrow i$.
2 [Increment k] Set $k \leftarrow k + 1$.
3 [Initialize SUM] Set $SUM \leftarrow 0$.
4 [Initialize j] Set $j \leftarrow 1$.
5 [Finished with number?] If $j < k$ then go to step 7.
6 [Is number perfect?] If SUM $= k$ then output k and Exit; otherwise go to step 2.
7 [Does j divide k?] If $j \mid k$ then set $SUM \leftarrow SUM + j$. Set $j \leftarrow j + 1$ and go to step 5.

The algorithm is an example of a semidecidable process. It can say yes, but can never say no, because the question of whether there are an infinite number of perfect numbers is not known. If there were a finite number of perfect numbers, then there would be a maximum perfect number and the algorithm could, in this case, answer yes or no to the question.   ////

In certain areas of mathematics we are interested in the existence of algorithms for solving problems which are not concerned with integers. The concept of solvability can be extended to domains other than the natural number system. We can set up a one-to-one correspondence between elements in the nonarithmetic system and the natural numbers. This type of numbering was discussed in Sec. 2-5.2. In so doing, statements about elements in the nonnumeric system can be transformed into corresponding statements concerning integers. The same notion applies to predicates.

EXERCISES 2-6.1

1 Show that the function

$$f(x) = \begin{cases} x/2 & \text{when } x \text{ is even} \\ (x-1)/2 & \text{when } x \text{ is odd} \end{cases}$$

is primitive recursive.
2 Show that the function $f \langle x, y \rangle = x - y$ is partial recursive.
3 Show that the function $x!$ (the factorial function) is primitive recursive, where $0! = 1$ and $n! = n * (n - 1)!$.
4 Show that the quotient function $g \langle x, y \rangle =$ quotient upon division of y by x is primitive recursive.
5 Show that the function $f(x) = k$, where k is a constant, is primitive recursive.
6 If $\Pi(x) =$ number of primes $\leq x$, show that $\Pi(x)$ is primitive recursive.
7 Show that every finite set is primitive recursive. (*Hint*: Use the fact that the union of primitive recursive sets is primitive recursive.)
8 Find a function $f(x)$ such that $f(2) = 3$, $f(4) = 5$, $f(7) = 2$, and $f(x)$ assumes any arbitrary value for other arguments. Show that $f(x)$ is primitive recursive.

2-6.2 Recursion in Programming Languages

In the previous section we defined the set of recursive functions. The basic idea is to define a function for all its argument values in a constructive manner by using induction. The value of a function for a particular argument value can be computed in a finite number of steps by using the recursive definition where at each step of recursion we get nearer to the solution. It should be noted that a recursive definition may not necessarily define a function. This is the reason why we imposed certain restrictions and obtained primitive recursive, recursive, and finally partial recursive functions.

An important facility available to the programmer is the procedure (function or subroutine). Procedures in programming languages are a convenience to the programmer since they enable the programmer to express just once an algorithm which is required in many places in a program. Corresponding to a recursive step in the definition of a function, in certain programming languages such as ALGOL, PL/I, and SNOBOL4 (but not FORTRAN) we have a procedure which may contain a procedure call to any procedure including itself. A procedure that contains a procedure call to itself, or a procedure call to a second procedure which eventually causes the first procedure to be called, is known as a *recursive procedure*.

There are two important conditions that must be satisfied by any recursive procedure. First, each time a procedure calls itself (either directly or indirectly) it must be "nearer," in some sense, to a solution. In the case of the factorial function (see Prob. 3 in Exercises 2-6.1), each time that the function calls itself, its argument is decremented by 1, and so the argument of the function is getting smaller. Second, there must be a decision criterion for stopping the process or computation. In the case of the factorial function, the value of n must be zero. The term "nearer" can therefore be defined in terms of the stopping condition.

As was discussed in the previous subsection, there are essentially two types of recursion. The first type is the class of primitive recursive functions, and an example of this kind is the factorial function. The second type of recursion is the class of functions which can be obtained by minimization.

Many people believe that recursion is an unnecessary luxury in a programming language. This view is based on the fact that any primitive recursive function can be solved iteratively.

An "iterative" process can be explained by the flowchart given in Fig. 2-6.1, There are four parts in the process, namely, initialization, decision, computation and update. The functions of the four parts are as follows:

1   Initialization. The parameters of the function and a decision parameter in this part are set to their initial values. The decision parameter is used to determine when to exit from the loop.

2   Computation. The required computation is performed in this part.

3   Decision. The decision parameter is to determine whether to remain in the loop.

4   Update. The decision parameter is updated, and a transfer to the next iteration results.

It is possible to transform mechanically any primitive recursive function into an equivalent iterative process. However, such is *not* the case for nonprimitive recursive functions. Although there does exist an iterative solution for Ackermann's function, in general there are many problems of that form for which iterative solutions either do not exist or are not easily found. Certain inherently recursive processes can be solved in programming languages which do not permit recursion only by essentially setting up a recursive framework. We will have occasion to return to this topic later. Recursion is becoming increasingly important in symbol manipulation and nonnumeric applications.

Throughout the text we encounter problems where recursion is *unavoidable* because of the recursive nature of the process or because of the recursive structure of the data which have to be processed. Even for cases where there is no inherent recursive structure, the recursive solution may be much simpler (though sometimes more time-consuming) than its iterative counterpart.

The drawbacks of recursion are that usually the execution of a recursive program is slower than that of its iterative counterparts, and a recursive program is more difficult to debug than a corresponding iterative one.

There are special problems associated with a recursive procedure that do not exist for a nonrecursive procedure. A recursive procedure can be called from

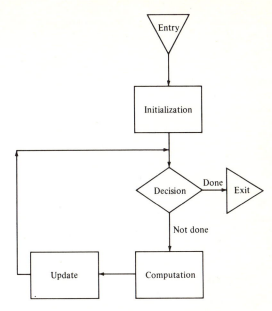

FIGURE 2-6.1 Model of iteration.

within or outside itself, and to ensure its proper functioning, it has to save, in some order, the return addresses so that a return to the proper location will result when return to a calling statement is made. The procedure must also save, in some order, the formal parameters, local variables, etc., upon entry and must restore these parameters and variables at completion.

The saving and restoring of return addresses, parameters, and local variables are incorporated in the flowchart model for a recursive procedure given in Fig. 2-6.2. The model consists of a prologue, a body, and an epilogue. The purpose of the prologue is to save the formal parameters, local variables, and return address, while that of the epilogue is to restore them. Note that the parameters, local variables, and return address which are restored are those which were most recently saved; i.e., the last saved are the first to be restored (Last In, First Out). The body of the procedure contains a procedure call to itself; in fact, there may be more than one call to itself in certain procedures.

It is rather difficult to understand a recursive procedure from its flowchart, and the best one can hope for is to acquire an intuitive understanding of the procedure. The key box contained in the body of the procedure is the one which invokes a call to itself. The dotted-line exit from this box indicates that a call to itself is being initiated within the same procedure. Each time a procedure call to itself is executed, the prologue of the procedure saves all necessary information required for proper functioning.

The procedure body contains two computation boxes, namely, the partial and final computation boxes. Frequently the partial computation box is combined with the procedure call box (this is the case for the computation of the factorial

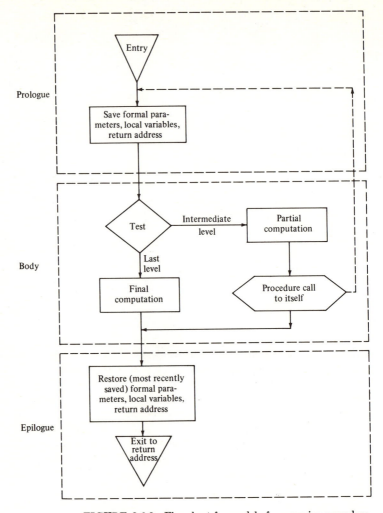

FIGURE 2-6.2 Flowchart for model of a recursive procedure.

function). The final computation box gives the explicit definition of the process for some value or values of the argument(s). The test box determines whether the argument value(s) are those for which an explicit definition of the process is given.

A flowchart for a procedure which computes the factorial function recursively is given in Fig. 2-6.3. The testing box checks n for a value of zero. If the test is successful, the argument (zero) for which the function is explicitly defined ($0! = 1$) has been found. The final computation box specifies the value of the factorial function for the argument $n = 0$. The partial computation box and the call box are combined into one. The prologue of the procedure saves the value of n and the return address on entering the procedure and the epilogue re-

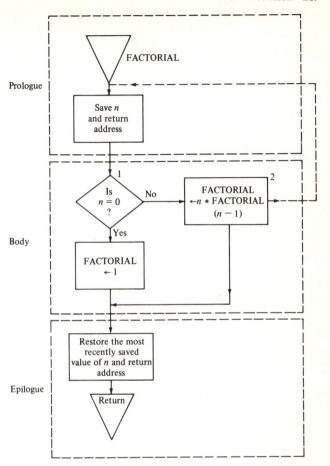

FIGURE 2-6.3   Flowchart for the factorial function.

stores the most recently stored value of n and the return address (on a Last In First Out basis).

A recursive PL/I formulation of the factorial function together with a main procedure to test the function is given in Fig. 2-6.4. Note that all variables used in the program are given the characteristics binary and fixed with precision of (31, 0). This assignment was necessary for proper execution of the procedure. Since the identifier FACTORIAL defaults to float decimal, the RETURNS attribute must be used both in a declaration of the function in the invoking procedure and in the PROCEDURE statement. This procedure, as well as all procedures which reactivate themselves, must be declared to have the RECURSIVE attribute.

Assume that this PL/I procedure is initially called from a main program with N equal to 2. We will associate a *level number* with each entry into the procedure FACTORIAL and in particular associate *level* 1 when the function is entered due to the initial call from the main program, which is assumed to have level 0. The following is a trace of the execution of the FACTORIAL procedure.

```
RUNFACT:
    PROCEDURE OPTIONS(MAIN);
    /* TEST THE RECURSIVE FACTRIAL FUNCTION */
    DECLARE
        FACTORIAL RETURNS(BINARY FIXED(31)),
        (I,K) BINARY FIXED(31);
    DO I = 3 TO 7 BY 2;
        PUT SKIP(2) EDIT('FACTORIAL(',I,') IS ',FACTORIAL(I))
            (A(10),F(1),A(5),F(5));
    END;

FACTRIAL:
        PROCEDURE (N) RECURSIVE RETURNS(BINARY FIXED(31));
        DECLARE
            N BINARY FIXED(31);
        IF N = 0
        THEN RETURN(1);
        ELSE RETURN(N * FACTORIAL(N - 1));
    END FACTORIAL;

    END RUNFACT;
```

```
FACTORIAL(3) IS      6

FACTORIAL(5) IS    120

FACTORIAL(7) IS   5040
```

FIGURE 2-6.4   PL/I program for the factorial function.

Enter level 1	called from the main program (level 0)	$\begin{cases} \text{Save N (initially garbage} \\ \text{as far as we are concerned)} \\ \text{N} \leftarrow 2 \end{cases}$
		$\begin{cases} \text{N} \neq 0 \\ \text{FACTORIAL(1) is called.} \end{cases}$
Enter level 2	first recursive call from N $*$ FACTORIAL (N − 1) with (N = 2)	$\begin{cases} \text{Save N, which has a value} \\ \text{of 2. N} \leftarrow 1 \end{cases}$
		$\begin{cases} \text{N} \neq 0 \\ \text{FACTORIAL(0) is called.} \end{cases}$
Enter level 3	second recursive call from N $*$ FACTO-RIAL(N − 1) (with N = 1)	$\begin{cases} \text{Save N, which has a value} \\ \text{of 1.} \\ \text{N} \leftarrow 0 \end{cases}$
		$\begin{cases} \text{N} = 0 \\ \text{Return 1.} \end{cases}$
		$\begin{cases} \text{Restore N} \leftarrow 1. \text{ The value} \\ 1 \text{ is passed to the expres-} \\ \text{sion in level 2, which called} \\ \text{the procedure.} \end{cases}$
Return to level 2		The expression N $*$ FAC-TORIAL(N − 1) is now 1 $*$ FACTORIAL(0) = 1.

$\left\{\begin{array}{l}\text{Restore N} \leftarrow 2. \text{ The value}\\ 1 \text{ computed above is passed}\\ \text{to the invoking expression}\\ \text{in level 1.}\end{array}\right.$

Return to level 1

The expression N $*$ FAC-TORIAL(N $-$ 1) is now 2 $*$ FACTORIAL(1) = 2.

$\left\{\begin{array}{l}\text{Restore N to garbage. Re-}\\ \text{turn the value 2 to invok-}\\ \text{ing statement.}\end{array}\right.$

Return to main
program (level 0)

$\left\{\begin{array}{l}\text{The call in the main pro-}\\ \text{gram has the value 2.}\end{array}\right.$

Let us now consider a more complex recursion example. A well-known algorithm for finding the greatest common divisor of two integers is Euclid's algorithm. The greatest common divisor function is denoted by the following:

$$\text{GCD}\ \langle m, n\rangle = \begin{cases} \text{GCD}\ \langle n, m\rangle & \text{if } n > m \\ m & \text{if } n = 0 \\ \text{GCD}\ \langle n, \text{MOD}\ \langle m, n\rangle\rangle & \text{otherwise} \end{cases}$$

Here MOD $\langle m, n\rangle$ is $m(\bmod n)$, the remainder on dividing m by n. The first part of the definition interchanges the order of the arguments if $n > m$ (the first argument must be greater than or equal to the second for the algorithm to work). If the second argument is zero, then the greatest common divisor is equal to the first argument (this defines the base values of the function). Finally, GCD is defined in terms of itself. Note that the process must terminate since MOD$\langle m, n\rangle$ will decrease to a value of zero in a finite number of steps. As an example, GCD $\langle 20, 6\rangle$ is obtained from the following computation:

$$20 = 6 * 3 + 2$$

By the euclidean algorithm, GCD$\langle 20, 6\rangle$ is the same as GCD$\langle 6, 2\rangle$. Therefore

$$6 = 2 * 3 + 0$$

and GCD $\langle 6, 2\rangle$ is the same as GCD $\langle 2, 0\rangle$, which is 2. If, instead, we were required to find GCD $\langle 6, 20\rangle$, this problem could be solved by finding a solution to GCD $\langle 20, 6\rangle$ instead.

The PL/I program for the GCD function is given in Fig. 2-6.5. The same comments given for the FACTORIAL procedure apply to the GCD procedure. Note also the use of the ON ENDFILE(SYSIN) statement which specifies the action required on exhaustion of the input card file. PL/I also has a MOD function which is a convenience in programming the GCD procedure.

In Sec. 2-6.1, Ackermann's function was briefly discussed. This classical function will be extensively studied in the remainder of this section. First, a recursive PL/I formulation is given, followed by an iterative solution in algorithmic notation and also in PL/I. Finally, this function will be programmed by faking recursion in FORTRAN.

A program to compute Ackermann's function recursively is simple to write

```
RUN_GCD:
     PROCEDURE OPTIONS(MAIN);
     /* TEST THE EUCLIDEAN ALGORITHM */
     DECLARE
         (I,J) BINARY FIXED(31),
         GCD RETURNS(BINARY FIXED(31));
     CN ENDFILE(SYSIN) GO TO END;
READ:   /* GET SOME VALUES TC TEST THE GCD FUNCTICN   */
     GET SKIP LIST(I,J);
     PUT SKIP(2) EDIT('THE GREATEST CCMMON DIVISOR OF ',I,' AND ',J,
         ' IS ',GCD(I,J))(A(31),F(5),A(5),F(5),A(4),F(5));
     GO TC READ;

GCD:
         PROCEDURE (M,N) RECURSIVE RETURNS(BINARY FIXED(31));
         DECLARE
             (M,N) BINARY FIXED(31);
         IF N > M /* REVERSE THE CALL */
         THEN RETURN(GCD(N,M));
         IF N = 0 /* M IS THE GREATEST COMMON DIVISOR */
         THEN RETURN(M);
         RETURN(GCD(N,MOD(M,N))); /* EQUIVALENT VALUE */
     END GCD;

END: END RUN_GCD;
```

THE GREATEST COMMON DIVISOR OF   84 AND   246 IS   6

THE GREATEST COMMON DIVISOR OF   6 AND   20 IS   2

THE GREATEST COMMON DIVISOR OF   121 AND   33 IS   11

FIGURE 2-6.5 PL/I program for the GCD function.

and is given in Fig. 2-6.6. It is essentially a one-one implementation of the clauses in the definition of the function embodied in a procedure with the RECURSIVE attribute.

Ackermann's function is theoretically significant in that it is a recursive function that is not primitive recursive. Ackermann provided the proof of the non-primitive recursive nature of this function when he established that it grows faster than any primitive recursive function. As an illustration of the growth rate, consider that if we define $g(x) = A \langle x, x \rangle$, then $g(x)$ for $x = 0, 1, 2, 3, 4, \ldots$ is $1, 3, 7, 61, 2^{2^{65,536}} - 3$.

To explain the iterative evaluation program for Ackermann's function, it is necessary first to redefine the function in a form which is more easily investigated. We can rewrite the original definition as

1 $A \langle 0, n \rangle = n + 1$
2 $A \langle m + 1, 0 \rangle = A \langle m, 1 \rangle$
3 $A \langle m + 1, n + 1 \rangle = A \langle m, A \langle m + 1, n \rangle \rangle$

We may think of this function as defining an entry in a table for each $\langle m, n \rangle$ argument pair. Let m designate the row number of the table and n the column number in which $A \langle m, n \rangle$ may be found. Row 0 is defined for each entry as the column number of that entry plus 1 (by clause (1)). Each entry of column 0 is defined (by (2)) as the column 1 entry of the previous row (except for $A \langle 0, 0 \rangle$

```
RECTEST:
    PROCEDURE OPTICNS(MAIN);
    /* TEST ACKERMANN'S FLNCTICN. */
    CECLARE
        A ENTRY(BINARY FIXED(31),BINARY FIXEC(31))
            RETURNS(BINARY FIXEC(31));
    PUT EDIT('THE SCLUTICN FCR ACKERMANN''S FUNCTION, A(2,2) IS ',
        A(2,2))(A(49),F(5));

A:
        PROCEDURE (M,N) RECLRSIVE RETURNS (BINARY FIXED(31));
        /* ACKERMANN'S FUNCTICN */
        DECLARE
            (M,N) BINARY FIXEC(31);
        IF M = 0
        THEN RETURN(N + 1);
        IF N = C
        THEN RETURN(A(M - 1,1));
        RETURN(A(M - 1,A(M,N - 1)));
    END A;

    END RECTEST;


THE SOLLTICN FOR ACKERMANN'S FUNCTION, A(2,2) IS     7
```

FIGURE 2-6.6   Recursive formulation of Ackermann's function.

which is defined by (1)). Part (3) states that the entry in row $m + 1$ and column
$n + 1$ is equal to the entry in the previous row in the column position given by
$A \langle m + 1, n \rangle$. These relationships are shown by arrows in Fig. 2-6.7.

Figure 2-6.7 gives an indication of the nature of the iterative solution by
showing all values which must be generated to calculate $A \langle 4, 0 \rangle$. Entries for row
0 are added one by one and, if necessary, are propagated to the following rows,
as shown by the arrows. Note that the last entry in each row is equal to $A \langle 4, 0 \rangle$.
The iterative solution can be performed without using a two-dimensional array
since there is no need to save an entry when another follows it in the same row.
Instead two vectors will be used. The ith elements of vectors *VALUE* and
PLACE will indicate the last number to be generated and its column position,
respectively, in row i. If $A \langle m, n \rangle$ is to be found, no more than $m + 1$ elements

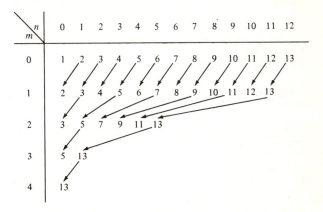

FIGURE 2-6.7

are required in each vector. On completion of the iterative solution to calculate $A \langle 4, 0 \rangle$, the vectors will contain the following:

i	$VALUE[i]$	$PLACE[i]$
0	13	12
1	13	11
2	13	5
3	13	1
4	13	0

With this introductory knowledge, we are now able to study the algorithm for the iterative solution.

Algorithm $ACKER$ Iteratively solve for $A \langle m, n \rangle$, the value of Ackermann's function for valid arguments m and n. The vectors $PLACE$ and $VALUE$ previously described are implemented. $ACKER$ is assigned the value of $A \langle m, n \rangle$ before return is made from the algorithm.

   1   [Trivial case] If $m = 0$ then set $ACKER \leftarrow n + 1$ and Exit.
   2   [Initialize for iteration] Set $VALUE[0] \leftarrow 1$, $PLACE[0] \leftarrow 0$. (This step initializes row 0.)
   3   [Iteration loop: get new value] Set $VALUE[0] \leftarrow$ VALUE$[0] + 1$ and $PLACE[0] \leftarrow PLACE[0] + 1$. (Here a new entry is made for row 0.)
   4   [Propagate $VALUE[0]$] Repeat steps 5 and 6 for $i = 0, \ldots, m - 1$.
   5   [Initiate new row] If $PLACE[i] = 1$ then set $VALUE[i + 1] \leftarrow VALUE[0]$ and $PLACE[i + 1] \leftarrow 0$; otherwise go to step 6. If $i = m - 1$ then go to step 7; otherwise go to step 3. (This step performs the assignment $A \langle i + 1, 0 \rangle \leftarrow A \langle i, 1 \rangle$. If $i + 1$ is equal to m, the algorithm may be complete. Otherwise we go to step 3 since no new rows may be started.)
   6   [Move $VALUE[0]$ to another row] If $VALUE[i + 1] = PLACE[i]$ then set $VALUE[i + 1] \leftarrow VALUE[0]$ and $PLACE[i + 1] \leftarrow PLACE[i + 1] + 1$; otherwise go to step 3. (If $VALUE[0]$ cannot be propagated to another row, leave the loop; otherwise the value is transferred according to $A \langle i + 1, j + 1 \rangle \leftarrow A \langle i, A \langle i + 1, j \rangle \rangle$ where j equals $PLACE[i + 1]$ before it is incremented. In this case, if $i + 1 < m$, we must remain in the loop.)
   7   [Check for end of iteration] If $PLACE[m] = n$ then set $ACKER \leftarrow VALUE[0]$ and Exit; otherwise go to step 3.

   It is important to note the correspondence between the steps of the algorithm and the three clauses used to redefine Ackermann's function:

Clause	Algorithm steps(s)
(1) $A \langle 0, n \rangle = n + 1$	2 and 3
(2) $A \langle m + 1, 0 \rangle = A \langle m, 1 \rangle$	5
(3) $A \langle m + 1, n + 1 \rangle = A \langle m, A \langle m + 1, n \rangle \rangle$	6

////

A PL/I program which tests this algorithm is given in Fig. 2-6.8.

```
ITERATE:
      PROCEDURE OPTIONS(MAIN);
      /* TEST THE ITERATIVE SOLUTION TO ACKERMANN'S FUNCTION */
      DECLARE
          ACKER ENTRY(BIN FIXED(31),BIN FIXED(31)) RETURNS(BIN FIXED(31))
                                                                        ;
      PUT SKIP(3) EDIT('THE SOLUTION TO ACKERMANN''S FUNCTION FOR M=2 A',
          'ND N=2 IS ',ACKER(2,2))(A(46),A(10),F(2));
      PUT SKIP(3) EDIT('THE SOLUTION TO ACKERMANN''S FUNCTION FOR M=3 A',
          'ND N=3 IS ',ACKER(3,3))(A(46),A(10),F(2));

ACKER:
          PROCEDURE (M,N) RETURNS(BINARY FIXED(31));
          /* AN ITERATIVE SOLUTION TO ACKERMANN'S FUNCTION DUE TO RICE,
             CACM VOLUME 8, NUMBER 2, (1965).
             COMPUTE ACKERMANN'S FUNCTION DEFINED BY
                        ACKER(0,N) = N + 1
                        ACKER(M + 1,0) = ACKER(M,1),
                        ACKER(M + 1,N + 1) = ACKER(M,ACKER(M + 1,N))
             FOR THE ARGUMENTS M AND N.                                */
          DECLARE
              (M,N) BINARY FIXED(31),
              (PLACE,VALUE)(0:M) BINARY FIXED (31);
          IF M = 0 /* TRIVIAL CASE - RETURN N + 1 */
          THEN RETURN(N + 1);
          VALUE(0) = 1; /* INITIALIZE FOR ITERATION */
          PLACE(0) = 0;
LOOP: /* ITERATION LOOP*/
          VALUE(0) = VALUE(0) + 1;  /* EXTEND ROW ZERO */
          PLACE(0) = PLACE(0) + 1;
          DO I = 0 TO M - 1; /* PROPAGATE NEW VALUE TO HIGHER LEVELS */
              IF PLACE(I) = 1
              THEN
                  DO; /* INITIATE NEW LEVEL */
                      VALUE(I + 1) = VALUE(0);
                      PLACE(I + 1) = 0;
                      IF I = M - 1 /* END OF PROPAGATION */
                      THEN GO TO CHECK_N;
                      ELSE GO TO LOOP;
                  END;
              IF VALUE(I + 1) = PLACE(I)
              THEN
                  DO; /* GET NEXT VALUE FOR LEVEL I + 1 FROM THE COLUMN
                         OF LEVEL I INDICATED BY VALUE(I+1) */
                      VALUE(I + 1) = VALUE(0);
                      PLACE(I + 1) = PLACE(I + 1) + 1;
                  END;
              ELSE GO TO LOOP; /* NO PROPAGATION SO GET NEXT VALUE */
          END; /* OF DO I = 0 TO M - 1 */
CHECK_N: /* CHECK FOR END OF ITERATIVE PROCESS */
          IF PLACE(M) = N /* NTH COLUMN AT LEVEL M HAS BEEN REACHED */
          THEN RETURN(VALUE(0));
          ELSE GO TO LOOP;
      END ACKER;

      END ITERATE;
```

THE SOLUTION TO ACKERMANN'S FUNCTION FOR M=2 AND N=2 IS 7

THE SOLUTION TO ACKERMANN'S FUNCTION FOR M=3 AND N=3 IS 61

FIGURE 2-6.8 Iterative formulation of Ackermann's function.

This algorithm could theoretically compute any value of Ackermann's function, but the majority of $\langle m, n \rangle$ pairs will result in function values which are too large for a computer word.

It was pointed out earlier that a FORTRAN subprogram could not contain a call to itself. It is an easy matter to program the recursion mechanism in

FORTRAN. This is an interesting exercise which gives an insight and understanding of recursion. Before starting the task of programming Ackermann's function in FORTRAN via the faking of recursion, it is necessary to discuss a data structure known as a *stack*. A stack is similar to a railway system for shunting cars, as shown in Fig. 2-6.9.

In this system, the last railway car to be placed on the stack is the first to leave. Repeatedly using the addition and deletion operations permits the cars to be arranged on the output railway line in some prescribed order. For our purposes, a stack will be represented by a vector consisting of some large number of elements which should be sufficient to handle all possible additions likely to be made to the stack. An approximate representation of such an allocation scheme is given in Fig. 2-6.10.

A pointer *TOP* keeps track of the top element in the stack. Initially, when the stack is empty, *TOP* has a value of zero; when the stack contains a single element, *TOP* has a value of 1; and so on. Each time a new element is inserted in the stack, the pointer is incremented by 1 before the element is placed on the stack. The pointer is decremented by 1 each time a deletion is made from the stack. The rightmost occupied element of the stack represents its top element. The leftmost element of the stack represents the bottom element of the stack.

When a recursive procedure is executed, a stack is used as storage for the items mentioned in the prologue and epilogue of Fig. 2-6.2. More specifically, the formal parameters, local variables, and return address are inserted on the stack in a specific order when the procedure is entered. In the epilogue, the most recently saved items are those which are currently on top of the stack because a stack is worked on a Last In, First Out basis. For this reason, a stack is ideally

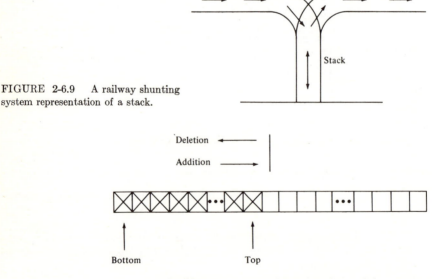

FIGURE 2-6.9 A railway shunting system representation of a stack.

FIGURE 2-6.10 Representation of a stack by a vector.

```
      SUBROUTINE INSERT(S,MAX,TCP,M,N,LABEL)
C   SUBROUTINE TO INSERT THE ARGUMENTS AND RETURN ADDRESS
C   OF ACKERMANN'S FUNCTION ON A STACK.
C   S IS A VECTOR REPRESENTING THE STACK.
C   MAX IS THE NUMBER OF ELEMENTS ALLOCATED TO THE STACK.
C   TOP IS THE POINTER TO THE TCP ELEMENT CF THE STACK.
C   M, N, AND LABEL ARE TO BE PLACED ON THE STACK.
C   ...
      INTEGER S(MAX),TOP
C   ...
C   WILL THE STACK CVERFLOW?
      IF(TOP + 3.GT.MAX) GO TO 1
C   ...
C   STORE NEW ELEMENTS CN STACK.
C   ...
      S(TOP + 1) = M
      S(TOP + 2) = N
      S(TOP + 3) = LABEL
      TCP = TOP + 3
      RETURN
C   ...
C   CUTPUT ERROR MESSAGE.
    1 WRITE(6,100)
      STOP
  100 FORMAT(' ',14HSTACK CVERFLCW)
      END
```

FIGURE 2-6.11   FORTRAN subprogram for stacking M, N, and LABEL.

suited for the handling of recursion. This stack processing, which is performed by the compiler for recursive procedures, must be simulated to permit the faking of recursion.

It should be noted that we have added flexibility in using a vector to represent a stack. We can access elements which are not indicated by *TOP*, a freedom which may not be allowed with other representations of stacks. This flexibility will be used to our advantage in the following FORTRAN subprograms.

For Ackermann's function, only three items, arguments m, n, and the return address, are stacked by the prologue of the procedure. A FORTRAN subroutine which is specifically written to handle the stacking of these items, denoted M, N, and LABEL in the subprogram, is given in Fig. 2-6.11. Stack overflow could occur if the initial choice of arguments M and N is unwise, and so this possibility is investigated in INSERT.

A second subprogram is required by the epilogue for deleting the triplet of items added to the stack by INSERT. This is an obvious procedure, but care must be taken that the proper elements are assigned to the variables M, N, and LABEL. Subroutine DELETE is given in Fig. 2-6.12.

Now that the two necessary stack operations are at our disposal, we must determine how to use them in faking the recursion process. It will be assumed that when execution is taking place at a certain level of recursion, the values of M and N pertaining to that level will be contained in the topmost elements of the stack. The associated return address will indicate the statement to which control is transferred on return to the next lowest level. Thus the arguments required at a certain level must be inserted on the stack immediately on entry, and deleted prior to transfer to a lower level.

The FORTRAN function in Fig. 2-6.13, ACKER, fakes the recursion process of Ackermann's function. The entire recursive framework of Ackermann's

```
      SUBROUTINE DELETE(S,MAX,TOP,M,N,LABEL)
C   SUBROUTINE TO DELETE THE ARGUMENTS AND RETURN ADDRESS OF A CALL
C   TO ACKERMANN'S FUNCTION FROM A STACK.
C   S IS THE NAME OF THE STACK.
C   MAX IS THE NUMBER OF ELEMENTS ALLOCATED TO THE STACK.
C   TOP IS THE NUMBER OF THE TOP ELEMENT OF THE STACK.
C   ...
      INTEGER S(MAX),TOP
C   ...
C   REMOVE ARGUMENTS AND RETURN ADDRESS.
C   ...
      LABEL = S(TOP)
      N = S(TOP - 1)
      M = S(TOP - 2)
      TOP = TOP - 3
      RETURN
      END
```

FIGURE 2-6.12 FORTRAN subprogram for deleting elements from a stack.

function is contained within this subprogram. The call to, entry into, and prologue of a level of the function are equivalent to a CALL INSERT statement followed by a transfer to the statement labeled 10. The first call to INSERT places the original values of M and N on the stack along with the number 60 corresponding to LABEL. When these values are unstacked, they will be recognized as corresponding to the initial call, and exit will be made from ACKER.

Statements 8, 9, 21, and 22 are used for tracing the levels of recursion. In statements 8 and 9, the level number from which a call has been made is calculated and printed. Note that the items used in the level being entered are currently on the stack. Thus, if the call was from level 0, there are 3 items on the stack; that is, level 1 is being entered. Similarly, if level $j + 1$ is the highest level entered, there will be $3 * (j + 1)$ items on the stack at that time, but the call to that level was made from level j. Note that the maximum level reached dictates the size of the stack which is necessary. For example, if the maximum level reached is 60, we need 180 elements in the S array. In statements 21 and 22, the level number to which return is being made is printed. If we are returning from level $k + 1$, then the generation of M, N, and return address effective at level $k + 1$ have already been deleted from the stack, and so the number of elements on the stack is $3k$, that is, 3 times the level number being returned to. Thus the level number is easily obtained on dividing TOP by 3.

In statements 6 and 7, the values of M and N to be used at the current level of recursion are retrieved. In statements 11 and 12, if M is zero, ACKER is set to N + 1 and a transfer is made to the statement labeled 50. Such a transfer is equivalent to a return, as will be seen later. Note that the current value of ACKER is always the result of the last completed call. In statements 14 and 15, if N is equal to zero, a recursive call is made by inserting M − 1, 1, and return address 50 on the stack. This procedure is in accordance with the definition $A \langle m, n \rangle = A \langle m - 1, 1 \rangle$, if $n = 0$, of Ackermann's function. The return address 50 is stacked since, when return is made from this recursive call, the program immediately returns from the level in which the call was made.

If M and N are nonzero, we have a situation where a recursive call must be made to calculate a value for use in another recursive call. That is,

$$A \langle m, n \rangle = A \langle m - 1, A \langle m, n - 1 \rangle \rangle$$

```
0001                    INTEGER FUNCTION ACKER(M,N)
          C   SUBPROGRAM TO EVALUATE ACKERMANN'S FUNCTION
          C   BY FAKING RECURSION IN FORTRAN.
          C   M AND N ARE ARGUMENTS OF ACKERMANN'S FUNCTION.
          C   S IS A VECTOR REPRESENTING THE STACK.
          C   TOP IS A POINTER TO THE TOP ELEMENT OF THE STACK.
          C   MAX IS THE MAXIMUM NUMBER OF ELEMENTS ALLOCATED TO THE
          C   STACK.
          C   LABEL REPRESENTS A RETURN ADDRESS.
          C   I IS THE LEVEL NUMBER OF A CALL OR RETURN.
0002                    INTEGER S(300),TOP
0003                    MAX = 300
          C   INITIALIZE THE STACK BY INSERTING THE INITIAL ARGUMENTS AND
          C   RETURN ADDRESS.  THESE VALUES WILL CAUSE RETURN TO THE
          C   INVOKING ROUTINE WHEN UNSTACKED.
0004                    TOP = 0
0005                    CALL INSERT(S,MAX,TOP,M,N,60)
          C   STATEMENTS 10, 20 AND 30 BEGIN SEGMENTS WHICH HANDLE THE
          C   THREE CASES OF ACKERMANN'S FUNCTION.
          C   ...
          C   OBTAIN M AND N VALUES CORRESPONDING TO THIS CALL.
0006             10 M = S(TOP - 2)
0007                N = S(TOP - 1)
          C   CALCULATE AND OUTPUT THE LEVEL NUMBER OF THE CALL.
0008                I = TOP / 3 - 1
0009                WRITE(6,101)I,M,N
          C   IF M=0 THEN A(M,N)=N+1 SO TRANSFER TO THE RETURN SEGMENT.
0010                IF(M.NE.0) GO TO 20
0011                ACKER = N + 1
0012                GO TO 50
          C   IF N = 0, A(M,N) = A(M - 1,1), SO STACK THE ARGUMENTS AND
          C   RETURN ADDRESS FOR THE NEXT CALL.
0013             20 IF(N.NE.0) GO TO 30
0014                CALL INSERT(S,MAX,TOP,M - 1,1,50)
0015                GO TO 10
          C   STACK THE ARGUMENTS AND RETURN ADDRESS FOR THE INNERMOST
          C   RECURSIVE CALL OF A(M,N) = A(M - 1, A(M,N - 1)).
0016             30 CALL INSERT(S,MAX,TOP,M,N - 1,40)
0017                GO TO 10
          C   RETURN FROM INNERMOST CALL IN A(M,N) = A(M - 1,A(M,N - 1)).
          C   NOW EXECUTE OUTER CALL.
0018             40 CALL INSERT(S,MAX,TOP,M - 1,ACKER,50)
0019                GO TO 10
          C   ...
          C   THIS SECTION SIMULATES A RETURN FROM A CALL
          C   TO ACKERMANN'S FUNCTION.
0020             50 CALL DELETE(S,MAX,TOP,M,N,LABEL)
          C   CALCULATE AND OUTPUT LEVEL NUMBER TO BE RETURNED TO.
0021                I = TOP / 3
0022                WRITE(6,100)I,ACKER
0023                IF(LABEL.EQ.40) GO TO 40
0024                IF(LABEL.EQ.50) GO TO 50
          C   RETURN TO INVOKING ROUTINE.
0025             60 RETURN
0026            100 FORMAT(' ',16HRETURN  TO LEVEL,I4,14H OF ACKER  =  ,I2)
0027            101 FORMAT(' ',16HCALL  FROM LEVEL,I4,10H OF ACKER(,I2,1H,
                   1,I2,1H))
0028                END
```

FIGURE 2-6.13   FORTRAN function for Ackermann's function.

The innermost call is made by inserting M and N − 1 on the stack with return address 40. The 40 indicates that on return from this call, transfer is made to the statement labeled 40 in which the outermost recursive call is made by stacking $M - 1$ and the previously returned value of ACKER. In this case, 50 is used as a return address, indicating that we return from the original level of invocation on completion of both calls.

```
C    PROGRAM TO TEST THE FUNCTION ACKER WHICH FAKES RECURSION
C    TO SOLVE ACKERMANN'S FUNCTION.
C    ...
     INTEGER ACKER,ANSWER
C    ...
C    CALL FROM LEVEL 0 WITH ARGUMENTS M=2 AND N=2.
C    ...
     ANSWER = ACKER(2,2)
     WRITE(6,100)ANSWER
     STOP
100  FORMAT(' ',13HACKER(2,2) = ,I3)
     END
```

```
                         CALL   FROM LEVEL   0 OF ACKER( 2, 2)
                         CALL   FROM LEVEL   1 OF ACKER( 2, 1)
                         CALL   FROM LEVEL   2 OF ACKER( 2, 0)
                         CALL   FROM LEVEL   3 OF ACKER( 1, 1)
                         CALL   FROM LEVEL   4 OF ACKER( 1, 0)
                         CALL   FROM LEVEL   5 OF ACKER( 0, 1)
                         RETURN TO LEVEL   5 OF ACKER   =    2
                         RETURN TO LEVEL   4 OF ACKER   =    2
                         CALL   FROM LEVEL   4 OF ACKER( 0, 2)
                         RETURN TO LEVEL   4 OF ACKER   =    3
                         RETURN TO LEVEL   3 OF ACKER   =    3
                         RETURN TO LEVEL   2 OF ACKER   =    3
                         CALL   FROM LEVEL   2 OF ACKER( 1, 3)
                         CALL   FROM LEVEL   3 OF ACKER( 1, 2)
                         CALL   FROM LEVEL   4 OF ACKER( 1, 1)
                         CALL   FROM LEVEL   5 OF ACKER( 1, 0)
                         CALL   FROM LEVEL   6 OF ACKER( 0, 1)
                         RETURN TO LEVEL   6 OF ACKER   =    2
                         RETURN TO LEVEL   5 OF ACKER   =    2
                         CALL   FROM LEVEL   5 OF ACKER( 0, 2)
                         RETURN TO LEVEL   5 OF ACKER   =    3
                         RETURN TO LEVEL   4 OF ACKER   =    3
                         CALL   FROM LEVEL   4 OF ACKER( 0, 3)
                         RETURN TO LEVEL   4 OF ACKER   =    4
                         RETURN TO LEVEL   3 OF ACKER   =    4
                         CALL   FROM LEVEL   3 OF ACKER( 0, 4)
                         RETURN TO LEVEL   3 OF ACKER   =    5
                         RETURN TO LEVEL   2 OF ACKER   =    5
                         RETURN TO LEVEL   1 OF ACKER   =    5
                         CALL   FROM LEVEL   1 OF ACKER( 1, 5)
                         CALL   FROM LEVEL   2 OF ACKER( 1, 4)
                         CALL   FROM LEVEL   3 OF ACKER( 1, 3)
                         CALL   FROM LEVEL   4 OF ACKER( 1, 2)
                         CALL   FROM LEVEL   5 OF ACKER( 1, 1)
                         CALL   FROM LEVEL   6 OF ACKER( 1, 0)
                         CALL   FROM LEVEL   7 OF ACKER( 0, 1)
                         RETURN TO LEVEL   7 OF ACKER   =    2
                         RETURN TO LEVEL   6 OF ACKER   =    2
                         CALL   FROM LEVEL   6 OF ACKER( 0, 2)
                         RETURN TO LEVEL   6 OF ACKER   =    3
                         RETURN TO LEVEL   5 OF ACKER   =    3
                         CALL   FROM LEVEL   5 OF ACKER( 0, 3)
                         RETURN TO LEVEL   5 OF ACKER   =    4
                         RETURN TO LEVEL   4 OF ACKER   =    4
                         CALL   FROM LEVEL   4 OF ACKER( 0, 4)
                         RETURN TO LEVEL   4 OF ACKER   =    5
                         RETURN TO LEVEL   3 OF ACKER   =    5
                         CALL   FROM LEVEL   3 OF ACKER( 0, 5)
                         RETURN TO LEVEL   3 OF ACKER   =    6
                         RETURN TO LEVEL   2 OF ACKER   =    6
                         CALL   FROM LEVEL   2 OF ACKER( 0, 6)
                         RETURN TO LEVEL   2 OF ACKER   =    7
                         RETURN TO LEVEL   1 OF ACKER   =    7
                         RETURN TO LEVEL   0 OF ACKER   =    7
                         ACKER(2,2) =    7
```

FIGURE 2-6.14 Mainline program and results for faking recursion of Ackermann's function.

In the statement labeled 50, the topmost three elements of the stack are deleted. In statements 23 and 24, control is transferred according to the unstacked return address. If that address is neither 40 nor 50, it must be 60, corresponding to the initial call, and thus we exit from ACKER.

A mainline program to test the FORTRAN function ACKER is given in Fig. 2-6.14, together with the results of computing $A \langle 2, 2 \rangle$.

A nontrivial application to which recursion can be easily applied is mechanical theorem proving. This is the topic of the following section.

EXERCISES 2-6.2

1 The usual method for evaluating a polynomial of the form

$$p_n(x) = a_0 x^n + a_1 x^{n-1} + a_2 x^{n-2} + \cdots + a_{n-1} x + a_n$$

uses the technique known as nesting or Horner's rule. This is an iterative method which can be described as follows:

$$b_0 = a_0$$

$$b_{i+1} = x \cdot b_i + a_{i+1} \qquad i = 0, 1, \ldots, n - 1$$

from which one can obtain $b_n = p_n(x)$.

An alternate solution to the problem is to write

$$p_n(x) = x \cdot p_{n-1}(x) + a_n$$

where

$$p_{n-1}(x) = a_0 x^{n-1} + a_1 x^{n-2} + \cdots + a_{n-2} x + a_{n-1}$$

which is a recursive formulation of the problem. Write a recursive function program to evaluate such a polynomial. Use as data $n = 3$, $a_0 = 1$, $a_1 = 3$, $a_2 = 3$, $a_3 = 1$ and $x = 2$.

2 Consider the set of all valid completely parenthesized infix arithmetic expressions consisting of single-letter variable names, nonnegative integers, and the four operators $+$, $-$, $*$, and $/$. The following recursive definition gives all such valid expressions:

1 Any single-letter variable (A to Z) or a nonnegative integer is a valid infix expression.

2 If γ and β are valid infix expressions, then $(\gamma + \beta)$, $(\gamma - \beta)$, $(\gamma * \beta)$, and (γ/β) are valid infix expressions.

3 The only valid infix expressions are those defined by steps 1 and 2.

Write a recursive function program which will have as input some string of symbols and which is to output "VALID EXPRESSION" if the input string is a valid infix expression and "INVALID EXPRESSION" otherwise. Write a main program to read the input data and invoke this function.

3 Write a recursive function program to compute the square root of a number. Read in triples of numbers N, A, and E, where N is the number for which the square root is to be found, A is an approximation of the square root, and E is the allowable error in the result. Use as your function

$$\text{ROOT}(N, A, E) = \begin{cases} A & \text{if } |A^2 - N| < E \\ \text{ROOT}\left(N, \dfrac{A^2 + N}{2A}, E\right) & \text{otherwise} \end{cases}$$

Use the following triples as test data.

2	1.0	0.001
3	1.5	0.001
8	2.5	0.001
225	14.2	0.001

4 Another common application for recursion is the problem of generating all possible permutations of a set of symbols. For the set consisting of symbols A, B, and C, there exist six permutations, namely, ABC, ACB, BAC, BCA, CBA, and CAB. The set of permutations of N symbols is generated by taking each symbol in turn and prefixing it to all the permutations which result from the remaining N − 1 symbols. It is therefore possible to specify the permutations of a set of symbols in terms of permutations of a smaller set of symbols. Write a recursive-function program for generating all possible permutations of a set of symbols.

5 In many applications it is required to know the number of different partitions of a given integer N, that is, how many different ways N can be expressed as a sum of integer summands. If we denote by Q_{MN} the number of ways in which an integer M can be expressed as a sum, each summand of which is no larger than N, then the number of partitions of N is given by Q_{NN}. The function Q_{MN} is defined recursively as

$$Q_{MN} = \begin{cases} 1 & \text{if } M = 1 \text{ and for all N} \\ 1 & \text{if } N = 1 \text{ and for all M} \\ Q_{MM} & \text{if } M < N \\ 1 + Q_{M,M-1} & \text{if } M = N \\ Q_{M,N-1} + Q_{M-N,N} & \text{if } M > N \end{cases}$$

Write a recursive-function program and use values of N = 3, 4, 5, 6 as data.

6 Recall from Sec. 1-2.7 the recursive definition of a well-formed formula (wff) for the propositional calculus. Develop algorithms and give a PL/I program for determining whether a formula is well-formed.

7 Formulate an algorithm and write a program for determining whether two statement formulas are equivalent. The approach which should be taken for solving this problem is to generate and compare the principal disjunctive (or conjunctive) normal forms for the statements. If they are the same, then the statement formulas are equivalent; otherwise they are not.

A procedure for manually obtaining the principal disjunctive normal form for a statement formula, as given in Sec. 1-3.3, consisted of the following steps:

1 Eliminate the unwanted connectives (such as → and ⇄).

2 Eliminate all occurrences of double negation and apply De Morgan's laws to distribute the negation operators. Repeat this step until De Morgan's laws can no longer be applied.

3 Distribute the conjunctions to obtain a disjunctive standard form.

4 In each term T_i of the standard form that has a variable missing, say Q, replace T_i by $(Q \lor \neg Q) \land T_i$. Duplicate terms and those containing $Q \land \neg Q$ are eliminated. This step is repeated until the principal disjunctive normal form is obtained.

This manual procedure can be formulated algorithmically by using string manipulation and recursion. The outline of an algorithm for generating the principal disjunctive normal form of a statement formula follows. It is assumed that the statement formula is well-formed.

The binary operators $\rightarrow$ and $\rightleftarrows$ are replaced by their equivalents in terms of operators $\vee$, $\wedge$, and $\neg$. Expressions in which a negation operator affects more than a single variable—for example, $\neg\neg(\neg(A \vee \neg B) \vee (\neg C \wedge D))$—must be dealt with. Occurrences of double negation are removed, and then De Morgan's laws are applied. Since this procedure may cause more occurrences of double negation, the procedure must be repeated until De Morgan's laws can no longer be applied.

When negation operators affect only single variables, it is possible to convert the statement formula to a disjunctive standard form by distributing conjunctions. For example, $((A \vee \neg B) \wedge (C \vee \neg D))$ must be converted to $(((A \wedge C) \vee (A \wedge \neg D)) \vee ((\neg B \wedge C) \vee (\neg B \wedge \neg D)))$. Recursion may prove useful for this step.

Finally, the disjunctive standard form must be converted to principal disjunctive normal form. Recursion should be used for generating the minterms, although the use of stacks is an alternative. Make sure that the duplicate or contradictory terms are eliminated. Since the normal form is to be compared with another normal form, both must depend on the same variables. It may therefore be necessary to include in a normal form variables which were not present in the original statement formula. Remember that the variables and minterms must be ordered to simplify the comparison of two normal forms.

This algorithm is the basis for determining the equivalence of two statement formulas. When both statements have been converted to their principal disjunctive normal form with ordering, they may easily be compared.

2-7 RECURSION IN MECHANICAL THEOREM PROVING

In Sec. 1-4.4 we presented a formulation of statement logic suitable for mechanical theorem proving. We now present algorithms that implement the mechanical theorem proving techniques based on this formulation.

Recall that in Sec. 1-4.4 when we were determining whether a particular argument was valid, we converted this problem to one of determining whether a proof existed for some formula corresponding to this argument. If a proof did exist, then the proof was constructed, thereby establishing the formula as a theorem. The procedure involved consisted of the following phases:

1 An analysis of the formula to determine if it had a proof
2 The construction of the proof if it was found to exist

The first phase was performed for all formulas, but for certain formulas (the nontheorems) the second phase could not take place. For the formulas which had proofs, the second phase consisted of merely retracing in reverse order the steps generated during the first phase. Therefore, the first phase was the important part of the procedure.

Let us consider in more detail this phase of analysis. Recall that each rule in this formulation of statement logic had one of the following forms:

1 If sequent α is a theorem, then sequent γ is a theorem.
2 If sequents α and β are theorems, then sequent γ is also a theorem.

Given a particular sequent, which we assumed to be a theorem, we selected a "rule" which converted this sequent to one or two simpler sequents which were also expected to be theorems. This process continued until the only sequents left were connective-free sequents. Since each of these sequents was expected to be a theorem (because of our original assumptions), and since every connective-free sequent that is a theorem is also an axiom (and conversely), it was then a simple matter to determine whether the original formula was a theorem. We simply determined if all these connective-free sequents were axioms. If they were, then the original formula was a theorem, and its proof consisted of the sequents generated by the analysis phase taken in reverse order (i.e., starting with the axioms and moving via the rules to the original formula).

However, what were the "rules" applied in the analysis phase to produce simpler sequents? The rules, as written, produced more complex sequents rather than simpler sequents; they introduced connectives. Yet, we were eliminating connectives in order to produce simpler formulas. Actually, we were applying the converse of the rules. The rules, as written, introduce connectives; but each rule has a converse rule which is also valid. These converse rules eliminate connectives, and it is these that were used during the analysis phase.

Another way of looking at this process is to observe that the application of rules of elimination generated all the conditions necessary for the given formula to be a theorem. If at least one of these conditions was not met (i.e., some connective-free sequent turned out to be a nonaxiom), then the given formula could not be a theorem. If all conditions were met, then, jointly, these conditions were a sufficient condition for the given formula to be a theorem.

It may already have been noticed that the proof of a formula in this presentation of statement logic can be represented by a treelike structure. The original formula is the root of the tree, and the axioms are the leaves. If we adhere to the convention suggested in Sec. 1-4.4, in which the main connective of the leftmost formula is always chosen for elimination, then this tree will be generated in what is known as a "preorder fashion" during the analysis (i.e., first the root, then the left branch, and finally the right branch, assuming that a root which has but one branch has a left branch). The proof of the formula, if it exists, is simply the steps of the analysis taken in reverse order. This corresponds to what we might call a converse-postorder traversal of this proof tree, i.e., first the right branch, then the left branch, and finally the root where a single branch leading to a root is assumed to be a right branch. Since the theory of graphs (which includes such trees) is discussed in Chap. 5, we will not discuss trees any further at this point.

The phase of analysis in this formulation of theorem proving is a good example of a recursive procedure. For any given sequent, there is a termination test—is this sequent connective-free? If it is, then recursion stops and some explicit value (e.g., *true* meaning "the sequent is a theorem" or *false* for "the sequent is not a theorem") is assigned, and then this value is returned to the step that generated this sequent.

If the sequent is not connective-free, then another connective is eliminated to produce one or two simpler sequents; these are then analyzed by a recursive call to the analysis procedure. The new sequents, because they are simpler, are one step nearer a successful application of the termination test.

We now present the algorithms that implement the form of mechanical theorem proving illustrated in Sec. 1-4.4. These algorithms are designed to perform the analysis phase. The construction of a proof (or synthesis phase), once it has been discovered to exist, reduces to the simple task of following, in reverse order, the steps produced during analysis. Consequently, we omit any treatment of actual proof construction. Since little tracing is used in explaining the algorithms, readers are encouraged to do their own tracing for sample inputs.

Note that the formulas in the sequents are all assumed to have no embedded blanks and to be in prefix form (see Sec. 1-3.6). Prefix formulas are used for two reasons:

1 The leftmost main connective is easier to determine for formulas in prefix form.

2 The determination of the operands of a connective is made easier when the formula is in prefix form.

This restriction to prefix formulas, though not affecting the validity of the technique, does require that the 10 rules of the system be expressed in a form modified to deal with prefix formulas.

Algorithm *DETECT* determines which connective, if any, is to be eliminated. The convention suggested in Sec. 1-4.4 is followed; namely, the main connective of the leftmost formula in the sequent is always chosen.

Algorithm *DETECT* Given a string of formulas, *FORM*, this procedure returns a numeric code for the type of leftmost connective found in *FORM*. Codes of 1, 2, 3, 4, and 5 are used for the symbols $\urcorner$, $\wedge$, $\vee$, $\rightarrow$, and $\rightleftarrows$ respectively. The code associated with no connective is 0. The position of the connective, i, is returned as a second parameter. *SYMBOLS* is defined in algorithm *MAIN* and is the string consisting of the five connectives $\urcorner$, $\wedge$, $\vee$, $\rightarrow$, and $\rightleftarrows$.

1 [Initialize position] Set $i \leftarrow 0$.
2 [Formulas exhausted?] If $i \geq LENGTH(FORM)$ then set $DETECT \leftarrow$ 0 and Exit.
3 [Get next symbol] Set $i \leftarrow i + 1$ and $DETECT \leftarrow INDEX(SYMBOLS, SUB(FORM, i, 1))$.
4 [Is it a connective?] If $DETECT > 0$ then Exit; otherwise go to step 2.

$////$

Algorithm *OPERANDS* uses the results of the previous algorithm to extract from the sequent the operands of this connective and to delete from the sequent the entire formula.

The method used in algorithm *OPERANDS* for isolating the operands of a connective is based on certain theorems (presented in Chap. 3) that deal with criteria for well-formed prefix expressions. These criteria make use of the notion of the rank of a formula. The *rank* of a formula is defined as the sum of the ranks of its component symbols. The ranks of a binary connective, a unary connective, and a variable are defined to be 1, 0, and -1 respectively. It can be shown that a prefix formula is well-formed if and only if its rank is -1 and the rank of every proper substring that includes the first symbol of the formula is nonnegative. Thus, starting with the symbols immediately after a connective and adding the ranks of these symbols one by one to a counter initially set to 1, as soon as the counter has a value of 0, we know that we have just taken the last symbol of a well-formed operand. To find a second operand (if the connective is a binary connective), we simply reset the counter to 1 and follow the same procedure.

To illustrate this method, we use it to determine the operands of the formula $\rightleftarrows P \wedge \vee P \neg QR$, the prefix form of $P \rightleftarrows ((P \vee \neg Q) \wedge R)$. The numbers below the symbols are the values of the counter as it is used to record rank totals for each operand.

$$\rightleftarrows \quad P \quad \wedge \quad \vee \quad P \quad \neg \quad Q \quad R$$

$$1 \quad 0$$

$$1 \quad 2 \quad 3 \quad 2 \quad 2 \quad 1 \quad 0$$

The first and second operands of the connective $\rightleftarrows$ are P and $\wedge \vee P \neg QR$ respectively.

Algorithm *OPERANDS* Given a string of formulas *FORM*, the position in the string of the leftmost connective, *POS*, and the number of operands appropriate to that connective, *NUM*, this procedure returns these operands as one of the parameters, the array *OPER*, and deletes the entire formula from *FORM*. *MAXL* serves two purposes in this algorithm. In the part that finds operands, it indicates the length of the string in which an operand must be found; in the part that deletes the entire formula, it indicates the length of the formula that must be deleted. Note that two blanks follow each formula within a string of formulas; these blanks, rather than commas, are used as separators. *LOC* is the position of the last symbol immediately preceding the substring that must be searched for an operand. *RANK* is the counter that records the total of the rank values, while j is an index counter used to select symbols one at a time from the substring to be searched. The symbol i is a counter that records the number of operands extracted, and *TEMP* is merely a temporary location holding one symbol from the substring. *SIGN* is a built-in function which returns a value of $-1, 0,$ or 1, depending on its argument being negative, zero, or positive, respectively. The symbol $''$ is used to denote a string of length 0.

1. [Initialize position and operand array] Set $LOC \leftarrow POS$, $OPER[1] \leftarrow ''$, $OPER[2] \leftarrow ''$.
2. [Operand-finding loop] Repeat steps 3 to 7 for $i = 1, 2, \ldots, NUM$.
3. [Initialize rank and index counters and set length limit] Set $RANK \leftarrow 1$, $j \leftarrow 0$, and $MAXL \leftarrow LENGTH(SUB(FORM, LOC + 1))$.
4. [Found an operand?] If $RANK = 0$ then go to step 7.
5. [Get next symbol if still a wff] Set $j \leftarrow j + 1$. If $j > MAXL$ then print error message and Exit; otherwise set $TEMP \leftarrow SUB(FORM, LOC + j, 1)$.
6. [Form new rank value if still a wff] If $TEMP = '\flat'$ then print error message and Exit; otherwise set $RANK \leftarrow RANK + SIGN(INDEX(SYMBOLS, TEMP) - 1)$ and go to step 4.
7. [Extract operand and reset position] Set $OPER[i] \leftarrow SUB(FORM, LOC + 1, j)$ and $LOC \leftarrow LOC + j$.

8 [Get length of formula to be deleted] Set $MAXL \leftarrow LENGTH$ $(OPER[1]) + LENGTH(OPER[2]) + 3$.

9 [Delete formula and exit] Set $FORM \leftarrow SUB(FORM, 1, POS - 1) \circ$ $SUB(FORM, POS + MAXL)$ and Exit. ////

Algorithm $HAO\text{-}WANG$ is the main algorithm that performs the recursive analysis, and it operates as follows:

> The sequent is printed. Algorithm $DETECT$ is invoked to find a connective to eliminate. If one is found, then algorithm $OPERANDS$ is used to isolate the operands of this connective and algorithm $HAO\text{-}WANG$ is recursively invoked in a manner appropriate for whichever rule is to be applied. If no connective is found, then the sequent is tested to determine if it is an axiom.

All the arguments for any invocation of the algorithm are assumed to be passed by value (see Sec. 1-1).

Algorithm $HAO\text{-}WANG$ This recursive procedure attempts to apply an elimination rule to a sequent which is presented as the pair of arguments $ANTE$, the antecedent, and $CONS$, the consequent. The sequent is printed, along with a nesting level number, $LEVEL$ (initialized in algorithm $MAIN$), which aids in grouping sequents of proof sequences. In following the "leftmost first" rule, the antecedent is searched for a connective to eliminate. $TYPE$ records the numeric code value for the connective found by algorithm $DETECT$, and POS is the position at which it is found in $ANTE$. If a connective is found, then algorithm $OPERANDS$ is invoked to isolate the operands of that connective. These operands are returned via the array parameter OP, and $ANTE$ is returned with this entire formula deleted from it. The appropriate elimination rule for the connective found in the antecedent is then applied by recursively invoking $HAO\text{-}WANG$ with arguments (passed by value) constructed to conform to the requirements of the chosen rule. If no connective is found in the antecedent, then the consequent, $CONS$, is checked in an identical manner.

Finding a leftmost connective in $CONS$ is followed by an invocation of $OPERANDS$ to isolate the operands and an application of the appropriate elimination rule for a connective found in the consequent. If $CONS$ should be connective-free, then the sequent is examined to determine whether it is an axiom. The variable i is an index of $ANTE$, while $TOKEN$ contains one symbol of $ANTE$ which is matched against each symbol of $CONS$. One successful match means the sequent was an axiom. In such a case, the procedure returns a value *true*. If the sequent was not an axiom, the procedure returns *false*.

1 [Increment level counter and print sequent] Set $LEVEL \leftarrow LEVEL + 1$ and print the sequent and level counter.

2 [Connective in antecedent?] Set $TYPE \leftarrow DETECT(ANTE, POS)$. If $TYPE = 0$ then go to step 4. If $TYPE = 1$ then call $OPERANDS$ (1, OP, $ANTE$, POS); otherwise call $OPERANDS$ (2, OP, $ANTE$, POS).

3 [Transfer to antecedent elimination rule] Go to the antecedent rule determined by the value of $TYPE$ (one of steps 10 to 14 below).

4 [Connective in consequent?] Set $TYPE \leftarrow DETECT(CONS, POS)$.

If $TYPE = 0$ then go to step 6. If $TYPE = 1$ then call $OPERANDS$ (1, OP, $CONS$, POS); otherwise call $OPERANDS$ (2, OP, $CONS$, POS).

    5 [Transfer to consequent elimination rule] Go to the consequent rule determined by the value of $TYPE$ (one of steps 15 to 19 below).

    6 [Axiom-test loop for connective-free sequent] Repeat steps 7 and 8 for $i = 1, \ldots, LENGTH(ANTE)$.

    7 [Get a symbol from antecedent] Set $TOKEN \leftarrow SUB(ANTE, i, 1)$.

    8 [If nonblank, test against consequent symbols] If $TOKEN \neq$ 'b̸' then if $INDEX(CONS, TOKEN) \neq 0$ print 'Axiom', set $HAO\text{-}WANG \leftarrow true$, and Exit.

    9 [A nonaxiom!] Print 'Nonaxiom', set $HAO\text{-}WANG \leftarrow false$, and Exit.

The next five steps are the antecedent rules. All arguments are passed by value.

    10 [$TYPE = 1$; $\neg\Rightarrow$: If $\alpha, \beta \stackrel{s}{\Rightarrow} X, \gamma$ then $\alpha, \neg X, \stackrel{s}{\Rightarrow} \gamma$] Set $HAO\text{-}WANG \leftarrow HAO\text{-}WANG(ANTE, OP[1] \circ$ 'b̸b̸' $\circ CONS)$, $LEVEL \leftarrow LEVEL - 1$, and Exit.

    11 [$TYPE = 2$; $\wedge \Rightarrow$: If $X, Y, \alpha, \beta \stackrel{s}{\Rightarrow} \gamma$ then $\alpha, \wedge XY, \beta \stackrel{s}{\Rightarrow} \gamma$] Set $HAO\text{-}WANG \leftarrow HAO\text{-}WANG(OP[1] \circ$ 'b̸b̸' $\circ OP[2] \circ$ 'b̸b̸' $\circ ANTE, CONS)$, $LEVEL \leftarrow LEVEL - 1$, and Exit.

    12 [$TYPE = 3$; $\vee \Rightarrow$: If $X, \alpha, \beta \stackrel{s}{\Rightarrow} \gamma$ and $Y, \alpha, \beta \stackrel{s}{\Rightarrow} \gamma$ then $\alpha, VXY, \beta \stackrel{s}{\Rightarrow} \gamma$] Set $HAO\text{-}WANG \leftarrow HAO\text{-}WANG(OP[1] \circ$ 'b̸b̸' $\circ ANTE, CONS)$, $LEVEL \leftarrow LEVEL - 1$. If $HAO\text{-}WANG$ is *false* then Exit; otherwise set $HAO\text{-}WANG \leftarrow HAO\text{-}WANG(OP[2] \circ$ 'b̸b̸' $\circ ANTE, CONS)$, $LEVEL \leftarrow LEVEL - 1$, and Exit.

    13 [$TYPE = 4$; $\to \Rightarrow$: If $Y, \alpha, \beta \stackrel{s}{\Rightarrow} \gamma$ and $\alpha, \beta \stackrel{s}{\Rightarrow} X, \gamma$ then $\alpha, \to XY, \beta \stackrel{s}{\Rightarrow} \gamma$] Set $HAO\text{-}WANG \leftarrow HAO\text{-}WANG(OP[2] \circ$ 'b̸b̸' $\circ ANTE, CONS)$, $LEVEL \leftarrow LEVEL - 1$. If $HAO\text{-}WANG$ is *false* then Exit; otherwise set $HAO\text{-}WANG \leftarrow HAO\text{-}WANG(ANTE, OP[1] \circ$ 'b̸b̸' $\circ CONS)$, $LEVEL \leftarrow LEVEL - 1$, and Exit.

    14 [$TYPE = 5$; $\rightleftarrows \Rightarrow$: If $X, Y, \alpha, \beta \stackrel{s}{\Rightarrow} \gamma$ and $\alpha, \beta \stackrel{s}{\Rightarrow} X, Y, \gamma$ then $\alpha, \rightleftarrows XY, \beta \stackrel{s}{\Rightarrow} \gamma$] Set $HAO\text{-}WANG \leftarrow HAO\text{-}WANG(OP[1] \circ$ 'b̸b̸' $\circ OP[2] \circ$ 'b̸b̸' $\circ ANTE, CONS)$, $LEVEL \leftarrow LEVEL - 1$. If $HAO\text{-}WANG$ is *false* then Exit, otherwise set $HAO\text{-}WANG \leftarrow HAO\text{-}WANG(ANTE, OP[1] \circ$ 'b̸b̸' $\circ OP[2] \circ$ 'b̸b̸' $\circ CONS)$, $LEVEL \leftarrow LEVEL - 1$, and Exit.

The next five steps are the consequent rules. All arguments are passed by value.

    15 [$TYPE = 1$; $\Rightarrow \neg$: If $X, \alpha \stackrel{s}{\Rightarrow} \beta, \gamma$ then $\alpha \stackrel{s}{\Rightarrow} \beta, \neg X, \gamma$] Set $HAO\text{-}WANG \leftarrow HAO\text{-}WANG(OP[1] \circ$ 'b̸b̸' $\circ ANTE, CONS)$, $LEVEL \leftarrow LEVEL - 1$, and Exit.

    16 [$TYPE = 2$; $\Rightarrow \wedge$: If $\alpha \stackrel{s}{\Rightarrow} X, \beta, \gamma$ and $\alpha \stackrel{s}{\Rightarrow} Y, \beta, \gamma$ then $\alpha \stackrel{s}{\Rightarrow} \beta, \wedge XY, \gamma$] Set $HAO\text{-}WANG \leftarrow HAO\text{-}WANG(ANTE, OP[1] \circ$ 'b̸b̸' $\circ CONS)$, $LEVEL \leftarrow LEVEL - 1$. If $HAO\text{-}WANG$ is *false* then Exit; otherwise set $HAO\text{-}WANG \leftarrow HAO\text{-}WANG(ANTE, OP[2] \circ$ 'b̸b̸' $\circ CONS)$, $LEVEL \leftarrow LEVEL - 1$, and Exit.

    17 [$TYPE = 3$; $\Rightarrow \vee$: If $\alpha \stackrel{s}{\Rightarrow} X, Y, \beta, \gamma$ then $\alpha \stackrel{s}{\Rightarrow} \beta, \vee XY, \gamma$] Set $HAO\text{-}WANG \leftarrow HAO\text{-}WANG(ANTE, OP[1] \circ$ 'b̸b̸' $\circ OP[2] \circ$ 'b̸b̸' $\circ CONS)$, $LEVEL \leftarrow LEVEL - 1$, and Exit.

    18 [$TYPE = 4$; $\Rightarrow \to$: If $X, \alpha \stackrel{s}{\Rightarrow} Y, \beta, \gamma$ then $\alpha \stackrel{s}{\Rightarrow} \beta, \to XY, \gamma$] Set $HAO\text{-}WANG \leftarrow HAO\text{-}WANG(OP[1] \circ$ 'b̸b̸' $\circ ANTE, OP[2] \circ$ 'b̸b̸' $\circ CONS)$, $LEVEL \leftarrow LEVEL - 1$, and Exit.

19 [*TYPE* = 5; ⇒⇄: If $X, \alpha \overset{s}{\Rightarrow} Y, \beta, \gamma$ and $Y, \alpha \overset{s}{\Rightarrow} X, \beta, \gamma$ then $\alpha \overset{s}{\Rightarrow} \beta$, ⇄*XY*, γ]Set *HAO-WANG* ← *HAO-WANG*(*OP*[1] ∘ '𝖻𝖻' ∘ *ANTE*, *OP*[2] ∘ '𝖻𝖻' ∘ *CONS*), *LEVEL* ← *LEVEL* − 1. If *HAO-WANG* is *false* then Exit; otherwise set *HAO-WANG* ← *HAO-WANG*(*OP*[2] ∘ '𝖻𝖻' ∘ *ANTE*, *OP*[1] ∘ '𝖻𝖻' ∘ *CONS*), *LEVEL* ← *LEVEL* − 1, and Exit.   ////

Algorithm *MAIN* This procedure reads in a well-formed prefix expression, *EXPRESSION*, prints it, and then calls algorithm *HAO-WANG* to analyze it. The results of the analysis are then printed. The variables *SYMBOLS* and

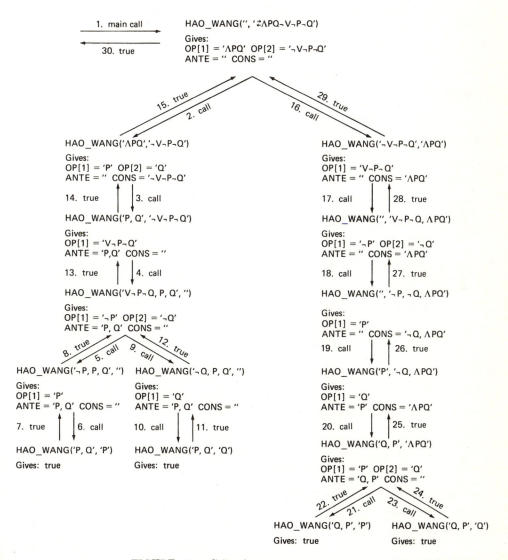

FIGURE 2-7.1 Call and return sequence of steps for algorithm HAO-WANG.

LEVEL, used in the other algorithms, are defined and initialized here. *SYM-BOLS* is simply a string formed from the valid connectives, while *LEVEL* indicates the depth to which recursive nesting of calls has occurred.

1 [Define the connectives] Set $SYMBOLS \leftarrow '\neg \wedge \vee \rightarrow \rightleftarrows '$.

2 [Finished processing?] If out of data then Exit.

3 [Set level counter and do I/O] Set $LEVEL \leftarrow -1$, read *EXPRESSION*, and print *EXPRESSION*.

4 [Process and print results] If $HAO\text{-}WANG('', EXPRESSION \circ '\not b\not b')$ is *true* then print 'Theorem'; otherwise print 'Nontheorem'. Go to step 2.   ////

Figure 2-7.1 is a flow-of-control diagram showing the call and return sequence of steps for algorithm *HAO-WANG* during the analysis of the theorem $\rightleftarrows \wedge PQ \neg \vee \neg P \neg Q$, the prefix form of $(P \wedge Q) \rightleftarrows \neg (\neg P \vee \neg Q)$. The transfers are numbered according to the order of their execution. The diagram also indicates, for each invocation of *HAO-WANG*, the operands that are found and the new antecedent and consequent pair from which the formula containing these operands has been deleted.

EXERCISES 2-7

1 Trace the operation of the theorem-proving program on the following formulas as input:

$$\rightleftarrows \neg \rightleftarrows PQ \vee \wedge \neg PQ \wedge P \neg Q \qquad \rightleftarrows \wedge SV P \neg PS$$

Do this by drawing the trees that could be associated with the analysis phase as it would be performed if these formulas were processed by the program.

2 Develop the appropriate rules for *NAND* and *NOR*, assuming their usual definitions in propositional logic (that is, $\uparrow \Rightarrow$, $\downarrow \Rightarrow$, $\Rightarrow \uparrow$, $\Rightarrow \downarrow$). Usng these rules, extend and modify the previous algorithms so that they are applicable to formulas that contain $\uparrow$ and $\downarrow$ as well as the usual connectives. (To do this, you will have to make minor changes in *DETECT*, *HAO-WANG*, and *MAIN*.)

3 Write a PL/I program which implements the algorithms *DETECT*, *HAO-WANG*, and *MAIN*.

BIBLIOGRAPHY

ABBOTT, JAMES C.: "Sets, Lattices, and Boolean Algebras," Allyn and Bacon, Inc., Boston, 1969.

BARRON, D. W.: "Recursive Techniques in Programming," American Elsevier Publishing Co., Inc., New York, 1968.

BERZTISS, A. T.: "Data Structures: Theory and Practice," Academic Press, Inc., New York, 1971.

D'IMPERIO, M. E.: Data Structures and Their Representation in Storage, "Annual Review in Automatic Programming," vol. 5, pp. 1–75, Pergamon Press, Oxford, 1969.

HARRISON, M. C.: "Data Structures and Programming," Scott, Foresman and Company, Glenview, Illinois, 1973.

KNUTH, D. E.: "The Art of Computer Programming, vol. 1, Fundamental Algorithms," Addison-Wesley Publishing Company, Inc., Reading, Mass., 1968.

LIPSCHUTZ, SEYMOUR: "Theory and Problems of Set Theory and Related Topics," Schaum Publishing Company, New York, 1964.

NELSON, RAYMOND J.: "Introduction to Automata," John Wiley & Sons, Inc., New York, 1968.

PRATHER, RONALD E.: "Introduction to Switching Theory," Allyn and Bacon, Inc., Boston, 1967.

RALSTON, ANTHONY: "Introduction to Programming and Computer Science," McGraw-Hill Book Company, New York, 1971.

RICE, H. G.: Recursion and Iteration, *Communications of the Association for Computing Machinery*, **8**(2): 114–115 (February, 1965).

STOLL, ROBERT R.: "Set Theory and Logic," W. H. Freeman and Company, Publishers, San Francisco, 1963.

SUPPES, E. H.: "Axiomatic Set Theory," D. Van Nostrand and Company, Inc., Princeton, N. J., 1960.

TREMBLAY, J. P., and P. G. SORENSON: "An Introduction to Data Structures with Applications," Lecture notes, University of Saskatchewan, Saskatoon, Saskatchewan, 1974. (To be published by the McGraw-Hill Book Company, New York, 1976.)

WANG, H.: Toward Mechanical Mathematics, *IBM J. Res. and Devel.*, **4**: 2–22 (January, 1960).

WELLS, CHARLES: "Mathematical Structures," Lecture notes, Case Western Reserve University, Cleveland, Ohio, 1968.

3

ALGEBRAIC STRUCTURES

INTRODUCTION

In this chapter we shall first explain what is meant by an algebraic system and then give several examples of familiar algebraic systems and discuss some of their properties. These examples show that different algebraic systems may have several properties in common. This observation provides a motivation for the study of abstract algebraic systems. For such algebraic systems, certain properties are taken as axioms of the system. Any result that is valid for an abstract system holds for all those algebraic systems for which the axioms are true.

Throughout the chapter we shall introduce certain important and useful concepts associated with algebraic systems. For example, the concept of isomorphism shows that two algebraic systems which are isomorphic to one another are structurally indistinguishable and that the results of operations in one system can be obtained from those of the other by simply relabeling the names of the elements and symbols for operations. This concept has useful applications in the sense that the results of one system permit an identical interpretation in the other system. Another important concept is that of a congruence relation which has a useful property known as substitution.

Semigroups are the simplest algebraic structures which satisfy the properties of closure and associativity. They are very important in the theory of sequential machines, formal languages, and in certain applications relating to computer arithmetic such as multiplication.

A monoid, in addition to being a semigroup, also satisfies the identity property. Monoids are used in a number of applications but most particularly in the area of syntactic analysis and formal languages.

Groups are monoids which also possess the inverse property. The application of group theory is important in the design of fast adders and error-correcting codes.

This chapter contains a number of applications dealing with topics such as the compilation of expressions in Polish notation, languages and grammars, the theory of fast adders, and error-detecting and -correcting codes.

3-1   ALGEBRAIC SYSTEMS: EXAMPLES AND GENERAL PROPERTIES

General algebraic systems and some of their basic properties are discussed in this Section. Examples of some familar algebraic systems are given. Also, the concepts of homomorphism, isomorphism, congruence relation, direct product, and subalgebras are introduced in general terms, that is, for any algebraic system. These concepts are repeatedly applied to particular algebraic systems discussed in the later sections.

3-1.1   Definition and Examples

Before we explain what we mean by an algebraic system, let us recall that an n-ary operation for $n = 1, 2, 3, \ldots$ on a set X was defined in Sec. 2-4.4 as a mapping from X^n to X. For $n = 1$ such an operation is called a unary operation. Similarly, for $n = 2$ it is called a binary operation. Any distinguished element of X such as an identity element or a zero element with respect to a binary operation is considered as a 0-ary operation. Accordingly, the result of a 0-ary operation is a particular distinguished element of the set. With this convention in mind, from now on we shall include a 0-ary operation as a particular case of an n-ary operation. In this chapter we are mostly concerned with n-ary operations for $n = 0, 1,$ and 2. For $n = 0$ we shall denote a 0-ary operation by means of a particular distinguished element. A binary operation will be denoted by means of a symbol such as $*$, Δ, $+$, $\oplus$, etc. and the result of a binary operation on the elements, say $x_1, x_2 \in X$, is expressed by writing $x_1 * x_2$. For a finite set X it is sometimes convenient to describe a binary operation by means of a composition table. For $n > 2$ we use the same notation for an n-ary operation as was used for a function of n variables. Thus, if f denotes an n-ary operation, then $f \langle x_1, x_2, \ldots, x_n \rangle$ is the image in X of the n-tuple $\langle x_1, x_2, \ldots, x_n \rangle \in X^n$. It may be more convenient to use the right composition for binary operations, as was done in the case of relations, than to use the left composition, as was done for functions.

For the purpose of our definition here, a system consisting of a set and one or more n-ary operations on the set will be called an *algebraic system*, or simply an *algebra*. We shall denote an algebraic system by $\langle S, f_1, f_2, \ldots \rangle$ where S is a nonempty set and f_1, f_2, ... are operations on S. As a part of the system, some authors include relations on S which are not necessarily operations. Since the operations and relations on the set S define a structure on the elements of S, an algebraic system is called an *algebraic structure*. It is also possible to consider more than one set as a part of the system and operations on these sets. Note that the different operations on the set S may be n-ary operations with different values of n. We shall restrict ourselves to $n = 0, 1$, and 2 and to algebraic systems containing one or two operations only. Occasionally, we shall consider two or more algebraic systems simultaneously. In such cases two algebraic systems $\langle X, \circ \rangle$ and $\langle Y, * \rangle$ are said to be of the same *type* whenever the n-ary operations $\circ$ and $*$ have the same value of n. Similarly, the systems $\langle X, \circ, + \rangle$ and $\langle Y, *, \oplus \rangle$ are of the same type provided that the operations $\circ$ and $*$, and the operations $+$ and $\oplus$, are of the same degree. We now give several examples of algebraic systems and discuss their properties. By a "property of an algebraic system" we mean a property possessed by any of its operations.

EXAMPLE 1 Let **I** be the set of integers. Consider the algebraic system $\langle \mathbf{I}, +, \times \rangle$ where $+$ and $\times$ are the operations of addition and multiplication on **I**. A list of important properties of these operations will now be given. The properties associated with the operations of addition and multiplication are labeled with the letters **A** and **M** respectively. Similarly, other appropriate labels are used to designate other properties. These properties will be repeatedly recalled for other algebraic systems.

(A-1) For any $a, b, c \in \mathbf{I}$

$$(a + b) + c = a + (b + c) \qquad (Associativity)$$

(A-2) For any $a, b \in \mathbf{I}$

$$a + b = b + a \qquad (Commutativity)$$

(A-3) There exists a distinguished element $0 \in \mathbf{I}$ such that for any $a \in \mathbf{I}$

$$a + 0 = 0 + a = a \qquad (Identity\ element)$$

Here $0 \in \mathbf{I}$ is the identity element with respect to addition.

(A-4) For each $a \in \mathbf{I}$, there exists an element in **I** denoted by $-a$ and called the *negative* of a such that

$$a + (-a) = 0 \qquad (Inverse\ element)$$

(M-1) For any $a, b, c \in \mathbf{I}$

$$(a \times b) \times c = a \times (b \times c) \qquad (Associativity)$$

(M-2) For any $a, b \in \mathbf{I}$

$$a \times b = b \times a \qquad (Commutativity)$$

(M-3) There exists a distinguished element $1 \in \mathbf{I}$ such that for any $a \in \mathbf{I}$

$$a \times 1 = 1 \times a = a \qquad (Identity\ element)$$

(**D**) For any $a, b, c \in \mathbf{I}$

$$a \times (b + c) = (a \times b) + (a \times c) \qquad (Distributivity)$$

The operation $\times$ distributes over $+$.

(**C**) For $a, b, c \in \mathbf{I}$ and $a \neq 0$

$$a \times b = a \times c \Rightarrow b = c \qquad (Cancellation\ property)$$

The algebraic system $\langle \mathbf{I}, +, \times \rangle$ should have been expressed as $\langle \mathbf{I}, +, \times, 0, 1 \rangle$ in order to emphasize the fact that 0 and 1 are distinguished elements of $\mathbf{I}$.

We shall now give examples of other algebraic systems with two binary operations which share most of the properties of $\langle \mathbf{I}, +, \times \rangle$ listed here.

EXAMPLE 2 Let $\mathbf{R}$ be the set of real numbers and $+$ and $\times$ be the operations of addition and multiplication on $\mathbf{R}$. The algebraic system $\langle \mathbf{R}, +, \times \rangle$ satisfies all the properties given for the system $\langle \mathbf{I}, +, \times \rangle$. There are certain other properties which distinguish the two systems from one another, but we shall not consider these properties here.

EXAMPLE 3 In the algebraic system $\langle \mathbf{N}, +, \times \rangle$ where $\mathbf{N}$ is the set of natural numbers and the operations $+$ and $\times$ have their usual meanings, all the properties listed for $\langle \mathbf{I}, +, \times \rangle$ except (**A-4**) are satisfied.

EXAMPLE 4 Let S be a nonempty set and $\rho(S)$ be its power set. For any sets $A, B \in \rho(S)$, define the operations $+$ and $\times$ on $\rho(S)$ as

$$A + B = (A - B) \cup (B - A) = (A \cap \sim B) \cup (B \cap \sim A)$$
$$A \times B = A \cap B \qquad (\times \text{ is not a cartesian product})$$

The algebraic system $\langle \rho(S), +, \times \rangle$ satisfies all the properties listed except (**C**). The elements $\varnothing$ and S are the identity elements for $+$ and $\times$ respectively. Note that for any set $A \in \rho(S)$ the inverse of A with respect to the operation $+$ is A itself because $A + A = \varnothing$, so that (**A-4**) is satisfied.

EXAMPLE 5 Let E be a universal set and $\rho(E)$ its power set. Denoting the union and intersection on $\rho(E)$ by $+$ and $\times$, we have an algebraic system $\langle \rho(E), +, \times \rangle$ with $\varnothing$ and E as distinguished elements in place of 0 and 1, and this system satisfies all the properties listed except (**A-4**) and (**C**).

EXAMPLE 6 Consider the set $B = \{0, 1\}$ and the operations $+$ and $\times$ on B given by the following tables:

+	0	1		×	0	1
0	0	1		0	0	0
1	1	0		1	0	1

The algebraic system $\langle B, +, \times \rangle$ satisfies all the properties listed for $\langle \mathbf{I}, +, \times \rangle$ earlier.

From these examples it is clear that a great variety of algebraic systems share some of the features of the system of integers. Instead of studying each individual system separately, it would be convenient to list a set of properties and to derive possible conclusions about any system that possesses those properties. The selected properties are considered as axioms, and any valid conclusion derived from the axioms will hold for any algebraic system for which the axioms hold. For such a discussion, we do not consider any particular set, nor do we attach any particular meaning to the operations involved. The set and the operations of the system are merely symbols, or more precisely, they are abstractions, and the corresponding algebraic system is called an abstract algebra. Such abstract systems are studied later in this chapter.

3-1.2 Some Simple Algebraic Systems and General Properties

The algebraic systems given in Sec. 3-1.1 contained two binary operations which were denoted by $+$ and $\times$ in each case. The choice of these examples was dictated by our familiarity with the systems of integers and real numbers. Similar remarks can be made about the choice of the symbols used to denote binary operations. These algebraic systems are not the simplest ones. In this section we give examples of algebraic systems consisting of a single unary or binary operation. It is possible to obtain such algebraic systems from those given earlier by simply considering one of the two binary operations; for example, $\langle \mathbf{I}, + \rangle$ and $\langle \mathbf{R}, \times \rangle$ are perfectly good examples of algebraic systems.

EXAMPLE 1   Let $M = \{1, 2, \ldots, m\}$ and τ be a unary operation on M given by

$$\tau(j) = \begin{cases} j + 1 & j \neq m \\ 1 & j = m \end{cases}$$

The algebra $\langle M, \tau \rangle$ is called a *clock algebra* for obvious reasons. The result of the operation τ on the elements of M can be illustrated as in Fig. 3-1.1. Observe that every element of M can be generated from the element $1 \in M$ by repeated ap-

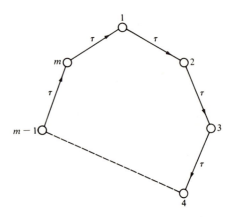

FIGURE 3-1.1   A clock algebra.

Table 3-1.1

$\circ$	f_1	f_2	f_3	f_4
f_1	f_1	f_2	f_3	f_4
f_2	f_2	f_2	f_2	f_2
f_3	f_3	f_3	f_3	f_3
f_4	f_4	f_3	f_2	f_1

plication of the operation τ. Therefore, 1 can be called a *generator* of the algebraic system $\langle M, \tau \rangle$.

EXAMPLE 2   Let $X = \{a, b\}$ and S denote the set of all mappings from X to X. Let us write $S = \{ f_1, f_2, f_3, f_4 \}$ where

$$f_1(a) = a \qquad f_1(b) = b \qquad f_2(a) = a \qquad f_2(b) = a$$
$$f_3(a) = b \qquad f_3(b) = b \qquad f_4(a) = b \qquad f_4(b) = a$$

Then $\langle S, \circ \rangle$, where $\circ$ denotes the operation of (left) composition of functions, is an algebraic system in which the operation is associative. The composition table for the operation $\circ$ is given in Table 3-1.1. Note that f_1 is the identity element with respect to the operation $\circ$. Furthermore, not all the elements of S are invertible. These remarks hold whether we choose $\circ$ to denote the left or right composition. This example can be generalized to the set of mappings from any set X to X. We shall return to this example in Sec. 3-2.

EXAMPLE 3   Let $X = \{1, 2, 3, 4\}$ and $f: X \to X$ be given by

$$f = \{ \langle 1, 2 \rangle, \langle 2, 3 \rangle, \langle 3, 4 \rangle, \langle 4, 1 \rangle \}$$

Let the identity mapping on X be denoted f^0. If we form the composite functions $f \circ f = f^2$, $f^2 \circ f = f^3$, $f^3 \circ f = f^4$, and so on, we find that $f^4 = f^0$. Let us denote f by f^1 and consider the set $F = \{ f^0, f^1, f^2, f^3 \}$. It is clear that the set F is closed under the operation of composition and that $\langle F, \circ \rangle$ is an algebraic system. The operation $\circ$ is both commutative and associative. Also the element f^0 is the identity element with respect to the operation of composition. The result of composition of any two functions of F is given by Table 3-1.2.

EXAMPLE 4   An equivalence relation called "congruence modulo m" on the set of integers was defined in Sec. 2-3.5. Let $m = 4$ and $\mathbf{Z}_4$ denote the set of equiv-

Table   3-1.2

$\circ$	f^0	f^1	f^2	f^3
f^0	f^0	f^1	f^2	f^3
f^1	f^1	f^2	f^3	f^0
f^2	f^2	f^3	f^0	f^1
f^3	f^3	f^0	f^1	f^2

Table 3-1.3

$+_4$	[0]	[1]	[2]	[3]
[0]	[0]	[1]	[2]	[3]
[1]	[1]	[2]	[3]	[0]
[2]	[2]	[3]	[0]	[1]
[3]	[3]	[0]	[1]	[2]

alence classes generated, so that

$$\mathbf{Z}_4 = \{[0], [1], [2], [3]\}$$

where $[j]$ denotes the set of all those integers which are equivalent to j. Let us define an operation $+_4$ on $\mathbf{Z}_4$ given by

$$[i] +_4 [j] = [(i + j)(\mathrm{mod}\ 4)]$$

for all $i, j = 0, 1, 2, 3$. The operation $+_4$ on $\mathbf{Z}_4$ is described in Table 3-1.3. Since the set $\mathbf{Z}_4$ is closed with respect to the operation $+_4$, we have the algebraic system $\langle \mathbf{Z}_4, +_4 \rangle$ in which the operation $+_4$ is commutative and associative. Also [0] is the identity element, and every element of $\mathbf{Z}_4$ is invertible.

It is easy to observe a similarity between Tables 3-1.2 and 3-1.3. One can obtain Table 3-1.3 from Table 3-1.2 by simply relabeling the entries f^0, f^1, f^2, and f^3 by [0], [1], [2], and [3] respectively and the operation $\circ$ by $+_4$. Let us now define a mapping $\psi \colon F \to \mathbf{Z}_4$ such that

$$\psi(f^j) = [j] \qquad \text{for } j = 0, 1, 2, 3$$

It is clear from the tables that

$$\psi(f^i \circ f^j) = \psi(f^i) +_4 \psi(f^j) \qquad \text{for all } i, j = 0, 1, 2, 3 \tag{1}$$

This equation shows that the image of ψ for the argument $f^i \circ f^j$ is the same as the result of the operation $+_4$ applied to the images $\psi(f^i)$ and $\psi(f^j)$ of the elements f^i and f^j. In other words, we can say that the mapping ψ preserves the operations $\circ$ and $+_4$. This property of the mapping ψ is demonstrated in Fig. 3-1.2, which clearly shows that the effect of applying the mapping $\circ$ from $F \times F$ to F and then applying the mapping ψ to the result is the same as the effect of the mapping $\psi \times \psi$ applied to $F \times F$ to obtain an ordered pair of $\mathbf{Z}_4 \times \mathbf{Z}_4$ and then applying the mapping $+_4$ to this ordered pair.

The existence of such a mapping shows that the two algebraic systems $\langle F, \circ \rangle$ and $\langle \mathbf{Z}_4, +_4 \rangle$ are not structurally different. They are only different in the names of the elements and the symbols used for the operations. Any result associated

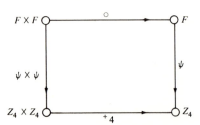

FIGURE 3-1.2

with any one system will also be true for the other system after the labels are changed. We shall now formalize these ideas for any two algebraic systems.

Definition 3-1.1 Let $\langle X, \circ \rangle$ and $\langle Y, * \rangle$ be two algebraic systems of the same type in the sense that both $\circ$ and $*$ are binary (n-ary) operations. A mapping $g: X \to Y$ is called a *homomorphism*, or simply morphism, from $\langle X, \circ \rangle$ to $\langle Y, * \rangle$ if for any $x_1, x_2 \in X$

$$g(x_1 \circ x_2) = g(x_1) * g(x_2) \tag{2}$$

If such a function g exists, then it is customary to call $\langle Y, * \rangle$ a homomorphic image of $\langle X, \circ \rangle$, although we must note that $g(X) \subseteq Y$.

The concept of homomorphism is not restricted to algebraic systems with one binary operation. One can extend this definition to any two algebraic systems of the same type. Since in a homomorphism the operations are preserved, we shall see that several properties of the operations are also preserved.

For the algebraic systems $\langle F, \circ \rangle$ and $\langle \mathbf{Z}_4, +_4 \rangle$, the mapping $\psi: F \to \mathbf{Z}_4$ given by Eq. (1) is a homomorphism. Any mapping which satisfies the condition given by Eq. (2) is a homomorphism. In the example of the algebraic systems $\langle F, \circ \rangle$ and $\langle \mathbf{Z}_4, +_4 \rangle$, the mapping is bijective, which is a special case of homomorphism as can be seen from Definition 3-1.2 which follows. It is possible to have more than one homomorphic mapping from one algebraic system to another.

Definition 3-1.2 Let g be a homomorphism from $\langle X, \circ \rangle$ to $\langle Y, * \rangle$. If $g: X \to Y$ is onto, then g is called an *epimorphism*. If $g: X \to Y$ is one-to-one, then g is called a *monomorphism*. If $g: X \to Y$ is one-to-one onto, then g is called an *isomorphism*.

Definition 3-1.3 Let $\langle X, \circ \rangle$ and $\langle Y, * \rangle$ be two algebraic systems of the same type. If there exists an isomorphic mapping $g: X \to Y$, then $\langle X, \circ \rangle$ and $\langle Y, * \rangle$ are said to be *isomorphic*.

In the case when $\langle X, \circ \rangle$ and $\langle Y, * \rangle$ are isomorphic, then the two algebraic systems are structurally indistinguishable in the sense that they differ only in the labels used to denote the elements of the sets and the operations involved. It is easy to see that the inverse of an isomorphism is also an isomorphism. Also all the properties of the operations are preserved in an isomorphism.

Definition 3-1.4 Let $\langle X, \circ \rangle$ and $\langle Y, * \rangle$ be two algebraic systems such that $Y \subseteq X$. A homomorphism g from $\langle X, \circ \rangle$ to $\langle Y, * \rangle$ in such a case is called an *endomorphism*. If $Y = X$, then an isomorphism from $\langle X, \circ \rangle$ to $\langle Y, * \rangle$ is called an *automorphism*.

EXAMPLE 5 Show that the algebraic systems of $\langle F, \circ \rangle$ and $\langle \mathbf{Z}_4, +_4 \rangle$ given in Examples 3 and 4 are isomorphic.

SOLUTION The mapping $\psi: F \to \mathbf{Z}_4$ defined by Eq. (1) is one-to-one onto and is a homomorphism; hence ψ is an isomorphism. ////

EXAMPLE 6   Let $\langle \mathbf{Z}_4, +_4 \rangle$ and $\langle B, + \rangle$ be the algebraic systems given in Example 4 of Sec. 3-1.2 and Example 6 of Sec. 3-1.1 respectively. Show that $\langle B, + \rangle$ is a homomorphic image of $\langle \mathbf{Z}_4, +_4 \rangle$.

SOLUTION   Let a mapping $g\colon \mathbf{Z}_4 \to B$ be given by

$$g([0]) = g([2]) = 0 \quad \text{and} \quad g([1]) = g([3]) = 1$$

It is easy to verify that g is an epimorphism from $\langle \mathbf{Z}_4, +_4 \rangle$ to $\langle B, + \rangle$ because for any $i, j = 0, 1, 2, 3$

$$g([i] +_4 [j]) = g([i]) + g([j]) \qquad \text{////}$$

EXAMPLE 7   Let $S = \{a, b, c\}$ and let $*$ denote a binary operation on S given by Table 3-1.4. Also let $P = \{1, 2, 3\}$ and $\oplus$ be a binary operation on P given by Table 3-1.4. Show that $\langle S, * \rangle$ and $\langle P, \oplus \rangle$ are isomorphic.

SOLUTION   Consider a mapping $g\colon S \to P$ given by

$$g(a) = 3 \quad g(b) = 1 \quad \text{and} \quad g(c) = 2$$

Obviously, g is one-to-one onto. Also a check of entries in Table 3-1.4 shows that g is a homomorphism. $\qquad$ ////

EXAMPLE 8   Given the algebraic system $\langle \mathbf{N}, + \rangle$ and $\langle \mathbf{Z}_4, +_4 \rangle$, where $\mathbf{N}$ is the set of natural numbers and $+$ is the operation of addition on $\mathbf{N}$, show that there exists a homomorphism from $\langle \mathbf{N}, + \rangle$ to $\langle \mathbf{Z}_4, +_4 \rangle$.

SOLUTION   Define $g\colon \mathbf{N} \to \mathbf{Z}_4$ given by

$$g(a) = [a(\mathrm{mod}\ 4)] \qquad \text{for any } a \in \mathbf{N}$$

For $a, b \in \mathbf{N}$, let $g(a) = [i]$ and $g(b) = [j]$; then

$$g(a + b) = [(i + j)(\mathrm{mod}\ 4)] = [i] +_4 [j] = g(a) +_4 g(b)$$

Observe that $g(0) = [0]$; that is, the mapping g also preserves the identity element. $\qquad$ ////

Let $\langle X, \circ \rangle$ be an algebraic system in which $\circ$ is a binary operation on X. Let us assume that E is an equivalence relation on X. The equivalence relation E is said to have the *substitution property* with respect to the operation $\circ$ iff for any $x_1, x_2 \in X$.

$$(x_1 E x_1') \wedge (x_2 E x_2') \Rightarrow (x_1 \circ x_2) E (x_1' \circ x_2') \qquad (3)$$

where $x_1', x_2' \in X$. Implication (3) states that in $x_1 \circ x_2$ if we substitute for x_1

Table 3-1.4

$*$	a	b	c	$\oplus$	1	2	3
a	a	b	c	1	1	2	1
b	b	b	c	2	1	2	2
c	c	b	c	3	1	2	3

any other element of X which is equivalent to it and similarly for x_2 any other element of X which is equivalent to x_2, then the resulting element is equivalent to $x_1 \circ x_2$; that is, the equivalence relationship is unaltered by such substitutions. The substitution property can be defined for any n-ary operation and also for any number of operations.

Definition 3-1.5 Let $\langle X, \circ \rangle$ be an algebraic system and E be an equivalence relation on X. The relation E is called a *congruence relation* on $\langle X, \circ \rangle$ if E satisfies the substitution property with respect to the operation $\circ$.

This definition of congruence relation can be generalized to any algebraic system, whenever the substitution property is satisfied with respect to all the operations of that system.

With the help of congruence relations it is possible to construct new and simpler algebraic systems from a given algebraic system. Also the concept of congruence relation is closely connected to that of homomorphism, as will be shown now.

Let $\langle X, \circ \rangle$ be an algebraic system in which $\circ$ is a binary operation on X. Let E be a congruence relation on $\langle X, \circ \rangle$. Since E is an equivalence relation on X, it partitions X into equivalence classes. The set of equivalence classes is the quotient set X/E. Let $x_1, x_2, y_1, y_2 \in X$ with $x_1 \, E \, y_1$ and $x_2 \, E \, y_2$. Since E is a congruence relation, $(x_1 \circ x_2) \, E \, (y_1 \circ y_2)$, so that $[x_1 \circ x_2] = [y_1 \circ y_2]$ where $[x_j]$ is used to denote the equivalence class in which x_j is a member. Corresponding to the operation $\circ$ on X, we now define a binary operation $*$ on X/E such that for any $x_1, x_2 \in X$

$$[x_1] * [x_2] = [x_1 \circ x_2] \qquad (4)$$

It is easy to see that the operation $*$ is well defined on X/E because $[x_1 \circ x_2]$ is independent of the elements chosen to represent the equivalence classes $[x_1]$ and $[x_2]$. We therefore have an algebraic system $\langle X/E, * \rangle$ called the *quotient algebra* which is of the same type as the algebra $\langle X, \circ \rangle$. In fact, several properties of the operation $\circ$ are preserved by the operation $*$.

In order to show a connection between a homomorphism and congruence relation, we first show that corresponding to a congruence relation E on $\langle X, \circ \rangle$ we can define a homomorphism g_E from $\langle X, \circ \rangle$ onto the quotient algebra $\langle X/E, * \rangle$ that is given by $g_E(x) = [x]$ for any $x \in X$. Obviously,

$$g_E(x_1 \circ x_2) = [x_1 \circ x_2] = [x_1] * [x_2] = g_E(x_1) * g_E(x_2) \qquad (5)$$

The homomorphism g_E is called the *natural homomorphism* associated with the congruence relation E.

As a next step, let us consider a homomorphism f from $\langle X, \circ \rangle$ onto $\langle Y, \oplus \rangle$. Now we show that corresponding to f we can define a congruence relation E_f on $\langle X, \circ \rangle$ by

$$x_1 \, E_f \, x_2 \Leftrightarrow f(x_1) = f(x_2) \qquad \text{for any } x_1, x_2 \in X \qquad (6)$$

This definition guarantees that E_f is an equivalence relation for any mapping

$f: X \to Y$. On the other hand, the fact that f is a homomorphism guarantees that E_f is a congruence relation on $\langle X, \circ \rangle$.

So far we have established that for *every* congruence relation E on $\langle X, \circ \rangle$, we can define a natural homomorphism g_E. Also, for any homomorphism f from $\langle X, \circ \rangle$ to $\langle Y, \oplus \rangle$, we can define a congruence relation E_f so that there is a one-to-one correspondence between the homomorphisms and congruence relations on $\langle X, \circ \rangle$. As a final step, we now show that if f is a homomorphism from $\langle X, \circ \rangle$ onto $\langle Y, \oplus \rangle$, if E is a congruence relation corresponding to f (called E_f earlier), and if g_E is the natural homomorphism from $\langle X, \circ \rangle$ to $\langle X/E, * \rangle$, then there exists an isomorphism h between $\langle X/E, * \rangle$ and $\langle Y, \oplus \rangle$. With the definitions of $E_f = E$ and g_E as given in Eqs. (5) and (6), let us now define a mapping $h: X/E \to Y$ such that

$$h[x_1] = f(x_1) \qquad \text{for any } x_1 \in X \qquad (7)$$

Observe that for $x_1, x_2 \in X$, $x_1 \circ x_2 \in X$ and

$$g_E(x_1 \circ x_2) = [x_1 \circ x_2] \qquad \text{from (5)}$$

This means

$$h(g_E(x_1 \circ x_2)) = h([x_1 \circ x_2]) = f(x_1 \circ x_2) \qquad \text{from (7)}$$

The mapping h is one-to-one onto, and

$$h([x_1] * [x_2]) = h(g_E(x_1 \circ x_2)) = f(x_1 \circ x_2) = f(x_1) \oplus f(x_2)$$

Hence h is an isomorphism. These mappings can be shown diagrammatically as given in Fig. 3-1.3. In particular, if $Y = X$, then

$$g_{E_f} = f$$

EXAMPLE 9 Let $\langle \mathbf{N}, + \rangle$ be the algebraic system of natural numbers as given in Example 8. Define an equivalence relation E on $\mathbf{N}$ such that $x_1 E x_2$ iff either $x_1 - x_2$ or $x_2 - x_1$ is divisible by 4. Show that E is a congruence relation and that the homomorphism g defined in Example 8 is the natural homomorphism associated with E.

SOLUTION Obviously E is an equivalence relation. Also E is a congruence relation because for $x_1 E x_1'$ and $x_2 E x_2'$, $(x_1 + x_2) E (x_1' + x_2')$ because $(x_1 + x_2) - (x_1' + x_2') = (x_1 - x_1') + (x_2 - x_2')$, and both $x_1 - x_1'$ as well as $x_2 - x_2'$ are divisible by 4. Observe also that the mapping $g(i) = [i]$ is the same as required in the definition of natural homomorphism in Eq. (5), so that $g = g_E$.   ////

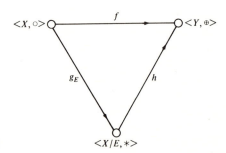

FIGURE 3-1.3

Definition 3-1.6   Let $\langle X, \circ \rangle$ be an algebraic system and $Y \subseteq X$ which is closed under the operation $\circ$. Then $\langle Y, \circ \rangle$ is called a *subalgebra* of $\langle X, \circ \rangle$.

The concept of a subalgebra can be applied to any algebraic system provided the subalgebra is closed under all the operations (including 0-ary operations) of the original system. Naturally a subalgebra is of the same type as the original system, and the operations of the systems being the same, most of their properties are also preserved.

Another useful concept associated with any algebraic system is that of direct product of algebras of the same type.

Definition 3-1.7   Let $\langle X, \circ \rangle$ and $\langle Y, * \rangle$ be two algebraic systems of the same type. The algebraic system $\langle X \times Y, \oplus \rangle$ is called the *direct product* of the algebras $\langle X, \circ \rangle$ and $\langle Y, * \rangle$ provided the operation $\oplus$ is defined for any $x_1, x_2 \in X$ and $y_1, y_2 \in Y$ as

$$\langle x_1, y_1 \rangle \oplus \langle x_2, y_2 \rangle = \langle x_1 \circ x_2, y_1 * y_2 \rangle$$

The algebraic systems $\langle X, \circ \rangle$ and $\langle Y, * \rangle$ are called the *factor algebras* of $\langle X \times Y, \oplus \rangle$.

The definition of direct product can be generalized on the one hand to any two algebraic systems of the same type. The operations in the direct product are defined in terms of the corresponding operations of the factor algebras. On the other hand, one can also define by repeated application of the above procedure the direct product of any finite number of algebraic systems of the same type.

The concepts of subalgebras as well as that of direct product of algebras will be used for almost every abstract algebraic system that we shall study in the next section.

EXERCISES 3-1

1 Which of the following systems satisfy the properties of $\langle \mathbf{I}, +, \times \rangle$ which are designated by (**A-1**) to (**A-4**), (**M-1**) to (**M-3**), (**D**), and (**C**)?
   (*a*) All odd integers
   (*b*) All even integers
   (*c*) All positive integers
   (*d*) All nonnegative integers
   (*e*) $\langle \mathbf{Z}_6, +_6, \times_6 \rangle$
   (*f*) $\langle \mathbf{Z}_7, +_7, \times_7 \rangle$

2 In Example 4, Sec. 3-1.1, let $S = \{a\}$. Given the composition tables for the operations $+$ and $\times$, show that the algebraic system $\langle \rho(S), +, \times \rangle$ in this case is isomorphic to the system given in Example 6, Sec. 3-1.2.

3 Show that if $g: A \to B$ is a homomorphism of an algebraic system $\langle A, * \rangle$ onto $\langle B, \Delta \rangle$ and $\langle A_1, * \rangle$ is a subalgebra of $\langle A, * \rangle$, then the image of A_1 under g is a subalgebra of $\langle B, \Delta \rangle$.

4 Show that the intersection of any two congruence relations on a set is also a congruence relation.

5 Show that the composition of two congruence relations on a set is not necessarily a congruence relation.

6 If $f: S \rightarrow T$ is a homomorphism from $\langle S, * \rangle$ to $\langle T, \Delta \rangle$ and $g: T \rightarrow P$ is also a homomorphism from $\langle T, \Delta \rangle$ to $\langle P, \nabla \rangle$, then $g \circ f: S \rightarrow P$ is a homomorphism from $\langle S, * \rangle$ to $\langle P, \nabla \rangle$.

3-2 SEMIGROUPS AND MONOIDS

Several examples of algebraic systems were given in the previous section. In this section and also in the remainder of this chapter, we study certain abstract algebraic systems. An abstract algebraic system is defined in terms of an arbitrary set and a number of operations on the set. These operations are assumed to have properties which are taken as axioms of the system. No other properties are assumed. Any valid conclusion which follows from these axioms is a theorem of the system. Such theorems are true for any algebraic system for which the axioms hold.

We shall restrict ourselves to algebraic systems with one binary operation. If no restriction is placed on the binary operation, we get an algebraic system which is too general to be of much use. As a next step, we consider an algebraic system consisting of a set and an associative binary operation on the set. After studying such a system, we consider those systems which possess an associative binary operation and an identity element. These algebraic systems are called semigroups and monoids respectively and have useful applications in the areas of computer arithmetic, formal languages, and sequential machines.

3-2.1 Definitions and Examples

Definition 3-2.1 Let S be a nonempty set and $\circ$ be a binary operation on S. The algebraic system $\langle S, \circ \rangle$ is called a *semigroup* if the operation $\circ$ is associative. In other words $\langle S, \circ \rangle$ is a semigroup if for any $x, y, z \in S$,

$$(x \circ y) \circ z = x \circ (y \circ z)$$

A semigroup can be described by giving the composition table of the operation $\circ$ when S is finite and when its order is not large; otherwise, it can be described by means of some rule for the operation $\circ$ on S. Several examples of semigroups are given here. These include some of the examples given in the previous section as special cases. Note that a semigroup may or may not have an identity element with respect to the operation $\circ$. If there is an identity element, then we have the following definition.

Definition 3-2.2 A semigroup $\langle M, \circ \rangle$ with an identity element with respect to the operation $\circ$ is called a *monoid*. In other words, an algebraic system $\langle M, \circ \rangle$ is called a monoid if for any $x, y, z \in M$,

$$(x \circ y) \circ z = x \circ (y \circ z)$$

and there exists an element $e \in M$ such that for any $x \in M$

$$e \circ x = x \circ e = x$$

It has already been shown in Sec. 2-4.4 that an identity element for any binary operation, if it exists, is unique. Therefore, a monoid has a unique or a distinguished element called the *identity* of the monoid. We shall sometimes represent a monoid as $\langle M, \circ, e \rangle$ to emphasize the fact that e is a distinguished element of such a monoid.

For a monoid $\langle M, * \rangle$, the existence of the identity element guarantees that no two columns or rows of the composition table are identical, because if e is the identity, then for $a_i, a_j \in M$ and $a_i \neq a_j$, $e * a_i = a_i \neq e * a_j = a_j$. Similarly, because $a_i * e = a_i$, no two rows are identical. This property will be used later in this section.

EXAMPLE 1   Let X be a nonempty set and X^X be the set of all mappings from X to X. Let $\circ$ denote the operation of composition of these mappings; i.e., for $f, g \in X^X, f \circ g$ given by $(f \circ g)(x) = f(g(x))$ for all $x \in X$ is in X^X. The algebra $\langle X^X, \circ \rangle$ is a monoid, because the operation of composition is associative and the identity mapping $f(x) = x$ for all $x \in X$ is the identity of the operation. (See also Example 3, Sec. 3-1.2.)

EXAMPLE 2   In Example 1, if we let $B(X)$ denote the set of all relations from X to X and we let the operation $\circ$ mean the composition of relations on $B(X)$, then we have a monoid $\langle B(X), \circ \rangle$ in which the identity relation is the identity of the monoid.

EXAMPLE 3   Let S be a nonempty set and $\rho(S)$ be its power set. The algebras $\langle \rho(S), \cup \rangle$ and $\langle \rho(S), \cap \rangle$ are monoids with the identities $\varnothing$ and S respectively.

EXAMPLE 4   Let **N** be the set of natural numbers. Then $\langle \mathbf{N}, + \rangle$ and $\langle \mathbf{N}, \times \rangle$ are monoids with the identities 0 and 1 respectively. On the other hand, if E denotes the set of positive even numbers, then $\langle E, + \rangle$ and $\langle E, \times \rangle$ are semigroups but not monoids.

EXAMPLE 5   Let **I** be the set of integers and $\mathbf{Z}_m$ be the set of equivalence classes generated by the equivalence relation "congruence modulo m" for any positive integer m. The algebraic systems $\langle \mathbf{Z}_m, +_m \rangle$ and $\langle \mathbf{Z}_m, \times_m \rangle$ are monoids in which the operations $+_m$ and $\times_m$ are defined in terms of the operations $+$ and $\times$ on **I** as follows. For any $[i], [j] \in \mathbf{Z}_m$

$$[i] +_m [j] = [(i + j) \pmod m]$$
$$[i] \times_m [j] = [(i \times j) \pmod m]$$

The composition tables for $m = 5$ and 6 are given in Table 3-2.1 (see also Example 4, Sec. 3-1.2). In this table $[i]$ is simply written as i. It may be noted that $[0]$ and $[1]$ are the identity elements with respect to the operations $+_m$ and $\times_m$ respectively. Note also that in the case of $m = 5$, the elements $[1], [2], [3]$, and $[4]$ have inverses with respect to the operation $\times_5$, while in the case of $m = 6$ only $[1]$ and $[5]$ are invertible.

Table 3-2.1

$$m = 5$$

$+_5$	0	1	2	3	4		$\times_5$	0	1	2	3	4
0	0	1	2	3	4		0	0	0	0	0	0
1	1	2	3	4	0		1	0	1	2	3	4
2	2	3	4	0	1		2	0	2	4	1	3
3	3	4	0	1	2		3	0	3	1	4	2
4	4	0	1	2	3		4	0	4	3	2	1

$$m = 6$$

$+_6$	0	1	2	3	4	5		$\times_6$	0	1	2	3	4	5
0	0	1	2	3	4	5		0	0	0	0	0	0	0
1	1	2	3	4	5	0		1	0	1	2	3	4	5
2	2	3	4	5	0	1		2	0	2	4	0	2	4
3	3	4	5	0	1	2		3	0	3	0	3	0	3
4	4	5	0	1	2	3		4	0	4	2	0	4	2
5	5	0	1	2	3	4		5	0	5	4	3	2	1

We shall now give some other examples of monoids which have useful applications. First, however, we introduce some terminology associated with grammars and formal languages. For this purpose, let V denote a nonempty set of symbols. Such a set V is called an *alphabet*. An alphabet need not be finite or even countable. However, for our purpose here we shall assume V to be finite. For example, we may have

$$V_1 = \{0, 1\} \qquad V_2 = \{a, b, \ldots, z\} \qquad V_3 = \{a, 1, *, +, A\}$$

$$V_4 = \{\text{cat, book, dog}, x\} \qquad V_5 = \{a, \ldots, z, 0, 1, \ldots, 9, ',, .\}$$

In alphabet V_4 we assume that each word is a symbol and is indivisible. An element of an alphabet is called a *letter*, a *character*, or a *symbol*. A *string* over an alphabet is an ordered set of symbols from the alphabet. A string is also called a *sequence*, a *word*, or a *sentence* depending upon its nature. A string consisting of m symbols ($m > 0$) is called a string of *length* m. For example, let $V = \{a, b\}$; then aa, bb, ab, and ba are all possible strings of length 2. If we admit an empty string, i.e., a string of length 0 ($m = 0$), which is usually denoted by Λ, then we can have strings of length m for $m \geq 0$. The set of strings over an alphabet V is generally denoted by V^* and the set of nonempty strings by $V^+ = V^* - \{\Lambda\}$. We shall assume that the strings in V^* are of finite length.

Let $\alpha, \beta \in V^*$. A binary operation $\circ$ on V^* is defined by $\alpha \circ \beta$, where $\alpha \circ \beta \in V^*$ is the string obtained by writing the string α on the left of the string β, that is, $\alpha \circ \beta = \alpha\beta$. The operation $\circ$ on V^* is called *concatenation*, or simply *catenation*. For example, let $V = \{a, b\}$ and consider the strings $abaab$ and bb. The concatenation of these strings produces the string $abaabbb$. It is easy to see that the concatenation is associative; therefore, $\langle V^+, \circ \rangle$ is a semigroup called a *free semigroup* generated by the alphabet V. If we admit the empty string Λ, then obviously for any string $\alpha \in V^*$

$$\alpha \Lambda = \Lambda \alpha = \alpha$$

so that Λ is the identity with respect to the operation of concatenation and $\langle V^*, \circ \rangle$ or $\langle V^*, \circ, \Lambda \rangle$ is a monoid.

From the definition it is clear that in general concatenation is not commutative except when V contains a single element. Also no element in V^* except Λ is invertible. No element of V^* is idempotent except the identity Λ. In the semigroup $\langle V^*, \circ \rangle$, every element satisfies the cancellation property. To see it, let us consider two strings α and β of V^* and let $\alpha = \alpha_1 x$ and $\beta = \beta_1 x$. If $\alpha = \beta$, then $\alpha_1 x = \beta_1 x$ which implies $\alpha_1 = \beta_1$. Here $\alpha, \beta \in V^*$ and $x \in V$.

We shall now describe certain monoids consisting of partitions of a set. These monoids are useful in the study of sequential machines. For this purpose, let S be any nonempty set and let $\Pi(S)$ denote the set of all partitions of S. For example, let

$$S_1 = \{a, b\} \qquad \Pi(S_1) = \{\{\bar{a}, \bar{b}\}, \{\overline{a, b}\}\}$$

$$S_2 = \{a, b, c\} \qquad \Pi(S_2) = \{\{\bar{a}, \bar{b}, \bar{c}\}, \{\overline{a, b}, \bar{c}\}, \{\bar{a}, \overline{b, c}\}, \{\overline{a, c}, \bar{b}\}, \{\overline{S_2}\}\}$$

Let $P = \{P_1, P_2, \ldots\}$ and $Q = \{Q_1, Q_2, \ldots\}$ be any two partitions of a set S, that is, $P, Q \in \Pi(S)$. We now define a binary operation $*$ on $\Pi(S)$ such that $P * Q$ consists of the set of intersections of every element of P with every element of Q, leaving out empty sets. For example, if we take

$$S = \{x_1, x_2, x_3, x_4, x_5, x_6\}$$

$$P = \{\overline{x_1, x_2}, \overline{x_3, x_4}, \overline{x_5, x_6}\} \qquad Q = \{\overline{x_1, x_2, x_3}, \overline{x_4}, \overline{x_5, x_6}\}$$

$$P * Q = \{\overline{x_1, x_2}, \overline{x_3}, \overline{x_4}, \overline{x_5, x_6}\}$$

It is easy to see that the operation $*$ is both associative and commutative. Also the partition $\{\bar{S}\}$ consisting of a single block is the identity of the operation $*$. Hence $\langle \Pi(S), * \rangle$ or $\langle \Pi(S), *, \{\bar{S}\} \rangle$ is a monoid. Note also that every element of $\Pi(S)$ is idempotent with respect to the operation $*$ since for any $P \in \Pi(S)$, $P * P = P$. The operation $*$ on $\Pi(S)$ is called the *product of partitions*.

It is possible to define another operation called the *sum of partitions*, which we denote by $\oplus$, such that $\langle \Pi(S), \oplus \rangle$ is also a monoid. The operation $\oplus$ is defined in the following manner.

For any $P, Q \in \Pi(S)$, a subset T of S is in $P \oplus Q$ if

1 T is the union of one or more elements of P,
2 T is the union of one or more elements of Q, and
3 no subset of T satisfies (1) and (2) except T itself.

An an example of this definition, let

$$P_1 = \{\overline{x_1, x_2}, \overline{x_3}, \overline{x_4, x_5, x_6}\} \qquad Q_1 = \{\overline{x_1, x_2, x_3}, \overline{x_4, x_5, x_6}\}$$

and P, Q be the partitions given earlier. Then

$$P_1 \oplus Q_1 = \{\overline{x_1, x_2, x_3}, \overline{x_4, x_5, x_6}\}$$

$$P \oplus Q = \{\overline{x_1, x_2, x_3, x_4, x_5, x_6}\}$$

The operation $\oplus$ is associative and commutative. Also the partition consisting of single elements of S is the identity for the operation $\oplus$ on $\Pi(S)$.

If in a semigroup (monoid) $\langle S, * \rangle$ the operation $*$ is commutative, then the semigroup (monoid) is called *commutative*. Similarly, if in a monoid $\langle M, *, e \rangle$ every element is invertible, then the monoid is called a *group*. We discuss groups in the next section.

In a monoid $\langle M, * \rangle$, the powers of any particular element, say $a \in M$, are defined as

$$a^0 = e \qquad a^1 = a \qquad a^2 = a * a \qquad \ldots \qquad a^{j+1} = a^j * a \qquad \text{for } j \in \mathbf{N}$$

By using the generalized associative law one can write

$$a^{j+k} = a^j * a^k = a^k * a^j \qquad \text{for all } j, k \in \mathbf{N}$$

A monoid $\langle M, *, e \rangle$ is said to be *cyclic* if there exists an element $a \in M$ such that every element of M can be written as some powers of a, that is, as a^n for some $n \in \mathbf{N}$. In such a case, the cylic monoid is said to be generated by the element a, and the element a is called the *generator* of the cyclic monoid. A cyclic monoid is commutative because for any $b, c \in M$, $b = a^m$ and $c = a^n$ for some m, $n \in \mathbf{N}$, so that

$$b * c = a^m * a^n = a^{m+n} = a^n * a^m = c * b$$

The monoid given in Example 1 of Sec. 3-1.2 is a finite cyclic monoid. On the other hand, $\langle \mathbf{N}, + \rangle$ is an infinite cyclic monoid generated by $1 \in \mathbf{N}$.

The cyclic semigroups or monoids considered so far were all generated by a single element. One can generalize this situation by considering a finite set of elements as the set of generators of a semigroup. For this purpose, let X be a set of n elements called the set of generators and let $*$ be a binary operation on X which is associative. The set of all elements generated by the elements of X by repeated application of $*$ is called the semigroup generated by X. We shall show in Sec. 3-2.2 that a semigroup generated by n generators is a homomorphic image of the free semigroup X^* generated by X.

EXAMPLE 6   Show that the semigroup $\langle X, * \rangle$ in which $X = \{a, b, p, q\}$ and the operation $*$ is given by Table 3-2.2 is generated by the set $\{a, b\}$.

SOLUTION   Note that $a * b = p$ and $a * a = q$. Therefore, every element of S involving p or q can be written in terms of a and b.   ////

Table 3-2.2

$*$	a	b	p	q
a	q	p	b	a
b	b	b	b	b
p	p	p	p	p
q	a	b	p	q

3-2.2 Homomorphism of Semigroups and Monoids

The concept of homomorphism for algebraic systems was introduced in Sec. 3-1.2. Now we apply this concept to semigroups and monoids. Homomorphisms of semigroups and monoids have useful applications in the economical design of sequential machines and in formal languages.

> **Definition 3-2.3** Let $\langle S, * \rangle$ and $\langle T, \Delta \rangle$ be any two semigroups. A mapping $g: S \to T$ such that for any two elements $a, b \in S$,
>
> $$g(a * b) = g(a) \, \Delta \, g(b) \qquad (1)$$
>
> is called a *semigroup homomorphism*.

As before, a semigroup homomorphism is called a semigroup monomorphism, epimorphism, or isomorphism depending on whether the mapping is one-to-one, onto, or one-to-one onto respectively. Two semigroups $\langle S, * \rangle$ and $\langle T, \Delta \rangle$ are said to be isomorphic if there exists a semigroup isomorphic mapping from S to T.

We have already seen in Example 8, Sec. 3-1.2, that there exists a semigroup homomorphism g from $\langle \mathbf{N}, + \rangle$ to $\langle \mathbf{Z}_m, +_m \rangle$ in which the identity of $\langle \mathbf{N}, + \rangle$ is mapped into the identity $[0]$ of $\langle \mathbf{Z}_m, +_m \rangle$.

Let us now examine some of the implications of Eq. (1). For this purpose, let us assume that $\langle S, * \rangle$ is a semigroup and $\langle T, \Delta \rangle$ is an algebraic structure of the same type, that is, Δ is a binary operation on T but it is not necessarily associative. If there exists an onto mapping $g: S \to T$ such that for any $a, b \in S$ Eq. (1) is satisfied, then we can show that Δ must be associative and hence $\langle T, \Delta \rangle$ must be a semigroup. In order to see this, let $a, b, c \in S$

$$g((a * b) * c) = g(a * b) \, \Delta \, g(c)$$
$$= (g(a) \, \Delta \, g(b)) \, \Delta \, (g(c))$$

On the other hand,

$$g(a * (b * c)) = g((a * b) * c)$$

but $g(a * (b * c))$ can be shown to be equal to $g(a) \, \Delta \, (g(b) \, \Delta \, g(c))$ by a similar argument. Hence Δ is associative, and $\langle T, \Delta \rangle$ must be a semigroup. This result shows that Eq. (1) preserves the semigroup character because it preserves associativity.

Next, note that if g is a semigroup homomorphism from $\langle S, * \rangle$ to $\langle T, \Delta \rangle$, then for any element $a \in S$ which is idempotent, we must have $g(a)$ idempotent, because

$$g(a * a) = g(a) = g(a) \, \Delta \, g(a)$$

The property of idempotency is preserved under the semigroup homomorphism. In a similar manner commutativity is also preserved.

If $\langle S, * \rangle$ is a semigroup with an identity e, that is, $\langle S, *, e \rangle$ is a monoid and g is a homomorphism from $\langle S, * \rangle$ to a semigroup $\langle T, \Delta \rangle$, then for any $a \in S$,

$$g(a * e) = g(e * a) = g(a) \, \Delta \, g(e) = g(e) \, \Delta \, g(a) = g(a)$$

However, this result does not guarantee that $g(e)$ is an identity with respect to the operation Δ in T. This lack of a guarantee is due to the fact that g is not necessarily onto and therefore there may be some elements of T which are not images of any elements of S. Let $y \in T$ be such an element; then $y \Delta g(e)$ is not necessarily equal to y, and hence $g(e)$ is not the identity element of $\langle T, \Delta \rangle$. Equation (1) alone does not guarantee that the identity is preserved. However, if g is an epimorphism, i.e., the semigroup homomorphism is onto and $\langle S, * \rangle$ is a monoid, then the identity is also preserved.

Definition 3-2.4 Let $\langle M, *, e_M \rangle$ and $\langle T, \Delta, e_T \rangle$ be any two monoids. A mapping $g: M \to T$ such that for any two elements $a, b \in M$

$$g(a * b) = g(a) \, \Delta \, g(b) \qquad (2)$$

and
$$g(e_M) = e_T \qquad (3)$$

is called a *monoid homomorphism*.

In the case where g is an onto mapping from M onto T, condition (2) implies (3).

As before, we can say that for any $\langle M, *, e_M \rangle$ and algebraic system $\langle T, \Delta \rangle$ (where Δ is a binary operation on T) where there exists a mapping $g: M \to T$ which is onto, the condition given by Eq. (2) guarantees that $\langle T, \Delta \rangle$ must be a monoid with $g(e_M)$ as its identity element.

The monoid homomorphism preserves not only associativity and the identity, but also commutativity. Moreover, if $a \in M$ is invertible and $a^{-1} \in M$ is its inverse, then $g(a^{-1})$ must be the inverse of $g(a)$; that is, $g(a^{-1}) = [g(a)]^{-1}$, because

$$g(a * a^{-1}) = g(e_M) = e_T = g(a) \, \Delta \, g(a^{-1})$$

and
$$g(a^{-1} * a) = g(e_M) = e_T = g(a^{-1}) \, \Delta \, g(a)$$

implying $g(a^{-1}) = [g(a)]^{-1}$. Thus the property of invertibility is also preserved and consequently so are the inverses.

For a monoid epimorphism, the zero element, if it exists, is also preserved. To verify this statement, let $g: M \to T$ be a monoid homomorphism of $\langle M, *, e_M \rangle$ onto $\langle T, \Delta, e_T \rangle$ and let $z \in M$ be the zero of M with respect to the operation $*$, so that for any $a \in M$,

$$z * a = a * z = z$$

and $g(z * a) = g(z) = g(z) \, \Delta \, g(a) = g(a * z) = g(a) \, \Delta \, g(z)$

Also any $t \in T$ can be written as $t = g(b)$ for some $b \in M$, and the above step, repeated for b, shows that $g(z)$ is the required zero of T.

EXAMPLE 1 Let $\langle \mathbf{N}, + \rangle$ be the semigroup of natural numbers and $\langle S, * \rangle$ be the semigroup on $S = \{e, 0, 1\}$ with the operation $*$ given by Table 3-2.3. A mapping $g: \mathbf{N} \to S$ given by $g(0) = 1$ and $g(j) = 0$ for $j \neq 0$ is a semigroup homomorphism. Although both $\langle \mathbf{N}, + \rangle$ and $\langle S, * \rangle$ are monoids with identities 0 and e respectively, g is not a monoid homomorphism because $g(0) \neq e$.

Table 3-2.3

$*$	e	0	1
e	e	0	1
0	0	0	0
1	1	0	1

The following theorem shows that the composition of semigroup homomorphisms is also a semigroup homomorphism.

Theorem 3-2.1 Let $\langle S, * \rangle$, $\langle T, \Delta \rangle$, and $\langle V, \oplus \rangle$ be semigroups and $g: S \to T$ and $h: T \to V$ be semigroup homomorphisms. Then $(h \circ g): S \to V$ is a semigroup homomorphism from $\langle S, * \rangle$ to $\langle V, \oplus \rangle$.

PROOF Let $a, b \in S$. Then

$$(h \circ g)(a * b) = h(g(a * b)) = h(g(a) \Delta g(b))$$
$$= h(g(a)) \oplus h(g(b))$$
$$= (h \circ g)(a) \oplus (h \circ g)(b) \qquad \qquad ////$$

A homomorphism of a semigroup into itself is called a *semigroup endomorphism*, while an isomorphism onto itself is called a *semigroup automorphism*.

From Theorem 3-2.1 we have the following theorem.

Theorem 3-2.2 The set of all semigroup endomorphisms of a semigroup is a semigroup under the operation of (left) composition.

Theorem 3-2.2 can be extended to automorphisms also. The identity mapping is the identity with respect to composition of functions. Hence the set of all the semigroup automorphisms of a semigroup is a monoid.

Our next theorem is first proved for semigroups and then extended to monoids.

Theorem 3-2.3 Let $\langle S, * \rangle$ be a given semigroup. There exists a homomorphism $g: S \to S^S$, where $\langle S^S, \circ \rangle$ is a semigroup of functions from S to S under the operation of (left) composition.

PROOF For any element $a \in S$, let $g(a) = f_a$ where $f_a \in S^S$ and f_a is defined by

$$f_a(b) = a * b \qquad \text{for any } b \in S$$

Now

$$g(a * b) = f_{a*b}$$

where

$$f_{a*b}(c) = (a * b) * c = a * (b * c)$$
$$= f_a(f_b(c)) = (f_a \circ f_b)(c)$$

Therefore, $g(a * b) = f_{a*b} = f_a \circ f_b = g(a) \circ g(b)$. The last step shows that $g: S \to S^S$ is a homomorphism of $\langle S, * \rangle$ into $\langle S^S, \circ \rangle$. Corresponding to an element $a \in S$, the function f_a is completely determined from the entries in the row corresponding to a in the composition table of $\langle S, * \rangle$. Since $f_a = g(a)$, every row of such a table determines the image under the homomorphism g.   ////

Let $g(S)$ be the image set of S under the homomorphism g of Theorem 3-2.3 such that $g(S) \subseteq S^S$. For $a, b \in S$, $g(a) = f_a$ and $g(b) = f_b$ are in $g(S)$. Also

$$f_a \circ f_b = g(a) \circ g(b) = g(a * b) = f_{a*b} \in g(S)$$

implying that $g(S)$ is closed under the operation of composition, and $g: S \to g(S)$ is an epimorphism from S onto $g(S)$.

EXAMPLE 2   Let $\langle S, * \rangle$ be a semigroup in which $S = \{a, b, c\}$ and the operation $*$ is given in Table 3-2.4. Let us define a mapping $g: S \to S^S$ given by $g(a) = f_a$, $g(b) = f_b$, and $g(c) = f_c$ where $f_a, f_b, f_c \in S^S$. Also

$$
\begin{array}{lll}
f_a(a) = a & f_a(b) = b & f_a(c) = c \\
f_b(a) = b & f_b(b) = c & f_b(c) = a \\
f_c(a) = c & f_c(b) = a & f_c(c) = b
\end{array}
$$

Obviously there are 3^3 elements in S^S and $\langle S^S, \circ \rangle$ is a monoid. However, $g: S \to S^S$ is a homomorphism from $\langle S, * \rangle$ to $\langle S^S, \circ \rangle$ and $g(S) = \{ f_a, f_b, f_c \}$. The composition table for $\langle g(S), \circ \rangle$ can be obtained from Table 3-2.4 by writing f_a, f_b, f_c for a, b and c respectively and by replacing $*$ by $\circ$.

The mapping $g: S \to g(S)$ is onto, so that g is an epimorphism from $\langle S, * \rangle$ onto $\langle g(S), \circ \rangle$. This fact does not guarantee that for any two elements $a, b \in S$ such that $a \neq b$ we will also have $g(a) \neq g(b)$. In fact, if any rows in the composition table are identical, then the functions defined by these rows will be equal. This idea suggests that if $\langle S, * \rangle$ is a monoid, then no two rows of the composition table can be identical. In that case, the mapping $g: S \to g(S)$ is one-to-one and onto; that is, g is an isomorphism.

Theorem 3-2.4   Let $\langle M, * \rangle$ be a monoid. Then there exists a subset $T \subseteq M^M$ such that $\langle M, * \rangle$ is isomorphic to the monoid $\langle T, \circ \rangle$.

It is easy to see that the identity element of $\langle T, \circ \rangle$ is $g(e)$ where e is the identity of M.

Theorem 3-2.4 establishes an isomorphism between any finite monoid and a monoid of functions under the operation of composition. Our next theorem establishes the existence of a homomorphism from the free semigroup with n generators to any semigroup with n generators.

Table 3-2.4

$*$	a	b	c
a	a	b	c
b	b	c	a
c	c	a	b

Theorem 3-2.5 Let X be a set containing n elements, let X^* denote the free semigroup generated by X, and let $\langle S, \oplus \rangle$ be any other semigroup generated by any n generators; then there exists a homomorphism $g: X^* \to S$.

PROOF Let Y be the set of n generators of S. Let $g: X \to Y$ be a one-to-one mapping given by $g(x_i) = y_i$ for $i = 1, 2, \ldots, n$. Now, for any string

$$\alpha = x_1 x_2 \ldots x_m$$

of X^*, we define

$$g(\alpha) = g(x_1) \oplus g(x_2) \oplus \cdots \oplus g(x_m)$$

From this definition it follows that for a string $\alpha\beta \in X^*$,

$$g(\alpha\beta) = g(\alpha) \oplus g(\beta)$$

so that g is the required homomorphism. ////

We shall now show that every semigroup homomorphism induces a congruence relation and conversely.

Theorem 3-2.6 Let $\langle S, * \rangle$ and $\langle T, \Delta \rangle$ be two semigroups and g be a semigroup homomorphism from $\langle S, * \rangle$ to $\langle T, \Delta \rangle$. Corresponding to the homomorphism g, there exists a congruence relation R on $\langle S, * \rangle$ defined by

$$x \, R \, y \qquad \text{iff} \qquad g(x) = g(y) \qquad \text{for } x, y \in S$$

PROOF It is easy to see that R is an equivalence relation on S. Let $x_1, x_2, x_1', x_2' \in S$ such that $x_1 \, R \, x_1'$ and $x_2 \, R \, x_2'$. From

$$g(x_1 * x_2) = g(x_1) \, \Delta \, g(x_2) = g(x_1') \, \Delta \, g(x_2') = g(x_1' * x_2')$$

it follows that R is a congruence relation on $\langle S, * \rangle$. ////

Our next theorem permits us to define a homomorphism from a semigroup to its quotient semigroup corresponding to a given congruence relation defined on the semigroup.

Theorem 3-2.7 Let $\langle S, * \rangle$ be a semigroup and R be a congruence relation on $\langle S, * \rangle$. The quotient set S/R is a semigroup $\langle S/R, \oplus \rangle$ where the operation $\oplus$ corresponds to the operation $*$ on S. Also, there exists a homomorphism from $\langle S, * \rangle$ onto $\langle S/R, \oplus \rangle$ called the *natural homomorphism*.

PROOF For any $a \in S$, let $[a]$ denote the equivalence class corresponding to the congruence relation R. For $a, b \in S$ define an operation $\oplus$ on S/R given by

$$[a] \oplus [b] = [a * b]$$

The associativity of the operation $*$ guarantees the associativity of the operation $\oplus$ on S/R, so that $\langle S/R, \oplus \rangle$ is a semigroup. Next, define a mapping $g: S \to S/R$ given by

$$g(a) = [a] \qquad \text{for any } a \in S$$

Then for $a, b \in S$,

$$g(a * b) = [a * b] = [a] \oplus [b] = g(a) \oplus g(b)$$

so that g is a homomorphism from $\langle S, * \rangle$ onto $\langle S/R, \oplus \rangle$. ////

EXAMPLE 3   Let $A = \{0, 1\}$ and A^* be the free semigroup generated by A by the operation of concatenation. Show that the relation R defined for $x, y \in A^*$ such that $x \, R \, y$ iff x and y contain the same number of 1s is a congruence relation. Suggest a homomorphism which induces R on A^*.

SOLUTION   It is easy to see that R is a congruence relation on $\langle A^*, \circ \rangle$ where $\circ$ denotes concatenation. Consider the semigroup $\langle N, + \rangle$ and a mapping g: $A^* \to \mathbf{N}$ such that for any $x \in A^*$, $g(x) = n$ where n is the number of 1s in x. Naturally, for any $x, y \in A^*$,

$$g(xy) = g(x) + g(y)$$

so that g is a homomorphism from $\langle A^*, \circ \rangle$ to $\langle \mathbf{N}, + \rangle$. Now for $x, y \in A^*$,

$$g(x) = g(y) \Leftrightarrow x \, R \, y$$

so that the congruence relation R is induced by the homomorphism g. ////

3-2.3   Subsemigroups and Submonoids

The concepts of subalgebras introduced in Sec. 3-1.2 can be applied to semigroups and monoids.

Definition 3-2.5   Let $\langle S, * \rangle$ be a semigroup and $T \subseteq S$. If the set T is closed under the operation, $*$, then $\langle T, * \rangle$ is said to be a *subsemigroup* of $\langle S, * \rangle$. Similarly, let $\langle M, *, e \rangle$ be a monoid and $T \subseteq M$. If T is closed under the operation $*$ and $e \in T$, then $\langle T, *, e \rangle$ is said to be a submonoid of $\langle M, *, e \rangle$.

The definition of subsemigroup requires that the subsemigroup also be a semigroup under the same operation as the original semigroup. The semigroup $\langle S, * \rangle$ itself is a trivial subsemigroup of $\langle S, * \rangle$. For any $a \in S$, the set consisting of all powers of a under the operation $*$ is a subsemigroup; i.e., if $T = \{a, a^2, a^3, \ldots\}$ where $a^2 = a * a$, etc., then $\langle T, * \rangle$ is a cyclic semigroup which is a subsemigroup of $\langle S, * \rangle$ generated by the element a. Similarly, we can consider the subsemigroups generated by any two elements $a, b \in S$, and so on.

EXAMPLE 1   For the semigroup $\langle \mathbf{N}, \times \rangle$, let T be the set of multiples of a positive integer m; then $\langle T, \times \rangle$ is a subsemigroup of $\langle \mathbf{N}, \times \rangle$.

EXAMPLE 2   For the semigroup $\langle \mathbf{N}, + \rangle$, the set E of all the even nonnegative integers is a subsemigroup $\langle E, + \rangle$ of $\langle \mathbf{N}, + \rangle$.

EXAMPLE 3   In Example 1 of Sec. 3-2.2, the semigroup $\langle \{0, 1\}, * \rangle$ is a subsemigroup of $\langle S, * \rangle$, but not a submonoid.

Theorem 3-2.8 For any commutative monoid $\langle M, * \rangle$, the set of idempotent elements of M forms a submonoid.

PROOF Since the identity element $e \in M$ is idempotent, $e \in S$, where S is the set of idempotents of M. Let $a, b \in S$, so that

$$a * a = a \quad \text{and} \quad b * b = b$$

Now $(a * b) * (a * b) = (a * b) * (b * a) \qquad (\langle M, * \rangle \text{ is commutative})$

$$= a * (b * b) * a$$

$$= a * b * a$$

$$= a * a * b = a * b$$

Hence $a * b \in S$ and $\langle S, * \rangle$ is a submonoid. ////

EXAMPLE 4 Recall the monoid $\langle \mathbf{Z}_m, \times_m \rangle$ for $m = 5$ and 6 given in Example 5 of Sec. 3-2.1. The sets of left invertibles of $\mathbf{Z}_5$ and $\mathbf{Z}_6$ are $\{[1], [2], [3], [4]\}$ and $\{[1], [5]\}$ respectively, which are submonoids. A similar result holds in general. ////

From any two given semigroups, we shall generate another semigroup called the direct product of the semigroups.

Definition 3-2.6 Let $\langle S, * \rangle$ and $\langle T, \Delta \rangle$ be two semigroups. The *direct product* of $\langle S, * \rangle$ and $\langle T, \Delta \rangle$ is the algebraic system $\langle S \times T, \circ \rangle$ in which the operation $\circ$ on $S \times T$ is defined by

$$\langle s_1, t_1 \rangle \circ \langle s_2, t_2 \rangle = \langle s_1 * s_2, t_1 \Delta t_2 \rangle$$

for any $\langle s_1, t_1 \rangle$ and $\langle s_2, t_2 \rangle \in S \times T$.

From the definition it follows that $\langle S \times T, \circ \rangle$ is a semigroup because the binary operation $\circ$ on $S \times T$ is defined in terms of the operations $*$ and Δ which are both associative. Therefore, the direct product of any two semigroups is a semigroup.

If $\langle S, * \rangle$ and $\langle T, \Delta \rangle$ are both commutative semigroups, then their direct product is also commutative.

If $\langle S, * \rangle$ and $\langle T, \Delta \rangle$ are monoids with e_S and e_T as their identity elements respectively, then their direct product $\langle S \times T, \circ \rangle$ is also a monoid with $\langle e_S, e_T \rangle$ as the identity element, because

$$\langle e_S, e_T \rangle \circ \langle s, t \rangle = \langle e_S * s, e_T \Delta t \rangle = \langle s, t \rangle$$

and

$$\langle s, t \rangle \circ \langle e_S, e_T \rangle = \langle s * e_S, t \Delta e_T \rangle = \langle s, t \rangle$$

It is easy to verify that if z_S and z_T are any zeros of $\langle S, * \rangle$ and $\langle T, \Delta \rangle$ respectively, then $\langle z_S, z_T \rangle$ is a zero of $\langle S \times T, \circ \rangle$. Similarly, if $s \in S$ and $t \in T$ have inverses, then $\langle s^{-1}, t^{-1} \rangle$ is the inverse of $\langle s, t \rangle$.

EXERCISES   3-2

1   Find the zeros of the semigroups $\langle P(X), \cap \rangle$ and $\langle P(X), \cup \rangle$ where X is any given set and $P(X)$ is its power set. Are these monoids? If so, what are the identities?

2   Let the alphabet $V = \{a, b\}$ and A be the set including Λ of all sequences on V beginning with a. Show that $\langle A, \circ, \Lambda \rangle$ is a monoid.

3   Show that the set **N** of natural numbers is a semigroup under the operation $x \ast y = \max \{x, y\}$. Is it a monoid?

4   Let $S = \{a, b\}$. Show that the semigroup $\langle S^S, \circ \rangle$ is not commutative.

5   Let $\langle S, \ast \rangle$ be a semigroup and $z \in S$ be a left zero. Show that for any $x \in S, x \ast z$ is also a left zero.

6   An element $a \in S$, where $\langle S, \ast \rangle$ is a semigroup, is called a *left-cancellable* element if for all $x, y \in S, a \ast x = a \ast y \Rightarrow x = y$. Show that if a and b are left-cancellable, then $a \ast b$ is also left-cancellable.

7   Show that every finite semigroup has an idempotent.

8   Show that a semigroup with more than one idempotent cannot be a group. Give an example of a semigroup which is not a group.

9   Show that the set of all the invertible elements of a monoid form a group under the same operation as that of the monoid.

10   Find all the subsemigroups of the semigroup $\langle X, \ast \rangle$ given in Example 6, Sec. 3-2.1.

11   In a monoid, show that the set of left-invertibles (right-invertibles) form a submonoid.

12   Find all the subsemigroups of $\langle \mathbf{Z}_6, \times_6 \rangle$ from Table 3-2.1. Then show that the subsemigroup of a monoid may be a monoid without being a submonoid.

13   Let **I** be the set of integers and $\cdot$ denote the operation of multiplication so that $\langle \mathbf{I}, \cdot, 1 \rangle$ is a monoid. Show that $\langle \{0\}, \cdot \rangle$ is a subsemigroup but not a submonoid.

14   Let $g: S \rightarrow T$ be an isomorphism of semigroups $\langle S, \ast \rangle$ and $\langle T, \Delta \rangle$. Show that if z is a zero of S, then $g(z)$ must be a zero of $\langle T, \Delta \rangle$.

15   Show that every monoid $\langle M, \ast, e \rangle$ is isomorphic to a submonoid of $\langle M^M, \circ, \Delta \rangle$ where Δ is the identity mapping of M. (*Hint*: See Theorem 3-2.4.)

16   Let $V = \{a, b\}$ be an alphabet. Show that $\langle V^*, \circ, \Lambda \rangle$ is an infinite monoid.

17   Let $\langle T, \ast \rangle$ be a subsemigroup of $\langle S, \ast \rangle$. T is called a *left ideal* of S if $S \ast T \subseteq T$. Similarly define a *right ideal*. If T is both a left and right ideal, then it is called an *ideal*. Show that in $\langle \mathbf{I}, \cdot \rangle$, where **I** is the set of integers under multiplication $\cdot$, the set of multiples of an integer n is an ideal.

3-3   GRAMMARS AND LANGUAGES

The basic machine instructions of a digital computer are very primitive compared with the complex operations that must be performed in various disciplines such as engineering, commerce, and mathematics. Although a complex procedure can be programmed in machine language, it is desirable to use a high-level language that contains instructions similar to those required in a particular application. For example, in a payroll application, one wants to manipulate employee records in a master file, generate complex reports, and perform rather simple arithmetic operations on certain data. A language such as COBOL which has high-level commands that manipulate records and generate reports is a definite asset to a programmer.

While high-level programming languages reduce much of the drudgery of machine language programming, they also introduce new problems. A program (compiler) which converts a program to some object language such as machine language must be written. Also, programming languages must be precisely defined. Sometimes it is the existence of a particular compiler which finally provides the precise definition of a language. The specification of a programming language involves the definition of the following:

1 The set of symbols (or alphabet) that can be used to construct correct programs
2 The set of all correct programs
3 The "meaning" of all correct programs

In this section we shall be concerned with the first two items in the specification of programming languages.

A language L can be considered a subset of the free monoid on an alphabet (see Sec. 3-2.1). The language consisting of the free monoid is not particularly interesting since it is too large. Our definition of a language L is a set of strings or sentences over some finite alphabet V_T, so that $L \subseteq V_T^*$.

How can a language be represented? A language consists of a finite or an infinite set of sentences. Finite languages can be specified by exhaustively enumerating all their sentences. However, for infinite languages, such an enumeration is not possible. On the other hand, any device which specifies a language should be finite. One method of specification which satisfies this requirement uses a generative device called a *grammar*. A grammar consists of a finite set of rules or productions which specify the syntax of the language. In addition, a grammar imposes structure on the sentences of a language. The study of grammars constitutes an important subarea of computer science called formal languages. This area emerged in the mid-1950s as a result of the efforts of Noam Chomsky who gave a mathematical model of a grammar in connection with his study of natural languages. In 1960, the concept of a grammar became important to programmers because the syntax of ALGOL 60 was described by a grammar.

A second method of language specification is to have a machine, called an acceptor, determine whether a given sentence belongs to the language. This approach is discussed further in Chap. 6, along with some very interesting and important relationships that exist between grammars and acceptors.

In this section we are concerned with a grammar as a mathematical system for defining languages and as a device for giving some useful structure to sentences in a language. The problem of syntactic analysis will be discussed briefly.

3-3.1 Discussion of Grammars

It was mentioned earlier that a grammar imposes a structure on the sentences of a language. For a sentence in English such a structure is described in terms of subject, predicate, phrase, noun, and so on. On the other hand, for a program, the structure is given in terms of procedures, statements, expressions, etc. In any case, it may be desirable to describe all such structures and to obtain a set of all the correct or admissible sentences in a language. For example, we may have a set of correct sentences in English or a set of valid ALGOL programs. The grammatical structure of a language helps us determine whether a particular sentence does or does not belong to the set of correct sentences. The grammatical structure of a sentence is generally studied by analyzing the various parts of a sentence and their relationships to one another; this analysis is called *parsing*.

Consider the sentence "a monkey ate the banana." Its structure, or parse, is shown in Fig. 3-3.1. This diagram of a parse displays the syntax of a sentence in a manner similar to a tree and is therefore called a syntax tree. Each node in the diagram represents a phrase of the syntax. The words such as "the," "monkey," etc., are the basic symbols, or primitives, of the language.

The syntax of a small subset of the English language can be described by using the symbols

S: sentence V: verb O: object A: article N: noun

SP: subject phrase VP: verb phrase NP: noun phrase

in the following rules:

$$S \rightarrow SP\ VP \qquad N \rightarrow \text{tree}$$
$$SP \rightarrow A\ N \qquad VP \rightarrow V\ O$$
$$A \rightarrow \text{a} \qquad V \rightarrow \text{ate}$$
$$A \rightarrow \text{the} \qquad V \rightarrow \text{climbs}$$
$$N \rightarrow \text{monkey} \qquad O \rightarrow NP$$
$$N \rightarrow \text{banana} \qquad NP \rightarrow A\ N$$

These rules state that a sentence is composed of a "subject phrase" followed by a "verb phrase"; the "subject phrase" is composed of an "article" followed by a "noun"; a verb phrase is composed of a "verb" followed by an "object"; and so on.

The structure of a language is discussed by using symbols such as "sen-

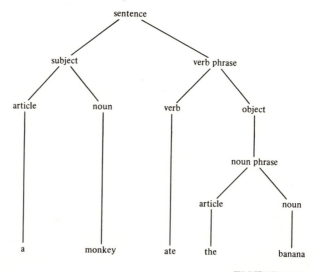

FIGURE 3-3.1

tence," "verb," "subject phrase," and "verb phrase," which represent *syntactic classes* of elements. Each syntactic class consists of a number of alternative structures, and each structure consists of an ordered set of items which are either primitives (of the language) or syntactic classes. These alternative structures are called *productions* or *rules of syntax*. For example, the production, $S \rightarrow SP\ VP$ defines a "sentence" to be composed of a "subject phrase" followed by a "verb phrase." The symbol $\rightarrow$ separates the syntactic class "sentence" from its definition.

The syntactic class and the arrow symbol along with the interpretation of a production enable us to describe a language. A system or language which describes another language is known as a *metalanguage*. The metalanguage used to teach German at most Canadian universities is English, while the metalanguage used to teach English is English. The diagram of a sentence describes its *syntax* but not its meaning or *semantics*. At this time, we are mainly concerned with the syntax of a language, and the device which we have just defined to give the syntactic definition of the language is called a *grammar*.

Using the grammatical rules for our example, we can either produce (generate) or derive a sentence in the language. A computer programmer is concerned with using the productions (grammatical rules) to produce syntactically correct programs. The compiler of a language, on the other hand, is faced with the problem of determining whether a given sentence (source program) is syntactically correct based upon the given grammatical rules. If the syntax is correct, then it produces object code.

Consider the problem of trying to generate or produce the sentence "a monkey ate the banana" from the set of productions given. It is accomplished by starting first with the syntactic class symbol S and looking for a production which has S to the left of the arrow. There is only one such production, namely,

$$S \rightarrow SP\ VP$$

We have replaced the class S by its only possible composition. We then take the string

$$SP\ VP$$

and look for a production whose left-hand side is SP and then replace it with the right-hand side of that production. The application of the only production possible produces the string

$$A\ N\ VP$$

We next look for a production whose left part is A, and two such productions are found. By selecting the production $A \rightarrow a$ and upon substituting its right-hand side in the string $A\ N\ VP$, we obtain the string

$$a\ N\ VP$$

This process is continued until we arrive at the correct sentence. At this point, the sentence contains only primitive or terminal elements of the language (no classes). A complete derivation or generation of the sentence "a monkey ate the banana" is as follows:

$$S \Rightarrow SP\ VP$$
$$\Rightarrow A\ N\ VP$$
$$\Rightarrow \text{a}\ N\ VP$$
$$\Rightarrow \text{a monkey}\ VP$$
$$\Rightarrow \text{a monkey}\ V\ O$$
$$\Rightarrow \text{a monkey ate}\ O$$
$$\Rightarrow \text{a monkey ate}\ NP$$
$$\Rightarrow \text{a monkey ate}\ A\ N$$
$$\Rightarrow \text{a monkey ate the}\ N$$
$$\Rightarrow \text{a monkey ate the banana}$$

Here the symbol $\Rightarrow$ denotes that the string on the right-hand side of the symbol can be obtained by applying one rewriting rule to the previous string.

The rules for the example language can produce a number of sentences. Examples of such sentences are

The monkey ate the banana.

The monkey climbs a tree.

The monkey climbs the tree.

The banana ate the monkey.

The last of these sentences, although grammatically correct, doesn't really make sense. This situation is often allowed in the specification of languages. There are many valid FORTRAN and PL/I programs that do not make sense. It is easier to define languages if certain sentences of questionable validity are allowed by the rewriting rules.

The set of sentences that can be generated by the example rules is finite. Any interesting language usually consists of an infinite set of sentences. As a matter of fact, the importance of a finite device such as a grammar is that it permits the study of the structure of a language consisting of an infinite set of sentences.

Let the symbols L, D, and I denote the classes L: letter, D: digit, and I: identifier. The productions which follow are recursive and produce an infinite set of names because the syntactic class I is present on both the left and the right sides of certain productions:

$$I \rightarrow L \qquad D \rightarrow 0$$
$$I \rightarrow ID \qquad D \rightarrow 1$$
$$I \rightarrow IL \qquad \cdots$$
$$L \rightarrow a \qquad D \rightarrow 9$$
$$L \rightarrow b$$
$$\cdots$$
$$L \rightarrow z$$

It is easily seen that the class I defines an infinite set of strings or names in which each name consists of a letter followed by any number of letters or digits. This set is a consequence of using recursion in the definition of the productions $I \rightarrow ID$ and $I \rightarrow IL$. In fact, recursion is fundamental to the definition of an infinite language by the use of a grammar.

3-3.2 Formal Definition of a Language

Let us now formalize the idea of a grammar and how it is used. For this purpose, let V_T be a finite nonempty set of symbols called the *alphabet*. The symbols in V_T are called *terminal symbols*. The *metalanguage* which is used to generate strings in the language is assumed to contain a set of syntactic classes or variables called *nonterminal symbols*. The set of nonterminal symbols is denoted by V_N, and the elements of V_N are used to define the syntax (structure) of the language. Furthermore, the sets V_N and V_T are assumed to be disjoint. The set $V_N \cup V_T$ consisting of nonterminal and terminal symbols is called the *vocabulary* of the language. We shall use capital letters such as A, B, C, ..., X, Y, Z to denote nonterminal symbols, while S_1, S_2, ... represent the elements of the vocabulary. The strings of terminal symbols are denoted by lowercase letters x, y, z, ..., while strings of symbols over the vocabulary are given by α, β, γ, ... The length of a string α will be denoted by $|\alpha|$.

> **Definition 3-3.1** A (phrase structure) *grammar* is defined by a 4-tuple $G = \langle V_N, V_T, S, \Phi \rangle$ where V_T and V_N are sets of terminal and nonterminal (syntactic class) symbols respectively. S, a distinguished element of V_N and therefore of the vocabulary, is called the starting symbol. Φ is a finite subset of the relation from $(V_T \cup V_N)^* V_N (V_T \cup V_N)^*$ to $(V_T \cup V_N)^*$. In general, an element $\langle \alpha, \beta \rangle$ is written as $\alpha \rightarrow \beta$ and is called a *production rule* or a *rewriting rule*.

For our example given earlier, we may write the grammar as $G_1 = \langle V_N, V_T, S, \Phi \rangle$ in which

$$V_N = \{I, L, D\}$$
$$V_T = \{a, b, c, d, e, f, g, h, i, j, k, l, m, n, o, p, q, r, s, t, u, v, w, x, y, z,$$
$$0, 1, 2, 3, 4, 5, 6, 7, 8, 9\}$$
$$S = I$$
$$\Phi = \{I \rightarrow L, I \rightarrow IL, I \rightarrow ID, L \rightarrow a, L \rightarrow b, \ldots, L \rightarrow z, D \rightarrow 0,$$
$$D \rightarrow 1, \ldots, D \rightarrow 9\}$$

> **Definition 3-3.2** Let $G = \langle V_N, V_T, S, \Phi \rangle$ be a grammar. For $\sigma, \psi \in (V_N \cup V_T)^* - \{\Lambda\}$, σ is said to be a *direct derivative* of ψ, written as $\psi \Rightarrow \sigma$, if there are strings ϕ_1 and ϕ_2 (including possibly empty strings) such that $\psi = \phi_1 \alpha \phi_2$ and $\sigma = \phi_1 \beta \phi_2$ and $\alpha \rightarrow \beta$ is a production of G.

If $\psi \Rightarrow \sigma$, we may also say that ψ directly produces σ or σ directly reduces to ψ. For grammar G_1 of our example, we have listed in Table 3-3.1 some illustrations of direct derivations.

Table 3-3.1

ψ	σ	**Rule used**	ϕ_1	ϕ_2
I	L	$I \to L$	Λ	Λ
Ib	Lb	$I \to L$	Λ	b
Lb	ab	$L \to a$	Λ	b
LD	$L1$	$D \to 1$	L	Λ
LD	aD	$L \to a$	Λ	D

These concepts can now be extended to produce a string σ not necessarily directly but in a number of steps from a string ψ.

Definition 3-3.3 Let $G = \langle V_N, V_T, S, \Phi \rangle$ be a grammar. The string ψ produces σ (σ reduces to ψ, or σ is the derivation of ψ), written as $\psi \overset{+}{\Rightarrow} \sigma$, if there are strings $\phi_0, \phi_1, \ldots, \phi_n$ ($n > 0$) such that $\psi = \phi_0 \Rightarrow \phi_1, \phi_1 \Rightarrow \phi_2, \ldots, \phi_{n-1} \Rightarrow \phi_n$ and $\phi_n = \sigma$. The relation $\overset{+}{\Rightarrow}$ is the transitive closure of the relation $\Rightarrow$. If we let $n = 0$, then we can define the reflexive transitive closure of $\Rightarrow$ as

$$\psi \overset{*}{\Rightarrow} \sigma \quad \Leftrightarrow \quad \psi \overset{+}{\Rightarrow} \sigma \quad \text{or} \quad \psi = \sigma$$

Returning to the grammar G_1, we show that the string $abc12$ is derived from I by following the derivation sequence:

$$I \Rightarrow ID \Rightarrow IDD \Rightarrow ILDD \Rightarrow ILLDD \Rightarrow LLLDD \Rightarrow aLLDD$$
$$\Rightarrow abLDD \Rightarrow abcDD \Rightarrow abc1D \Rightarrow abc12$$

Note that as long as we have a nonterminal character in the string, we can produce a new string from it. On the other hand, if a string contains only terminal symbols, then the derivation is complete, and we cannot produce any further strings from it.

Definition 3-3.4 A *sentential form* is any derivative of the unique nonterminal symbol S. The language L generated by a grammar G is the set of all sentential forms whose symbols are terminal, i.e.,

$$L(G) = \{\sigma \mid S \overset{*}{\Rightarrow} \sigma \text{ and } \sigma \in V_T^*\}$$

Therefore, the language is merely a subset of the set of all terminal strings over V_T.

We shall now give a number of examples of grammars.

EXAMPLE 1 Let $G_2 = \langle \{E, T, F\}, \{a, +, *, (,)\}, E, \Phi \rangle$ where Φ consists of the productions

$$E \to E + T$$
$$E \to T$$
$$T \to T * F$$
$$T \to F$$
$$F \to (E)$$
$$F \to a$$

where the variables E, T, and F represent the names "expression," "term," and "factor" commonly used in conjunction with arithmetic expressions. A derivation for the expression $a * a + a$ is

$$E \Rightarrow E + T$$
$$\Rightarrow T + T$$
$$\Rightarrow T * F + T$$
$$\Rightarrow F * F + T$$
$$\Rightarrow a * F + T$$
$$\Rightarrow a * a + T$$
$$\Rightarrow a * a + F$$
$$\Rightarrow a * a + a$$

EXAMPLE 2 The language $L(G_3) = \{a^n b^n c^n \mid n \geq 1\}$ is generated by the following grammar.

$$G_3 = \langle \{S, B, C\}, \{a, b, c\}, S, \Phi \rangle$$

where Φ consists of the productions

$$S \rightarrow aSBC$$
$$S \rightarrow aBC$$
$$CB \rightarrow BC$$
$$aB \rightarrow ab$$
$$bB \rightarrow bb$$
$$bC \rightarrow bc$$
$$cC \rightarrow cc$$

The following is a derivation for the string $a^2 b^2 c^2$:

$$S \Rightarrow aSBC$$
$$\Rightarrow aaBCBC$$
$$\Rightarrow aaBBCC$$
$$\Rightarrow aabBCC$$
$$\Rightarrow aabbCC$$
$$\Rightarrow aabbcC$$
$$\Rightarrow aabbcc$$

EXAMPLE 3 The language $L(G_4) = \{a^n b a^n \mid n \geq 1\}$ is generated by the grammar

$$G_4 = \langle \{S, C\}, \{a, b\}, S, \Phi \rangle$$

where Φ is the set of productions

$$S \rightarrow aCa$$
$$C \rightarrow aCa$$
$$C \rightarrow b$$

A derivation for a^2ba^2 consists of the following steps:

$$S \Rightarrow aCa$$
$$\Rightarrow aaCaa$$
$$\Rightarrow aabaa$$

EXAMPLE 4   The language $L(G_5) = \{a^nba^m \mid n, m \geq 1\}$ is generated by the grammar

$$G_5 = \langle\{S, A, B, C\}, \{a, b\}, S, \Phi\rangle$$

where the set of productions is

$$S \rightarrow aS$$
$$S \rightarrow aB$$
$$B \rightarrow bC$$
$$C \rightarrow aC$$
$$C \rightarrow a$$

The sentence a^2ba^3 has the following derivation:

$$S \Rightarrow aS$$
$$\Rightarrow aaB$$
$$\Rightarrow aabC$$
$$\Rightarrow aabaC$$
$$\Rightarrow aabaaC$$
$$\Rightarrow aabaaa$$

Chomsky classified grammars into four classes by imposing restrictions on the productions.

Definition 3-3.5   A *context-sensitive grammar* contains only productions of the form $\alpha \rightarrow \beta$ where $|\alpha| \leq |\beta|$.

This restriction on a production prevents β from being empty. Because of this restriction the set of sentences generated by such a grammar is recursively solvable. The restriction on the productions of a context-sensitive grammar can be equivalently stated as follows:

α and β in the production $\alpha \rightarrow \beta$ can be expressed as $\alpha = \phi_1 A \phi_2$ and $\beta = \phi_1 \psi \phi_2$ (ϕ_1 and/or ϕ_2 are possibly empty) where ψ must be nonempty.

The meaning of "context-sensitive" becomes clearer with this reformulation. The application of a production $\phi_1 A \phi_2 \rightarrow \phi_1 \psi \phi_2$ to a sentential form means that A is rewritten as ψ in the context ϕ_1 and ϕ_2. Context-sensitive grammars are said to generate context-sensitive languages. G_3 is an example of a context-sensitive grammar.

We now impose a further restriction on productions to obtain a context-free grammar.

Definition 3-3.6 A *context-free grammar* contains productions of only the form $\alpha \rightarrow \beta$ where $|\alpha| \leq |\beta|$ and $\alpha \in V_N$.

With such grammars, the rewriting variable in a sentential form is rewritten regardless of the other symbols in its vicinity or context. It has led to the term "context-free" for grammars consisting of productions whose left-hand side consists of a single class symbol. Context-free grammars do not have the power to represent even significant parts of the English language since context dependency is often required in order to properly analyze the structure of a sentence. Context-free grammars are not capable of specifying (or determining) that a certain variable was declared when it is used in some expression in a subsequent statement of a source program. However, these grammars can specify most of the syntax for computer or artificial languages since these are, by and large, simple in structure. Context-free grammars are said to generate context-free languages. Grammars G_1, G_2, and G_4 are examples of context-free grammars.

A final restriction leads to the definition of regular grammars.

Definition 3-3.7 A *regular grammar* contains only productions of the form $\alpha \rightarrow \beta$ where $|\alpha| \leq |\beta|$, $\alpha \in V_N$, and β has the form aB or a where $a \in V_T$ and $B \in V_N$.

The set of languages generated by such grammars is said to be regular. G_5 is an example of a regular grammar.

Let the unrestricted, context-sensitive, context-free, and regular grammars be denoted by the class symbols T_0, T_1, T_2, and T_3 respectively. If $L(T_i)$ represents the class of languages that can be generated by the class of T_i grammars, it can be shown that

$$L(T_3) \subset L(T_2) \subset L(T_1) \subset L(T_0)$$

and therefore the four classes of grammars form a hierarchy. Corresponding to each class of grammars there is a class of machines (acceptors) that will accept the class of languages generated by the former. We return to this problem in Chap. 6.

We conclude this subsection by introducing a different metalanguage from the one which was previously used. The metavariables or syntactic classes will be enclosed by the symbols $\langle$ and $\rangle$. Using this terminology, the symbol $\langle$sentence$\rangle$ is a symbol of V_N and the symbol "sentence" is an element of V_T. In this way, no confusion or ambiguity arises when attempting to distinguish the two symbols. This metalanguage is known as *Backus Naur Form* (*BNF*) and has been used extensively in the formal definition of many programming languages. A popular language described using BNF is ALGOL. For example, the definition of an identifier in BNF is given as

$\langle$identifier$\rangle$ :: = $\langle$letter$\rangle$ | $\langle$identifier$\rangle\langle$letter$\rangle$ | $\langle$identifier$\rangle\langle$digit$\rangle$

$\langle$letter$\rangle$ :: = $a \mid b \mid c \mid \cdots \mid y \mid z$

$\langle$digit$\rangle$ :: = $0 \mid 1 \mid 2 \mid \cdots \mid 8 \mid 9$

The symbol :: = replaces the symbol $\rightarrow$ in the grammar notation, and $\mid$ is used to separate different right-hand sides of productions corresponding to the same left-hand side. The symbol :: = is interpreted as "is defined as" and | as "or." BNF gives a much more compact description of a language than could be achieved with the previous metalanguage.

3-3.3 Notions of Syntax Analysis

In the following pages we briefly discuss the problem of syntax analysis or parsing. The *parse* of a sentence is the construction of a derivation for that sentence; that is, a sequence of productions used in generating a given sentence from the starting symbol is required.

An important aid to understanding the syntax of a sentence is a *syntax tree*. The structural relationships between the parts of a sentence are easily seen from its syntax tree. Consider the grammar described earlier for the set of valid identifiers or variable names. The derivation of the identifier $a1$ is ⟨identifier⟩ ⟹ ⟨identifier⟩⟨digit⟩ ⟹ ⟨letter⟩⟨digit⟩ ⟹ a ⟨digit⟩ ⟹ $a1$. Let us now illustrate how to construct a syntax tree corresponding to this derivation. This process is shown as a sequence of diagrams in Fig. 3-3.2, where each diagram corresponds to a

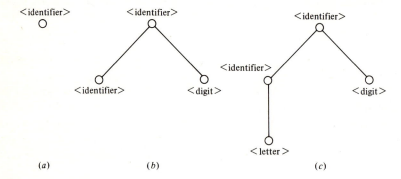

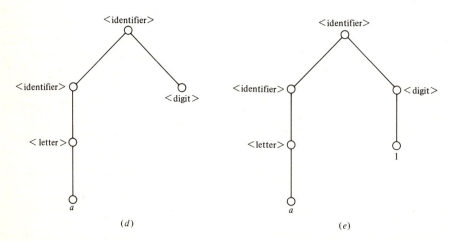

FIGURE 3-3.2 Syntax tree for sentence a1.

sentential form in the derivation of the sentence. The syntax tree has a distinguished point called its root, which is labeled by the starting symbol ⟨identifier⟩ of the grammar. From the root we draw two downward branches (see Fig. 3-3.2*b*) corresponding to the rewriting of ⟨identifier⟩ by ⟨identifier⟩⟨digit⟩. The symbol ⟨identifier⟩ in the sentential form ⟨identifier⟩⟨digit⟩ is then rewritten as ⟨letter⟩ by using the production ⟨identifier⟩ :: = ⟨letter⟩ (see Fig. 3-3.2*c*). This process continues for each production applied until Fig. 3-3.2*e* is obtained.

Given a sentence in the language, the construction of a parse can be described pictorially in Fig. 3-3.3 where the root and leaves (which represent the terminal symbols in the sentence) of the tree are known and the rest of the syntax tree must be found. There are a number of ways by which this construction can be accomplished. First, an attempt to construct the tree can be initiated by starting at the root and proceeding downward toward the leaves. This method is called a *top-down parse*. Alternatively, the completion of the tree can be attempted by starting at the leaves and moving upward toward the root. This method is called a *bottom-up parse*. The top-down and bottom-up approaches can be combined to yield other possibilities.

Let us briefly discuss top-down parsing. Consider the identifier $c2$ generated by the BNF grammar of the previous subsection. The first step is to construct the direct derivation ⟨identifier⟩ $\Rightarrow$ ⟨identifier⟩⟨digit⟩. At each successive step, the leftmost variable A of the current sentential form $\phi_1 A \phi_2$ is replaced by the right part of a production $A :: = \psi$ to obtain the next sentential form. This process is shown for the identifier $c2$ by the five trees of Fig. 3-3.4.

We have very conveniently chosen the rules which generate the given identifier. If the first step had been the construction of the direct derivation ⟨identifier⟩ $\Rightarrow$ ⟨identifier⟩⟨letter⟩, then we would have eventually produced the sentential form c⟨letter⟩ where it would have been impossible to obtain $c2$. At this point, a new alternative would have to be tried by restarting the procedure and choosing the rule ⟨identifier⟩ :: = ⟨identifier⟩⟨digit⟩.

A bottom-up parsing technique begins with a given string and tries to reduce it to the starting symbol of the grammar. The first step in parsing the identifier $c2$ is to reduce c to ⟨letter⟩, resulting in the sentential form ⟨letter⟩2. The direct derivation ⟨letter⟩2 $\Rightarrow c2$ has now been constructed, as shown in Fig. 3-3.5*d*. The next step is to reduce ⟨letter⟩ to ⟨identifier⟩, as represented by Fig. 3-3.5*c*. The process continues until the entire syntax tree of Fig. 3-3.5*a* is constructed. Note that it is possible to construct other derivations, but the re-

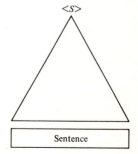

FIGURE 3-3.3

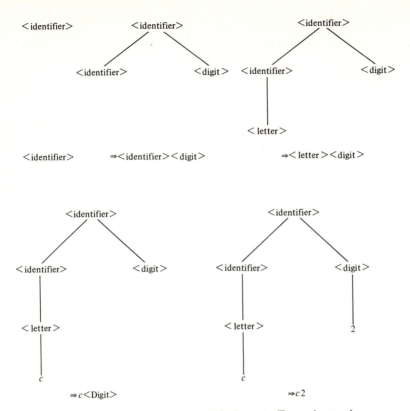

FIGURE 3-3.4   Trace of a top-down parse.

sulting syntax tree is the same. We will return to the very important problem of bottom-up parsing in Chap. 5.

We now turn to a more general discussion of language translation. A compiler for a certain language is concerned with a number of tasks, namely, determining whether a sentence belongs to the language, constructing a syntax tree for the sentence, and generating object code for the given sentence if its syntax and semantics are valid. This process can be represented by Fig. 3-3.6.

The source program is input to a scanner whose purpose is to separate the incoming text into pieces such as constants, variable names, key words (such as DO, IF, and the like in FORTRAN), and operators. This type of analysis is quite simple to perform. Usually the scanner constructs tables which contain variable names, constants, and labels.

The scanner feeds the syntax analyzer whose task is essentially to construct a syntax tree (or its equivalent) for the given sentence. The syntax analyzer is much more complicated than the scanner. The output of the syntax analyzer is fed to the code generation block which uses the syntax tree for the sentence and other things (which are not specified for simplicity) to generate object code for that sentence.

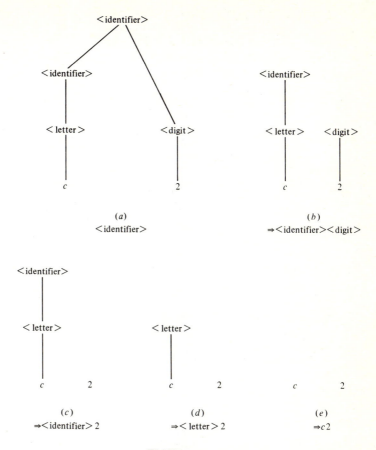

FIGURE 3-3.5   Trace of a bottom-up parse.

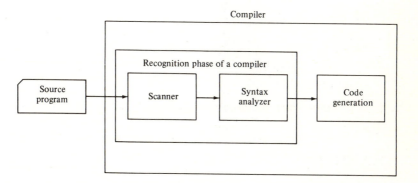

FIGURE 3-3.6   Block diagram of a compiler.

Consider the following scanner problem. It is required to construct a scanner that will split up a sentence into a number of parts. These parts are strings such as identifiers, literal constants, adding operators, multiplying operators, and exponential operators. The syntax of these primitive classes is now given. An identifier is described by the following rules:

$\langle$identifier$\rangle$ :: = $\langle$identifier$\rangle\langle$letter$\rangle$ | $\langle$identifier$\rangle\langle$digit$\rangle$ | $\langle$letter$\rangle$

$\langle$letter$\rangle$ :: = $A \mid B \mid C \mid \cdots Y \mid Z$

$\langle$digit$\rangle$ :: = $0 \mid 1 \mid \cdots 8 \mid 9$

Literal constants are described by the rules

$\langle$literal constant$\rangle$ :: = $\langle$digit string$\rangle$ | $\langle$digit string$\rangle$.$\langle$digit string$\rangle$ | $\langle$digit string$\rangle$.

$\langle$digit string$\rangle$:: = $\langle$digit$\rangle$ | $\langle$digit string$\rangle$ $\langle$digit$\rangle$

The different classes of operators are described by the productions

$$\langle\text{adding operator}\rangle :: = + \mid -$$

$$\langle\text{multiplying operator}\rangle :: = * \mid /$$

$$\langle\text{exponentiation operator}\rangle :: = **$$

The syntactic classes $\langle$identifier$\rangle$, $\langle$literal constant$\rangle$, $\langle$adding operator$\rangle$, $\langle$multiplying operator$\rangle$, $\langle$exponentiation operator$\rangle$ in a line of text are to be singled out. For example, an input statement such as

$$\text{ANSWER} + 15.5 * G + H * * F/12 - Q$$

would break down to the following table:

ANSWER	$\langle$identifier$\rangle$
+	$\langle$adding operator$\rangle$
15.5	$\langle$literal constant$\rangle$
*	$\langle$multiplying operator$\rangle$
G	$\langle$identifier$\rangle$
+	$\langle$adding operator$\rangle$
H	$\langle$identifier$\rangle$
**	$\langle$exponentiation operator$\rangle$
F	$\langle$identifier$\rangle$
/	$\langle$multiplying operator$\rangle$
12	$\langle$literal constant$\rangle$
−	$\langle$adding operator$\rangle$
Q	$\langle$identifier$\rangle$

A PL/I program which performs this scanning is left as an exercise.

EXERCISES 3-3

1 Obtain a grammar which will generate the language $L = \{xx \text{ where } x = x_1 x_2 \cdots x_n$ and $x_i \in \{a, b\}$ for all $1 \leq i \leq n\}$. For example, if $x = ab$, then $abab$ is in the language.

2 Consider the following grammar with the set of terminal symbols $\{a, b\}$:

$$S \rightarrow a \qquad S \rightarrow Sa \qquad S \rightarrow b \qquad S \rightarrow bS$$

Describe (in a closed form) the set of strings generated by the grammar.

3 Write grammars for the following languages:
 (*a*) The set of nonnegative odd integers
 (*b*) The set of nonnegative even integers with no leading zeros permitted

4 Give a grammar which generates

$$L = \{w \mid w \text{ consists of an equal number of } a\text{'s and } b\text{'s}\}$$

5 Give a context-free grammar which generates

$$L = \{w \mid w \text{ contains twice as many 0s as 1s}\}$$

6 Construct a regular grammar which will generate all strings of 0s and 1s having both an odd number of 0s and an odd number of 1s.

7 Obtain a grammar for the language

$$L = \{0^i 1^j \mid i \neq j \quad \text{and} \quad i, j > 0\}$$

8 Obtain a context-sensitive grammar for the language $\{a^{m^2} \mid m \geq 1\}$.

9 Construct a context-sensitive grammar for the language $\{w \mid w \in \{a, b, c\}^* - \{\Lambda\}$, where w contains the same number of a's, b's and c's$\}$.

3-4 POLISH EXPRESSIONS AND THEIR COMPILATION

In this section we are primarily concerned with the mechanical evaluation or compilation of infix expressions. A brief introduction to this topic was given in Sec. 1-3.6 where it was found to be more efficient to evaluate an infix logical expression by first converting it to a prefix expression and then evaluating the latter. This approach eliminated the repeated scanning of an infix expression in order to obtain its logical value. We shall use examples of expressions found in scientific programming languages in this section although the theory developed applies to any type of expression.

It was seen in the previous section that a language consisting of the set of all valid infix expressions can be precisely described by a grammar. The same can be done for the corresponding set of all valid Polish expressions (suffix or prefix). When we convert a sentence in a language, say L_1, to a sentence in another language L_2 by some mapping, it is required that L_2 have many of the properties possessed by L_1. This requirement brings up the very important concept of a language homomorphism. Properties such as "well-formed expression," associativity, and commutativity of operators in the conversion of expressions from one type to another must be preserved by the mapping.

Initially, a theorem which permits us to determine whether a Polish expression is well-formed (and consequently its corresponding infix counterpart) will be given. This theorem will be followed by a brief introduction to language homomorphisms. The translation of infix expressions to Polish notation is examined in detail and represents one of the classical applications of a stack (see Sec. 2-6).

3-4.1 Polish Notation

The Polish notation for expressions was introduced in Sec. 1-3.6 in connection with the evaluation of infix logical expressions. The discussion was concerned mostly with prefix expressions since these were subsequently used as input to the mechanical theorem proving algorithm given in Sec. 2-7. We are primarily concerned with suffix Polish expressions throughout this section although analogous results hold for prefix Polish expressions as well. First let us describe by induction the set of well-formed suffix Polish expressions.

Suppose S is a set of symbols $\{s_1, s_2, \ldots s_q\}$ (typically variable names and literals) and the set $\{o_1, o_2, \ldots, o_m\}$ consists of connectives or operators for constructing formulas using elements of S. A *formula* is defined by the following:

1 A single symbol s_i is a formula.
2 If $x_1, x_2, \ldots, x_n$ are formulas and o_i is of order n, then $x_1 x_2 \cdots x_n o_i$ is a formula.
3 The only well-formed formulas are those obtained by steps 1 and 2.

To determine whether a formula is well-formed, we next associate with each formula a *rank* which is determined as follows:

4 The rank of a symbol s_i is 1.
5 The rank of a connective o_j is $1 - n$, where n is the order of o_j.
6 The rank of an arbitrary sequence of symbols and connectives is the sum of the ranks of the individual symbols and connectives.

For example, let the sets of symbols and connectives consist of single-letter variables (a to z) and the four arithmetic operators respectively. The rank function which is denoted by r is given as

$$r(s_j) = 1 \qquad \text{for } 1 \le j \le 26$$
$$r(+) = r(-) = -1 \qquad r(*) = r(/) = -1$$

The rank of the formula $ab+cd-*$ is obtained from the computation

$$r(a) + r(b) + r(+) + r(c) + r(d) + r(-) + r(*) = 1$$

The following theorem is very important since it can be used to determine whether a given formula is well-formed. Before we state the theorem, some mention of the terminology required is in order. The *length* of a formula or an expression is taken to be equal to the number of symbols and operators appearing in the expression. We shall denote the length of an x by $l(x)$. If $z = x \circ y$ is a string, then x is a *head* of z. Finally, x is a proper head if y is not empty (y is not Λ).

Theorem 3-4.1 The rank of any well-formed Polish formula is 1, and the rank of any proper head of a Polish formula is greater than or equal to 1. Conversely, if the ranks are as described earlier, then the formula is well-formed.

PROOF The proof will be by induction on the length of formulas.
If we have a formula of length 1, then it must be a symbol and by (4) it has a rank of 1. This completes the basis step. We now proceed to the induction

step. Assume that every formula of length $\leq n$ has a rank of 1. Consider the form

$$x_1 x_2 \cdots x_p o_i \qquad l(x_j) \leq n \qquad j = 1, 2, \ldots, p$$

where each x_j is well-formed. By the inductive hypothesis each x_j, therefore, has a rank of 1. Moreover, by (5) o_i has a rank of $1 - p$. Consequently, by (5) and (6) the rank of $x_1 x_2 \cdots x_p o_i$ must be

$$1 - p + [1 + 1 + \cdots + 1 \ (p \text{ times})] = 1$$

Also, if y is a proper head of $x_1 x_2 \cdots x_p o_i$, then

$$r(y) \geq 1$$

This completes the first part of the proof. The converse is left as an exercise.

$$////$$

This theorem is very important in the compilation of infix expressions since it permits us to detect a Polish expression that is not well-formed (and consequently a corresponding infix expression not well-formed). Table 3-4.1 contains a number of well-formed and not well-formed expressions.

We shall next consider the mechanical conversion of infix expressions to Polish notation.

3-4.2 Conversion of Infix Expressions to Polish Notation

In this section we discuss certain mappings on languages and in particular we are concerned with mappings of infix expressions to suffix Polish expressions. Of course, in all such mappings, we are interested in preserving certain properties of the language, and, therefore, we shall be concerned with homomorphisms. In the image set, we would like to preserve the commutativity and associativity of the operators appearing in the expressions. In addition, we also want the expressions which are well-formed to remain well-formed under the mapping.

Let S_1 and S_2 be alphabets. Then $h: S_1 \to S_2^*$ is a mapping from the elements of S_1 to strings on S_2. The domain of h can be extended to S_1^* by letting

$$h(\Lambda) = \Lambda$$

and
$$h(xa) = h(x) \circ h(a) \qquad \text{for all } x \in S_1^* \text{ and } a \in S_1$$

This new mapping $h: S_1^* \to S_2^*$ is a homomorphism where the operation in both

Table 3-4.1

Infix	Suffix Polish	Rank	Well-formed or not well-formed
$a + *b$	$ab*+$	0	Not well-formed
$a - b*c$	$ab-c*$	1	Well-formed
$ab + c$	$abc+$	2	Not well-formed
$(a + b)*(c - d)$	$ab+cd-*$	1	Well-formed
$a + b/d-$	$ab+d/-$	0	Not well-formed

instances is that of concatenation. The image of a homomorphism h of a language L is a language $h(L)$ where $h(L) = \{h(y) \mid y \in L\}$.

EXAMPLE 1 Suppose that it is required to change every instance of 0 in a string to a and every 1 to bb. We can define a mapping h such that $h(0) = a$ and $h(1) = bb$. If L is the language $\{0^n 1^n \mid n \geq 1\}$, then $h(L) = \{a^n b^{2n} \mid n \geq 1\}$.

We shall now discuss a homomorphic mapping which transforms the language of infix expressions to the language of suffix Polish expressions. Let us recall that in an infix expression we can reduce the number of parentheses (see Sec. 1-3.6) by prescribing certain precedence rules for the operators. A homomorphic mapping in such a case will have to take into consideration both the precedence requirements of the operators appearing as well as those due to parentheses. For this reason, it is more difficult to express the required homomorphism than was the case in the previous example. The homomorphic mapping for the translation process will be specified by an algorithm. We shall first develop an algorithm for translating unparenthesized infix expressions to suffix Polish. This algorithm will be subsequently modified to handle parenthesized expressions. Note that there can also be completely parenthesized infix expressions which do not require any rules of precedence except the usual rule for parentheses. Such expressions are inconvenient to use because of the large number of parentheses which are required.

The evaluation of an infix expression as well as of a prefix Polish expression was discussed in Sec. 1-3.6. A similar process can be described for a suffix Polish expression. Recall that in an unparenthesized infix expression the evaluation is performed in such a manner that the operator with the highest precedence is evaluated before the others. If more than one operator has the same precedence in the expression, then the leftmost operator (for left-associative operators) or rightmost operator (for right-associative operators such as exponentiation and negation) with that precedence is evaluated first. Of course, in such an evaluation process, we need to do repeated scanning of the expression, thereby making the process inefficient. The same idea can be applied to partially parenthesized infix expressions. The subexpression that is evaluated first is located by scanning up to the first right parenthesis and moving left until a left parenthesis is detected. The subexpression can then be evaluated by using the rules of precedence.

Let us now define in BNF the infix expression containing single-letter variables, integer constants, and the four binary arithmetic operators $+$, $-$, $*$, and $/$.

$\langle \text{identifier} \rangle ::= a \mid b \mid c \cdots \mid z$

$\langle \text{digit} \rangle ::= 0 \mid 1 \mid 2 \cdots \mid 9$

$\langle \text{digit string} \rangle ::= \langle \text{digit string} \rangle \langle \text{digit} \rangle \mid \langle \text{digit} \rangle$

$\langle \text{primary} \rangle ::= \langle \text{identifier} \rangle \mid \langle \text{digit string} \rangle \mid (\langle \text{infix expression} \rangle)$

$\langle \text{term} \rangle ::= \langle \text{primary} \rangle \mid \langle \text{term} \rangle * \langle \text{primary} \rangle \mid \langle \text{term} \rangle / \langle \text{primary} \rangle$

$\langle \text{infix expression} \rangle ::= \langle \text{term} \rangle \mid \langle \text{infix expression} \rangle + \langle \text{term} \rangle \mid$
$\qquad\qquad\qquad \langle \text{infix expression} \rangle - \langle \text{term} \rangle$

The above grammar *inherently* specifies that the operators $*$ and $/$ have equal precedence which is greater than the precedence of $+$ and $-$. We shall discuss this topic further in Chap. 5.

On the other hand, in a parenthesis-free suffix expression the subexpressions have the form

$$\langle \text{operand } 1 \rangle \langle \text{operand } 2 \rangle \langle \text{operator} \rangle$$

and a suffix Polish expression can be specified by the following rules.

$$\langle \text{reverse Polish} \rangle ::= \langle \text{reverse Polish} \rangle \langle \text{reverse Polish} \rangle \langle \text{operator} \rangle \mid$$
$$\langle \text{identifier} \rangle \mid \langle \text{digit string} \rangle$$

$$\langle \text{operator} \rangle ::= + \mid - \mid * \mid /$$

For example, the following expressions are equivalent:

Infix	*Reverse Polish*
b	b
$a + b$	$ab+$
$a + b + c$	$ab+c+$
$a + b * c$	$abc*+$
$a * (b + c)$	$abc+*$
$a/b * c$	$ab/c*$

It may be mentioned here again that in the reverse Polish equivalent of an infix expression, the identifiers (or variables) and constants are in the same relative order as in the infix form. The only difference between the two forms is that reverse Polish is parenthesis-free and that the operators in this form have been rearranged according to the rules of precedence for the operators and the overruling of precedence rules by the use of parentheses.

Continuing our discussion of mechanically converting a parenthesis-free infix expression into reverse Polish, the leftmost infix operator having the highest precedence will be the first operator to be encountered in the reverse Polish string. The next-highest precedence operator will be the second operator to be encountered in the reverse Polish expression. Note that if we do not specify that a leftmost (or rightmost in certain cases) operator has precedence over other operators of equal precedence in an infix expression, then the reverse Polish equivalent is not unique. For example, the expression

$$a + b + c$$

would be converted to $ab+c+$ or $abc++$ if no mention was made that the leftmost operator $+$ has precedence over the remaining operator.

The evaluation of prefix Polish expressions was described at the end of Sec. 1-3.6. The same evaluation process can be applied to suffix Polish expressions except that we replace "prefix" by "suffix," "left" by "right," and "right" by "left" throughout the process. As an example, consider the Polish expression $abc/d * +$ which corresponds to the infix expression $a + (b / c) * d$ and which is evaluated here for values of $a = 5$, $b = 4$, $c = 2$, and $d = 2$:

Reverse Polish	*Current operator*	*Current operands*
$abc/d*+$	$/$	b, c
$a2d*+$	$*$	$2, d$
$a4+$	$+$	$a, 4$
9	$-$	$-$

It is an easy matter to devise an algorithm which will convert an infix expression without parentheses into Polish. This conversion is based on the precedence of the operators and requires the use of a stack. The Polish expression will be stored in some output string which will be used later in the generation of object code. Recall that all variables and constants are not reordered in any way when the infix expression is converted to Polish. The operators, however, are reordered in the output string depending on their relative precedence, and it is for this reason that a stack is required.

Let us initially assign precedence values to the four arithmetic operators as displayed in Table 3-4.2. The precedence associated with multiplication and division is greater than the precedence of addition and subtraction. Also included in Table 3-4.2 is a precedence value for variables (which are restricted to a single letter for simplicity) and the rank function. The reason for this will be explained shortly.

Assume that the stack contents have been initialized to some symbol ($\mapsto$ in Table 3-4.2) which has a precedence value less than all other precedence values given in Table 3-4.2.

Algorithm *BASIC*   Given an input string *INFIX* containing an infix expression whose symbols have precedence values and ranks given in Table 3-4.2, a vector S which is used as a stack, and a function *NEXTCHAR* which, when invoked, returns the next character of the mentioned string, it is required to convert the string *INFIX* to reverse Polish and store it in a vector called *POLISH*. The variable *RANK* is used to compute the ranks of the Polish string. A special symbol shown as $\mapsto$ is added to the end of string *INFIX*.

   1   [Initialize stack] Set $TOP \leftarrow 1$, $S[TOP] \leftarrow$ '$\mapsto$'.

   2   [Initialize output string pointer and *RANK*] Set $RANK \leftarrow i \leftarrow 0$.

   3   [Get next input symbol] Set $NEXT \leftarrow NEXTCHAR(INFIX)$.

   4   [End of *INFIX*?] If $NEXT =$ '$\mapsto$' then go to step 7.

   5   [Stack *NEXT*?] If $f(NEXT) > f(S[TOP])$ then set $TOP \leftarrow TOP + 1$, $S[TOP] \leftarrow NEXT$, go to step 3.

   6   [Output stack symbol and update rank of *POLISH*] Set $i \leftarrow i + 1$,

Table 3-4.2

Symbol	Precedence f	Rank r
$+, -$	1	-1
$*, /$	2	-1
$a, b, c, \ldots$	3	1
$\mapsto$	0	$-$

$POLISH[i] \leftarrow S[TOP]$, $RANK \leftarrow RANK + r(S[TOP])$. If $RANK \leq 0$ then 'INVALID' and Exit; otherwise, set $TOP \leftarrow TOP - 1$, go to step 5.

    7 [Is top element of stack a '$\mapsto$'?] If $S[TOP] = $ '$\mapsto$' then go to step 9.

    8 [Pop stack and place in $POLISH$] Set $i \leftarrow i + 1$, $POLISH[i] \leftarrow S[TOP]$, $RANK \leftarrow RANK + r(S[TOP])$, $TOP \leftarrow TOP - 1$, go to step 7.

    9 [Is the expression valid?] If $RANK = 1$ then 'VALID'; otherwise, print 'INVALID'. Exit.

The algorithm operates in a straightforward manner. Initially a special symbol $\mapsto$ is placed on the stack. The purpose of this symbol is that upon the detection of $\mapsto$ at the end of the string $INFIX$, the remaining elements of the stack (except $\mapsto$) are put in $POLISH$. The main portion of the algorithm is concerned with the precedence-value comparison of the incoming symbol $NEXT$ and the top element of the stack. If the precedence value of $NEXT$ is greater than that of the top element of the stack, then the symbol $NEXT$ is inserted on the stack and the next input symbol is scanned. If, on the other hand, the precedence value of $NEXT$ is less than or equal to that of the top element of the stack, then the latter element is removed from the stack and placed in string $POLISH$, after which the precedence values for $NEXT$ and the new top element of the stack are compared, etc. The rank of the Polish string is updated each time a symbol is written in $POLISH$.

Note that since a variable has the highest precedence, it will be placed on the top of the stack; and on scanning the very next input symbol, the variable will be deleted from the stack and copied into $POLISH$ (since in a valid infix expression no two consecutive variables are permitted). Actually, it is a very easy matter to alter the algorithm so that the precedence value of $NEXT$ is tested for a value of 3. If this test succeeds, then $NEXT$ is a variable and it can be written out directly into $POLISH$ without being placed on the stack. We do not do this, however, for reasons of simplicity which become important as the infix expression is permitted to be more complex than that which we are presently considering.

An incoming symbol with a precedence value greater than that of the top element of the stack will result in that operator (or variable) being inserted in the stack. This is understandable since the operation corresponding to this incoming operator should be performed before any other operations corresponding to the other operators on the stack. This pattern will be reflected in the last operator to be placed on the stack being the first to be deleted from the stack and placed in string $POLISH$. Notice that when the precedence of an incoming operator is equal to the precedence of the operator on the top of the stack, then the latter is placed in the string $POLISH$. This process preserves the property that in an expression containing operators with the same precedence, the leftmost operator is executed first. Therefore, this algorithm will convert $a + b + c$ to $ab+c+$ and *not* to $abc++$. The Polish string $ab+c+$ corresponds to the infix $(a + b) + c$, and $abc++$ to $a + (b + c)$. A trace of the stack contents and the Polish string $POLISH$ for the infix expression $a + b * c - d / e * h$ is given in Table 3-4.3.   ////

Let us now consider the problem of converting an infix expression containing parenthesized subexpressions. When a programmer writes an expression con-

Table 3-4.3

Character scanned	Contents of stack (rightmost symbol is top of stack)	Reverse Polish expression	Rank
	$\mapsto$		
a	$\mapsto a$		
$+$	$\mapsto +$	a	1
b	$\mapsto +b$	a	1
$*$	$\mapsto +*$	ab	2
c	$\mapsto +*c$	ab	2
$-$	$\mapsto -$	$abc*+$	1
d	$\mapsto -d$	$abc*+$	1
$/$	$\mapsto -/$	$abc*+d$	2
e	$\mapsto -/e$	$abc*+d$	2
$*$	$\mapsto -*$	$abc*+de/$	2
h	$\mapsto -*h$	$abc*+de/$	2
$\mapsto$	$\mapsto$	$abc*+de/h*-$	1

taining parentheses, it is not normally written in a completely parenthesized form. Intuitively, when a left parenthesis is encountered in the infix expression, it should be placed on the stack regardless of the present contents. However, when it is in the stack, it should only be removed and discarded when a right parenthesis is encountered in the infix expression, at which time the right parenthesis is also ignored. A left parenthesis can be forced on the stack by assigning to it a precedence value greater than that of any other operator. Once on the stack, the left parenthesis should have another precedence value (called its stack precedence) which is smaller than that of any other operator. We can get rid of the left parenthesis on the stack by checking for an incoming right parenthesis in the infix expression. The right parenthesis is never inserted on the stack.

Actually, we can modify the previous algorithm in such a manner that the left and right parentheses can perform the same function as the special symbol $\mapsto$ used earlier. The original table of precedence values of Table 3-4.2 can be revised to have both an input and stack precedence value for each operator and operand. This revision is done, in addition to getting rid of the symbol $\mapsto$, in order to make the algorithm more general in the sense that the algorithm does not grow significantly in complexity when we add other operators such as relational, logical, unary, and ternary operators. Table 3-4.4 is a revised table which

Table 3-4.4

Symbol	Precedence		Rank function r
	Input precedence function f	Stack precedence function g	
$+, -$	1	2	-1
$*, /$	3	4	-1
$\uparrow$	6	5	-1
variables	7	8	1
(	9	0	—
)	0	—	—

includes parentheses. Each symbol has both an input symbol and stack symbol precedence except for a right parenthesis which does not possess a stack precedence since it is never placed on the stack. The table also contains the exponentiation operator, denoted here by the symbol $\uparrow$. All arithmetic operators except exponentiation have input precedences which are lower in value than their stack precedences. This .preserves the left-to-right processing of operators of equal precedence in an expression. The exponentiation operator in mathematics is right-associative. The expression $a \uparrow b \uparrow c$ is equivalent to the parenthesized expression $a \uparrow (b \uparrow c)$ and not to the expression $(a \uparrow b) \uparrow c$.

The conversion of an infix expression into reverse Polish operates in much the same way as the previous algorithm. A left parenthesis is initially placed on the stack, and the infix expression is padded on the right with a right parenthesis. The new algorithm is formulated as follows.

Algorithm *REVPOL*   Given an input string *INFIX* containing an infix expression which has been padded on the right with a ")" and whose symbols have precedence values given by Table 3-4.4, a vector S used as a stack, and a function *NEXTCHAR* which when invoked returns the next character of its argument, it is required to convert the string *INFIX* to reverse Polish and to store it in a vector called *POLISH*. The variable *RANK* is used to compute the rank of the Polish string.

1   [Initialize stack] Set $TOP \leftarrow 1$, $S[TOP] \leftarrow$ '('.

2   [Initialize output string pointer and *RANK*] Set $RANK \leftarrow i \leftarrow 0$.

3   [Get next input symbol] Set $NEXT \leftarrow NEXTCHAR(INFIX)$.

4   [End of *INFIX*?] If $NEXT = \Lambda$ then go to step 7.

5   [Stack *NEXT*?] If $f(NEXT) > g(S[TOP])$ then set $TOP \leftarrow TOP + 1$, $S[TOP] \leftarrow NEXT$, go to step 3.

6   [Move stack element to *POLISH*?] If $f(NEXT) = g(S[TOP])$ then set $TOP \leftarrow TOP - 1$, go to step 3; otherwise, set $i \leftarrow i + 1$, $POLISH[i] \leftarrow S[TOP]$, $RANK \leftarrow RANK + r(S[TOP])$, if $RANK \leq 0$ then 'INVALID' and Exit; otherwise, set $TOP \leftarrow TOP - 1$, go to step 5.

7   [Is the expression valid?] If $TOP \neq 0$ or $RANK \neq 1$ then print 'INVALID'; otherwise, print 'VALID'. Exit.   ////

A trace of the stack contents and the Polish string *POLISH* for the infix expression

$$(a + b \uparrow c \uparrow d) * (e + f / d)$$

is given in Table 3-4.5. The reader is encouraged to trace the algorithm for the not well-formed expression $((a * x + b) * x) + c))$.

It is possible to extend precedence functions to handle relational operators, conditional statements, unconditional transfers (GO TO), subscripted variables, and many other features found in present programming languages. Some exercises at the end of this section will deal with these extensions.

We have been concerned until now with the conversion of an infix expression to reverse Polish. The purpose of this conversion was that reverse Polish could be converted into object code by linearly scanning the Polish string once.

The problem of converting infix expressions to prefix Polish will not be dis-

Table 3-4.5   Translation of Infix String $(a + b \uparrow c \uparrow d) * (e + f/d)$ to Polish

Character scanned	Contents of stack (rightmost symbol is top of stack)	Reverse Polish expression	Rank
	(		
(	((		
a	((a		
+	((+	a	1
b	((+b	a	1
↑	((+↑	ab	2
c	((+↑c	ab	2
↑	((+↑↑	abc	3
d	((+↑↑d	abc	3
)	(	abcd ↑ ↑ +	1
*	(*	abcd ↑ ↑ +	1
(	(*(	abcd ↑ ↑ +	1
e	(*(e	abcd ↑ ↑ +	1
+	(*(+	abcd ↑ ↑ +e	2
f	(*(+f	abcd ↑ ↑ +e	2
/	(*(+/	abcd ↑ ↑ +ef	3
d	(*(+/d	abcd ↑ ↑ +ef	3
)	(*	abcd ↑ ↑ +efd/+	2
)		abcd ↑ ↑ +efd/+*	1

cussed in this section. A simple algorithm, which was based on the scanning of an infix expression from right to left, was given in Sec. 1-3.6. In many cases the entire infix string is not available, but it is obtained one symbol at a time in a left-to-right manner (because this is the way we write programs). Therefore, a practical algorithm for converting infix to prefix must be based on a left-to-right scan of the infix string. To obtain such an algorithm, however, two stacks instead of the usual one are normally required. This construction is left as an exercise.

The area of compiling has been introduced only in this discussion. We pursue this topic further in Chap. 5.

EXERCISES 3-4

1 Write a recursive routine which will recognize if a particular expression is well-formed reverse Polish. Assume that the expression consists of single-letter variable names and the four basic arithmetic operators.

2 Prove the converse of Theorem 3-4.1.

3 Thus far, we have only been concerned with the binary subtraction operator. In mathematics there are three uses of the minus sign, namely, to indicate the binary subtraction operator, the unary minus operator (such as $-x$), and to indicate the sign of a constant [such as $x + (-5)$]. Obtain a precedence table capable of handling assignment statements containing the unary minus and the assignment operator (denoted by ←).

Hint: It is an easy matter to distinguish the different occurrences of minus. A minus symbol will denote a binary operator if it does not occur either at the beginning of an expression or immediately after a left parenthesis. A minus symbol at the beginning of an expression or immediately after a left parenthesis will be a unary operator unless it is followed by a digit or decimal point.

4 Consider expressions which can contain relational and logical operators. Formulate the precedence functions required to convert such expressions to reverse Polish.

5 As mentioned in the text, for certain applications the scanning of the infix expression is restricted to a left-to-right one-character-at-a-time scan. In an infix-to-prefix conversion, two stacks instead of one (for infix-to-suffix conversion) are required, namely, an operator stack and an operand stack (to store temporarily the intermediate operands). Recall from Sec. 1-3.6 that all variables and constants retain their relative order when an infix expression is converted to prefix form. The operators, however, are reordered according to their relative precedence, and the operator stack is used in this reordering. The operand stack is used for temporary storage of intermediate operands, so that when finally the operator which connects them is found to be applicable, it can be placed in front of the concatenated operands. Formulate an algorithm to perform the translation, assuming infix expressions consisting of single-letter variables and the four arithmetic operators.

6 Can you point out how conditional and unconditional statements might be implemented in the reverse Polish framework?

3-5 GROUPS

In this section we study an abstract algebraic system called a group. Group theory is a well-developed branch of abstract algebra, and there are many books which are exclusively devoted to the study of groups. Group theory is applied in various branches of the physical sciences and in computer science. In this section we discuss some basic properties of groups and give certain well-known examples of them. The application of group theory in the design of fast adders and error-correcting codes is discussed in Secs. 3-6 and 3-7. Concepts of subgroups and group homomorphisms are studied. Some important theorems of group theory which have useful applications will be proved here.

3-5.1 Definitions and Examples

Recall that an algebraic system $\langle S, * \rangle$ is called a semigroup if the binary operation $*$ is associative. If, in addition, there exists an identity element $e \in S$, then $\langle S, * \rangle$ is a monoid. A further restriction imposed on the elements of the monoid, viz., the existence of an inverse for each element, results in an algebraic system called a group.

Definition 3-4.1 A *group* $\langle G, * \rangle$ is an algebraic system in which the binary operation $*$ on G satisfies three conditions:

1 For all $x, y, z \in G$,

$$x * (y * z) = (x * y) * z \quad (Associativity)$$

2 There exists an element $e \in G$ such that for any $x \in G$

$$x * e = e * x = x \quad (Identity)$$

3 For every $x \in G$, there exists an element denoted by $x^{-1} \in G$ such that

$$x^{-1} * x = x * x^{-1} = e \quad (Inverse)$$

Since a group is a special case of a semigroup and a monoid, it must satisfy all the properties of the latter systems. In particular, the identity element of a group is unique and is called the *identity of the group*. Also the existence of the identity guarantees that no two rows or columns in the composition table of $\langle G, * \rangle$ are identical (see Sec. 3-2.1).

Let us now examine some of the properties of a group that follow from condition (3). In fact, this condition distinguishes a group from a monoid.

From the associativity of the operation $*$, it follows that the inverse of any element of $\langle G, * \rangle$ must be unique (see Theorem 2-4.5). The existence of a unique inverse of every element of G also guarantees the unique solvability of any equation of the type $a * x = b$, where $a, b \in G$. The solution is given by $x = a^{-1} * b$. Also, the existence of the inverse of every element implies that the cancellation property holds, i.e.,

$$a * b = a * c \Rightarrow b = c$$

$$\text{for any } a, b, c \in G$$

$$b * a = c * a \Rightarrow b = c$$

A group cannot have a zero element because every element in a group is invertible. Also a group cannot have any element which is idempotent except the identity element. To see this, let us assume that $a \in G$ is idempotent. Then $a * a = a$, and

$$e = a^{-1} * a = a^{-1} * (a * a) = (a^{-1} * a) * a = e * a = a$$

We shall now examine the rows and columns of the composition table of a group $\langle G, * \rangle$. Before we do this, let us define a permutation.

Definition 3-5.2 Any one-to-one mapping of a set S onto S is called a *permutation* of S.

Theorem 3-5.1 Every row or column in the composition table of a group $\langle G, * \rangle$ is a permutation of the elements of G.

PROOF   As a first step, we shall show that no row or column in the composition table can have an element of G more than once. Let us assume, to the contrary, that the row corresponding to an element $a \in G$ has two entries which are both k; that is, assume that

$$a * b_1 = a * b_2 = k \qquad b_1, b_2, k \in G \text{ and } b_1 \neq b_2$$

From the cancellation property we have $b_1 = b_2$, which is a contradiction. A similar result holds for any column.

As a next step of our proof, we show that every element of G appears in each row and column of the table of composition. For this step, again consider the row corresponding to the element $a \in G$, and let b be any element of G. Since $b = a * (a^{-1} * b)$, b must appear in the row corresponding to the element $a \in G$. The same argument applies to every column of the table as well.

From the above result and the fact that no two rows or columns are identical, it follows that every row of the composition table is obtained by a permutation of the elements of G and that each row is a distinct permutation. The same result applies to the columns of the composition table.   ////

Table 3-5.1

$*$	e	a
e	e	a
a	a	e

Definition 3-5.3 The *order* of a group $\langle G, * \rangle$, denoted by $|G|$, is the number of elements of G, when G is finite.

Definition 3-5.4 A group $\langle G, * \rangle$ in which the operation $*$ is commutative is called an *abelian group*.

EXAMPLE 1   Let **I** be the set of integers. The algebra $\langle \mathbf{I}, + \rangle$ is an abelian group.

EXAMPLE 2   The set of rational numbers excluding zero is an abelian group under multiplication.

EXAMPLE 3   The set $\{ f^0, f^1, f^2, f^3 \}$ of functions under the operation of composition given in Table 3-1.2 is an abelian group of order 4.

Let us now examine groups of order 1, 2, 3, and 4. Obviously, a group of order 1 has only the identity element, that is, $\langle \{e\}, * \rangle$. A group of order 2 has one more element, besides the identity element. Let $\langle \{e, a\}, * \rangle$ be such a group. Table 3-5.1 is the required composition table. No other table is possible because of the requirements of Theorem 3-5.1. We can easily say that all the groups of order 2 are isomorphic to the group given here. We shall return to this point later when we define isomorphism of groups.

As a next step, let us consider $G = \langle \{e, a, b\}, * \rangle$ in which e is the identity element. The operation $*$ on G is given in Table 3-5.2. No other composition table is possible because of the conditions of Theorem 3-5.1. Obviously, any group of order 3 must be isomorphic to the group given here.

The examples of groups of orders 2 and 3 show that all such groups are abelian. In fact, the groups of orders 4 and 5 are also abelian. We shall see that groups of order 6 are not necessarily abelian.

EXAMPLE 4   Let $G = \{\alpha, \beta, \gamma, \delta\}$ and the operation $*$ on G is given in Table 3-5.3. Observe that α is the identity, and the inverses of β, γ, and δ are

Table 3-5.2

$*$	e	a	b
e	e	a	b
a	a	b	e
b	b	e	a

Table 3-5.3

$*$	α	β	γ	δ
α	α	β	γ	δ
β	β	α	δ	γ
γ	γ	δ	β	α
δ	δ	γ	α	β

β, δ, and γ respectively. It is not easy to verify that the operation $*$ is associative. In order to do this, we must consider $3^3 = 27$ combinations of β, γ, and δ. Observe that the group of order 4 given in Example 3 is not isomorphic to the group given here. In fact, all the groups of order 4 are isomorphic to one of these two groups. ////

The nonnegative power of an element of a group is defined in the same way as was done for a monoid. However, in the case of a group we can extend this concept to all the integral powers of an element in the following manner.

Let $\langle G, * \rangle$ be a group and $a \in G$. Define

$$a^0 = e \qquad a^{n+1} = a^n * a \qquad \text{for } n \in \mathbf{N}$$

Also define

$$(a^{-1})^n = a^{-n} \qquad \text{for } n \in \mathbf{N}$$

so that we have defined a^r for $r \in \mathbf{I}$, where $\mathbf{I}$ is the set of integers. Furthermore,

$$a^m * a^k = a^{m+k} \qquad \text{for } m, k \in \mathbf{I}$$

Recall the definition of permutation given earlier. We shall consider the set of all permutations of the elements of a finite set and define a binary operation on them. We shall consider those sets of permutations which form a group under this operation. Such groups are called *permutation groups*.

Let $S = \{a, b, c\}$ be a set, and let p denote a permutation of the elements of S; that is, $p: S \rightarrow S$ is a bijective mapping. There are two convenient ways of describing the permutation p. Suppose that

$$p(a) = c \qquad p(b) = a \qquad \text{and} \qquad p(c) = b$$

then we may represent p as

$$p = \begin{pmatrix} a & b & c \\ c & a & b \end{pmatrix}$$

where the image of any element of S is entered below the element. According to this notation

$$p = \begin{pmatrix} a & b & c \\ c & a & b \end{pmatrix} = \begin{pmatrix} a & c & b \\ c & b & a \end{pmatrix} = \begin{pmatrix} b & a & c \\ a & c & b \end{pmatrix} \qquad \text{and so on}$$

Another method is to show p diagrammatically as in Fig. 3-5.1.

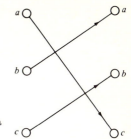

FIGURE 3-5.1 Representation of a permutation.

Consider now a set $S = \{a, b\}$ consisting of only two elements, and let the permutations on the elements of this set be denoted by p_1 and p_2, where

$$p_1 = \begin{pmatrix} a & b \\ a & b \end{pmatrix} \quad \text{and} \quad p_2 = \begin{pmatrix} a & b \\ b & a \end{pmatrix}$$

It is easy to see that $S_2 = \{p_1, p_2\}$ is the set of all possible permutations of the elements of $\{a, b\}$.

Let $\diamondsuit$ denote a binary operation on S_2 representing the (right) *composition of permutations*. For $i, j = 1, 2$ we mean by $p_i \diamondsuit p_j$ the permutation obtained by permuting the elements of S by an application of p_i followed by an application of the permutation p_j. It is convenient to use the right composition for permutations. If we consider p_i and p_j as functions and let $\circ$ denote the left composition of functions, then

$$p_i \diamondsuit p_j = p_j \circ p_i \quad \text{for } i, j = 1, 2$$

Accordingly, $(p_i \diamondsuit p_j)(a) = (p_j \circ p_i)(a) = p_j(p_i(a))$, and similarly for b. The composition of permutations is associative because $\circ$ is associative. Also p_1 is the identity element with respect to the operation $\diamondsuit$. The operation $\diamondsuit$ on S_2 is described in Table 3-5.4. A comparison with Table 3-5.1 immediately shows that $\langle S_2, \diamondsuit \rangle$ is a group of order 2.

Note that $\langle S_2, \diamondsuit \rangle$ is independent of the elements of the set $\{a, b\}$ but depends upon the number of elements in this set. Any other set of two elements will generate the same permutation group $\langle S_2, \diamondsuit \rangle$. We therefore say that the *degree* of a permutation group is the cardinality of the set on which the permutations are defined. Accordingly, the degree of $\langle S_2, \diamondsuit \rangle$ is 2.

Next, consider the $3! = 6$ permutations of the elements of the set $\{1, 2, 3\}$. Let us denote the set of all permutations by $S_3 = \{p_1, p_2, \ldots, p_6\}$. The elements $p_1, \ldots, p_6$ are described in Fig. 3-5.2. The composition of permutations on S_3

Table 3-5.4

$\diamondsuit$	p_1	p_2
p_1	p_1	p_2
p_2	p_2	p_1

$$p_1 = \begin{pmatrix} 1 & 2 & 3 \\ 1 & 2 & 3 \end{pmatrix} \qquad p_2 = \begin{pmatrix} 1 & 2 & 3 \\ 2 & 1 & 3 \end{pmatrix} \qquad p_3 = \begin{pmatrix} 1 & 2 & 3 \\ 3 & 2 & 1 \end{pmatrix}$$

$$p_4 = \begin{pmatrix} 1 & 2 & 3 \\ 1 & 3 & 2 \end{pmatrix} \qquad p_5 = \begin{pmatrix} 1 & 2 & 3 \\ 2 & 3 & 1 \end{pmatrix} \qquad p_6 = \begin{pmatrix} 1 & 2 & 3 \\ 3 & 1 & 2 \end{pmatrix}$$

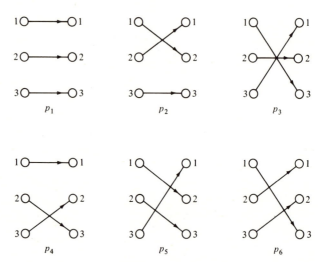

FIGURE 3-5.2   Permutations of $\{1, 2, 3\}$.

is given in Table 3-5.5. Any entry in the table can easily be obtained; for example,

$$p_3 \diamond p_5 = \begin{pmatrix} 1 & 2 & 3 \\ 3 & 2 & 1 \end{pmatrix} \diamond \begin{pmatrix} 1 & 2 & 3 \\ 2 & 3 & 1 \end{pmatrix} = \begin{pmatrix} 1 & 2 & 3 \\ 3 & 2 & 1 \end{pmatrix} \diamond \begin{pmatrix} 3 & 2 & 1 \\ 1 & 3 & 2 \end{pmatrix} = \begin{pmatrix} 1 & 2 & 3 \\ 1 & 3 & 2 \end{pmatrix}$$

$$= p_4$$

Table 3-5.5

$\diamond$	p_1	p_2	p_3	p_4	p_5	p_6
p_1	p_1	p_2	p_3	p_4	p_5	p_6
p_2	p_2	p_1	p_5	p_6	p_3	p_4
p_3	p_3	p_6	p_1	p_5	p_4	p_2
p_4	p_4	p_5	p_6	p_1	p_2	p_3
p_5	p_5	p_4	p_2	p_3	p_6	p_1
p_6	p_6	p_3	p_4	p_2	p_1	p_5

Note that $\langle S_3, \diamond \rangle$ is not an abelian group. It is our first example of a group of order 6. The degree of this permutation group is 3, because S_3 consists of permutations of a set of three elements. It is easy to see from Table 3-5.5 that $\langle \{p_1, p_2\}, \diamond \rangle$, $\langle \{p_1, p_3\}, \diamond \rangle$, $\langle \{p_1, p_4\}, \diamond \rangle$, and $\langle \{p_1, p_5, p_6\}, \diamond \rangle$ are all permutation groups of degree 3.

In general, the set S_n of all permutations of n elements is a permutation group $\langle S_n, \diamond \rangle$, also called the *symmetric group*. The group $\langle S_n, \diamond \rangle$ is of order $n!$ and degree n.

In Sec. 3-5.2 it is shown that every finite group of order n is isomorphic to a permutation group of degree n. This theorem is similar to Theorem 3-2.4 on monoids.

By considering the symmetries of regular polygons we obtain certain other permutation groups known as *dihedral groups*. For this purpose, let us first consider an equilateral triangle whose vertices are denoted by 1, 2, and 3, as shown in Fig. 3-5.3. Now consider all possible rotations and reflections which leave the final position of the triangle unchanged from its original position except for the renaming of vertices. We shall denote such rotations by $p_1, p_2, \ldots$. A rotation is described as a transformation of the set of vertices $\{1, 2, 3\}$. For example, let p_1 denote either no rotation or a rotation of the triangle about the center of gravity O through 360°. We may describe p_1 by writing, as before,

$$p_1 = \begin{pmatrix} 1 & 2 & 3 \\ 1 & 2 & 3 \end{pmatrix}$$

Similarly, let us denote the counterclockwise rotation of the triangle about 0 and through 120 and 240° by p_5 and p_6 respectively. Observe that

$$p_5 = \begin{pmatrix} 1 & 2 & 3 \\ 2 & 3 & 1 \end{pmatrix} \qquad p_6 = \begin{pmatrix} 1 & 2 & 3 \\ 3 & 1 & 2 \end{pmatrix}$$

All other rotations of the triangle through any multiple of 120°, whether clockwise or counterclockwise, will result in one of the rotations p_1, p_5, or p_6. In fact, p_1 can be considered as a rotation p_5 followed by the rotation p_6. We may express this idea by writing $p_1 = p_5 \diamond p_6$ where $\diamond$ denotes the composition of rotation. Accordingly, $p_5 \diamond p_5 = p_6$, $p_6 \diamond p_6 = p_5$, $p_6 \diamond p_5 = p_5 \diamond p_6 = p_1$, and so on. The composition of the rotations on $\{p_1, p_5, p_6\}$ is given in Table 3-5.6. It is easy to see that $\langle \{p_1, p_5, p_6\}, \diamond \rangle$ is a group (see Table 3-5.2).

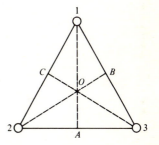

FIGURE 3-5.3

Table 3-5.6

$\diamondsuit$	p_1	p_5	p_6
p_1	p_1	p_5	p_6
p_5	p_5	p_6	p_1
p_6	p_6	p_1	p_5

Note, however, that the rotations p_1, p_5, and p_6 do not exhaust all possible rigid rotations of the triangle which result in the triangle's returning to its original position. For example, a rotation through 180° about any one of the lines $1A$, $2B$, or $3C$ is not described by p_1, p_5, or p_6. Any such rotation can also be considered as a reflection of the triangle. Let us denote these rotations by p_4, p_3, and p_2, respectively, where all the rotations p_1, p_2, ..., p_6 are the same as described in Fig. 3-5.2. Note that after the rotations or reflections p_2, p_3, or p_4, only two of the vertices are interchanged. There are no other rotations which return the triangle to the original position. The set of all such rotations, $\{p_1, p_2, \ldots, p_6\}$, can also be interpreted as the set of all the symmetries of the equilateral triangle. This set under the operation of composition is denoted by $\langle D_3, \diamondsuit \rangle$ and is called a dihedral group. $\langle D_3, \diamondsuit \rangle$ is of order 6 and degree 3 because it is a permutation group obtained from the permutation of the vertices of the triangle. In fact, in this case the dihedral group is the same as the group $\langle S_3, \diamondsuit \rangle$.

We shall now obtain the dihedral group $\langle D_4, \diamondsuit \rangle$ by considering the symmetries of a square shown in Fig. 3-5.4. There are four rotations about the point O given by

$$r_1 = \begin{pmatrix} 1 & 2 & 3 & 4 \\ 2 & 3 & 4 & 1 \end{pmatrix} \qquad r_2 = \begin{pmatrix} 1 & 2 & 3 & 4 \\ 3 & 4 & 1 & 2 \end{pmatrix}$$

$$r_3 = \begin{pmatrix} 1 & 2 & 3 & 4 \\ 4 & 1 & 2 & 3 \end{pmatrix} \qquad r_4 = \begin{pmatrix} 1 & 2 & 3 & 4 \\ 1 & 2 & 3 & 4 \end{pmatrix}$$

which are obtained by rotating the square counterclockwise through 90, 180, 270, and other multiples of 90°. These rotations include clockwise rotations of the same type. Other rigid rotations are obtained by rotating the square about the lines AA, BB, and the diagonals 13 and 24. Note that these rotations are reflec-

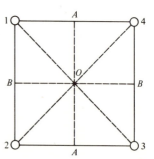

FIGURE 3-5.4

tions. These reflections are given by

$$r_5 = \begin{pmatrix} 1 & 2 & 3 & 4 \\ 4 & 3 & 2 & 1 \end{pmatrix} \qquad r_6 = \begin{pmatrix} 1 & 2 & 3 & 4 \\ 2 & 1 & 4 & 3 \end{pmatrix}$$

$$r_7 = \begin{pmatrix} 1 & 2 & 3 & 4 \\ 1 & 4 & 3 & 2 \end{pmatrix} \qquad r_8 = \begin{pmatrix} 1 & 2 & 3 & 4 \\ 3 & 2 & 1 & 4 \end{pmatrix}$$

Denoting the set of rotations of the square by $D_4 = \{r_1, r_2, \ldots, r_8\}$, the composition of the rotations of D_4 is given by Table 3-5.7. Note that $\langle D_4, \diamond \rangle$ is a group of order 8 and a permutation group of degree 4.

In general, the set of all rigid rotations of a regular polygon of n sides under the composition $\diamond$ is a group $\langle D_n, \diamond \rangle$ where D_n is of order $2n$. The group $\langle D_n, \diamond \rangle$ is a permutation group of degree n. The group D_n ($n = 1, 2, \ldots$) is called a *dihedral group*. Since $\langle D_n, \diamond \rangle$ is a permutation group of degree n, we shall see that $\langle D_n, \diamond \rangle$ is a subgroup of $\langle S_n, \diamond \rangle$. For $n = 3$, the orders of both $\langle S_3, \diamond \rangle$ and $\langle D_3, \diamond \rangle$ are 6, but for $n = 4$, D_4 is of order 8 and S_4 of order 4!

A group $\langle G, * \rangle$ is said to be *cyclic* if there exists an element $a \in G$ such that every element of G can be written as some power of a, that is, a^n for some integer n. In such a case, a cyclic group is said to be generated by a, or a is a generator of the group G. A cyclic group is abelian, because for any $p, q \in G$, $p = a^r$ and $q = a^s$ for some $r, s \in \mathbf{I}$ and

$$p * q = a^r * a^s = a^{r+s} = a^{s+r} = a^s * a^r = q * p$$

Consider the group $\langle G, * \rangle$ of Example 4. From Table 3-5.3 we have

$$\alpha * \alpha = \alpha \qquad\qquad \beta * \beta = \alpha$$

$$\gamma * \gamma = \gamma^2 = \beta \qquad \gamma^3 = \delta \qquad\qquad \gamma^4 = \alpha$$

$$\delta * \delta = \delta^2 = \beta \qquad \delta^3 = \gamma \qquad\qquad \delta^4 = \alpha$$

Table 3-5.7

$\diamond$	r_1	r_2	r_3	r_4	r_5	r_6	r_7	r_8
r_1	r_2	r_3	r_4	r_1	r_8	r_7	r_5	r_6
r_2	r_3	r_4	r_1	r_2	r_6	r_5	r_8	r_7
r_3	r_4	r_1	r_2	r_3	r_7	r_8	r_6	r_5
r_4	r_1	r_2	r_3	r_4	r_5	r_6	r_7	r_8
r_5	r_7	r_6	r_8	r_5	r_4	r_2	r_1	r_3
r_6	r_8	r_5	r_7	r_6	r_2	r_4	r_3	r_1
r_7	r_6	r_8	r_5	r_7	r_3	r_1	r_4	r_2
r_8	r_5	r_7	r_6	r_8	r_1	r_3	r_2	r_4

Therefore, the group $\langle G, * \rangle$ is generated by γ or δ, any one of which can be considered as the generator, and $\langle G, * \rangle$ is cyclic. Note that β generates $\langle \{\alpha, \beta\}, * \rangle$ while α generates $\langle \{\alpha\}, * \rangle$; these are subgroups of $\langle G, * \rangle$. Subgroups are defined in the next section.

Similarly, from Table 3-5.7 we find that r_1 and r_3 are both generators of the group $\langle \{r_1, r_2, r_3, r_4\}, \diamondsuit \rangle$, and r_2 generates $\langle \{r_2, r_4\}, \diamondsuit \rangle$. Similarly, each of the elements r_5, r_6, r_7, and r_8 generates two-element subgroups of $\langle D_4, \diamondsuit \rangle$.

EXAMPLE 5 Consider the group $\langle \mathbf{Z}_m, +_m \rangle$ where $\mathbf{Z}_m$ is the set of equivalence classes for the relation congruence modulo m (see Example 5, Sec. 3-2.1) over the set of integers. For any m, $\mathbf{Z}_m$ can be considered as a cyclic group generated by $[1]$. There may be other elements of $\mathbf{Z}_m$ which generate the same group. For example, in the case of $m = 5$, the group $\langle \mathbf{Z}_5, +_5 \rangle$ is generated by $[1]$, $[2]$, $[3]$, or $[4]$, while for $m = 6$ the group $\langle \mathbf{Z}_6, +_6 \rangle$ is generated by $[1]$ or $[5]$ only. The elements $[2]$, $[3]$, and $[4]$ only generate subgroups of $\langle \mathbf{Z}_6, +_6 \rangle$.

For a finite cyclic group we have the following theorem.

Theorem 3-5.2 Let $\langle G, * \rangle$ be a finite cyclic group generated by an element $a \in G$. If G is of order n, that is, $|G| = n$, then $a^n = e$, so that

$$G = \{a, a^2, a^3, \ldots, a^n = e\}$$

Furthermore, n is the least positive integer for which $a^n = e$.

PROOF Let us assume that for some positive integer $m < n$, $a^m = e$. Since G is a cyclic group, any element of G can be written as a^k for some $k \in \mathbf{I}$. Now from Euclid's algorithm, we can write $k = mq + r$, where q is some integer and $0 \leq r < m$. This means $a^k = a^{mq+r} = (a^m)^q * a^r = a^r$, so that every element of G can be expressed as a^r for some $0 \leq r < m$, thus implying that G has at most m distinct elements, that is, $|G| = m < n$ which is a contradiction. Hence $a^m = e$ for $m < n$ is not possible. As a next step, we show that the elements $a, a^2, a^3, \ldots, a^n$ are all distinct, where $a^n = e$. Assume to the contrary that $a^i = a^j$ for $i < j \leq n$. This means that $a^{j-i} = e$ where $j - i < n$, which again is a contradiction. ////

In the following subsections we shall often use the cyclic groups, dihedral groups, and the symmetric groups as examples.

EXERCISES 3-5.1

1 If $\langle G, * \rangle$ is an abelian group, then for all $a, b \in G$ show that $(a * b)^n = a^n * b^n$.
2 In the symmetric group S_3 (see Table 3-5.5) find all those elements a and b such that
   (a) $(a * b)^2 \neq a^2 * b^2$
   (b) $a^2 = e$
   (c) $a^3 = e$
3 Show that in a group $\langle G, * \rangle$, if for any $a, b \in G$, $(a * b)^2 = a^2 * b^2$, then $\langle G, * \rangle$ must be abelian.

4 Show that if every element in a group is its own inverse, then the group must be abelian.

5 Write down the composition tables for $\langle \mathbf{Z}_7, +_7 \rangle$ and $\langle \mathbf{Z}_7^*, \times_7 \rangle$ where $\mathbf{Z}_7^* = \mathbf{Z}_7 - \{[0]\}$.

6 Let the permutations of the elements of $\{1, 2, 3, 4, 5\}$ be given by

$$\alpha = \begin{pmatrix} 1 & 2 & 3 & 4 & 5 \\ 2 & 3 & 1 & 4 & 5 \end{pmatrix} \qquad \beta = \begin{pmatrix} 1 & 2 & 3 & 4 & 5 \\ 1 & 2 & 3 & 5 & 4 \end{pmatrix}$$

$$\gamma = \begin{pmatrix} 1 & 2 & 3 & 4 & 5 \\ 5 & 4 & 3 & 1 & 2 \end{pmatrix} \qquad \delta = \begin{pmatrix} 1 & 2 & 3 & 4 & 5 \\ 3 & 2 & 1 & 5 & 4 \end{pmatrix}$$

Find $\alpha\beta$, $\beta\alpha$, α^2, $\gamma\beta$, δ^{-1}, and $\alpha\beta\gamma$. Solve the equation $\alpha x = \beta$.

7 Show that $\langle \{1\}, \times \rangle$ and $\langle \{1, -1\}, \times \rangle$ are the only finite groups of nonzero real numbers under the operation of multiplication.

8 For $P = \{p_1, p_2, \ldots, p_5\}$ and $Q = \{q_1, q_2, \ldots, q_5\}$ explain why $\langle P, * \rangle$ and $\langle Q, \Delta \rangle$ are not groups. The operations $*$ and Δ are given in the following table:

$*$	p_1	p_2	p_3	p_4	p_5	Δ	q_1	q_2	q_3	q_4	q_5
p_1	p_1	p_2	p_3	p_4	p_5	q_1	q_4	q_1	q_5	q_3	q_2
p_2	p_2	p_1	p_4	p_5	p_3	q_2	q_3	q_5	q_2	q_1	q_4
p_3	p_3	p_5	p_1	p_2	p_4	q_3	q_1	q_2	q_3	q_4	q_5
p_4	p_4	p_3	p_5	p_1	p_2	q_4	q_2	q_4	q_1	q_5	q_3
p_5	p_5	p_4	p_2	p_3	p_4	q_5	q_5	q_3	q_4	q_2	q_1

9 Show that the set of all polynomials in x under the operation of addition is a group.

3-5.2 Subgroups and Homomorphisms

The general notions of subalgebra and homomorphism will be applied to groups in this section. The idea of a subgroup is similar to that of a subsemigroup and a submonoid given earlier.

Definition 3-5.5 Let $\langle G, * \rangle$ be a group and $S \subseteq G$ be such that it satisfies the following conditions:

 1 $e \in S$, where e is the identity of $\langle G, * \rangle$.
 2 For any $a \in S$, $a^{-1} \in S$.
 3 For $a, b \in S$, $a * b \in S$.

Then $\langle S, * \rangle$ is called a *subgroup* of $\langle G, * \rangle$.

Note that $\langle S, * \rangle$ itself is a group with the same identity element as that of $\langle G, * \rangle$. Also the operation $*$ on S is the same as the operation $*$ on G, but restricted to S.

For any group $\langle G, * \rangle$, naturally $\langle \{e\}, * \rangle$ and $\langle G, * \rangle$ are trivial subgroups of $\langle G, * \rangle$. All other subgroups of $\langle G, * \rangle$ are called *proper subgroups*.

Let $\langle G, * \rangle$ be a group and let a be any element of G. Obviously, G must contain all the integral powers of a, that is, $a^r \in G$ for $r \in \mathbf{I}$. This means that the cyclic group generated by a must be a subgroup of $\langle G, * \rangle$. Similarly, there are other subgroups generated by the elements of G.

It was shown in Example 4 of Sec. 3-5.1 that the group $\langle G, * \rangle$ was generated by the elements γ or δ, while the element β generates the subgroup $\langle \{\alpha, \beta\}, * \rangle$ and the element α generates the trivial subgroup $\langle \{\alpha\}, * \rangle$. One can write the subgroups generated by the elements of the dihedral group $\langle D_4, \diamond \rangle$ from Table 3-5.7.

Let us return to Example 5 of Sec. 3-5.1 and make the following interesting observation. For a group $\langle \mathbf{Z}_m, +_m \rangle$ certain elements of $\mathbf{Z}_m$ generate the group $\langle \mathbf{Z}_m, +_m \rangle$ itself, while certain other elements generate only some proper subgroups. For example, with $m = 5$, the elements [1], [2], [3], and [4] generate $\langle \mathbf{Z}_5, +_5 \rangle$, but for $m = 6$ only [1] and [5] generate $\langle \mathbf{Z}_6, +_6 \rangle$. The elements [2] and [4] generate the subgroup $\langle \{[0], [2], [4]\}, +_6 \rangle$ while [3] generates the subgroup $\langle \{[3], [0]\}, +_6 \rangle$. In the case of $m = 14$, only the elements [1], [3], [5], [9], [11], and [13] generate the group $\langle \mathbf{Z}_{14}, +_{14} \rangle$, while the other elements generate proper subgroups which are equal to the subgroup generated by either the element [2] or the element [7].

The observation made here about the subgroups of $\langle \mathbf{Z}_m, +_m \rangle$ generated by the elements of $\mathbf{Z}_m$ is a special case of an interesting theorem, proved in Sec. 3-5.3, which asserts that for a group G of order n, the subgroups are precisely those cyclic groups which are generated by a^m, where $a \in G$ and m divides n. According to this theorem, $\langle \mathbf{Z}_{14}, +_{14} \rangle$ is of order 14, and the elements [2] and [7] generate proper subgroups of $\langle \mathbf{Z}_{14}, +_{14} \rangle$, while the elements [1] and [0] generate the trivial subgroups. All other elements generate the group $\langle \mathbf{Z}_{14}, +_{14} \rangle$ or its subgroups, as was pointed out before.

Sometimes a convenient criterion to determine whether a subset $S \subseteq G$ is a subgroup of $\langle G, * \rangle$ is provided by the following theorem.

Theorem 3-5.3 A subset $S \neq \varnothing$ of G is a subgroup of $\langle G, * \rangle$ iff for any pair of elements $a, b \in S$, $a * b^{-1} \in S$.

PROOF Assuming that S is a subgroup, it is clear that if $a, b \in S$, then $b^{-1} \in S$ and $a * b^{-1} \in S$. To prove the converse, let us assume that $a, b \in S$ and $a * b^{-1} \in S$ for any pair a, b. Taking $b = a$, $a * a^{-1} = e \in S$. From e, a, $b \in S$, we have $e * a^{-1} = a^{-1} \in S$. Similarly, $b^{-1} \in S$. Finally, because a and b^{-1} are in S, we have $a * b \in S$. Hence $\langle S, * \rangle$ is a subgroup of $\langle G, * \rangle$.   ////

Definition 3-5.6 Let $\langle G, * \rangle$ and $\langle H, \Delta \rangle$ be two groups. A mapping g: $G \to H$ is called a *group homomorphism* from $\langle G, * \rangle$ to $\langle H, \Delta \rangle$ if for any $a, b \in G$

$$g(a * b) = g(a) \, \Delta \, g(b) \qquad (1)$$

We shall now show that (1) guarantees that a group homomorphism preserves identities, inverses, and subgroups. In other words, if e_G and e_H are the identities of $\langle G, * \rangle$ and $\langle H, \Delta \rangle$ respectively, then

$$g(e_G) = e_H \qquad (2)$$

Also for any $a \in G$

$$g(a^{-1}) = [g(a)]^{-1} \qquad (3)$$

If $\langle S, * \rangle$ is a subgroup of $\langle G, * \rangle$ and $g(S)$ denotes the image set of S under the homomorphism g, then $\langle g(S), \Delta \rangle$ is a subgroup of $\langle H, \Delta \rangle$. We shall now prove these statements.

From (1) we have $g(e_G * e_G) = g(e_G) = g(e_G) \Delta g(e_G)$, so that $g(e_G)$ is idempotent. But the only idempotent element of a group is the identity; hence $g(e_G) = e_H$.

For any $a \in G$, $a^{-1} \in G$ and hence

$$g(a * a^{-1}) = g(e_G) = e_H = g(a) \Delta g(a^{-1})$$
$$g(a^{-1} * a) = g(e_G) = e_H = g(a^{-1}) \Delta g(a)$$

which implies (3).

Finally, let $\langle S, * \rangle$ be a subgroup of $\langle G, * \rangle$ with $e_G \in S$. Therefore, $g(e_G) = e_H \in g(S)$. For any $a \in S$, $a^{-1} \in S$ and $g(a)$ as well as $g(a^{-1}) = [g(a)]^{-1}$ are in $g(S)$. Also for $a, b \in S$, $a * b \in S$ and consequently for $g(a), g(b) \in g(S)$, $g(a) \Delta g(b) \in g(S)$. This guarantees that $\langle g(S), \Delta \rangle$ is a subgroup of $\langle H, \Delta \rangle$ because every element of $g(S)$ can be written as $g(b)$ for some $b \in S$.

Recall that in the case of a monoid homomorphism we required both conditions (1) and (2) to be satisfied. However, for a group homomorphism, condition (1) alone guarantees (2) and (3).

As before, a group homomorphism g is called a *monomorphism, epimorphism,* or *isomorphism* depending upon whether g is one-to-one, onto, or one-to-one and onto, respectively.

Let $\langle G, * \rangle$ be a group and $\langle H, \Delta \rangle$ be an algebraic system in which Δ is a binary operation. If there exists a mapping $g\colon G \to H$ which is onto and satisfies condition (1), then $\langle H, \Delta \rangle$ must be a group. We leave the proof of this statement as an exercise and note here that condition (1) preserves the group property as well.

A homomorphism from a group $\langle G, * \rangle$ to $\langle G, * \rangle$ is called an *endomorphism,* while an isomorphism of $\langle G, * \rangle$ to $\langle G, * \rangle$ is called an *automorphism.*

Definition 3-5.7 Let g be a group homomorphism from $\langle G, * \rangle$ to $\langle H, \Delta \rangle$. The set of elements of G which are mapped into e_H, the identity of H, is called the *kernel* of the homomorphism g and denoted by $\ker(g)$.

Theorem 3-5.4 The kernel of a homomorphism g from a group $\langle G, * \rangle$ to $\langle H, \Delta \rangle$ is a subgroup of $\langle G, * \rangle$.

PROOF Since $g(e_G) = e_H$, $e_G \in \ker(g)$. Also, if $a, b \in \ker(g)$, that is, $g(a) = g(b) = e_H$, then

$$g(a * b) = g(a) \Delta g(b) = e_H \Delta e_H = e_H$$

so that $a * b \in \ker(g)$. Finally, if $a \in \ker(g)$, then $g(a^{-1}) = [g(a)]^{-1} = e_H^{-1} = e_H$. Hence $a^{-1} \in \ker(g)$ and $\ker(g)$ is a subgroup of $\langle G, * \rangle$. ////

EXAMPLE 1 Let $\mathbf{Z}_5^* = \{[1], [2], [3], [4]\}$ in which $[1], [2], \ldots$ have the same meaning as in $\mathbf{Z}_5$ (see Example 5, Sec. 3-2.1), except that $\mathbf{Z}_5^*$ is $\mathbf{Z}_5 - \{[0]\}$. Also let $\times_5$ denote the operation $\times_5$ defined in Table 3-2.1. Show that $g\colon \mathbf{Z}_4 \to \mathbf{Z}_5^*$

given by

$$g([0]) = [1] \qquad g([1]) = [2] \qquad g([2]) = [4] \qquad \text{and} \qquad g([3]) = [3]$$

defines a homomorphism from the group $\langle \mathbf{Z}_4, +_4 \rangle$ to $\langle \mathbf{Z}_5^*, \times_5 \rangle$. Hence show that $\langle \mathbf{Z}_5^*, \times_5 \rangle$ is a group isomorphic to $\langle \mathbf{Z}_4, +_4 \rangle$.

SOLUTION   In Table 3-1.3 replace [0] by [1], [1] by [2], [2] by [4], and rearrange the rows and columns and compare the resulting table with the one for $\langle \mathbf{Z}_5^*, \times_5 \rangle$. It follows immediately that $\langle \mathbf{Z}_5^*, \times_5 \rangle$ is a group. Since $g \colon \mathbf{Z}_4 \to \mathbf{Z}_5^*$ is one-to-one onto, we have the required isomorphism.   ////

EXAMPLE 2   Show that every cyclic group of order n is isomorphic to the group $\langle \mathbf{Z}_n, +_n \rangle$.

SOLUTION   Let the cyclic group $\langle G, * \rangle$ of order n be generated by an element $a \in G$, so that the elements of g are $a, a^2, \ldots, a^n = e$. Define $g \colon \mathbf{Z}_n \to G$ such that $g([1]) = a$. Note that $[1]$ is the generator of $\langle \mathbf{Z}_n, +_n \rangle$. Then $g([j]) = a^j$ for $j = 0, 1, \ldots, n - 1$, and hence the isomorphism is established.   ////

A representation theorem similar to Theorem 3-2.4 for monoids will now be proved for groups. Our method of proof is similar to that used in Theorem 3-2.4.

Theorem 3-5.5   Every finite group of order n is isomorphic to a permutation group of degree n.

PROOF   Let $\langle G, * \rangle$ be a group of order n. From Theorem 3-5.1 we know that every row and column in the composition table of $\langle G, * \rangle$ represents a permutation of the elements of G. Corresponding to an element $a \in G$ we denote by p_a the permutation given by the column under a in the composition table. Thus

$$p_a(c) = c * a \qquad \text{for any } c \in G$$

For every column we can define permutations of the elements of G. Let the set of permutations be denoted by P. Obviously, P has n elements. We shall now show that $\langle P, \diamond \rangle$ is a group, where $\diamond$ denotes the right composition of the permutations of P. Note that since $e \in G$, $p_e \in P$, and

$$p_e \diamond p_a = p_a \diamond p_e = p_a \qquad \text{for any } a \in G$$

Also for any $a \in G$,

$$p_{a^{-1}} \diamond p_a = p_e$$

Also for $a, b \in G$

$$p_a \diamond p_b = p_{a*b} \qquad\qquad (4)$$

Equation (4) follows from the fact that for any element $c \in G$, $p_a(c) = c * a$, so that $(p_a \diamond p_b)(c) = (c * a) * b = c * (a * b) = p_{a*b}(c)$. Hence $\langle P, \diamond \rangle$ is a group. The last step is sufficient to guarantee that $\langle P, \diamond \rangle$ is a group, because it shows that $\langle P, \diamond \rangle$ is isomorphic to $\langle G, * \rangle$. Consider a mapping $f \colon G \to P$ given by $f(a) = p_a$ for any $a \in G$. Naturally, f is one-to-one onto according to Theorem 3-5.1. Equation (4) can be written as

$$f(a \ast b) = f(a) \Diamond f(b)$$

showing that f is an isomorphism.   ////

Example 2 of Sec. 3-2.2 is an illustration of the representation theorem. This representation theorem is also known as Cayley's representation theorem. It was proposed by Arthur Cayley in 1854. This theorem shows that the structure of a group is determined solely by its composition table.

EXERCISES 3-5.2

1 Find all the subgroups of (a) $\langle \mathbf{Z}_{12}, +_{12} \rangle$; (b) $\langle \mathbf{Z}_5, +_5 \rangle$; (c) $\langle \mathbf{Z}_7^*, \times_7 \rangle$; and (d) $\langle \mathbf{Z}_{11}^*, \times_{11} \rangle$.

2 Find the group of rigid rotations of a rectangle which is not a square. Show that this is a subgroup of $\langle D_4, \Diamond \rangle$ given in Table 3-5.7.

3 Find all the subgroups of S_4 generated by the permutations

$$\begin{pmatrix} 1 & 2 & 3 & 4 \\ 1 & 3 & 2 & 4 \end{pmatrix} \quad \text{and} \quad \begin{pmatrix} 1 & 2 & 3 & 4 \\ 1 & 3 & 4 & 2 \end{pmatrix}$$

4 Show that the set of all elements a of a group $\langle G, \ast \rangle$ such that $a \ast x = x \ast a$ for every $x \in G$ is a subgroup of G.

5 Show that if $\langle G, \ast \rangle$ is a cyclic group, then every subgroup of $\langle G, \ast \rangle$ must be cyclic.

6 Show that $\langle \{1, 4, 13, 16\}, \times_{17} \rangle$ is a subgroup of $\langle \mathbf{Z}_{17}^*, \times_{17} \rangle$.

7 Let $\langle G, \ast \rangle$ be a group and $a \in G$. Let $f: G \to G$ be given by $f(x) = a \ast x \ast a^{-1}$ for every $x \in G$. Prove that f is an isomorphism of G onto G.

8 Show that the groups $\langle G, \ast \rangle$ and $\langle S, \Delta \rangle$ given by the following table are isomorphic.

$\ast$	p_1	p_2	p_3	p_4
p_1	p_1	p_2	p_3	p_4
p_2	p_2	p_1	p_4	p_3
p_3	p_3	p_4	p_1	p_2
p_4	p_4	p_3	p_2	p_1

Δ	q_1	q_2	q_3	q_4
q_1	q_3	q_4	q_1	q_2
q_2	q_4	q_3	q_2	q_1
q_3	q_1	q_2	q_3	q_4
q_4	q_2	q_1	q_4	q_3

3-5.3 Cosets and Lagrange's Theorem

From the definition of a subgroup it is clear that not every subset of a group is a subgroup. The problem that we try to solve here is to find those subsets which can qualify to become subgroups. An important relationship exists between the subgroups and the group itself. This relationship is explained by a theorem known as Lagrange's theorem, which is proved in this section. This theorem has important applications in the development of efficient group codes required in the transmission of information. Such group codes are discussed in Sec. 3-8. Another application of subgroups is in the construction of computer modules which perform group operations. Such modules are constructed by joining various subgroup modules that do operations in subgroups. The application of these to the design of fast adders is discussed in Sec. 3-7.

Let $\langle G, * \rangle$ be a group and $\langle H, * \rangle$ be a subgroup of $\langle G, * \rangle$. We shall define an equivalence relation on G called a *left coset relation* with respect to the subgroup $\langle H, * \rangle$, or a left coset relation modulo H, denoted by the symbol $\equiv$, such that for $a, b \in G$, $a \equiv b$, or more precisely $a \equiv b \pmod H$ if $b^{-1} * a \in H$. We now show that this relation is an equivalence relation.

Since H is a subset of G, $e_G \in H$. For any $a \in G$, $a^{-1} * a = e_G \in H$; therefore $a \equiv a \pmod H$. Also, if $b^{-1} * a \in H$, then $(b^{-1} * a)^{-1} = a^{-1} * b \in H$, implying that if $a \equiv b \pmod H$, then $b \equiv a \pmod H$. Similarly, one can see that if $b^{-1} * a \in H$ and $c^{-1} * b \in H$, then $c^{-1} * a = (c^{-1} * b) * (b^{-1} * a) \in H$, implying that from $a \equiv b \pmod H$ and $b \equiv c \pmod H$ we have $a \equiv c \pmod H$. Hence a left coset modulo H relation is an equivalence relation on G.

Obviously, the left coset equivalence relation defined here partitions G into equivalence classes. For any $a \in G$, we shall denote the equivalence class containing a by $[a]$, that is,

$$[a] = \{x \in G \mid x \equiv a \pmod H \}$$
$$= \{x \in G \mid a^{-1} * x \in H \}$$
$$= \{a * h \mid h \in H \}$$

The last step follows from the fact that if $a^{-1} * x = h$, where h is some element of H, then $a * h = x$. This step also leads us to the definition of a left coset.

Definition 3-5.8 Let $\langle H, * \rangle$ be a subgroup of $\langle G, * \rangle$. For any $a \in G$, the set aH defined by

$$aH = \{a * h \mid h \in H \}$$

is called the *left coset of H in G* determined by the element $a \in G$. The element a is called the *representative element* of the left coset aH.

It is immediately clear that the left coset of H in G determined by $a \in G$ is the same as the equivalence class $[a]$ determined by the relation left coset modulo H. We may formulate this statement as a theorem.

Theorem 3-5.6 Let $\langle H, * \rangle$ be a subgroup of $\langle G, * \rangle$. The set of left cosets of H in G form a partition of G. Every element of G belongs to one and only one left coset of H in G.

One can define right cosets in the same manner and denote the right coset of H in G determined by a as

$$Ha = \{h * a \mid h \in H \}$$

It can then be shown that the right cosets of H in G again partition G. Naturally, this partition corresponds to a right coset equivalence relation such that $a \overset{R}{\equiv} b \pmod H$ iff $a * b^{-1} \in H$. The remaining discussion follows on the same lines; however, we shall not pursue it any further.

EXAMPLE 1 The subset $H = \{[0], [2]\}$ is a subgroup of $\langle \mathbf{Z}_4, +_4 \rangle$, as can be seen from Table 3-1.3. The left cosets of H in G determined by the elements of G are $\{[1], [3]\}$ and $\{[0], [2]\}$, which is a partition of $\mathbf{Z}_4$.

EXAMPLE 2 Recall the symmetric group $\langle S_3, \diamond \rangle$ given by its composition table, Table 3-5.5. Let $\langle H, \diamond \rangle$ be the subgroup of $\langle S_3, \diamond \rangle$, where $H = \{p_1, p_2\}$. The left cosets of H in G are $\{p_1, p_2\}$, $\{p_3, p_6\}$, and $\{p_4, p_5\}$. Here

$$p_1 H = p_2 H = \{p_1, p_2\} \qquad p_3 H = p_6 H = \{p_3, p_6\} \qquad p_4 H = p_5 H = \{p_4, p_5\}$$

Let us now examine the left cosets of H in G determined by various elements of G. If an element $a \in H$, then the left coset determined by a is H itself. As a next step, consider any element $a \in G$ and examine how different elements of H contribute to the left coset aH. Let $h_1, h_2 \in H$; since $a * h_1 = a * h_2 \Rightarrow h_1 = h_2$, distinct elements of H contribute to distinct elements of aH. Therefore, the number of elements in aH is the same as the number of elements in H. This means that every left coset of H in G determined by any element of G must have the same number of elements as the number of elements in H. This fact explains why in Examples 1 and 2 the number of elements in each left coset is the same.

Let $\langle G, * \rangle$ be a group of order n, and let H be a subgroup of G of order m. According to the previous discussion, every left coset of H in G has exactly m elements, and the left cosets partition G; therefore we must have n/m left cosets. From this observation we have the following theorem, known as Lagrange's theorem.

Theorem 3-5.7 The order of a subgroup of a finite group divides the order of the group.

The number of left cosets of H in G is called the *index* of H in G. From Lagrange's theorem we have the index k of G given by

$$k = |G|/|H|$$

It immediately follows from Lagrange's theorem that any group of prime order has only trivial subgroups, while a group of order n which has divisors other than 1 and n has proper subgroups.

Recall the group $\langle D_4, \diamond \rangle$ of order 8 given in Table 3-5.7. $\langle D_4, \diamond \rangle$ has five different subgroups of order 2 and one subgroup of order 4. Similarly the symmetric group $\langle S_3, \diamond \rangle$ has subgroups of orders 2 and 3 besides the trivial subgroups.

For a group $\langle G, * \rangle$ we know that the cyclic group generated by any element of G must be a subgroup of G. Let $a \in G$ and the cyclic subgroup generated by a be denoted by H, that is, $H = \{a^i \mid i \in \mathbf{I}\}$. If H is of order m, then according to Lagrange's theorem m must divide n where n is the order of the group G. Hence from $a^m = e$ we also have $a^n = a^{mk} = (a^m)^k = e^k = e$. We therefore have the following corollary of Lagrange's theorem.

Corollary If $\langle G, * \rangle$ is a finite group of order n, then for any $a \in G$, we must have $a^n = e$, where e is the identity of the group G. ////

3-5.4 Normal Subgroups

It was shown in Sec. 3-1.2 that corresponding to a congruence relation on an algebraic system, we can define a homomorphism onto its quotient algebra. This correspondence was discussed for both semigroups and monoids. Instead of repeating the same arguments for groups, we shall now investigate whether the left or right coset relation defined by a subgroup is a congruence relation. It was shown that such a relation is an equivalence relation and that the corresponding equivalence classes are the left and right cosets. In general, this relation is not a congruence relation. We therefore determine conditions on the subgroup such that the left coset relation determined by it is a congruence relation. Once a congruence relation is available, the existence of a homomorphism follows.

Let $\langle H, * \rangle$ be a subgroup of $\langle G, * \rangle$ and $a, b, p, q \in G$ be such that

$$a \equiv p \pmod{H} \qquad \text{and} \qquad b \equiv q \pmod{H} \qquad (1)$$

We wish to determine whether condition (1) implies

$$(a * b) \equiv (p * q) \pmod{H} \qquad (2)$$

If relation (2) is satisfied for any $a, b, p, q \in G$ for which (1) holds, then the left coset relation determined by H is a congruence relation on G.

Condition (1) can be written as

$$p^{-1} * a \in H \qquad \text{and} \qquad q^{-1} * b \in H$$

Let us denote $p^{-1} * a = h_1$ and $q^{-1} * b = h_2$ for some $h_1, h_2 \in H$. In a similar manner, (2) can be rewritten as

$$(p * q)^{-1} * (a * b) \in H \qquad \text{or} \qquad (q^{-1} * p^{-1}) * (a * b) \in H$$

or

$$q^{-1} * h_1 * b \in H \qquad (3)$$

Condition (3) is clearly satisfied if $h_1 * b = b * h_3$ where h_3 is some element of H. In that case, $q^{-1} * h_1 * b = q^{-1} * b * h_3 = h_2 * h_3 \in H$.

We can restate our last result by saying that a left coset relation determined by H is a congruence relation provided that for any $a \in G$ and $h_1 \in H$, there exists an element $h_2 \in H$ such that

$$h_1 * a = a * h_2 \qquad (4)$$

or equivalently

$$a^{-1} * h_1 * a \in H \qquad (4a)$$

Condition (4) or (4a) is automatically satisfied if G is an abelian group. This means for an abelian group the left coset relation is a congruence relation no matter what subgroup is used to generate the left cosets.

We shall now show that conditions (4) or (4a) are equivalent to the condition

$$aH = Ha \qquad (4b)$$

where aH and Ha are the left and right cosets, respectively, of H in G determined by an element $a \in G$.

If we assume (4b) and choose an element $h_2 \in H$, we have $a * h_2 \in aH$, and (4b) says that $a * h_2 \in Ha$; that is, there exists an element in H, say h_1, such that $a * h_2 = h_1 * a$. Hence (4b) $\Rightarrow$ (4). Let us assume (4) and consider different values of $h_1 \in H$. Then $h_1 * a$ are the elements of Ha, and from (4) we have $Ha \subseteq aH$ because $a * h_2 \in aH$. By considering a^{-1} in place of a in (4), we can see that (4) implies $aH \subseteq Ha$. Hence $aH = Ha$ and (4) $\Rightarrow$ (4b).

Definition 3-5.9 A subgroup $\langle H, * \rangle$ of $\langle G, * \rangle$ is called a *normal subgroup* if for any $a \in G$, $aH = Ha$.

Note that $aH = Ha$ does not necessarily mean that $a * h = h * a$ for any $h \in H$. It only means that $a * h = h_1 * a$ for some, $h, h_1 \in H$. If H is a normal subgroup, then both the left and right cosets of H in G are equal, and therefore we may simply call them cosets. Note that every subgroup of an abelian group is normal. The trivial subgroups are also normal.

EXAMPLE 1 Determine all the proper subgroups of the symmetric group $\langle S_3, \diamond \rangle$ described in Table 3-5.5.

SOLUTION From the table it is clear that $\{p_1, p_2\}$, $\{p_1, p_3\}$, $\{p_1, p_4\}$, and $\{p_1, p_5, p_6\}$ are subgroups of $\langle S_3, \diamond \rangle$. The left cosets of $\{p_1, p_2\}$ are $\{p_1, p_2\}$, $\{p_3, p_6\}$, and $\{p_4, p_5\}$, while the right cosets of $\{p_1, p_2\}$ are $\{p_1, p_2\}$, $\{p_3, p_5\}$, and $\{p_4, p_6\}$. Hence $\{p_1, p_2\}$ is not a normal subgroup. Similarly, we can show that $\{p_1, p_3\}$ and $\{p_1, p_4\}$ are also not normal subgroups. On the other hand, the left and right cosets of $\{p_1, p_5, p_6\}$ are $\{p_1, p_5, p_6\}$ and $\{p_2, p_3, p_4\}$. Hence $\{p_1, p_5, p_6\}$ is a normal subgroup. ////

EXAMPLE 2 Let $\langle \mathbf{I}, + \rangle$ be the group of integers and m be any positive integer. The set of multiples of m forms a subgroup which we may denote by $\langle H_m, + \rangle$. Naturally H_m is a normal subgroup, because $\mathbf{I}$ is abelian. The cosets of H_m are clearly the equivalence classes generated by the relation congruence modulo m; that is, the cosets are the elements of $\mathbf{Z}_m$.

It was shown in the previous section that the left coset relation is an equivalence relation, and therefore it partitions the group into equivalence classes which are the left cosets. Let us denote the set of left cosets of subgroup H in G by G/H; that is, G/H is the quotient set with respect to the equivalence relation. If H is a normal subgroup, then the coset relation is a congruence relation, and corresponding to the operation $*$ in the group $\langle G, * \rangle$ we can define an operation $\circledast$ on G/H as follows. For any $a, b \in G$, let

$$(a * b)H = aH \circledast bH \qquad (5)$$

Naturally $\circledast$ is a binary operation on G/H. One can directly prove that $\langle G/H, \circledast \rangle$ is a group; however, we shall show that there exists a homomorphism $g: G \to G/H$ which is onto, and this demonstration will guarantee that $\langle G/H, \circledast \rangle$ is a group.

Let us define $g: G \to G/H$ such that for any $a \in G$

$$g(a) = aH$$

Naturally, for $a * b \in G$,

$$g(a * b) = (a * b)H = aH \circledast bH = g(a) \circledast g(b) \qquad (6)$$

Hence g is a homomorphism. Since every left coset is an image of some element of G, g is an onto mapping and hence g is an epimorphism. The group $\langle G/H, \circledast \rangle$ is called a *factor group*.

Recall that every left coset of H in G has the same number of elements as the order of H. Therefore, the order of G/H is simply the order of G divided by the order of H.

EXAMPLE 3   In Example 1, it was shown that $\{p_1, p_5, p_6\}$ is a normal subgroup of $\langle S_3, \diamond \rangle$. Let $H = \{p_1, p_5, p_6\}$; then the quotient set is given by $\{H, H_1\}$, where $H_1 = \{p_2, p_3, p_4\}$. A binary operation Δ on S_3/H corresponding to the operation $\diamond$ on S_3 is given in Table 3-5.8.

Our next theorem shows that the kernel of every group homomorphism is a normal subgroup.

Theorem 3-5.8   Let $\langle G, * \rangle$ and $\langle H, \Delta \rangle$ be groups and $g: G \to H$ be a homomorphism. Then the kernel of g is a normal subgroup.

PROOF   From Theorem 3-5.4 we know that

$$K = \ker(g) = \{a \mid a \in G \text{ and } g(a) = e_H\}$$

is a subgroup of $\langle G, * \rangle$. Now, for any $a \in G$ and $k \in K$,

$$g(a^{-1} * k * a) = g(a^{-1}) \Delta g(k) \Delta g(a)$$
$$= g(a^{-1}) \Delta e_H \Delta g(a)$$
$$= [g(a)]^{-1} \Delta g(a) = e_H$$

Hence $a^{-1} * k * a \in K$, which shows that K is a normal subgroup [see Eq. (4)].
////

If H is a normal subgroup of $\langle G, * \rangle$, then it was shown in Eq. (6) that corresponding to the coset relation which is a congruence relation we have a homomorphism from G to G/H. In general, this is true for any congruence relation on G. We shall now give a theorem which is known as the *fundamental theorem of group homomorphisms*.

Theorem 3-5.9   Let g be a homomorphism from a group $\langle G, * \rangle$ to a group $\langle H, \Delta \rangle$, and let K be the kernel of g and $H' \subseteq H$ be the image set of g in H. Then G/K is isomorphic to H'.

PROOF   Since K is a kernel of a homomorphism, it must be a normal subgroup of G, according to Theorem 3-5.8. Also we can define a mapping $f: G \to G/K$ which is an epimorphism from $\langle G, * \rangle$ to the factor group $\langle G/K, \circledast \rangle$ where $\circledast$ is defined according to Eq. (5), that is,

$$f(a) = aK \qquad \text{for any } a \in G$$

Table 3.5.8

Δ	H	H_1
H	H	H_1
H_1	H_1	H

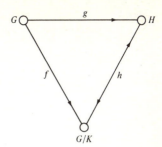

FIGURE 3-5.5

Let us define a mapping $h: G/K \rightarrow H'$ such that

$$h(aK) = g(a)$$

The image set of the mapping h is the same as the image set of the mapping g, so that $h: G/K \rightarrow H'$ is onto. Further, for any $a, b \in G$ such that $aK = bK$, we have $a * k_1 = b * k_2$ for some k_1 and k_2 in K. Thus

$$g(a * k_1) = g(a) \, \Delta \, g(k_1) = g(a) = g(b * k_2) = g(b)$$

which implies that $h(aK) = h(bK)$. Also $f(a) = f(b)$. Hence the mapping is one-to-one onto. These mappings are shown in Fig. 3-5.5. ////

We shall now introduce the concept of the direct product of two or more groups to form groups of higher order. Such direct products of groups are used in Sec. 3-7.2.

Definition 3-5.10 Let $\langle G, * \rangle$ and $\langle H, \Delta \rangle$ be two groups. The *direct product* of these two groups is the algebraic structure $\langle G \times H, \circ \rangle$ in which the binary operation $\circ$ on $G \times H$ is given by

$$\langle g_1, h_1 \rangle \circ \langle g_2, h_2 \rangle = \langle g_1 * g_2, h_1 \, \Delta \, h_2 \rangle$$

for any $\langle g_1, h_1 \rangle, \langle g_2, h_2 \rangle \in G \times H$.

Let e_G and e_H be the identity elements of $\langle G, * \rangle$ and $\langle H, \Delta \rangle$ respectively. It is easy to show that $\langle G \times H, \circ \rangle$ is a group with $\langle e_G, e_H \rangle$ as its identity element and that the associativity of the operation $\circ$ follows from the associativity of the operations $*$ and Δ. The inverse of any element $\langle g, h \rangle$ is $\langle g^{-1}, h^{-1} \rangle$.

Consider now the subsets $\{\langle a, e_H \rangle \mid a \in G\}$ and $\{\langle e_G, b \rangle \mid b \in H\}$ of $G \times H$. These are subgroups of $\langle G \times H, \circ \rangle$ which are isomorphic to the groups $\langle G, * \rangle$ and $\langle H, \Delta \rangle$ respectively. It is often possible to detect whether a group is a direct product of two groups by observing the subgroups of the direct product.

EXAMPLE 4 Let $\langle G, * \rangle$ be a group of order 2 in which $G = \{e, a\}$. Find $\langle G \times G, \circ \rangle$, the direct product of $\langle G, * \rangle$ with itself.

SOLUTION From the composition table of $\langle G, * \rangle$ one can easily write the direct product, which is shown in Table 3-5.9. Note that the group of order 4 obtained here is not isomorphic to the cyclic group of order 4 given in Example 4,

Table 3-5.9

∘	$\langle e, e \rangle$	$\langle e, a \rangle$	$\langle a, e \rangle$	$\langle a, a \rangle$
$\langle e, e \rangle$	$\langle e, e \rangle$	$\langle e, a \rangle$	$\langle a, e \rangle$	$\langle a, a \rangle$
$\langle e, a \rangle$	$\langle e, a \rangle$	$\langle e, e \rangle$	$\langle a, a \rangle$	$\langle a, e \rangle$
$\langle a, e \rangle$	$\langle a, e \rangle$	$\langle a, a \rangle$	$\langle e, e \rangle$	$\langle e, a \rangle$
$\langle a, a \rangle$	$\langle a, a \rangle$	$\langle a, e \rangle$	$\langle e, a \rangle$	$\langle e, e \rangle$

Sec. 3-5.1. However, all the cyclic groups of order 4 are isomorphic to one of these two groups of order 4. ////

EXAMPLE 5 Consider the groups $\langle G, \ast \rangle$ and $\langle H, \Delta \rangle$ where $G = \{e_1, a\}$ and $H = \{e_2, b, c\}$. The composition tables for both these groups can easily be written (see Tables 3-5.1 and 3-5.2). The direct product $\langle G \times H, \circ \rangle$ is given in Table 3-5.10. Note that $\{ \langle e_1, e_2 \rangle, \langle a, e_2 \rangle \}$ and $\{ \langle e_1, e_2 \rangle, \langle e_1, b \rangle, \langle e_1, c \rangle \}$ are two subgroups of $\langle G \times H, \circ \rangle$ which are isomorphic to the groups $\langle G, \ast \rangle$ and $\langle H, \Delta \rangle$ respectively. Also note that $\langle G \times H, \circ \rangle$ is isomorphic to a cyclic group of order 6. This isomorphism can easily be seen by replacing

$$\langle e_1, e_2 \rangle \text{ by } e \qquad \langle e_1, b \rangle \text{ by } \alpha^2 \qquad \langle e_1, c \rangle \text{ by } \alpha^4$$
$$\langle a, e_2 \rangle \text{ by } \alpha^3 \qquad \langle a, b \rangle \text{ by } \alpha^5 \qquad \langle a, c \rangle \text{ by } \alpha$$

This example is a special case of a theorem which we shall state here without proof.

Theorem 3-5.10 Let C_n be a cyclic group of order n and $n = p_1^{n_1} p_2^{n_2} \cdots p_k^{n_k}$ where p_i are distinct primes. Then C_n is isomorphic to the direct product of $C_1, C_2, \ldots, C_k$ where C_i is a cyclic group of order $p_i^{n_i}$.

Theorem 3-5.11 Every abelian group G is isomorphic to a group which is a direct product of cyclic groups $H_1, H_2, \ldots, H_k$ whose orders are powers of primes, the primes are not necessarily distinct.

Table 3-5.10

∘	$\langle e_1, e_2 \rangle$	$\langle e_1, b \rangle$	$\langle e_1, c \rangle$	$\langle a, e_2 \rangle$	$\langle a, b \rangle$	$\langle a, c \rangle$
$\langle e_1, e_2 \rangle$	$\langle e_1, e_2 \rangle$	$\langle e_1, b \rangle$	$\langle e_1, c \rangle$	$\langle a, e_2 \rangle$	$\langle a, b \rangle$	$\langle a, c \rangle$
$\langle e_1, b \rangle$	$\langle e_1, b \rangle$	$\langle e_1, c \rangle$	$\langle e_1, e_2 \rangle$	$\langle a, b \rangle$	$\langle a, c \rangle$	$\langle a, e_2 \rangle$
$\langle e_1, c \rangle$	$\langle e_1, c \rangle$	$\langle e_1, e_2 \rangle$	$\langle e_1, b \rangle$	$\langle a, c \rangle$	$\langle a, e_2 \rangle$	$\langle a, b \rangle$
$\langle a, e_2 \rangle$	$\langle a, e_2 \rangle$	$\langle a, b \rangle$	$\langle a, c \rangle$	$\langle e_1, e_2 \rangle$	$\langle e_1, b \rangle$	$\langle e_1, c \rangle$
$\langle a, b \rangle$	$\langle a, b \rangle$	$\langle a, c \rangle$	$\langle a, e_2 \rangle$	$\langle e_1, b \rangle$	$\langle e_1, c \rangle$	$\langle e_1, e_2 \rangle$
$\langle a, c \rangle$	$\langle a, c \rangle$	$\langle a, e_2 \rangle$	$\langle a, b \rangle$	$\langle e_1, c \rangle$	$\langle e_1, e_2 \rangle$	$\langle e_1, b \rangle$

3-5.5   Algebraic Systems with Two Binary Operations

In the beginning of this chapter, several examples of algebraic systems with two binary operations were given. These examples were motivated by our familiarity with the system of real numbers or integers which involve two basic operations of addition and multiplication. The algebraic systems with one binary operation which have been studied so far are not adequate to describe the system of real numbers. We shall therefore consider an abstract algebraic system called a ring, which is a special case of a group on which an additional binary operation satisfying certain properties could be defined. Other algebraic systems with two binary operations will be obtained by imposing further restrictions on rings.

> **Definition 3-5.11** An algebraic system $\langle S, +, \cdot \rangle$ is called a *ring* if the binary operations $+$ and $\cdot$ on S satisfy the following three properties:
>
> *1* $\langle S, + \rangle$ is an abelian group.
> *2* $\langle S, \cdot \rangle$ is a semigroup.
> *3* The operation $\cdot$ is distributive over $+$; that is, for any $a, b, c \in S$,
>
> $$a \cdot (b + c) = a \cdot b + a \cdot c \qquad \text{and} \qquad (b + c) \cdot a = b \cdot a + c \cdot a$$

Familiar examples of rings are the sets of integers, real numbers, rational numbers, even numbers, and complex numbers under the operations of addition and multiplication. Because of these examples, it is customary to refer to the operation $+$ as addition and the operation $\cdot$ as multiplication in a ring $\langle S, +, \cdot \rangle$ although these operations may not necessarily mean additions and multiplications. In keeping with this convention, we shall also refer to the identity of $\langle S, + \rangle$ as the *additive identity* and denote it by 0. Similarly, if $\langle S, \cdot \rangle$ is a monoid, then the identity with respect to $\cdot$ will be called the *multiplicative identity* and will be denoted by 1. The additive inverse of an element $a \in S$ will be denoted by $-a$, while the multiplicative inverse, if it exists, will be denoted by a^{-1}. It must be emphasized at this point that the use of this terminology does not mean that the operations $+$ and $\cdot$ on the ring $\langle S, +, \cdot \rangle$ have all the properties that $+$ and $\cdot$ have in the system of real numbers.

Depending upon the structure of $\langle S, \cdot \rangle$, various special cases of rings will be defined.

If $\langle S, \cdot \rangle$ is commutative, then the ring $\langle S, +, \cdot \rangle$ is called a *commutative ring*. Similarly, if $\langle S, \cdot \rangle$ is a monoid, then $\langle S, +, \cdot \rangle$ is called a *ring with identity*.

Naturally, we cannot expect $\langle S, \cdot \rangle$ to be a group, because a group with more than one element cannot have a zero element. We therefore inquire first whether $\langle S - \{0\}, \cdot \rangle$ is closed with respect to the operation $\cdot$. If it is closed, then we have for any $a, b \in S$ such that $a \neq 0$ and $b \neq 0$, $a \cdot b \neq 0$, and we call $\langle S, +, \cdot \rangle$ a *ring without divisors of zero*. It is possible to show that in a ring without divisors of zero $a \cdot b = 0 \Rightarrow (a = 0 \text{ or } b = 0)$.

A commutative ring $\langle S, +, \cdot \rangle$ with identity and without divisors of zero is called an *integral domain*.

It is assumed in the definition of integral domain that the ring $\langle S, +, \cdot \rangle$ has more than one element; i.e., it has at least one nonzero element.

Our next condition is to inquire whether $\langle S - \{0\}, \cdot \rangle$ is a group. This ques- leads to the following definition.

Definition 3-5.12 A commutative ring $\langle S, +, \cdot \rangle$ which has more than one element such that every nonzero element of S has a multiplicative inverse in S is called a *field*.

The ring of integers is an example of an integral domain which is not a field. The rings of real numbers and rational numbers are examples of fields.

EXAMPLE 1 The algebraic system $\langle \mathbf{Z}_n, +_n, \times_n \rangle$ consisting of equivalence classes generated by the relation congruence modulo n for some fixed integer n over the set of integers is a ring. The operations $+_n$ and $\times_n$ were defined earlier in Example 5, Sec. 3-2.1, and correspond to the operations of addition and multiplication over integers.

Observe that for $n = 6$, $\langle \mathbf{Z}_6, +_6, \times_6 \rangle$ is not an integral domain, since $[3] * [2] = [0]$. On the other hand, $\langle \mathbf{Z}_7, +_7, \times_7 \rangle$ is an integral domain. In fact $\langle \mathbf{Z}_n, +_n, \times_n \rangle$ is a field iff n is a prime integer. We shall not prove this result here.

EXAMPLE 2 Let $R = \{a, b, c, d\}$ and define the operations $+$ and $\cdot$ on R, as shown in the Table 3-5.11. Then $\langle R, +, \cdot \rangle$ is a ring.

EXAMPLE 3 Let S be a set and $\rho(S)$ its power set. On $\rho(S)$ we define operations $+$ and $\cdot$ as follows:

$$A + B = \{x \in S \mid (x \in A \vee x \in B) \wedge (x \notin A \cap B)\}$$

$$A \cdot B = A \cup B$$

for all $A, B \in \rho(S)$. It is easy to verify that $\langle \rho(S), +, \cdot \rangle$ is a ring called the ring of subsets of S.

Using the definition of a ring one can prove the following results for a ring $\langle R, +, \cdot \rangle$ in which 0 is the additive identity and $-a$ denotes the additive inverse of an element $a \in R$.

1 $\quad a \cdot 0 = 0 \cdot a = 0$
2 $\quad a \cdot (-b) = -(a \cdot b)$
3 $\quad (-a) \cdot (b) = -(a \cdot b)$
4 $\quad (-a) \cdot (-b) = a \cdot b$
5 $\quad a \cdot (b - c) = a \cdot b - a \cdot c$
6 $\quad (a - b) \cdot c = a \cdot c - b \cdot c$

In (5) we write $b - c$ in place of $b + (-c)$ and $a \cdot b - a \cdot c$ for $a \cdot b + [-(a \cdot c)]$.

Table 3-5.11

+	a	b	c	d		$\cdot$	a	b	c	d
a	a	b	c	d		a	a	a	a	a
b	b	a	d	c		b	a	a	b	a
c	c	d	b	a		c	a	b	c	d
d	d	c	a	b		d	a	a	d	a

Definition 3-5.12 A subset $R \subseteq S$ where $\langle S, +, \cdot \rangle$ is a ring is called a *subring* if $\langle R, +, \cdot \rangle$ is itself a ring with the operations $+$ and $\cdot$ restricted to R.

EXAMPLE 4 The ring of even integers is a subring of the ring of integers.

In fact, if $R \subseteq S$, if we determine that R is closed with respect to addition and that for any $a \in R$, $-a \in R$, and finally if R is closed with respect to the operation $\cdot$, then R is a subring of S. All other properties of a ring are satisfied by R. It may happen that R may not have some aditional properties which S may possess. For example, note that the ring of even integers is not a ring with identity, while the ring of integers is a ring with identity.

Definition 3-5.13 Let $\langle R, +, \cdot \rangle$ and $\langle S, \oplus, \odot \rangle$ be rings. A mapping $g \colon R \to S$ is called a *ring homomorphism* from $\langle R, +, \cdot \rangle$ to $\langle S, \oplus, \odot \rangle$ if for any $a, b \in R$,

$$g(a + b) = g(a) \oplus g(b) \qquad \text{and} \qquad g(a \cdot b) = g(a) \odot g(b)$$

Notice that the first condition is a group homomorphism from $\langle R, + \rangle$ to $\langle S, \oplus \rangle$ while the second is a semigroup homomorphism from $\langle R, \cdot \rangle$ to $\langle S, \odot \rangle$. These two conditions guarantee that the distributive property is preserved; i.e., for any $a, b, c \in R$,

$$
\begin{aligned}
g[a \cdot (b + c)] &= g(a) \odot g(b + c) = g(a) \odot [g(b) \oplus g(c)] \\
&= [g(a) \odot g(b)] \oplus [g(a) \odot g(c)] \\
&= g(a \cdot b + a \cdot c)
\end{aligned}
$$

We have given here a very brief outline of algebraic systems such as rings and fields. These systems have been studied in great detail, and some of the results are useful in the study of computer arithmetic. Also the theory of finite fields is applied in the study of sequential machines.

EXERCISES 3-5.5

1 We are given the ring $\langle \{a, b, c, d\}, +, \cdot \rangle$ whose operations are given by the following table:

+	a	b	c	d		$\cdot$	a	b	c	d
a	a	b	c	d		a	a	a	a	a
b	b	c	d	a		b	a	c	a	c
c	c	d	a	b		c	a	a	a	a
d	d	a	b	c		d	a	c	a	a

Is it a commutative ring? Does it have an identity? What is the zero of this ring? Find the additive inverse of each of its elements.

2 In Example 3, take $S = \{a\}$ and find the ring $\langle \rho(S), +, \cdot \rangle$. Compare this ring with $\langle \{0, 1\}, +, \cdot \rangle$ given in Example 6 of Sec. 3-1.1.

3 Show that $\langle \mathbf{I}, \oplus, \odot \rangle$ is a commutative ring with identity, where the operations $\oplus$ and $\odot$ are defined, for any $a, b \in \mathbf{I}$, as $a \oplus b = a + b - 1$ and $a \odot b = a + b - ab$.

4 For any integer m, show that $\{xm \mid x \in \mathbf{I}\}$ is a subring of the ring of integers.

5 Prove that if $a, b \in \mathbf{R}$ where $\langle \mathbf{R}, +, \cdot \rangle$ is a ring, then

$$(a + b)^2 = a^2 + a \cdot b + b \cdot a + b^2$$

where $a^2 = a \cdot a$.

EXERCISES 3-5

1 Find the left cosets of $\{[0], [3]\}$ in the group $\langle \mathbf{Z}_6, +_6 \rangle$.

2 Find the left cosets of $\{p_1, p_5, p_6\}$ in the group $\langle S_3, \diamondsuit \rangle$ given in Table 3-5.5.

3 Find the left cosets of $\{r_2, r_4\}$ and $\{r_1, r_2, r_3, r_4\}$ in the dihedral group $\langle D_4, \diamondsuit \rangle$ given in Table 3-5.7.

4 Find the normal subgroup of the dihedral group $\langle D_4, \diamondsuit \rangle$ given in Table 3-5.7.

5 Show that every subgroup of a cyclic group is normal.

6 Show that the intersection of two normal subgroups is a normal subgroup.

7 Let $\langle H_1, * \rangle$ and $\langle H_2, * \rangle$ be subgroups of a group $\langle G, * \rangle$ and $H_1 \cdot H_2 = \{h_1 * h_2 \mid h_1 \in H_1 \wedge h_2 \in H_2\}$. Is $\langle H_1 \cdot H_2, * \rangle$ a subgroup? Is $\langle H_1 \cdot H_2, * \rangle$ a normal subgroup if either H_1 or H_2 is normal?

8 Let $\langle H_1, * \rangle$ and $\langle H_2, * \rangle$ be subgroups of a group $\langle G, * \rangle$. Show that $\langle H_1 \cap H_2, * \rangle$ is also a subgroup of $\langle G, * \rangle$. Show that, in general, $\langle H_1 \cup H_2, * \rangle$ is not a subgroup of $\langle G, * \rangle$ except when $H_1 \subseteq H_2$ or $H_2 \subseteq H_1$.

9 Find the direct product of $\langle \mathbf{Z}_3, +_3 \rangle$ and $\langle \mathbf{Z}_3^*, \times_3 \rangle$.

10 Show that the direct product of groups $\langle G, * \rangle$ and $\langle H, \Delta \rangle$ contains two normal subgroups which are isomorphic to $\langle G, * \rangle$ and $\langle H, \Delta \rangle$ respectively.

11 Show that if a group $\langle G, * \rangle$ is of order n and $a \in G$ is such that $a^m = e$ for some integer $m \leq n$, then m must divide n.

12 Show that if a group $\langle G, * \rangle$ is of even order, then there must be an element $a \in G$ such that $a \neq e$ and $a * a = e$.

13 If an abelian group has subgroups of orders m and n, then show that it has a subgroup whose order is the least common multiple of m and n.

14 Show that among the cosets determined by a subgroup S in a group $\langle G, * \rangle$, only one of the cosets is a subgroup.

15 Let the order of a cyclic group be n, and let m be a positive integer that divides n. Show that there is only one cyclic subgroup of order m. Show by an example that this result is not true for finite groups which are not cyclic.

16 Prove that in an abelian group if an element a has order k and an element b has an order j and if k and j are relatively prime, then the element $a * b$ has the order kj.

17 Show that $\langle \mathbf{Z}_7, +_7, \times_7 \rangle$ is a commutative ring with identity.

18 If for every element a in a ring, $a^2 = a$, then the ring is called a *Boolean ring*. Show that a Boolean ring is always commutative.

19 Show that in the ring $\langle \mathbf{Z}_6, +_6, \times_6 \rangle$, both $S = \{[0], [2], [4]\}$ and $T = \{[0], [3]\}$ are subrings and that every element of $\mathbf{Z}_6$ can be expressed as $s +_6 t$ where $s \in S$ and $t \in T$. What is $s \times_6 t$?

3-6 THE APPLICATION OF RESIDUE ARITHMETIC TO COMPUTERS

This section is concerned with the topic of residue arithmetic and its application to the organization of digital computers. We will be concerned with the description of the residue number system as an alternative to the fixed-base weighted number systems of which the decimal and binary systems are classical examples. Although fixed-base number systems have many advantages, they also have disadvantages that restrict the speed of performing arithmetic operations. In the residue number system, however, all arithmetic operations except division are inherently carry-free; i.e., each digit in the result is a function of only the corresponding digits of the operands. Consequently, addition, subtraction, and multiplication can be performed on a "residue computer" in less time than would be possible in an equivalent (as to operating speed and number range) binary computer.

The first part of the section gives a brief introduction to number systems and their applicability to digital computers. The remainder of the section deals with the residue number system and its computational advantages.

3-6.1 Introduction to Number Systems

Number systems may be classed into *nonpositional* and *positional* types. The Roman numerals are a classical example of a nonpositional system. The positional systems were not possible until the concept of a number zero was introduced by the Hindus in approximately the twelfth century A.D. In these systems, the position of a digit in a number implies a certain weight by which this digit is multiplied. Thus any nonnegative integer x in a general positional number system can be represented as

$$x = a_n w_n + a_{n-1} w_{n-1} + \cdots + a_1 w_1 + a_0 w_0 = \sum_{i=0}^{n} a_i w_i$$

where the a_i are a set of permissible digits and the w_i are a set of weights.

If we let the values of w_i be successive powers of some fixed number, then the number system is said to have a *fixed-base* or *fixed-radix*. For example, if $w_i = 10^i$ or $w_i = 2^i$, we obtain the familiar decimal or binary number systems respectively. The binary number system is used in computers much more frequently than its decimal counterpart. A number system which is not fixed-base is said to be *mixed*-base. In this section we will give an example of a mixed-base number system called the residue number system.

There are other properties that number systems can possess that will be mentioned at this time. In particular, a number system can have the properties of range, uniqueness, and nonredundancy.

The range of a number system is defined as the maximum interval in which each integer can be uniquely represented. Systems such as the binary and decimal number system can represent any integer and are said to have an unlimited range. However, in digital computers where only a limited number of digit positions are allowed, the range of the number system used is necessarily finite.

A number system has the uniqueness property if each number in the system can be represented in only one way. The decimal and binary number systems for nonnegative integers are unique. If we extend the set of numbers to be represented to all integers, then the sign-magnitude representation of zero can be $+00\cdots0$ or $-00\cdots0$. Similarly, using 1s complement representation in the binary system yields two possible representations for zero, namely $11\cdots1$ and $000\cdots0$.

A number system is said to be *redundant* if there exist fewer numbers than the number of possible combinations of the digits. A redundant number system implies that for certain combinations of digits no corresponding number exists or that perhaps many combinations of digits correspond to the same number.

An example of a weighted mixed-base number system is given in Table 3-6.1 with $w_0 = 1$, $w_1 = 2$, $w_2 = 6$, $0 \le a_0 < 2$, $0 \le a_1 < 3$, and $0 \le a_2 < 5$.

Certain weighted number systems are important because the magnitude comparison of two numbers can be performed by simply comparing their corresponding digits according to position. The decimal and binary number systems exhibit this property. Consider, on the other hand, the number system defined by

$$x = 5a_4 + 4a_3 + 3a_2 + 2a_1 + a_0$$

where $0 \le a_i < 10$. Let x and y be the following numbers:

$$x = 2 * 5 + 1 * 4 + 0 * 3 + 0 * 2 + 0 * 1$$
$$y = 0 * 5 + 2 * 4 + 2 * 3 + 0 * 2 + 0 * 1$$

It is not possible to compare these numbers algebraically by merely performing a digit-by-digit comparison.

The decimal and binary number systems have been used to perform arithmetic on digital computers because of the following advantages:

1 Algebraic comparison of two numbers can be easily mechanized.

2 The range of these number systems can be easily extended by adding more digit positions.

3 Multiplication and division by the fixed radix can be achieved by shifting digit positions in memory.

4 The logic required for performing a particular arithmetic operation (such as addition) is more or less the same for all digit positions.

5 Overflow detection is easy.

Table 3-6.1

Number	a_2	a_1	a_0
0	0	0	0
1	0	0	1
2	0	1	0
3	0	1	1
4	0	2	0
5	0	2	1
6	1	0	0
7	1	0	1
8	1	1	0
9	1	1	1
10	1	2	0
....			
29	4	2	1

The decimal and binary number systems possess properties which are directly responsible for the aforementioned advantages, but these same properties restrict the speed at which arithmetic operations can be performed. In both systems, a fully parallel arithmetic operation, i.e., an operation which processes all digits simultaneously, is not feasible because of a carry propagation. For any arithmetic operation, each digit of the result depends on all digits of equal or lower order. This phenomenon imposes a limitation on the speed with which arithmetic operations can be performed.

In order to eliminate the carry-propagation problem, one can use the following alternatives:

1 Using special "look-ahead" carry circuitry
2 Choosing a number system which has special carry attributes

In the next section, we concern ourselves with the residue number system and show how it can be used to reduce the carry-propagation problem. However, before we discuss this subject in detail, we will first give a brief description of conventional arithmetic adders and their hardware restrictions as far as the speed of the operations is concerned.

Most digital computers perform arithmetic operations in binary. There are instances of decimal machines, but each digit is necessarily encoded as a sequence of binary bits because of the two-state-device makeup of computers. Many computers have a certain maximum number of bits or word size for the representation of an integer. The number of bits usually varies from a minimum of 8 to a maximum of 64. The upper bound represents an integer of approximately 20 decimal digits. Let us consider the case in which only 30 bits are available for the representation of the magnitude of a number. Obviously, in such a system we can only represent $m = 2^{30}$ distinct numbers, and every real number can be considered to be equivalent to one of the 2^{30} numbers; i.e., the numbers are reduced to the system $\langle \mathbf{Z}_m, +_m \rangle$ where $+_m$ denotes addition modulo m and $m = 2^{30}$.

Since computers consist of two-state devices, addition in the system $\langle \mathbf{Z}_m, +_m \rangle$ cannot be performed directly; it must be simulated. This simulation can be achieved by first encoding each element of $\mathbf{Z}_m$ by a distinct sequence of n bits, $n = \lceil log_2 m \rceil$ where $\lceil \ \rceil$ denotes the ceiling function and then by performing binary addition on the bit sequences. In other words, we obtain a structure $\langle (\mathbf{Z}_2)^n, \oplus \rangle$ where $(\mathbf{Z}_2)^n = \mathbf{Z}_2 \times \mathbf{Z}_2 \times \cdots \times \mathbf{Z}_2$ (n times) and $\oplus$ denotes binary addition. We set up a correspondence between systems $\langle \mathbf{Z}_m, +_m \rangle$ and $\langle (\mathbf{Z}_2)^n, \oplus \rangle$ by finding a one-to-one onto function g defined as

$$g: \mathbf{Z}_m \to (\mathbf{Z}_2)^n \qquad \text{or} \qquad g(x) = \langle g_1(x), g_2(x), \ldots, g_n(x) \rangle$$

with $g_i(x) \in \mathbf{Z}_2$ for all $1 \le i \le n$ such that the following relationship holds

$$g(x +_m y) = g(x) \oplus g(y) \qquad \text{for all } x, y \in \mathbf{Z}_m$$

Therefore, addition modulo m is isomorphic to addition of binary n-tuples. For example, if $m = 8$, then it would take 3 bits to encode each element of $\mathbf{Z}_8$, and letting $x = 3$ and $y = 2$, we obtain

$$g(3) = \langle 0, 1, 1 \rangle \qquad \text{and} \qquad g(2) = \langle 0, 1, 0 \rangle$$

$$g(3 +_8 2) = g(3) \oplus g(2) = \langle 0, 1, 1 \rangle \oplus \langle 0, 1, 0 \rangle = \langle 1, 0, 1 \rangle = 5$$

Notice that the first bit in the result is determined by the carry bit generated from the second bit values of the operands.

In Sec. 1-2.15 we discussed logical components or gates which can be used to realize certain functions. In Chap. 4 we show how adders can be constructed by using such gates. At this point, however, we wish to investigate what other restrictive properties, besides carry propagation, the implementation of the above isomorphic system might have. No restriction as to the number of inputs was placed on gates in Sec. 1-2.15. From physical realization considerations, it is not possible to let these gates have an arbitrary number of inputs. Actually, most gates produced permit no more than four inputs. Also, such gates have associated time delays; i.e., there is a time lapse between the time when input signals are applied to the gate and the time at which the output of the gate becomes available. Although delay times are in the order of nanoseconds, these can become significant when performing arithmetic operations (at the rate of millions of operations per second) on modern digital computers. If the output of one gate is used as input to another, and the output of the latter as an input to a third, and so on, these time delays are additive. For example, the realization of some function T described by Fig. 3-6.1 would result in a time delay of 3 units at the output. If we allowed the gates to have an arbitrary number of inputs, most functions could theoretically (though expensively) be realized with two levels of gates, and only minimal delays would result. Since the word size on certain computers can be as high as 64 bits, the level of gates required to perform addition is significantly greater than the theoretical minimum when a maximum number of inputs is specified.

It can be shown that the time required to compute an n-ary function with gates restricted to p inputs is at least $\lceil \log_p n \rceil$. Furthermore, the addition time attainable in $\langle \mathbf{Z}_m, +_m \rangle$ by simulation using binary n-tuples is an increasing function of p and m.

We shall next investigate the residue number system as a means of eliminating carry propagation. Also, the time-delay problem can be reduced significantly when this alternate number system is used.

3-6.2 Residue Arithmetic

This section is concerned with the description of the residue number system as an alternative to the binary and decimal number systems. As pointed out earlier, fixed-base number systems in digital computers have many advantages; however, these systems have disadvantages that restrict the speed of performing arithmetic operations. The residue number system is not a weighted system, and, consequently, it does not have many of the advantages of fixed-base systems. We shall show that in the residue number system all arithmetic operations except division are inherently carry-free; i.e., each digit in the result is a function of only the corresponding digits of the operands. Consequently, addition, subtraction, and multiplication can be performed on a "residue computer" in less time than would be possible in an equivalent (as to operating speed and number range) binary computer.

Some disadvantages of the residue number system when compared to fixed-

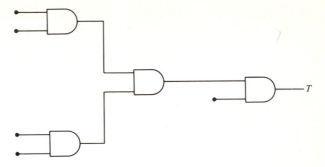

FIGURE 3-6.1   A three-level network.

base number systems are as follows:

1   Comparison of numbers is difficult.
2   It is difficult to determine whether an overflow occurred.
3   Division is complex.
4   The residue number system is not convenient for the representation of fractions.
5   Residue arithmetic can be justified only if efficient means of conversion into and out of the residue number system are available.

Let m be a positive integer. By the unique factorization theorem, it is possible to factorize m as

$$m = p_1^{n_1} p_2^{n_2} \cdots p_r^{n_r} = m_1 m_2 \cdots m_r \qquad (1)$$

where $p_1, p_2, \ldots, p_r$ are prime numbers, $n_1, n_2, \ldots, n_r$ are positive integers, and $m_1 = p_1^{n_1}$, $m_2 = p_2^{n_2}$, $\ldots$, and $m_r = p_r^{m_r}$. Clearly, $m_1, m_2, \ldots, m_r$ are pairwise relatively prime; that is, $\mathrm{GCD}(m_i, m_j) = 1$ for $i \neq j$.

Our aim in this section is to show that the arithmetic operations of addition, subtraction, and multiplication in $\mathbf{Z}_m$ can be carried out more efficiently in terms of the operations in $\mathbf{Z}_{m_i}$ for each m_i and that the conversion from one system to another can also be done efficiently. These ideas can be used in the construction of adders and other arithmetic units which are faster than the conventional units described in the previous section.

The decomposition in Eq. (1) can be used to represent any number in $\mathbf{Z}_m$ in terms of the numbers in $\mathbf{Z}_{m_i}$ for $i = 1, 2, \ldots, r$. For this purpose, let x be any number in $\mathbf{Z}_m$ and let $x_i = x \bmod m_i$ for $i = 1, 2, \ldots, r$; then the r-tuple

$$\langle x_1, x_2, \ldots, x_r \rangle = \langle x \bmod m_1, x \bmod m_2, \ldots, x \bmod m_r \rangle \qquad (2)$$

is called the *residue* or the *modular representation* of x. Note that for any $x \in \mathbf{Z}_m$, we have as its modular representation an r-tuple which is an element of $\mathbf{Z}_m^*$ where

$$\mathbf{Z}_m^* = \mathbf{Z}_{m_1} \times \mathbf{Z}_{m_2} \times \cdots \times \mathbf{Z}_{m_r}$$

The number of elements in $\mathbf{Z}_m^*$ is clearly $m_1 m_2 \cdots m_r = m$.

We shall now prove a theorem which states that there exists a one-to-one correspondence between $\mathbf{Z}_m$ and $\mathbf{Z}_m^*$. This theorem is known as the *Chinese Remainder theorem*. A constructive proof of this theorem is given later.

Let $g: \mathbf{Z}_m \to \mathbf{Z}_m^*$ be such that for any $x \in \mathbf{Z}_m$,

$$g(x) = \langle x_1, x_2, \ldots, x_r \rangle$$
$$= \langle x \bmod m_1, x \bmod m_2, \ldots, x \bmod m_r \rangle$$

We shall now show that g is one-to-one onto. In order to show that g is one-to-one, let us assume, to the contrary, that the residue representation of x and $y \in \mathbf{Z}_m$ is identical and $x \neq y$, so that

$$x \bmod m_i = y \bmod m_i \qquad \text{for } i = 1, 2, \ldots, r$$

Obviously, this means that $x - y$ is divisible by m_i for each i or $x - y$ is divisible by m since the m_i are pairwise relatively prime. But $x - y$ is not divisible by m according to our assumption. Therefore, we have a contradiction, showing that the mapping g is one-to-one. Note that both $\mathbf{Z}_m^*$ and $\mathbf{Z}_m$ are of cardinality m; therefore, the mapping g must be bijective. Consequently, the residue representation of any number in $\mathbf{Z}_m$ is unique, and conversely.

As an example, let $m = 30$, so that $m_1 = 2$, $m_2 = 3$, and $m_3 = 5$ with $\mathbf{Z}_{30}^* = \mathbf{Z}_2 \times \mathbf{Z}_3 \times \mathbf{Z}_5$. The residue representations of the numbers in $\mathbf{Z}_{30}$ are given in Table 3-6.2.

We now define operations of addition, subtraction, and multiplication on $\mathbf{Z}_m^*$ in terms of the corresponding operations in $\mathbf{Z}_m$, for $i = 1, 2, \ldots, r$, and denote these operations by $\oplus_m$, $\ominus_m$, and $\otimes_m$ respectively.

Recall that $\langle \mathbf{Z}_m, +_m \rangle$ and $\langle \mathbf{Z}_{m_i}, +_{m_i} \rangle$ are cyclic groups. Let us now define an operation $\oplus_m$ on $\mathbf{Z}_m^*$ such that for any two numbers $\langle x_1, x_2, \ldots, x_r \rangle$ and $\langle y_1, y_2, \ldots, y_r \rangle$ in $\mathbf{Z}_m^*$ which are residue representations of $x, y \in \mathbf{Z}_m$,

$$\langle x_1, \ldots, x_r \rangle \oplus_m \langle y_1, \ldots, y_r \rangle = g(x) \oplus_m g(y)$$
$$= \langle x_1 +_{m_1} y_1, \ldots, x_r +_{m_r} y_r \rangle \qquad (3)$$

Table 3-6.2

x	Residue digits Moduli			x	Residue digits Moduli		
	2	3	5		2	3	5
0	0	0	0	15	1	0	0
1	1	1	1	16	0	1	1
2	0	2	2	17	1	2	2
3	1	0	3	18	0	0	3
4	0	1	4	19	1	1	4
5	1	2	0	20	0	2	0
6	0	0	1	21	1	0	1
7	1	1	2	22	0	1	2
8	0	2	3	23	1	2	3
9	1	0	4	24	0	0	4
10	0	1	0	25	1	1	0
11	1	2	1	26	0	2	1
12	0	0	2	27	1	0	2
13	1	1	3	28	0	1	3
14	0	2	4	29	1	2	4

Clearly $\langle \mathbf{Z}_m^*, \oplus_m \rangle$ is also a cyclic group because it is the direct product of the cyclic groups $\langle \mathbf{Z}_{m_1}, +_{m_1} \rangle, \langle \mathbf{Z}_{m_2}, +_{m_2} \rangle, \ldots, \langle \mathbf{Z}_{m_r}, +_{m_r} \rangle$.

Similar equations can be given for subtraction and multiplication, as follows:

$$\langle x_1, \ldots, x_r \rangle \ominus_m \langle y_1, \ldots, y_r \rangle = g(x) \ominus_m g(y)$$

$$= \langle x_1 -_{m_1} y_1, \ldots, x_r -_{m_r} y_r \rangle \tag{4}$$

$$\langle x_1, \ldots, x_r \rangle \otimes_m \langle y_1, \ldots, y_r \rangle = g(x) \otimes_m g(y)$$

$$= \langle x_1 \times_{m_1} y_1, \ldots, x_r \times_{m_r} y_r \rangle \tag{5}$$

We shall now show that the mapping $g \colon \mathbf{Z}_m \to \mathbf{Z}_m^*$ which was shown to be bijective also preserves the operations $+_m$ and $\oplus_m$ in $\mathbf{Z}_m$ and $\mathbf{Z}_m^*$ respectively. This would imply that $\langle \mathbf{Z}_m, +_m \rangle$ and $\langle \mathbf{Z}_m^*, \oplus_m \rangle$ are isomorphic and addition $+_m$ in $\mathbf{Z}_m$ can be done in $\mathbf{Z}_m^*$ by means of the operation $\oplus_m$ or equivalently in terms of the operations $+_{m_i}$ for $i = 1, 2, \ldots, r$. This was our aim, although we shall study its actual implementation later in this section. The isomorphism follows from the definition of the operation $\oplus_m$ given in Eq. (3) and the following observations.

Let

$$x = pm_i + x_i \quad \text{and} \quad y = qm_i + y_i$$

then

$$x + y = (p + q)m_i + (x_i + y_i)$$

and

$$(x + y) \bmod m_i = (x_i + y_i) \bmod m_i = x_i +_{m_i} y_i$$

Further, since m_i divides m,

$$[(x + y) \bmod m] \bmod m_i = (x + y) \bmod m_i$$

or

$$(x +_m y) \bmod m_i = x_i +_{m_i} y_i$$

Hence

$$g(x +_m y) = g(x) \oplus_m g(y)$$

As an example, let us take $m = 30$, $x = 14$, and $y = 11$. From Table 3-6.2,

$$g(x) = g(14) = \langle 0, 2, 4 \rangle$$

$$g(y) = g(11) = \langle 1, 2, 1 \rangle$$

$$g(x) \oplus_{30} g(y) = \langle 0 +_2 1, 2 +_3 2, 4 +_5 1 \rangle = \langle 1, 1, 0 \rangle$$

$$= g(25) = g(x +_{30} y)$$

Similarly,

$$g(x) \otimes_{30} g(y) = \langle 0 \times_2 1, 2 \times_3 2, 4 \times_5 1 \rangle = \langle 0, 1, 4 \rangle = g(4)$$

$$= g(x \times_{30} y)$$

In the example given here, we have been able to determine x from its residue representation with the help of Table 3-6.2. In general, such a table is neither available nor convenient to construct if m is large. We shall consider certain theorems which will permit us to obtain the element of $\mathbf{Z}_m$ which corresponds to an element of $\mathbf{Z}_m^*$.

Before continuing the discussion, let us verify that the decomposition of $\mathbf{Z}_m$ yields a system which can perform fast arithmetic when compared with conventional binary computers. Note that the arithmetic operations performed modulo m_i, where m_i is substantially less than m, will certainly reduce the carry-propagation problem since fewer binary digits are required to represent m_i than to represent m. The largest carry-propagation time will be due to the subgroup which has the largest m_i. Since each residue digit in the result can be computed directly from only the corresponding residue digits of the operands, a model for addition, subtraction, and multiplication can be represented by Fig. 3-6.2.

It was shown that one could get a residue representation of any number in $\mathbf{Z}_m$ in terms of the moduli $m_1, m_2, \ldots, m_r$ and that such a representation is unique. Furthermore, it is also possible to do the operations of addition, subtraction, and multiplication by performing such operations on the residue components. We shall now give certain definitions and theorems which will allow us to convert the result of any such operation from the residue number system to an element of $\mathbf{Z}_m$. This conversion capability will lead to a constructive proof of the Chinese Remainder theorem and will enable the explicit computation of the element of $\mathbf{Z}_m$ corresponding to its residue representation.

An important property of modular arithmetic is the cancellation law of multiplication. If the greatest common divisor of an element $c \in \mathbf{Z}_m$ and m is 1, that is, $\mathrm{GCD}(c, m) = 1$, then for any two elements $a, b \in \mathbf{Z}_m$

$$(ca) \bmod m = (cb) \bmod m \quad \Rightarrow \quad a \bmod m = b \bmod m \qquad (6)$$

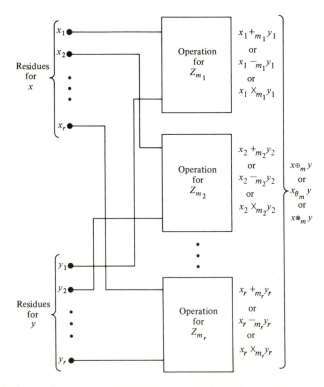

FIGURE 3-6.2 A residue system for performing addition, subtraction, or multiplication.

By definition of congruence,

$$ca = pm + r_1$$

and
$$cb = qm + r_2$$

Since $(ca) \bmod m = (cb) \bmod m$, then $r_1 = r_2$, and it therefore follows that

$$ca - pm - cb = -qm \quad \text{or} \quad c(a - b) = (p - q)m$$

Consequently, $c(a - b)$ must be divisible by m, and because $GCD(c, m) = 1$, it then follows that $a - b$ is a multiple of m, that is,

$$a \bmod m = b \bmod m$$

As a consequence of this fact, we can say that if $GCD(a, m) = 1$, then an equation of the form

$$(ax) \bmod m = b \bmod m$$

has a unique solution for $x \bmod m$.

Definition 3-6.1 For $0 \le a < m$, if there exists an a' such that $(a'a) \bmod m = 1$, then a' is the *multiplicative inverse* of a.

Theorem 3-6.1 The quantity a' exists and is unique if and only if $GCD(a, m) = 1$ and $a \ne 0$.

PROOF Consider the set of numbers $\{a^n \bmod m \mid n > 0\}$ which consists of at most m distinct elements. There must exist two positive integers n_1 and n_2 with $n_1 > n_2$ such that

$$a^{n_1} \bmod m = a^{n_2} \bmod m$$

However, this equation can be rewritten as

$$(a^{n_1-n_2} a^{n_2}) \bmod m = a^{n_2} \bmod m$$

Since $GCD(a, m) = 1$, it directly follows that $GCD(a^{n_2}, m) = 1$. Furthermore, by the cancellation law of multiplication, we obtain

$$a^{n_1-n_2} \bmod m = 1 \quad \text{or} \quad (a^{n_1-n_2-1}a) \bmod m = 1$$

which implies that $a^{n_1-n_2-1} \bmod m$ is the inverse of a. This inverse is unique by the cancellation law of multiplication.

Assume to the contrary that $GCD(a, m) = q$ where $q > 1$. Then a and m can be written as

$$a = c_1 q \quad \text{and} \quad m = c_2 q \quad c_1 \text{ and } c_2 \text{ integers}$$

It therefore follows that

$$(a'a) \bmod m = (a'c_1 q) \bmod m = (a'c_1 q) \bmod c_2 q = q(a'c_1) \bmod c_2$$

since $(c_1 q) \bmod c_2 q = q(c_1 \bmod c_2)$. Since $q > 1$ by assumption, it is impossible for $(a'a) \bmod m$ to be 1, and consequently a has no inverse. ////

As an example, Table 3-6.3 contains the inverses of elements in $\mathbf{Z}_5$ and $\mathbf{Z}_8$.

Table 3-6.3

$m=5$		$m=8$	
a	a'	a	a'
1	1	1	1
2	3	2	none
3	2	3	3
4	4	4	none
		5	5
		6	none
		7	7

We would like to have an explicit formula for computing the multiplicative inverse of an integer. The following theorem provides such a formula when m is a prime.

Theorem 3-6.2 Fermat's Theorem If a is an integer and m is a prime, then

$$a^m \bmod m = a \bmod m$$

PROOF We shall give an inductive proof. Clearly, the theorem is true for $a = 0$. Assume that the theorem holds for a, that is,

$$a^m \bmod m = a \bmod m$$

We must now show that it holds for $a + 1$. By the binomial theorem, $(a + 1)^m$ can be expanded as

$$(a + 1)^m = a^m + \frac{m}{1!} a^{m-1} + \frac{m(m - 1)}{2!} a^{m-2} + \cdots + 1$$

Because m is a prime, each term except the first and the last is a multiple of m, and it follows that

$$(a + 1)^m \bmod m = (a^m + 1) \bmod m$$

and by the inductive hypothesis this equation further reduces to

$$(a + 1)^m \bmod m = (a + 1) \bmod m$$

Therefore by the law of finite induction the theorem is true for any nonnegative integer a. This theorem can be extended to all integers. ////

By using Fermat's theorem and Theorem 3-6.1, the inverse of a can be evaluated by the formula

$$a' = a^{m-2} \bmod m \qquad (7)$$

For example, by using Table 3-6.3 with $m = 5$, the inverses of 2, 3, and 4 can be obtained explicitly by the following computations:

$$2^3 \bmod 5 = 8 \bmod 5 = 3 \bmod 5$$

$$3^3 \bmod 5 = 27 \bmod 5 = 2 \bmod 5$$

$$4^3 \bmod 5 = 64 \bmod 5 = 4 \bmod 5$$

Note that the multiplicative inverse given by Eq. (7) is true only if m is a prime, because Theorem 3-6.2 is true only if m is a prime. The formula does not hold in the case when m is not a prime. For example, let $m = 8$ and $a = 3$; then

$$a^{m-2} \bmod m = 3^6 \bmod 8 = 729 \bmod 8 = 1 \bmod 8$$

On the other hand, $a' = 3 \bmod 8$.

We would like to generalize Eq. (7) so that the inverse of an element, if it existed, could be computed even when m was not a prime. In pursuit of this goal, let $f(p)$ be defined as the number of elements from the set $\{1, 2, \ldots, p - 1\}$ which are relatively prime to p. Thus $f(2) = 1$, $f(3) = 2$, $f(4) = 2$, etc. If p is a prime, then $f(p) = p - 1$. Suppose that it is required to evaluate $f(p^n)$ for some positive integer n. Note that a number is relatively prime to p^n if and only if it is not a multiple of p. The number of such elements which are multiples of p and less than or equal to p^n is p^{n-1}. Hence

$$f(p^n) = p^n - p^{n-1} \tag{8}$$

As an example, $f(8) = 4$, indicating that there are four numbers that are relatively prime to 8 and less than 8, namely, 1, 3, 5, and 7. The following theorem permits us to explicitly compute the inverse of an element, if it exists.

Theorem 3-6.3 Euler's Theorem Let a and m be relatively prime. Then for any a,

$$a^{f(m)} \bmod m = 1$$

for any positive integer m, and hence

$$a' = a^{f(m)-1} \bmod m$$

PROOF Suppose that a and b are both relatively prime to m, that is,

$$\mathrm{GCD}(a, m) = \mathrm{GCD}(b, m) = 1$$

We first want to show that this assumption implies that $(ab) \bmod m$ is also relatively prime to m. Assume, to the contrary, that

$$\mathrm{GCD}[(ab) \bmod m, m] = d \qquad \text{where } d > 1$$

This implies that d divides both $(ab) \bmod m$ and m. Furthermore, d dividing $(ab) \bmod m$ implies that either d divides a or d divides b, in which case either $\mathrm{GCD}(a, m) = d$ or $\mathrm{GCD}(b, m) = d$, and a contradiction follows. Therefore, $(ab) \bmod m$ is relatively prime to m.

Now, let $z_1, z_2, \ldots, z_{f(m)}$ be the set of distinct elements which are relatively prime to m. Then the set

$$\{(az_1) \bmod m, \ldots, (az_{f(m)}) \bmod m\}$$

where $0 < a < m$ and a is relatively prime to m, enumerates the elements z_1, $z_2, \ldots, z_{f(m)}$ in some order [because each $(az_i) \bmod m$ must be some z_j since $\mathrm{GCD}[(az_i) \bmod m, m] = 1$ and each $(az_i) \bmod m$ is unique by the cancellation property]. This means the set $\{z_1, z_2, \ldots, z_{f(m)}\}$ is a group of order $f(m)$ with respect to multiplication. Also, by the corollary of Lagrange's theorem (Theorem 3-5.7 in Sec. 3-5.3) every element a in this group satisfies the formula

$$a^{f(m)} \bmod m = 1$$

and the theorem is established. The inverse of an element a can be directly computed from the equation

$$a' = a^{f(m)-1} \bmod m \qquad ////$$

For example, for $m = 8$ and $a = 3$, the inverse is

$$a' = 3^{4-1} \bmod 8 = 27 \bmod 8 = 3$$

Note that Fermat's theorem is a special case of Euler's theorem with $f(m) = m - 1$ when m is prime.

We have already shown that there exists a one-to-one correspondence between the elements of $\mathbf{Z}_m$ and those of $\mathbf{Z}_m^*$. For a given $x \in \mathbf{Z}_m$, its residue representation, viz., $\langle x_1, x_2, \ldots, x_r \rangle \in \mathbf{Z}_m^*$ can be easily obtained from $x_i = x \bmod m_i$ for $i = 1, 2, \ldots, r$. However, no such explicit procedure has been given so far for determining the $x \in \mathbf{Z}_m$ which corresponds to a given element in $\mathbf{Z}_m^*$. We shall now show, with the help of Euler's theorem, how it can be done.

Let us first determine a set of r numbers $\hat{m}_i \in \mathbf{Z}_m$ for $i = 1, 2, \ldots, r$ such that their residue representation has a 1 in the ith component and a 0 in all other components; that is, $\hat{m}_i \bmod m_i = 1$ and $\hat{m}_i \bmod m_j = 0$ for $i \neq j$. According to this, the residue representations of $\hat{m}_1, \hat{m}_2, \ldots, \hat{m}_r$ are given by the r-tuples

$$\langle 1, 0, \ldots, 0 \rangle, \langle 0, 1, \ldots, 0 \rangle, \ldots, \langle 0, 0, \ldots, 1 \rangle$$

Note that m/m_i and m_i are relatively prime. Therefore from Euler's theorem

$$\left(\frac{m}{m_i}\right)^{f(m_i)} \bmod m_i = 1$$

Also

$$\left(\frac{m}{m_i}\right)^{f(m_i)} \bmod m_j = 0$$

This means that the number

$$\left(\frac{m}{m_i}\right)^{f(m_i)} \bmod m$$

satisfies all the conditions that the number $\hat{m}_i$ must satisfy. We therefore choose

$$\hat{m}_i = \left(\frac{m}{m_i}\right)^{f(m_i)} \bmod m \qquad \text{for } i = 1, 2, \ldots, r \qquad (9)$$

For any number $\langle x_1, x_2, \ldots, x_r \rangle \in \mathbf{Z}_m^*$, we can immediately write the corresponding number $x \in \mathbf{Z}_m$ as

$$x = \left(\sum_{i=1}^{r} \hat{m}_i x_i\right) \bmod m \qquad (10)$$

thereby obtaining an explicit expression, once all the $\hat{m}_i$ are known.

As an example, let $m = 30$, so that $m_1 = 2$, $m_2 = 3$, and $m_3 = 5$. The values of $\hat{m}_i$ for $i = 1, 2, 3$ are given by

$$\hat{m}_1 = 15 \qquad \hat{m}_2 = 10^2 \bmod 30 = 10 \qquad \hat{m}_3 = 6^4 \bmod 30 = 6$$

Hence for $\langle x_1, x_2, x_3 \rangle \in \mathbf{Z}_{30}^*$,

$$x = (15x_1 + 10x_2 + 6x_3) \bmod 30$$

For $x_1 = 1$, $x_2 = 1$, and $x_3 = 4$, say, we get

$$x = (15 * 1 + 10 * 1 + 6 * 4) \bmod 30 = 19 \bmod 30$$

From Table 3-6.2 one can easily see that the residue representation of 19 is $\langle 1, 1, 4 \rangle$.

Observe that the conversion from the residue representation of a number to its positional form as given by Eq. (10) does require arithmetic operations modulo m. Therefore, this procedure is not usable on a computer which may be able to perform operations modulo m_i but not modulo m. The reason for using the residue number system was to avoid performing operations modulo m in the first place! An alternative procedure is therefore required if we are to have a useful method for converting from $\langle x_1, x_2, \ldots, x_r \rangle$ to x. This new formulation will be based on the mixed-base number system in which only operations modulo m_i are required. The mixed-base representation of numbers is important in residue arithmetic because it is a weighted number system and consequently numbers can be easily compared. Furthermore, the method of conversion from residue to certain mixed-base systems is reasonably rapid in a residue computer.

Any integer $x \in \mathbf{Z}_m$ can be represented in a mixed-base number system by

$$x = a_r \prod_{i=1}^{r-1} m_i + \cdots + a_3 m_1 m_2 + a_2 m_1 + a_1 \qquad (11)$$

where $m = m_1 m_2 \cdots m_r$, each mixed-based digit a_i is in the interval $0 \le a_i < m_i$, and the weight w_i of each a_i is given by

$$\prod_{j=1}^{i-1} m_j \qquad \text{for } i = 2, 3, \ldots, r$$

Any positive integer in the interval

$$0 \le x < \prod_{i=1}^{r} m_i$$

can be represented in this system and each such integer has a unique representation. Note that this system reduces to the decimal number system when $m_i = 10$ for all i. The residue number and the mixed-base systems are equivalent in the sense that both are capable of representing any integer in $\mathbf{Z}_m$; that is, they have the same range. We want a conversion process which will transform a number from the residue system to the mixed-base system. This can be achieved by solving Eq. (11) for all a_i, $1 \le i \le r$. The mixed-base digits can be obtained sequentially in the following way by starting with a_1. Taking both sides of Eq. (11) modulo m_1, we obtain

$$a_1 = x \bmod m_1 = x_1$$

where $\langle x_1, x_2, \ldots, x_r \rangle \in \mathbf{Z}_m^*$ is the residue representation of x, since all terms on the right side except the last are multiples of m_1. To obtain a_2, we reformulate

Eq. (11) as

$$x - a_1 = a_r \prod_{i=1}^{r-1} m_i + \cdots + a_3 m_1 m_2 + a_2 m_1$$

and rewrite it as

$$\frac{x - a_1}{m_1} = a_r \prod_{i=2}^{r-1} m_i + \cdots + a_3 m_2 + a_2$$

Taking both sides of this equation modulo m_2 yields

$$a_2 = \left(\frac{x - a_1}{m_1}\right) \bmod m_2$$

since all terms on the right side except the last are multiples of m_2. The problem now is to evaluate the right part of this formula. It is already known that $x - a_1$ is a multiple of m_1. Furthermore, since m_1 and m_2 are relatively prime to each other, a_2 can be obtained from the equation

$$a_2 = (x_2 - a_1) c_{12} \bmod m_2$$

where c_{12} denotes the multiplicative inverse of m_1 modulo m_2. Similarly, a_3 can be computed from the equation

$$a_3 = \left[\frac{(x_3 - a_1)/m_1 - a_2}{m_2}\right] \bmod m_3$$

or, equivalently from

$$a_3 = [(x_3 - a_1) c_{13} - a_2] c_{23} \bmod m_3$$

where c_{13} is the multiplicative inverse of m_1 modulo m_3. Continuing in this manner, a_i is given by

$$a_i = ((\cdots (x_i - a_1) c_{1i} - a_2) c_{2i} - \cdots - a_{i-1}) c_{i-1,i} \bmod m_i \qquad \text{for } 1 < i \leq r$$

The element c_{ij} in this equation can be computed by Euler's theorem as

$$c_{ij} = m_i^{f(m_j)-1} \bmod m_j \qquad 1 \leq i < j \leq r$$

Note that since we are now using a weighted number system, the magnitude comparison of numbers can be performed more easily.

As an example, let $m = 30$, $m_1 = 2$, $m_2 = 3$, $m_3 = 5$, and $x = \langle x_1, x_2, x_3 \rangle = \langle 1, 1, 4 \rangle$. The coefficients c_{12}, c_{13}, and c_{23} are computed as follows:

$$c_{12} = m_1^{f(m_2)-1} \bmod m_2 = 2 \bmod 3$$

$$c_{13} = m_1^{f(m_3)-1} \bmod m_3 = 2^3 \bmod 5 = 3 \bmod 5$$

$$c_{23} = m_2^{f(m_3)-1} \bmod m_3 = 3^3 \bmod 5 = 2 \bmod 5$$

The following sequence of evaluations yields a_1, a_2, and a_3:

$$a_1 = x_1 = 1$$

$$a_2 = (1 - 1)2 = 0$$

$$a_3 = [(4 - 1)3 - 0]2 \bmod 5 = 3$$

Equation (11) then reduces to the equation

$$x = 6a_3 + 2a_2 + a_1 = 6 \cdot 3 + 1 = 19$$

which gives the correct result.

The previous discussion has shown that we can transform integers in $\mathbf{Z}_m$ from conventional notation to residue notation, and conversely, with relative ease. The residue number system can be used with significant advantage when the operations of addition, subtraction, and multiplication predominate and where few or no divisions are required. Further, there should be little demand for the comparison of numbers and the testing of results for overflow.

Residue arithmetic has been used successfully in a number of applications. In particular, the exact solutions to sets of simultaneous linear equations with rational coefficients have been obtained with greater efficiency than previously realized using conventional arithmetic. The same procedure has also been applied to systems of linear equations with an ill-conditioned matrix of floating-point coefficients. This procedure can more generally be applied to obtaining the inverse of an ill-conditioned matrix.

EXERCISES 3-6

1 Find all integers x which satisfy the conditions $x \bmod 7 = 1$, $x \bmod 9 = 6$, $x \bmod 11 = 5$, and $0 \le x \le 1{,}000$.
2 Give the residue representation of all integers in $\mathbf{Z}_{60}$ for moduli $m_1 = 4$, $m_2 = 3$, and $m_3 = 5$.
3 Give a proof of Eq. (5).
4 Compute the inverse of each element in $\mathbf{Z}_7$, using Fermat's theorem.
5 Compute the inverse of each element of $\mathbf{Z}_{12}$, if it exists, using Euler's theorem.
6 For moduli $m_1 = 8$, $m_2 = 3$, and $m_3 = 5$, find the number whose residue representation is $\langle 4, 2, 3 \rangle$ without the use of mixed-base arithmetic.
7 For moduli $m_1 = 8$, $m_2 = 3$, and $m_3 = 5$, find the associated mixed-base digits of $\langle 4, 2, 3 \rangle$, where the mixed-base expression is

$$x = a_3(8 \times 3) + a_2(8) + a_1$$

3-7 GROUP CODES

Error-detection and -correction techniques have become increasingly important in the design of computer systems. Most systems today contain telephone and communication lines which cause transmitted messages to be corrupted by the presence of noise. Peripheral equipment associated with such systems is by far the most unreliable component of these systems, and both error detection and error correction are frequently performed.

Structure in the design of error-correcting codes is important. First, it facilitates finding the properties of a code; second, and more importantly, it makes the hardware realization of such codes practical. Algebraic structures have been the basis of the most important codes which have been designed.

The first part of this section is concerned with a simple communication model and the basic notions of error correction. The second part of the section deals with the design of codes. The last subsection is concerned with the topic of error recovery in which Lagrange's theorem and the theory of cosets play an important role.

3-7.1 The Communication Model and Basic Notions of Error Correction

A communication process may take place in a variety of ways, e.g., by making a telephone call, sending a message by a telegram or a letter, using a sign language, etc. In all such cases, the process involves the flow of some information-carrying commodity which is conveyed from a sender to a receiver. The information-carrying commodity can vary from music to speech to electricity to water to a sequence of binary digits, etc., or it may be as intangible as anything by which one human mind may affect another. In any case, a communication process involves the flow of a commodity through a system.

An ideal communication system can be represented by at least three essential parts, as shown in Fig. 3-7.1, namely,

1 Transmitter, sender, or source
2 Channel or storage medium
3 Receiver

The channel conveys the message sent by the transmitter to the receiver. This system is perhaps one of the simplest that one can visualize. In practical situations, a system may consist of a number of transmitters and receivers, such as in a telephone exchange or a large computer center. In the latter example, there may be a number of computers connected by communication lines. Such a system will consist of many users that can function both as transmitters and receivers of information.

In practice, a communication channel is subjected to a variety of disturbances which results in a distortion of the commodity being transmitted. Any such disturbance is called *noise*. The form in which noise may appear depends on the channel. For example, in a conversation between two individuals, the channel can be subjected to noises, such as the wind, a passing car, other voices, etc. On the other hand, these noises may not affect a radio transmission. In any case, the important task of a communication system designer is to minimize the losses due to noise and to recover in some optimal manner the original commodity when it is corrupted by the presence of noise. A device that can be used to improve the efficiency of the communication channel is an *encoder* which transforms the incoming messages in such a way that the presence of noise on the transformed messages is detectable. The use of an encoder requires that a *decoder* be employed to transform the encoded messages into their original form that is acceptable to the receiver. It may be possible not only to detect the distortion due to the noise

FIGURE 3-7.1   A model of a general data communication system.

in the channel but also to correct the messages by using a proper encoder and decoder and thus transmit the messages in a perfect manner, at least in an ideal case. In practice, it may not be possible or feasible to eliminate all the noise. The model of the communication system given in Fig. 3-7.1 can now be modified to include the encoder and decoder and to show the presence of noise in the channel. Such a model is given in Fig. 3-7.2.

We shall be concerned here with communication channels which deal with symbols from a specified set called the alphabet of the communication language. Any element of the alphabet will be called a *symbol*, a *letter*, or a *character*. A finite sequence of characters of the alphabet is called a *message* or a *word*. The *length* of a word [denoted by $l(x)$ for the word x] is the number of symbols in the word.

When messages, originally expressed in some language (such as letters of printed text), are transformed into messages in another language, in a manner which is understood by both the transmitter and the receiver and such that these messages can be unambiguously transformed back again, then such messages are said to be *coded*. The *encoding* or *enciphering* process is a procedure for associating words from one language with given words of another language in a one-to-one fashion. Similarly, the *decoding* or *deciphering* process is either the inverse operation or some other one-to-one mapping.

There are many examples of codes used in everyday life. For example, the Morse code is a well-known code that is used in telegraphy. A number of codes are used in digital computer systems. The punch-card code is one that invariably comes to mind. The ASCII (American Standard Code for Information Interchange) expresses each symbol of a 64-character set (consisting of letters, decimal digits, and certain special characters) as a sequence of 6 or 7 binary digits. Another code used in computers is EBCDIC (Extended Binary Coded Decimal Interchange Code).

In most applications the communication channel is restricted to a binary-valued alphabet, whose signals may be designated by 0 and 1. Such a channel is called a *binary channel*. For example, let us code the simple alphabet of eight symbols denoted by the set $\{A, B, C, \ldots, H\}$. Each of the letters can be represented by a sequence of three binary digits. A possible code is given in Table 3-7.1. If a message carried by a channel in this example is changed, owing to disturbances or noise, then the receiver will make an uncorrectable and undetectable mistake because any interchange of 0 or 1 in a particular code sequence results

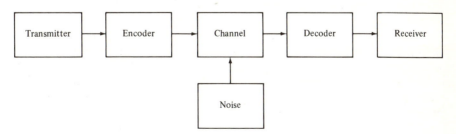

FIGURE 3-7.2 General structure of a typical data communication system with noise.

Table 3-7.1

Symbol	Original code			Code with redundancy			
A	0	0	0	0	0	0	0
B	0	0	1	0	0	1	1
C	0	1	0	0	1	0	1
D	0	1	1	0	1	1	0
E	1	0	0	1	0	0	1
F	1	0	1	1	0	1	0
G	1	1	0	1	1	0	0
H	1	1	1	1	1	1	1

in a different code sequence. For example, if the sequence 000 for A is changed by noise to 100, then it will be simply decoded as E.

We shall now modify our code by adding one extra or redundant digit to each sequence of 3 bits as shown in Table 3-7.1. This additional digit is chosen to be 1 if the sum of the three digits of the original code is odd; otherwise, it is chosen to be 0. A single mistake in a particular code sequence produces another sequence which does not belong to the code. For example, the code sequence 0000 for A might be transformed by noise to any of the sequences 0001, 0010, 0100, or 1000. None of these resulting sequences appear in the code, and an error is immediately detected. Thus, the redundancy in the example code permits us to detect one digit error per code sequence. Observe that the sequence 0001 may be produced by an error in a single digit of the sequences for A, B, C, or E. Therefore, it is not possible to correct the error. By introducing further redundancies, it is possible to both detect and correct one or more errors per code sequence. In order to understand how such codes can be selected, we shall first introduce a method of representing binary codes where each code sequence consists of n binary digits.

Let us first consider a binary code consisting of sequences of 2 digits. There are 2^2 such sequences, and consequently an alphabet of four letters can be coded. Let the alphabet be $\{A, B, C, D\}$ and the code be given by

$$A = 00 \qquad B = 01 \qquad C = 10 \qquad \text{and} \qquad D = 11$$

The four-element code can be represented by a diagram shown in Fig. 3-7.3a where each code sequence occupies a corner of a square. Note that the sequences which differ from another in two digit positions are at opposite ends of the diagonals, while those sequences which differ in one digit position are at the ends of a side. An analogous representation of an eight-element code is given in Fig. 3-7.3b.

Observe again that the sequences which differ from another only in a single digit position are located at the ends of a side, while those which differ by two digits are located at the ends of the diagonal of a square (2 cube) surface. Finally, those sequences which differ from one another in three digits are located at the ends of a diagonal of the cube (3 cube). In general, a 2^n-element code consisting of sequences of n binary digits can be represented by an n cube with sequences properly located at the vertices such that the sequences differing from one another in d digits can be reached from one to the other by going along d edges (sides) of the n cube. In other words, they are a distance d apart, where distance is

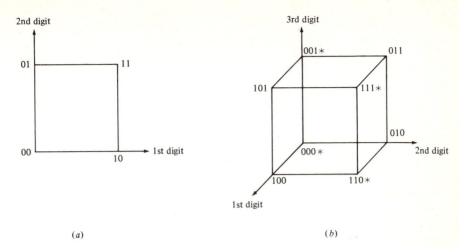

FIGURE 3-7.3 Binary coding.

meant in terms of going along the edges only. It is clear that no detection of error is possible in any such code because a single error in any digit of a code word results in another code word. We now show how this representation can be used to design codes for which the detection as well as the correction of errors up to a certain number of digits in each code sequence is possible.

Let us consider a two-element code consisting of the elements 000 and 111. These two sequences differ in all three digit positions. It is clear that one or two errors in the transmission of these code words will be detectable. Also, in the case when a single digit is being altered by noise, it would be possible to correct the error as well. From Fig. 3-7.3*b* it is evident that the sequence 111 could change to 110, 101, or 011 by a single error in one of the digit positions, while an error of a single digit in 000 will not change it to any of the sequences obtained from 111. Hence, on detection of an error, it is also possible to correct it. Note that in order to detect and correct only one error in each code word, we must have code words that differ from one another in at least three digit positions. It may be pointed out that if two digits are changed by a noisy channel and if error correction is applied in this case, an error will result. For example, if 111 is changed to 100, then the error-correcting code will decode it as 000. Although such a code will not be perfect, it may still prove useful, if we assume that it is much more likely that only one digit will be changed instead of two. It is not unreasonable to consider such probabilities in order to make the design of systems economical.

As mentioned earlier, most communication channels in digital computers carry symbols that are chosen from a binary alphabet, namely, 0 and 1. The symbols in such signals are transmitted sequentially through the channel to a receiver. Let p be the probability that a given symbol will be transmitted correctly by the channel, and let $q = 1 - p$ be the probability that an error due to noise will occur as shown in Fig. 3-7.4. We shall assume that the errors in transmitting successive digits occur independently of the symbols transmitted earlier by the channel. Accordingly, the probability that no errors occur in the trans-

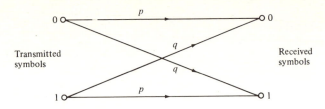

FIGURE 3-7.4   A binary symmetric channel.

mission of a symbol with a three-digit code word is given by p^3. Similarly, the probability that exactly one error occurs in one of the three digits is given by $3p^2q$ because there are three possible ways in which one error can occur. For example, 111 may be received as $101, 011$, or 110. The probability that two errors occur is $3pq^2$, and finally, the probability that all three binary digits are received in error is q^3.

In general, for a sequence of n binary digits, the probability of receiving exactly $n - r$ correct digits, or equivalently, exactly r erroneous digits, is

$$P(r \text{ errors}) = \binom{n}{r} p^{n-r} q^r$$

where

$$\binom{n}{r} = \frac{n!}{(n - r)!\,r!} = \frac{n(n - 1)\cdots(n - r + 1)}{1 \cdot 2 \cdot 3 \cdots \cdots r}$$

So far we have introduced some basic notions of coding. In general, there are three main aspects associated with the problem of obtaining codes, namely,

1 Finding codes that permit error correction
2 Finding practical encoding methods
3 Finding error-correction methods

In the next section we show that the codes with error-correcting properties have a certain mathematical structure. This structure is then used to formulate coding and decoding algorithms.

3-7.2   Generation of Codes by Using Parity Checks

This section is concerned with a formal description of the first complete error-detecting and error-correcting encoding procedure developed by Hamming in 1950. This procedure is rather simple as far as encoding procedures are concerned, and it has been frequently used in computer systems. Indeed, it is still a popular method of detecting and correcting errors today. The discussion in Sec. 3-7.1 provided an intuitive justification for the formal approach that we will follow in this subsection.

Hamming codes were constructed by introducing redundant digits called *parity digits*. In a message that is n digits long, m digits ($m < n$) are used to represent the information part of the message, and the remaining $k = n - m$

digits are used for the detection and correction of errors. The latter digits are called *parity checks*.

Hamming's single-error detecting codes can be described as follows: The information contents of the message is contained in the first $n - 1$ digits of a code word, and the last digit position is set to 0 or to 1 so as to make the entire message contain an even number of 1s. Such an encoding procedure is called an *even parity check*. Alternatively, an odd parity check can be used. For example, the messages 00, 01, 10, 11 become 000, 011, 101, 110 when a single even-parity digit is added and become 001, 010, 100, 111 in the case of an odd parity check. Hamming developed an error-correcting method, based on these parity checks, that enabled the detection of the positions of erroneous digits. As a special case, a single-error detection and correction method will enable

1 The detection of a single or double error in the encoded message

2 The positional identification of a single error in the coded message

We will now present certain definitions and theorems that lead to this encoding method.

We discussed in the previous subsection how encoded messages consisting of n digits could be viewed as a point in an n-dimensional space. For the case of a binary alphabet, points in this space have either 0 or 1 as each of their coordinate values. Let S_n be the set of all n-digit sequences. Let $\oplus$ be a binary operation on S_n such that for any $x, y \in S_n$, when

$$x = \langle x_1, x_2, \ldots, x_n \rangle \quad \text{and} \quad y = \langle y_1, y_2, \ldots, y_n \rangle$$
$$x \oplus y = \langle x_1 \bigtriangledown y_1, x_2 \bigtriangledown y_2, \ldots, x_n \bigtriangledown y_n \rangle$$

where the operation $\bigtriangledown$ on $\{0, 1\}$ is given by Table 3-7.2. It is easy to see that the algebraic system $\langle S_n, \oplus \rangle$ is a group in which $\langle 0, 0, \ldots, 0 \rangle$ or $00 \cdots 0$ is the identity and each element is its own inverse. In general, any code which is a group under the operation $\oplus$ as just defined is called a *group code*. This geometric model, which was first employed by Hamming, is very useful in discussing binary encoding techniques. We will now introduce the concept of Hamming distance.

Definition 3-7.1 Let $x = \langle x_1, x_2, \ldots, x_n \rangle$ and $y = \langle y_1, y_2, \ldots, y_n \rangle$ be n-tuples representing messages $x_1 x_2 \cdots x_n$ and $y_1 y_2 \cdots y_n$ respectively, where $x_i, y_i \in \{0, 1\}$ for all i. The *Hamming distance* between x and y, denoted by $H(x, y)$, is the number of coordinates for which all x_i and y_i are different. Clearly

$$H(x, y) = \sum_{i=1}^{n} (x_i \bigtriangledown y_i) \tag{1}$$

Table 3-7.2

$\bigtriangledown$	0	1
0	0	1
1	1	0

For example, the Hamming distance between $\langle 1, 1, 1, 0, 1 \rangle$ and $\langle 0, 1, 1, 1, 0 \rangle$ is 3. Our definition of distance satisfies a number of useful mathematical properties, namely, that for all $x, y, z \in S_n$

$$H(x, y) \geq 0 \tag{2}$$

$$H(x, y) = 0 \Leftrightarrow x = y \tag{3}$$

$$H(x, y) = H(y, x) \tag{4}$$

$$H(x, y) + H(y, z) \geq H(x, z) \tag{5}$$

The validity of these properties is intuitively obvious, and their proofs are left as exercises.

Definition 3-7.2   The *minimum distance* of a code, whose words are n-tuples, is the minimum of the Hamming distances between all pairs of code words in that code.

As an example, let

$$
\begin{aligned}
x &= \langle 1, 0, 0, 1 \rangle & H(x, y) &= 3 \\
y &= \langle 0, 1, 0, 0 \rangle & H(y, z) &= 2 \\
z &= \langle 1, 0, 0, 0 \rangle & H(x, z) &= 1
\end{aligned}
$$

then the minimum distance between these words is 1.

Theorem 3-7.1   A code can detect all combinations of k or fewer errors if and only if the minimum distance between any two code words is at least $k + 1$.

PROOF   We are unable to detect a combination of errors if and only if that particular combination transforms a code word u into some code word v. With a minimum distance of at least $k + 1$, it would take a combination of at least $k + 1$ errors to change code word u into code word v. Hence, all combinations of k or fewer errors can be detected.   ////

As an example, let $n = 3$ and take our code to be the words $\langle 0, 0, 0 \rangle$ and $\langle 1, 1, 1 \rangle$; the minimum distance is obviously 3. Furthermore, from Fig. 3-7.3, it is clear that this code can detect any combinations of two errors or one error.

We now turn to the problem of error correction. When an error is detected and corrective action is to be taken, the question of what corrective criteria to use is encountered. Our criterion will be simple, namely, that a noisy message will be decoded as the code word that is nearest to it in terms of Hamming distance. In other words, our decoding rule will be to choose the most probable code word based on the occurrence of the most probable error, i.e., the occurrence of the fewest single errors. The following theorem is concerned with error correction and is analogous to Theorem 3-7.1.

Theorem 3-7.2   A code can correct all combinations of k or fewer errors if and only if the minimum distance between any two code words is at least $2k + 1$.

PROOF We shall first prove that if the code can correct all combinations of k or fewer errors, then the minimum distance between any two codes must be at least $2k + 1$. Let us assume, to the contrary, that there is at least one pair of words u and v such that $H(u, v) < 2k + 1$. We may assume that $H(u, v) \geq k + 1$; otherwise, one cannot even detect k errors. Let us consider a word u' which differs from u in exactly k digits. These k digits are chosen to be any subset of those digits in which u and v differ from one another. This means $H(u, u') = k$. Obviously, by our choice $H(u', v) \leq k$ because u and v only differ in at most $2k$ digits. Therefore, u' cannot be decoded with certainty, since code word v is at least as close to u' as u is. Thus we have established a contradiction.

We shall now prove the converse of the theorem by assuming that the minimum code distance is $2k + 1$ and from this assumption deducing that the code can correct all sets of k errors. Let u be a code word, and let u' be a received erroneous record that has no more than k error digits. If a decoding rule correctly decodes u' as u, then we know that u' is nearer to the code word u than any other code word v. From property (5) of the Hamming distance, we have

$$H(u, u') + H(u', v) \geq H(u, v)$$

Since $H(u, v) \geq 2k + 1$ and $H(u, u') \leq k$, it then follows that $H(u', v) \geq k + 1$. This implies that every code word v is farther away from u' than u, and consequently u' can be correctly decoded. ////

So far, we have discussed codes, but nothing has been said about their design. A good code C will contain as many code words as possible which satisfy the minimum distance chosen for the desired code. Codes can be designed in a number of ways. One of the more general and powerful methods of choosing codes is based on elements of group theory. In essence, we want to find the largest subset C which is a subgroup of S_n, the set of all n-digit sequences, and which satisfies the minimum distance specified. Before describing how group theory can be used to design single-error correcting codes, we give a less elegant method of generating such codes.

Recall that the minimum distance required between any pair of code words for correcting a single error, according to Theorem 3-7.2, is 3. Therefore, the procedure for transmitting a word $\langle x_1, x_2, \ldots, x_m \rangle$ of length m is first to find the parity-check digits $x_{m+1}, x_{m+2}, \ldots, x_n$ and then to transmit $\langle x_1, x_2, \ldots, x_n \rangle$. In addition, we need a device for determining the position of any possible error in $\langle x_1, x_2, \ldots, x_n \rangle$ and then correcting it.

We shall now show by means of an example how we can determine the parity-check digits for any given word of length m. For our example we choose $m = 4$ and $k = 3$, because at least three parity-check digits are required for a single-error correcting code. Later we shall generalize the procedure to any $k \geq 3$ and m. Let x_i denote that ith digit in the code word. The parity-check word $\langle x_5, x_6, x_7 \rangle$ can be derived from the following modulo 2 equations:

$$x_1 + x_2 + x_3 + x_5 = 0 \qquad\qquad (6)$$

$$x_1 + x_2 + x_4 + x_6 = 0 \quad \text{all mod 2} \qquad (7)$$

$$x_1 + x_3 + x_4 + x_7 = 0 \qquad\qquad (8)$$

These equations define the desired code. It can be obtained by solving the three simultaneous equations for the dependent variables x_5, x_6, and x_7 in terms of the independent variables x_1, x_2, x_3, and x_4. The equations can be rewritten as

$$\left.\begin{array}{l} x_5 = -(x_1 + x_2 + x_3) \\[2ex] x_6 = -(x_1 + x_2 + x_4) \\[2ex] x_7 = -(x_1 + x_3 + x_4) \end{array}\right\} \quad \text{all mod 2}$$

These equations can be rewritten as follows:

$$\left.\begin{array}{l} x_5 = x_1 + x_2 + x_3 \\[2ex] x_6 = x_1 + x_2 + x_4 \\[2ex] x_7 = x_1 + x_3 + x_4 \end{array}\right\} \quad \text{all mod 2}$$

because $-x_i \bmod 2 = (-x_i + 2x_i) \bmod 2 = x_i \bmod 2$, $1 \le i \le 4$. Now, each independent variable has two possible values (0 or 1), and consequently there are 16 possible solutions. Each solution is a code word of the desired code. The code is given in Table 3-7.3, and it should be observed that the distance between any two code words is at least 3.

In order to develop a decoding procedure for the code given in Table 3-7.3, we consider Eqs. (6) to (8). Obviously, for any correct message these equations will be satisfied. However, if there is any single error in any one of the seven binary digits of the coded messages, then one or the other of these equations will not be satisfied. There are only seven possible ways in which one or more of these equations will not be satisfied, and one of these ways will clearly indicate

Table 3-7.3 A Single-Error Correcting Code with
$m = 4$ and $n = 7$

Bit position

x_1	x_2	x_3	x_4	x_5	x_6	x_7
0	0	0	0	0	0	0
0	0	0	1	0	1	1
0	0	1	0	1	0	1
0	0	1	1	1	1	0
0	1	0	0	1	1	0
0	1	0	1	1	0	1
0	1	1	0	0	1	1
0	1	1	1	0	0	0
1	0	0	0	1	1	1
1	0	0	1	1	0	0
1	0	1	0	0	1	0
1	0	1	1	0	0	1
1	1	0	0	0	0	1
1	1	0	1	0	1	0
1	1	1	0	1	0	0
1	1	1	1	1	1	1

the location of the digit in error. We shall now explain how this observation can be used for determining the error.

Let P_1, P_2, and P_3 be the propositions that Eqs. (6) to (8) are *true*, respectively (i.e., the sum of the variables in each of the equations is even). Furthermore, let the sets S_1, S_2, and S_3 be the extension sets of the propositions P_1, P_2, and P_3 respectively. For any word received, these sets corresponding to the equations can be interpreted as in Fig. 3-7.5 where there are seven disjoint nonempty sets, each being associated with a variable x_i. The variable x_1 belongs to the intersection of sets S_1, S_2, and S_3, while the variable x_3 belongs to the set $S_1 \cap \sim S_2 \cap S_3$, and similarly for the other variables. The decoding rule for this code is summarized in Table 3-7.4 where the symbol "x" in the ith column ($i \leq 3$) denotes that proposition P_i is *false*. For example, if 1000011 is received, then P_1 has failed and x_5 is in error. If 0111111 is received, all propositions are false and x_1 is in error. The validity of this decoding method that we have described is based on the fact that the sets S_1, S_2, and S_3 have seven disjoint nonempty subsets, each subset being in a one-to-one correspondence with a proposition concerning the truth or falseness of P_1, P_2, and P_3.

The previous discussion has shown that error-correcting codes can be generated without too much difficulty. The method used, however, was somewhat ad hoc. The remaining pages in this subsection will show how the theory of groups can facilitate the design of single-error correcting codes.

The group code $\langle S_n, \oplus \rangle$ was previously defined in Table 3-7.2. In practice, we are looking for the largest subgroup C of S_n which satisfies the minimum-distance requirements. It will be shown that the error-correcting ability of a group code depends on the number of 1s possessed by each code word. The *weight*, denoted as $W(x)$, of a code word is simply the number of 1s in that word. The words $\langle 1, 1, 0, 1, 0 \rangle$ and $\langle 0, 1, 1, 0, 0 \rangle$ have weights of 3 and 2 respectively. If we let the code word $\langle 0, 0, \ldots, 0 \rangle$ be denoted by 0, then $W(x) = H(x, 0)$. We can also express the Hamming distance between two words as the weight of their sum with respect to the group operation. That is,

$$H(x, y) = H(x \oplus y, 0) = W(x \oplus y) \tag{9}$$

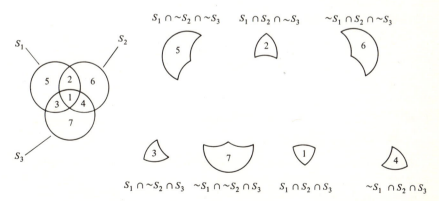

FIGURE 3-7.5 A set-theoretic approach to Hamming's single-error correcting code.

Table 3-7.4 **Decoding Rule for a Single-Error
Correction Code**

Propositions			
P_1	P_2	P_3	**Incorrect digit**
			None
x			x_5
	x		x_6
		x	x_7
x	x		x_2
x		x	x_3
	x	x	x_4
x	x	x	x_1

We will now prove an interesting statement concerning the minimum distance of a group code.

Theorem 3-7.3 The minimum weight of the nonzero code words in a group code is equal to its minimum distance.

PROOF   Assume that code word z has the minimum weight of the code. We want to show that there exist two code words whose Hamming distance is this minimum weight. Since, for any x, $x \oplus x = 0$, it follows that 0 is a code word. Using Eq. (9), we have $W(z) = H(z, 0)$, and therefore z and 0 are the two required code words.

Conversely, let x and y be code words such that $H(x, y)$ is equal to the minimum distance for the code. Since $\langle S_n, \oplus \rangle$ is a group, it follows because of closure that $x \oplus y = z \in S_n$. Consequently, $W(x \oplus y) = W(z) = H(x, y)$, and we have found a code word whose weight is equal to the minimum distance of the code.   ////

In our example of the group code given in Table 3-7.3, observe that the minimum weight of the code is 3. This group code was obtained by solving the set of three simultaneous linear equations (modulo 2). The coefficient matrix for these equations is given by

$$H = \begin{pmatrix} 1 & 1 & 1 & 0 & 1 & 0 & 0 \\ 1 & 1 & 0 & 1 & 0 & 1 & 0 \\ 1 & 0 & 1 & 1 & 0 & 0 & 1 \end{pmatrix} \quad (10)$$

If we write $\langle x_1, x_2, \ldots, x_7 \rangle = x$, then Eqs. (6) to (8) can be written as

$$x \cdot H^t = 0$$

where H^t denotes the transpose of the matrix H and the right-hand side of the equation is a row vector containing three zeros. We will now show that the matrix H always defines a group code and, furthermore, that the minimum weight of the code can be obtained from the matrix. We shall assume throughout our discussion here that matrix H has elements which are binary digits, that is, 0 and 1.

Theorem 3-7.4 Let H be a matrix which consists of k rows and n columns. Then the set of words $x = \langle x_1, x_2, \ldots, x_n \rangle$ which belong to the following set

$$C = \{x \mid (x \cdot H^t = 0) \bmod 2\}$$

is a group code under the operation $\oplus$.

PROOF Observe that $0 \cdot H^t = 0$, and hence $0 \in C$. If x, $y \in C$, then $x \cdot H^t = y \cdot H^t = 0$

$$(x \oplus y) \cdot H^t = (x \cdot H^t) \oplus (y \cdot H^t) = 0$$

so that $x \oplus y \in C$. The associativity of the operation $\oplus$ follows along the same lines. Since $x \oplus x = 0$, every element in C is its own inverse. Hence $\langle C, \oplus \rangle$ is a group code. ////

Observe that each row of the matrix in Eq. (10) represents an even parity check for different combinations of variables; therefore, each row is called a *parity-check row*, and the matrix H is called the *parity-check matrix*. We will show that the minimum weight of the group code defined by a parity-check matrix can be directly obtained from the matrix.

Let us assume as before that the parity-check matrix H is a $k \times n$ matrix. We shall denote the columns of H by $h_1, h_2, \ldots, h_n$, and $h_i \oplus h_j$ will represent the k-tuple sum of the columns h_i and h_j. The same notion can be extended to the sum of more than two columns. Any solution of $x \cdot H^t = 0$ in which $x = \langle x_1, x_2, \ldots, x_n \rangle$ is called a code word generated by H.

Theorem 3-7.5 The parity-check matrix H generates a code word of weight q iff there exists a set of q columns of H such that their k-tuple sum is zero.

PROOF Let us assume that in a code word x generated by H the components $x_{i_1}, x_{i_2}, \ldots, x_{i_q}$ are 1s and the remaining components are zero, so that the weight of this word is q. From $x \cdot H^t = 0$ it follows that

$$h_{i_1} \oplus h_{i_2} \oplus \cdots \oplus h_{i_q} = 0$$

Conversely, if we assume that there is a set of q distinct columns of H viz., $h_{i_1}, h_{i_2}, \ldots, h_{i_q}$ such that

$$h_{i_1} \oplus h_{i_2} \oplus \cdots \oplus h_{i_q} = 0$$

then we can choose an n-tuple x such that $x_{i_1}, x_{i_2}, \ldots, x_{i_q}$ are 1s and the other components are 0. This n-tuple will satisfy $x \cdot H^t = 0$, implying that x is a code word of weight q generated by H. ////

Observe that the preceding theorem enables us to determine the minimum weight of a group code. This determination can be achieved by looking for the minimum number of columns in H that have a zero sum. It then follows from the theorem that there exists a code word which has a weight equal to this number of columns.

If we examine the parity-check matrix H of our example, then it is obvious that the minimum weight of the code cannot be 1 since there is no zero column in the matrix. Furthermore, it cannot be 2 since such a result could be obtained only from a matrix having two identical columns. Therefore, the minimum weight of the example code can be no less than 3. Suppose that the following columns are chosen:

$$h_{i_1} = h_2 = \langle 1, 1, 0 \rangle \qquad h_{i_2} = h_3 = \langle 1, 0, 1 \rangle \qquad h_{i_3} = h_4 = \langle 0, 1, 1 \rangle$$

Then, it is obvious that $h_2 \oplus h_3 \oplus h_4 = \langle 0, 0, 0 \rangle$ and consequently that the minimum weight of the code is 3. There are other combinations of three columns that will yield the same result.

The matrix H of our example is a 3×7 matrix, and the number of words generated by it is 16. We shall now show that if the parity-check matrix is a $k \times n$ matrix, then the maximum number of code words generated by it is 2^{n-k}. We shall also discuss a generalization of the method used in the previous example to determine the parity-check digits.

For our discussion, let m be the number of binary digits representing the information portion of the code and k be the number of parity bits which are needed to augment the encoded word so that it is of length $k + m = n$. Since there are k parity bits to be determined, we need to solve k linear equations. The parity-check matrix H contains k rows and n columns. If we wish to express each parity bit explicitly in terms of the m binary information digits, it is best to choose the parity-check matrix H such that it can be partitioned as

$$\left(\begin{array}{c|c} Q & I_k \end{array} \right)$$

where Q is an arbitrary $k \times m$ matrix and I_k is a $k \times k$ identity matrix. Although there is no unique way of choosing Q, there are certain restrictions which will be imposed on Q so that the parity-check matrix H may generate a single-error correcting code. For the moment, let Q be an arbitrary matrix with entries 0 and 1. Recall that every code word is a solution of $x \cdot H^t = 0$ where $x = \langle x_1, x_2, \ldots, x_n \rangle$ in which the bits $x_{m+1}, x_{m+2}, \ldots, x_n$ are the parity-check bits. Using the partition of H, we can write immediately that

$$x_{m+i} = \sum_{j=1}^{m} x_j \, q_{ij} \pmod{2} \qquad \text{for } i = 1, 2, \ldots, k$$

where q_{ij} is the element of the matrix Q in the ith row and jth column. Once the matrix Q is chosen, one can obtain the parity bits from the equations obtained for every m-tuple of the information code. For m bits of information, we can have at most $2^m = 2^{n-k}$ code words.

So far, the matrix Q which is $k \times n$ is arbitrary. Since the parity matrix H generates a single-error correcting code, we must have the weight of each code word to be at least 3, as shown in Theorem 3-7.3. Thus it is required, according to Theorem 3-7.5, that no column of H be zero. Furthermore, we also require that no two columns of H be identical. For the matrix H, we can choose $2^k - 1$ distinct columns, none of which is zero. We have already chosen from these k columns for matrix I_k; therefore, we are left with $2^k - k - 1$ possible columns for Q. This means

$$m \le 2^k - k - 1 \qquad \text{or } 2^k \ge m + k + 1 = n + 1 \tag{11}$$

For our example $n = 7$, so that $2^k \geq 8$, or $k \geq 3$, and the smallest number of parity-check bits is 3.

We may summarize our results by saying that for a single-error correcting code of length n containing k parity bits, the number of information bits is given by Eq. (11) and the number of different information code words is $2^m = 2^{n-k}$.

We have been concerned in this subsection with the design of single-error correcting codes and the problem of encoding. The important topic of decoding was briefly mentioned. The next subsection deals with error recovery of a code word that has been corrupted by a noisy channel.

3-7.3 Error Recovery in Group Codes

When a code word is transmitted across a noisy channel, some of the digit positions in the code word can be altered during transmission. The problem of a decoder at the receiver end is to find the original code word that was transmitted. The criterion used in many cases is to choose a code word which is nearest to the noisy word received. In this section we shall apply basic group theory to this decoding problem.

Let us assume for our discussion that the code words transmitted contain n binary digits in which the first m digits contain the information part and the last k [$k + m = n$] digits are the parity-check bits. Not all the n-tuples are code words. Let S_n be the set of all n-tuples and C be the set of all code words. It was shown in Theorem 3-7.4 that the group code $\langle C, \oplus \rangle$ is a proper subgroup of $\langle S_n, \oplus \rangle$.

Let us consider a code word $c_i \in C$ being transmitted through a noisy channel. Let e_i be the error n-tuple consisting of 1s in the digit positions in which an error occurs; therefore the transmitted word is no longer c_i but $c_i \oplus e_i$. Our problem is to recover c_i from $c_i \oplus e_i$ which is actually received. If we denote $c_i \oplus e_i = y_i \in S_n$, then $e_i = y_i \oplus c_i$ or $c_i = y_i \oplus e_i$. Recall that the code word we will be looking for is an element of C which is closest in terms of the Hamming distance to the word y_i received. This means that we shall be looking for the error with the least weight.

We know that the set of left cosets (or right cosets, since the groups we are considering are abelian) of C in S_n form a partition of S_n. Every element of S_n belongs to one and only one left coset of C in S_n. Let us consider an element $y \in S_n$. Clearly y is in the left coset $y \oplus C$. Among all the elements of the coset $y \oplus C$, we can determine the one with the least weight. Such an n-tuple will be called the *coset leader*. Let us denote a particular coset leader by e. Naturally, the coset of C generated by y or by any other element of the coset, and in particular by e, will remain the same. For each coset we thus have a coset leader. For the coset C itself we have 0 as the coset leader. Since C has 2^m elements, we have 2^{n-m} cosets. A method of constructing a decoding table will now be described. An important point that may be noticed at this stage is that if e is a coset leader, then the elements of the coset of which e is an element are given by $e \oplus c_i$ where $c_i \in C$. Furthermore, the element of C which is closest to $e \oplus c_i$ is c_i.

The first step in the procedure is to construct a row of elements consisting of all code words in C with the zero code word in its leftmost position; thus

$$0 = c_1 \quad c_2 \quad c_3 \quad \cdots \quad c_{2^m}$$

where it is assumed that $c_1 = \langle 0, 0, \ldots, 0 \rangle = 0$ for convenience.

In the second step, we select some word $y_j \in S_n$ but not in C and construct a new row or coset $y_j \oplus c_i$ for all $1 \leq i \leq 2^m$; that is, we add each code word c_i to y_j. We now have the following two rows of the desired table:

$$0 = c_1 \quad c_2 \quad c_3 \quad \cdots \quad c_{2^m}$$
$$y_j \oplus 0 \quad y_j \oplus c_2 \quad y_j \oplus c_3 \quad \cdots \quad y_j \oplus c_{2^m}$$

The second row is rewritten (if necessary) with the leftmost element in the row being chosen on the basis of least weight (i.e., the element $y_j \oplus c_i$ with the least number of 1s). This element is the coset leader. Let this coset leader be denoted by y_2 ($y_1 = 0$ is the coset leader of the first row); then the rows obtained so far can be rewritten as

$$0 = c_1 \quad c_2 \quad c_3 \quad \cdots \quad c_{2^m}$$
$$y_2 \quad y_2 \oplus c_2 \quad y_2 \oplus c_3 \quad \cdots \quad y_2 \oplus c_{2^m}$$

We now form a third row by selecting some $y_k \in S_n$ which is not in the preceding two rows. This third row is also rewritten with its leftmost element being the word in that row with the least weight. This coset leader is called y_3.

This process is continued until all elements in S_n are accounted for in the table. The complete decoding table has the form

$$0 = c_1 \quad c_2 \quad c_3 \quad \cdots \quad c_{2^m}$$
$$y_2 \quad y_2 \oplus c_2 \quad y_2 \oplus c_3 \quad \cdots \quad y_2 \oplus c_{2^m}$$
$$y_3 \quad y_3 \oplus c_2 \quad y_3 \oplus c_3 \quad \cdots \quad y_3 \oplus c_{2^m}$$
$$\cdots\cdots\cdots\cdots\cdots\cdots\cdots\cdots\cdots\cdots\cdots\cdots$$
$$y_{2^{n-m}} \quad y_{2^{n-m}} \oplus c_2 \quad y_{2^{n-m}} \oplus c_3 \quad \cdots \quad y_{2^{n-m}} \oplus c_{2^m}$$

A received word x can be decoded by first finding x in a row of the decoding table. Let it be the kth row. Then the decoded word c_i is given by

$$c_i = y_k \oplus x = x \oplus y_k$$

where y_k is the coset leader for that row (and is the same as the error word e mentioned at the beginning of this subsection). Also, if no error has occurred in transmission, then the coset leader will be the zero word $\langle 0, 0, \ldots, 0 \rangle$.

As an example, let $m = 3$, $n = 6$, and the parity-check matrix be

$$H = \begin{pmatrix} 1 & 1 & 0 & 1 & 0 & 0 \\ 1 & 0 & 1 & 0 & 1 & 0 \\ 1 & 1 & 1 & 0 & 0 & 1 \end{pmatrix}$$

The parity-check positions can be obtained from the equations

$$\left.\begin{array}{l} x_4 = x_1 + x_2 \\[1em] x_5 = x_1 + x_3 \\[1em] x_6 = x_1 + x_2 + x_3 \end{array}\right\} \quad \text{all mod } 2$$

The single-error correcting code generated by H is

$$C = \{ \langle 0, 0, 0, 0, 0, 0 \rangle, \langle 0, 0, 1, 0, 1, 1 \rangle, \langle 0, 1, 0, 1, 0, 1 \rangle, \langle 0, 1, 1, 1, 1, 0 \rangle,$$
$$\langle 1, 0, 0, 1, 1, 1 \rangle, \langle 1, 0, 1, 1, 0, 0 \rangle, \langle 1, 1, 0, 0, 1, 0 \rangle, \langle 1, 1, 1, 0, 0, 1 \rangle \}$$

The decoding table for this code is given in Table 3-7.5 where, for convenience, each word $\langle x_1, x_2, \ldots, x_n \rangle$ has been rewritten as the sequence $x_1 x_2 \cdots x_n$. To decode a received word $c_i \oplus e$, we locate it in the table, and the code word at the top of the column in which the received word occurs is taken to be the transmitted code word. For example, if $\langle 0, 0, 0, 0, 1, 1 \rangle$ is received, then the code word transmitted is taken to be $\langle 0, 0, 1, 0, 1, 1 \rangle$; if $\langle 1, 0, 1, 1, 1, 0 \rangle$ is received, then the code word transmitted is taken to be $\langle 1, 0, 1, 1, 0, 0 \rangle$.

The error patterns that will be corrected by such a decoding table consist of only those error words which occur as coset leaders. In the example given,

$$\text{Parity-check matrix } H = \begin{pmatrix} 1 & 1 & 0 & 1 & 0 & 0 \\ 1 & 0 & 1 & 0 & 1 & 0 \\ 1 & 1 & 1 & 0 & 0 & 1 \end{pmatrix}$$

the error patterns can be any element in the set

$$\{ \langle 0, 0, 0, 0, 0, 0 \rangle, \langle 1, 0, 0, 0, 0, 0 \rangle, \langle 0, 1, 0, 0, 0, 0 \rangle, \langle 0, 0, 1, 0, 0, 0 \rangle,$$
$$\langle 0, 0, 0, 1, 0, 0 \rangle, \langle 0, 0, 0, 0, 1, 0 \rangle, \langle 0, 0, 0, 0, 0, 1 \rangle, \langle 0, 0, 0, 1, 1, 0 \rangle \}$$

Observe that only those errors which are shown as coset leaders can be

Table 3-7.5 A Decoding Table for a Single-error Correcting Code with $m = 3$ and $n = 6$

Coset leaders ↓							
Row of → 000000	001011	010101	011110	100111	101100	110010	111001
code 100000	101011	110101	111110	000111	001100	010010	011001
words 010000	011011	000101	001110	110111	111100	100010	101001
001000	000011	011101	010110	101111	100100	111010	110001
000100	001111	010001	011010	100011	101000	110110	111101
000010	001001	010111	011100	100101	101110	110000	111011
000001	001010	010100	011111	100110	101101	110011	111000
000110	001101	010011	011000	100001	101010	110100	111111

corrected. From the column of coset leaders, it is clear that in addition to all occurrences of single errors, this code will correct the double error $\langle 0, 0, 0, 1, 1, 0 \rangle$ which is the coset leader of the last row in Table 3-7.5. It is also clear from the table that not all double errors can be corrected.

From the column of coset leaders it is easy to determine the type of errors that can be corrected. In the case of a binary channel, one can obtain the probability that a transmitted word can be correctly decoded by simply adding all the probabilities of the occurrences of the errors given by the coset leaders. In our example, the probability of correct transmission of a 6-tuple word is

$$p^6 + 6p^5q + p^4q^2$$

which includes the correct transmission of a code word and the correction of all single errors as well as one type of double error.

We have been concerned in this subsection with only the basic notions of encoding and decoding. Advanced discussions of error-detecting and error-correcting codes invariably involve topics from abstract algebra such as vector spaces and polynomial rings.

EXERCISES 3-7

1 Prove that the Hamming distance satisfies the following properties for all $x, y, z \in S_n$.
  (*a*) $H(x, y) \geq 0$
  (*b*) $H(x, y) = 0 \Leftrightarrow x = y$
  (*c*) $H(x, y) = H(y, x)$
  (*d*) $H(x, y) + H(y, z) \geq H(x, z)$
2 Show that a binary code can detect all combinations of $k + 1$ to q errors, where $k \leq q$, and correct all combinations of k or fewer errors if and only if this code has at least $k + q + 1$ as its minimum distance.
3 Prove that in a binary group code either half of its code words have odd weight and half even weight, or all have even weight. (*Hint:* Prove that the code words of even weight are a subgroup.)
4 Devise a single-error correcting group code and the associated decoding table for the following cases:
  (*a*) $m = 3, n = 7$
  (*b*) $m = 4, n = 8$
For a binary symmetric channel obtain the probability of correct transmission for each case.

BIBLIOGRAPHY

ABBOTT, J. C.: "Sets, Lattices, and Boolean Algebras," Allyn and Bacon, Inc., Boston, 1969.

ABRAMSON, N.: "Information Theory and Coding," McGraw-Hill Book Company, New York, 1963.

ANDREE, R. V.: "Selection from Modern Abstract Algebra," 2d ed., Holt, Rinehart and Winston, Inc., New York, 1971.

BERZTISS, A. T.: "Data Structures: Theory and Practice," Academic Press, Inc., New York, 1971.

BIRKHOFF, G. and T. C. BARTEE: "Modern Applied Algebra," McGraw-Hill Book Company, New York, 1970.

———— and S. MACLANE: "A Survey of Modern Algebra," 3d ed., MacMillan & Co., Ltd., London, 1965.

CHOMSKY, N.: On Certain Formal Properties of Grammars, *Information and Control*, **2**(2): 137–167 (1959).

GRIES, D. E.: "Compiler Construction for Digital Computers," John Wiley & Sons, Inc., New York, 1971.

HERSTEIN, I. N.: "Topics in Algebra," Blaisdell Publishing Company, New York, 1964.

HOPCROFT, J. E., and J. D. ULLMAN: "Formal Languages and Their Relation to Automata," Addison-Wesley Publishing Company, Inc., Reading, Mass., 1969.

KNUTH, D. E.: "The Art of Computer Programming," vol. 2, Seminumerical Algorithms, Addison-Wesley Publishing Company, Inc., Reading, Mass., 1969.

LARSEN, M. D.: "Introduction to Modern Algebraic Concepts," Addison-Wesley Publishing Company, Inc., Reading, Mass., 1969.

McCOY, N. H.: "Introduction to Modern Algebra," Allyn and Bacon, Inc., Boston, 1960.

NELSON, RAYMOND J.: "Introduction to Automata," John Wiley & Sons, Inc., New York, 1968.

PETERSON, W. W., and E. J. WELDON: "Error-Correcting Codes," 2d ed., The M.I.T. Press, Cambridge, Mass., 1972.

PREPARATA, F. P., and R. T. YEH: "Introduction to Discrete Structures," Addison-Wesley Publishing Company, Inc., Reading, Mass., 1973.

REZA, F. M.: "An Introduction to Information Theory," McGraw-Hill Book Company, New York, 1961.

STONE, H. S.: "Discrete Mathematical Structures and Their Applications," Science Research Associates, Inc., Chicago, 1973.

SZABO, N. S., and R. I. TANAKA: "Residue Arithmetic and Its Application to Computer Technology," McGraw-Hill Book Company, New York, 1967.

WELLS, CHARLES: "Mathematical Structures," Lecture notes, Case Western Reserve University, Cleveland, Ohio, 1968.

4

LATTICES AND BOOLEAN ALGEBRA

INTRODUCTION

The statement algebra of Chap. 1 and the algebra of sets given in Chap. 2 provide a motivation for the study of an abstract algebraic system possessing all the essential properties of these algebras. Such an algebraic system was introduced by George Boole in 1854 and is known as Boolean algebra. Before we study Boolean algebra in this chapter, we consider a more general algebraic system called a lattice. A Boolean algebra is then introduced as a special lattice.

A basic difference between the algebraic systems studied in this chapter and those given in Chap. 3 is the fact that the ordering relation plays a significant role in the algebraic systems studied here. In order to emphasize the role of an ordering relation, a lattice is first introduced as a partially ordered set, followed by the definition of a lattice as an algebraic system.

Both lattices and Boolean algebra have important applications in the theory and design of computers. There are many other areas such as engineering and science to which Boolean algebra is applied.

4-1 LATTICES AS PARTIALLY ORDERED SETS

In this section we introduce a lattice as a partially ordered set satisfying certain properties. Partially ordered sets, their properties, and associated terminology given in Sec. 2-3.9 will be used throughout our discussion here. In particular, the notion of the least upper bound (LUB) and the greatest lower bound (GLB) of a subset of a partially ordered set will be used repeatedly.

4-1.1 Definition and Examples

Definition 4-1.1 A *lattice* is a partially ordered set $\langle L, \leq \rangle$ in which every pair of elements $a, b \in L$ has a greatest lower bound and a least upper bound.

The greatest lower bound of a subset $\{a, b\} \subseteq L$ will be denoted by $a * b$ and the least upper bound by $a \oplus b$. It is customary to call the GLB $\{a, b\} = a * b$ the *meet* or *product* of a and b, and the LUB $\{a, b\} = a \oplus b$ the *join* or *sum* of a and b. Other symbols such as $\wedge$ and $\vee$ or $\cdot$ and $+$ are also used to denote the meet and join of two elements respectively. When using the symbols $\cdot$ and $+$ it is not uncommon to supress the dot and write $a \cdot b$ simply as ab. In certain cases, the symbols $\cap$ and $\cup$ are also used to denote the meet and join respectively. It follows from the definition of a lattice that both $*$ and $\oplus$ are binary operations on L because of the uniqueness of the least upper bound and greatest lower bound of any subset of a partially ordered set.

A totally ordered set is trivially a lattice, but not all partially ordered sets are lattices, as can be seen from the Hasse diagrams of some of the partially ordered sets given in Figs. 4-1.1 and 4-1.2. For the sake of brevity, throughout this chapter we shall refer to the Hasse diagrams simply as the diagrams of partially ordered sets. Naturally, the diagram of a totally ordered set is a chain.

The following are some examples of lattices. These examples will be referred to frequently throughout this chapter.

EXAMPLE 1 Let S be any set and $\rho(S)$ be its power set. The partially ordered set $\langle \rho(S), \subseteq \rangle$ is a lattice in which the meet and join are the same as the operations $\cap$ and $\cup$ respectively. In particular, when S has a single element, the corresponding lattice is a chain containing two elements. When S has two and three elements, the diagrams of the corresponding lattices are as shown in Fig. 4-1.1b and f respectively.

EXAMPLE 2 Let $\mathbf{I}_+$ be the set of all positive integers, and let D denote the relation of "division" in $\mathbf{I}_+$ such that for any $a, b \in \mathbf{I}_+$, $a \, D \, b$ iff a divides b. Then $\langle \mathbf{I}_+, D \rangle$ is a lattice in which the join of a and b is given by the least common multiple (LCM) of a and b, that is, $a \oplus b = $ LCM of a and b, and the meet of a and b, that is, $a * b$ is the greatest common divisor (GCD) of a and b.

EXAMPLE 3 Let n be a positive integer and S_n be the set of all divisors of n; for example, $n = 6$, $S_6 = \{1, 2, 3, 6\}$ and for $n = 24$, $S_{24} = \{1, 2, 3, 4, 6, 8, 12, 24\}$. Let D denote the relation of "division" as defined in Example 2. The

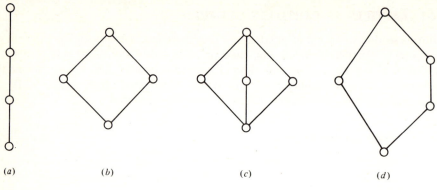

(a)   (b)   (c)   (d)

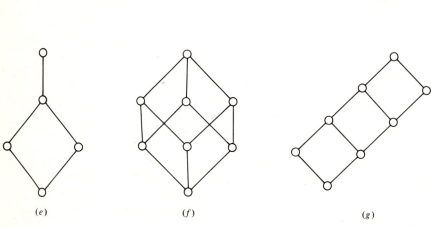

(e)   (f)   (g)

FIGURE 4-1.1   Lattices.

lattices $\langle S_6, D \rangle$, $\langle S_{24}, D \rangle$, $\langle S_8, D \rangle$, and $\langle S_{30}, D \rangle$ are given in Fig. 4-1.1b, g, a, and f respectively.

EXAMPLE 4   Let S be a nonempty set and $\Pi(S)$ be the set of all partitions of S. Two binary operations $*$ and $\oplus$ on $\Pi(S)$ were introduced in Sec. 3-2.1. We can also define a corresponding partial ordering relation $\leq$ on $\Pi(S)$ such that for $\Pi_1, \Pi_2 \in \Pi(S)$, $\Pi_1 \leq \Pi_2$ iff every block of Π_1 is a subset of some block of Π_2. It is easy to see that $\langle \Pi(S), \leq \rangle$ is a lattice in which the operations $*$ and $\oplus$ are the required meet and join respectively.

In particular, let $S = \{a, b, c\}$; then

$$\Pi(S) = \{\Pi_1, \Pi_2, \Pi_3, \Pi_4, \Pi_5\}$$

where $\Pi_1 = \{\overline{a, b, c}\}$ $\Pi_2 = \{\overline{a, b}, \overline{c}\}$ $\Pi_3 = \{\overline{a, c}, \overline{b}\}$

$\Pi_4 = \{\overline{a}, \overline{b, c}\}$ and $\Pi_5 = \{\overline{a}, \overline{b}, \overline{c}\}$

The diagram of $\langle \Pi(S), \leq \rangle$ is given in Fig. 4-1.1c.

One can show that there are 15 partitions of a set of four elements, 52 partitions of a set of five elements, and so on.

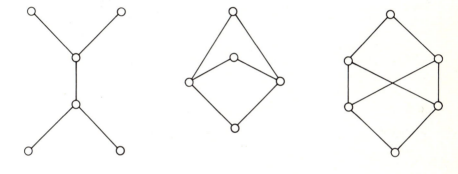

FIGURE 4-1.2 Partially ordered
sets which are not lattices.

The previous examples show that different lattices can be represented by
the same diagram except that the nodes have different labels. We show in Sec.
4-1.4 that different partially ordered sets may be represented by the same diagram if they are order-isomorphic.

Recall that for any partial ordering relation $\leq$ on a set S, the converse
relation $\geq$ is also a partial ordering relation on S. The diagram of $\langle S, \geq \rangle$ can
be obtained from that of $\langle S, \leq \rangle$ by simply turning it upside down. The partially
ordered sets $\langle S, \leq \rangle$ and $\langle S, \geq \rangle$ are called duals of each other. If $A \subseteq S$, then
LUB A with respect to the relation $\leq$ is the same as GLB A with respect to the
relation $\geq$, and vice versa. In other words, the GLB and LUB are interchanged
if we interchange the relations $\leq$ and $\geq$. In terms of lattices, we can say that the
operations of meet and join on $\langle L, \leq \rangle$ become the operations of join and meet
on $\langle L, \geq \rangle$. In any case, $\langle L, \geq \rangle$ is a lattice if $\langle L, \leq \rangle$ is a lattice. We may now
formulate the *principle of duality* of lattices as follows.

Any statement about lattices involving the operations $*$ and $\oplus$ and the relations $\leq$ and $\geq$ remains true if $*$ is replaced by $\oplus$, $\oplus$ by $*$, $\leq$ by $\geq$, and $\geq$ by $\leq$.

The operations $*$ and $\oplus$ are called *duals* of each other as are the relations $\leq$ and $\geq$. Similarly, the lattices $\langle L, \leq \rangle$ and $\langle L, \geq \rangle$ are called duals of each other.

EXERCISES 4-1.1

1 Explain why the partially ordered sets given in Fig. 4-1.2 are not lattices.

2 Draw the diagrams of lattices $\langle S_n, D \rangle$ given in Example 3 for $n = 4, 6, 10, 12, 15, 45, 60, 75,$ and 210. For what values of n do you expect $\langle S_n, D \rangle$ to be a chain?

3 Show that there are 15 partitions of a set of four elements. Draw the diagram of the corresponding lattice.

4 Show that the operations of meet and join on a lattice are commutative, associative, and idempotent.

5 Let $S = \{a, b, c\}$. Draw the diagram of $\langle \rho(S), \subseteq \rangle$.

6 Let **R** be the set of real numbers in $[0, 1]$ and $\leq$ be the usual operation of "less than or equal to" on **R**. Show that $\langle \mathbf{R}, \leq \rangle$ is a lattice. What are the operations of meet and join on this lattice?

7 Let the sets $S_0, S_1, \ldots, S_7$ be given by

$$S_0 = \{a, b, c, d, e, f\} \qquad S_1 = \{a, b, c, d, e\} \qquad S_2 = \{a, b, c, e, f\}$$

$$S_3 = \{a, b, c, e\} \qquad S_4 = \{a, b, c\} \qquad S_5 = \{a, b\} \qquad S_6 = \{a, c\} \qquad S_7 = \{a\}$$

Draw the diagram of $\langle L, \subseteq \rangle$ where $L = \{ S_0, S_1, \ldots, S_7 \}$.

4-1.2 Some Properties of Lattices

We shall first list some of the properties of the two binary operations of meet and join denoted by $*$ and $\oplus$ on a lattice $\langle L, \leq \rangle$. For any $a, b, c \in L$, we have

(L-1) $a * a = a$	**(L-1)**$'$ $a \oplus a = a$
	(Idempotent)
(L-2) $a * b = b * a$	**(L-2)**$'$ $a \oplus b = b \oplus a$
	(Commutative)
(L-3) $(a * b) * c = a * (b * c)$	**(L-3)**$'$ $(a \oplus b) \oplus c = a \oplus (b \oplus c)$
	(Associative)
(L-4) $a * (a \oplus b) = a$	**(L-4)**$'$ $a \oplus (a * b) = a$
	(Absorption)

The identities **(L-1)** to **(L-4)** can be proved using the definitions of the operators $*$ and $\oplus$. The identities **(L-1)**$'$ to **(L-4)**$'$ then follow from the principle of duality. The latter identities can also be proved directly. We shall prove the identity **(L-4)**.

For any $a \in L$, $a \leq a$ and $a \leq a \oplus b$ by definition of $\oplus$; hence $a \leq a * (a \oplus b)$. On the other hand, $a * (a \oplus b) \leq a$ by the definition of $*$. Therefore, $a * (a \oplus b) = a$.

These identities along with the following theorem will be used in defining a lattice as an algebraic system in the next section.

Theorem 4-1.1 Let $\langle L, \leq \rangle$ be a lattice in which $*$ and $\oplus$ denote the operations of meet and join respectively. For any $a, b \in L$,

$$a \leq b \Leftrightarrow a * b = a \Leftrightarrow a \oplus b = b$$

PROOF We shall first prove that $a \leq b \Leftrightarrow a * b = a$. In order to do this, let us assume that $a \leq b$. We also know that $a \leq a$. Therefore $a \leq a * b$. But from the definition of $a * b$, we have $a * b \leq a$. Hence $a \leq b \Rightarrow a * b = a$. Next, assume that $a * b = a$; but it is only possible if $a \leq b$, that is, $a * b = a \Rightarrow a \leq b$. Combining these two results, we get the required equivalence.

It is possible to show that $a \leq b \Leftrightarrow a \oplus b = b$ in a similar manner. Alternatively, from $a * b = a$, we have

$$b \oplus (a * b) = b \oplus a = a \oplus b$$

but

$$b \oplus (a * b) = b$$

Hence $a \oplus b = b$ follows from $a * b = a$. By repeating similar steps, we can show that $a * b = a$ follows from $a \oplus b = b$, and hence these are equivalent.

$$////$$

Theorem 4-1.1 establishes a connection between the partial ordering relation $\leq$ and the two binary operations $*$ and $\oplus$ on the meet and join in a lattice $\langle L, \leq \rangle$. We shall use this result in Sec. 4-1.3 to show that a lattice can be defined as an algebraic system. We now prove some basic inequalities that hold between the elements of a lattice.

Theorem 4-1.2 Let $\langle L, \leq \rangle$ be a lattice. For any $a, b, c \in L$, the following properties called *isotonicity* hold.

$$b \leq c \quad \Rightarrow \quad \begin{cases} a * b \leq a * c \\ \\ a \oplus b \leq a \oplus c \end{cases}$$

PROOF From Theorem 4-1.1,

$$b \leq c \Leftrightarrow b * c = b$$

To show that $a * b \leq a * c$, we shall show that

$$(a * b) * (a * c) = a * b$$

Note that

$$(a * b) * (a * c) = (a * a) * (b * c) = a * (b * c) = a * b$$

The second result can be proved in a similar manner. $////$

We shall now list some implications which hold for any $a, b, c \in L$ where $\langle L, \leq \rangle$ is a lattice. These implications follow from the definitions of the operations $*$ and $\oplus$ on L. They can also be proved by using the properties of isotonicity.

$$a \leq b \wedge a \leq c \Rightarrow a \leq b \oplus c \qquad (1)$$

$$a \leq b \wedge a \leq c \Rightarrow a \leq b * c \qquad (2)$$

Of course (1) is obvious from the definition of $\oplus$. Implication (2) can also be proved from the definition of $*$ and from the fact that both b and c are comparable to a. It can also be proved by using Theorem 4-1.2. In a similar manner, we can write the duals of (1) and (2) as

$$a \geq b \wedge a \geq c \Rightarrow a \geq b * c \qquad (3)$$

$$a \geq b \wedge a \geq c \Rightarrow a \geq b \oplus c \qquad (4)$$

We shall frequently employ these implications in our proofs.

Theorem 4-1.3 Let $\langle L, \leq \rangle$ be a lattice. For any $a, b, c \in L$, the following inequalities, called the *distributive inequalities*, hold:

$$a \oplus (b * c) \leq (a \oplus b) * (a \oplus c)$$

$$a * (b \oplus c) \geq (a * b) \oplus (a * c)$$

PROOF From $a \leq a \oplus b$ and $a \leq a \oplus c$ we have, using (2),

$$a \leq (a \oplus b) * (a \oplus c) \qquad (5)$$

$$b * c \leq b \leq a \oplus b$$

and

$$b * c \leq c \leq a \oplus c$$

Hence, by using (2) again we get

$$b * c \leq (a \oplus b) * (a \oplus c) \qquad (6)$$

From (5) and (6) and by using (4), we get the required inequality

$$a \oplus (b * c) \leq (a \oplus b) * (a \oplus c)$$

The second distributive inequality can be proved in a similar manner or by using the principle of duality. ////

Theorem 4-1.4 Let $\langle L, \leq \rangle$ be a lattice. For any $a, b, c \in L$ the following holds:

$$a \leq c \Leftrightarrow a \oplus (b * c) \leq (a \oplus b) * c \qquad (7)$$

PROOF Since $a \leq c \Leftrightarrow a \oplus c = c$ from Theorem 4-1.1, we get the required result by substituting c for $a \oplus c$ in the first distributive inequality. One could prove the above equivalence directly using an argument similar to the one given in the proof of Theorem 4-1.3. ////

The inequality given in Theorem 4-1.4 is called the *modular inequality*. There are other ways in which the modular inequalities are expressed:

$$(a * b) \oplus (a * c) \leq a * [b \oplus (a * c)] \qquad (8)$$

$$(a \oplus b) * (a \oplus c) \geq a \oplus [b * (a \oplus c)] \qquad (9)$$

The method of proof is similar to the one used in proving Theorem 4-1.3. We shall leave it as an exercise.

EXERCISES 4-1.2

1 Show that the identities (**L-1**) and (**L-1**)′ follow from the identities (**L-2**) to (**L-4**) and their duals.

2 Complete the proof of Theorem 4-1.1 by showing that in a lattice

$$a \leq b \Leftrightarrow a \oplus b = b$$

3 Show that in a lattice if $a \leq b \leq c$, then

$$a \oplus b = b * c$$

and
$$(a * b) \oplus (b * c) = b = (a \oplus b) * (a \oplus c)$$

4 Show that in a lattice if $a \leq b$ and $c \leq d$, then $a * c \leq b * d$.

5 In a lattice, show that

$$(a * b) \oplus (c * d) \leq (a \oplus c) * (b \oplus d)$$

$$(a * b) \oplus (b * c) \oplus (c * a) \leq (a \oplus b) * (b \oplus c) * (c \oplus a)$$

6 Show that a lattice with three or fewer elements is a chain.

7 Prove that every finite subset of a lattice has an LUB and a GLB. (*Hint:* Use the principle of mathematical induction.) What can you say about a finite lattice?

8 Prove inequalities (8) and (9).

9 Show that Theorem 4-1.4 is a self-dual.

4-1.3 Lattices as Algebraic Systems

In this section we define a lattice as an algebraic system on which it is possible to define a partial ordering relation. The advantage of considering a lattice as an algebraic system is that many concepts which are associated with algebraic systems can be applied to lattices as well. Thus it is possible to define sublattices, direct product of lattices, and also lattice homomorphisms.

> **Definition 4-1.2** A *lattice* is an algebraic system $\langle L, *, \oplus \rangle$ with two binary operations $*$ and $\oplus$ on L which are both (1) commutative and (2) associative and (3) satisfy the absorption laws. In other words, the operations $*$ and $\oplus$ satisfy the identities (**L-2**) to (**L-4**) and (**L-2**)′ to (**L-4**)′ given in Sec. 4-1.2.

The absence of the identities (**L-1**) and (**L-1**)′ in the definition here is due to the fact that (**L-4**) and its dual imply the identities (**L-1**) and (**L-1**)′ as follows. For any $a \in L$,

$$a * a = a * [a \oplus (a * a)] = a$$

where we have replaced the second a in $a * a$ by $a \oplus (a * a)$ and then from (**L-4**)′ obtained a in the second step. The identity $a \oplus a = a$ can be proved in a similar manner or by the principle of duality.

Note that Definition 4-1.2 does not assume the existence of any partial ordering on L. We shall now show that a partial ordering relation on L follows as a consequence of the properties of the operations $*$ and $\oplus$.

Let us define a relation R on L such that for $a, b \in L$

$$a \, R \, b \Leftrightarrow a * b = a$$

Obviously, for any $a \in L$, $a * a = a$, so that $a \, R \, a$, or the relation R is reflexive. Now for some $a, b \in L$ let us assume that $a \, R \, b$ and $b \, R \, a$, so that $a * b = a$ and $b * a = b$. But $a * b = b * a$, and so $a = b$. The assumptions $a \, R \, b$ and $b \, R \, a$ imply $a = b$, or that the relation R is antisymmetric. Finally, let us assume that for some $a, b, c \in L$, $a \, R \, b$ and $b \, R \, c$. This requires that $a * b = a$ and $b * c = b$. Thus, $a * c = (a * b) * c = a * (b * c) = a * b = a$, or $a \, R \, c$. The last step shows that the relation R is transitive. From this we can conclude that R is a partial ordering relation.

It is easy to show that $a * b = a \Leftrightarrow a \oplus b = b$. Hence we could have defined the same partial ordering relation R on L as

$$a \, R \, b \Leftrightarrow a \oplus b = b \qquad \text{for any } a, b \in L$$

Our next step is to show that for any two elements $a, b \in L$, the greatest lower bound and the least upper bound of $\{a, b\} \subseteq L$ with respect to the partial ordering R are $a * b$ and $a \oplus b$, respectively.

From the absorption laws $a * (a \oplus b) = a$ and $b * (a \oplus b) = b$, we have $a \, R \, (a \oplus b)$ and $b \, R \, (a \oplus b)$. Let us now assume that there exists an element $c \in L$ such that $a \, R \, c$ and $b \, R \, c$. This means that

$$a \oplus c = c \qquad \text{and} \qquad b \oplus c = c$$

or
$$(a \oplus c) \oplus (b \oplus c) = (a \oplus b) \oplus c = c \oplus c = c$$

implying that $(a \oplus b) \, R \, c$. The last step shows that $a \oplus b$ is the least upper bound of a and b. In a similar manner, we can show that $a * b$ is the greatest lower bound of $\{a, b\}$ with respect to the partial ordering relation R. We can summarize the discussion by saying that on a lattice $\langle L, *, \oplus \rangle$ it is possible to define a partial ordering relation R such that for any $a, b \in L$

$$a \, R \, b \Leftrightarrow a * b = a \Leftrightarrow a \oplus b = b$$

and that LUB $\{a, b\} = a \oplus b$ and GLB $\{a, b\} = a * b$ with respect to the relation R on L.

On the other hand, it was shown earlier in Sec. 4-1.1 that in a lattice $\langle L, \leq \rangle$ defined as a partially ordered set, it is possible to define two binary operations $*$ and $\oplus$ such that for any $a, b \in L$

$$a * b = \text{GLB } \{a, b\} \qquad \text{and} \qquad a \oplus b = \text{LUB } \{a, b\}$$

and

$$a \leq b \Leftrightarrow a * b = a \Leftrightarrow a \oplus b = b$$

where the operations $*$ and $\oplus$ are both commutative and associative and satisfy the absorption laws. This establishes the equivalence of the two definitions where the relation R is the same as the relation $\leq$ on L.

4-1.4 Sublattices, Direct Product, and Homomorphism

The advantage of defining a lattice as an algebraic system is that we can introduce the concept of sublattices in a natural way.

> **Definition 4-1.3** Let $\langle L, *, \oplus \rangle$ be a lattice and let $S \subseteq L$ be a subset of L. The algebra $\langle S, *, \oplus \rangle$ is a *sublattice* of $\langle L, *, \oplus \rangle$ iff S is closed under both operations $*$ and $\oplus$.

From the definition it follows that a sublattice itself is a lattice. However, any subset of L which is a lattice need not be a sublattice, as will be shown by an example. Note that for a partially ordered set the situation is simpler in the sense that every subset of a partially ordered set is also a partially ordered set under the same partial ordering relationship. Thus, if $\langle P, \leq \rangle$ is a partially ordered set and $Q \subseteq P$, then $\langle Q, \leq \rangle$ is also a partially ordered set.

For a lattice $\langle L, *, \oplus \rangle$ and for any two elements $a, b \in L$ such that $a \leq b$, the closed *interval* $[a, b]$ consisting of all the elements $x \in L$ such that $a \leq x \leq b$ is a sublattice of L.

EXAMPLE 1 Let $\langle L, \leq \rangle$ be a lattice in which $L = \{a_1, a_2, \ldots, a_8\}$ and S_1, S_2, and S_3 be the subsets of L given by $S_1 = \{a_1, a_2, a_4, a_6\}$, $S_2 = \{a_3, a_5, a_7, a_8\}$, and $S_3 = \{a_1, a_2, a_4, a_8\}$. The diagram of $\langle L, \leq \rangle$ is given in Fig. 4-1.3. Observe that $\langle S_1, \leq \rangle$ and $\langle S_2, \leq \rangle$ are sublattices of $\langle L, \leq \rangle$, but $\langle S_3, \leq \rangle$ is not a sublattice, because $a_2, a_4, \in S_3$ but $a_2 * a_4 = a_6 \notin S_3$. Note that $\langle S_3, \leq \rangle$ is a lattice.

EXAMPLE 2 The lattice of divisors of any positive integer n given in Example 3, Sec. 4-1.1, and denoted by $\langle S_n, D \rangle$ is a sublattice of $\langle I_+, D \rangle$ given in Example 2 of the same section.

EXAMPLE 3 Let S be any set and $\rho(S)$ be its power set. It was shown in Example 1, Sec. 4-1.1, that $\langle \rho(S), \subseteq \rangle$ is a lattice in which the meet and join are the usual operations of intersection and union respectively. A family of subsets of S such that for any two subsets A and B in this family both $A \cap B$ and $A \cup B$ are in the family, is obviously a sublattice of $\langle \rho(S), \subseteq \rangle$. Such a family is called a *ring of subsets* of S and is denoted by $\langle R(S), \subseteq \rangle$. The lattice $\langle R(S), \cap, \cup \rangle$ is not a ring in the sense of the definition of a ring given in Sec. 3-5.5; that is why some authors prefer to call it a *lattice of subsets*.

As a particular case of Example 3, let $S = \{p, q, r\}$. The diagram of the lattice $\langle \rho(S), \cap, \cup \rangle$ is the same as given in Fig. 4-1.3 in which $a_1 = S = \{p, q, r\}$, $a_2 = \{p, q\}$, $a_3 = \{p, r\}$, $a_4 = \{q, r\}$, $a_5 = \{p\}$, $a_6 = \{q\}$, $a_7 = \{r\}$, and $a_8 = \varnothing$. The sets S_1 and S_2 given in Example 1 are both examples of a ring of subsets of S and are sublattices of $\langle \rho(S), \cap, \cup \rangle$.

> **Definition 4-1.4** Let $\langle L, *, \oplus \rangle$ and $\langle S, \wedge, \vee \rangle$ be two lattices. The algebraic system $\langle L \times S, \cdot, + \rangle$ in which the binary operations $+$ and $\cdot$ on $L \times S$

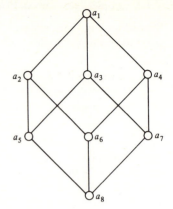

FIGURE 4-1.3

are such that for any $\langle a_1, b_1 \rangle$ and $\langle a_2, b_2 \rangle$ in $L \times S$

$$\langle a_1, b_1 \rangle \cdot \langle a_2, b_2 \rangle = \langle a_1 * a_2, b_1 \wedge b_2 \rangle$$

$$\langle a_1, b_1 \rangle + \langle a_2, b_2 \rangle = \langle a_1 \oplus a_2, b_1 \vee b_2 \rangle$$

is called the *direct product* of the lattices $\langle L, *, \oplus \rangle$ and $\langle S, \wedge, \vee \rangle$.

The operations $+$ and $\cdot$ on $L \times S$ are commutative and associative and satisfy the absorption laws because they are defined in terms of the operations $*$, $\oplus$ and $\wedge$, $\vee$. Therefore, the direct product is itself a lattice. Since $\langle L \times S, \cdot, + \rangle$ is a lattice, we can form a direct product of this lattice with another lattice, and so on. As before, we shall write $L \times L$ as L^2 and $L \times L \times L$ as L^3. The order of the lattice formed by the direct product of two lattices is equal to the product of the orders of the lattices appearing in the direct product. It should be noted that not all lattices can be written as a direct product of other lattices. The direct product of lattices can be used to construct large lattices from smaller ones.

EXAMPLE 4 Let $L = \{0, 1\}$ and the lattice $\langle L, \leq \rangle$ be as shown in Fig. 4-1.4. The lattices $\langle L^2, \leq_2 \rangle$, $\langle L^3, \leq_3 \rangle$ are shown in Fig. 4-1.4. In general, the diagram of $\langle L^n, \leq_n \rangle$ is an n cube.

Note that in the lattice $\langle L^n, \leq_n \rangle$ any element can be written as $\langle a_1, a_2, \ldots, a_n \rangle$ in which a_i is either 0 or 1 for $i = 1, 2, \ldots, n$. The partial ordering relation $\leq_n$ on L^n can be defined for any $a, b \in L^n$, where $a = \langle a_1, a_2, \ldots, a_n \rangle$ and $b = \langle b_1, b_2, \ldots, b_n \rangle$, as

$$a \leq_n b \Leftrightarrow a_i \leq b_i \qquad \text{for all } i = 1, 2, \ldots, n$$

where $\leq$ means the relation of "less than or equal to" on $\{0, 1\}$. The operations $*$ and $\oplus$ on L^n can also be defined easily. The lattice $\langle L^n, \leq_n \rangle$ will be called the *lattice of n-tuples of 0 and 1*.

EXAMPLE 5 Consider the chains of divisors of 4 and 9, that is, $L_1 = \{1, 2, 4\}$ and $L_2 = \{1, 3, 9\}$, and the partial ordering relation of "division" on L_1 and L_2. The lattice $L_1 \times L_2$ is shown in Fig. 4-1.5. Notice that the diagram of the lattice

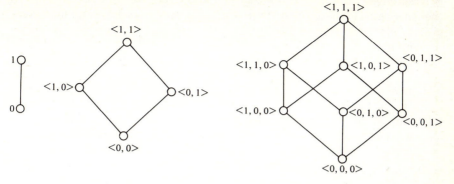

FIGURE 4-1.4

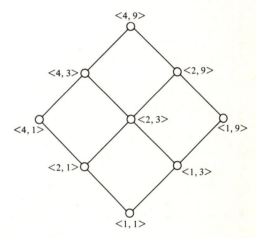

FIGURE 4-1.5

of divisors of 36 is the same as the one given in Fig. 4-1.5 except that the node $\langle a, b \rangle$ is replaced by the product ab.

Definition 4-1.5 Let $\langle L, *, \oplus \rangle$ and $\langle S, \wedge, \vee \rangle$ be two lattices. A mapping $g: L \to S$ is called a *lattice homomorphism* from the lattice $\langle L, *, \oplus \rangle$ to $\langle S, \wedge, \vee \rangle$ if for any $a, b \in L$,

$$g(a * b) = g(a) \wedge g(b) \qquad \text{and} \qquad g(a \oplus b) = g(a) \vee g(b)$$

Observe that both the operations of meet and join are preserved. There may be mappings which preserve only one of the two operations. Such mappings are not lattice homomorphisms.

Let $\langle L, *, \oplus \rangle$ and $\langle S, \wedge, \vee \rangle$ be two lattices and the partial ordering relations on L and S corresponding to the operations of meet and join be $\leq$ and

$\leq'$ respectively. If $g: L \to S$ is a homomorphism, then we show that g preserves the ordering relations also; i.e., for any $a, b \in L$ such that $a \leq b$, we must have $g(a) \leq' g(b)$.

From $a \leq b \Leftrightarrow a * b = a$, we have

$$g(a * b) = g(a) \wedge g(b) = g(a) \Leftrightarrow g(a) \leq' g(b)$$

This means $a \leq b \Rightarrow g(a) \leq' g(b)$ if g is a homomorphism.

If a homomorphism $g: L \to S$ of two lattices $\langle L, *, \oplus \rangle$ and $\langle S, \wedge, \vee \rangle$ is bijective, i.e., one-to-one onto, then g is called an *isomorphism*. If there exists an isomorphism between two lattices, then the lattices are called *isomorphic*.

If the lattices $\langle L, *, \oplus \rangle$ and $\langle S, \wedge, \vee \rangle$ are isomorphic and g denotes an isomorphism, then g preserves the ordering relation; i.e., for any $a, b \in L$, $a \leq b \Rightarrow g(a) \leq' g(b)$. In addition to this, we also have $g(a) \leq' g(b) \Rightarrow a \leq b$. This result also shows that the two lattices which are isomorphic can be represented by the same diagram in which the nodes are replaced by the images. This fact explains why we found that several different lattices could be represented by the same diagram.

EXAMPLE 6 Let S be any set containing n elements and $\rho(S)$ be its power set. The lattice $\langle \rho(S), \cap, \cup \rangle$ or $\langle \rho(S), \subseteq \rangle$ is isomorphic to the lattice $\langle L^n, \leq_n \rangle$ given in Example 4.

It is interesting to observe that the lattices with one, two, or three elements are isomorphic to the chains containing one, two, or three elements, respectively. On the other hand, any lattice of order 4 must be isomorphic to one of the two lattices given in Figs. 4-1.1 a and b. Similarly, any lattice of order 5 is isomorphic to one of the lattices whose diagrams are given in Fig. 4-1.6.

A homomorphism $g: L \to L$ where $\langle L, *, \oplus \rangle$ is a lattice is called an *endomorphism*. If $g: L \to L$ is an isomorphism, then g is called an *automorphism*.

It is interesting to observe that if $g: L \to L$ is an endomorphism, then the image set of g is a sublattice of L.

Although the concepts of homomorphism and isomorphism are associated with any algebraic system, we shall now show how these concepts can be applied to partially ordered sets also.

Definition 4-1.6 Let $\langle P, \leq \rangle$ and $\langle Q, \leq' \rangle$ be two partially ordered sets. A mapping $f: P \to Q$ is said to be *order-preserving* relative to the ordering $\leq$ in P and $\leq'$ in Q iff for any $a, b \in P$ such that $a \leq b$, $f(a) \leq' f(b)$ in Q.

If $\langle P, \leq \rangle$ and $\langle Q, \leq' \rangle$ are lattices and $g: P \to Q$ is a lattice homomorphism, then g is order-preserving.

Definition 4-1.7 Two partially ordered sets $\langle P, \leq \rangle$ and $\langle Q, \leq' \rangle$ are called *order-isomorphic* if there exists a mapping $f: P \to Q$ which is bijective and if both f and f^{-1} are order-preserving.

It may happen that a mapping $f: P \to Q$ is bijective and order-preserving, but that f^{-1} is not order-preserving (see Example 7). In such a case, P and Q are not order-isomorphic. For lattices $\langle L, \leq \rangle$ and $\langle S, \leq' \rangle$, an order isomorphism

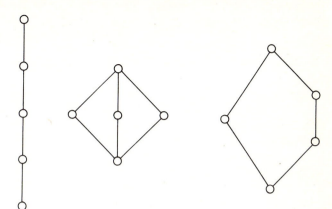

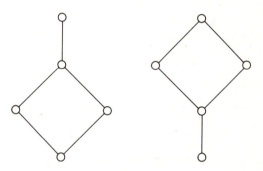

FIGURE 4-1.6   Lattices of order 5.

is equivalent to lattice isomorphism. Hence lattices which are order-isomorphic as partially ordered sets are isomorphic. The importance of order isomorphism lies in the fact that two partially ordered sets which are order-isomorphic can be represented by the same diagram.

EXAMPLE 7   Consider the lattice $\langle S_n, D \rangle$ for $n = 12$, that is, the lattice of divisors of 12 in which the partial ordering relation D means "division" as given in Example 3, Sec. 4-1.1. Consider another lattice $\langle S_n, \leq \rangle$ in which $\leq$ denotes the ordering relation "less than or equal to." A mapping $f\colon S_n \to S_n$ given by $f(x) = x$ is order-preserving and bijective, but f^{-1} is not order-preserving. Hence $\langle S_n, D \rangle$ and $\langle S_n, \leq \rangle$ are neither order-isomorphic nor isomorphic.

EXERCISES   4-1.4

1   For the lattice $\langle L, \subseteq \rangle$ given in Prob. 7 of Exercises 4-1.1, what are the operations of meet and join?

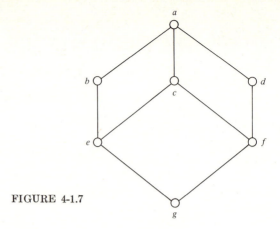

FIGURE 4-1.7

2 Show that the diagram given in Fig. 4-1.7 is a lattice, and it is not a sublattice of the lattice given in Fig. 4-1.1*f*.

3 Show that every interval of a lattice is a sublattice.

4 Find all the sublattices of the lattice $\langle S_n, D \rangle$ for $n = 12$.

5 Draw the diagram of a lattice which is the direct product of the five-element lattice shown in Fig. 4-1.1*c* and a two-element chain.

6 Show that the lattice $\langle S_n, D \rangle$ for $n = 216$ is isomorphic to the direct product of lattices for $n = 8$ and $n = 27$.

7 Show that there exists a mapping from the five-element lattice given in Fig. 4-1.1*c* to a three-element chain and that this mapping is order-preserving. Is it a homomorphism?

4-1.5 Some Special Lattices

In a lattice every pair of elements has a least upper bound and a greatest lower bound. As a consequence of this fact, one can show by using the principle of mathematical induction that every finite subset of a lattice has a least upper bound and a greatest lower bound. This, however, may not be the case for an infinite subset of a lattice. Consider, for example, the lattice $\langle \mathbf{I}_+, \leq \rangle$ in which $\mathbf{I}_+$ is the set of positive integers. The subset consisting of even positive integers has no least upper bound.

Let $\langle L, *, \oplus \rangle$ be a lattice and $S \subseteq L$ be a finite subset of L where $S = \{a_1, a_2, \ldots, a_n\}$. The greatest lower bound and the least upper bound of S can be expressed as

$$\text{GLB } S = \overset{n}{\underset{i=1}{*}} a_i \quad \text{and} \quad \text{LUB } S = \overset{n}{\underset{i=1}{\oplus}} a_i \qquad (1)$$

where

$$\overset{2}{\underset{i=1}{*}} a_i = a_1 * a_2 \quad \text{and} \quad \overset{k}{\underset{i=1}{*}} a_i = \overset{k-1}{\underset{i=1}{*}} a_i * a_k \qquad k = 3, 4, \ldots$$

A similar representation can be given for $\overset{n}{\underset{i=1}{\oplus}} a_i$. Because of the associativity of the operations $*$ and $\oplus$, we can write

$$\overset{n}{\underset{i=1}{*}} a_i = a_1 * a_2 * \cdots * a_n \qquad \text{and} \qquad \overset{n}{\underset{i=1}{\oplus}} a_i = a_1 \oplus a_2 \oplus \ldots \oplus a_n$$

Definition 4-1.8 A lattice is called *complete* if each of its nonempty subsets has a least upper bound and a greatest lower bound.

Obviously, every finite lattice must be complete. Also every complete lattice must have a least element and a greatest element. The least and the greatest elements of a lattice, if they exist, are called the *bounds* (*units, universal bounds*) of the lattice and are denoted by 0 and 1 respectively. A lattice which has both elements 0 and 1 is called a bounded lattice. For the lattice $\langle L, *, \oplus \rangle$ with $L = \{a_1, \ldots, a_n\}$,

$$\overset{n}{\underset{i=1}{*}} a_i = 0 \qquad \text{and} \qquad \overset{n}{\underset{i=1}{\oplus}} a_i = 1 \tag{2}$$

The bounds 0 and 1 of a lattice $\langle L, *, \oplus, 0, 1 \rangle$ satisfy the following identities. For any $a \in L$,

$$a \oplus 0 = a \qquad a * 1 = a \tag{3}$$

$$a \oplus 1 = 1 \qquad a * 0 = 0 \tag{4}$$

Obviously, 0 is the identity of the operation $\oplus$, and 1 is the identity of the operation $*$. Similarly, 0 and 1 are zeros with respect to the operations $*$ and $\oplus$ respectively. In a bounded lattice, 1 and 0 are duals of each other, and the principle of duality can now be extended to include the interchanges of 0 and 1. The identities in (3) are duals of each other, and so also are the identities in (4).

For bounded lattices it is possible to introduce the notion of a complement of an element in the following manner.

Definition 4-1.9 In a bounded lattice $\langle L, *, \oplus, 0, 1 \rangle$, an element $b \in L$ is called a *complement* of an element $a \in L$ if

$$a * b = 0 \qquad \text{and} \qquad a \oplus b = 1$$

Note that the definition of a complement is symmetric in a and b, so that b is a complement of a if a is a complement of b. Any element $a \in L$ may or may not have a complement. Furthermore, an element of L may have more than one complement in L.

From the identities (3) and (4) we have

$$0 * 1 = 0 \qquad \text{and} \qquad 0 \oplus 1 = 1 \tag{5}$$

which show that 0 and 1 are complements of each other. It is easy to show that 1 is the only complement of 0. Let us assume that $c \neq 1$ is a complement of 0 and $c \in L$; then

$$0 * c = 0 \qquad \text{and} \qquad 0 \oplus c = 1$$

However, $0 \oplus c = c$ from (3), and $c \neq 1$ leads to a contradiction. In a similar manner we can show that 0 is the only complement of 1.

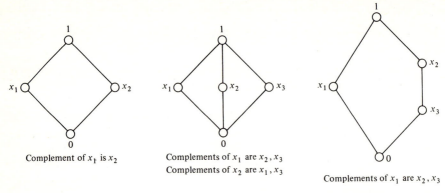

FIGURE 4-1.8   Complements in lattices.

Definition 4-1.10   A lattice $\langle L, *, \oplus, 0, 1 \rangle$ is said to be a *complemented lattice* if every element of L has at least one complement.

In Fig. 4-1.8 some lattices are shown, and the complements of some of the elements are noted below the diagrams.

EXAMPLE 1   Let $\langle L^n, \leq_n \rangle$ be the lattice of n-tuples of 0 and 1 given in Example 4, Sec. 4-1.4. This is a complemented lattice in which every element has a unique complement. The complement of an element of L^n can be obtained by interchanging 1 by 0 and 0 by 1 in the n-tuple representing the element. As a special case, let $n = 3$. The bounds of $\langle L^3, \leq_3 \rangle$ are $\langle 0, 0, 0 \rangle$ and $\langle 1, 1, 1 \rangle$. The complement of $\langle 1, 0, 1 \rangle$ is $\langle 0, 1, 0 \rangle$.

EXAMPLE 2   The lattice $\langle \rho(S), \subseteq \rangle$ of the power set of any set S is isomorphic to the lattice $\langle L^n, \leq_n \rangle$ provided S has n elements. The meet and join operations on $\rho(S)$ are $\cap$ and $\cup$ respectively, while the bounds are $\varnothing$ and S. The lattice $\langle \rho(S), \subseteq \rangle$ is a complemented lattice in which the complement of any subset A of S is the set $S - A$.

It was shown in Theorem 4-1.3 that the elements of any lattice satisfy the distributive inequalities. We shall now define a special class of lattices as follows.

Definition 4-1.11   A lattice $\langle L, *, \oplus \rangle$ is called a *distributive lattice* if for any $a, b, c \in L$,

$$a * (b \oplus c) = (a * b) \oplus (a * c) \qquad (6)$$

and
$$a \oplus (b * c) = (a \oplus b) * (a \oplus c) \qquad (7)$$

In other words, in a distributive lattice the operations $*$ and $\oplus$ distribute over each other.

It may be mentioned here that the equalities (6) and (7) are equivalent to one another (see Prob. 7, Exercises 4-1.5), and it is sufficient to verify any

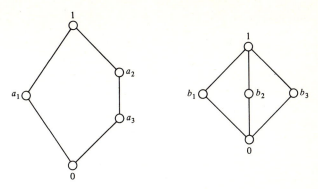

FIGURE 4-1.9 Lattices which are not distributive.

one of these two equalities for all possible combinations of the elements of a lattice. Note that the distributive equalities may be satisfied by some elements of a lattice, but this does not guarantee that the lattice is distributive (see Example 3).

The lattices given in Examples 1 and 2 are distributive lattices.

EXAMPLE 3 Show that the lattices given by the diagrams in Fig. 4-1.9 are not distributive.

SOLUTION

$$a_3 * (a_1 \oplus a_2) = a_3 * 1 = a_3 = (a_3 * a_1) \oplus (a_3 * a_2)$$
$$a_1 * (a_2 \oplus a_3) = 0 = (a_1 * a_2) \oplus (a_1 * a_3)$$

but

$$a_2 * (a_1 \oplus a_3) = a_2 * 1 = a_2$$
$$(a_2 * a_1) \oplus (a_2 * a_3) = 0 \oplus a_3 = a_3$$

Hence the lattice is not distributive. In the other case, $b_1 * (b_2 \oplus b_3) = b_1$ while $(b_1 * b_2) \oplus (b_1 * b_3) = 0$, which shows that the lattice is not distributive.

////

The two five-element lattices given in Fig. 4-1.9 are important because of a theorem which states that a lattice is distributive iff no sublattice is isomorphic to either of the two five-element lattices given there. We shall not prove this theorem.

The following theorems show that certain lattices are always distributive.

Theorem 4-1.5 Every chain is a distributive lattice.

PROOF Let $\langle L, \leq \rangle$ be a chain and $a, b, c \in L$. Consider the following possible cases: (1) $a \leq b$ or $a \leq c$, and (2) $a \geq b$ and $a \geq c$. We shall now show that the distributive law (6) is satisfied by a, b, c.

For (1),

$$a * (b \oplus c) = a \quad \text{and} \quad (a * b) \oplus (a * c) = a$$

For (2),

$$a * (b \oplus c) = b \oplus c \quad \text{and} \quad (a * b) \oplus (a * c) = b \oplus c \qquad ////$$

Theorem 4-1.6 The direct product of any two distributive lattices is a distributive lattice.

PROOF   The proof of the theorem follows from the definition of direct product. ////

In addition to these distributive lattices, we also have that any sublattice of a distributive lattice is distributive.

Observe that the distributive laws as stated in Eqs. (6) and (7) are duals of each other; therefore, the principle of duality holds for all distributive lattices.

The following are some examples of distributive lattices.

EXAMPLE 4   The ring of subsets of a given set S defined in Example 3, Sec. 4-1.4, and denoted by $\langle R(S), \cap, \cup \rangle$ is a distributive lattice, because of the fact that both set union and set intersection satisfy the distributive laws.

EXAMPLE 5   The lattice $\langle \mathbf{I}_+, D \rangle$ given in Example 2, Sec. 4-1.1, is a distributive lattice, and so also are the sublattices $\langle S_n, D \rangle$ for any positive integer n.

The following interesting theorem holds for a distributive lattice.

Theorem 4-1.7 Let $\langle L, *, \oplus \rangle$ be a distributive lattice. For any a, b, $c \in L$,

$$(a * b = a * c) \wedge (a \oplus b = a \oplus c) \Rightarrow b = c$$

PROOF

$$(a * b) \oplus c = (a * c) \oplus c = c$$

$$(a * b) \oplus c = (a \oplus c) * (b \oplus c) = (a \oplus b) * (b \oplus c)$$

$$= b \oplus (a * c) = b \oplus (a * b) = b \qquad ////$$

An important consequence of this theorem is that in a distributive lattice, if an element $a \in L$ has a complement, then it must be unique. Suppose that b and c are complements of a; then

$$a * b = a * c = 0 \quad \text{and} \quad a \oplus b = a \oplus c = 1$$

But from Theorem 4-1.7 this means $b = c$.

Recall that a lattice is called complemented if every element of the lattice has at least one complement. If we now consider those lattices which are complemented as well as distributive, then we are assured that every element of such a lattice has a unique complement, and we denote the complement of an element $a \in L$ by a'. Lattices which are complemented and distributive are called Boolean algebras. We shall study such lattices in detail in the next section.

It may be mentioned here that the converse of Theorem 4-1.7 also holds. We shall, however, omit the proof.

EXERCISES 4-1.5

1 Find the complements of every element of the lattice $\langle S_n, D \rangle$ for $n = 75$.
2 Show that in a lattice with two or more elements, no element is its own complement.
3 Show that a chain of three or more elements is not complemented.
4 Which of the two lattices $\langle S_n, D \rangle$ for $n = 30$ and $n = 45$ are complemented? Are these lattices distributive?
5 Show that De Morgan's laws, given by

$$(a * b)' = a' \oplus b' \quad \text{and} \quad (a \oplus b)' = a' * b'$$

hold in a complemented, distributive lattice.
6 Show that in a complemented, distributive lattice

$$a \le b \Leftrightarrow a * b' = 0 \Leftrightarrow a' \oplus b = 1 \Leftrightarrow b' \le a'$$

7 Show that Eqs. (6) and (7) are equivalent.
8 Show that a lattice is distributive iff

$$(a * b) \oplus (b * c) \oplus (c * a) = (a \oplus b) * (b \oplus c) * (c \oplus a)$$

9 Show that in a distributive lattice, the distributive laws can be generalized as

$$a * \left(\bigoplus_{i=1}^{n} b_i \right) = \bigoplus_{i=1}^{n} (a * b_i) \quad \text{and} \quad a \oplus \left(\mathop{*}_{i=1}^{n} b_i \right) = \mathop{*}_{i=1}^{n} (a \oplus b_i)$$

10 Show that in a bounded distributive lattice, the elements which have complements form a sublattice.
11 A lattice is said to be *modular* if

$$a \le c \Rightarrow a \oplus (b * c) = (a \oplus b) * c$$

Show that every distributive lattice is modular, but not conversely.

4-2 BOOLEAN ALGEBRA

The example of the power set $\rho(S)$ of a nonempty set S appeared throughout our discussion of lattices. It is not accidental. In fact, we first started with a general algebraic system called a lattice and gradually imposed those conditions on lattices which are satisfied by the lattice of the power set. Our aim was to arrive at an algebraic system which has all the essential characteristics of the lattice of the power set. Once this is done, we arrive at an abstract algebraic system which will be shown to be isomorphic to the lattice of the power set of a set. Many other algebraic systems such as the statement algebra and switching algebra are also special cases of such an algebraic system called Boolean algebra. We shall be concerned with only finite Boolean algebras in this chapter.

4-2.1 Definition and Examples

Definition 4-2.1 A *Boolean algebra* is a complemented, distributive lattice.

A Boolean algebra will generally be denoted by $\langle B, *, \oplus, ', 0, 1 \rangle$ in which $\langle B, *, \oplus \rangle$ is a lattice with two binary operations $*$ and $\oplus$ called the meet and join respectively. The corresponding partially ordered set will be denoted by $\langle B, \leq \rangle$. The bounds of the lattice are denoted by 0 and 1, where 0 is the least element and 1 the greatest element of $\langle B, \leq \rangle$. Since $\langle B, *, \oplus \rangle$ is complemented and because of the fact that it is a distributive lattice, each element of B has a unique complement. We shall denote the unary operation of complementation by $'$, so that for any $a \in B$, the complement of a is denoted by $a' \in B$.

Most of the properties of a Boolean algebra have been derived in the previous section. We shall list some of the important properties here. It may be mentioned that the properties listed here are not independent of each other. There are redundancies, but our list is chosen because of the importance of these properties.

A Boolean algebra $\langle B, *, \oplus, ', 0, 1 \rangle$ satisfies the following properties in which a, b, and c denote any elements of the set B.

1 $\langle B, *, \oplus \rangle$ is a lattice in which the operations $*$ and $\oplus$ satisfy the following identities:

(L-1) $a * a = a$	**(L-1)'** $a \oplus a = a$
(L-2) $a * b = b * a$	**(L-2)'** $a \oplus b = b \oplus a$
(L-3) $(a * b) * c = a * (b * c)$	**(L-3)'** $(a \oplus b) \oplus c = a \oplus (b \oplus c)$
(L-4) $a * (a \oplus b) = a$	**(L-4)'** $a \oplus (a * b) = a$

(See Sec. 4-1.2 for these identities.)

2 $\langle B, *, \oplus \rangle$ is a distributive lattice and satisfies these identities:

(D-1) $a * (b \oplus c) = (a * b) \oplus (a * c)$

(D-2) $a \oplus (b * c) = (a \oplus b) * (a \oplus c)$

(D-3) $(a * b) \oplus (b * c) \oplus (c * a) = (a \oplus b) * (b \oplus c) * (c \oplus a)$

(D-4) $a * b = a * c$, and $a \oplus b = a \oplus c \Rightarrow b = c$

(See Definition 4-1.11, Theorem 4-1.7, and Prob. 8 of Exercises 4-1.5.)

3 $\langle B, *, \oplus, 0, 1 \rangle$ is a bounded lattice in which for any $a \in B$, the following hold:

(B-1) $0 \leq a \leq 1$

(B-2) $a * 0 = 0$ **(B-2)'** $a \oplus 1 = 1$

(B-3) $a * 1 = a$ **(B-3)'** $a \oplus 0 = a$

[See identities (3) and (4) in Sec. 4-1.5.]

4 $\langle B, *, \oplus, ', 0, 1 \rangle$ is a uniquely complemented lattice in which the complement of any element $a \in B$ is denoted by $a' \in B$ and satisfies the following identities:

(**C-1**) $a * a' = 0$ (**C-1**)′ $a \oplus a' = 1$

(**C-2**) $0' = 1$ (**C-2**)′ $1' = 0$

(**C-3**) $(a * b)' = a' \oplus b'$ (**C-3**)′ $(a \oplus b)' = a' * b'$

(See Definition 4-1.9 and Prob. 5, Exercises 4-1.5.)

  5 There exists a partial ordering relation $\leq$ on B such that

(**P-1**) $a * b = \text{GLB } \{a, b\}$ (**P-1**)′ $a \oplus b = \text{LUB } \{a, b\}$

(**P-2**) $a \leq b \Leftrightarrow a * b = a \Leftrightarrow a \oplus b = b$

(**P-3**) $a \leq b \Leftrightarrow a * b' = 0 \Leftrightarrow b' \leq a' \Leftrightarrow a' \oplus b = 1$

(See Theorem 4-1.1 and Prob. 6, Exercises 4-1.5.)

As pointed out earlier, not all the identities given here are independent of one another. These identities arose by looking at a Boolean algebra as a special lattice. It is possible to define a Boolean algebra as an abstract algebraic system satisfying certain properties which are independent of each other. In fact, even the two binary operations $*$ and $\oplus$, the unary operation $'$, and the two distinguished elements are not all independent. One can define a Boolean algebra in terms of the operations $*$ and $'$ and a set of independent properties satisfied by these operations. We shall not, however, concern ourselves with this approach.

EXAMPLE 1 Let $B = \{0, 1\}$ be a set. The operations $*$, $\oplus$, and $'$ on B are given by Table 4-2.1. The algebra $\langle B, *, \oplus, ', 0, 1 \rangle$ satisfies all the properties listed here and is one of the simplest examples of a two-element Boolean algebra. A two-element Boolean algebra is the only Boolean algebra whose diagram is a chain.

EXAMPLE 2 Let S be a nonempty set and $\rho(S)$ be its power set. The set algebra $\langle \rho(S), \cap, \cup, \sim, \varnothing, S \rangle$ is a Boolean algebra in which the complement of any subset $A \subseteq S$ is $\sim A = S - A$, the relative complement of the set A. If S has n elements, then $\rho(S)$ has 2^n elements and the diagram of the Boolean algebra is an n cube. The partial ordering relation on $\rho(S)$ corresponding to the operations $\cap$ and $\cup$ is the subset relation $\subseteq$. The diagrams for the Boolean algebra $\langle \rho(S), \cap, \cup \rangle$ when S has 1, 2, and 3 elements are given in Fig. 4-2.1. If S is an empty set, then $\rho(S)$ has only one element, viz., $\varnothing$, so that $\varnothing = 0 = 1$, and the corresponding Boolean algebra is a degenerate Boolean algebra. We shall consider nondegenerate Boolean algebras only.

Table 4-2.1

$*$	0	1	$\oplus$	0	1	x	x'
0	0	0	0	0	1	0	1
1	0	1	1	1	1	1	0

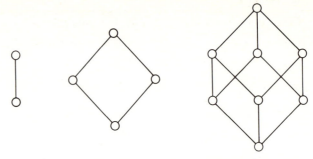

FIGURE 4-2.1   Boolean algebra of power sets.

EXAMPLE 3   Let S denote the set of statement formulas involving n statement variables. The algebraic system $\langle S, \wedge, \vee, \daleth, \mathbf{F}, \mathbf{T} \rangle$ is a Boolean algebra in which $\wedge$, $\vee$, and $\daleth$ denote the operations of conjunction, disjunction, and negation respectively. The elements $\mathbf{F}$ and $\mathbf{T}$ denote the formulas which are contradictions and tautologies respectively. Two statement formulas which are equivalent to one another are considered as equal. The partial ordering relation corresponding to the operations $\wedge$ and $\vee$ is the implication $\Rightarrow$ defined in Chap. 1.

EXAMPLE 4   Let B_n be the set of n-tuples whose members are either 0 or 1. Thus $a \in B_n$ iff $a = \langle a_1, a_2, \ldots, a_n \rangle$ where $a_i = 0$ or 1 for $i = 1, 2, \ldots, n$. Let us define for any $a = \langle a_1, a_2, \ldots, a_n \rangle$, $b = \langle b_1, b_2, \ldots, b_n \rangle$, and $a, b \in B_n$

$$a * b = \langle a_1 \wedge b_1, a_2 \wedge b_2, \ldots, a_n \wedge b_n \rangle$$

$$a \oplus b = \langle a_1 \vee b_1, a_2 \vee b_2, \ldots, a_n \vee b_n \rangle$$

$$a' = \langle \daleth a_1, \daleth a_2, \ldots, \daleth a_n \rangle$$

where $\wedge$, $\vee$, and $\daleth$ are the usual logical operations on $\{0, 1\}$. The algebra $\langle B_n, *, \oplus, ', 0_n, 1_n \rangle$ is a Boolean algebra in which 0_n and 1_n are n-tuples whose members are all 0s and 1s respectively. This algebra is known as a *switching algebra* and represents a switching network with n inputs and one output.

In a Boolean algebra it is possible to show that the associativity laws (**L-3**) and (**L-3**)$'$, the distributive laws (**D-1**) and (**D-2**), and De Morgan's laws (**C-3**) and (**C-3**)$'$ can be generalized over any finite number of elements by using the principle of mathematical induction. We shall simply state these generalized laws. For this purpose, let $S = \{a_1, a_2, \ldots, a_n\}$ and $T = \{b_1, b_2, \ldots, b_m\}$ and let $a_1, a_2, \ldots, a_n, b_1, b_2, \ldots, b_m$ be the elements of a Boolean algebra; then

$$\left(\underset{S}{*} a_i \right) * \left(\underset{T}{*} b_j \right) = \underset{S \cup T}{*} c_k$$

where

$$\underset{S}{*} a_i = a_1 * a_2 * \cdots * a_n$$

$$\underset{T}{*} b_j = b_1 * b_2 * \cdots * b_m$$

$$\underset{S \cup T}{*} c_k = a_1 * a_2 * \cdots * a_n * b_1 * b_2 * \cdots * b_m$$

The order in which the elements $a_1, a_2, \ldots, b_1, b_2, \ldots$ appear in these expressions is unimportant. Similarly, the generalized distributive laws are

$$(\underset{S}{*} a_i) \oplus (\underset{T}{*} b_j) = \underset{S \times T}{*} (a_i \oplus b_j)$$

$$(\underset{S}{\oplus} a_i) * (\underset{T}{\oplus} b_j) = \underset{S \times T}{\oplus} (a_i * b_j)$$

The generalized De Morgan's laws are

$$(\underset{S}{*} a_i)' = \underset{S}{\oplus} a_i' \quad \text{and} \quad (\underset{S}{\oplus} a_i)' = \underset{S}{*} a_i'$$

Using the above results, we can also write

$$[(\underset{S}{*} a_i) \oplus (\underset{T}{*} b_j)]' = \underset{S \times T}{\oplus} (a_i' * b_j')$$

$$[(\underset{S}{\oplus} a_i) * (\underset{T}{\oplus} b_j)]' = \underset{S \times T}{*} (a_i' \oplus b_j')$$

4-2.2 Subalgebra, Direct Product, and Homomorphism

Definition 4-2.2 Let $\langle B, *, \oplus, ', 0, 1 \rangle$ be a Boolean algebra and $S \subseteq B$. If S contains the elements 0 and 1 and is closed under the operations $*$, $\oplus$, and $'$, then $\langle S, *, \oplus, ', 0, 1 \rangle$ is called a *sub-Boolean algebra*.

In practice it is not necessary to check for closure with respect to all three operations $*$, $\oplus$, and $'$, nor is it necessary to check whether 0 and 1 are in S. Only closure with respect to the set of operations $\{ *, ' \}$ or $\{ \oplus, ' \}$ is enough to guarantee that S is a subalgebra. This argument follows from the fact that these sets of operations are functionally complete in a Boolean algebra, because for any $a, b \in B$

$$a \oplus b = (a' * b')' \qquad \text{also} \qquad 1 = (a * a')' \qquad \text{and} \qquad 0 = a * a'$$

so that closure with respect to $*$ and $'$ guarantees closure with respect to $\oplus$ as well as the existence of 0 and 1 in the subalgebra, and similarly for the set $\{ \oplus, ' \}$.

Our definition of a sub-Boolean algebra implies that it is a Boolean algebra. A subset of a Boolean algebra can be a Boolean algebra; however, it may not be a sub-Boolean algebra because it is not closed with respect to the operations in B. We shall show this fact by means of an example (see Example 1 in this subsection).

For any Boolean algebra $\langle B, *, \oplus, ', 0, 1 \rangle$, the subsets $\{0, 1\}$ and the set B are both sub-Boolean algebras. In addition to these sub-Boolean algebras, consider now any element $a \in B$ such that $a \neq 0$ and $a \neq 1$ and consider the set $\{a, a', 0, 1\}$. Obviously this set is a sub-Boolean algebra of the given Boolean algebra. Every element of B generates a sub-Boolean algebra. More generally, any subset of B generates a sub-Boolean algebra. We shall study Boolean algebras generated by a set of elements later in Sec. 4-3.1.

EXAMPLE 1 Consider the Boolean algebra given in Fig. 4-2.2. Let the subsets be

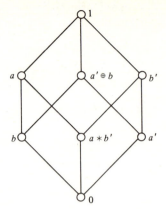

FIGURE 4-2.2

$$S_1 = \{a, a', 0, 1\}$$
$$S_2 = \{a' \oplus b, a * b', 0, 1\}$$
$$S_3 = \{a * b', b', a, 1\}$$
$$S_4 = \{b', a * b', a', 0\}$$
$$S_5 = \{a, b', 0, 1\}$$

The subsets S_1 and S_2 are sub-Boolean algebras. The subsets S_3 and S_4 are Boolean algebras, but not sub-Boolean algebras of the given algebra. The subset S_5 is not even a Boolean algebra.

Let $\langle B_1, *_1, \oplus_1, {}', 0_1, 1_1 \rangle$ and $\langle B_2, *_2, \oplus_2, {}'', 0_2, 1_2 \rangle$ be two Boolean algebras. The *direct product* of the two Boolean algebras is defined to be a Boolean algebra that is given by $\langle B_1 \times B_2, *_3, \oplus_3, {}''', 0_3, 1_3 \rangle$ in which the operations are defined for any $\langle a_1, b_1 \rangle$ and $\langle a_2, b_2 \rangle \in B_1 \times B_2$ as

$$\langle a_1, b_1 \rangle *_3 \langle a_2, b_2 \rangle = \langle a_1 *_1 a_2, b_1 *_2 b_2 \rangle$$
$$\langle a_1, b_1 \rangle \oplus_3 \langle a_2, b_2 \rangle = \langle a_1 \oplus_1 a_2, b_1 \oplus_2 b_2 \rangle$$
$$\langle a_1, b_1 \rangle''' = \langle a_1', b_1'' \rangle$$
$$0_3 = \langle 0_1, 0_2 \rangle \qquad \text{and} \qquad 1_3 = \langle 1_1, 1_2 \rangle$$

The direct product of Boolean algebras enables us to generate new Boolean algebras. Thus from the 2-element Boolean algebra given in Example 1, Sec. 4-2.1, we can generate $B \times B = B^2$, $B \times B \times B = B^3$, etc., and finally the Boolean algebra of n-tuples given in Example 4, Sec. 4-2.1, which is B^n.

Let $\langle B, *, \oplus, {}', 0, 1 \rangle$ and $\langle P, \cap, \cup, -, \alpha, \beta \rangle$ be two Boolean algebras. A mapping $f: B \to P$ is called a *Boolean homomorphism* if all the operations of the Boolean algebra are preserved, i.e., for any $a, b \in B$

$$f(a * b) = f(a) \cap f(b) \qquad f(a \oplus b) = f(a) \cup f(b)$$
$$f(a') = \overline{f(a)} \qquad f(0) = \alpha \qquad \text{and} \qquad f(1) = \beta$$

As before, the above definition of homomorphism can be simplified by asserting that $f: B \to P$ preserves either the operations $*$ and $'$ or the operations $\oplus$ and $'$. It is easy to see that this definition implies the previous definition.

Suppose that, instead of preserving the operations which are functionally complete, we now consider a mapping $g: B \to P$ in which the operations $*$ and $\oplus$ are preserved. In other words, let g be a lattice homomorphism. Naturally, g preserves the order, and hence it maps the bounds 0 and 1 into the least and the greatest elements respectively of the image set $g(B) \subseteq P$. It is, however, not necessary that $g(0) = \alpha$ and $g(1) = \beta$. The complements, if defined in terms of $g(0)$ and $g(1)$ in $g(B)$, are preserved, and $\langle g(B), \cap, \cup, -, g(0), g(1) \rangle$ is a Boolean algebra. Note that $g: B \to P$ is not a Boolean homomorphism, although $g: B \to g(B)$ is. In any case, for any mapping from a Boolean algebra which preserves the operations $*$ and $\oplus$, the image set is a Boolean algebra.

We shall now consider some properties of a Boolean algebra that will eventually lead us to an important theorem in Boolean algebra. This theorem states that any Boolean algebra is isomorphic to a power set algebra $\langle \rho(S), \cap, \cup, \sim, \varnothing, S \rangle$ for some set S. This theorem is known as *Stone's representation theorem* and is valid for any Boolean algebra. We shall, however, restrict our discussion to finite Boolean algebras.

Let $\langle B, *, \oplus, ', 0, 1 \rangle$ be a Boolean algebra and $a_1, a_2, \ldots$ denote the elements of B. It is possible to write well-formed expressions involving the elements of B, the operations $*$, $\oplus$, and $'$, and the parentheses wherever necessary. The following are some of the examples of such expressions:

$$a_1 \qquad a_1 * a_2' \qquad (a_1 * a_3)' \oplus (a_3' \oplus a_4)' \qquad (a_1 \oplus a_2) * (a_1 \oplus a_3) * a_2'$$

Because of the fact that B is closed under the operations $*$, $\oplus$, and $'$, each expression represents a particular element of the Boolean algebra B. Every such expression represents a definite element, although various different expressions may represent the same element. We study the general problem of equality of expressions in Sec. 4-3.1. For the present, let us confine our attention to only those elements of B which can be expressed as the join of two or more elements of B. Naturally, there are elements of B which cannot be expressed as the join of two or more elements. Such elements are called *join-irreducible*. In fact the idea of join-irreducible is more general, and we define it as follows.

Definition 4-2.3 Let $\langle L, *, \oplus \rangle$ be a lattice. An element $a \in L$ is called *join-irreducible* if it cannot be expressed as the join of two distinct elements of L. In other words, $a \in L$ is join-irreducible if for any $a_1, a_2 \in L$

$$a = a_1 \oplus a_2 \Rightarrow (a = a_1) \lor (a = a_2)$$

In the case of a Boolean algebra, it can be shown that the only elements which are join-irreducible are those which cover the least element 0. Such elements are called the *atoms* of the Boolean algebra. It is also possible to show that except for the least element 0 and the atoms, every other element of a Boolean algebra can be represented as the join of two or more atoms of the algebra and that this representation is unique. We shall demonstrate this idea by some examples of Boolean algebras whose diagrams are given in Fig. 4-2.3.

Let us consider the set $S = \{a_1, a_2, \ldots, a_n\}$ of the atoms of a Boolean

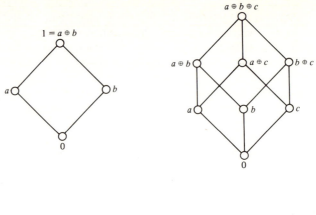

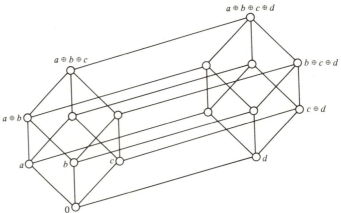

FIGURE 4-2.3

algebra $\langle B_n, *, \oplus, ', 0, 1\rangle$. Note that every element of B_n, except the atoms themselves and the least element 0, can be expressed as the join of some of its atoms. In fact, every such join represents an element of B_n. Consider all possible subsets of S and associate with each subset of S a Boolean expression consisting of the join of the elements of the subset. This means that we associate an element of B_n with every subset consisting of two or more elements of S. Let us now associate the element $a_i \in B_n$ with the subsets such as $\{a_i\} \subseteq S$ and the element $0 \in B_n$ with the subset $\varnothing \subseteq S$. In this way, we have associated with each subset of S a Boolean expression consisting of the join of the elements of the subset, and each such expression is distinct and represents an element of B_n. This association establishes a one-to-one correspondence between the subsets of S and the elements of B_n. It is possible to show that such a one-to-one correspondence preserves the operations $*$, $\oplus$, and $'$; that is, the Boolean algebra $\langle B_n, *, \oplus, ', 0, 1\rangle$ is isomorphic to the power set algebra $\langle \rho(S), \cap, \cup, \sim, \varnothing, S\rangle$. This result explains why the diagrams of Boolean algebras given so far are all n cubes containing 2^n elements for $n = 1, 2, \ldots$. This also shows that a Boolean algebra is completely specified by its atoms.

Let us now determine those atoms which are present in the join representation of a particular element of the Boolean algebra $\langle B_n, *, \oplus, ', 0, 1 \rangle$ for which the set of atoms is $S = \{a_1, a_2, \ldots, a_n\}$. Let $a \in B_n$ be any element of B_n such that $a = a_i \oplus a_j \oplus a_k$ for some $a_i, a_j, a_k \in S$. Obviously, $a_i \leq a$, $a_j \leq a$, and $a_k \leq a$. Next, let $a_h \in S$ be such that $a_h \leq a$ and such that $a_h \neq a_i, a_h \neq a_j,$ and $a_h \neq a_k$. This means

$$a_h = a_h * a = a_h * (a_i \oplus a_j \oplus a_k) = (a_h * a_i) \oplus (a_h * a_j) \oplus (a_h * a_k) = 0$$

But $a_h \neq 0$ because it is an atom; hence we have a contradiction, showing that any atom which is $\leq a$ must appear in the join representation of the element a. Also no atom is $\geq a$ unless $a = 0$. This result shows that for any element of B_n only those atoms appear in the join representation which are $\leq$ the element. Those atoms which are incomparable with the element do not appear in such a join representation.

The atoms of a Boolean algebra are also called its *minterms*. It follows from the previous discussion that every element of a Boolean algebra except the element 0 can be expressed as the join of its minterms. The use of the term "minterm" will become clear in Sec. 4-3.1 when we discuss the Boolean forms.

Instead of representing the elements of a Boolean algebra in terms of the join of their atoms, we could also represent the elements in terms of the meet of their *antiatoms*, where the antiatoms which are also called the *maxterms* are those elements of the Boolean algebra which are covered by the greatest element 1. In fact, the antiatoms are the complements of the atoms. Because of the principle of duality, the whole discussion can be repeated by interchanging $*$ by $\oplus$, 0 by 1, maxterm by minterm, and $\leq$ by $\geq$. We shall not pursue this idea any further.

EXERCISES 4-2

1 Prove the following Boolean identities:
   (a) $a \oplus (a' * b) = a \oplus b$
   (b) $a * (a' \oplus b) = a * b$
   (c) $(a * b) \oplus (a * b') = a$
   (d) $(a * b * c) \oplus (a * b) = a * b$

2 It is conventional in switching theory to use the symbols $+$ and $\cdot$ in place of the symbols $\oplus$ and $*$. Further simplifications of the Boolean expressions are introduced by assuming the order of precedence of the operators $'$, $\cdot$, and $+$ and also by suppressing the dot and writing $a \cdot b$ as ab. Write all the identities of Sec. 4-2.1 and those given in Prob. 1 by using these conventions and notations.

3 In any Boolean algebra, show that
   (a) $a = b \Leftrightarrow ab' + a'b = 0$
   (b) $a = 0 \Leftrightarrow ab' + a'b = b$
   (c) $(a + b')(b + c')(c + a') = (a' + b)(b' + c)(c' + a)$
   (d) $(a + b)(a' + c) = ac + a'b = ac + a'b + bc$
   (e) $a \leq b \Rightarrow a + bc = b(a + c)$

4 Simplify the following Boolean expressions:
   (a) $(a * b)' \oplus (a \oplus b)'$
   (b) $(a' * b' * c) \oplus (a * b' * c) \oplus (a * b' * c')$

    (c) $(a * c) \oplus c \oplus [(b \oplus b') * e]$
    (d) $(1 * a) \oplus (0 * a')$

5 Let $\langle \rho(S), \cap, \cup, \sim, \varnothing, S \rangle$ be the algebra of the subsets of $S = \{a, b, c\}$, and let $g: \rho(S) \to B$ be a mapping onto the two-element Boolean algebra given in Example 1 of Sec. 4-2.1, such that $g(x) = 1$ if x contains the element b, otherwise $g(x) = 0$. Show that g is a Boolean homomorphism.

6 Show that a mapping from one Boolean algebra to another which preserves the operations $\oplus$ and $'$ also preserves the operation $*$.

7 Show that a lattice homomorphism on a Boolean algebra which preserves 0 and 1 is a Boolean homomorphism.

8 Let $\langle B, *, \oplus, ', 0, 1 \rangle$ be a Boolean algebra. Define the operations $+$ and $\cdot$ on the elements of B by

$$a + b = (a * b') \oplus (a' * b)$$

$$a \cdot b = a * b$$

    Show that $\langle B, +, \cdot, 1 \rangle$ is a Boolean ring with identity 1.

9 For the operation $+$ defined in Prob. 8, show that
    (a) $(a + b) + b = a$
    (b) $a \cdot (b + c) = (a \cdot b) + (a \cdot c)$
    (c) $a + a = 0$
    (d) $a + 0 = a$
    (e) $a + 1 = a'$

4-3 BOOLEAN FUNCTIONS

Several identities and expressions involving the elements of a Boolean algebra were given in Sec. 4-2. In this section we shall first introduce well-formed expressions involving Boolean variables. It will be shown that these expressions form a Boolean algebra called a free Boolean algebra. An equivalence relation on the set of Boolean expressions in a certain number of variables is then introduced. As a next step, it is shown that every Boolean expression is equivalent to another expression which possesses a certain standard, or normal, form. The idea of the equivalence of Boolean expressions is effectively used in the design of economical switching circuits, as is shown later in Secs. 4-4 and 4-5. In this section, we next introduce the concept of the value of a Boolean expression and a valuation process over a given Boolean algebra. It is then shown that if certain statements about Boolean expressions are true for a Boolean algebra, then they are true for all Boolean algebras. This finally permits us to define Boolean functions associated with Boolean expressions.

4-3.1 Boolean Forms and Free Boolean Algebra

In our discussion so far, we have assumed that we are given a Boolean algebra $\langle B, *, \oplus, ', 0, 1 \rangle$ in which the elements 0 and 1 are the distinguished elements, or the bounds, and the operations $*$, $\oplus$, and $'$ are defined on the elements of B and satisfy the identities given in Sec. 4-2.1. Let us now consider a set of n variables or literals $x_1, x_2, \ldots, x_n$ and operator symbols $*$, $\oplus$, and $'$. With the help of these symbols and variables we form strings according to certain rules which will now be given.

Definition 4-3.1 A *Boolean expression, form,* or *formula* in n variables $x_1, x_2, \ldots, x_n$ is any finite string of symbols formed in the following manner:

1 0 and 1 are Boolean expressions.

2 $x_1, x_2, \ldots, x_n$ are Boolean expressions.

3 If α_1 and α_2 are Boolean expressions, then $(\alpha_1) * (\alpha_2)$ and $(\alpha_1) \oplus (\alpha_2)$ are also Boolean expressions.

4 If α is a Boolean expression, then $(\alpha)'$ is also a Boolean expression.

5 No strings of symbols except those formed in accordance with rules 1 to 4 are Boolean expressions.

We shall generally denote a Boolean expression by $\alpha, \beta, \gamma, \ldots$, or more explicitly as $\alpha(x_1, x_2, \ldots, x_n)$. The only exception that we shall make in practice from that given in the definition is to drop some of the parentheses, wherever possible. With this convention, the following are examples of Boolean expressions in three variables $x_1, x_2,$ and x_3.

$$x_1 \qquad x_1' \oplus x_2 \qquad (x_2' \oplus x_1)' * (x_3 \oplus x_1) \qquad (x_1' \oplus x_1) * x_2 * x_3'$$

Notice that a Boolean expression in n variables may or may not contain all the n variables.

Obviously one can construct an infinite number of Boolean expressions in n variables. However, if we assume that the operations $*$, $\oplus$, and $'$ satisfy all the identities of a Boolean algebra, then it is possible to define an equivalence relation on the set of Boolean expressions in n variables.

Definition 4-3.2 Two Boolean forms $\alpha(x_1, x_2, \ldots, x_n)$ and $\beta(x_1, x_2, \ldots, x_n)$ are called *equivalent* (or *equal*) if one can be obtained from the other by a finite number of applications of the identities of a Boolean algebra.

It is easy to see that the relation given by Definition 4-3.2 is an equivalence relation on the set of Boolean expressions in n variables and therefore partitions the set into equivalence classes. All those Boolean expressions which are in the same equivalence class are equivalent, or equal, to one another. We shall now show that the number of these equivalence classes is finite. Let us first consider certain special Boolean expressions called minterms. It will be convenient to call the operations $*$ and $\oplus$ "product" and "sum" respectively in the rest of our discussion.

Definition 4-3.3 A Boolean form in n variables $x_1, x_2, \ldots, x_n$ consisting of the product of n terms such as

$$x_1{}^{a_1} * x_2{}^{a_2} * \cdots * x_n{}^{a_n} = \underset{i=1}{\overset{n}{*}} x_i{}^{a_i}$$

in which a_i is either 0 or 1, $x_i{}^0$ stands for x_i', and $x_i{}^1$ stands for x_i for $i = 1, 2, \ldots, n$ is called a *minterm, complete product,* or a *fundamental product* of the n variables.

Note the similarity in the definition of "minterm" given here and that given in Sec. 1-3.3. In fact, most of our discussion that follows will be similar to the discussion in Sec. 1-3.5. We shall denote a particular minterm by $\min_j$ or $\min_j^n$ or simply as m_j where j is the decimal representation of the binary number $a_1 a_2 \cdots a_n$. Since for each i $(i = 1, 2, \ldots, n)$, a_i can be either 0 or 1, we have 2^n minterms which we denote as $m_0, m_1, \ldots, m_{2^n-1}$. These minterms satisfy the following properties:

$$\min_i * \min_j = 0 \qquad \text{for } i \neq j \tag{1}$$

$$\bigoplus_{i=0}^{2^n-1} \min_i = 1 \tag{2}$$

For $i \neq j$, there is at least one variable and its complement that appear in the product $\min_i * \min_j$ in Eq. (1), and hence it is equal to 0. Equation (2) can be proved by the principle of mathematical induction. Note also that any two minterms $\min_i$ and $\min_j$ for $i \neq j$ cannot be equivalent to each other.

We have assumed that the operations $*$, $\oplus$, and $'$ along with the bounds 0 and 1 satisfy all the identities given in Sec. 4-2.1 when the operations are applied to the variables x_1, x_2, $\ldots$, x_n. Therefore, one can show that every Boolean expression except 0 can be expressed in an equivalent form consisting of the sums of minterms. Such an equivalent form is called the *sum-of-products canonical* form. For every Boolean expression in n variables, a canonical form exists and is unique in some sense. This statement can be proved in the same manner as was done in Sec. 1-3.3.

Observe that in a sum-of-products canonical form any particular minterm may or may not be present. Since there are 2^n minterms, we can have only 2^{2^n} different sum-of-products canonical forms. These canonical forms include the sum-of-products canonical form of 0 in which no minterm is present in the sum and also the sum-of-products canonical form of 1 where all the minterms are present in the sum. In any case, every Boolean expression in n variables is equivalent to exactly one of the 2^{2^n} Boolean expressions which have the sum-of-products canonical form. This fact allows us to partition the set of all the Boolean expressions into 2^{2^n} equivalence classes.

Equations (1) and (2) suggest that the 2^n minterms behave as the atoms of a Boolean algebra. Let us denote this Boolean algebra by $\langle B_{2^n}, *, \oplus, ', 0, 1 \rangle$. All the elements of B_{2^n} can be obtained from the minterms by the operation of join ($\oplus$). This means that the 2^{2^n} sum-of-products canonical forms are the elements of this Boolean algebra. In fact, any Boolean expression in the variables x_1, x_2, $\ldots$, x_n is equal to one of the elements of B_{2^n} and hence represents an element of this algebra. For this reason, $\langle B_{2^n}, *, \oplus, ', 0, 1 \rangle$ is called a *free Boolean algebra* generated by x_1, x_2, $\ldots$, x_n. The order of B_{2^n} is clearly 2^{2^n}, and the equality of two elements of B_{2^n} is understood to mean their equivalence as Boolean expressions.

EXAMPLE 1   Write the following Boolean expressions in an equivalent sum-of-products canonical form in three variables x_1, x_2, and x_3: (a) $x_1 * x_2$; (b) $x_1 \oplus x_2$; and (c) $(x_1 \oplus x_2)' * x_3$.

SOLUTION

(a) $x_1 * x_2 = x_1 * x_2 * (x_3 \oplus x_3')$

$\qquad = (x_1 * x_2 * x_3) \oplus (x_1 * x_2 * x_3')$

$\qquad = \min_6 \oplus \min_7 = \oplus\, 6, 7$

(b) $x_1 \oplus x_2 = [x_1 * (x_2 \oplus x_2')] \oplus [x_2 * (x_1 \oplus x_1')]$

$\qquad = (x_1 * x_2) \oplus (x_1 * x_2') \oplus (x_2 * x_1) \oplus (x_1' * x_2)$

$\qquad = (x_1 * x_2) \oplus (x_1 * x_2') \oplus (x_1' * x_2)$

$\qquad = [(x_1 * x_2) * (x_3 \oplus x_3')] \oplus (x_1 * x_2') * (x_3 \oplus x_3')$

$\qquad\qquad\qquad\qquad\qquad \oplus [(x_1' * x_2) * (x_3 \oplus x_3')]$

$\qquad = (x_1 * x_2 * x_3) \oplus (x_1 * x_2 * x_3') \oplus (x_1 * x_2' * x_3)$

$\qquad\quad \oplus (x_1 * x_2' * x_3') \oplus (x_1' * x_2 * x_3) \oplus (x_1' * x_2 * x_3')$

$\qquad = \min_7 \oplus \min_6 \oplus \min_5 \oplus \min_4 \oplus \min_3 \oplus \min_2$

$\qquad = \oplus\, 2, 3, 4, 5, 6, 7$

(c) $(x_1 \oplus x_2)' * x_3 = (x_1' * x_2') * x_3 = \min_1$ ////

EXAMPLE 2 Show that

$$(x_1' * x_2' * x_3' * x_4') \oplus (x_1' * x_2' * x_3' * x_4) \oplus (x_1' * x_2' * x_3 * x_4)$$
$$\oplus (x_1' * x_2' * x_3 * x_4') = x_1' * x_2'$$

SOLUTION

$$(x_1' * x_2' * x_3' * x_4') \oplus (x_1' * x_2' * x_3' * x_4) = x_1' * x_2' * x_3'$$
$$(x_1' * x_2' * x_3 * x_4) \oplus (x_1' * x_2' * x_3 * x_4') = x_1' * x_2' * x_3$$

Hence the given formula is equal to

$$(x_1' * x_2' * x_3') \oplus (x_1' * x_2' * x_3) = x_1' * x_2' \qquad ////$$

Examples 1 and 2 show that for a given Boolean expression its equivalent sum-of-products canonical form is not necessarily simpler or shorter as a string. However, if we wish to determine whether any two given Boolean expressions are equivalent to one another, it may be easier to obtain their sum-of-products canonical forms and compare these forms, rather than trying to reduce one Boolean form into another. The process of obtaining the sum-of-products canonical form of a Boolean expression can be made mechanical.

In Sec. 1-2.15 it was shown that a switching circuit can be built to perform a certain task, which is first described by a number of statements. These statements are replaced by switches and gates, and the description of the circuit is obtained in terms of Boolean expressions. A circuit based upon such an expression may not be the most economical in a certain sense. Therefore, one may seek equivalent Boolean expressions which may be simpler (or more economical as a circuit from the point of view of the components used). Therefore, one is generally interested in obtaining either equivalent Boolean expressions which are simpler in that either the number of variables is smaller or the number of operations is fewer, or an expression in which only certain types of operations appear but not others. The final expression to be obtained will depend upon the criteria used. We shall discuss some such methods in Sec. 4-4.

It is possible to repeat our discussion of canonical form using maxterms in place of minterms and showing that every Boolean expression in n variables is equivalent to a Boolean expression consisting of the product of maxterms only. Such a canonical form is known as the *product-of-sums canonical form*. The representation of maxterms and the method of obtaining the product-of-sums canonical form of a Boolean expression follow on the same lines as given in Secs. 1-3.3 to 1-3.5. One can also obtain these results by using the principle of duality.

EXAMPLE 3 Obtain the product-of-sums canonical forms of the Boolean expressions given in Example 1.

SOLUTION

$$x_1 * x_2 = [x_1 \oplus (x_2 * x_2')] * [x_2 \oplus (x_1 * x_1')]$$
$$= (x_1 \oplus x_2) * (x_1 \oplus x_2') * (x_1 \oplus x_2) * (x_1' \oplus x_2)$$
$$= (x_1 \oplus x_2) * (x_1 \oplus x_2') * (x_1' \oplus x_2)$$
$$= (x_1 \oplus x_2 \oplus x_3) * (x_1 \oplus x_2 \oplus x_3') * (x_1 \oplus x_2' \oplus x_3)$$
$$\quad * (x_1 \oplus x_2' \oplus x_3') * (x_1' \oplus x_2 \oplus x_3) * (x_1' \oplus x_2 \oplus x_3')$$
$$= \max_0 * \max_1 * \max_2 * \max_3 * \max_4 * \max_5$$
$$= * \, 0, 1, 2, 3, 4, 5$$

One could obtain this result directly from the sum-of-products form given in Example 1. It is easier to obtain the sum-of-products form than the product-of-sums canonical form in this case. On the other hand, for $x_1 \oplus x_2$, one can obtain the product-of-sums form directly as

$$x_1 \oplus x_2 = x_1 \oplus x_2 \oplus (x_3 * x_3') = (x_1 \oplus x_2 \oplus x_3) * (x_1 \oplus x_2 \oplus x_3')$$
$$= \max_0 * \max_1$$

In any case, if one of the canonical forms is known, then the other canonical form can be obtained directly. ////

4-3.2 Values of Boolean Expressions and Boolean Functions

Let $\alpha(x_1, x_2, \ldots, x_n)$ be a Boolean expression in n variables and $\langle B, *, \oplus, ', 0, 1 \rangle$ be any Boolean algebra whose elements are denoted by $a_1, a_2, \ldots$. Let $\langle a_1, a_2, \ldots, a_n \rangle$ be an n-tuple of B^n. If we replace x_1 by a_1, x_2 by a_2, $\ldots$, and x_n by a_n in the Boolean expression $\alpha(x_1, x_2, \ldots, x_n)$, we obtain an expression which represents an element of B. We shall denote the resulting expression by $\alpha(a_1, a_2, \ldots, a_n) \in B$ and call it the *value* of the Boolean expression $\alpha(x_1, x_2, \ldots, x_n)$ for the n-tuple $\langle a_1, a_2, \ldots, a_n \rangle \in B^n$. It is possible to determine the values of the Boolean expression $\alpha(x_1, x_2, \ldots, x_n)$ for every n-tuple of B^n. The process of determining all such values is called a *valuation process* over the Boolean algebra

$\langle B, *, \oplus, ', 0, 1 \rangle$. In particular, if $B = \{0, 1\}$, the valuation process over the two-element Boolean algebra is called a *binary valuation process*.

We shall now interpret the equivalence of two Boolean expressions in terms of the valuation process over any Boolean algebra. Recall that two Boolean expressions are equivalent to one another if one can be obtained from the other by using the identities of a Boolean algebra. Let $\alpha(x_1, x_2, \ldots, x_n)$ and $\beta(x_1, x_2, \ldots, x_n)$ be two Boolean expressions which are equivalent to one another, and let $\langle B, *, \oplus, ', 0, 1 \rangle$ be a Boolean algebra over which we evaluate the two expressions. Let $\langle a_1, a_2, \ldots, a_n \rangle$ be any n-tuple of B^n and $\alpha(a_1, a_2, \ldots, a_n)$ be the value of $\alpha(x_1, x_2, \ldots, x_n)$ for this n-tuple. Since all the identities of a Boolean algebra hold for the given Boolean algebra, it is possible to transform $\alpha(a_1, a_2, \ldots, a_n)$ into $\beta(a_1, a_2, \ldots, a_n)$ by the use of the identities. This implies that the values of the two Boolean expressions which are equivalent will be equal for any n-tuple of B^n, or that the valuation process over any Boolean algebra results in identical values of the expressions. We shall see later in this section that the converse result also holds.

This discussion suggests that the values of a given Boolean expression can be obtained either by directly replacing the variables with the members of the n-tuple or by first obtaining an equivalent expression which is simpler in some sense and then replacing the variables. These two procedures will be demonstrated by examples.

EXAMPLE 1 Find the value of

$$x_1 * x_2 * [(x_1 * x_4) \oplus x_2' \oplus (x_3 * x_1')]$$

for $x_1 = a$, $x_2 = 1$, $x_3 = b$, and $x_4 = 1$, where $a, b, 1 \in B$ and the Boolean algebra $\langle B, *, \oplus, ', 0, 1 \rangle$ is shown in Fig. 4-3.1.

SOLUTION By substituting the required elements in the expression, we get

$$a * 1 * [(a * 1) \oplus 1' \oplus (b * a')] = a * [a \oplus 0 \oplus (b * b)]$$

$$= a * (a \oplus b) = a * 1 = a$$

Alternatively, the given expression can be written in an equivalent form as

$$(x_1 * x_2 * x_1 * x_4) \oplus (x_1 * x_2 * x_2') \oplus (x_1 * x_2 * x_3 * x_1')$$

$$= (x_1 * x_2 * x_4) \oplus 0 \oplus 0 = x_1 * x_2 * x_4$$

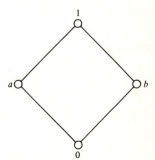

FIGURE 4-3.1

Now, replacing the variables, we get

$$a * 1 * 1 = a \qquad ////$$

EXAMPLE 2   Obtain the values of the Boolean forms

$$x_1 * (x_1' \oplus x_2) \qquad x_1 * x_2 \qquad \text{and} \qquad x_1 \oplus (x_1 * x_2)$$

over the ordered pairs of the two-element Boolean algebra.

SOLUTION   Let $B = \{0, 1\}$. The elements of B^2 are listed in the first column of Table 4-3.1, and the values of the given Boolean expressions are given in the remaining columns. Observe that

$$x_1 * (x_1' \oplus x_2) = (x_1 * x_1') \oplus (x_1 * x_2) = 0 \oplus (x_1 * x_2) = x_1 * x_2$$

and

$$x_1 \oplus (x_1 * x_2) = x_1$$

This explains why the values of $x_1 * x_2$ and $x_1 * (x_1' \oplus x_2)$ are identical. Similarly, the values of x_1 and $x_1 \oplus (x_1 * x_2)$ are also identical.   ////

We shall now examine the binary valuation process of a minterm. For this purpose let us consider the minterm

$$x_1{}^{m_1} * x_2{}^{m_2} * \cdots * x_n{}^{m_n}$$

in which $m_i = 0$ or 1 for $i = 1, 2, \ldots, n$. For the n-tuple $\langle m_1, m_2, \ldots, m_n \rangle \in \{0, 1\}^n$, the value of the minterm is 1, while for every other n-tuple of $\{0, 1\}^n$, its value is 0. For every minterm this is the case; viz., the value of the minterm is equal to 1 for exactly one n-tuple of $\{0, 1\}^n$ and 0 for all other n-tuples. Distinct minterms have the value 1 for distinct n-tuples of $\{0, 1\}^n$, and one can establish a one-to-one correspondence between the minterms and the n-tuples of $\{0, 1\}^n$ by associating with each minterm the n-tuple for which its value is 1.

Since the set $\{0, 1\}$ is a sub-Boolean algebra of any Boolean algebra, the values of a Boolean expression for any n-tuple of $\{0, 1\}^n$ must be either 0 or 1. Furthermore, the binary valuation process of a Boolean expression determines the minterms that are present in its sum-of-products canonical form. More precisely, appearing in the sum-of-products canonical form of a Boolean expression are only those minterms which are associated with the n-tuples of $\{0, 1\}^n$ for which the value of the Boolean expression is 1. This result shows that for a given Boolean expression, its equivalent sum-of-products canonical form can be completely determined by its binary valuation process.

Table 4-3.1

$\langle x_1, x_2 \rangle$	$x_1 * x_2$	x_1'	$x_1' \oplus x_2$	$x_1 * (x_1' \oplus x_2)$	$x_1 \oplus (x_1 * x_2)$
$\langle 0, 0 \rangle$	0	1	1	0	0
$\langle 0, 1 \rangle$	0	1	1	0	0
$\langle 1, 0 \rangle$	0	0	0	0	1
$\langle 1, 1 \rangle$	1	0	1	1	1

We know that any two Boolean expressions in n variables which are equivalent have the same sum-of-products canonical form. It is therefore possible to determine the equivalence of two Boolean expressions simply by their binary valuation process. However, once the equivalence is established, we can say that the values of two equivalent Boolean expressions must be equal for every n-tuple of B^n, where $\langle B, *, \oplus, ', 0, 1 \rangle$ is any Boolean algebra. Thus, from a binary valuation process alone it is possible to make a statement about the valuation process over any Boolean algebra. It is easy to generalize this statement by saying that if two Boolean expressions have equal values for every n-tuple of a Boolean algebra, then they must have equal values for every n-tuple of any other Boolean algebra. This result follows from the fact that the equality of the values of two Boolean expressions over the n-tuples of any Boolean algebra implies their equality over the n-tuples of a two-element Boolean algebra which is a sub-Boolean algebra. These remarks can be rephrased by saying that any Boolean identity which holds for every n-tuple of one Boolean algebra holds for every Boolean algebra.

EXAMPLE 3 Show that the following Boolean expressions are equivalent to one another. Obtain their sum-of-products canonical form.

(a) $(x \oplus y) * (x' \oplus z) * (y \oplus z)$
(b) $(x * z) \oplus (x' * y) \oplus (y * z)$
(c) $(x \oplus y) * (x' \oplus z)$
(d) $(x * z) \oplus (x' * y)$

SOLUTION   The binary valuations of the expressions are given in Table 4-3.2. Since the values of the given Boolean expressions are equal over every triple of the two-element Boolean algebra, they are equivalent.

We can show the equivalence of the Boolean expression alternatively as follows.

$$(c) = [(x \oplus y) * x'] \oplus [(x \oplus y) * z] = (x * x')$$
$$\oplus (y * x') \oplus (x * z) \oplus (y * z)$$
$$= (b)$$

From the principle of duality or in a similar manner we can show that $(a) = (d)$.

Table 4-3.2

x	y	z	$x \oplus y$	$x' \oplus z$	$y \oplus z$	(a)	(c)	$x * z$	$x' * y$	$y * z$	(b)	(d)
0	0	0	0	1	0	0	0	0	0	0	0	0
0	0	1	0	1	1	0	0	0	0	0	0	0
0	1	0	1	1	1	1	1	0	1	0	1	1
0	1	1	1	1	1	1	1	0	1	1	1	1
1	0	0	1	0	0	0	0	0	0	0	0	0
1	0	1	1	1	1	1	1	1	0	0	1	1
1	1	0	1	0	1	0	0	0	0	0	0	0
1	1	1	1	1	1	1	1	1	0	1	1	1

Finally, we show that

$$
\begin{aligned}
(a) &= (x \oplus y) * [(x' * y) \oplus z] \\
&= [(x \oplus y) * (x' * y)] \oplus [(x \oplus y) * z] \\
&= \{[(x \oplus y) * y] * x'\} \oplus [(x * z) \oplus (y * z)] \\
&= (y * x') \oplus (x * z) \oplus (y * z) = (b)
\end{aligned}
$$

All the four Boolean forms have been shown to be equivalent to one another. They all have the same sum-of-products canonical form which can be obtained either directly from the table as $\min_2 \oplus \min_3 \oplus \min_5 \oplus \min_7$ or from (d) as

$$
\begin{aligned}
(d) &= [(x * z) * (y \oplus y')] \oplus [(x' * y) * (z \oplus z')] \\
&= (x * z * y) \oplus (x * z * y') \oplus (x' * y * z) \oplus (x' * y * z') \qquad ////
\end{aligned}
$$

Given a Boolean expression $\alpha(x_1, x_2, \ldots, x_n)$ and a Boolean algebra $\langle B, *, \oplus, ', 0, 1 \rangle$, we can obtain the values of the Boolean expression for every n-tuple of B^n. Let us now consider a function $f_{\alpha, B} : B^n \to B$ such that for any n-tuple $\langle a_1, a_2, \ldots, a_n \rangle \in B^n$, the value of $f_{\alpha, B}$ is equal to the value of the Boolean expression $\alpha(x_1, x_2, \ldots, x_n)$, that is,

$$
f_{\alpha, B}(a_1, a_2, \ldots, a_n) = \alpha(a_1, a_2, \ldots, a_n)
$$

for all $\langle a_1, a_2, \ldots, a_n \rangle \in B^n$. We shall call $f_{\alpha, B}$ the *function associated with* (or *described by*) the Boolean expression $\alpha(x_1, x_2, \ldots, x_n)$.

It follows from the definition that any two Boolean expressions which are equivalent to one another describe the same function irrespective of the Boolean algebra under consideration; that is, if $\alpha(x_1, x_2, \ldots, x_n) = \beta(x_1, x_2, \ldots, x_n)$, then $f_{\alpha, B} = f_{\beta, B}$ for every Boolean algebra B. Conversely, if for any two Boolean expressions $\alpha(x_1, x_2, \ldots, x_n)$ and $\beta(x_1, x_2, \ldots, x_n)$, the functions described by them over any Boolean algebra are equal, that is, if $f_{\alpha, B} = f_{\beta, B}$, then $\alpha(x_1, x_2, \ldots, x_n) = \beta(x_1, x_2, \ldots, x_n)$. This result shows that a function associated with a Boolean expression is defined over any Boolean algebra, if it is defined over a Boolean algebra. In such cases, it is most convenient to define the function over a two-element Boolean algebra.

Let us see how we can determine the values of such a function which is associated with a Boolean expression, say $\alpha(x_1, x_2, \ldots, x_n)$, and whose values are given over the n-tuples of a two-element Boolean algebra. To determine its values for an n-tuple of some other Boolean algebra, all we need to do is write the sum-of-products canonical form of the Boolean expression from its binary valuation, which is given in this case. The values of the given expression are the same as the values of its sum-of-products canonical form, which in turn are the values of the function. This idea is demonstrated by the following example.

EXAMPLE 4 Find the value of the function $f_{\alpha, B} : B^3 \to B$ for $x_1 = a$, $x_2 = 1$, and $x_3 = b$ where $a, b, 1$ are the elements of the Boolean algebra given in Example 1 and $\alpha(x_1, x_2, x_3)$ is the expression whose binary valuation is given in Table 4-3.3.

Table 4-3.3

$\langle x_1, x_2, x_3 \rangle$	$\alpha(x_1, x_2, x_3)$
$\langle 0, 0, 0 \rangle$	1
$\langle 0, 0, 1 \rangle$	0
$\langle 0, 1, 0 \rangle$	1
$\langle 0, 1, 1 \rangle$	1
$\langle 1, 0, 0 \rangle$	0
$\langle 1, 0, 1 \rangle$	1
$\langle 1, 1, 0 \rangle$	0
$\langle 1, 1, 1 \rangle$	0

SOLUTION   From the table we can immediately obtain the sum-of-products form of $\alpha(x_1, x_2, x_3)$ by selecting for each value 1 a corresponding minterm

$$(x_1' * x_2' * x_3') \oplus (x_1' * x_2 * x_3') \oplus (x_1' * x_2 * x_3) \oplus (x_1 * x_2' * x_3)$$

The value of $\alpha(a, 1, b)$ is the same as the value of the corresponding canonical form, viz.,

$$\alpha(a, 1, b) = (b * 0 * a) \oplus (b * 1 * a) \oplus (b * 1 * b) \oplus (a * 0 * b) = b$$

$////$

Definition 4-3.4   Let $\langle B, *, \oplus, ', 0, 1 \rangle$ be a Boolean algebra. A function $f: B^n \to B$ which is associated with a Boolean expression in n variables is called a *Boolean function*.

Observe that not every function $g: B^n \to B$ is a Boolean function. If we assume that the Boolean algebra B is of order 2^m for $m > 1$, then it is easy to see that the number of functions from B^n to B is greater than 2^{2^n} showing that there are functions from B^n to B which are not Boolean functions. On the other hand, for $m = 1$, that is, for a two-element Boolean algebra, the number of functions from B^n to B is 2^{2^n}, which is the same as the number of distinct Boolean expressions in n variables. Hence every function from B^n to B in this case is a Boolean function.

From the definition of a Boolean function it is clear that there exists a one-to-one correspondence between the set of Boolean functions and the elements of a free Boolean algebra. Let us denote the set of Boolean functions in n variables by F_n. For any $f \in F_n$ associated with a Boolean expression α in n variables, let us denote the Boolean function associated with $(\alpha)'$ by $\bar{f}$. Clearly $\bar{f} \in F_n$. Next, for any two Boolean functions f, $g \in F_n$ associated with Boolean expressions α and β respectively, denote the Boolean functions corresponding to $(\alpha) * (\beta)$ and $(\alpha) \oplus (\beta)$ by $f \wedge g$ and $f \vee g$. Again, $f \wedge g, f \vee g \in F_n$. Finally, let us denote the Boolean functions associated with the Boolean expressions 1 and 0 by f_1 and f_0 respectively. Since the operations $\wedge$, $\vee$, and $-$ as well as the elements f_0 and f_1 on F_n are defined in terms of the operations $*$, $\oplus$, $'$ and the elements 0 and 1 of the free Boolean algebra, it is easy to see that $\langle F_n, \wedge, \vee, -, f_0, f_1 \rangle$ is a Boolean algebra of order 2^{2^n}. Furthermore, if we define a mapping

$g: F_n \to B_{2^n}$ such that for any $f \in F_n$, $g(f) = \alpha$, where α is the Boolean expression associated with the function f, then clearly g is an isomorphism. The two Boolean algebras $\langle F_n, \wedge, \vee, -, f_0, f_1 \rangle$ and $\langle B_{2^n}, *, \oplus, ', 0, 1 \rangle$ are isomorphic to one another. Because of this isomorphism the terms "Boolean expression" and "Boolean function" are often used interchangeably.

In the remaining part of this section we discuss a special class of Boolean expressions or functions which are symmetric in some of the variables. Recognition of such symmetries permits considerable simplification in the design of circuits which such functions may represent. We shall discuss only some basic notions of symmetries here.

A Boolean expression in n variables $x_1, x_2, \ldots, x_n$ is said to be *pairwise symmetric* with respect to the variables x_i and x_j, if by interchanging the variables x_i and x_j throughout the expression we obtain an equivalent expression. Accordingly, a Boolean expression $\alpha(x_1, x_2, \ldots, x_n)$ is symmetric in x_i and x_j if

$$\alpha(x_1, x_2, \ldots, x_i, \ldots, x_j, \ldots, x_n) = \alpha(x_1, x_2, \ldots, x_j, \ldots, x_i, \ldots, x_n)$$

For example, the expression

$$(x_1 * x_2) \oplus (x_2' * x_3') \oplus (x_1 * x_3)$$

is symmetric in x_2 and x_3 but not symmetric in x_1 and x_3. Similarly, the expression

$$(x_1 * x_2) \oplus (x_3 * x_4')$$

is symmetric in x_1 and x_2. It is also symmetric in x_3 and x_4'. We shall, however, restrict ourselves to the consideration of symmetries in the variables and not in their complements.

The definition of symmetry can be generalized to include symmetry with respect to all the variables.

Definition 4-3.5 A Boolean expression in n variables $x_1, x_2, \ldots, x_n$ is called *symmetric* if interchanging any two variables results in an equivalent expression.

Note that the definition permits the interchange of any number of variables, and the resulting expression will still remain equivalent to the original symmetric expression. The following are some examples of symmetric Boolean expressions in two and three variables:

(a) $(x_1 * x_2') \oplus (x_1' * x_2)$

(b) $(x_1' * x_2') \oplus (x_1 \oplus x_2)$

(c) $(x_1 * x_2' * x_3') \oplus (x_1' * x_2 * x_3') \oplus (x_1' * x_2' * x_3) \oplus (x_1 * x_2 * x_3)$

(d) $(x_1 * x_2 * x_3') \oplus (x_1 * x_2' * x_3) \oplus (x_1' * x_2 * x_3)$

Let us now consider the binary valuation of a symmetric expression in n variables. Clearly, its value will not change if the number of variables which are assigned the value 1 remains fixed. This means that its value remains independent of the particular variables which are assigned the value 1 because of the fact that the value of a symmetric function remains unchanged with interchanges of variables. This leads to a simple criterion which will now be stated as a theorem.

Theorem 4-3.1 A necessary and sufficient condition that a Boolean expression in n variables is symmetric is that there exists a set of numbers $n_1, n_2, \ldots, n_k$ such that the value of the expression is 1 if any number n_i of the variables for $i = 1, 2, \ldots, k$ is assigned the value 1 in a binary valuation process.

The numbers $n_1, n_2, \ldots, n_k$ are called the *characteristic numbers* of the symmetric function. The proof of the theorem depends upon the definition of symmetry and is straightforward. We shall, however, omit it. Observe that the characteristic numbers of the symmetric functions are 1 in (a), 0 and 2 in (b), 1 and 3 in (c), and 2 in (d).

An important consequence of the theorem is the fact that in the sum-of-products canonical form of a symmetric function only certain combinations of minterms must appear. If there is a minterm in the sum-of-products form of a symmetric expression whose value is 1, if m of the variables are assigned the value 1, then all those minterms must also be present whose values are 1 for exactly m variables. Obviously, m is one of the characteristic numbers in this case. Using this information, one can easily write symmetric functions with a given set of characteristic numbers. For example, with $n = 3$, the expression with characteristic number 0 and 2 is given by

$$(x_1' \ast x_2' \ast x_3') \oplus (x_1 \ast x_2 \ast x_3') \oplus (x_1 \ast x_2' \ast x_3) \oplus (x_1' \ast x_2 \ast x_3)$$

EXERCISE 4-3

1 Obtain the sum-of-products canonical forms of the following Boolean expressions.
  (a) $x_1 \oplus x_2$
  (b) $x_1 \oplus (x_2 \ast x_3')$
  (c) $(x_1 \oplus x_2)' \oplus (x_1' \ast x_3)$
  (d) $(x_1 \ast x_2') \oplus x_4$ (assuming that this is an expression in four variables x_1, x_2, x_3, and x_4)

2 Obtain the sum-of-products and product-of-sums canonical forms of the following expressions.
  (a) $x_1 x_2' + x_3$
  (b) $[(x_1 + x_2)(x_3 x_4)']'$
  (c) $x_2' + [x_3' + x_1 + (x_2 x_3)'](x_3 + x_1' x_2)$
  Here we have used the notations and conventions given in Prob. 2, Exercises 4-2.

3 If $\beta(x_1, x_2, \ldots, x_n)$ is the dual of $\alpha(x_1, x_2, \ldots, x_n)$, then show that

$$[\alpha(x_1, x_2, \ldots, x_n)]' = \beta(x_1', x_2', \ldots, x_n')$$

Show how this result is used in obtaining the product-of-sums canonical form of a given expression from its sum-of-products canonical form.

4 Show that
  (a) $[a \ast (b' \oplus c)]' \ast [b' \oplus (a \ast c')']' = a \ast b \ast c'$
  (b) $a' \ast [(b' \oplus c)' \oplus (b \ast c)] \oplus [(a \oplus b')' \ast c] = a' \ast b$

5 Given an expression $\alpha(x_1, x_2, x_3)$ defined to be $\sum 0, 3, 5, 7$, determine the value of

$\alpha(a, b, 1)$ where $a, b, 1 \in B$ and $\langle B, *, \oplus, 0, 1 \rangle$ is the Boolean algebra given in Fig. 4-1.1b.

6 Obtain simplified Boolean expressions which are equivalent to these expressions:
(a) $m_0 + m_7$
(b) $m_0 + m_1 + m_2 + m_3$
(c) $m_5 + m_7 + m_9 + m_{11} + m_{13}$
where m_j are the minterms in the variables $x_1, x_2, x_3,$ and x_4.

7 Let B be a Boolean algebra with 2^n elements. Show that the number of sub-Boolean algebras of B is equal to the number of partitions of a set with n elements.

8 Let n be an integer $(n > 1)$ and B be the set of divisors of n. For any $a, b \in B$, let $a \oplus b = \text{LCM } (a, b)$, $a * b = \text{GCD } (a, b)$, and $a' = n/a$. Show that $\langle B, *, \oplus, ', 0, 1 \rangle$ is a Boolean algebra if n is not divisible by a square greater than 1. What are the sub-Boolean algebras of this algebra? Draw the diagram of the Boolean algebras for $n = 30$.

9 Show that the symmetric functions form a Boolean algebra.

10 Determine whether the following functions are symmetric.
(a) $a'bc' + a'c'd + a'bcd + abc'd$
(b) $a'bcd + a'c' + b'c'd' + ad'$
(c) $abc' + ab'c + a'bc + ab'c' + a'bc' + a'b'c$

4-4 REPRESENTATION AND MINIMIZATION OF BOOLEAN FUNCTIONS

In this section we are primarily concerned with the problem of obtaining a Boolean function which is minimal according to some criterion, such as the minimum numbers of gates and/or inputs, and which is equivalent to a given Boolean function. Such problems arise in the design of switching circuits. In a typical situation, the operational requirements of the circuit are stated in verbal form. These statements are subsequently transformed into a Boolean equation for the required output. The next step is to obtain an equation which is logically equivalent to the output equation which will result in a least expensive physical realization. The desired circuit is finally obtained by replacing the Boolean connectives in the minimal equation by appropriate logic blocks such as *OR* gates, *AND* gates, inverters, etc. The ideas of physical realization and logic blocks were introduced in Sec. 1-2.15. Furthermore, the notion of equivalent Boolean functions was introduced in Sec. 4-3.1 where examples of algebraic simplification were also given.

The first part of this section discusses a number of useful ways for representing Boolean functions. The remainder of the section is concerned with systematic ways of simplifying Boolean functions. In particular, an algorithm is given for one such method.

4-4.1 Representation of Boolean Functions

As previously mentioned, we will use the notions of Boolean algebra as a tool for expressing a problem of circuit design. Moreover, this tool will also be used in the analysis, simplification, and development of a solution to such a problem. However, in order to gain understanding of the various relationships that may exist among the particular elements of a problem, we will often represent the appropriate Boolean function in various forms. A further advantage in using these representations is that certain operations and simplifications upon Boolean functions are far more easily performed when one representation is used rather than another. Here we are concerned with producing solutions that are either minimal or at least reasonably close to being minimal. The ease of simplifying functions will be quite important in any technique.

In Sec. 4-3.2 we defined a Boolean function and showed the existence of a one-to-one correspondence between every Boolean function $f: B^n \rightarrow B$ and a Boolean expression in n variables. Because of this correspondence, we can represent a Boolean function by any one of the Boolean expressions to which the function corresponds. Such a representation of a Boolean function will be found convenient for our purpose.

This way of representing a Boolean function is simply to give the Boolean equation for the values of the symbol(s) in the output combination in terms of some subset of the elements of the input combinations. For example, the function

$$p = f(m, r, g, s) = m \cdot [r + (g \cdot \bar{s})]$$

gives the output p in terms of the input variables m, r, g, and s.

Another method of representing Boolean functions is to form a table which lists exhaustively all the possible combinations of input variables and which, for each such input configuration, records a functional value. An example of this approach was given in the system problem in Sec. 1-2.15.

The tabular representation is perhaps easier to use than Boolean equations for determining values of outputs for specified inputs. There is no computation involved, only a table to look up. Boolean equations are, of course, a far more concise way of expressing relationships. Such tables, just like truth tables for propositional expressions, suffer from the disadvantage of being overly cumbersome for expressions of five or more variables.

A third representation of Boolean functions is the n-space representation. The ordered n-tuple that is some particular input combination is presumed to define a point in n-dimensional space. A similar representation of codes was given in Sec. 3-7. The set of all possible n-tuple inputs defines a figure in n-space with the vertices corresponding to each of the different n-tuples. The mapping which associates input n-tuples to the appropriate output value may most conveniently be done by showing vertices which correspond to an output value of 1 in some emphasized fashion.

For example, consider the Boolean function $f(a, b, c) = a \cdot (b + \bar{c})$. Since the function has three input variables, there are eight possible input combinations. These correspond to the vertices of a three-dimensional cube as shown in Fig. 4-4.1. Each vertex is labeled to indicate to which input triple it corresponds, and each vertex that corresponds to an input triple which has a functional value of 1 is denoted by a bold dot. The geometrical interpretation of Boolean functions leads to the concept of Hamming distance which was introduced in Sec. 3-7.2. Recall that the Hamming distance between two n-tuples or vertices is equal to the number of positions in which these n-tuples differ. The concepts of adjacency (a separation distance of 1) and of distance in general will be important in the discussion of minimization of Boolean functions.

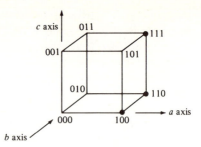

FIGURE 4-4.1   A cube representation of a function.

As might be expected, this n-space topological representation becomes visually confusing when n exceeds 4. For this reason, the n-space representation as we have described here is not often used for functions that are relatively complex. One modification that is sometimes used is to draw diagrams that do not include those vertices which correspond to a functional value of 0. For example, the function $p = m \cdot [r + (g \cdot \bar{s})]$ would appear as

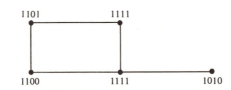

In this form of n-space representation, the diagram preserves the adjacency relation and distance values between vertices that correspond to a functional value of 1, but the relation between these vertices and those which correspond to a functional value of 0 is no longer apparent.

A fourth commonly used form of representation for Boolean functions is an outgrowth of the previous representation. Perhaps the greatest importance of the n-space representation is, first, that it gives us a picture of the function—something we can use in an intuitive manner to discover relationships—and second, that it provides us with a convenient notation to use. However, if we are willing to give up the advantage of a visual picture, then a Boolean function can be represented by what is often called *cube notation*. To express a Boolean function in cube representation, one simply gives the array of n-tuple input combinations for which the function has a value of 1.

In cube representation, the example function $p = m \cdot (r + g \cdot \bar{s})$ would be represented as $\{1010, 1100, 1101, 1110, 1111\}$. This set of n-tuples is called a *cube array*, and each element is called a cube. To be more precise, each element is a 0 cube; this notational precision will be made clear later.

It is still possible to determine which cubes are adjacent. One simply looks for cubes that differ in exactly one position in the sequences of 0s and 1s. A further advantage of cube notation is that clarity and understandability are not dependent on the number of input variables in any significant way. This is true because the understanding is no longer tied to any pictorial representation, which naturally undergoes great complications in order to display higher-dimensional figures. A final advantage of cube notation is the ease with which such a representation can be simplified with the aid of a computer.

A fifth method of representing Boolean functions is by *Karnaugh maps*. This method is very widely used for the representation of Boolean functions, and it lends itself quite readily to manual simplifications of functions (as opposed to computer simplifications).

A Karnaugh map structure is an area which is subdivided into 2^n cells— one for each possible input combination for a Boolean function of n variables. Of these cells, half are associated with an input value of 1 for one of the variables, and the other half are associated with an input value of 0 for the same variable. This association of cells is done for each variable, with the splitting of the 2^n cells yielding a different pair of halves for each distinct variable.

For example, a function, say a, in one variable would have the Karnaugh map representation of Fig. 4-4.2, where the cells labeled a and $\bar{a}$ are the halves that are associated with input values of 1 and 0 for a respectively. The Boolean function of two variables a and b would have the Karnaugh map given in Fig. 4-4.3, where one half of the cells (the left column) are assigned to the input value of 0 for a and where the right column is the half assigned to the input value of 1 for a. Note that the four cells were split into halves in two different ways—one for each variable. Usually, to avoid cluttering the diagram, the labels $\bar{a}$ and $\bar{b}$ are omitted since it is obvious which half is associated with a 0 input value once the other half is known. A 3-variable Karnaugh map could be like Fig. 4-4.4, and a 4-variable map is given in Fig. 4-4.5. A 5-variable Karnaugh map can be represented by two 4-variable maps as shown in Fig.

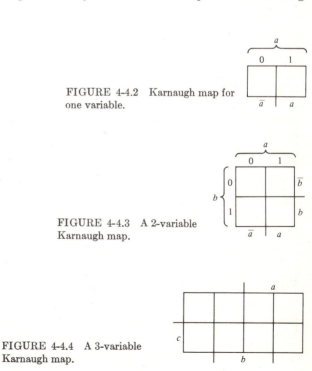

FIGURE 4-4.2 Karnaugh map for one variable.

FIGURE 4-4.3 A 2-variable Karnaugh map.

FIGURE 4-4.4 A 3-variable Karnaugh map.

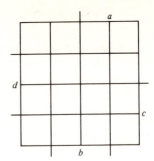

FIGURE 4-4.5   A 4-variable
Karnaugh map.

4-4.6—one of them associated with a 0 value for a (the unlabeled map in the diagram) and the other associated with the value 1 for a. A 6-variable map would be two 5-variable maps, and so on. One problem with Karnaugh maps is that for functions of more than 6 variables, they become more difficult to use in minimization simply because of the greater complexity of the map.

Observe that the labeling used in Karnaugh maps may appear to be arbitrary. However, there is one important concept of adjacency involved in these maps; i.e., those n-tuples which are adjacent to one another should also appear in adjacent cells. This arrangement, however, is not always possible because of the planar representation of Karnaugh maps. We can overcome this difficulty easily, if we interpret as adjacent not only those internal cells which are adjacent to one another, but also the cells on opposite edges. For example, the map in Fig. 4-4.7 has cell d adjacent to cells a, g, f, and e, and cell a is adjacent to cells h, d, b, and c. In other words, this map is assumed to act as if it were inscribed on the surface of a sphere. The top edge wraps around the back to connect to the bottom edge, and the left edge wraps around to connect to the right edge. Similar remarks hold for 2- and 3-variable maps. For a 5-variable map, each of the 4-variable maps is assumed to be connected as we have described, but also one of the maps is assumed to be on top of the other, so that each cell in one map is adjacent to the corresponding cell in the other map. The geometrical model might be two fixed concentric hollow spheres—the inner one having one 4-variable map in its outer surface and the outer sphere having the other 4-variable map

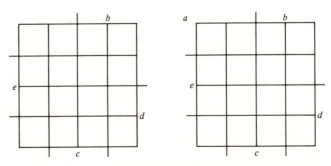

FIGURE 4-4.6   A 5-variable Karnaugh map.

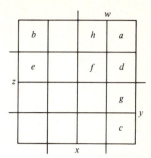

FIGURE 4-4.7

on its inner surface in the same orientation. Similar remarks hold for higher-order maps.

To this point we have discussed Karnaugh map structures, indicating what form they take for functions of different numbers of variables and describing how they are to be interpreted. To represent a Boolean function by means of a Karnaugh map, we select the Karnaugh map structure appropriate for that function and place 0s and 1s in the cells according to whether the functional value is 0 or 1 for the input combination associated with that cell. (Because one half of the map is associated with a 1 input value for a variable and the other half of the map with a 0 input value for that same variable, the input combinations are mapped one-to-one onto the cells of the Karnaugh map structure. The input combination serves as a sort of "address" for a cell within a Karnaugh map structure.) The Karnaugh map for the Boolean function $f = x_1 \cdot [x_2 + (x_3 \cdot \bar{x}_4)]$ is given in Fig. 4-4.8 (see also Fig. 4-4.5). Observe that only the functional values of 1 have been written in the appropriate cells; a blank cell is presumed to have a 0 in it. Also, for convenience, the map of the function f has had each of its cells labeled with the input combination to which it corresponds.

The last method for representing Boolean functions is one that was previously encountered in Sec. 1-2.15, namely, *circuit diagrams*. This representation does seem appropriate since Boolean functions can express the functioning of circuits. Because a circuit diagram actually shows which circuits are to be connected to which other circuits, it is occasionally possible to make use of a circuit diagram to eliminate unnecessary connectives and thus yield a simpler circuit.

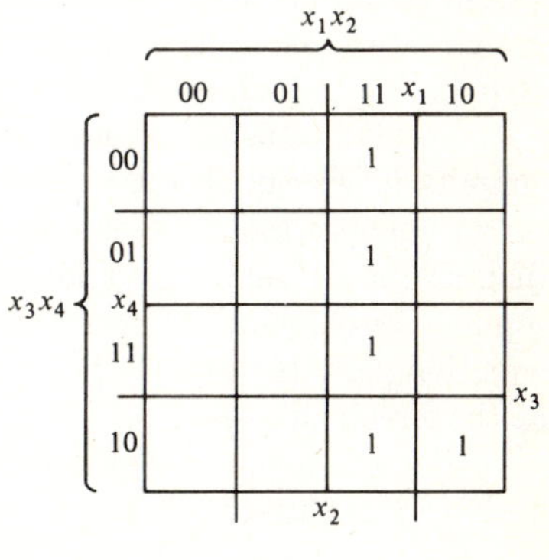

FIGURE 4-4.8

All the representations of Boolean functions discussed thus far can be used. In practice, however, Karnaugh maps, cubes, and Boolean equations are most often used in minimization.

We may also express Boolean functions as sums of minterms (or products of maxterms). For example, the function $f = x_1 \cdot (x_2 + x_3 \cdot \bar{x}_4)$ can be expressed in the sum-of-products form as

$$f = \sum (10, 12, 13, 14, 15)$$

or we may write the sum-of-products form of f explicitly as

$$f = x_1 \bar{x}_2 x_3 \bar{x}_4 + x_1 x_2 \bar{x}_3 \bar{x}_4 + x_1 x_2 \bar{x}_3 x_4 + x_1 x_2 x_3 \bar{x}_4 + x_1 x_2 x_3 x_4$$

The advantage of using a sum-of-products form for the function given here is that such a form is quite amenable to simplification—either directly or in one of the previously discussed representations.

4-4.2 Minimization of Boolean Functions

One very important use of Boolean algebra is the expression of circuit design problems in a form that lends itself to being more readily understood and simplified. A very general algorithm that describes how particular circuits are produced is as follows:

1 A person indicates a desire to have a particular circuit built. The person specifies (often in a rather vague manner) what this circuit is supposed to do.

2 A circuit designer (often after further discussions with the requestor to specify more precisely and carefully the operation of the desired circuit) produces a preliminary design which is often a set of Boolean functions.

3 The preliminary design of step 2 is then simplified and modified in such a way that a reliable circuit that performs to specifications without waste of circuit elements is produced.

4 The circuit is built according to step 3.

Boolean algebra is often used to express a particular circuit that has been requested. A natural-language description may not be very easily understood, and it certainly does not lend itself to simplification. The same problem expressed in Boolean equations indicates the formal relations among its elements, and it is in a language that permits simplifications of operations. Steps 1, 2, and 4 in the design procedure have been discussed in Sec. 1-2.15, and further examples of designs are given in Sec. 4-5. In this subsection, we are concerned primarily with step 3, viz., the minimization of the design equations.

Instead of using Boolean algebra to synthesize a circuit and subsequently simplify it, we can also use the algebra to analyze and simplify existing circuits. As an analytic tool, Boolean algebra can be used to express some given circuit diagram in a form which relates the circuit output as a function of the circuit inputs. Once again, having the operation of the circuit expressed as a Boolean equation permits simplification that may not be at all obvious by simply looking at the circuit diagram.

For example, consider the circuit given in Fig. 4-4.9. The approach used here to determine the output for z starts with the output gate and expresses the inputs

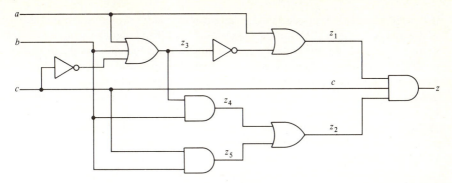

FIGURE 4-4.9 A circuit to be analyzed.

to this gate as outputs of earlier subcircuits. These intermediate outputs are treated in a similar fashion, until all the paths to the original inputs have been traced.

Using this approach, we can write the equation for z as

$$z = z_1 \cdot c \cdot z_2$$
$$= (a + \bar{z}_3) \cdot c \cdot (z_4 + z_5)$$
$$= (a + \overline{a + b + \bar{c}}) \cdot c \cdot (bz_3 + bc)$$
$$= (a + \overline{a + b + \bar{c}}) \cdot c \cdot [b \cdot (a + b + \bar{c}) + bc]$$

We can simplify this equation considerably by applying certain Boolean identities given in Sec. 4-2.1. Therefore,

$$z = [a + (\overline{a + b + \bar{c}})]c[b(a + b + \bar{c}) + bc]$$
$$= (a + \bar{a}\bar{b}c)cb(a + b + \bar{c} + c)$$
$$= (acb + \bar{a}b\bar{b}c)(a + b + 1)$$
$$= (acb)$$
$$= abc$$

The use of Boolean equations should be obvious. Not only do they provide a precise description of the functioning of each subcircuit, but they also permit the reduction of the original circuit to one three-input *AND* gate, a reduction that is not immediately obvious by looking at the circuit diagram.

This procedure of minimization is important in circuit design, particularly if many circuits of one kind are to be built, because the cost of a circuit depends, to a degree, on the number of gates in the circuit. The goal of minimization is to reduce to a minimum the number of gates required by a circuit. (It must be noted, however, that as the cost of gates decreases because of newer technologies, the goal of minimizing the number of gates becomes less important, as the price component due to connections becomes a larger fraction of the total cost.)

The importance of Boolean algebra is that it makes minimization more readily possible. The reason for this fact is that Boolean algebra is a language whose rules and permissible operations are known and understood. Consequently, if a problem can be expressed in this language, we have available all the mathematical operations and techniques associated with the language. Hence, we are more readily able to minimize because defined operations and identities can be applied to equations. These formal manipulative techniques are lacking for a switching function represented as a circuit. In more formal terms, we may characterize minimization as the selection of the simplest representative expression of an equivalence class to serve as our circuit. Recall that there are 2^{2^n} distinct Boolean functions of n variables, but there is a denumerably infinite number of well-formed Boolean expressions. However, these Boolean expressions form a partition consisting of 2^{2^n} equivalence classes. We commonly take the "simplest" expression and use it as the representative of the equivalence class, all members of which designate the same function. Unfortunately, the choice of which Boolean identities to use in any particular minimization operation is primarily determined by the skill one has in performing Boolean manipulations, and this skill is partly a matter of experience. Thus, there are no real guarantees that one will choose the right identities to reduce a Boolean equation to minimal form.

Because of the difficulty in reducing certain Boolean expressions to their simplest forms by purely algebraic means, other methods of minimization have been developed. These methods make use of certain representations of switching functions.

We shall now discuss two minimization methods. The first method will be based on the cube-array representation of a function, while the second will be based on Karnaugh maps.

Consider the Boolean identity $ab + a\bar{b} = a$ which permits variables b and $\bar{b}$ to be deleted, thus yielding an equivalent simpler expression. In a more generalized form, the identity would be $abc + a\bar{b}c = ac$. This transformation, in cube notation, can be represented as the replacement of the cube array $\{111, 101\}$ by the array $\{1x1\}$ where the x indicates the place of the missing variable. Repeated application of $ab + a\bar{b} = a$ to the expression $abcd + a\bar{b}cd + ab\bar{c}d + a\bar{b}\bar{c}d$ yields ad as a final result. In cube notation, this transformation can be represented as the replacement of the array $\{1111, 1011, 1101, 1001\}$ by the array $\{1x11, 1x01\}$ and then the replacement of this second array by the array $\{1xx1\}$, where now the x's mark the places in the ordered 4-tuple of the missing b and c variables. In short, this transformation is really the replacement of two adjacent terms by one term which covers them both. The terminology used suggests this intuitive concept. The cube $1x1$ is said to *cover* each of the cubes 111 and 101 (the decomposition products of $1x1$), and the set of cubes $\{111, 101\}$ is the base of cube $1x1$. A cube, such as $1x1$, is decomposed into its base cubes by replacing each x by a 1 and then by a 0.

The geometrical interpretation of this covering relationship in the n-space representation of switching functions is the replacement of adjacent vertices by the line that joins them, or the replacement of adjacent lines by the plane they define, or the replacement of adjacent planes by the cube they define, etc. A number of examples of this interpretation are given in Fig. 4-4.10.

Before we describe how the absorption law can be used in minimization, let us refer to cubes such as $1x0$, $x111$, $010x0$, etc., as "1 cubes" since each such cube has one variable missing. Cubes such as $1xx0$, $x0x$, etc., are called 2 cubes because two variables are missing in each cube; $10xxx$ is a 3 cube; etc. It should

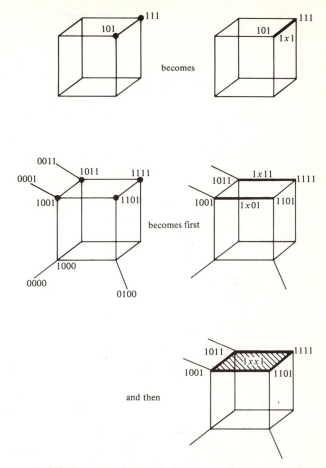

FIGURE 4-4.10   Geometrical interpretation of cube cover.

now be clear why earlier minterms were called 0 cubes—they have no variables missing. A minterm, or 0 cube, is a cube of 0 dimensions; it is a point or vertex. A 1 cube, 2 cube, and 3 cube can be represented by a line, plane, and three-dimensional cube respectively. Furthermore, recall that the cube $1x0$ covers 110 and 100, while $11xx1$ covers 11001, 11011, 11101, and 11111.

From the absorption law we have $ab + a = a$. Similarly, $abc + ac = ac$, etc. This latter transformation expressed in cube notation would be the replacement of $\{111, 1x1\}$ by $1x1$. In other words, the Boolean sum of two terms, one of which covers the other, is equivalent to the one covering term. In n-space form, this would appear as shown in Fig. 4-4.11 because the line $1x1$ already includes the vertex 111.

This fact implies that cubes which are covered by cubes of a higher order need not be retained. In any expression, we need to retain only the cubes of highest order which are not covered by any other cube, and which taken together cover all the vertices that have a functional value of 1 associated with them.

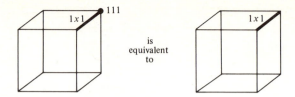

FIGURE 4-4.11   Geometrical interpretation of absorption law.

By using the two Boolean identities described here, it is possible to reduce a switching function to an equivalent form consisting of all those cubes which are not covered by any other cubes. Any such cube is called a *prime implicant*. After this reduction is done, we may find among the cubes that are present one or more cubes which are redundant in the sense that the removal of such cubes would not delete any of the 0 cubes present. The minimization process can now be restated as the selection of the smallest subset of the set of prime implicants that still covers the set of 0 cubes.

As an example, consider the function

$$z = \bar{x}_1\bar{x}_2\bar{x}_3\bar{x}_4 + \bar{x}_1x_2\bar{x}_3\bar{x}_4 + \bar{x}_1x_2\bar{x}_3x_4 + \bar{x}_1\bar{x}_2\bar{x}_3x_4 + x_1\bar{x}_2\bar{x}_3x_4 + x_1\bar{x}_2x_3x_4$$

$$= \sum (0, 1, 4, 5, 9, 11)$$

which appears in its 4-space representation in Fig. 4-4.12. By inspection, there are six 0 cubes, six 1 cubes ($10x1$, $x001$, $0x01$, $010x$, $0x00$, $000x$), and one 2 cube ($0x0x$). Now, the set of prime implicants will contain the 2 cube $0x0x$ and the two 1 cubes $10x1$ and $x001$ because there are no cubes that cover these cubes. Again, by inspection, we can see that the 1 cube $x001$ is redundant because the two vertices it covers are also covered by the other two prime implicants (0001 by the 2 cube $0x0x$ and 1001 by the 1 cube $10x1$). Hence the minimal equation is $z = \bar{x}_1\bar{x}_3 + x_1\bar{x}_2x_4$ which is obtained by rewriting the minimal covering set $\{0x0x,\ 10x1\}$ as a sum-of-products expression (with each cube corresponding to a product term).

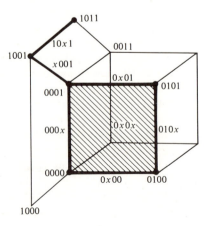

FIGURE 4-4.12   Cover representation of $f = \sum(0, 1, 4, 5, 9, 11)$.

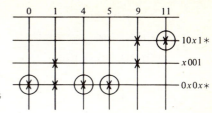

FIGURE 4-4.13 Prime implicant chart for $f = \sum(0, 1, 4, 5, 9, 11)$.

An alternate method for selecting a suitable minimum sum from the group of prime implicants is to construct a prime-implicant chart which for this problem is given in Fig. 4-4.13. The chart contains a number of columns, each of which has a number at the top that corresponds to a minterm in the sum-of-products form of the function. Each row corresponds to one of the prime implicants, as identified by $10x0$, $x001$, and $0x0x$ at the right. In each row we mark a cross under each minterm contained in the prime implicant represented by that row. Thus, in the example the first prime implicant $10x1$ contains or covers minterms 11 and 9. The remainder of the chart is completed in a similar manner.

The first step in using the prime-implicant chart is to examine the columns to see whether any column has exactly one cross in it. This is true for columns 0, 4, 5, and 11. We place circles around each of the crosses which stand alone in a column, and then we rule a line through all the crosses in each row containing a circled cross. The significance of this maneuver is that the particular prime implicant which has been marked is the only one which can cover the required encircled minterm. However, since it also covers all other minterms designated by a cross in the same row, no other prime implicants need be chosen to cover these minterms. A single asterisk is placed at the end of each prime implicant thus required. Such rows are called *primary basis rows*. In addition to covering the minterms under which the crosses are circled, each primary basis row covers other minterms where other crosses lie in that row. Thus row $0x0x$ in Fig. 4-4.13 covers not only minterms 0, 4, and 5 but also minterm 1.

We continue this process for the columns containing crosses which are in the other primary basis row, and at the end we have covered all minterms. Hence we have determined the minimum sum $\bar{x}_1\bar{x}_3 + x_1\bar{x}_2x_4$.

A general method that can be used to generate automatically all the prime implicants that cover a given set of minterms is the *Quine-McCluskey algorithm*. First, the 0 cubes are used to generate all the possible 1 cubes; then these 1 cubes are used to generate all possible 2 cubes; this process continues until the r cubes are generated for some r such that there are no $(r + 1)$ cubes. The cubes that remain after the elimination of all cubes covered by higher-order cubes are the prime implicants.

Consider the example of $g = x_1 \cdot (x_2 + x_3\bar{x}_4)$ which can be represented by the standard sum $\sum(10, 12, 13, 14, 15)$. Writing the minterms in cube form, grouping them in order of increasing number of 1s in each 0 cube, and finally applying the Quine-McCluskey algorithm to this set of ordered cubes gives the result shown in Fig. 4-4.14. The arrows in the diagram have been drawn and labeled to indicate which cubes generated the higher-order cubes. Observe that

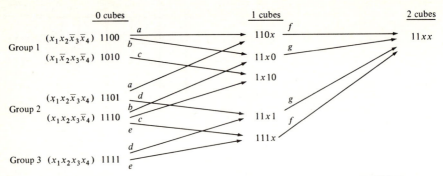

FIGURE 4-4.14

cubes within one grouping are compared only with cubes in the next higher grouping in order to determine which higher cubes are possible.

The entire set of cubes is known as the *complex* of the function, while the minterms (0 cubes) are the *base* of the function. To eliminate redundant cubes, we simply ignore every cube which has an arrow leading from it to another higher cube. The cubes that are left, $1x10$ and $11xx$, form the set of prime implicants. If Fig. 4-4.14 is turned on its side so that the arrows are pointing upward, then we have a Hasse diagram. Hasse diagrams show all the covering relationships that exist among the elements of the complex of a function, with the prime implicants being those cubes which are not connected to any cube above them.

By examination, we see that both prime implicants are required in order to cover the base of the function. Hence the minimum sum is $g = \{11xx, 1x10\} = x_1x_2 + x_1x_3\bar{x}_4$.

The Quine-McCluskey procedure for finding the cover of a set of minterms, or 0 cubes, can be performed on a computer by using bit strings to represent cubes. The algorithm for doing this is now described.

In the Quine-McCluskey method, all pairs of 0 cubes are first combined, if possible, to form 1 cubes. For example, 1001 and 1011 are covered by $10x1$. Since only values 0 and 1 can appear in a bit string, a different convention must be adopted for the representation of cubes. If 1 and 0 are written as 10 and 01 respectively, then the above 0 cubes become 10010110 and 10011010. Similarly, x can be represented by 11, so that $10x1$ is written as 10011110. Since every 2 bits may represent a 0, 1, or x, this may be thought of as a ternary representation. Note that each odd-even pair of bits, for example, the first and second, third and fourth, etc., can represent 0, 1, or x, but there is no relationship between even-odd pairs such as the second and third bits.

Two operations must be performed on the ternary representations of cubes. The first is to determine whether two cubes can be combined. Note that for the cubes 1001 and 1011,

$$10010110 \ \bigtriangledown \ 10011010 = 00001100$$

The cubes $101x$ and $10x1$ when combined with the exclusive OR operation yield

$$10011011 \ \bigtriangledown \ 10011110 = 00000101$$

These examples illustrate that two cubes can be combined if and only if the exclusive OR of their ternary representation yields 11 in one odd-even pair of bit positions and 0 in all other positions. In the following algorithm, two cubes will be combined if their exclusive OR is equal to $2^i + 2^{i+1}$ for one i belonging to $\{0, 2, \ldots, 2 * n - 2\}$, where n is the number of variables on which the cubes depend.

The second operation which must be performed on the ternary representations is to combine two i cubes to form the $(i + 1)$ cube that covers them. This can be accomplished by using the logical OR. For example, 1001 and 1011 give

$$10010110 \lor 10011010 = 10011110$$

which represents $10x1$, the required result. Two cubes which differ in one ternary position, one cube having a 01, the other a 10, will always yield 11 in that position when the logical OR is performed, and all other positions remain unchanged.

In the following algorithm, cubes will be contained in simple linked lists. Each node will have the format

CUBE	COVERED	LINK

NODE

where *CUBE* is the ternary representation of a cube and *COVERED* has value T or F if the cube is covered or not covered respectively. *LINK* indicates the following node in a list. Each element of an array of pointers denoted *CUBELIST* and having subscripts 0 to n, where n is the number of variables on which the cubes are based, will indicate a list of i cubes if its subscript is i. Initially *CUBELIST*[0] points to a list of 0 cubes, and all other lists are empty.

Algorithm *COVER* Given a set of 0 cubes dependent on n variables and contained in the list indicated by *CUBELIST*[0], this algorithm determines the set of prime implicants by using the Quine-McCluskey procedure. Each i cube that is generated is placed in the list pointed to by *CUBELIST*[i]. Pointers P, Q, and R and counters i and j are used.

1 [Initialize] Set $i \leftarrow 0$.

2 [Scan list i] Set $P \leftarrow CUBELIST[i]$. If $P = NULL$, then Exit. If $LINK(P) = NULL$, then Exit.

3 [Scan successors of P] Set $Q \leftarrow LINK(P)$.

4 [Test for a possible combination] Set $TEST \leftarrow CUBE(P) \lor CUBE(Q)$. Repeat for $j = 0, 2, \ldots, 2 * n - 2$: If $TEST = 2^{j+1} + 2^j$, then go to step 5. Go to step 9.

5 [Mark cubes to be combined and form a new cube] Set $COVERED(P) \leftarrow COVERED(Q) \leftarrow T$ and $NEWCUBE \leftarrow CUBE(P) \lor CUBE(Q)$.

6 [Scan the next cube list for duplicates] Set $R \leftarrow CUBELIST[i + 1]$.

7 [End of list or equal cubes?] If $R = NULL$, then go to step 8. If $NEWCUBE = CUBE(R)$, then go to step 9; otherwise set $R \leftarrow LINK(R)$ and repeat this step.

8 [Add an $(i + 1)$ cube to the list] Set $R \leftarrow NODE$, $CUBE(R) \leftarrow NEWCUBE$, $COVERED(R) \leftarrow F$, $LINK(R) \leftarrow CUBELIST[i + 1]$, and $CUBELIST[i + 1] \leftarrow R$.

9 [Next successor of P] Set $Q \leftarrow LINK(Q)$. If $Q \neq NULL$, then go to step 4.

10 [Get next cube for comparison with successors] Set $P \leftarrow LINK(P)$. If $LINK(P) = NULL$, then set $i \leftarrow i + 1$ and go to step 2; otherwise go to step 3.   ////

Algorithm *COVER* scans each list of cubes, comparing each cube to its successors in the list. In step 4, it is determined whether two cubes can be combined. If they can, steps 5 to 8 combine them using the OR operation, mark them as being covered, and enter the new cube in the $(i + 1)$st list if that cube was not previously formed.

Turning to Karnaugh maps, which are perhaps the easiest to use for functions of six or fewer variables, we can make similar interpretations of minimization techniques as were observed in using the cube notation. The application of the identity $ab + a\bar{b} = a$, when seen in the context of a Karnaugh map, becomes the replacement of two adjacent cells containing 1s by a larger area containing two cells. Thus, replacing $abc + a\bar{b}c$ by ac becomes the replacement shown in Fig. 4-4.15, where the ellipse indicates that the two cells are considered to be one area. A pair of adjacent 2-cell areas can be joined into a 4-cell area, and two adjacent 4-cell areas can be combined into one 8-cell area, etc.

A minterm, so-called because it occupies a minimum nonzero area on a Karnaugh map, is associated with one cell. A 1 cube is associated with two adjacent cells, a 2 cube is associated with four adjacent cells, and, in general, an r cube is associated with 2^r adjacent cells.

The absorption operation, $abc + ab = ab$, or its cube counterpart, the replacement of cubes by cubes that cover them, has its counterpart on a Karnaugh map as well. In this case, it is simply the grouping of adjacent cells into the largest possible block of such cells, and the use of the block of cells instead of the individual cells.

Minimization then becomes the search for the largest areas composed of the adjacent cells with 1s in them. From the set of these largest areas, the minimum number of areas is chosen such that every original 0 cube is part of at least one such area.

For example, consider the function

$$z = \bar{c}(\bar{e} + abc) + b \cdot [a\bar{c}d + \bar{d} \cdot (a + ce)]$$

This function is a 5-variable function, and so a 5-variable map structure is required. For convenience, the cells have been numbered with the decimal equiv-

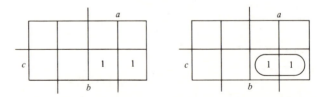

FIGURE 4-4.15 Map simplification of $abc + a\bar{b}c = ac$.

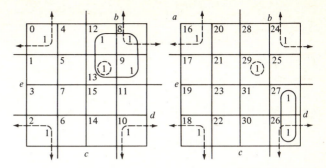

FIGURE 4-4.16 Minimization with a Karnaugh map.

alent of the 5-tuple input that they correspond to, as shown in Fig. 4-4.16. Also, those cells that correspond to functional values of 1 have been appropriately designated in the diagram. The largest groups of adjacent cells have been designated by lines enclosing the 1s in these cells. Solid-line encirclements designate groupings that are wholly within the a or $\bar{a}$ half. Dotted-line encirclements join groups that cross over the $a - \bar{a}$ boundary, with cells being adjacent to their counterparts in the other half. Lines that extend over a map edge are connected around the back to a matching line that is over the edge of the opposite edge.

The important consideration in using Karnaugh maps is to enclose cells in the largest possible areas. Thus, cell 12 could have been paired with cell 8 or with cell 13. Either one of these pairs would have been a 2-cell grouping. But we chose to enclose cell 12 with cells 8, 9, and 13 because it gave us a 4-cell grouping. Always forming the largest possible areas is equivalent to forming the highest possible cubes—those with the greatest number of variables missing.

From the marked diagram, we see that one 3 cube, one 2 cube, and two 1 cubes have been formed. All these are necessary to completely cover the minterm base of the function, and so the minimized function becomes

$$z = \bar{c}\bar{e} + \bar{a}b\bar{d} + bc\bar{d}e + ab\bar{c}d$$

We have examined, in some detail, two popular minimization methods. In general, there may be more than one minimum sum. The Quine-McCluskey method can be modified and extended to generate all such minimum sums. However, we do not give such an algorithm here.

EXERCISES 4-4

1 For each of the following functions give (1) the circuit diagram representation, (2) the cube representation, (3) the truth table representation, and (4) the Karnaugh map representation.
   (a) $f_1 = x + y + z$
   (b) $f_2 = \bar{x}\bar{y}z + \bar{x}y\bar{z} + xy\bar{z}$
   (c) $f_3 = \bar{w} + y(\bar{x} + \bar{z})$

2 The cube representation of three switching functions is given in Fig. 4-4.17. Write

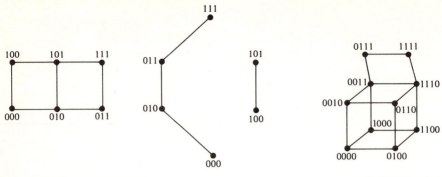

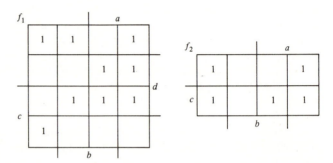

FIGURE 4-4.17

FIGURE 4-4.18

a Boolean expression for each function, and then simplify it by using theorems of Boolean algebra.

3 Karnaugh maps of two switching functions are given in Fig. 4-4.18.

(a) Write a Boolean expression for each function, draw its cube representation, and draw a gate circuit that realizes the function.

(b) Simplify the Boolean expression using theorems of Boolean algebra and repeat part (a).

4 Analyze the gate network given in Fig. 4-4.19 by expressing f as a function of the input variables w, x, y, and z. Try to find an equivalent network which is simpler. Assume that only the variables w, x, y, and z can appear as input terminals.

5 Expand the following functions into their canonical sum-of-products form.

(a) $f_1(x, y, z) = xy + y\bar{z}$

(b) $f_2(w, x, y, z) = xy + y\bar{w}z$

(c) $f_3(w, x, y, z) = w + \bar{y}z + \bar{x}y$

6 Use the Karnaugh map representation to find a minimal sum-of-products expression of each of the following functions.

(a) $f(a, b, c) = \sum (0, 1, 4, 6)$

(b) $f(a, b, c, d) = \sum (0, 5, 7, 8, 12, 14)$

(c) $f(a, b, c, d) = \sum (0, 1, 2, 3, 13, 15)$

(d) $f(a, b, c, d, e) = \sum (0, 1, 3, 8, 9, 13, 14, 15, 16, 17, 19, 24, 25, 27, 31)$

7 Use the Quine-McCluskey algorithm to find the prime implicants of the following expressions. In each case, also obtain a minimal expression for each function.

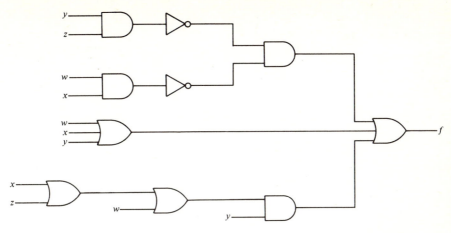

FIGURE 4-4.19

(a) $f(a, b, c) = \sum (0, 2, 3, 7)$
(b) $f(a, b, c, d) = \sum (5, 7, 10, 13, 15)$
(c) $f(a, b, c, d) = \sum (0, 2, 6, 7, 8, 9, 13, 15)$
(d) $f(a, b, c, d, e) = \sum (9, 20, 21, 29, 30, 31)$

8 From the prime-implicant charts of Fig. 4-4.20, obtain a minimal expression for each of the functions.

9 Write a PL/I program for algorithm *COVER*. The program input is to consist of a set of 0 cubes, or minterms, expressed in decimal form; for example, 3, 8, and 9 represent $\bar{x}_1 \bar{x}_2 x_3 x_4$, $x_1 \bar{x}_2 \bar{x}_3 \bar{x}_4$, and $x_1 \bar{x}_2 \bar{x}_3 x_4$ respectively.

10 Formulate an algorithm and write a program which will produce the numbers of the minterms for any Boolean expression.

The required algorithm is similar to the procedure described in Prob. 6, Exercises 2-6, for generating the minterms of a statement formula. Assume that letters A to Z represent Boolean variables and that $*$, $+$, and $-$ represent the Boolean product, sum, and negation respectively. Furthermore, assume the input expressions are well-formed. The algorithm would consist of the following steps.

1 For expressions in which a negation operator affects more than a single variable, occurrences of double negation are first removed, and then De Morgan's laws are applied. Since this may cause more occurrences of double negation, repeat this step until De Morgan's laws can no longer be applied.

2 Distribute the Boolean product to obtain an expression which is the sum of products of variables or of their negations; for example,

$$(\{(A * D) + [(-C * B) * C]\} + [(E * -A) * -A])$$

Recursion may prove useful.

3 Convert the products in this sum of products to 0 cubes. Make sure that contradictory products and duplicate 0 cubes are eliminated. Use recursion to replace each term T_i missing a variable, say B, by $T_i * B$ and $T_i * -B$. Be sure that variables within minterms are in some predetermined order.

4 Scan each minterm and determine its decimal representation.

11 Algorithm *COVER* determines the prime implicants of a set of 0 cubes, but this cover may contain redundant cubes. Formulate an algorithm and write a program which

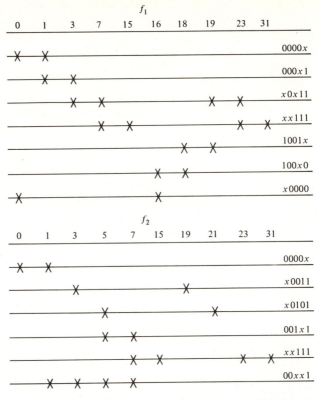

FIGURE 4-4.20

will find all possible minimal covers of a set of 0 cubes, where minimal means that the cover does not contain redundant cubes.

The first step that should be taken in your algorithm is to determine the essential prime implicants. Then the problem reduces to finding the minimal covers of nonessential prime implicants for cubes not yet covered. A brute-force solution would be to test all combinations of nonessential prime implicants. There are other solutions to this problem however.

4-5 DESIGN EXAMPLES USING BOOLEAN ALGEBRA

In this section we illustrate how Boolean algebra is used in the design of some simple switching circuits that perform various arithmetic operations on numbers. We are concerned with fixed-length binary numbers, since in general most digital computers manipulate binary numbers of fixed length.

Initially, we give a brief discussion of arithmetic operations that can be performed on integral binary numbers. Let $a = \langle a_1, a_2, \ldots, a_n \rangle$ and $b = \langle b_1, b_2, \ldots, b_n \rangle$ denote two binary numbers. The binary addition table given in Table 4-5.1 is simple. Note, however, that in the case of two 1s, a 2-digit sequence is

Table 4-5.1

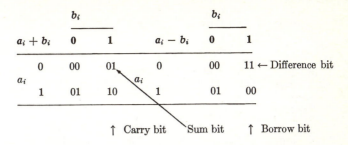

| | b_i | | | b_i | |
$a_i + b_i$	**0**	**1**	$a_i - b_i$	**0**	**1**
0	00	01	**0**	00	11 ← Difference bit
1	01	10	**1**	01	00

↑ Carry bit　　Sum bit　　↑ Borrow bit

required to express their sum. The left digit in this sequence is called the *carry* bit. In hand calculations, this carry bit creates no problems, but in fixed-length computer words, a carry may require an extra bit position which does not exist. Such a condition is called an *overflow*, and it must be detected since its occurrence signifies an incorrect sum. Subtraction is equally simple, and its table is also given in Table 4-5.1. Note that in the case of $0 - 1$, a 2-digit sequence is again required, with the left digit representing a borrow bit. In hand calculations, if $b > a$, we merely form $b - a$ instead and prefix the result with a minus sign. The determination of whether $b > a$ on a digital computer is time-consuming and is generally not done. In such cases, a borrow may "propagate" out of the high-order end of the result, indicating that the result as it exists is incorrect and must be corrected.

The operations described in Table 4-5.1 can easily handle signed binary numbers. The addition of a negative number to a positive number can be accomplished by merely subtracting them. The subtraction of a negative number from a positive number can be obtained by adding them and placing a plus sign on the result. The subtraction of a positive number from a negative number can be performed by adding them and placing a minus sign on the result.

By examining a number of examples, we can formulate rules that govern the handling of signs and propagating borrows (borrows that carry into a non-existent bit position). Assuming 4-bit numbers, we have

```
    (+) 1001        (+) 1001        (−) 1001        (−) 1001
 + (+) 0101     + (+) 0111     + (−) 0101     + (−) 0111
 ────────────   ────────────   ────────────   ────────────
    (+) 1110        (+)10000        (−) 1110        (−)10000
                       ↑                               ↑
                    overflow                        overflow


    (+) 1001        (+) 1001        (−) 0101        (−) 0101
 + (−) 0101     − (+) 0101     + (+) 1001     − (−) 1001
 ────────────   ────────────   ────────────   ────────────
  Change to        (+) 0100      Change to         11100 ⇒ (+) 0100
                                                       ↑
                                                    borrow


    (−) 1001        (−) 1001        (+) 0101        (+) 0101
 + (+) 0101     − (−) 0101     + (−) 1001     − (+) 1001
 ────────────   ────────────   ────────────   ────────────
  Change to        (−) 0100      Change to         11100 ⇒ (−) 0100
                                                       ↑
                                                    borrow
```

(+) 1001	(+) 0101		(−) 1001	(−) 0101
− (+) 0101	− (+) 1001		− (−) 0101	− (−) 1001

(+) 0100	11100 ⟹ (−) 0100		(−) 0100	11100 ⟹ (+) 0100
	↑			↑
	borrow			borrow

(+) 1001	(+) 1001	(+) 0101	(+) 0101
− (−) 0101	+ (+) 0101	− (−) 1001	+ (+) 1001

Change to	(+) 1110	Change to	(+) 1110

(−) 1001	(−) 1001	(−) 0101	(−) 0101
− (+) 0101	+ (−) 0101	− (+) 1001	+ (−) 1001

Change to	(−) 1110	Change to	(−) 1110

From these examples, observe first that in certain cases the actual operation performed is not the original one intended. For example, we add numbers of opposite signs by actually subtracting them, and we subtract numbers of opposite signs by actually adding them. Notice, also, that overflow and a propagating borrow can occur only when we are actually adding and subtracting numbers, respectively. Furthermore, the sign of the result is always equal to the sign of the first operand, except when a propagating borrow occurs. The reason for doing these equivalent operations is that it eliminates the need to compare two numbers in order to determine which one should be subtracted from the other. The second number is always subtracted from the first and if something goes wrong (i.e., if the larger is taken from the smaller), this fact is indicated by a propagating borrow, and we can apply a correction. This correction is to form the $2s$ complement of the result and affix the sign opposite to that of the first operand. We shall discuss methods of forming $2s$ complement shortly. In the case of an overflow, we can make no correction. These observations can be summarized in Table 4-5.2.

Note that an overflow and a propagating borrow manifest themselves in the same manner—an attempt to set a bit beyond the leftmost end of the number to 1. We distinguish between overflows and propagating borrows by observing whether an addition or a subtraction is actually performed.

Now, it has been noted that on certain occasions a result is in 2s complement form. This fact introduces the problem of how negative numbers can be represented in a computer. The numeric part of a number can be represented simply by the regular 0 and 1 bit pattern that records it as a binary number. But how is a sign to be represented? A computer can use only 0s and 1s; it has

Table 4-5.2

Desired operation	Form	Signs of operands	Actual operation	Results
addition	$a + b$	same	addition	(1)*
addition	$a + b$	different	subtraction	(2)†
subtraction	$a - b$	same	subtraction	(2)†
subtraction	$a - b$	different	addition	(1)*

* The sign is the sign of a; an overflow indicates that the result is too large to be represented.
† If no propagating borrow is present, then the sign is the sign of a; otherwise, the result is in $2s$ complement form, and the sign is the opposite to that of a.

no other symbols at its disposal. Consequently, the sign portion of a number will also have to be represented as some 0 or 1 coded pattern. For reasons of simplicity, 0 and 1 are chosen to represent the plus and minus signs respectively.

How are we to distinguish between a 1 representing the sign bit and a 1 that is part of a numeric (magnitude) representation for a number? One approach is to treat the sign bit differently from the remaining magnitude bits. Since the length of a computer word is known, we can always save the first bit at the high-order end of the word for the sign and treat it accordingly.

This approach is called the *sign-magnitude representation* of signed binary numbers. For example, the representation of $+1001$ and -1001 would be 01001 and 11001 respectively. In our previous examples, where a computer word length 4 was assumed, it would now be increased to 5 bits, 1 bit for the sign and the remaining 4 bits for the magnitude. An overflow or propagating borrow is now seen as an attempt to use the sign-bit position to store a numeric-bit value.

Sign-magnitude arithmetic is conceptually straightforward, but it has the disadvantage of requiring separate circuitry for handling sign bits. This difficulty has led to other methods of representing numbers that avoid the need for distinguishing between sign bits and magnitude bits.

One such method is the 1s complement representation. A negative number in 1s complement form appears as the corresponding positive number of the same magnitude (including the sign bit) complemented. Thus, -9 would appear as 10110, which is the result of complementing every bit in 01001, the representation of $+9$. Note that positive numbers are identical both in the sign-magnitude representation and in the 1s complement form; it is the negative numbers that appear different in these two forms.

One minor point to note about 1s complement representation is that there are two ways of representing zero—either by 00000 or by 11111 ($+0$ and -0), assuming a total word length of 5. (Actually the sign-magnitude representation shares this same problem; 00000 and 10000 represent $+0$ and -0 respectively.)

The advantage of using 1s complement representation lies in the fact that the sign bits are treated as numeric bits. No special circuitry for generating the sign is required; the sign comes out correct. Furthermore, the operation of subtraction becomes unnecessary. In order to perform a subtraction, just form the 1s complement of the second operand and add. To detect an uncorrectable overflow condition, observe the signs of the operands that are actually added. If both operand signs are the same and the sign of the result differs, then there is an overflow and no correction is possible. On the other hand, if there is a propagating carry out of the sign-bit position, then this carry of 1 must be added to the result in order to get the correct answer. This is called an *end-around carry*. Evidently, if there is both a propagating carry and an overflow, then the result is still in error even with the application of the end-around carry. The following examples demonstrate these points.

9	01001	9	01001	01001
+ +5	+ 00101	+ −5	+ −00101	+ 11010
14	01110	4	Change to	$100011 \Rightarrow 00100$
				↑
				end-around carry

5	00101	00101	−9	10110
+ −9	+ −01001	+ 10110	+ −5	+ 11010
−4	Change to	11011	−14	110000 → 10001

           ↑

           end-around carry,
           no overflow

7	00111	−7	11000	−7	11000	11000
+ +9	+ 01001	+ −9	+ 10110	− −9	− 10110	+ 01001
16	10000		101110	2	Change to	100001 ⇒ 00010

    ↑   ↑   ↑

   overflow   end-around carry   end-around
                  but also overflow   carry

Another form by which signed binary numbers can be represented is the 2s complement representation. Again, numbers represented in this fashion have all the bits (including the sign bit) taking part in the arithmetic operation, and, as in the case of 1s complement, subtraction is unnecessary. Addition of the second operand in 2s complement form yields the same result as the subtraction of the second operand from the first operand. There are no end-around carries. The sign bit always comes out correct, except in the case of an overflow, for which no correction is possible. Except for one case, overflows are detected by checking the signs of the operands. If, when actually adding, the two operands have the same sign and the result has the opposite sign, then an overflow has occurred. The one exceptional case that cannot be detected by this method is the following: if a and b are n-bit words representing negative binary numbers (that is, 1 sign bit and $n - 1$ magnitude bits), then if $|a| + |b| = 2^{n-1}$, an unused word is generated $(100 \cdots 0)$ with a carry of 1 out of the sign bit. To detect this overflow, we must check for the magnitude bits being all 0 and for the carry-out bit value of 1.

To form the 2s complement representation of a number, first form the 1s complement representation of it (including the sign bit in the scope of the 1s complementation operation) and then add 1 to the low-order bit position. Another method is to copy bits from the original number, starting at the low-order end until the first 1 bit is encountered. After copying this first 1 bit, then the complements of each of the remaining bits are copied. Thus to form the 2s complement representation of $+9$, we have $01001 \Rightarrow 10110 + 00001 = 10111$. Using the alternate method, we would have

      01001 ⇒   1   (copy until first 1 is copied)

          10111   (copy complements of remaining bits)

Again, in the 2s complement representation, positive numbers are identical to positive numbers in sign-magnitude form or in 1s complement form. Negative numbers are represented as the result of performing a 2s complementation of the corresponding positive number of the same magnitude. Some examples of 2s complement arithmetic are as follows:

01001	01001	01001	5	00101	00101
+ 00101	− 00101	+ 11011	−9	− 01001	+ 10111

01110	Change to	00100	−4	Change to	11100

−9	10111	7	00111	−7	11001	11001
+ −5	+ 11011	+ 9	01001	− −9	− 10111	+ 01001

−14	110010	16	10000	2	Change to	100010

      ↑   ↑   ↑

ignore (remember   overflow   ignore
that all carries
out are ignored)

−7	11001
+ −9	+ 10111

−16	110000

      ↑

overflow (erroneous answer because this is the exceptional
case that the simple overflow test cannot detect)

    Having now briefly discussed arithmetic operations as they might be performed manually on fixed-length binary numbers, we turn to the design of some circuits that incorporate the logic involved in performing these operations. We shall restrict ourselves primarily to circuits that perform sign-magnitude arithmetic. We will, however, construct complementers that form the 2s complement and 1s complement of certain numbers. In general, the approach will be modular; i.e., we shall design modules that correctly perform the arithmetic operations on one bit position. To use these modules to process an entire word of n bits, n such modules would be connected in series or parallel.

    We shall first formulate a design for a 1s complementer. Assume that a data signal (a bit) is input to the complementer module. The required output is the complement of the data signal if a control signal is 1, or the unchanged data signal otherwise (a control signal is used simply to permit selective complementation). These requirements can be expressed in the form of a table where x_i is the input signal, c is the control signal, and s is the output. This is done in Table 4-5.3. From this table it is easy to see that

$$s = c \oplus x_i$$

Table 4-5.3

c	x_i	s
0	0	0
0	1	1
1	0	1
1	1	0

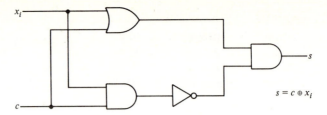

FIGURE 4-5.1   A module of a 1s complementer.

where $\oplus$ is the exclusive OR (*EX-OR*) operation. The circuit realization of this function in terms of gates consists of two inverters, two *AND* gates, and one *OR* gate. The following properties of the operator $\oplus$ will be required in this section. For any a and b,

$$a \oplus b = a\bar{b} + \bar{a}b = (a + b) \cdot \overline{ab} \qquad (1)$$

Also

$$\overline{a \oplus b} = \bar{a}\bar{b} + ab \qquad (2)$$

Thus, the equation that will be used for the 1s complementer is $s = c \oplus x_i = (c + x_i) \cdot \overline{cx_i}$. The reasons for choosing this realization (which is not a two-level circuit) over the earlier one (which is a two-level circuit) are that one inverter is saved and, more important, this circuit is almost identical to a half-adder circuit, which will be described later. A 1s complementer module is given in Fig. 4-5.1.

For a word size of 32 bits, for example, each of the 32 bits of a word would be an x_i input into an array of 32 such modules in parallel. One control line, c, would serve as the control signal into each of these modules, and the array modules would either form the 1s complement of the 32-bit input or just output it unchanged, depending on the value of c at the time.

We shall now design a 2s complementer. As previously mentioned, one method of forming the 2s complement of a number was first to copy all the low-order bits until a 1 had been copied, and second, to copy the 1s complement of all remaining bits. This method will be used here. Again, we shall design a module which will work properly for a single bit position. In this case, however, since it must be known whether a 1 has already been copied to the right, the modules when connected in parallel will be interdependent. This means that in addition to the input control signal c, which indicates whether complementation is to take place, there will also be an input bit indicator, b, which has a value of 1 if some bit to the right was 1.

We shall design the ith module of the array. This typical module receives a data bit, x_i, a bit indicator, b_i, and the control signal, c. The input b_i is the output bit indicator from the $(i - 1)$st module, and b_{i+1} is the bit indicator generated by the ith module for transmission to the $(i + 1)$st module. The input to the 0th module (the module for the lowest-order bit), b_0, will be connected to a switch that is set to 0. Figure 4-5.2 illustrates such a module with its interface to other modules in the iterative network.

The requirements for the ith module can be stated as follows. If c is 0, then no complementation takes place. In this case, s_i equals x_i, and the bit indicator,

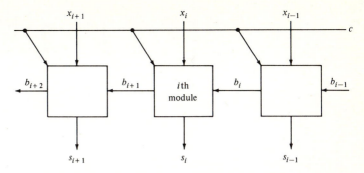

FIGURE 4-5.2   Typical module interface in a 2s complementer.

b_{i+1}, generated for the $(i + 1)$st module is 0. Let c have a value of 1. If the bit indicator, b_i, from the previous module is 0, then $s_i = x_i$ and b_{i+1} for the next module equals x_i; but if the bit indicator $b_i = 1$, then $s_i = \bar{x}_i$ and $b_{i+1} = 1$. In tabular form, these requirements can be expressed by Table 4-5.4.

To generate the equation for s_i and b_{i+1}, let us turn to Karnaugh maps. See Fig. 4-5.3. From the maps the equations can be written as

$$s_i = \bar{c}x_i + cb_i\bar{x}_i + c\bar{b}_ix_i$$
$$= \bar{c}x_i + c(b_i\bar{x}_i + \bar{b}_ix_i)$$
$$= \bar{c}x_i + c(b_i \oplus x_i)$$

and
$$b_{i+1} = b_ic + cx_i = c(b_i + x_i)$$

Note that the *EX-OR* function is required again, and we can simply use the same circuit that was used for the 1s complement module. Another reason for the choice of module made earlier in the 1s complementer becomes apparent. We are now able to obtain $b_i + x_i$ directly from that module by simply making another connection. Had we chosen $b_i \oplus x_i = b_i\bar{x}_i + \bar{b}_ix_i$ and constructed a circuit exactly according to this equation, separate circuitry would have been necessary to produce $b_i + x_i$. The circuit for the module is given in Fig. 4-5.4.

If we had desired to produce a circuit that could perform only a 2s complement operation, the circuit would have been simpler. In particular, we could

Table 4-5.4

c	b_i	x_i	s_i	b_{i+1}
0	0	0	0	0
0	0	1	1	0
0	1	0	0	0
0	1	1	1	0
1	0	0	0	0
1	0	1	1	1
1	1	0	1	1
1	1	1	0	1

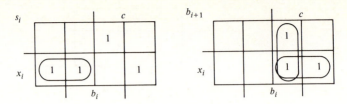

FIGURE 4-5.3   Karnaugh map for 2s complement module.

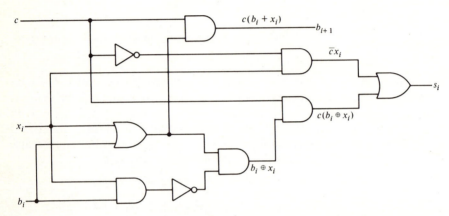

FIGURE 4-5.4   Circuit for a module in 2s complementer.

have forced b_0 to be zero, which in effect would have removed the third and fourth rows from Table 4-5.4, and this maneuver would have yielded a simpler equation for s_i, namely $s_i = b_i \oplus x_i$. The circuit we have designed, however, will do either 2s complementation or 1s complementation. It works as follows: If the value of c is 1, then for a value of $b_0 = 0$, the 2s complement of x_i is formed, while for $b_0 = 1$, the 1s complement of x_i is formed.

Consequently, with this circuit, we have made expendable our first circuit, though at a cost of slower operation. This multipurpose complementer is slower than the 1s complementer circuit.

The next example will be to design a full-adder. The initial step in this design is to first design a half-adder. A half-adder will accept two data input bits and output their sum and carry bit. Let x_i and y_i be the input bits and s_i and c_{i+1} be the sum and carry bits respectively. A tabulation of this function is given in Table 4-5.5. From this table it is obvious that $s_i = x_i \oplus y_i$ and $c_{i+1} = x_iy_i$.

Table 4-5.5

x_i	y_i	s_i	c_{i+1}
0	0	0	0
0	1	1	0
1	0	1	0
1	1	0	1

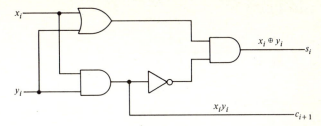

FIGURE 4-5.5   Circuit diagram for a half-adder module.

Again, we can use the circuit developed for the 1s complementer. In fact, that circuit with one extra connection is the required half-adder circuit. This circuit is given in Fig. 4-5.5.

Half-adders are not of much use by themselves in actually performing arithmetic operations because they cannot handle carry bits, and, in general, carry bits must be processed when an addition is performed. However, half-adders are very useful as components from which we can construct larger units that do perform arithmetic operations, e.g., a full-adder.

A full-adder module accepts two input data bits and a carry bit from the preceding full-adder module and generates the proper sum and carry bits. Figure 4-5.6 illustrates such a module with its interface to other modules in the iterative network. In tabular form, the requirements for a full-adder module are given in Table 4-5.6. From this table, we can construct equations as follows:

$$s_i = \bar{x}_i\bar{y}_ic_i + \bar{x}_iy_i\bar{c}_i + x_i\bar{y}_i\bar{c}_i + x_iy_ic_i$$

$$c_{i+1} = \bar{x}_iy_ic_i + x_i\bar{y}_ic_i + x_iy_i\bar{c}_i + x_iy_ic_i$$

These equations can be simplified or modified in such a manner that previous circuits, such as half-adders, can be used to construct new circuits. Formally,

$$s_i = \bar{x}_i\bar{y}_ic_i + \bar{x}_iy_i\bar{c}_i + x_i\bar{y}_i\bar{c}_i + x_iy_ic_i$$
$$= \bar{x}_i(\bar{y}_ic_i + y_i\bar{c}_i) + x_i(\bar{y}_i\bar{c}_i + y_ic_i) \qquad \text{(using the distributive law)}$$
$$= \bar{x}_i(y_i \oplus c_i) + x_i(\bar{y}_i\bar{c}_i + y_ic_i) \qquad \text{(from the definition of } \oplus\text{)}$$
$$= x_i \oplus (y_i \oplus c_i) \qquad \text{[using Eq. (2)]}$$

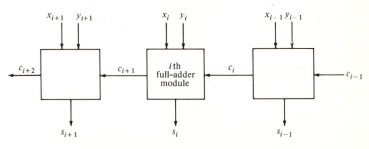

FIGURE 4-5.6   Typical module interface in a full-adder.

Table 4-5.6

x_i	y_i	c_i	s_i	c_{i+1}
0	0	0	0	0
0	0	1	1	0
0	1	0	1	0
0	1	1	0	1
1	0	0	1	0
1	0	1	0	1
1	1	0	0	1
1	1	1	1	1

and

$$c_{i+1} = \bar{x}_i y_i c_i + x_i \bar{y}_i c_i + x_i y_i \bar{c}_i + x_i y_i c_i$$

$$= y_i c_i (\bar{x}_i + x_i) + x_i (\bar{y}_i c_i + y_i \bar{c}_i)$$

$$= y_i c_i + x_i (y_i \oplus c_i)$$

Note that terms such as $y_i c_i$ and $y_i \oplus c_i$ are required, and these can be obtained from a half-adder whose inputs are y_i and c_i. The terms $x_i(y_i \oplus c_i)$ and $x_i \oplus (y_i \oplus c_i)$ are also required, and these can be obtained from another half-adder whose inputs are x_i and $y_i \oplus c_i$ (one of the outputs of the first half-adder). Thus, a half-adder is "sort of" half of a full-adder.

For convenience, let us symbolize the half-adder circuit, previously described, by Fig. 4-5.7. Note that c_0 is 0. Then a full-adder circuit diagram is given in Fig. 4-5.8.

We will next design a circuit that will do proper sign-magnitude addition or subtraction, depending on the value of a control signal a (0 for addition and 1 for subtraction). The highest-order bit is presumed to be a sign bit in each of the $(n + 1)$-bit operands, and the circuit is to produce the correct sign for the result, as well as signaling if an overflow has occurred. Consequently, we are required to design a basic adder-subtractor module for bits 0 to $n - 1$ and to design separate sign-handling circuitry for the nth bits of the input operands. (We

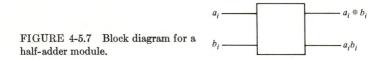

FIGURE 4-5.7 Block diagram for a half-adder module.

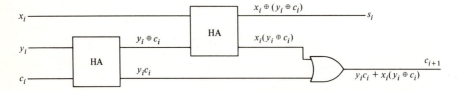

FIGURE 4-5.8 A full-adder module.

Table 4-5.7

x_i	y_i	b_i	d_i	b_{i+1}
0	0	0	0	0
0	0	1	1	1
0	1	0	1	1
0	1	1	0	1
1	0	0	1	0
1	0	1	0	0
1	1	0	0	0
1	1	1	1	1

are numbering the $n + 1$ bits in the computer word as n, $n - 1$, $n - 2$, $\ldots$, 1, 0 from left to right with the sign bit being bit n.)

The truth table for a module of a full-adder was given in Table 4-5.6. The truth table for a full-subtractor, where d_i is the difference bit and b_i is the borrow bit, is remarkably similar, as is shown in Table 4-5.7. From this table it is immediately obvious that the column for d_i is identical to the column for s_i in Table 4-5.6. Hence $d_i = x_i \oplus (y_i \oplus b_i)$. The equation for b_{i+1} is given by

$$b_{i+1} = \bar{x}_i\bar{y}_ib_i + \bar{x}_iy_i\bar{b}_i + \bar{x}_iy_ib_i + x_iy_ib_i$$
$$= \bar{x}_i(\bar{y}_ib_i + y_i\bar{b}_i) + y_ib_i(\bar{x}_i + x_i)$$
$$= \bar{x}_i(y_i \oplus b_i) + y_ib_i$$

Observe that this equation is identical to the equation for c_{i+1} in a full-adder except for having $\bar{x}_i$ instead of x_i and b_i rather than c_i. Now, if we had some way of deciding whether to use b_i or c_i, and $\bar{x}_i$ or x_i, we could use the same circuit for both addition and subtraction. The control signal a can be used for this purpose where a value of 0 denotes addition and 1 subtraction. Since it is now possible to distinguish between a bit representing a sum bit or a difference bit and between a bit representing a carry bit or a borrow bit, the notation used can be further simplified. The result bit, whether it represents a sum or difference bit, will be denoted by s_i; and the propagating bit, whether it is a carry or a borrow, will be denoted by c_i. The equations which also contain the control signal reduce to

$$s_i = x_i \oplus (y_i \oplus c_i)$$

and
$$c_{i+1} = y_ic_i + (\bar{a}x_i + a\bar{x}_i) \cdot (y_i \oplus c_i)$$

since

$$\bar{a}x_i + a\bar{x}_i \equiv x_i \qquad \text{when } a = 0$$
$$\equiv \bar{x}_i \qquad \text{when } a = 1$$

But then

$$c_{i+1} = y_ic_i + (a \oplus x_i) \cdot (y_i \oplus c_i)$$

A diagram for a typical module that processes numeric bits (bits 0 to $n - 1$) is given in Fig. 4-5.9. Note that c_0 will have a value of 0.

Recalling that in sign-magnitude arithmetic the actual operation performed is not necessarily the operation that was originally desired, the proper control

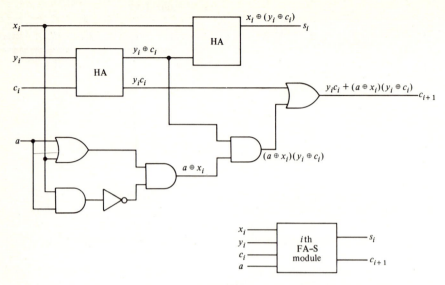

FIGURE 4-5.9 A full-adder-subtracter module.

signal, a, must be generated. In particular, for an addition, if the signs are the same, then we actually add; otherwise, we subtract. In the case of a subtraction, if the signs are the same, then we actually subtract; otherwise, we add. Let r denote a signal that represents the original operation, namely $r = 0$ denoting $x + y$ and $r = 1$ denoting $x - y$. By examining the bits x_n and y_n, the sign bits of the two operands, the truth table for the control signal a can be formed as shown in Table 4-5.8. From this table, the equation for a is

$$
\begin{aligned}
a &= \bar{r}\bar{x}_n y_n + \bar{r} x_n \bar{y}_n + r\bar{x}_n \bar{y}_n + r x_n y_n \\
&= \bar{r}(\bar{x}_n y_n + x_n \bar{y}_n) + r(\bar{x}_n \bar{y}_n + x_n y_n) \\
&= \bar{r}(x_n \oplus y_n) + r(\overline{x_n \oplus y_n}) \\
&= r \oplus (x_n \oplus y_n)
\end{aligned}
$$

An overflow can occur only when an addition is actually performed and there is a carry out of the highest-order numeric bit position (i.e., module $n - 1$

Table 4-5.8

r	x_n	y_n	a
0	0	0	0
0	0	1	1
0	1	0	1
0	1	1	0
1	0	0	1
1	0	1	0
1	1	0	0
1	1	1	1

produces a value of 1 for c_n). If we recall that we actually add when $a = 0$ and if we let e (for "error") be the overflow indicator, then $e = \bar{a}c_n$, and it has a value of 1 iff an overflow occurs.

Similarly, a propagating borrow can occur only if an actual subtraction is performed and the value of c_n is 1. Thus, letting p be the propagating-borrow indicator, we have $p = ac_n$, and it has a value of 1 iff a propagating borrow occurs.

In general, the sign of the result is the same as the sign of x, the first operand. (In the case of an overflow, it doesn't really matter what the sign is since the answer is wrong anyway.) The only exception to this rule occurs when a propagating borrow has occurred where the result bits are in 2s complement form and therefore must be complemented in order to assume their sign-magnitude form. In addition, the sign to be associated with the result is opposite to that of x. Both of these operations can be achieved with a single complementation operation. All $n + 1$ bits of the result are passed to the complementer, thus forming the 2s complement of the result. The output from this transformation is then in sign-magnitude form (remember that both $00\cdots0$ and $10\cdots0$ represent numeric 0 in sign-magnitude conventions).

Let the symbols in Fig. 4-5.10 represent an *EX-OR* module and one module of a 2s complementer, where b_i signals whether we are to complement the remaining bits (because we have already copied the first 1 bit) rather than a borrow bit in a full-subtractor.

A full-adder-subtractor for $(n + 1)$-bit sign-magnitude numbers, with $s'_n s'_{n-1} \cdots s'_1 s'_0$ as the proper signed result for all cases except overflow, is given in Fig. 4-5.11.

It should be noted that most computers today have much more sophisticated circuitry for developing sums and differences that operates considerably more rapidly than this circuit. This circuit is fairly slow because of $5n$ gates that must be traversed before the final sum bit, s_{n-1}, and carry bit, c_n, which govern the overflow testing and complementation (if required), are generated. This type of circuit was assumed in the discussion of fast-adders in Sec. 3-6.

As a last example, a parity-bit generator will be designed. As previously mentioned in Sec. 3-7, the use of parity bits is a method of determining whether errors have occurred in transmission. We shall be concerned with the generation of a single parity bit, although the method could easily be extended.

Assume that we are working with data words under an odd parity convention. What is required for a parity-bit generator is a circuit that will scan an input word, keeping track of whether there is an even or odd number of 1 bits and generate the appropriate parity bit.

The *EX-OR* function is admirably suited for this operation. If, among the two inputs to the *EX-OR* gate, there is an odd number of 1s, then the output is 1; otherwise, the output is 0.

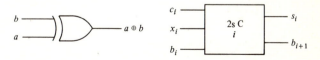

FIGURE 4-5.10   An exclusive-OR gate and 2s complementer module.

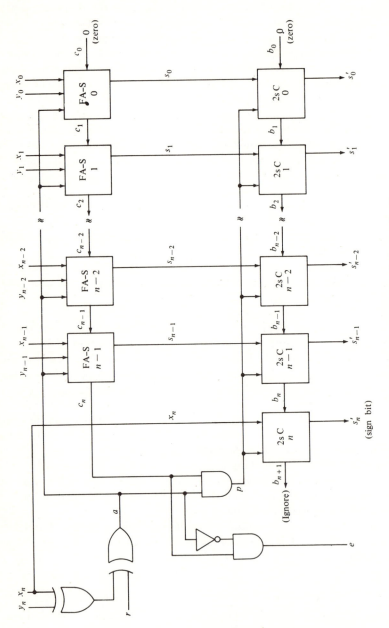

FIGURE 4-5.11 A full-adder-subtracter circuit.

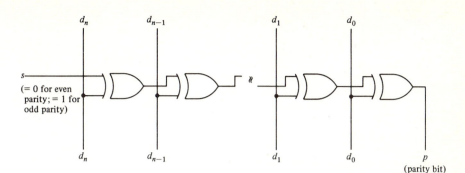

FIGURE 4-5.12 A single parity-bit generator.

One method of implementing such a check is to do it bit by bit. One input to an *EX-OR* gate is a bit from the data word, and the other input is the output from the previous *EX-OR* gate, which is 0 or 1 depending on whether an even or an odd number of 1 bits have been encountered to that point. The output from the last *EX-OR* gate is the required bit. The input to the first gate, corresponding to the input from a previous *EX-OR* gate which does not exist for the first gate, is a value set by a switch. This value is set to 0 and 1 for even and odd parity-bit generation respectively. Such a configuration is shown in Fig. 4-5.12.

The advantage of this type of serial modular circuit is that it can be easily varied with the value of n. More modules can be added or deleted as n varies. A disadvantage is that it is slow and costly in gates. If the number of bits in data words is fixed, then faster circuitry can be designed.

In this section we have discussed a number of simple design examples in which Boolean algebra and simple minimization procedures were used. Many more complex functions of digital computers can be designed by using similar techniques.

EXERCISES 4-5

1 Give three 7-bit (including sign) representations of each integer.

Number	Sign magnitude	1s complement	2s complement
−13			
+17			
−30			
+53			

2 (*a*) Represent the numbers in 1's-complement form, and perform the indicated operations in binary.

$$x = +11 \qquad y = -23$$

(1) $x - y$

(2) $x + y$

(3) $-x + y$

(b) Repeat part (a), performing subtraction by complementing and adding.

(c) Repeat part (a), using 2s complement representation of signed numbers.

3 Design a gate network that will have as input two 2-bit numbers and present the 4-bit product on four output terminals.

4 One form of an old puzzle requires a farmer (f) to transport a wolf (w), a goose (g), and a sack of corn (c) across a river, subject to the condition that if left unattended, the wolf will eat the goose, or the goose will eat the corn. Let $f = 0$ indicate the presence of the farmer on the west bank, $f = 1$ indicate his presence on the east bank, and similarly for w, g, and c.

(a) Write the table of combinations describing a switching circuit which has a transmission of 1 if and only if the farmer is in danger of losing the goose or corn. Assume that if an object is not on one side of the river, it must be on the other side.

(b) Design a two-level minimal circuit having the required transmission, and show the circuit.

5 Design a circuit which determines whether four signals on four input lines represent a valid BCD (Binary Coded Decimal) code word. The BCD code is given in Table 4-5.9.

Table 4-5.9

Decimal number	Inputs			
	a	b	c	d
0	0	0	0	0
1	0	0	0	1
2	0	0	1	0
3	0	0	1	1
4	0	1	0	0
5	0	1	0	1
6	0	1	1	0
7	0	1	1	1
8	1	0	0	0
9	1	0	0	1

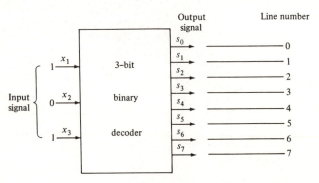

FIGURE 4-5.13 A 3-bit binary decoder.

6 A binary decoder is a circuit with n input lines and 2^n output lines arranged so that for each of the possible 2^n combinations of the input lines, a single output line is 1, with all others 0. Figure 4-5.13 is an example of a 3-bit binary decoder with an input of 1, 0, 1 and a corresponding output of 1 for line number 5, while all others are 0. Design a minimum circuit for this decoder.

4-6 FINITE-STATE MACHINES

In Secs. 1-2.15, 4-4, and 4-5 we have discussed switching circuits in which the outputs at a particular instant in time were functions of only the inputs at that time. Such circuits were called combinational circuits. In most digital computers, however, a number of circuits (or elements) are required which enable operations to be performed in a sequential manner. This sequencing of operations is achieved by means of a timed sequence of clock signals. The outputs of these circuits at any given time are functions of the external inputs and the stored information in the computer at that time. Such circuits are called sequential circuits. A computer can be viewed as a network consisting of a finite set of elements. Each of these elements can be in only one of a finite number of states at any one time, so that we may also consider a computer as a network consisting of a finite set of states.

The first subsection briefly introduces the concept of a sequential circuit. The finite-state machine is then introduced as an abstract model for sequential circuits. For reasons such as costs, reliability, etc., it is desirable to obtain a reduced or minimal machine which is equivalent to a given (and usually not minimal) machine. In pursuit of this goal, the second subsection gives a definition of equivalent machines and proceeds to develop an algorithm for determining a minimal machine which is equivalent to a given machine.

4-6.1 Introductory Sequential Circuits

Many sequential circuits are encountered in daily activities. Most people on their way to work encounter the sequential and usually predictable operation of traffic lights; the elevator control which causes the elevator to drop us at some point on the way up before taking on passengers on the way down; the sequential aspects of a combination lock which remembers the sequence of combinational digits; etc. We now proceed to give a concrete example of a sequential circuit for a serial adder.

In Sec. 4-5 a combinational circuit for a binary full-adder was discussed. Each bit position in a 32-bit number, for example, was made available at the same time. Therefore the adder had 64 external inputs available at one time. Let us now consider a binary adder which consists of two external inputs, each corresponding to a binary number. Each number consists of a sequence of bits, but the availability of the bits depends on time. An adder to perform the indicated operation necessarily operates in a sequential manner and is consequently called a *serial binary adder*. The block diagram of such an adder is given in Fig. 4-6.1, where the sequences of bits for x, y, and z are represented by $x_{n-1}x_{n-2}\cdots x_1x_0$, $y_{n-1}y_{n-2}\cdots y_1y_0$ and $z_{n-1}z_{n-2}\cdots z_1z_0$, respectively. The two inputs, x and y, and the output, z, each consists of n bits. The addition of x and y is to be done in a serial

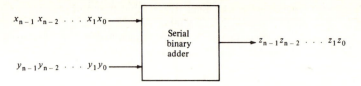

FIGURE 4-6.1   A block diagram of a serial adder.

manner; i.e., the least significant digits, x_0 and y_0, of the inputs arrive simultaneously at the input terminals at time t_0; a unit of time later (typically from 10^{-6} to 10^{-9} sec), the next least significant digits x_1 and y_1 arrive, etc. Finally, the bits x_{n-1} and y_{n-1} arrive at time t_{n-1}. The time interval between the arrival of pairs of input bits is controlled by a very precise clock signal. It will be assumed that the combinational circuit delay is insignificant as compared to the clock frequency. Accordingly, we may say that z_i appears at the output of the adder at the same time that x_i and y_i appear at the input terminals.

Consider the addition, according to Table 4-5.1, of the following binary numbers:

	t_4	t_3	t_2	t_1	t_0
$x =$	0	1	1	1	1
$y =$	0	1	0	1	0
$z =$	1	1	0	0	1

Note the difference between a combinational circuit and the serial adder. In the former case, the output at time t_i is determined from the inputs at that time, while in the latter circuit the output required at a particular time is different from that required at another even though the input combinations are the same. For example, at times t_1 and t_3 the inputs are both 1s, but the required outputs are $z_1 = 0$ and $z_3 = 1$, respectively. A similar situation exists for the input combination at times t_0 and t_2. From these observations, it is evident that the output of the serial adder cannot be specified as merely a function of its inputs.

It is obvious that the output of the adder at time t_i is a function of its inputs x_i and y_i at that time and of the carry bit which was generated at time t_{i-1}. This carry bit will depend on the inputs at time t_{i-2}, and so on. Therefore the serial adder must be able to remember or store information regarding its inputs from time t_0 to t_{i-1}. It is impractical to store all the previously encountered input bits, and we therefore try to establish a relationship between the inputs x_i and y_i and the output z_i.

Observe that in the serial adder there are two different cases arising from past input histories; the first case involves a carry bit of 0, and the second a carry bit of 1. These cases represent the states that the adder can be in at any given time. Of course, the circuit can be in only one state at one time. By having the adder remember the carry digit from the previous time interval, the adder has essentially remembered all its past inputs.

Let s_0 and s_1 denote the state of the adder at time t_i if a carry of 0 and 1 was generated at time t_{i-1}, respectively. We shall denote the *present state* of the adder

Table 4-6.1

Present state	$x_iy_i =$	Next-state function				Output function			
		Input symbols				Input symbols			
		00	01	11	10	00	01	11	10
s_0		s_0	s_0	s_1	s_0	0	1	0	1
s_1		s_0	s_1	s_1	s_1	1	0	1	0

as the state of the circuit when the present inputs are applied to the input terminals. The *next state* of the adder is defined as the state to which it goes after the present inputs and the previous carry bit have been examined. The output z_i at time t_i will then be a function of the inputs x_i and y_i and the state of the adder at time t_i. Also, the next state of the adder depends only on the present inputs and the carry bit (denoted by the present state). The behavior of the serial adder can be conveniently described by means of a table as shown in Table 4-6.1.

The table consists of two functions—the next-state function and the output function. Each row of the table corresponds to a state in the adder, and every column for each function corresponds to a combination of inputs. The entries for the next-state function denotes a state transition, and the corresponding entries in the output function denote the output symbols written on the output tape. For example, if the adder is in state s_0, that is, the present carry bit is 0, and it receives the input combination $x_iy_i = 11$, then the adder will go to state s_1, indicating that a carry bit of 1 has been set, and an output bit $z_i = 0$ is generated. The other entries of the table can be interpreted in a similar manner. It now becomes evident that the table completely specifies the operation of the serial adder.

We can easily implement such an adder if some storage device to represent the presence or absence of a carry is used. A number of such devices are available, but we shall only mention one—the unit delay element whose delay is equal to the time interval between two successive clock pulses. The state of the

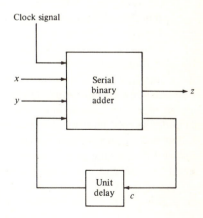

FIGURE 4-6.2 A serial binary adder.

delay element will be represented by c, and it will assume a value of 0 or 1, corresponding to the absence or presence of a carry bit. Since the present value at the input of the unit delay at time t_i is equal to its output at time t_{i+1}, this input is called the next state of the delay element. A block-diagram representation of the adder is given in Fig. 4-6.2, where an additional input line denoting the clock signal is also included. This additional input indicates that the serial adder is a synchronous circuit and that all events occur at discrete points in time.

We have given a very brief introduction to sequential circuits. In the next subsection we formalize these ideas and proceed with the development of an algorithm for determining a minimal equivalent sequential circuit for a given sequential circuit.

4-6.2 Equivalence of Finite-state Machines

In the previous subsection the basic notions of sequential circuits were introduced. We now wish to formalize these concepts by defining a finite-state machine. Furthermore, the important question of equivalent machines is discussed. In particular, we shall define what is meant by equivalent machines and show that for any given machine there exists a minimal equivalent machine. This reduced machine is homomorphic to the given machine. An algorithm for obtaining a minimal machine is developed. Finite-state machines have interesting algebraic properties based on the theory of semigroups, but we will not be concerned with such properties in this subsection. Finite-state machines can do many things, but there are certain operations such as multiplication which are beyond their range. We now proceed to the definition of a finite-state machine.

Definition 4-6.1 A *sequential machine*, or *finite-state machine*, is a system $N = \langle I, S, O, \delta, \lambda \rangle$, where the finite sets I, S, and O are alphabets that represent the input, state, and output symbols of the machine respectively. The alphabets I and O are not necessarily disjoint, but $I \cap S = O \cap S = \varnothing$. We shall denote the alphabets by

$$I = \{a_0, a_1, \ldots, a_n\} \qquad S = \{s_0, s_1, \ldots, s_m\} \qquad O = \{o_0, o_1, \ldots, o_r\}$$

δ is a mapping of $S \times I \to S$ which denotes the next-state function, and λ is a mapping $S \times I \to O$ which denotes the output function. We assume that the machine is in an initial state s_0.

Formally, a finite-state machine therefore consists of three not necessarily distinct alphabets and two functions. An abstract representation of a finite-state machine is given in Fig. 4-6.3. The machine reads a sequence of input symbols that are stored on an *input tape* and stores a sequence of output symbols on an *output tape*. Let the machine be in some state s_i and reading the input symbol a_p under its reading head. The mapping λ is then applied to s_i and a_p, thus causing the writing head to record a symbol o_k on the output tape. The function δ then causes the machine to go into state s_j. The machine proceeds to read the next input symbol and continues its operation until all symbols on the input tape are processed. Observe that the tapes are allowed to move only in one direction. In Fig. 4-6.3 the input symbols are processed from left to right. It should be

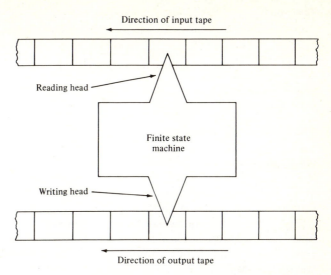

FIGURE 4-6.3 Model of a finite-state machine.

noted, however, that in the serial-adder example the input was assumed to have been read right to left. This is due to the positional property of fixed-radix number systems.

The mappings δ and λ are defined for all ordered pairs in $S \times I$, and in such a case the finite-state machine is said to be *completely specified*. A machine of this type, when starting in a given initial state s_0, will read the input tape and write a uniquely determinable sequence of symbols on the output tape.

The serial-adder example given in the previous subsection can be described within the framework of this definition as

$$I = \{00, 01, 11, 10\} \qquad S = \{s_0, s_1\} \qquad 0 = \{0, 1\}$$
$$\delta = \{\langle s_0, 00, s_0 \rangle, \langle s_0, 01, s_0 \rangle, \langle s_0, 11, s_1 \rangle, \langle s_0, 10, s_0 \rangle,$$
$$\langle s_1, 00, s_0 \rangle, \langle s_1, 01, s_1 \rangle, \langle s_1, 11, s_1 \rangle, \langle s_1, 10, s_1 \rangle\}$$
$$\lambda = \{\langle s_0, 00, 0 \rangle, \langle s_0, 01, 1 \rangle, \langle s_0, 11, 0 \rangle, \langle s_0, 10, 1 \rangle,$$
$$\langle s_1, 00, 1 \rangle, \langle s_1, 01, 0 \rangle, \langle s_1, 11, 1 \rangle, \langle s_1, 10, 0 \rangle\}$$

The starting state of the machine is s_0.

As a second example, consider the construction of a finite-state machine which will operate like a pulse divider. The pulse divider is to have as input a sequence of bits. The output, which is also a sequence of bits, is to be determined as follows:

A 1 is to be written out at time t if and only if the number of 1s on the input tape up to time t is a nonzero even number.

The specification of a machine to perform this task is given in Table 4-6.2, and the initial state is assumed to be s_0. Suppose that the input tape contains the string 101011. The machine starts in state s_0, and when it reads the first input symbol 1, it goes to state s_1 and writes 0 on the output tape. When the second

Table 4-6.2

Present state ↓	δ		λ	
	Input symbols		Input symbols	
	0	1	0	1
s_0	s_0	s_1	0	0
s_1	s_1	s_0	0	1

input symbol 0 is read, the machine remains in state s_1. The third symbol causes the machine to enter s_0 and output a 1. This process is continued until the end of the input tape is encountered. It is easily verified that the input 101011 is transformed to the output 001001.

It is frequently convenient to use a directed graph instead of describing the functions δ and λ by means of a table called the *transition table*, as was just done. In the design of a finite-state machine, it is usually easier to formulate a design based on a graph rather than one based on a state table. The graph associated with a machine is called its transition diagram.

Definition 4-6.2 The *transition diagram* of a finite-state machine M is a directed graph in which there is a node for each state symbol in S, and each node is labeled by the state symbol with which it is associated. Furthermore, for each ordered pair $\langle s_i, s_j \rangle$ such that there exist the 3-tuples $\langle s_i, a_p, s_j \rangle$ and $\langle s_i, a_p, o_k \rangle$, there is a branch originating at node s_i and terminating at node s_j, and each such branch is labeled by the pair a_p/o_k.

As an example, the transition diagram of our serial adder is shown in Fig. 4-6.4.

Any finite-state machine can be viewed as a "black box" which reads input words and generates output words. It is natural to think of a finite-state machine as a device which transforms words into words. More precisely, if I^* and O^* are the sets of words on the input and output alphabets, I and O, respectively, the operation of the machine can be described by the function $g: I^* \to O^*$. Observe that this function has an infinite domain and range. Since machine equivalence

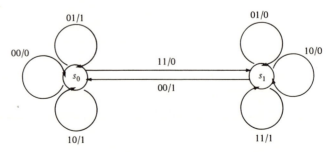

FIGURE 4-6.4 Transition diagram for serial adder.

can be described in terms of such a mapping, we proceed to generalize the functions δ and λ.

Consider a sequence $x = x_0 x_1 x_2 \cdots$ of input symbols. Let s_0 be the initial state of the machine. The state s_1 of the machine for the input x_0 is given by

$$s_1 = \delta(s_0, x_0) = \delta_1(s_0, x_0)$$

where $\delta = \delta_1 : S \times I \to S$. The reason for introducing δ_1 will become obvious as we proceed. Next, consider the change in state due to the second input symbol x_1; the next state s_2 is given by

$$s_2 = \delta(s_1, x_1) = \delta(\delta_1(s_0, x_0), x_1) = \delta_2(s_0, x_0 x_1)$$

where $\delta_2 : S \times I^2 \to S$. The next state after the input x_2 is

$$s_3 = \delta(s_2, x_2) = \delta(\delta_2(s_0, x_0 x_1), x_2) = \delta_3(s_0, x_0 x_1 x_2)$$

where $\delta_3 : S \times I^3 \to S$. Continuing this procedure, one can now define a function $\delta_n : S \times I^n \to S$ such that

$$s_n = \delta_n(s_0, x_0 x_1 \cdots x_{n-1}) = \delta(\delta_{n-1}(s_0, x_0 x_1 \cdots x_{n-2}), x_{n-1})$$

Similarly, the output symbols $o_0, o_1, \ldots$ can also be described with the help of the function λ, such that

$$o_0 = \lambda(s_0, x_0) = \lambda_1(s_0, x_0)$$

$$o_1 = \lambda(s_1, x_1) = \lambda(\delta_1(s_0, x_0), x_1) = \lambda_2(s_0, x_0 x_1)$$

$$o_2 = \lambda(s_2, x_2) = \lambda(\delta_2(s_0, x_0 x_1), x_2) = \lambda_3(s_0, x_0 x_1 x_2)$$

$$\vdots$$

$$o_{n-1} = \lambda(s_{n-1}, x_{n-1}) = \lambda(\delta_{n-1}(s_0, x_0 x_1 \cdots x_{n-2}), x_{n-1})$$

$$= \lambda_n(s_0, x_0 x_1 \cdots x_{n-1})$$

Continuing in this manner, we can therefore define a function $\lambda_n : S \times I^n \to 0$.

There is no likelihood of any ambiguity if we suppress the subscript n from δ_n and λ_n and write these functions as δ and λ. It would be clear from the length of the string as to what function is involved.

Definition 4-6.3 Let $x = x_0 x_1 \cdots x_{n-1}$ be any input sequence containing n symbols, and let a be any input symbol. Then the mappings δ and λ can be extended recursively as follows:

(a) $\delta(s_i, xa) = \delta(\delta(s_i, x), a)$
(b) $\lambda(s_i, xa) = \lambda(\delta(s_i, x), a)$
(c) $g(s_i, x_0 x_1 \cdots x_{n-1}) = \lambda(s_i, x_0) \lambda(s_i, x_0 x_1) \cdots \lambda(s_i, x_0 x_1 \cdots x_{n-1})$

As an example, consider the pulse-divider example of Table 4-6.2 when it is subjected to an input sequence of 11011. Computing the output function g, starting in state s_0, we have

$$g(s_0, 11011) = \lambda(s_0, 1)\lambda(s_0, 11)\lambda(s_0, 110)\lambda(s_0, 1101)\lambda(s_0, 11011)$$

$$= \lambda(s_0, 1)\lambda(\delta(s_0, 1), 1)\lambda(\delta(s_0, 11), 0)\,\lambda(\delta(s_0, 110), 1)\lambda(\delta(s_0, 1101), 1)$$

$$= \lambda(s_0, 1)\lambda(\delta(s_0, 1), 1)\lambda(\delta(\delta(s_0, 1), 1), 0)\,\lambda(\delta(\delta(\delta(s_0, 1), 1), 0), 1)$$

$$\lambda(\delta(\delta(\delta(\delta(s_0, 1), 1), 0), 1), 1)$$

$$= 01001$$

Since our ultimate goal in this subsection is to develop an algorithm for obtaining an equivalent minimal machine for some given machine, we first formulate what is meant by equivalent states. Intuitively, two states are equivalent iff they produce the same output for any input sequence.

Definition 4-6.4 Let $M = \langle I, S, O, \delta, \lambda \rangle$ be a finite-state machine. Two states $s_i, s_j \in S$ are said to be *equivalent*, written $s_i \equiv s_j$, iff $\lambda(s_i, x) = \lambda(s_j, x)$ for every word $x \in I^*$.

It is easy to show that the relation $\equiv$ is an equivalence relation.

Theorem 4-6.1 Let s be any state in a finite-state machine and x and y be any words. Then

$$\delta(s, xy) = \delta(\delta(s, x), y) \qquad \text{and} \qquad \lambda(s, xy) = \lambda(\delta(s, x), y)$$

PROOF The proof will be by induction on the length of y. Let $y = a$. Then

$$\delta(s, xa) = \delta(\delta(s, x), a) \qquad \text{by Definition 4-6.3}a$$

Assume that the equation is true for any y of length n; that is, the induction hypothesis is

$$\delta(s, xy) = \delta(\delta(s, x), y)$$

We want to show that it is true for y having $n + 1$ symbols. From Definition 4-6.3a we can write

$$\delta(s, xya) = \delta(\delta(s, xy), a)$$

The right side of this identity can be rewritten as

$$\delta(\delta(s, xy), a) = \delta(\delta(\delta(s, x), y), a)$$

by the induction hypothesis. By letting $s' = \delta(s, x)$, the right side of this equation can be expressed as

$$\delta(\delta(\delta(s, x), y), a) = \delta(\delta(s', y), a)$$
$$= \delta(s', ya) \qquad \text{by Definition 4-6.3}a$$
$$= \delta(\delta(s, x), ya)$$

The other part of the proof can be obtained in a similar manner. ////

We next prove an important theorem which states that if two states are equivalent, then their next states will also be equivalent.

Theorem 4-6.2 If $s_i \equiv s_j$, then for any input sequence x, $\delta(s_i, x) \equiv \delta(s_j, x)$.

PROOF It is clear from Definition 4-6.3 that if $s_i \equiv s_j$, then $\lambda(s_i, xy) = \lambda(s_j, xy)$ for any input word xy. Moreover, from Theorem 4-6.1, we have

$$\lambda(\delta(s_i, x), y) = \lambda(\delta(s_j, x), y)$$

for any $y \in I^*$. It therefore follows by the definition of equivalence that

$$\delta(s_i, x) \equiv \delta(s_j, x) \qquad ////$$

Table 4-6.3

Present state ↓	δ Input symbols		λ Input symbols	
	0	1	0	1
s_0	s_5	s_3	0	1
s_1	s_1	s_4	0	0
s_2	s_1	s_3	0	0
s_3	s_1	s_2	0	0
s_4	s_5	s_2	0	1
s_5	s_4	s_1	0	1

Definition 4-6.4, which defines equivalent states in a finite-state machine, makes the identification of equivalent states virtually impossible. The definition implies that the equivalence of s_i and s_j can be determined by placing an input tape into the machine when it is in an initial state s_i, repeating the operation for an initial state s_j, and comparing the output tapes. Since the number of possible input words is infinite, this exhaustive procedure of comparing corresponding output words for every input word is endless. Therefore, a more realistic and efficient method for determining state equivalence must be used.

Definition 4-6.5 Let $M = \langle I, S, O, \delta, \lambda \rangle$ be a finite-state machine. Then for some positive integer k, s_i is said to be *k-equivalent* to s_j, that is, $s_i \overset{k}{\equiv} s_j$, if

$$s_i \overset{k}{\equiv} s_j \Leftrightarrow \lambda(s_i, x) = \lambda(s_j, x) \qquad \text{for all } x \text{ such that } |x| \leq k$$

Clearly, Definition 4-6.4 is a generalization of Definition 4-6.5 for all k, and hence $s_i \equiv s_j$ implies $s_i \overset{k}{\equiv} s_j$, but not conversely.

The k-equivalence relation is also an equivalence relation, and it defines a corresponding k-partition P_k on the set of states S whose k-equivalence is described as follows:

$$[s_i]_k = \{s_j \mid s_i \overset{k}{\equiv} s_j\} \qquad \text{and} \qquad P_k = \bigcup_{s \in S} [s]_k$$

As an example, consider the machine given in Table 4-6.3. Let us compute the partition P_1. It can be easily done by placing all states that have the same outputs for all input words of length 1 in the same equivalence class. From Table 4-6.3 we obtain

$$[s_0]_1 = \{s_0, s_4, s_5\} \qquad \text{and} \qquad [s_1]_1 = \{s_1, s_2, s_3\}$$

and $P_1 = \{\{s_0, s_4, s_5\}, \{s_1, s_2, s_3\}\}$.

Let P represent the partition generated by the equivalence relation $\equiv$; then we have the following.

Theorem 4-6.3 If for some integer k, $P_{k+1} = P_k$, then $P_k = P$ and conversely.

PROOF It is obvious that $P_k = P$ implies $P_{k+1} = P_k$ for any k; therefore the converse is established.

We next want to prove that $P_{k+1} = P_k \Rightarrow P_k = P$. This will be done by contradiction. Assume that $P_k \neq P$ and then show that $P_{k+1} \neq P_k$. By definition, there exist states s_i and s_j such that $s_i \overset{k}{\equiv} s_j$ but $s_i \neq s_j$. Let q be the smallest integer such that $s_i \overset{q}{\not\equiv} s_j$. It is obvious that $q > k$. If $q = k+1$, then $s_i \overset{k+1}{\not\equiv} s_j$, and consequently $P_{k+1} \neq P_k$.

Now suppose that $q > k+1$. Let x be an input sequence of length q, and let $x = wy$ with w and y having lengths of $q - k - 1$ and $k + 1$, respectively. Because q was chosen to be the smallest integer such that $s_i \overset{q}{\not\equiv} s_j$, it directly follows that

$$\lambda(s_i, wy) \neq \lambda(s_j, wy)$$

Then by Theorem 4-6.1 with $s_i' = \delta(s_i, w)$ and $s_j' = \delta(s_j, w)$, we obtain

$$\lambda(s_i', y) \neq \lambda(s_j', y)$$

Since y contains $k + 1$ symbols, we have shown that $s_i' \overset{k+1}{\not\equiv} s_j'$.

Finally, assume that y consists of k or fewer symbols. Since q was the smallest integer violating the definition of k-equivalence, it follows that

$$\lambda(s_i, wy) = \lambda(s_j, wy)$$

Again by Theorem 4-6.1 we obtain $s_i' \overset{k}{\equiv} s_j'$. In summary, we have found two states s_i' and s_j' such that $s_i' \overset{k+1}{\not\equiv} s_j'$ and $s_i' \overset{k}{\equiv} s_j'$, and it therefore follows that $P_{k+1} \neq P_k$. ////

This theorem provides us with a simple algorithm for obtaining the partition of the states of a finite-state machine induced by the equivalence relation $\equiv$. The algorithm consists of the following steps.

1 Obtain P_1 from the output function (λ) for the finite-state machine.
2 $i \leftarrow 2$.
3 Obtain P_i from P_{i-1}.
4 If $P_i = P_{i-1}$, then Halt.
5 $i \leftarrow i + 1$, go to step 3.

The only step in this algorithm that we are unable to perform is step 3. The following theorem shows how to construct P_i from P_{i-1}.

Theorem 4-6.4 Let s_i, $s_j \in S$. Then $s_i \overset{k+1}{\equiv} s_j$ iff $s_i \overset{k}{\equiv} s_j$ and for all $a \in I$, $\delta(s_i, a) \overset{k}{\equiv} \delta(s_j, a)$.

PROOF Clearly $s_i \overset{k+1}{\equiv} s_j$ implies $s_i \overset{k}{\equiv} s_j$. We need only prove that

$$s_i \overset{k+1}{\equiv} s_j \qquad \text{if and only if} \qquad \delta(s_i, a) \overset{k}{\equiv} \delta(s_j, a)$$

By Definition 4-6.5, Theorem 4-6.1, and Theorem 4-6.2, this statement is equivalent to

$$\lambda(s_i, ax) = \lambda(s_j, ax) \qquad \text{if and only if} \qquad \delta(s_i, a) \overset{k}{\equiv} \delta(s_j, a)$$

where the string ax is of length $k + 1$. ////

Let us now apply the previous algorithm to the finite-state machine described in Table 4-6.3. We have already obtained $P_1 = \{\{s_0, s_4, s_5\}, \{s_1, s_2, s_3\}\}$. The next step is to obtain partition P_2 whose equivalence classes are 2-equivalent, i.e., equivalent for any input sequence of length 2. From Theorem 4-6.4, two states are 2-equivalent if and only if they are 1-equivalent and their next-state successors are 1-equivalent for all $a \in \{0, 1\}$. This step is performed by splitting equivalence classes in P_1 whenever their next-state successors do not all fall within an equivalence class of P_1. Therefore $P_2 = \{\{s_0, s_4, s_5\}, \{s_1\}, \{s_2, s_3\}\}$. Similarly, we can obtain P_3 by using the fact that two states are 3-equivalent if and only if they are 2-equivalent and their next-state successors are 2-equivalent for all $a \in \{0, 1\}$. Such a computation yields $P_3 = \{\{s_0, s_4\}, \{s_1\}, \{s_2, s_3\}, \{s_5\}\}$. This process is continued for one more step, giving $P_4 = P_3$. Therefore the required partition is

$$P = \{\{s_0, s_4\}, \{s_1\}, \{s_2, s_3\}, \{s_5\}\}$$

A question of considerable importance concerning this algorithm is whether the process will always terminate. It can be shown that for any finite-state machine with $n > 1$ states, there exists some integer $k \leq n - 1$ such that $P_k = P$. This proof is left as an exercise.

We have discussed at some length the notion of state equivalence. In the remainder of this subsection we will be concerned with machine equivalence.

Definition 4-6.6 Let $M = \langle I, S, O, \delta, \lambda \rangle$ and $M' = \langle I, S', O, \delta', \lambda' \rangle$ be finite-state machines. Then M and M' are *equivalent*, written $M \equiv M'$, iff for all $s_i \in S$ there exists an $s_j \in S'$ such that $s_i \equiv s_j$, and for all $s_j \in S'$ there exists an $s_i \in S$ such that $s_i \equiv s_j$.

Again it is easily shown that $\equiv$ is an equivalence relation.

Table 4-6.4 contains a finite-state machine which is equivalent to the machine given in Table 4-6.3. Observe that s_0' in M' is equivalent to s_0 and s_4 in M; s_1' in M' is equivalent to s_1 in M; s_2' in M' is equivalent to s_2 and s_3 in M; and s_3' in M' is equivalent to s_5 in M. Also note that the functions λ and λ' are the same for the indicated correspondence, but this is only a necessary condition for equivalence, not a sufficient one.

Table 4-6.4

Present state ↓	δ' Input symbols		λ' Input symbols	
	0	1	0	1
s_0'	s_3'	s_2'	0	1
s_1'	s_1'	s_0'	0	0
s_2'	s_1'	s_2'	0	0
s_3'	s_0'	s_1'	0	1

Definition 4-6.7   A finite-state machine $M = \langle I, S, O, \delta, \lambda \rangle$ is said to be *reduced* if and only if $s_i \equiv s_j$ implies that $s_i = s_j$ for all states $s_i, s_j \in S$.

In other words, a reduced finite-state machine is one in which each state is equivalent to itself and to no other. The partition of S in such a machine has all its equivalence classes consisting of a single element.

We shall now show how to construct a reduced finite-state machine M' which is equivalent to some given machine M. Let S in M be partitioned in a set of equivalence classes $[s]$ such that $P = \cup [s]$. Let the function ϕ be defined on the partition P such that $\phi([s]) = s'$, where s' is an arbitrary fixed element of $[s]$, called a representative. It is clear that $s' \equiv s$ in M. Let S' in M' be defined as

$$S' = \{ s' \mid (\exists s)[s \in S \text{ and } \phi([s]) = s'] \}$$

and let $I' = I$ and $O' = O$; that is, both machines will have the same input and output alphabets. The functions δ' and λ' are defined as follows:

$$\delta'(s', a) = \phi([\delta(s', a)])$$

and

$$\lambda'(s', a) = \lambda(s', a)$$

where s' is both in S and S'. Therefore the reduced machine is $M' = \langle I, S', O, \delta', \lambda' \rangle$.

Applying this procedure to the machine given in Table 4-6.3 gives the equivalent reduced machine in Table 4-6.4.

We shall now state a theorem without proof which shows the existence of a reduced equivalent machine.

Theorem 4-6.5   Let $M = \langle I, S, O, \delta, \lambda \rangle$ be a finite-state machine. Then there exists an equivalent machine M' with a set of states S' such that $S' \subseteq S$ and M' is reduced.

The idea of one finite-state machine simulating another is very important in a number of applications. This notion is formalized in the next definition.

Definition 4-6.8   Let $M = \langle I, S, O, \delta, \lambda \rangle$ and $M' = \langle I, S', O, \delta', \lambda' \rangle$ be two finite-state machines. Let function ϕ be a mapping from S into S'. A *finite-state homomorphism* is defined as

$$\left. \begin{aligned} \phi(\delta(s, a)) &= \delta'(\phi(s), a) \\[2mm] \lambda(s, a) &= \lambda'(\phi(s), a) \end{aligned} \right\} \quad \text{for all } a \in I$$

If ϕ is a one-one and onto function, then M is *isomorphic* to M'.

Finite-state machines are often used in compilers where they usually perform the task of a scanner (Sec. 3-3). The machine in such a case does lower-level syntax analysis such as identifying variable names, operators, constants, etc. A machine which performs this scanning task is called an *acceptor*. In Chap. 6 we show that the set of languages that can be recognized by an acceptor is exactly the set of those languages that can be generated by a regular grammar.

EXERCISES 4-6

1 Design a parity-check machine which is to read a sequence of 0s and 1s from an input tape. The machine is to output a 1 if the input tape contains an even number of 1s, or 0 otherwise.

2 Design a sequential machine which has one input line x in addition to a clock input and one output line z. z is to have a value of 0 unless the input contains three consecutive 1s or three consecutive 0s. z must be 1 at the time of the third consecutive identical input.

3 A sequential circuit is to be designed which will identify a particular sequence of inputs and provide an output to trigger a combinational lock. The inputs to the circuit are three switches labeled x_1, x_2, and x_3. The output of the circuit is to be 0 unless the input switches are in the position 010 where this position occurs at the conclusion of a sequence of input positions 101, 111, 011, 010. Design a sequential machine which will have only one output of 1 at the conclusion of the described sequence of switch positions. A correct sequence may begin every time the switches are set to 101.

4 The output of a sequential machine is to be 1 if and only if the last four input symbols are of the following form:

Time	t_i	t_{i+1}	t_{i+2}	t_{i+3}
Input symbol	1	0	1	1

Design such a machine.

5 Draw transition diagrams for the single-input, single-output sequential machines whose operations are specified as follows:

(a) An output $z = 1$ is to be written if on the input tape a 1 is preceded by exactly two 0s, for example, $\cdots 1001 \cdots$.

(b) An output $z = 1$ is to be produced if a 1 on the input tape follows two or more 0s.

6 Prove the second part of Theorem 4-6.1.

7 A serial parity-bit machine is to be designed. This machine is to receive coded messages and is to add a parity bit to every 4-bit message, so that the output of the machine is an error-detecting coded message. The machine is to have a single input consisting of strings of four symbols spaced apart by a single time unit. The parity bits are to be inserted at the appropriate spaces, so that the resulting output is a continuous sequence of symbols without spaces. Odd parity is to be used; i.e., a parity bit is inserted if and only if the number of 1s in the preceding four input symbols is even.

8 Reduce the following machine, if possible.

Present state $\downarrow$	δ Input symbols $x = 0$	1	λ Input symbols $x = 0$	1
s_0	s_1	s_7	0	0
s_1	s_7	s_0	0	1
s_2	s_8	s_7	0	1
s_3	s_7	s_5	0	1
s_4	s_3	s_2	0	0
s_5	s_6	s_7	0	0
s_6	s_8	s_5	0	1
s_7	s_3	s_7	0	1
s_8	s_2	s_0	0	1

9 Obtain a reduced machine for the machine obtained in Prob. 3.

10 Determine the reduced equivalent machine which corresponds to the machine described by the following table:

Present state ↓	δ Input symbols				λ Input symbols			
	a	b	c	d	a	b	c	d
s_0	s_4	s_2	s_1	s_4	1	0	1	1
s_1	s_2	s_5	s_4	s_1	0	1	1	0
s_2	s_1	s_0	s_3	s_5	1	0	1	1
s_3	s_6	s_5	s_4	s_1	0	1	1	0
s_4	s_2	s_5	s_3	s_4	0	1	1	0
s_5	s_2	s_5	s_3	s_7	1	1	0	0
s_6	s_3	s_0	s_1	s_5	1	0	1	1
s_7	s_1	s_2	s_4	s_5	1	0	1	1

11 Prove that $g(s_i, x) = g(s_j, x)$ for every x if and only if $\lambda(s_i, x) = \lambda(s_j, x)$, that is, if and only if $s_i \equiv s_j$.

12 Prove that if $P_k \neq P$, then the cardinality of P is greater than or equal to $k + 1$.

13 Prove that if a finite-state machine has n states where $n \geq 2$, then there exists an integer $k \leq n - 1$ such that $P_k = P$.

14 Prove Theorem 4-6.5.

BIBLIOGRAPHY

ABBOTT, J. C.: "Sets, Lattices, and Boolean Algebras," Allyn and Bacon, Inc., Boston, 1969.

ARNOLD, B. H.: "Logic and Boolean Algebra," Prentice-Hall, Inc., Englewood Cliffs, N. J., 1962.

CALDWELL, S. H.: "Switching Circuits and Logical Design," John Wiley & Sons, Inc., New York, 1958.

DIETMEYER, DONALD L.: "Logic Design of Digital Systems," Allyn and Bacon, Inc., Boston, 1971.

DONNELLAN, T.: "Lattice Theory," Pergamon Press, Oxford, 1968.

FLEGG, H. G.: "Boolean Algebra and Its Applications," John Wiley & Sons, Inc., New York, 1964.

GERICKE, H.: "Lattice Theory," George G. Harrap & Co., Ltd., London, English translation, 1966.

HILL, F. J., and G. R. PETERSON: "Introduction to Switching Theory and Logical Design," John Wiley & Sons, Inc., New York, 1968.

HOHN, F. E.: "Applied Boolean Algebra," MacMillan & Co., Ltd., London, 1969.

KAIN, R. Y.: "Automata Theory: Machines and Languages," McGraw-Hill Book Company, New York, 1972.

KOHAVI, ZVI: "Switching and Finite Automata Theory," McGraw-Hill Book Company, New York, 1970.

KORFHAGE, ROBERT R.: "Logic and Algorithms," John Wiley & Sons, Inc., New York, 1966.

NELSON, RAYMOND J.: "Introduction to Automata," John Wiley & Sons, Inc., New York, 1968.

PREPARATA, F. P., and R. T. YEH: "Introduction to Discrete Structures," Addison-Wesley Publishing Company, Inc., Reading, Mass., 1973.

STONE, H. S.: "Discrete Mathematical Structures and Their Applications," Science Research Associates, Inc., Chicago, 1973.

WELLS, CHARLES: "Mathematical Structures," Lecture notes, Case Western Reserve University, Cleveland, Ohio, 1968.

WHITESITT, J. E.: "Boolean Algebra and Its Applications," Addison-Wesley Publishing Company, Inc., Reading, Mass., 1961.

5

GRAPH THEORY

INTRODUCTION

We have already encountered some idea of graph theory in Chap. 2 where we discussed the graph of a relation. Of course, there a graph was used as a pictorial device to represent a relation, and as such, it served only a limited purpose. In this chapter we shall extend, and in some cases, generalize these ideas. A graph will be introduced as an abstract mathematical system. Graph theory is applied in such diverse areas as social sciences, linguistics, physical sciences, communication engineering, and others. Because of this diversity of application, it is useful to develop and study the subject in abstract terms and to interpret its results in terms of the objects of any particular system in which one may be interested. Graph theory also plays an important role in several areas of computer science, such as switching theory and logical design, artificial intelligence, formal languages, computer graphics, operating systems, compiler writing, and information organization and retrieval.

In this chapter first we introduce some of the basic terminology of graph theory. In the beginning we discuss graphs in general, but finally we concentrate on the theory of directed graphs. The results obtained here will be applied to formal syntax analysis and fault detection and diagnosis.

5-1   BASIC CONCEPTS OF GRAPH THEORY

The terminology used in graph theory is not standard. It is not uncommon to find several different terms being used as synonyms. This situation, however, becomes more complicated when we find that a particular term is used by different authors to describe different concepts. This situation is natural because of the diversity of the fields in which graph theory is applied. Wherever possible, we shall indicate the alternative terms which are frequently used. We shall generally select alternatives that are often used in the literature in computer science.

In this section we shall define a graph as an abstract mathematical system. However, in order to provide some motivation for the terminology used and also to develop some intuitive feelings, we shall represent graphs diagrammatically. Any such diagram will also be called a graph. Our definitions and terms are not restricted to those graphs which can be represented by means of diagrams, even though this may appear to be the case because these terms have strong associations with such a representation. We shall see later on that a diagrammatic representation is only suitable in some very simple cases. Alternative methods of representing graphs will also be discussed. After introducing the terminology, we shall also discuss some of the basic results and theorems of graph theory.

5-1.1   Basic Definitions

Recall that in Chap. 2 a binary relation in a set V was defined as a subset of $V \times V$. It was shown that such a relation could be represented at least in some cases by a diagram which was called the graph of the relation. An alternative method of representing a relation was given by means of a relation or an incidence matrix. In this section we shall extend these ideas and in some ways generalize them.

We first consider several graphs which are represented by means of diagrams. Some of these graphs may be considered as graphs of certain relations, but there are others which cannot be interpreted in this manner.

Consider the diagrams shown in Fig. 5-1.1. For our purpose here, these diagrams represent graphs. Notice that every diagram consists of a set of points which are shown by dots or circles and are sometimes labeled v_1, v_2, ..., or 1, 2, ... Also in every diagram certain pairs of such points are connected by lines or arcs. The other details, such as the geometry of the arcs, their lengths, the position of the points etc., are of no importance at present. Notice that every arc starts at one point and ends at another point. A definition of the graph which is essentially an abstract mathematical system will now be given. Such a mathematical system is an abstraction of the graphs given in Fig. 5-1.1.

> **Definition 5-1.1**   A *graph* $G = \langle V, E, \phi \rangle$ consists of a nonempty set V called the set of *nodes* (*points*, *vertices*) of the graph, E is said to be the set of *edges* of the graph, and ϕ is a mapping from the set of edges E to a set of ordered or unordered pairs of elements of V.

We shall assume throughout that both the sets V and E of a graph are finite. It would be convenient to write a graph G as $\langle V, E \rangle$, or simply as G. Notice

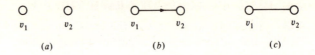

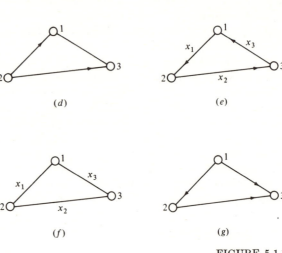

FIGURE 5-1.1

that the definition of a graph implies that to every edge of the graph G we can associate an ordered or unordered pair of nodes of the graph. If an edge $x \in E$ is thus associated with an ordered pair $\langle u, v \rangle$ or an unordered pair (u, v) where $u, v \in V$, then we say that the edge x connects or joins the nodes u and v. Any pair of nodes which are connected by an edge in a graph is called *adjacent* nodes.

Definition 5-1.2 In a graph $G = \langle V, E \rangle$, an edge which is associated with an ordered pair of $V \times V$ is called a *directed edge* of G, while an edge which is associated with an unordered pair of nodes is called an *undirected edge*. A graph in which every edge is directed is called a *digraph*, or a *directed graph*. A graph in which every edge is undirected is called an *undirected graph*. If some edges are directed and some are undirected in a graph, the graph is called *mixed*.

In the diagrams the directed edges are shown by means of arrows which also show the directions. The graphs given in Fig. 5-1.1*b*, *e*, and *g* are directed graphs. Those given in *c* and *f* are undirected, while the one given in *d* is mixed. The graph given in Fig. 5-1.1*a* could be considered as either directed or undirected. Notice that the edges x_1, x_2, and x_3 in Fig. 5-1.1*e* are associated with the ordered pairs $\langle 1, 2 \rangle$, $\langle 2, 3 \rangle$, and $\langle 3, 1 \rangle$ respectively, while the edges x_1, x_2, and x_3 in *f* are associated with the unordered pairs $(1, 2)$, $(2, 3)$, and $(3, 1)$ respectively. In Fig. 5-1.1*f* the node 1 is adjacent to nodes 2 and 3.

A city map showing only the one-way streets is an example of a directed graph in which the nodes are the intersections and the edges are the streets. A map showing only the two-way streets is an example of an undirected graph, while a map showing all the one-way and two-way streets is an example of a mixed graph.

Let $\langle V, E \rangle$ be a graph and let $x \in E$ be a directed edge associated with the ordered pair of nodes $\langle u, v \rangle$. Then the edge x is said to be *initiating* or *originating* in the node u and *terminating* or *ending* in the node v. The nodes u and v are also called the *initial* and *terminal* nodes of the edge x. An edge $x \in E$ which joins the nodes u and v, whether it be directed or undirected, is said to be *incident* to the nodes u and v.

An edge of a graph which joins a node to itself is called a *loop* (*sling*) (not to be confused with a loop in a program). The direction of a loop is of no significance; hence it can be considered either a directed or an undirected edge. Some authors do not admit any loops in the definition of a graph. We shall see that the presence or absence of a loop does not significantly change the theorems of graph theory.

The graphs given in Fig. 5-1.1 have no more than one edge between any pair of nodes. In the case of directed edges, the two possible edges between a pair of nodes which are opposite in direction are considered distinct. In some directed as well as undirected graphs, we may have certain pairs of nodes joined by more than one edge, as shown in Fig. 5-1.2a and b. Such edges are called *parallel*. Note that there are no multiple edges in the graph of Fig. 5-1.2c. In Fig. 5-1.2a there are two parallel edges joining the nodes 1 and 2, two parallel edges joining the nodes 2 and 3, while there are two parallel loops at 2. In 5-1.2b there are two parallel edges associated with the ordered pair $\langle v_1, v_2 \rangle$.

Any graph which contains some parallel edges is called a *multigraph*. On the other hand, if there is no more than one edge between a pair of nodes (no more than one directed edge in the case of a directed graph), then such a graph is called *a simple graph*. The graphs given in Fig. 5-1.1 are all simple graphs.

The graphs in Fig. 5-1.2a and b may be represented by the diagrams given in Fig. 5-1.3a and b in which the number on any edge shows the multiplicity of the edge. We may also consider the multiplicity as a weight assigned to an edge. This interpretation allows us to generalize the concept of weight to numbers which are not necessarily integers. We may thus have graphs as shown in Fig.

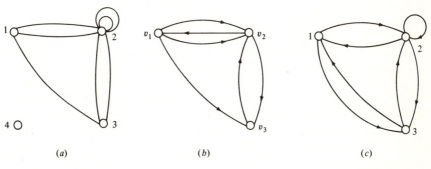

(a)   (b)   (c)

FIGURE 5-1.2

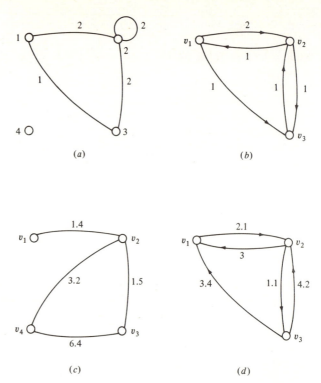

(a)

(b)

(c)

(d)

FIGURE 5-1.3

5-1.3c and d in which the numbers on the edges show the weights of the edges. A graph in which weights are assigned to every edge is called a *weighted graph*.

A graph representing a system of pipelines in which the weights assigned indicate the amount of some commodity transferred through the pipe is an example of a weighted graph. Similarly, a graph of city streets may be assigned weights according to the traffic density on each street.

In a graph a node which is not adjacent to any other node is called an *isolated node*. A graph containing only isolated nodes is called a *null graph*. In other words, the set of edges in a null graph is empty. The graph in Fig. 5-1.1a is a null graph, while that in Fig. 5-1.2a has an isolated node. In practice, an isolated node in a graph has very little importance.

The definition of graph contains no reference to the length or the shape and positioning of the arc joining any pair of nodes, nor does it prescribe any ordering of positions of the nodes. Therefore, for a given graph, there is no unique diagram which represents the graph. We can obtain a variety of diagrams by locating the nodes in an arbitrary number of different positions and also by showing the edges by arcs or lines of different shapes. Because of this arbitrariness, it can happen that two diagrams which look entirely different from one another may represent the same graph, as in Fig. 5-1.4a, a', also in b, b', and c, c'. The graphs in c and c' need further explanation, because the nodes are also labeled differently in these two graphs.

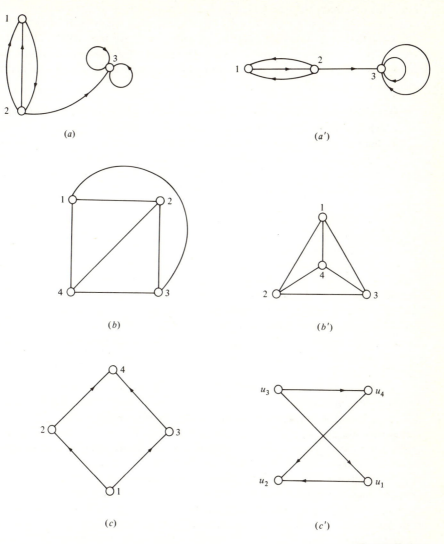

FIGURE 5-1.4

Definition 5-1.3 Two graphs are *isomorphic* if there exists a one-to-one correspondence between the nodes of the two graphs which preserves adjacency of the nodes as well as the directions of the edges, if any.

According to the definition of isomorphism we note that any two nodes in one graph which are joined by an edge must have the corresponding nodes in the other graph also joined by an edge, and hence a one-to-one correspondence exists between the edges as well. The graphs given in Fig. 5-1.4c and c' are isomorphic because of the existence of a mapping

$$1 \rightarrow u_3 \qquad 2 \rightarrow u_1 \qquad 3 \rightarrow u_4 \qquad \text{and} \qquad 4 \rightarrow u_2$$

Under this mapping, the edges $\langle 1, 3 \rangle$, $\langle 1, 2 \rangle$, $\langle 2, 4 \rangle$, and $\langle 3, 4 \rangle$ are mapped into $\langle u_3, u_4 \rangle$, $\langle u_3, u_1 \rangle$, $\langle u_1, u_2 \rangle$, and $\langle u_4, u_2 \rangle$ which are the only edges of the graph in c'.

Note that it is essential that two graphs which are isomorphic have the same number of nodes and edges; however, this is not a sufficient condition for an isomorphism to exist, as can be seen from the graphs given in Fig. 5-1.1e and g which are not isomorphic.

Definition 5-1.4 In a directed graph, for any node v the number of edges which have v as their initial node is called the *outdegree* of the node v. The number of edges which have v as their terminal node is called the *indegree* of v, and the sum of the outdegree and the indegree of a node v is called its *total degree*. In case of an undirected graph, the *total degree* or the *degree* of a node v is equal to the number of edges incident with v.

The total degree of an isolated node is 0.

The concept of the degree of a node can be generalized to a set of nodes. Let $G = \langle V, E \rangle$ be a directed graph and $X \subseteq V$ be a subset of nodes. The number of edges of G which have their initial node in X but their terminal node not in X is called the *outdegree* of X. Similarly, the number of edges of G which have their terminal nodes in X but their initial nodes not in X is called the *indegree* of X. The indegree and outdegree of a node are a special case of this definition.

A simple result involving the notion of the degree of nodes of a graph is that the sum of the degrees (or total degrees in the case of a directed graph) of all the nodes of a graph must be an even number which is equal to twice the number of edges in the graph.

Let $V(H)$ be the set of nodes of a graph H and $V(G)$ be the set of nodes of a graph G such that $V(H) \subseteq V(G)$. If, in addition, every edge of H is also an edge of G, then the graph H is called a *subgraph* of the graph G, which is expressed by writing $H \subseteq G$. Naturally, the graph G itself, as well as the null graph obtained from G by deleting all the edges of G, is also a subgraph of G. Other subgraphs of G can be obtained by deleting certain modes and edges of G.

We shall end this section by showing how the theory of binary relations given in Chap. 2 is closely linked to the theory of simple digraphs.

Let $G = \langle V, E \rangle$ be a simple digraph. Then every edge of E can be expressed by means of an ordered pair of elements of V. Such an ordered pair uniquely defines the edge; hence $E \subseteq V \times V$. On the other hand, any subset of $V \times V$ defines a relation in V. Accordingly, E is a binary relation in V whose graph is the same as the simple digraph G. This observation permits us to carry over the terminology and the results developed in Chap. 2 on binary relations.

A simple digraph $G = \langle V, E \rangle$ is called *reflexive, transitive, symmetric, anti-symmetric*, etc., if the relation E is reflexive, transitive, symmetric, antisymmetric, etc. We can also define the *converse of a digraph* $G = \langle V, E \rangle$ to be a digraph $\tilde{G} = \langle V, \tilde{E} \rangle$ in which the relation $\tilde{E}$ is the converse of the relation E. The diagram of $\tilde{G}$ is obtained from that of G by simply reversing the directions of the edges in G. The converse $\tilde{G}$ is also called the *reversal* or *directional dual* of a digraph G.

If a simple digraph $G = \langle V, E \rangle$ is reflexive, symmetric, and transitive, then the relation E must be an equivalence relation on V, and hence V can be partitioned into equivalence classes. If we consider any such equivalence class of nodes along with the edges that join these nodes, we have subgraphs of G. These subgraphs are such that every node in the subgraph is adjacent to every other node of the subgraph. However, no node of any one subgraph is adjacent to any node of another subgraph. In this sense the graph G is partitioned into subgraphs which are disjoint.

EXERCISES 5-1.1

1 Show that the sum of indegrees of all the nodes of a simple digraph is equal to the sum of outdegrees of all its nodes and that this sum is equal to the number of edges of the graph.

2 Draw all possible simple digraphs having three nodes. Show that there is only one digraph with no edges, one with one edge, four with two edges, four with three edges, four with four edges, one with five edges, and one with six edges. Assume that there are no loops and that graphs which are isomorphic are not distinguishable.

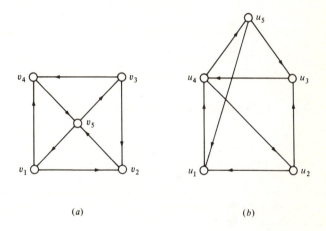

(a)   (b)

FIGURE 5-1.5

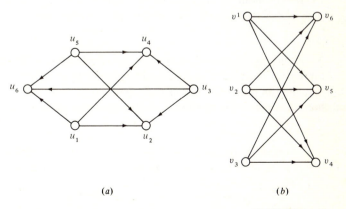

(a)   (b)

FIGURE 5-1.6

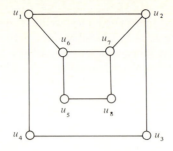 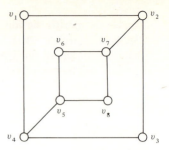

FIGURE 5-1.7

State the properties of these digraphs such as symmetry, transitivity, antisymmetry, etc.

3 Show that the digraphs given in Fig. 5-1.5a and b are isomorphic.

4 Show that the digraphs given in Fig. 5-1.6a and b are isomorphic.

5 Show that the digraphs in Fig. 5-1.7 are not isomorphic.

6 A simple digraph $G = \langle V, E \rangle$ is said to be *complete* if every node is adjacent to all other nodes of the graph. Show that a complete digraph with n nodes has the maximum number of edges viz., $n(n-1)$ edges, assuming that there are no loops.

7 The *complement* of a simple digraph $G = \langle V, E \rangle$ is the digraph $\bar{G} = \langle V, \bar{E} \rangle$ where $\bar{E} = V \times V - E$. Find the complements of the graphs given in Prob. 2.

5-1.2 Paths, Reachability, and Connectedness

In this section we introduce some additional terminology associated with a simple digraph. During the course of our discussion we shall also indicate how the same terminology and concepts can be extended to simple undirected graphs as well as to multigraphs.

Let $G = \langle V, E \rangle$ be a simple digraph. Consider a sequence of edges of G such that the terminal node of any edge in the sequence is the initial node of the next edge, if any, in the sequence. An example of such a sequence is

$$(\langle v_{i_1}, v_{i_2} \rangle, \langle v_{i_2}, v_{i_3} \rangle, \ldots, \langle v_{i_{k-2}}, v_{i_{k-1}} \rangle, \langle v_{i_{k-1}}, v_{i_k} \rangle)$$

where it is assumed that all the nodes and edges appearing in the sequence are in V and E respectively. It is customary to write such a sequence as

$$(v_{i_1}, v_{i_2}, \ldots, v_{i_{k-1}}, v_{i_k})$$

Note that not all edges and nodes appearing in a sequence need be distinct. Also, for a given graph any arbitrary set of nodes written in any order do not give a sequence as required. In fact each node appearing in the sequence must be adjacent to the nodes appearing just before and after it in the sequence, except in the case of the first and last nodes.

Definition 5-1.5 Any sequence of edges of a digraph such that the terminal node of any edge in the sequence is the initial node of the edge, if any, appearing next in the sequence defines a *path* of the graph.

A path is said to *traverse* through the nodes appearing in the sequence, *orig-*

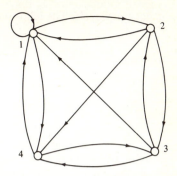

FIGURE 5-1.8

inating in the initial node of the first edge and *ending* in the terminal node of the last edge in the sequence.

Definition 5-1.6 The number of edges appearing in the sequence of a path is called the *length* of the path.

Consider the simple digraph given in Fig. 5-1.8. Some of the paths originating in node 1 and ending in node 3 are

$$P_1 = (\langle 1, 2 \rangle, \langle 2, 3 \rangle)$$

$$P_2 = (\langle 1, 4 \rangle, \langle 4, 3 \rangle)$$

$$P_3 = (\langle 1, 2 \rangle, \langle 2, 4 \rangle, \langle 4, 3 \rangle)$$

$$P_4 = (\langle 1, 2 \rangle, \langle 2, 4 \rangle, \langle 4, 1 \rangle, \langle 1, 2 \rangle, \langle 2, 3 \rangle)$$

$$P_5 = (\langle 1, 2 \rangle, \langle 2, 4 \rangle, \langle 4, 1 \rangle, \langle 1, 4 \rangle, \langle 4, 3 \rangle)$$

$$P_6 = (\langle 1, 1 \rangle, \langle 1, 1 \rangle, \ldots, \langle 1, 2 \rangle, \langle 2, 3 \rangle)$$

Definition 5-1.7 A path in a digraph in which the edges are all distinct is called a *simple path* (*edge simple*). A path in which all the nodes through which it traverses are distinct is called an *elementary path* (*node simple*).

Naturally, every elementary path of a digraph is also simple. The paths P_1, P_2, and P_3 of the digraph in Fig. 5-1.8 are elementary, while the path P_5 is simple but not elementary. We shall show here that if there exists a path from a node say, u, to another node v, then there must also be an elementary path from u to v.

Definition 5-1.8 A path which originates and ends in the same node is called a *cycle* (*circuit*). A cycle is called *simple* if its path is simple, i.e., no edge in the cycle appears more than once in the path. A cycle is called *elementary* if it does not traverse through any node more than once.

Note that in a cycle the initial node appears at least twice even if it is an elementary cycle. The following are some of the cycles in the graph of Fig. 5-1.8:

$$C_1 = (\langle 1, 1 \rangle)$$
$$C_2 = (\langle 1, 2 \rangle, \langle 2, 1 \rangle)$$
$$C_3 = (\langle 1, 2 \rangle, \langle 2, 3 \rangle, \langle 3, 1 \rangle)$$
$$C_4 = (\langle 1, 4 \rangle, \langle 4, 3 \rangle, \langle 3, 1 \rangle)$$
$$C_5 = (\langle 1, 4 \rangle, \langle 4, 3 \rangle, \langle 3, 2 \rangle, \langle 2, 1 \rangle)$$

Observe that any path which is not elementary contains cycles traversing through those nodes which appear more than once in the path. By deleting such cycles one can obtain elementary paths. For example, in the path P_5, if we delete the cycle $(\langle 1, 2 \rangle, \langle 2, 4 \rangle, \langle 4, 1 \rangle)$, we obtain the path P_2, which also originates at 1 and ends in 3 and is an elementary path. Similarly, if in the path P_4 we delete the same cycle, we get the elementary path P_1. Likewise, it is possible to obtain elementary cycles at any node from a cycle at that node. Because of this property, some authors use the term "path" to mean only the elementary paths, and they likewise apply the notion of the length of a path to only elementary paths.

A simple digraph which does not have any cycles is called *acyclic*. Naturally, such graphs cannot have any loops. We consider a class of digraphs which are acyclic in Sec. 5-1.4.

Definition 5-1.9 A node v of a simple digraph is said to be *reachable (accessible)* from the node u of the same digraph, if there exists a path from u to v.

Note that the concept of reachability is independent of the number of alternate paths from u to v and also of their lengths. For the graph given in Fig. 5-1.8, we have given paths P_1 to P_5 from node 1 to node 3. Any one of these paths is sufficient to establish the reachability of node 3 from node 1. For the sake of completeness we shall assume that every node is reachable from itself.

If a node v is reachable from the node u, then a path of minimum length from u to v is called a *geodesic*. The length of a geodesic from the node u to the node v is called the *distance* and is denoted by $d \langle u, v \rangle$. It is assumed that $d \langle u, u \rangle = 0$ for any node u.

It is clear from the definition that reachability is a binary relation on the set of nodes of a simple digraph. By our definition, reachability is reflexive. If there exists a path from a node u to a node v, and a path from the node v to a node w, then clearly there is a path from u to w. In other words, reachability is also a transitive relation. In general, it is not true that if there is a path from u to v, then there exists a path from v to u. Therefore, reachability is not necessarily symmetric, nor is it antisymmetric.

The distance from a node u to a node v, if v is reachable from u, is written as $d \langle u, v \rangle$ and satisfies the following properties:

$$d \langle u, v \rangle \geq 0$$
$$d \langle u, u \rangle = 0$$
$$d \langle u, v \rangle + d \langle v, w \rangle \geq d \langle u, w \rangle$$

The last inequality is called the *triangle inequality*. If v is not reachable from u, then it is customary to write $d \langle u, v \rangle = \infty$. Note also that if v is reachable from u and u is reachable from v, then $d \langle u, v \rangle$ is not necessarily equal to $d \langle v, u \rangle$.

The following theorem about the length of an elementary path between two nodes of a simple digraph will be used in Sec. 5-1.3.

Theorem 5-1.1 In a simple digraph, the length of any elementary path is less than or equal to $n - 1$, where n is the number of nodes in the graph. Similarly, the length of any elementary cycle does not exceed n.

PROOF The proof is based upon the fact that in any elementary path the nodes appearing in the sequence are distinct. The number of distinct nodes in any elementary path of length k is $k + 1$. Since there are only n distinct nodes in the graph, we cannot have an elementary path of length greater than $n - 1$. For an elementary cycle of length k, the sequence contains k distinct nodes; hence the result.   ////

Let us now briefly consider how the concepts of path and cycle can be extended to undirected graphs. Notice that the definition of a path requires that the edges appearing in the sequence must have a definite initial and terminal node. In the case of a simple undirected graph, an edge is given by an unordered pair, and any one of the nodes in the ordered pair can be considered as the initial or the terminal node of the edge. In order to apply the same definition of a path to an undirected graph, we consider every edge in an undirected graph to be replaced by two directed edges in opposite directions. Once this is done, we have a directed graph, and all the definitions of path, cycle, elementary path, reachability, etc., are carried over to undirected graphs. In the case of an undirected graph, the reachability relation is symmetric and so also is the distance. Theorem 5-1.1 holds for undirected graphs.

For a directed graph $G = \langle V, E \rangle$ we shall now extend the concept of reachability of a node. The set of nodes which are reachable from a given node v is said to be the *reachable set* of v. The reachable set of v is written as $R(v)$. For any subset $S \subseteq V$, the *reachable set* of S is the set of nodes which are reachable from any node of S, and this set is denoted by $R(S)$.

For the digraph given in Fig. 5-1.9, some of the reachable sets are as follows:

$R(v_1) = \{v_1, v_2, v_3, v_4, v_5, v_6\} = R(v_2) = R(v_3) = R(v_4) = R(v_5)$

$R(v_6) = \{v_6\}$ $R(v_7) = \{v_6, v_7\}$ $R(v_8) = \{v_6, v_7, v_8\}$

$R(v_9) = \{v_9\}$ $R(v_{10}) = \{v_{10}\}$ $R(v_5, v_8, v_9, v_{10}) = V = R(v_1, v_8, v_9, v_{10})$

In a digraph $G = \langle V, E \rangle$, a subset $X \subseteq V$ is called a *node base* if its reachable set is V and if no proper subset of X has this property.

In the digraph of Fig. 5-1.9, the set $\{v_1, v_8, v_9, v_{10}\}$ is a node base and so is the set $\{v_5, v_8, v_9, v_{10}\}$. There are several interesting facts about a node base of a simple digraph. We shall mention here a few of these facts, but we shall not prove these statements for the proofs are quite simple and straightforward.

Every isolated point of a digraph must be present in a node base. Any node whose indegree is zero must be present in any node base. From the definition

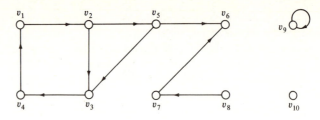

FIGURE 5-1.9

of a node base, it is clear that no node in the node base is reachable from another node in the node base. From the nodes lying on an elementary cycle any one node could be chosen as an element of a node base. Consequently, any node that does not have indegree zero and that does not lie on a cycle cannot be present in a node base. In a acyclic graph, a node base consists of only those nodes whose indegree is zero.

For a given simple digraph, we may have more than one node base; however, every node base has the same number of nodes. This statement is proved by showing that for any two node bases S_1 and S_2, every node of S_2 is reachable from exactly one node of S_1, and conversely. Thus a one-to-one correspondence is established between S_1 and S_2.

We shall now introduce an important concept, viz., that of the connectedness of nodes in a graph.

An undirected graph is said to be *connected* if for any pair of nodes of the graph the two nodes are reachable from one another. This definition cannot be applied to directed graphs without some further modifications, because in a directed graph if a node u is reachable from another node v, the node v may not be reachable from u. In order to overcome this difficulty, we call a digraph *connected* (*weakly connected*) if it is connected as an undirected graph in which the direction of the edges is neglected, i.e., if the graph when treated as an undirected graph is connected.

Definition 5-1.10   A simple digraph is said to be *unilaterally connected* if for any pair of nodes of the graph at least one of the nodes of the pair is reachable from the other node. If for any pair of nodes of the graph both the nodes of the pair are reachable from one another, then the graph is called *strongly connected*.

Observe that a unilaterally connected digraph is weakly connected, but a weakly connected digraph is not necessarily unilaterally connected. In fact, in a weakly connected digraph we may find that for any pair of nodes, say u and v, neither u is reachable from v nor v is reachable from u. A strongly connected digraph is both unilaterally and weakly connected.

For the digraphs given in Fig. 5-1.10, the digraph in Fig. 5-1.10a is strongly connected, b is weakly connected but not unilaterally connected, while c is unilaterally connected but not strongly connected.

Let $G = \langle V, E \rangle$ be a simple digraph and $X \subseteq V$. A subgraph whose nodes

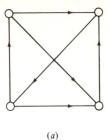
(a)

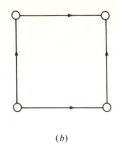
(b)

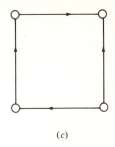
(c)

FIGURE 5-1.10

are given by the set X and whose edges consist of all those edges of G which have their initial and terminal nodes in X is called the *subgraph generated by X*. A subgraph G_1 is said to be maximal with respect to some property if no other subgraph has the property and also includes G_1.

Definition 5-1.11 For a simple digraph, a maximal strongly connected subgraph is called a *strong component*. Similarly, a maximal unilaterally connected or maximal weakly connected subgraph is called a *unilateral* or *weak component* respectively.

For the digraph given in Fig. 5-1.11, $\{1, 2, 3\}$, $\{4\}$, $\{5\}$, $\{6\}$ are the strong components. $\{1, 2, 3, 4, 5\}$, $\{6\}$ are the unilateral components, and $\{1, 2, 3, 4, 5, 6\}$ is the weak component because the graph is weakly connected.

Theorem 5-1.2 In a simple digraph, $G = \langle V, E \rangle$, every node of the digraph lies in exactly one strong component.

PROOF Let $v \in V$ and S be the set of all those nodes of G which are mutually reachable with v. The set S naturally contains v and is a strong component of G. This shows that every node of G is contained in a strong component.

Assume now that a node v is in two strong components. It would imply that any node in one strong component which contains v is reachable from any node in the other strong component which also contains v, because every such path is easily established through v. This, however, is impossible. Hence every node is contained in exactly one strong component. Thus the strong components partition V.   ////

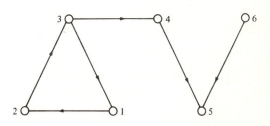

FIGURE 5-1.11

Note that any edge $x \in E$ of a simple digraph may or may not be contained in a strong component. If $x = \langle u, v \rangle$ and both u and v are in a strong component S, then x is in a strong component. If an edge $x \in E$ is in a strong component, then x must be a part of a cycle because if $\langle u, v \rangle \in S$, then $\langle v, u \rangle$ is also in S.

Similar results can be proved for weak and unilateral components. We shall simply state these results. The proof is similar to the one given for Theorem 5-1.2.

Every node and edge of a simple digraph is contained in exactly one weak component.

Every node and edge of a simple digraph lies in at least one unilateral component.

We shall now show how a simple digraph can be used to represent the resource allocation status of an operating system.

In a multiprogrammed computer system, it appears that several programs are executed at one time. In reality, the programs are sharing the resources of the computer system, such as tape units, disc devices, the central processor, main memory, and compilers. A special set of programs called an operating system controls the allocation of these resources to the programs. When a program requires the use of a certain resource, it issues a request for that resource, and the operating system must ensure that the request is satisfied.

It may happen that requests for resources are in conflict. For example, program A may have control of resource r_1 and require resource r_2, but program B has control of resource r_2 and requires resource r_1. In such a case, the computer system is said to be in a state known as *deadlock*, and the conflicting requests must be resolved. A directed graph can be used to model resource requests and assist in the detection and correction of deadlocks.

It is assumed that all resource requests of a program must be satisfied before that program can complete execution. If any requested resources are unavailable at the time of the request, the program will assume control of the resources which are available, but must wait for the unavailable resources.

Let $P_t = \{p_1, p_2, \ldots, p_m\}$ represent the set of programs in the computer system at time t. Let $A_t \subseteq P_t$ be the set of active programs, or programs that have been allocated at least a portion of their resource requests at time t. Finally, let $R_t = \{r_1, r_2, \ldots, r_n\}$ represent the set of resources in the system at time t. An allocation graph G_t is a directed graph representing the resource allocation status of the system at time t and consisting of a set of nodes $V = R_t$ and a set of edges E. Each resource is represented by a node of the graph. There is a directed edge from node r_i to r_j if and only if there is a program p_k in A_t that has been allocated resource r_i but is waiting for r_j.

For example, let $R_t = \{r_1, r_2, r_3, r_4\}$, $A_t = \{p_1, p_2, p_3, p_4\}$, and the resource allocation status be

p_1 has resource r_4 and requires r_1

p_2 has resource r_1 and requires r_2 and r_3

p_3 has resource r_2 and requires r_3

p_4 has resource r_3 and requires r_1 and r_4

Then the allocation graph at time t is given in Fig. 5-1.12.

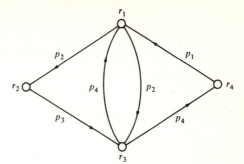

FIGURE 5-1.12 Allocation graph for detecting deadlocks.

It can be shown that the state of deadlock exists in a computer system at time t if and only if the allocation graph G_t contains strongly connected components. In the case of our example, the graph G_t is strongly connected. In fact, in Sec. 5-1.3 we discuss methods which will identify the nodes in a strong component and thus detect the resources and programs which are involved in the deadlock.

EXERCISES 5-1.2

1 Give three different elementary paths from v_1 to v_3 for the digraph given in Fig. 5-1.13. What is the shortest distance between v_1 and v_3? Is there any cycle in the graph? Is the digraph transitive? In case it is not transitive, find the transitive closure (see Sec. 2-3.7) of the digraph.

2 Find all the indegrees and outdegrees of the nodes of the graph given in Fig. 5-1.14. Give all the elementary cycles of this graph. Obtain an acyclic digraph by deleting one edge of the given digraph. List all the nodes which are reachable from another node of the digraph.

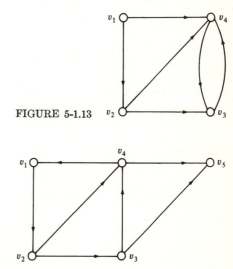

FIGURE 5-1.13

FIGURE 5-1.14

3 Given a simple digraph $G = \langle V, E \rangle$, under what condition is the equation

$$d(v_1, v_2) + d(v_2, v_3) = d(v_1, v_3)$$

satisfied for v_1, v_2, and $v_3 \in V$?

4 Find the reachable sets of $\{v_1, v_4\}$, $\{v_4, v_5\}$, and $\{v_3\}$ for the digraph given in Fig. 5-1.14.

5 Find a node base for each of the digraphs given in Figs. 5-1.13 and 5-1.14.

6 Explain why no node in a node base is reachable from another node in the node base.

7 Prove that in an acyclic simple digraph a node base consists of only those nodes whose indegree is zero.

8 For the digraphs given in Figs. 5-1.13 and 5-1.14, determine whether they are strongly, weakly, or unilaterally connected.

9 Show that a simple digraph is strongly connected iff there is a cycle in G which includes each node at least once and no isolated node.

10 The *diameter* of a simple digraph $G = \langle V, E \rangle$ is given by δ, where

$$\delta = \max_{u,\, v\epsilon V} d(u, v)$$

Find the diameter of the digraphs given in Figs. 5-1.13 and 5-1.14.

11 Find the strong components of the digraph given in Fig. 5-1.14. Also find its unilateral and weak components.

12 Show that every node and edge of a graph are contained in exactly one weak component.

5-1.3 Matrix Representation of Graphs

A diagrammatic representation of a graph has limited usefulness. Furthermore, such a representation is only possible when the number of nodes and edges is reasonably small. In this subsection we shall present an alternative method of representing graphs using matrices. Such a method of representation has several advantages. It is easy to store and manipulate matrices and hence the graphs represented by them in a computer. Well-known operations of matrix algebra can be used to calculate paths, cycles, and other characteristics of a graph.

Given a simple digraph $G = \langle V, E \rangle$, it is necessary to assume some kind of ordering of the nodes of the graph in the sense that a particular node is called a first node, another a second node, and so on. Our matrix representation of G depends upon the ordering of the nodes.

Definition 5-1.12 Let $G = \langle V, E \rangle$ be a simple digraph in which $V = \{v_1, v_2, \ldots, v_n\}$ and the nodes are assumed to be ordered from v_1 to v_n. An $n \times n$ matrix A whose elements a_{ij} are given by

$$a_{ij} = \begin{cases} 1 & \text{if } \langle v_i, v_j \rangle \in E \\ 0 & \text{otherwise} \end{cases}$$

is called the *adjacency matrix* of the graph G.

Recall that the adjacency matrix is the same as the relation matrix or the incidence matrix of the relation E in V. Any element of the adjacency matrix is either 0 or 1. Any matrix whose elements are either 0 or 1 is called a *bit matrix* or a *Boolean matrix*. Note that the ith row in the adjacency matrix is determined by the edges which originate in the node v_i. The number of elements in the ith row whose value is 1 is equal to the outdegree of the node v_i. Similarly, the number of elements whose value is 1 in a column, say the jth column, is equal to the indegree of the node v_j. An adjacency matrix completely defines a simple digraph.

For a given digraph $G = \langle V, E \rangle$, an adjacency matrix depends upon the ordering of the elements of V. For different orderings of the elements of V we get different adjacency matrices of the same graph G. However, any one of the adjacency matrices of G can be obtained from another adjacency matrix of the same graph by interchanging some of the rows and the corresponding columns of the matrix. We shall neglect the arbitrariness introduced in an adjacency matrix because of the ordering of the elements of V and take any adjacency matrix of the graph to be the adjacency matrix of the graph. In fact, if two digraphs are such that the adjacency matrix of one can be obtained from the adjacency matrix of the other by interchanging some of the rows and the corresponding columns, then the digraphs are isomorphic.

As an example, consider the digraph given in Fig. 5-1.15 in which first we order the nodes as v_1, v_2, v_3, and v_4 and write its adjacency matrix. Next we reorder the rows as v_2, v_3, v_1, and v_4 and write its adjacency matrix. The two adjacency matrices are A_1 and A_2 as shown. If we interchange the first row and the first column with the third row and the third column of A_2, and then we interchange the second row with the third row and similarly the second column with the third column, we get A_1.

$$A_1 = \begin{pmatrix} 0 & 1 & 0 & 0 \\ 0 & 0 & 1 & 1 \\ 1 & 1 & 0 & 1 \\ 1 & 0 & 0 & 0 \end{pmatrix} \qquad A_2 = \begin{pmatrix} 0 & 1 & 0 & 1 \\ 1 & 0 & 1 & 1 \\ 1 & 0 & 0 & 0 \\ 0 & 0 & 1 & 0 \end{pmatrix}$$

Some of the properties of a simple digraph are immediately seen from its adjacency matrix. If a digraph is reflexive, then the diagonal elements of the adjacency matrix are 1s. For a symmetric digraph, the adjacency matrix is also symmetric; that is, $a_{ij} = a_{ji}$ for all i and j. Similarly, if a digraph is antisymmetric, then $a_{ij} = 1$ implies $a_{ji} = 0$, and $a_{ij} = 0$ implies that $a_{ji} = 1$ for all i and j.

We can extend the idea of matrix representation to multigraphs and weighted graphs. For simple undirected graphs, such an extension simply gives

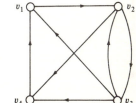

FIGURE 5-1.15

a symmetric adjacency matrix. In the case of a multigraph or a weighted graph, we write $a_{ij} = w_{ij}$ where w_{ij} denotes either the multiplicity or the weight of the edge $\langle v_i, v_j \rangle$. If $\langle v_i, v_j \rangle \notin E$, then we write $w_{ij} = 0$.

For a null graph which consists of only n nodes but no edges, the adjacency matrix has all its elements zero; i.e., the adjacency matrix is a null matrix. If there are loops at each node but no other edges in the graph, then the adjacency matrix is the identity or the unit matrix. If $G = \langle V, E \rangle$ is a simple digraph whose adjacency matrix is A, then the adjacency matrix of $\tilde{G}$, the converse of G, is the transpose of A, that is, A^T. For an undirected graph or for a symmetric graph, $A = A^T$.

We shall now consider the matrices AA^T, A^TA, and A^n for $n = 2, 3, 4, \ldots$. As an example, let us choose $A = A_1$, the first adjacency matrix of the digraph given in Fig. 5-1.15. Some of the matrices obtained from A are as follows:

$$A^T = \begin{pmatrix} 0 & 0 & 1 & 1 \\ 1 & 0 & 1 & 0 \\ 0 & 1 & 0 & 0 \\ 0 & 1 & 1 & 0 \end{pmatrix} \qquad AA^T = \begin{pmatrix} 1 & 0 & 1 & 0 \\ 0 & 2 & 1 & 0 \\ 1 & 1 & 3 & 1 \\ 0 & 0 & 1 & 1 \end{pmatrix}$$

$$A^TA = \begin{pmatrix} 2 & 1 & 0 & 1 \\ 1 & 2 & 0 & 1 \\ 0 & 0 & 1 & 1 \\ 1 & 1 & 1 & 2 \end{pmatrix} \qquad A^2 = \begin{pmatrix} 0 & 0 & 1 & 1 \\ 2 & 1 & 0 & 1 \\ 1 & 1 & 1 & 1 \\ 0 & 1 & 0 & 0 \end{pmatrix}$$

$$A^3 = \begin{pmatrix} 2 & 1 & 0 & 1 \\ 1 & 2 & 1 & 1 \\ 2 & 2 & 1 & 2 \\ 0 & 0 & 1 & 1 \end{pmatrix} \qquad A^4 = \begin{pmatrix} 1 & 2 & 1 & 1 \\ 2 & 2 & 2 & 3 \\ 3 & 3 & 2 & 3 \\ 2 & 1 & 0 & 1 \end{pmatrix}$$

Let us consider the elements of AA^T. For the sake of simplicity, write $B = AA^T$ and denote by b_{ij} the element in the ith row and jth column of B or AA^T. In general, for $i, j = 1, 2, \ldots, n$

$$b_{ij} = \sum_{k=1}^{n} a_{ik}a_{jk}$$

The value of $a_{ik}a_{jk} = 1$ iff both a_{ik} and a_{jk} are 1; otherwise $a_{ik}a_{jk} = 0$. Now $a_{ik} = 1$ if $\langle v_i, v_k \rangle \in E$, and $a_{jk} = 1$ if $\langle v_j, v_k \rangle \in E$. If both $\langle v_i, v_k \rangle$ and $\langle v_j, v_k \rangle$ are the edges of the graph for some fixed k, then we get a contribution of 1 in the summation expressing b_{ij}. The value of b_{ij} shows the number of nodes which are terminal nodes of edges from both v_i and v_j. In the graph G of Fig. 5-1.15, choose $i = 2$ and $j = 3$ and note that only the node v_4 is such that the edges from both

v_2 and v_3 terminate in v_4. Hence the entry is 1 in the second row and third column. If $i = j$, then

$$b_{ii} = \sum_{k=1}^{n} a_{ik}^2$$

and $a_{ik}^2 = 1$ if $a_{ik} = 1$, that is, if $\langle v_i, v_k \rangle \in E$. The diagonal entries of AA^T simply show the outdegree of the nodes.

A similar discussion shows that the element in the ith row and jth column of $A^T A$ shows the number of nodes of the graph which are such that the edges initiating from these nodes terminate in both v_i and v_j. Also the diagonal entries show the indegrees of the nodes.

Consider now the powers of an adjacency matrix. Naturally an entry of 1 in the ith row and jth column of A shows the existence of an edge $\langle v_i, v_j \rangle$, that is, a path of length 1 from v_i to v_j. Let us denote the elements of A^2 by $a_{ij}^{(2)}$. Then

$$a_{ij}^{(2)} = \sum_{k=1}^{n} a_{ik} a_{kj}$$

For any fixed k, $a_{ik} a_{kj} = 1$ iff both a_{ik} and a_{kj} equal 1, that is, iff $\langle v_i, v_k \rangle$ and $\langle v_k, v_j \rangle$ are the edges of the graph. For each such k we get a contribution of 1 in the sum. Now $\langle v_i, v_k \rangle$ and $\langle v_k, v_j \rangle$ imply that there is a path from v_i to v_j of length 2. Therefore, $a_{ij}^{(2)}$ is equal to the number of different paths of exactly length 2 from v_i to v_j. Similarly, the diagonal element $a_{ii}^{(2)}$ shows the number of cycles of length 2 at the node v_i for $i = 1, 2, \ldots, n$.

By a similar argument, one can show that the element in the ith row and jth column of A^3 gives the number of paths of exactly length 3 from v_i to v_j. In general, we have the following theorem.

Theorem 5-1.3 Let A be the adjacency matrix of a digraph G. The element in the ith row and jth column of A^n (n is a nonnegative integer) is equal to the number of paths of length n from the ith node to the jth node.

Theorem 5-1.3 can be proved for any positive integer n by using mathematical induction and an argument similar to the one given here.

For the graph given in Fig. 5-1.15 we see that there are two paths of length 2 from v_2 to v_1, hence the entry 2 in the second row and first column of A^2. Similarly, there are two paths of length 4 from v_2 to v_1, hence the corresponding entry in A^4.

Given a simple digraph $G = \langle V, E \rangle$, let v_i and v_j be any two nodes of G. From the adjacency matrix of A we can immediately determine whether there exists an edge from v_i to v_j in G. Also from the matrix A^r, where r is some positive integer, we can establish the number of paths of length r from v_i to v_j. If we add the matrices $A, A^2, A^3, \ldots, A^r$ to get B_r

$$B_r = A + A^2 + \cdots + A^r$$

then from the matrix B_r we can determine the number of paths of length less than or equal to r from v_i to v_j. If we wish to determine whether v_j is reachable from v_i, it would be necessary to investigate whether there exists a path of any length from v_i to v_j. In order to decide this, with the help of the adjacency matrix we would have to consider all possible A^r for $r = 1, 2, \ldots$ This method is neither practical nor necessary, as we shall show.

Recall that in a simple digraph with n nodes, the length of an elementary path or cycle does not exceed n (see Theorem 5-1.1). Also for a path between any two nodes one can obtain an elementary path by deleting certain parts of the path which are cycles. Similarly (for cycles), we can always obtain an elementary cycle from a given cycle. If we are interested in determining whether there exists a path from v_i to v_j, all we need to examine are the elementary paths of length less than or equal to $n - 1$. In the case of $v_i = v_j$ and the path is a cycle, we need to examine all possible elementary cycles of length less than or equal to n. Such cycles or paths are easily determined from the matrix B_n where

$$B_n = A + A^2 + A^3 + \cdots + A^n$$

The element in the ith row and jth column of B_n shows the number of paths of length n or less which exist from v_i to v_j. If this element is nonzero, then it is clear that v_j is reachable from v_i. Of course, in order to determine reachability, we need to know the existence of a path, and not the number of paths between any two nodes. In any case, the matrix B_n furnishes the required information about the reachability of any node of the graph from any other node.

Definition 5-1.13 Let $G = \langle V, E \rangle$ be a simple digraph in which $|V| = n$ and the nodes of G are assumed to be ordered. An $n \times n$ matrix P whose elements are given by

$$p_{ij} = \begin{cases} 1 & \text{if there exists a path from } v_i \text{ to } v_j \\ 0 & \text{otherwise} \end{cases}$$

is called the *path matrix (reachability matrix)* of the graph G.

Note that the path matrix only shows the presence or absence of at least one path between a pair of points and also the presence or absence of a cycle at any node. It does not, however, show all the paths that may exist. In this sense a path matrix does not give complete information about a graph as does the adjacency matrix. The path matrix is important in its own right.

The path matrix can be calculated from the matrix B_n by choosing $p_{ij} = 1$ if the element in the ith row and jth column of B_n is nonzero and $p_{ij} = 0$ otherwise. We shall apply this method of calculating the path matrix to our sample problem, whose graph is given in Fig. 5-1.15. The adjacency matrix $A = A_1$ and its powers A^2, A^3, A^4 have already been calculated. We thus have B_4 and the path matrix P given by

$$B_4 = \begin{pmatrix} 3 & 4 & 2 & 3 \\ 5 & 5 & 4 & 6 \\ 7 & 7 & 4 & 7 \\ 3 & 2 & 1 & 2 \end{pmatrix} \qquad P = \begin{pmatrix} 1 & 1 & 1 & 1 \\ 1 & 1 & 1 & 1 \\ 1 & 1 & 1 & 1 \\ 1 & 1 & 1 & 1 \end{pmatrix}$$

It may be remarked that if we are interested in knowing the reachability of one node from another, it is sufficient to calculate B_{n-1}, because a path of length n cannot be elementary. The only difference between P calculated from B_{n-1} and P calculated from B_n is in the diagonal elements. For the purpose of reachability, every node is assumed to be reachable from itself. Some authors calculate the path matrix from B_{n-1}, while others do it from B_n.

The method of calculating the path matrix P of a graph by calculating first $A, A^2, \ldots, A^n$ and then B_n is cumbersome. We shall now describe another method based upon a similar idea but which is more efficient in practice. Observe that we are not interested in the number of paths of any particular length from a node, say v_i, to a node v_j. This information is obtained during the course of our calculation of the powers of A, and later it is suppressed because these actual numbers are not needed. To reduce the amount of calculation involved, this unwanted information is not generated. This is achieved by using Boolean matrix operations in our calculations, which will now be defined.

A matrix whose entries are the elements of a two-element Boolean algebra $\langle B, \wedge, \vee, ^{-}, 0, 1 \rangle$ where $B = \{0, 1\}$ is called a Boolean matrix. The operations $\wedge$ and $\vee$ on B are given in Table 5-1.1. For any two $n \times n$ Boolean matrices A and B, the Boolean sum and Boolean product of A and B are written as $A \vee B$ and $A \wedge B$, which are also Boolean matrices, say C and D. The elements of C and D are given by

$$c_{ij} = a_{ij} \vee b_{ij} \quad \text{and} \quad d_{ij} = \bigvee_{k=1}^{n} (a_{ik} \wedge b_{kj}) \quad \text{for all } i, j = 1, 2, \ldots, n$$

Note that the element d_{ij} is easily obtained by scanning the ith row of A from left to right and simultaneously the jth column of B from top to bottom. If, for any k, the kth element in the row and kth element in the column are both 1, then $d_{ij} = 1$; otherwise $d_{ij} = 0$.

The adjacency matrix is a Boolean matrix, and so also is the path matrix. Let us write $A \wedge A = A^{(2)}$, $A \wedge A^{(r-1)} = A^{(r)}$ for any $r = 2, 3, \ldots$. The only difference between A^2 and $A^{(2)}$ is that $A^{(2)}$ is a Boolean matrix and the entry in the ith row and jth column of $A^{(2)}$ is 1 if there is at least one path of length 2 from v_i to v_j, while in A^2 the entry in the ith row and jth column shows the number of paths of length 2 from v_i to v_j. Similar remarks apply to A^3 and $A^{(3)}$ or in general A^r and $A^{(r)}$ for any positive integer r. From this description, it is clear that the path matrix P is given by

$$P = A \vee A^{(2)} \vee A^{(3)} \vee \cdots \vee A^{(n)} = \bigvee_{k=1}^{n} A^{(k)}$$

If we take the sum from $k = 1$ to $k = n - 1$, we get a matrix which may differ if at all from P in the diagonal terms only.

Table 5-1.1

$\wedge$	0	1		$\vee$	0	1
0	0	0		0	0	1
1	0	1		1	1	1

For our sample example of the graph given in Fig. 5-1.15,

$$A^{(2)} = \begin{pmatrix} 0 & 0 & 1 & 1 \\ 1 & 1 & 0 & 1 \\ 1 & 1 & 1 & 1 \\ 0 & 1 & 0 & 0 \end{pmatrix} \qquad A^{(3)} = \begin{pmatrix} 1 & 1 & 0 & 1 \\ 1 & 1 & 1 & 1 \\ 1 & 1 & 1 & 1 \\ 0 & 0 & 1 & 1 \end{pmatrix} \qquad A^{(4)} = \begin{pmatrix} 1 & 1 & 1 & 1 \\ 1 & 1 & 1 & 1 \\ 1 & 1 & 1 & 1 \\ 1 & 1 & 0 & 1 \end{pmatrix}$$

$$A \vee A^{(2)} \vee A^{(3)} = \begin{pmatrix} 1 & 1 & 1 & 1 \\ 1 & 1 & 1 & 1 \\ 1 & 1 & 1 & 1 \\ 1 & 1 & 1 & 1 \end{pmatrix} = A \vee A^{(2)} \vee A^{(3)} \vee A^{(4)} = P$$

The matrices A, $A^{(2)}$, $A^{(3)}$, ... can be interpreted in a different way. In a simple digraph, $G = \langle V, E \rangle$, $E \subseteq V \times V$ so that E can be interpreted as a relation in V. The adjacency matrix A is the relation matrix of the relation E. Recall that the composite relation $E \circ E = E^2$ was defined in Sec. 2-3.7 as the relation such that $v_i E^2 v_j$ if there exists a v_k such that $v_i E v_k$ and $v_k E v_j$. In other words, the relation matrix of E^2 has 1 in the ith row and jth column if there is at least a path of length 2 from v_i to v_j. This shows that $A^{(2)}$ is the relation matrix of the relation E^2. Similarly, $A^{(3)}$, $A^{(4)}$, ... are the relation matrices of the relations $E \circ E \circ E = E^3, E^4, \ldots$ in V.

Next, let E_1 and E_2 be two relations in V and A_1 and A_2 be the corresponding relation matrices. For the relations $E_1 \cup E_2$ and $E_1 \cap E_2$, the relation matrices are given by $A_1 \vee A_2$ and $A_1 \wedge A_2$ respectively.

For a given relation E in V, a relation E^+, called the transitive closure of E, was defined in Sec. 2-3.7 as

$$E^+ = E \cup E^2 \cup \cdots$$

Clearly, the relation matrix of E^+ is given by

$$A^+ = A \vee A^{(2)} \vee A^{(3)} \vee \cdots$$

where A is the relation matrix of E. It has been shown that if the number of elements in V is n, then no path or cycle exceeds n in length; therefore A^+ can be obtained by simply considering the sum up to $A^{(n)}$, for powers higher than n will not change A^+. Therefore

$$A^+ = A \vee A^{(2)} \vee A^{(3)} \vee \cdots \vee A^{(n)} = P$$

The matrix A^+ is the same as the path matrix. This method of obtaining the transitive closure of a relation as well as the path matrix of a simple digraph can easily be programmed by using the following algorithm due to Warshall.

Algorithm $WARSHALL$ Given the adjacency matrix A, the following steps produce the path matrix P or A^+:

1 $P \leftarrow A$.
2 $k \leftarrow 1$.

3 $i \leftarrow 1$.

4 $p_{ij} \leftarrow p_{ij} \lor (p_{ik} \land p_{kj})$ for all j from 1 to n.

5 $i \leftarrow i + 1$. If $i \le n$, go to step 4.

6 $k \leftarrow k + 1$. If $k \le n$, go to step 3; otherwise, halt.

To show that this algorithm produces the required matrix, note that for $k = 0$, step 1 produces a matrix in which $p_{ij} = 1$ if there is a path of length 1 from v_i to v_j. Assume that for a fixed k, the intermediate matrix p_{ij} produced by steps 3 to 5 of the algorithm is such that the element in the ith row and jth column is 1 iff there is a path from v_i to v_j through the nodes $v_1, v_2, \ldots, v_k$, or an edge from v_i to v_j. In the next step, $k \leftarrow k + 1$ and we find that $p_{ij} = 1$ either if $p_{ij} = 1$ earlier or if there is a path from p_i to p_j which traverses through v_{k+1}. This means that $p_{ij} = 1$ iff there is a path from v_i to v_j through the nodes $v_1, v_2, \ldots v_{k+1}$ or an edge from v_i to v_j, which completes the proof.   ////

A different algorithm due to Warshall which also permits the calculation of the path matrix P from a given adjacency matrix is obtained from algorithm $WARSHALL$ by replacing step 4 by step 4$'$:

4$'$ If $p_{ik} = 1$, then $p_{ij} = p_{ij} \lor p_{kj}$ for all j from 1 to n.

The other steps remain the same. The proof that this algorithm produces the path matrix is rather involved, and we shall omit it.

Algorithm $WARSHALL$ can be modified further to obtain a matrix which gives the lengths of shortest paths between the nodes. For this purpose, let A be the adjacency matrix of the graph. Replace all those elements of A which are zero by ∞, which shows that there is no edge between the nodes in question. The following algorithm produces the required matrix which shows the lengths of minimum paths.

Algorithm $MINIMA$ Given the adjacency matrix in which the zero elements are replaced by infinity or by some very large number, let this matrix be denoted by B. The matrix C produced by the following steps shows the minimum lengths of paths between the nodes.

1 $C \leftarrow B$.

2 $k \leftarrow 1$.

3 $i \leftarrow 1$.

4 $c_{ij} \leftarrow \min(c_{ij}, c_{ik} + c_{kj})$ for all j from 1 to n.

5 $i \leftarrow i + 1$. If $i \le n$, go to step 4.

6 $k \leftarrow k + 1$. If $k \le n$, go to step 3; otherwise, halt.

Here $+$ in step 4 means the ordinary adding of integers. In practice we are often interested not only in the length of the minimum path between any two nodes, but also in the actual path. It is a simple matter to modify the previous algorithm to obtain such a path, and therefore it is left as an exercise.   ////

Many other properties of a graph can be determined by using the adjacency matrix and the path matrix of a graph. As an example, we shall show how the path matrix can be used to obtain the strong component containing any particular node of the graph.

Let v_i be any node of a simple digraph G and P be its path matrix. If P' is the transpose of the matrix P, then the ith row of the matrix $P \wedge P'$ which is obtained by the elementwise product of the elements gives the strong component containing v_i.

Notice that if v_j is reachable from v_i, then clearly $p_{ij} = 1$; also, if v_i is reachable from v_j, then $p_{ji} = 1$ or $p'_{ij} = 1$. Therefore, the element in the ith row and jth column of $P \wedge P'$ is 1 iff v_i and v_j are mutually reachable. This is true for all j. Hence the result.

We shall end this subsection by showing how the path matrix of a digraph can be used in determining whether certain procedures in a program are recursive.

In some programming languages, a programmer must explicitly state that a procedure is recursive. For example, in PL/I the RECURSIVE option must be specified. In other languages which do not require any such specification, it is possible to use concepts from graph theory to determine which procedures are recursive. A recursive procedure is not necessarily one which invokes itself directly. If procedure p_1 invokes p_2, procedure p_2 invokes p_3, ..., procedure p_{n-1} invokes p_n, and procedure p_n invokes p_1, then procedure p_1 is recursive.

Let $P = \{p_1, p_2, \ldots, p_n\}$ be the set of procedures in a program. In a directed graph consisting of nodes representing elements of P, there is an edge from p_i to p_j if procedure p_i invokes p_j. Figure 5-1.16 shows a directed graph representing the calls made by the set of procedures $P = \{p_1, p_2, \ldots, p_5\}$. The adjacency matrix of the graph is

$$
A = \begin{array}{c} \\ p_1 \\ p_2 \\ p_3 \\ p_4 \\ p_5 \end{array}
\begin{array}{c} \begin{array}{ccccc} p_1 & p_2 & p_3 & p_4 & p_5 \end{array} \\
\begin{pmatrix}
0 & 1 & 0 & 0 & 0 \\
0 & 0 & 0 & 1 & 0 \\
1 & 0 & 0 & 0 & 0 \\
0 & 0 & 0 & 0 & 1 \\
0 & 1 & 0 & 0 & 0
\end{pmatrix}
\end{array}
$$

A procedure p_i is recursive if there exists a cycle involving p_i in the graph. Such cycles can be detected from the diagonal elements of the path matrix

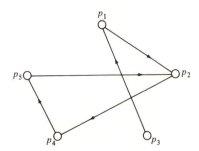

FIGURE 5-1.16 Procedure calls among $p_1, p_2, p_3, p_4,$ and p_5.

$Q = A^+$ of the graph. Thus p_i is recursive iff $q_{ii} = 1$. The matrix Q can be obtained by using Warshall's algorithm. The matrix Q is given by

$$Q = \begin{pmatrix} 0 & 1 & 0 & 1 & 1 \\ 0 & 1 & 0 & 1 & 1 \\ 1 & 1 & 0 & 1 & 1 \\ 0 & 1 & 0 & 1 & 1 \\ 0 & 1 & 0 & 1 & 1 \end{pmatrix}$$

which shows that the procedures p_2, p_4, and p_5 are recursive.

EXERCISES 5-1.3

1 Obtain the adjacency matrix A of the digraph given in Fig. 5-1.17. Find the elementary paths of lengths 1 and 2 from v_1 to v_4. Show that there is also a simple path of length 4 from v_1 to v_4. Verify the results by calculating A^2, A^3, and A^4.

2 For the digraph of Fig. 5-1.17 determine A', AA', and $A'A$. Interpret the entries of the matrix $A \wedge A'$. (A' is the transpose of A.)

3 For any $n \times n$ Boolean matrix A, show that

$$(I + A)^{(2)} = (I + A) \wedge (I + A) = I + A + A^{(2)}$$

where I is the $n \times n$ identity matrix and $A^{(2)} = A \wedge A$. Show also that for any positive integer r

$$(I + A)^{(r)} = I + A + A^{(2)} + \cdots + A^{(r)}$$

4 Using the result obtained in Prob. 3, show that the path matrix of a simple digraph is given by $P = (I + A)^{(n)}$ where A is the adjacency matrix of the digraph which has n nodes.

5 Given the adjacency matrix A of the digraph in Fig. 5-1.16, obtain the path matrix $Q = A^+$.

6 For a simple digraph $G = \langle V, E \rangle$ whose adjacency matrix is denoted by A, its *distance*

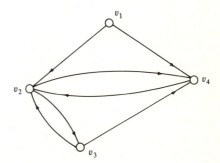

FIGURE 5-1.17

matrix is given by

$$d_{ij} = \infty \qquad \text{if } \langle v_i, v_j \rangle \notin E$$
$$d_{ii} = 0 \qquad \text{for all } i = 1, 2, \ldots, n$$
$$d_{ij} = k \qquad \text{where } k \text{ is the smallest integer for which}$$
$$a_{ij}{}^{(k)} \neq 0$$

Determine the distance matrix of the digraph given in Fig. 5-1.17. What does $d_{ij} = 1$ mean?

7 Show that a digraph G is strongly connected if all the entries of the distance matrix except the diagonal entries are nonzero. How will you obtain the path matrix from a distance matrix? How will you modify the diagonal entries?

8 Modify algorithm $MINIMA$ so that all minimal paths are computed.

5-1.4 Trees

An important class of diagraphs called directed trees will be introduced in this section along with the terminology associated with such trees. Trees are useful in describing any structure which involves hierarchy. Familiar examples of such structures are family trees, the decimal classification of books in a library, the hierarchy of positions in an organization, an algebraic expression involving operations for which certain rules of precedence are prescribed, etc. We shall describe here how trees can be represented by diagrams and other means. Representation of trees in a computer is discussed in Sec. 5-2.1. Applications of trees to grammars is given in Sec. 5-3.1.

> **Definition 5-1.14** A *directed tree* is an acyclic digraph which has one node called its *root* with indegree 0, while all other nodes have indegree 1.

Note that every directed tree must have at least one node. An isolated node is also a directed tree.

> **Definition 5-1.15** In a directed tree, any node which has outdegree 0 is called a *terminal node* or a *leaf*; all other nodes are called *branch nodes*. The *level* of any node is the length of its path from the root.

The level of the root of a directed tree is 0, while the level of any node is equal to its distance from the root. Observe that all the paths in a directed tree are elementary, and the length of a path from any node to another node, if such a path exists, is the distance between the nodes, because a directed tree is acyclic.

Figure 5-1.18 shows three different diagrams of a directed tree. Several other diagrams of the same tree can be drawn by choosing different relative positions of the nodes with respect to its root. The directed tree of our example has two nodes at level 1, five nodes at level 2, and three nodes at level 3. Figure 5-1.18a shows a natural way of representation, viz., the way a tree grows from its root up and ending in leaves at different levels. Figure 5-1.18b shows the same tree drawn upside down. This is a convenient way of drawing a directed tree and is commonly used in the literature. Figure 5-1.18c differs from b in the order in which the nodes appear at any level from left to right. According to our defini-

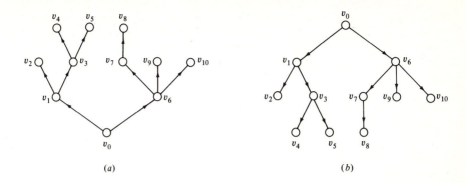

(a)

(b)

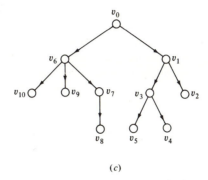

(c)

FIGURE 5-1.18

tion of a directed tree, such an order is of no significance. We shall, however, consider certain modifications so that an ordering of the nodes become relevant to a tree.

In many applications the relative order of the nodes at any particular level assumes some significance. In a computer representation such an order, even if it is arbitrary, is automatically implied. It is easy to impose an order on the nodes at a level by referring to a particular node as the first node, to another node as the second, and so on. In the diagrams the ordering may be done from left to right. Instead of ordering the nodes, we may prescribe an order on the edges. If, in a directed tree, an ordering of the nodes at each level is prescribed, then such a tree is called an *ordered tree*. According to this definition, the diagrams given in Fig. 5-18b and c represent the same directed tree but different ordered trees. Note that ordered trees as such are no longer directed graphs because the concept of order does not exist in a directed graph. We are mostly concerned with ordered trees in this section, and therefore we use the term "tree" to mean ordered tree unless stated otherwise. If we label the nodes as 1, 2, ... or in some other way from left to right in an ordered tree, then such a tree is said to be *canonically labeled*.

In both directed and ordered trees it is important to decide whether the root is shown on top or at the bottom, because certain other terminology used to describe the relative positions of the nodes as above or below may assume different meanings according to the choice made for locating the root. In our discussion we shall assume that the root is at the top and that all other nodes are below the root.

From the structure of the directed tree it is clear that every node of a tree is the root of some subtrees contained in the original tree. In fact, if we delete the root and the edges connecting the root to the nodes at level 1, we get subtrees with roots which are the nodes at level 1. For the tree in Fig. 5-1.18, the node v_6 is the root of the subtree $\{v_6, v_7, v_8, v_9, v_{10}\}$, v_1 is the root of $\{v_1, v_2, v_3, v_4, v_5\}$, v_3 is the root of $\{v_3, v_4, v_5\}$, v_5 is the root of $\{v_5\}$, and v_7 is the root of $\{v_7, v_8\}$, etc. The number of subtrees of a node is called the *degree* of the node. Naturally, the degree of a terminal node is 0. The degree of v_3 is 2 because $\{v_4\}$ and $\{v_5\}$ are its subtrees, while the degree of v_1 is also 2 because $\{v_2\}$ and $\{v_3, v_4, v_5\}$ are its subtrees.

If we delete the root and the edges connecting the nodes at level 1, we obtain a set of disjoint trees. A set of disjoint trees is called a *forest*. We have also seen that any node of a directed tree is a root of some subtree. Therefore, subtrees immediately below a node form a forest.

At this stage we shall give a recursive definition of directed trees. According to this definition, a tree contains one or more nodes such that one of the nodes is called the root while all other nodes are partitioned into a finite number of trees called subtrees.

Here a tree with n nodes has been defined in terms of trees with less than n nodes. For the tree in Fig. 5-1.18, the tree $\{v_0, \ldots, v_{10}\}$ is defined in terms of trees $\{v_1, \ldots, v_5\}$ and $\{v_6, \ldots, v_{10}\}$, while the tree $\{v_1, \ldots, v_5\}$ can be defined in terms of $\{v_2\}$ and $\{v_3, v_4, v_5\}$, and so on. Finally, we get trees with one node each, which are its terminal nodes.

There are several other ways in which a directed tree can be represented graphically. These methods of representation for the directed tree of Fig. 5-1.18 are given in Fig. 5-1.19a, b, and c. The first method uses the familiar technique of Venn diagrams to show subtrees, the second uses the convention of nesting parentheses, and the last method is the one used in the list of contents of books.

The method of representation given in Fig. 5-1.19b immediately shows how any completely parenthesized algebraic expression or a well-formed formula in statement logic can be represented by a tree structure. Naturally, it is not necessary to have a completely parenthesized expression if we prescribe a set of precedence rules as discussed in Sec. 1-3.6. As an example, consider the expression

$$v_1 v_2 + \left(v_4 + \frac{v_5}{v_6}\right)v_3$$

The tree corresponding to this expression is shown in Fig. 5-1.20.

In the diagrams representing trees we have chosen to show the roots on top and the edges pointing downward. All the nodes at any particular level are shown on a horizontal line. In the case of an ordered tree, the nodes at any particular level are ordered from left to right. This ordering distinguishes an ordered tree from other directed trees. It is sometimes convenient to borrow some ter-

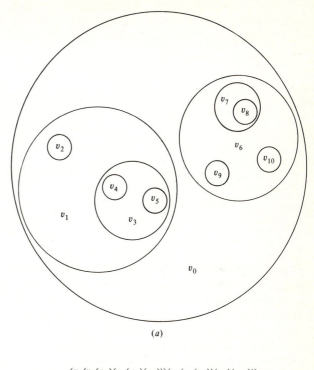

(a)

$$(v_0(v_1(v_2)(v_3(v_4)(v_5)))(v_6(v_7(v_8))(v_9)(v_{10})))$$

(b)

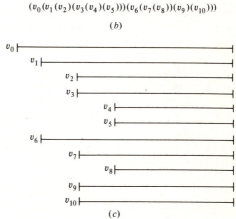

(c)

FIGURE 5-1.19   Different representations of trees.

minology from a family tree. Accordingly, every node that is reachable from a node, say u, is called a *descendent* of u. Also the nodes which are reachable from u through a single edge are called the *sons* of u.

So far we have not placed any restriction on the outdegree of any node in a directed or an ordered tree. If, in a directed tree, the outdegree of every node is less than or equal to m, then the tree is called an *m-ary tree*. If the outdegree

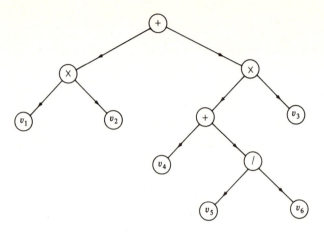

FIGURE 5-1.20

of every node is exactly equal to m or 0, then the tree is called a *full* or *complete* *m-ary tree*. For $m = 2$, the trees are called *binary* and *full binary* trees. We shall now consider m-ary trees in which the m (or fewer) sons of any node are assumed to have m distinct positions. If such positions are taken into account, then the tree is called a *positional m-ary tree*.

Figure 5-1.21a shows a binary tree, b shows a full binary tree, and c shows all four possible arrangements of sons of a node in a binary tree. The binary trees shown in Fig. 5-1.21a and d are distinct positional trees although they are not distinct ordered trees. In a positional binary tree, every node is uniquely

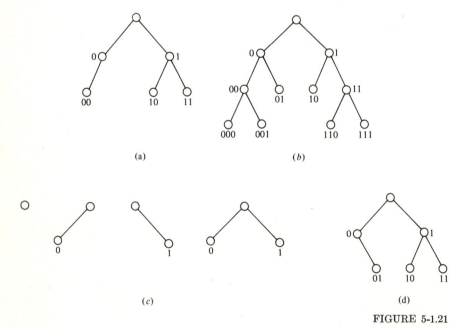

FIGURE 5-1.21

represented by a string over the alphabet {0, 1}, the root being represented by an empty string. Any son of a node u has a string which is prefixed by the string of u. The string of any terminal node is not prefixed to the string of any other node. The set of strings which correspond to terminal nodes form a *prefix* code. Thus the prefix code of the binary tree in Fig. 5-1.21b is {000, 001, 01, 10, 110, 111}. A similar representation of nodes of a positional m-ary tree by means of strings over an alphabet {0, 1, ..., $m - 1$} is possible.

The string representation of the nodes of a positional binary tree immediately suggests a natural method of representing a binary tree in a computer. It is sufficient for our purpose at this stage simply to recognize that such a natural representation exists.

Binary trees are useful in several applications. We shall now show that every tree can be uniquely represented by a binary tree, so that for the computer representation of a tree it is possible to consider the representation of its

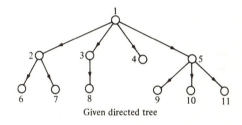

Given directed tree

Stage 1

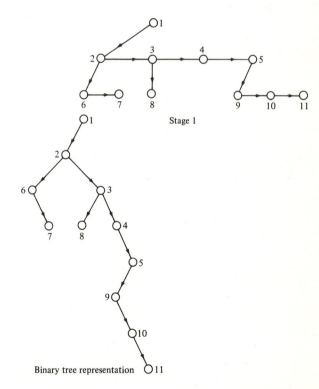

Binary tree representation

FIGURE 5-1.22

corresponding binary tree. Furthermore a forest can also be represented by a binary tree.

In Fig. 5-1.22 we show in two stages how one can obtain a binary tree which represents a given ordered tree. As a first step, we delete all the branches originating in every node except the leftmost branch. Also, we draw edges from a node to the node on the right, if any, which is situated at the same level. Once this is done then for any particular node, we choose its left and right sons in the following manner. The left son is the node which is immediately below the given node, and the right son is the node to the immediate right of the given node on the same horizontal line. Such a binary tree will not have a right subtree.

The above method of representing any ordered tree by a unique binary tree can be extended to an ordered forest as shown in Fig. 5-1.23. Both these repre-

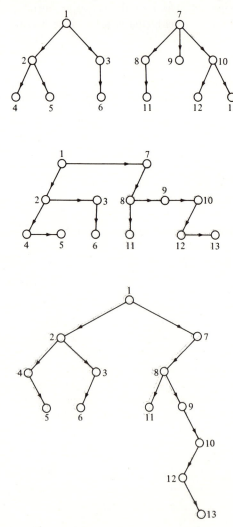

FIGURE 5-1.23   Binary tree representation of a forest.

sentations can be defined mathematically. This correspondence is called the natural correspondence between ordered trees and positional binary trees and also between ordered forests and positional binary trees.

EXERCISES 5-1.4

1 Show by means of an example that a simple digraph in which exactly one node has indegree 0 and every other node has indegree 1 is not necessarily a directed tree.

2 How many different directed trees are there with three nodes? How many different ordered trees are there with three nodes?

3 Give a directed tree representation of the following formula:

$$(P \vee (\neg P \wedge Q)) \wedge ((\neg P \vee Q) \wedge \neg R)$$

From this representation obtain the corresponding prefix formula.

4 Show that in a complete binary tree the total number of edges is given by $2(n_t - 1)$, where n_t is the number of terminal nodes.

5 From the adjacency matrix of a simple digraph, how will you determine whether it is a directed tree? If it is a directed tree, how will you determine its root and terminal nodes?

6 Obtain the binary tree corresponding to the tree given in Fig. 5-1.18.

5-2 STORAGE REPRESENTATION AND MANIPULATION OF GRAPHS

Recall that in Sec. 2-2 the computer representation of certain elementary discrete structures such as sets and arrays was discussed. We now wish to extend these concepts to more complex structures such as trees and graphs. Since trees are probably the most important nonlinear structure, their representations and manipulation will be emphasized in this section.

More particularly, our discussion will be limited to binary trees because their representation and manipulation are relatively simple when compared to those for general trees. Any general tree, as discussed at the end of Sec. 5-1.4, can be conveniently transformed into an equivalent binary tree.

The tree structures will be represented by using linked allocation. There are a number of storage methods that are based on sequential allocation, but we will not be concerned with them here.

The remainder of this section defines a list structure and describes a storage representation for it. These list structures are capable of representing certain digraphs. Finally, a storage method for representing a general graph is given.

5-2.1 Trees: Their Representation and Operations

The advantages and disadvantages in the use of linked allocation as opposed to sequential allocation in the representation of simple structures were discussed in Sec. 2-2. Although there are ways of representing trees based on sequential allocation techniques, we will not discuss them here. Computer representation of trees based on linked allocation seems to be more popular because of the ease with which nodes can be inserted in and deleted from a tree, and because tree structures can grow to an arbitrary size, a size which is often unpredictable.

We will restrict our discussions to binary trees since they are easily represented and manipulated. A general tree can be readily converted into an equivalent binary tree by using the natural correspondence algorithm discussed in Sec. 5-1.4. Therefore linked allocation techniques will be used to represent binary trees. A number of possible traversals which can be performed on binary trees are described. The subsection ends with a symbol table algorithm based on a tree structure.

We now turn to the task of using linked allocation techniques to represent binary trees. Recall that a binary tree has one root node with no descendants or else a left, or a right, or a left and right subtree descendant(s). Each subtree descendant is also a binary tree, and we do make the distinction between its left and right branches. A convenient way of representing binary trees is to use linked allocation techniques involving nodes with structure

$$\boxed{LLINK} \quad \boxed{DATA} \quad \boxed{RLINK}$$

where *LLINK* or *RLINK* contain a pointer to the left subtree or right subtree respectively of the node in question. *DATA* contains the information which is to be associated with this particular node. Each pointer can have a value of *NULL*.

An example of a binary tree as a graph and its corresponding linked representation in memory are given in Fig. 5-2.1*a* and *b* respectively. Observe the very close similarity between the figures as drawn. Such a similarity illustrates that the linked storage representation of a tree is closer to the logical structuring of the data involved. This property can be useful in designing algorithms which process tree structures.

Let us now examine a number of operations which are performed on trees. One of the most common operations performed on tree structures is that of traversal. This is a procedure by which each node is processed exactly once in some systematic manner. Using the terminology popularized by Knuth, we can traverse a binary tree in three ways, namely, in preorder, in inorder, and in postorder. The following are recursive definitions for these traversals.

Preorder traversal
    Process the root node.
    Traverse the left subtree in preorder.
    Traverse the right subtree in preorder.

Inorder traversal
    Traverse the left subtree in inorder.
    Process the root node.
    Traverse the right subtree in inorder.

Postorder traversal
    Traverse the left subtree in postorder.
    Traverse the right subtree in postorder.
    Process the root node.

If a particular subtree is empty (i.e., when a node has no left or right descendant), the traversal is performed by doing nothing. In other words, a null subtree is considered to be fully traversed when it is encountered.

If the words "left" and "right" are interchanged in the preceding definitions, then we have three new traversal methods which are called *converse preorder, converse inorder,* and *converse postorder,* respectively.

The preorder, inorder, and postorder traversals of the tree given in Fig. 5-2.1 will process the nodes in the following order:

$ABCDEFGH$ (preorder)

$CBDAEGHF$ (inorder)

$CDBHGFEA$ (postorder)

(The respective converse traversals would be $AEFGHBDC$, $FHGEADBC$, and $HGFEDCBA$.)

Although recursive algorithms would probably be the simplest to write for the traversals of binary trees, we will formulate algorithms which are nonrecursive. Since in traversing a tree it is required to descend and subsequently ascend parts of the tree, pointer information which will permit movement up the tree must be temporarily stored. Observe that the structural information that is already present in the tree permits downward movement from the root of the tree. Because movement up the tree must be made in a reverse manner from that taken in descending the tree, a stack is required to save pointer values as the tree is traversed. We will now give an algorithm for traversing a tree in preorder.

Algorithm *PREORDER* Given a binary tree whose root node address is given by a variable T and whose node structure is the same as previously described, this algorithm traverses the tree in preorder. An auxiliary stack S is used, and TOP is the index of the top element of S. P is a temporary variable which denotes where we are in the tree.

1 [Initialize] If $T = NULL$, then Exit (the tree has no root and therefore is not a proper binary tree); otherwise set $P \leftarrow T$ and $TOP \leftarrow 0$.

2 [Visit node, stack right branch address, and go left] Process node P. If $RLINK(P) \neq NULL$, then set $TOP \leftarrow TOP + 1$ and $S[TOP] \leftarrow RLINK(P)$. Set $P \leftarrow LLINK(P)$.

3 [End of chain?] If $P \neq NULL$, then go to step 2.

4 [Unstack a right branch address] If $TOP = 0$, then Exit; otherwise set $P \leftarrow S[TOP]$, $TOP \leftarrow TOP - 1$, and go to step 2.

In the second and third steps of the algorithm, we visit and process a node. The address of the right branch of such a node, if it exists, is stacked, and a chain of left branches is followed until this chain ends. At this point, we enter step 4 and delete from the stack the address of the root node of the most recently encountered right subtree and process it according to steps 2 and 3. A trace of the algorithm for the binary tree given in Fig. 5-2.1 appears in Table 5-2.1, where the rightmost element in the stack is considered to be its top element and the

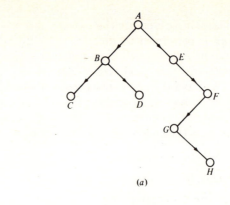

(a)

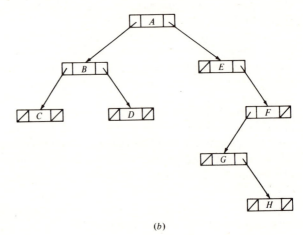

(b)

FIGURE 5-2.1   Graph and linked representation of a binary tree.

Table 5-2.1   TRACE OF ALGORITHM *PREORDER* FOR FIG. 5-2.1

Stack contents	*P*	Visit *P*	Output string
	NA	*A*	*A*
NE	*NB*	*B*	*AB*
NE ND	*NC*	*C*	*ABC*
NE ND	*NULL*		
NE	*ND*	*D*	*ABCD*
NE	*NULL*		
	NE	*E*	*ABCDE*
NF	*NULL*		
	NF	*F*	*ABCDEF*
	NG	*G*	*ABCDEFG*
NH	*NULL*		
	NH	*H*	*ABCDEFGH*
	NULL		

notation "*NE*," for example, denotes the address of node *E*. The visit of a node in this case merely involves the output of the label for that node.　　　////

　　The next algorithm traverses a tree in postorder.

Algorithm *POSTORDER* The same node structure described previously is assumed, and *T* is again a variable which contains the address of the root of the tree. A stack *S* with its top element pointer is also required, but in this case, each node will be stacked twice, namely, once when its left subtree is traversed and once when its right subtree is traversed. On completion of these two traversals, the particular node being considered is processed. Hence, we must be able to distinguish two types of stack entries. The first type of entry indicates that a left subtree is being traversed, while the second indicates the traversal of a right subtree. For convenience, we will use negative pointer values for the second type of entry. This, of course, assumes that valid pointer data is always nonzero and positive.

　　1 [Initialize] If $T = NULL$, then Exit (the tree has no root and therefore is not a proper binary tree); otherwise set $P \leftarrow T$ and $TOP \leftarrow 0$.

　　2 [Stack node address and go left] Set $TOP \leftarrow TOP + 1$, $S[TOP] \leftarrow P$, and $P \leftarrow LLINK(P)$.

　　3 [End of chain?] If $P \neq NULL$, then go to step 2.

　　4 [Unstack a node address] If $TOP = 0$, then Exit; otherwise set $P \leftarrow S[TOP]$ and $TOP \leftarrow TOP - 1$.

　　5 [Restack address if right subtree is not traversed] If $P < 0$, then go to step 6; otherwise set $TOP \leftarrow TOP + 1$, $S[TOP] \leftarrow -P$, $P \leftarrow RLINK(P)$, and go to step 3.

　　6 [Visit node] Set $P \leftarrow -P$, process node *P*, and go to step 4.

In the second and third steps, a chain of left branches is followed and the address of each node which is encountered is stacked. At the end of such a chain, the stack entry for the last node encountered is checked against zero. If it is positive, the negative address of that node is restacked and the right branch of this node is taken and processed according to steps 2 and 3. If the stack value is negative, however, we have finished traversing the right subtree of that node. The node is then processed, and the next stack entry is subsequently checked.

　　　////

　　If the terms '*RLINK*' and '*LLINK*' are interchanged in the previous algorithms, then algorithms for converse preorder and converse postorder traversals result.

　　Binary trees have already been encountered in a number of instances. Recall that the theorem proving algorithm in Sec. 2-7 generated a binary tree in a preorder manner. A converse postorder traversal of this tree would construct the proof sequence required to establish a propositional logic formula as a theorem.

　　Also, in Sec. 3-4 we observed that formulas in reverse Polish notation are very useful in the compilation process. There is a close relationship between binary trees and formulas in prefix or suffix notation. Let us write an infix formula as a binary tree, where a node has an operator as a value and where the left

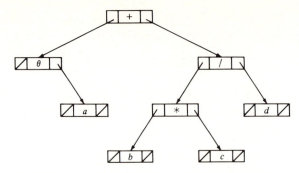

FIGURE 5-2.2   The formula $\ominus a + b * c/d$ as a binary tree.

and right subtrees are the left and right operands of that operator. The leaves of the tree will be the variables and constants in the expression. Let θ represent the unary minus. There are rules given in Exercises 3-4 that can distinguish a unary minus from a binary minus and the negative sign of a constant. The operand of θ will be considered to be a right subtree. The binary tree in Fig. 5-2.2 represents the formula $\theta a + b * c/d$. If we traverse this tree in preorder, we visit the nodes in the order $+\theta a/*bcd$, and this is merely the prefix form of the infix formula. On the other hand, if we traverse the tree in postorder, then we visit the nodes in the order $a\theta bc*d/+$, which is the formula written in suffix notation. Observe that if we had represented the formula as a general tree and then applied the natural correspondence algorithm of Sec. 5-1.4 to convert this tree into an equivalent binary tree, we would have the structures shown in Fig. 5-2.3. The prefix form of the formula is obtained by traversing the binary tree

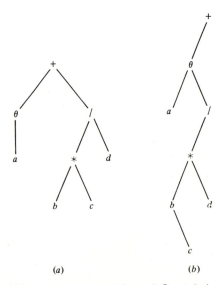

(a)   (b)

FIGURE 5-2.3   The general and binary tree representations of $\ominus a + b *$ c/d. (a) General tree; (b) binary tree.

in preorder, while the suffix form is generated by an inorder traversal of the binary tree (not a postorder traversal!).

As an application of binary trees, we will formulate an algorithm that will maintain a tree-structured symbol table. (See Sec. 2-4.6.) One of the criteria that a symbol table routine must meet is that table searching be performed efficiently. This requirement originates in the compilation phase where many references to the entries of a symbol table are made. The two required operations that must be performed on a symbol table are insertion and "look-up," each of which involves searching. A binary tree structure was chosen for two reasons. The first reason is because if the symbol entries as encountered are randomly distributed according to lexicographic order, then table searching becomes approximately equivalent to a binary search as long as the tree is maintained in lexicographic order. Second, a binary tree structure is easily maintained in lexicographic order (in the sense that only a few pointers need be changed).

For simplicity, we assume a relatively sophisticated system which allows variable-length character strings to be used without much effort on the part of the programmer to handle them. We further assume that the symbol table routine is used to create trees that are local to a block of program code. This implies that an attempt to insert a duplicate entry is an error. In a global context, duplicate entries would be permitted as long as they were at different block levels. In a sense, the symbol table is a set of trees, one for each block level.

A binary tree will be constructed whose typical node is of the form

| LLINK | SYMBOLS | INFO | RLINK |

where *LLINK* and *RLINK* are pointer fields, *SYMBOLS* is the field for the character string which is the identifier or variable name (note that string descriptors might well be used here to allow fixed-length nodes, but it is assumed that this use is clear to the user), and *INFO* is some set of fields containing additional information about the identifier, such as its type. A node will be created by the execution of the statement $P \leftarrow NODE$ where the address of the new node is stored in P.

Finally, it is assumed that prior to any use of the symbol table routine at a particular block level, the appropriate tree head node is created with the *SYMBOLS* field set to a value that is greater lexicographically than any valid identifier. $HEAD[n]$ will point to this node where n designates the nth block level. Hence, the existence of an appropriate main routine which administers to the creation of tree heads as a new block is entered and to the deletion of tree heads as a block is exited, is assumed.

Because both the insertion and look-up operations involve many of the same actions (e.g., searching), we will actually produce only one routine, *TABLE*, and distinguish between insertion and look-up by the value of a global logical variable, *FLAG*. On invoking algorithm *TABLE*, if *FLAG* is *true*, then the requested operation is insertion; *NAME* and *DATA* contain the identifier name and additional information respectively. If the insertion is successful, then *FLAG* retains its original value; otherwise the value of *FLAG* is negated to indicate an error (because the identifier is already present in the table at that level), and an exit from the algorithm is made. On the other hand, if the algorithm is invoked with *FLAG* set to *false*, then the requested operation is look-up. In this case, $NAME$ contains the identifier name to be searched for, and $DATA$ is irrelevant. On a successful search, $DATA$ is set to the $INFO$ fields of the matching $SYMBOLS$ entry, $FLAG$ retains its value, and a return is made to the invoking program. An unsuccessful search during a look-up operation causes the value of $FLAG$ to be negated and an exit to be made. In this latter case, it is the responsibility of the invoking main routine to try the look-up procedure at lower block levels (trees headed by $HEAD[n - 1]$, $HEAD[n - 2]$, etc.).

Algorithm $TABLE$ Given n, a global variable indicating the block level of current interest, and $FLAG$, a global variable which indicates the required operation, this algorithm performs the requested operation on the tree-structured symbol table local to level n. The parameters $DATA$ and $NAME$ are used for data communications between the algorithm and the invoking routine. $FLAG$ is used as a success or failure indicator in the algorithm.

1 [Initialize] Set $T \leftarrow HEAD[n]$.

2 [Compare] If $NAME < SYMBOLS(T)$, then go to step 4. If $NAME > SYMBOLS(T)$, then go to step 5.

3 [A match] If $FLAG$, then set $FLAG \leftarrow \neg FLAG$ and Exit; otherwise, set $DATA \leftarrow INFO(T)$ and Exit.

4 [Go left?] If $LLINK(T) \neq NULL$, then set $T \leftarrow LLINK(T)$ and go to step 2;
   otherwise, if $\neg FLAG$, then set $FLAG \leftarrow \neg FLAG$ and Exit;
      otherwise, set $P \leftarrow NODE$, $SYMBOLS(P) \leftarrow NAME$, $INFO(P) \leftarrow DATA$, $LLINK(P) \leftarrow NULL$, $RLINK(P) \leftarrow NULL$, $LLINK(T) \leftarrow P$, and Exit.

5 [Go right?] If $RLINK(T) \neq NULL$, then set $T \leftarrow RLINK(T)$ and go to step 2;
   otherwise, if $\neg FLAG$ then set $FLAG \leftarrow \neg FLAG$ and Exit;
      otherwise, set $P \leftarrow NODE$, $SYMBOLS(P) \leftarrow NAME$, $INFO(P) \leftarrow DATA$, $LLINK(P) \leftarrow NULL$, $RLINK(P) \leftarrow NULL$, $RLINK(T) \leftarrow P$, and Exit.

The algorithm is basically simple. In step 2 we compare $NAME$ against a symbol table entry. If they match, either we have found the required entry or we have attempted to enter a duplicate name. In either case we exit. If no match is found, we go to either step 4 or step 5 depending on whether $NAME$ was less than or greater than the symbol table entry being examined, and we next prepare to take the left or right node descendant and return to step 2 for further comparison. However, since a tree ordered in this manner is such that every node in a left subtree precedes lexicographically the root node and every node in a right subtree follows lexicographically the root node, we know that whenever an attempt is made to go down an empty subtree, then no match can be found. Thus, we have determined where the entry should be, but it is not there. In such a case, an error flag is set if the requested operation was a look-up; otherwise a new node is created, pertinent information is copied into it, and it is inserted to either the left or the right of the current node being examined in the existing tree structure. ////

5-2.2 List Structures and Graphs

This subsection will first be concerned with the representation of a structure which is more general than a tree. Such a structure is called a list structure, and several programming languages have been developed to allow easy processing of structures similar to those that will be described. The need for list processing arose from the high cost of rapid computer storage and the unpredictable nature of the storage requirements of computer programs and data. There are many symbol manipulation applications in which this unpredictability is particularly acute. It will be shown that a list structure can be used to represent a directed graph. Second, we will give a brief introduction to the representation of a general graph structure. Such representations are based not only on the nature of the data, but also on the operations which are to be performed on the data. A specific representation for a particular application of graphs is given in Sec. 5-5.

In the context of list processing, we define a *list* to be any finite sequence of zero or more *atoms* or *lists*, where an atom is taken to be any object (e.g., a string of symbols) which is distinguishable from a list by treating the atom as structurally indivisible. If we enclose lists within parentheses and separate elements of lists by commas, then the following can be considered lists:

$$(a, (b, c), d, (e, f, g))$$

$$(\ )$$

$$(((a)))$$

The first list contains four elements, namely, the atom a, the list (b, c) which contains the atoms b and c, the atom d, and the list (e, f, g) whose elements are the atoms e, f, and g. The second list has no elements, but the null list is still a valid list according to our definition. The third list has one element—the list $((a))$ which contains the single element (a), which in turn contains the atom a.

There is a distinct relationship between graphs and lists. A list is a directed graph with one *source* node (a node whose indegree is 0) corresponding to the entire list, and with every node immediately connected to the source node corresponding to an element of the list—either by being a node with outdegree 0 (for atoms) or by being a node that has branches (for elements which are lists) emanating from it. Every node except the source node has an indegree of 1. The edges leaving a node are considered to be ordered lists. This means that we distinguish the first edge, second edge, etc., which corresponds to the ordering of list elements by the first element, second element, etc. Furthermore, there are no cycles in the graph.

The preceding discussion could apply equally well to trees. However, lists are, in fact, extensions of trees in that a list can contain itself as an element and a tree cannot. Hence, there are some lists which cannot be represented as trees, but every tree can be represented as a list. Lists can have an essentially recursive nesting structure that no tree can have. Thus there are some lists that have a finite representation in our parentheses-comma notation, but which correspond to infinite graphs.

The graphs of some examples of lists appear in Fig. 5-2.4. If, however, M is the list (a, b, M), then we have an "infinite" graph for M, as shown in Fig. 5-2.5.

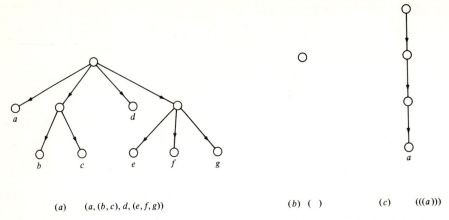

(a)   (a, (b, c), d, (e, f, g))   (b) ( )   (c)   (((a)))

FIGURE 5-2.4   Graph of list structures.

Linked allocation techniques can be used to represent lists in the memory of a computer. In such a representation there are two types of nodes—one for atoms and one for list elements. An atom node contains two fields: the first contains the value of the atom (e.g., a string of symbols), and the second contains a pointer to the next element in the list. A list node also contains two fields: the first field points to the storage representation of the list, and the second points to the element which follows this particular list element. It is assumed that an atom node and a list node are distinguishable.

Observe that in addition to order, a list also has *depth*. The list

$$(a, (b, c), d)$$

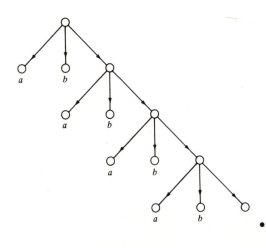

FIGURE 5-2.5   A recursive list structure and its graph.

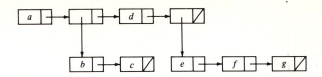

FIGURE 5-2.6   Storage representation of $(a, (b, c), d, (e, f, g))$.

has a depth of 2. The depth of a list is the number of levels it contains. The elements a and d are at level 1, and b and c are at level 2. The number of pairs of parentheses surrounding an element indicates its level. The element d in the list $(a, (b, (c, (d))))$ has a level of 4.

Order and depth are more easily understood in terms of our storage representation, where order is indicated by horizontal arrows and depth by vertical (downward-pointing) arrows. Thus, the list $(a, (b, c), d, (e, f, g))$ would be represented by the storage structure in Fig. 5-2.6. In storage, several lists may share common sublists. For example, the lists $(a, (b, c), d)$ and $(1, 5.2, (b, c))$ could be represented as in Fig. 5-2.7.

The recursive list M, where M is (a, b, M), can be represented as shown in Fig. 5-2.8. We would naturally use this storage representation where the common structure is shared rather than generating an infinite number of nodes to correspond to an infinite graph, but great care must be taken when manipulating such recursive structures in order to avoid programming oneself into an infinite loop.

A list structure occurs quite frequently in the processing of information, although it is not always evident. Consider a simple English sentence which consists of a subject, verb, and object. Any such sentence can be interpreted as a three-element list, whose elements can be atoms (single words) or lists (word phrases). The following sentences and their corresponding list representations are examples:

Man bites dog. = (Man, bites, dog)

The man bites the dog. = ((The, man), bites, (the, dog))

The big man is biting the small dog. = ((The, big, man), (is, biting), (the, small, dog))

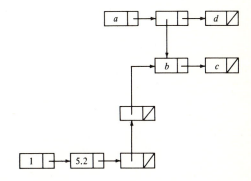

FIGURE 5-2.7   Two lists sharing a common sublist.

FIGURE 5-2.8 The representation of a recursive list M.

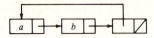

The subject and object of the last example can be further separated into nouns and qualifiers as in

(((The, big), (man)), (is, biting), ((the, small), (dog)))

The storage representation of this sentence is given in Fig. 5-2.9.

Observe that both order and level are significant. In this list structure, it is clear that the first node at level 1 either contains a noun which is the subject, or points to a list which contains a noun phrase which is the subject. If the latter is the case, we know that the first node (at level 2) of the list that is pointed to either contains a single qualifier or points to a list containing multiple qualifiers, and that the second node points to the noun. Thus, it is a simple matter to locate the noun subject of a sentence represented in this manner. Other elements of the sentence may be as easily isolated. Most list processing systems have features which facilitate such parsing operations.

List structures can therefore be used to represent digraphs, and a property of such representations is that sublists can be shared. As an example, a digraph and its list representation are given in Fig. 5-2.10.

As mentioned previously, several programming languages have been developed to allow easy processing of list structures. LISP 1.5 is one of the most powerful of these.

We will now discuss another storage method for graphs. The best storage representation for some general graph depends on the nature of the data and on the operations which are to be performed on these data. Furthermore, the choice of a suitable representation is affected by other factors such as the number of nodes, the average number of edges leaving a node, whether a graph is directed, the frequency of insertions and/or deletions to be performed, etc.

Arrays can sometimes be used (when there is at most one edge between any pair of nodes and there are no slings) to represent graphs. In this case the nodes are numbered from 1 to n, and a two-dimensional array with n rows and

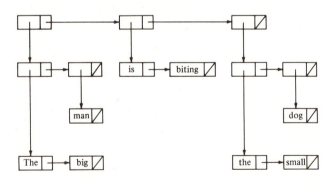

FIGURE 5-2.9 Storage representation of (((The, big), (man)), (is, biting), ((the, small), (dog))).

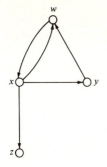

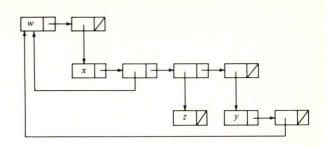

FIGURE 5-2.10 A digraph and its list structure representation.

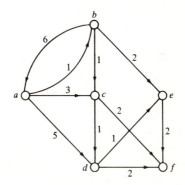

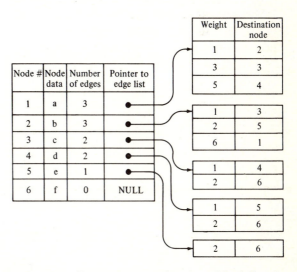

FIGURE 5-2.11 Storage representation of a weighted digraph.

n columns is used to represent the graph. Also, vectors could be required to store data on nodes in such a representation. This approach is not very suitable for a graph that has a large number of nodes or many nodes which are connected to only a few edges, nor when the graph must be continually altered.

If there are a number of branches between a pair of nodes and a considerable number of nodes that are connected to only a few other nodes, then a storage structure representation for such a graph could be the one shown in Fig. 5-2.11. Observe that the graph is weighted and that the storage representation consists of a node table directory, and associated with each entry in this directory we can have an edge list. A typical node directory entry consists of a node number, the data associated with it, the number of edges emanating from it, and a pointer field which gives the address of the edge list associated with this node. Each edge list, in this case, is stored as a sequential table whose typical entry consists of the weight of an edge and the node number at which that particular edge terminates. For a graph which is continually being changed, a representation which stores each edge list as a linked list is more desirable. In such a case it is not necessary to have the field which denotes the number of edges in the node table directory.

EXERCISES 5-2

1 Prove that a binary tree with n nodes has exactly $n + 1$ null branches.
2 Trace through algorithm *POSTORDER* using the binary tree of Fig. 5-2.1, and construct a table similar to Table 5-2.1.
3 Formulate an algorithm for the inorder traversal of a binary tree.
4 Trace through algorithm *TABLE* using a suitable set of seven variable names.
5 Given the binary tree in Fig. 5-2.12, determine the order in which the nodes will be visited if the tree is traversed in inorder, in postorder, and in preorder. Repeat this exercise for the converse traversals.

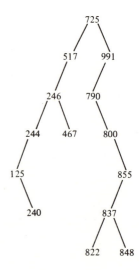

FIGURE 5-2.12

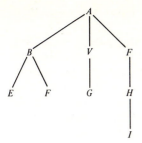
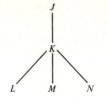
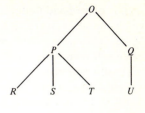

FIGURE 5-2.13   A forest of trees.

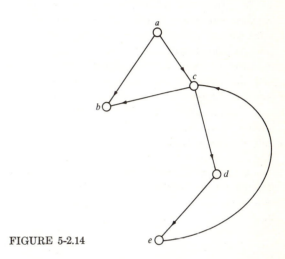

FIGURE 5-2.14

6   Develop an algorithm that converts a forest of trees into a single binary tree according to the natural correspondence. Illustrate the working of your algorithm by converting the forest in Fig. 5-2.13 to the binary tree corresponding to it.

7   Give a storage representation for the following lists:

$$(a, (b, (c, d)), e, f)$$

$$((x), y, A, z) \quad \text{where } A = (a, b, (c, d))$$

8   Represent the graph of Fig. 5-2.14 by a list structure. Draw its storage representation.

5-3   SIMPLE PRECEDENCE GRAMMARS

In Sec. 3-3 the notions of a grammar as a mathematical system for defining languages and as a device for giving some useful structure to sentences of a language were discussed. Also, the problem of obtaining a parse for a particular sentence of a language was introduced. Recall that a parse consisted of finding a sequence of productions which would generate a given sentence from the starting symbol of the grammar. The concept of a syntax tree and its relationship to the parse of a sentence of a language were mentioned briefly. The syntax tree (or derivation) corresponding to a sentence of a language could be found in a top-down or bottom-up manner.

This section deals with the use of grammars in syntax analysis or parsing. We will therefore be concerned with the syntax recognition phase of a compiler. The discrete structure which is central to syntax analysis is the syntax tree. From such a tree can be derived the meaning of a sentence. Furthermore, a syntax tree is a convenient representation which can be used in the derivation of many important relations for certain classes of grammars. A number of such instances will arise in this section. Although we will not do it here, a grammar can be represented as a directed graph (with cycles to denote recursion) from which it is possible to recognize many properties of the grammar. The syntax analysis method that will be developed is of the bottom-up type. Furthermore, this method will apply to a class of grammars called the simple precedence grammars. This class of grammars is a proper subset of the class of context-free grammars. The parsing algorithm is the same for any such grammar; only the parsing tables (relations) which can be obtained directly from the grammar change. These parsing tables are sometimes analogous to the input and stack precedence functions discussed in Sec. 3-4.

Before we describe the set of simple precedence grammars and its associated syntax analyzer, additional terminology dealing with parsing is introduced. The important concept of syntactic ambiguity and its relationship to the parsing problem are mentioned. Then follows a discussion of what relations can be obtained directly from the productions of a grammar. These preliminaries permit the introduction of precedence relations. From these relations simple precedence grammars are defined, and an associated parsing algorithm is formulated.

5-3.1 Syntax Terminology

A number of terms such as production rule (or production), terminal symbol, nonterminal symbol, grammar, sentential form, etc., were introduced in Sec. 3-3.2. We now introduce additional terms that will facilitate the discussion of syntax analysis.

Definition 5-3.1 Let $G = \langle V_N, V_T, S, \Phi \rangle$ be a grammar, and let $\sigma = \phi_1 \beta \phi_2$ be a sentential form. Then β is called a *phrase* of the sentential form σ for some nonterminal A if

$$S \stackrel{*}{\Rightarrow} \phi_1 A \phi_2 \quad \text{and} \quad A \stackrel{+}{\Rightarrow} \beta$$

Furthermore, β is called a *simple phrase* if $S \stackrel{*}{\Rightarrow} \phi_1 A \phi_2$ and $A \Rightarrow \beta$.

Care must be exercised when applying this definition. $A \stackrel{+}{\Rightarrow} \beta$ does not necessarily imply that β is a phrase of $\phi_1 \beta \phi_2$; one must also have $S \stackrel{*}{\Rightarrow} \phi_1 A \phi_2$. For example, consider the sequence $\langle \text{digit} \rangle \langle \text{letter} \rangle \langle \text{digit} \rangle$ in relation to the following grammar:

$$G_1 = \langle \{ \langle \text{identifier} \rangle, \langle \text{letter} \rangle, \langle \text{digit} \rangle \}, \{ a \text{ to } z, 0 \text{ to } 9 \}, \langle \text{identifier} \rangle, \Phi \rangle$$

where Φ is

$\langle\text{identifier}\rangle ::= \langle\text{letter}\rangle \mid \langle\text{identifier}\rangle\langle\text{letter}\rangle \mid \langle\text{identifier}\rangle\langle\text{digit}\rangle$

$\langle\text{letter}\rangle ::= a \mid b \mid \cdots \mid y \mid z$

$\langle\text{digit}\rangle ::= 0 \mid 1 \mid \cdots \mid 8 \mid 9$

The existence of the rule $\langle\text{identifier}\rangle ::= \langle\text{letter}\rangle$ does not imply that $\langle\text{letter}\rangle$ is a phrase since we cannot generate $\langle\text{digit}\rangle\langle\text{identifier}\rangle\langle\text{digit}\rangle$ from the starting symbol $\langle\text{identifier}\rangle$. What are the phrases of $\langle\text{letter}\rangle$ 1? A derivation for this sentential form is

$$\langle\text{identifier}\rangle \Rightarrow \langle\text{identifier}\rangle\langle\text{digit}\rangle \Rightarrow \langle\text{letter}\rangle\langle\text{digit}\rangle \Rightarrow \langle\text{letter}\rangle 1$$

Therefore

$$\langle\text{identifier}\rangle \overset{*}{\Rightarrow} \langle\text{letter}\rangle\langle\text{digit}\rangle \qquad \text{and} \qquad \langle\text{digit}\rangle \overset{+}{\Rightarrow} 1$$

Consequently, 1 is a simple phrase. Another derivation for the given sentential form is

$$\langle\text{identifier}\rangle \Rightarrow \langle\text{identifier}\rangle\langle\text{digit}\rangle \Rightarrow \langle\text{identifier}\rangle 1 \Rightarrow \langle\text{letter}\rangle 1$$

where

$$\langle\text{identifier}\rangle \overset{*}{\Rightarrow} \langle\text{identifier}\rangle 1 \qquad \text{and} \qquad \langle\text{identifier}\rangle \overset{+}{\Rightarrow} \langle\text{letter}\rangle$$

Again, the only phrase which is also a simple phrase is $\langle\text{letter}\rangle$.

In the subsequent discussion the leftmost simple phrase of a sentential form will be required. We therefore formulate the following definition.

Definition 5-3.2 The *handle* of a sentential form is its leftmost simple phrase.

In the current example, we have two possible simple phrases, namely, $\langle\text{letter}\rangle$ and 1, and since $\langle\text{letter}\rangle$ is the leftmost phrase, it is also the handle.

As previously discussed in Sec. 3-3.3, syntax trees are an important aid to understanding the syntax of a sentence. A syntax tree for a sentence of some language has a distinguished node called its *root* which is labeled by the starting symbol of the grammar. The leaf nodes of the syntax tree represent the terminal symbols in the sentence being diagramed. All nonleaf nodes correspond to nonterminal symbols. Each nonterminal node has a number of branches emanating downward, each of which represents a symbol in the right side of the production being applied at that point in the syntax tree.

The syntax tree corresponding to the following derivation of the sentence $c1$ in grammar G_1 is given in Fig. 5-3.1.

$$\langle\text{identifier}\rangle \Rightarrow \langle\text{identifier}\rangle\langle\text{digit}\rangle \Rightarrow \langle\text{letter}\rangle\langle\text{digit}\rangle \Rightarrow c\langle\text{digit}\rangle \Rightarrow c1$$

Note that another possible derivation for the same sentence is

$$\langle\text{identifier}\rangle \Rightarrow \langle\text{identifier}\rangle\langle\text{digit}\rangle \Rightarrow \langle\text{identifier}\rangle 1 \Rightarrow \langle\text{letter}\rangle 1 \Rightarrow c1$$

and that this derivation has the same syntax tree as that given in Fig. 5-3.1. Therefore for each syntax tree there exists at least one derivation.

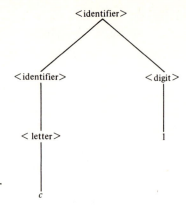

FIGURE 5-3.1 Syntax tree for sentence $c1$ in G_1.

More generally, any sentential form can have a syntax tree. The leaf nodes in such a tree can designate terminal and nonterminal symbols. Let A be the root of a subtree for a sentential form $\sigma = \phi_1 \beta \phi_2$ where β forms the string of leaf nodes emanating from that subtree. Then β is the phrase for A of the sentential form σ. β is a simple phrase if the subtree whose root is A consists of the application of the single production $A \rightarrow \beta$.

Consider the example grammar

$$G_2 = \langle \{\langle\text{expression}\rangle, \langle\text{factor}\rangle, \langle\text{term}\rangle\}, \{i, +, *, (,)\}, \langle\text{expression}\rangle, \Phi\rangle$$

where Φ consists of the productions

$$\langle\text{factor}\rangle ::= i \mid (\langle\text{expression}\rangle)$$

$$\langle\text{term}\rangle ::= \langle\text{factor}\rangle \mid \langle\text{term}\rangle * \langle\text{factor}\rangle$$

$$\langle\text{expression}\rangle ::= \langle\text{term}\rangle \mid \langle\text{expression}\rangle + \langle\text{term}\rangle$$

and i stands for an identifier or variable name. The syntax tree for the sentential form $\langle\text{expression}\rangle + \langle\text{term}\rangle * \langle\text{factor}\rangle$ is given in Fig. 5-3.2, where $\langle\text{expression}\rangle + \langle\text{term}\rangle * \langle\text{factor}\rangle$ and $\langle\text{term}\rangle * \langle\text{factor}\rangle$ are its phrases while $\langle\text{term}\rangle * \langle\text{factor}\rangle$ is a simple phrase.

An important question which arises in formal languages is whether a sen-

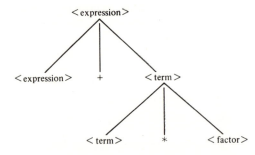

FIGURE 5-3.2 Syntax tree for $\langle\text{expression}\rangle + \langle\text{term}\rangle * \langle\text{factor}\rangle$ in G_2.

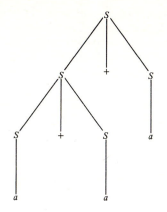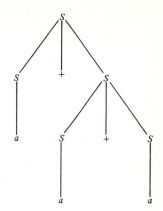

FIGURE 5-3.3   Two distinct syntax trees for the sentence $a + a + a$ in G_3.

tential form has a unique syntax tree. Consider the simple grammar G_3 which has the following productions:

$$S \rightarrow S + S$$
$$S \rightarrow a$$

where a is a terminal symbol. Let us find a derivation for the sentence $a + a + a$. One such derivation is

$$S \Rightarrow S + S \Rightarrow S + S + S \Rightarrow a + S + S \Rightarrow a + a + S \Rightarrow a + a + a$$

where the leftmost S in the second step has been rewritten as $S + S$. Another possibility, of course, is that the rightmost S in the same step was rewritten as $S + S$. Both possibilities are diagramed in Fig. 5-3.3. It is clear that the two syntax trees are different. That is, we have two different parses for the same sentence. The existence of more than one parse for some sentence in a language can cause a compiler to generate a different set of instructions (object code) for different parses. Usually, this phenomenon is intolerable. If a compiler is to perform valid translations of sentences in a language, then that language must be unambiguously defined. This concept leads us to the following definition.

Definition 5-3.3   A sentence generated by a grammar is *ambiguous* if there exists more than one syntax tree for it. A grammar is ambiguous if it generates at least one ambiguous sentence; otherwise it is *unambiguous*.

It should be noted that we called the grammar ambiguous and not the language which it generates. There are many grammars which can generate the same language; some are ambiguous and some are not. However, there are certain languages for which no unambiguous grammars can be found. Such languages are said to be *inherently ambiguous*. For example, the language $\{x^i y^j z^k \mid i = j$ or $j = k\}$ is an inherently ambiguous context-free language.

The question which naturally arises at this point is, Does there exist an algorithm which can accept any context-free grammar and determine, in some finite time, whether it is ambiguous? The answer is no! A simple set of sufficient conditions can be developed such that when they are applied to a grammar and are found to hold, then the grammar is guaranteed to be unambiguous. We wish to point out that these conditions are sufficient but not necessary. In other words, even if a grammar does not satisfy the conditions, it may still be unambiguous. We will formulate such a set of conditions in Sec. 5-3.4.

Let us examine another example of an ambiguous grammar. In particular, consider the grammar G_4 for arithmetic expressions consisting of the operators $+$ and $*$ with single-letter variables:

$\langle \text{expression} \rangle ::= i \mid \langle \text{expression} \rangle + \langle \text{expression} \rangle \mid \langle \text{expression} \rangle * \langle \text{expression} \rangle$

Assume that the sentence $i * i + i$ is to be diagramed. Two possible derivations are as follows:

$$\langle \text{expression} \rangle \Rightarrow \langle \text{expression} \rangle * \langle \text{expression} \rangle$$
$$\Rightarrow \langle \text{expression} \rangle * \langle \text{expression} \rangle + \langle \text{expression} \rangle$$
$$\Rightarrow i * \langle \text{expression} \rangle + \langle \text{expression} \rangle$$
$$\Rightarrow i * i + \langle \text{expression} \rangle$$
$$\rightarrow i * i + i$$

$$\langle \text{expression} \rangle \Rightarrow \langle \text{expression} \rangle + \langle \text{expression} \rangle$$
$$\Rightarrow \langle \text{expression} \rangle * \langle \text{expression} \rangle + \langle \text{expression} \rangle$$
$$\Rightarrow i * \langle \text{expression} \rangle + \langle \text{expression} \rangle$$
$$\Rightarrow i * i + \langle \text{expression} \rangle$$
$$\Rightarrow i * i + i$$

Their corresponding syntax trees are given in Fig. 5-3.4. Since there exist two distinct syntax trees for the sentence $i * i + i$, the grammar is ambiguous. Intuitively, this grammar is ambiguous because it is not known whether to evaluate $*$ before $+$ or conversely. The grammar can be rewritten in such a manner that the multiplication will have precedence over addition. This revision is accomplished in the following grammar G_4:

$$\langle \text{expression} \rangle ::= \langle \text{term} \rangle \mid \langle \text{expression} \rangle + \langle \text{term} \rangle$$
$$\langle \text{term} \rangle ::= \langle \text{factor} \rangle \mid \langle \text{term} \rangle * \langle \text{factor} \rangle$$
$$\langle \text{factor} \rangle ::= i \mid (\langle \text{expression} \rangle)$$

5-3.2 A View of Parsing

In Sec. 3-3 the problem of obtaining a parse for a sentence of a language was briefly introduced. A parse consisted of finding a sequence of production rules which would generate a given sentence from the starting symbol of the grammar. A syntax tree is frequently associated with a parse of a sentence. The parse (or syntax tree) can be constructed in a top-down or bottom-up manner.

In addition to the relation $\Rightarrow$, which was defined in connection with a grammar in Sec. 3-3, we can also define the following leftmost canonical direct

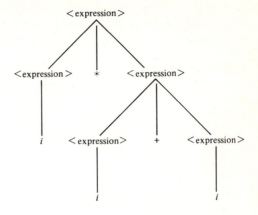

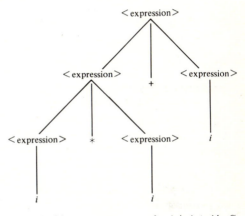

FIGURE 5-3.4 Ambiguous syntax trees for $i * i + i$ in G_4.

derivation:

$$\phi_1 A \phi_2 \underset{L}{\Rightarrow} \phi_1 \beta \phi_2$$

if $A \to \beta$ is a rule of the grammar and $\phi_1 \in V_T^*$. This relation can be easily extended as before to $\underset{L}{\overset{+}{\Rightarrow}}$ and $\underset{L}{\overset{*}{\Rightarrow}}$ where the relation $\psi \underset{L}{\overset{+}{\Rightarrow}} \sigma$ may be read, "ψ left-produces σ."

There are, in general, many sequences of strings $\phi_1, \phi_2, \ldots, \phi_n$ such that

$$S \Rightarrow \phi_1 \Rightarrow \phi_2 \Rightarrow \cdots \Rightarrow \phi_n \Rightarrow \sigma$$

is a derivation of a sentence σ in the language. Whenever ϕ_i contains at least two nonterminal symbols, we have a choice as to which nonterminal will be replaced first. The relation $\underset{L}{\overset{+}{\Rightarrow}}$ specifies that there is exactly one $\underset{L}{\Rightarrow}$ derivation.

Similarly, we can define a rightmost canonical direct derivation

$$\phi_1 A \phi_2 \underset{R}{\Rightarrow} \phi_1 \beta \phi_2$$

If $A \rightarrow \beta$ is a rule of the grammar and $\phi_2 \in V_T^*$. Again the relation is easily extended to $\underset{R}{\overset{+}{\Rightarrow}}$ and $\underset{R}{\overset{*}{\Rightarrow}}$ where the relation $\psi \underset{R}{\overset{+}{\Rightarrow}} \sigma$ may be read as "ψ right-produces σ." The relation $\underset{R}{\overset{+}{\Rightarrow}}$ specifies that there is exactly one $\Rightarrow$ derivation. For example, the leftmost and rightmost derivations for $i + i * i$ in G_4 are

$$\langle\text{expression}\rangle \underset{L}{\Rightarrow} \langle\text{expression}\rangle + \langle\text{expression}\rangle \underset{L}{\Rightarrow} \langle\text{term}\rangle + \langle\text{expression}\rangle$$
$$\underset{L}{\Rightarrow} \langle\text{factor}\rangle + \langle\text{expression}\rangle \underset{L}{\Rightarrow} i + \langle\text{expression}\rangle$$
$$\underset{L}{\Rightarrow} i + \langle\text{term}\rangle \underset{L}{\Rightarrow} i + \langle\text{term}\rangle * \langle\text{factor}\rangle$$
$$\underset{L}{\Rightarrow} i + \langle\text{factor}\rangle * \langle\text{factor}\rangle \underset{L}{\Rightarrow} i + i * \langle\text{factor}\rangle$$
$$\underset{L}{\Rightarrow} i + i * i$$

and

$$\langle\text{expression}\rangle \underset{R}{\Rightarrow} \langle\text{expression}\rangle + \langle\text{expression}\rangle \underset{R}{\Rightarrow} \langle\text{expression}\rangle + \langle\text{term}\rangle$$
$$\underset{R}{\Rightarrow} \langle\text{expression}\rangle + \langle\text{term}\rangle * \langle\text{factor}\rangle$$
$$\underset{R}{\Rightarrow} \langle\text{expression}\rangle + \langle\text{term}\rangle * i$$
$$\underset{R}{\Rightarrow} \langle\text{expression}\rangle + \langle\text{factor}\rangle * i$$
$$\underset{R}{\Rightarrow} \langle\text{expression}\rangle + i * i \underset{R}{\Rightarrow} \langle\text{term}\rangle + i * i$$
$$\underset{R}{\Rightarrow} \langle\text{factor}\rangle + i * i \underset{R}{\Rightarrow} i + i * i$$

respectively. The leftmost and the rightmost derivations correspond to a left-to-right and right-to-left top-down parse, respectively.

The general problem of parsing is to start with a string σ of terminal symbols, for example, $i + i * i$, and to find a sequence of productions such that $\langle\text{expression}\rangle \overset{*}{\Rightarrow} \sigma$. The bottom-up method (proceeding from left to right) attacks the problem by first "reducing" the above string to

$$\langle\text{factor}\rangle + i * i$$

then reducing this string to

$$\langle\text{term}\rangle + i * i$$

and then

$$\langle\text{expression}\rangle + i * i$$

and

$$\langle\text{expression}\rangle + \langle\text{factor}\rangle * i$$

etc., where a reduction is the opposite of a production. This process continues until everything is reduced to $\langle\text{expression}\rangle$ or until it is shown that it cannot be done. Note that the sequence of reductions is the reverse of the right canonical derivation. In general, bottom-up parsing from left to right proceeds by right reductions.

In a left-to-right bottom-up parse, the handle is to be reduced at each step in the parse. The questions which arise are, How do we find the handle of a sentential form and to what do we reduce it?

One obvious approach is merely to select one of the possible alternatives. If a mistake is subsequently detected, then we must retrace our steps to the location of the error and try some other alternative. This process is called "back-up," and it can be very time-consuming.

A more efficient solution involves looking at the context around the substring which is currently being considered as a potential handle. This evaluation is done mechanically by humans when they evaluate an expression like $i + i * i$. The question of whether to evaluate $i + i$ first is answered by looking ahead at the symbol $*$ which denotes that we should not. We will formulate in the next subsection a strategy which will guarantee that we can parse any sentence in a given language without backup if certain conditions are imposed on the grammar.

In the remainder of this section it will be assumed that a grammar is reduced.

Definition 5-3.4 A grammar $G = \langle V_N, V_T, S, \Phi \rangle$ is said to be *reduced* if it satisfies the following conditions:

(*a*) The grammar does not contain rules of the form

$$A ::= A$$

(*b*) First, each nonterminal A (other than S) must occur in some sentential form $S \overset{*}{\Rightarrow} \phi_1 A \phi_2$, and second, some terminal string must be derivable from each A (including S), that is, $A \overset{+}{\Rightarrow} \sigma$ for some $\sigma \in V_T{}^+$.

5-3.3 Notion and Use of Precedence Relations

In Sec. 3-4 the technique of establishing precedence relations between symbols was used to convert infix expressions to their reverse Polish equivalents. This conversion was based on the use of the input and stack precedence functions (f and g functions respectively).

In this section we are concerned with a left-to-right bottom-up parsing technique which involves no backup. This method constructs the parse for a sentence by repeatedly finding the handle in each sentential form. As was previously mentioned, once the handle has been found, we must also determine which production to apply, i.e., to which nonterminal the handle should be reduced. This parsing method will work for a class of grammars (which is a proper subset of the context-free grammars) called the simple precedence grammars. Since the proposed method proceeds in a left-to-right bottom-up manner, all the sentential forms will be rightmost canonical. In the remainder of the discussion on precedence grammars, all derivations are understood to be rightmost canonical.

Let us now investigate how the handle in a sentential form might be found. Since the parsing method is left to right, we want to scan the sentential form from left to right, looking at only two adjacent symbols at one time so as to be able to determine the rightmost symbol of the handle which is called its *tail*. Starting at the tail of the handle, and again using only two adjacent symbols, we will then scan from right to left and find the leftmost symbol in the handle which is called its *head*. We are then faced with the following problem. Given some sentential form

$$\alpha = \cdots S_1 S_2 \cdots$$

where $\cdots$ denotes a possibly empty string of symbols, four possibilities are obvious, namely, S_2 is the tail of the handle, both S_1 and S_2 are in the handle, S_2 is in the handle but S_1 is not, and neither S_1 nor S_2 are in the handle. This last case is impossible because the grammar is reduced and we are in the process of obtaining a right canonical parse.

We would like to develop certain relations from the grammar which would permit us to make such a decision. For any pair of symbols S_1 and S_2 in the vocabulary of the grammar, assume there is a sentential form $\cdots S_1 S_2 \cdots$. At some stage in the canonical parse, either S_1 or S_2 or both must be in the handle. The following three cases can occur:

1 S_1 is part of the handle (actually its tail) and S_2 is not. This relationship is denoted as $S_1 \cdot > S_2$ which signifies that S_1 has precedence over S_2 because S_1 must be reduced before S_2. Formally, if $\alpha = \phi_1 \beta \phi_2$ where β is the handle of α and there is a rule $A \rightarrow \beta$, then S_1 is the tail of β.

2 S_1 and S_2 are both contained in the handle. This relationship is specified as $S_1 \doteq S_2$ which means that both symbols have the same precedence and are to be reduced at the same time. This implies that there is a rule of the form $A \rightarrow \cdots S_1 S_2 \cdots$ in the grammar.

3 S_2 is contained in the handle (actually its head) and S_1 is not. We denote such a relationship as $S_1 < \cdot S_2$ which signifies that S_2 has precedence over S_1. The grammar must contain a rule of the form $A \rightarrow S_2 \cdots$.

These three cases can be interpreted pictorially in Fig. 5-3.5a to c respectively.

As an example, consider the grammar $G_5 = \langle \{E, U, T, V, F\}, \{i, +, *, (,)\}, E, \Phi \rangle$ where Φ is the set of productions

$$E \rightarrow U \qquad V \rightarrow F$$
$$U \rightarrow T \qquad V \rightarrow V * F$$
$$U \rightarrow U + T \qquad F \rightarrow i$$
$$T \rightarrow V \qquad F \rightarrow (E)$$

and i represents a variable name. The language generated by this grammar is the set of parenthesized arithmetic expressions consisting of variables and the operations of addition and multiplication. Each column given in Fig. 5-3.6 represents a sentential form, a syntax tree for it, the handle of the sentential form, and the

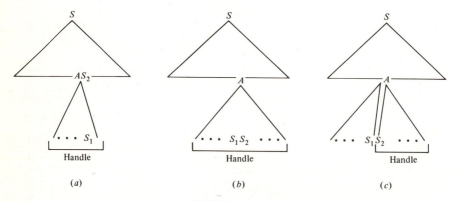

FIGURE 5-3.5 Interpretation of precedence relations.

Sentential form: $U + i * i$ $\qquad\qquad\qquad V * (U + T)$

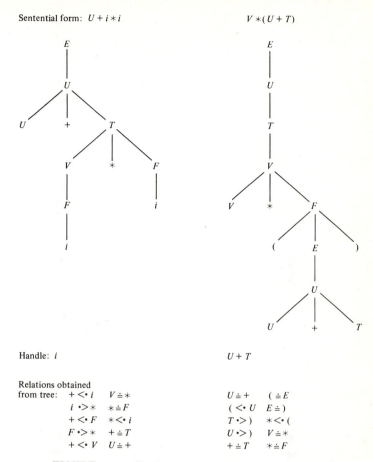

Handle: i $\qquad\qquad\qquad\qquad\qquad U + T$

Relations obtained
from tree:
$+ <\cdot\, i$ $\quad V \doteq *$ $\qquad\qquad U \doteq + \quad (\,\doteq E$
$i \,\cdot\!> *$ $\quad * \doteq F$ $\qquad\qquad (\, <\cdot\, U \quad E \doteq)$
$+ <\cdot\, F$ $\quad * <\cdot\, i$ $\qquad\qquad T \cdot\!>) \quad * <\cdot\, ($
$F \cdot\!> *$ $\quad + \doteq T$ $\qquad\qquad U \cdot\!>) \quad V \doteq *$
$+ <\cdot\, V$ $\quad U \doteq +$ $\qquad\qquad + \doteq T \quad * \doteq F$

FIGURE 5-3.6 Obtaining precedence relations from syntax trees.

precedence relations that can be derived from the tree after repeated reductions. For example, the handle of the sentential form $U + i * i$ in Fig. 5-3.6 is i, and the relations $i \cdot\!> *$ and $+ <\cdot\, i$ hold. When the reduction $F \to i$ is made, then F is the handle of the sentential form $U + F * i$ which yields the relations $+ <\cdot\, F$ and $F \cdot\!> *$. Continuing in this manner, we can obtain other relations between other pairs of symbols. A matrix which displays all the precedence relations for G_5 is given in Table 5-3.1 where a blank entry indicates that no relationship exists between a pair of symbols.

The approach used in Fig. 5-3.6 has yielded a number of relations for the symbols of the example grammar; however, it can be seen from the table that not all were obtained from the two trees considered. We could examine other syntax trees until all such relations were obtained. We shall show in the next subsection that all these relations can be obtained rather easily.

The obvious question which arises at this point is, How do these relations

Table 5-3.1 PRECEDENCE RELATIONS FOR G_5

	E	U	T	F	V	$+$	$*$	i	$($	$)$
E										$\doteq$
U						$\doteq$				$\cdot >$
T						$\cdot >$				$\cdot >$
F						$\cdot >$	$\cdot >$			$\cdot >$
V						$\cdot >$	$\doteq$			$\cdot >$
$+$			$\doteq$	$< \cdot$	$< \cdot$			$< \cdot$	$< \cdot$	
$*$				$\doteq$				$< \cdot$	$< \cdot$	
i						$\cdot >$	$\cdot >$			$\cdot >$
$($	$\doteq$	$< \cdot$	$< \cdot$	$< \cdot$	$< \cdot$			$< \cdot$	$< \cdot$	
$)$						$\cdot >$	$\cdot >$			$\cdot >$

help us to obtain the parse of a sentence? It turns out that if at most one relation holds between any pair of symbols, then the precedence relations can be used to determine the handle of a sentential form. If, however, more than one relation holds between a pair of symbols, then this approach may not work. In the former case the handle of the sentential form $S_1 S_2 \cdots S_n$ is the leftmost substring $S_i \cdots S_j$ such that

$$S_{i-1} < \cdot \; S_i$$
$$S_i \doteq S_{i+1} \doteq S_{i+2} \doteq \cdots \doteq S_j \qquad (1)$$
$$S_j \cdot > S_{j+1}$$

It is nontrivial to show that the leftmost substring satisfying these equations is the handle. We will return to this problem in the next subsection. To ensure that this approach will work even when the handle is the first or last symbol in the sentential form, we introduce a special symbol # such that

$$\# < \cdot \; x \qquad \text{and} \qquad x \cdot > \# \qquad \text{for any } x \text{ in the vocabulary}$$

As an example, Table 5-3.2 gives a parse for the sentence $i + i * i$ for G_5. Each step in the table gives the sentential form along with the relations that exist between the symbols according to Table 5-3.1.

5-3.4 Formal Definition of Precedence Relations

In the previous subsection the precedence relations were defined in terms of syntax trees. We will now redefine these relations in terms of the productions of the grammar. It will be shown that these relations can be computed easily from the grammar.

We first define two relations associated with any grammar that will be important when defining precedence relations. For some particular grammar and nonterminal U, the set of head symbols of the strings that can be produced by U will be required. The set of such symbols, $h(U)$, is defined as

$$h(U) = \{X \mid U \overset{+}{\Rightarrow} X\beta\}$$

Since the mechanical evaluation of $h(U)$ may be cumbersome, we redefine it in terms of another relation over a finite set in the following manner. Let L be a

Table 5-3.2 EXAMPLE PARSE FOR $i + i \ast i$ IN G_5

Step	Sentential form	Handle	Reduction	Direct derivation obtained
1	$\# \;\lessdot\; i \;\gtrdot\; + \;\lessdot\; i \;\gtrdot\; \ast \;\lessdot\; i \;\gtrdot\; \#$	i	$F \rightarrow i$	$\#F+i\ast i\# \Rightarrow \#i+i\ast i\#$
2	$\# \;\lessdot\; F \;\gtrdot\; + \;\lessdot\; i \;\gtrdot\; \ast \;\lessdot\; i \;\gtrdot\; \#$	F	$V \rightarrow F$	$\#V+i\ast i\# \Rightarrow \#F+i\ast i\#$
3	$\# \;\lessdot\; V \;\gtrdot\; + \;\lessdot\; i \;\gtrdot\; \ast \;\lessdot\; i \;\gtrdot\; \#$	V	$T \rightarrow V$	$\#T+i\ast i\# \Rightarrow \#V+i\ast i\#$
4	$\# \;\lessdot\; T \;\gtrdot\; + \;\lessdot\; i \;\gtrdot\; \ast \;\lessdot\; i \;\gtrdot\; \#$	T	$U \rightarrow T$	$\#U+i\ast i\# \Rightarrow \#T+i\ast i\#$
5	$\# \;\lessdot\; U \;\doteq\; + \;\lessdot\; i \;\gtrdot\; \ast \;\lessdot\; i \;\gtrdot\; \#$	i	$F \rightarrow i$	$\#U+F\ast i\# \Rightarrow \#U+i\ast i\#$
6	$\# \;\lessdot\; U \;\doteq\; + \;\lessdot\; F \;\gtrdot\; \ast \;\lessdot\; i \;\gtrdot\; \#$	F	$V \rightarrow F$	$\#U+V\ast i\# \Rightarrow \#U+F\ast i\#$
7	$\# \;\lessdot\; U \;\doteq\; + \;\lessdot\; V \;\doteq\; \ast \;\lessdot\; i \;\gtrdot\; \#$	i	$F \rightarrow i$	$\#U+V\ast F\# \Rightarrow \#U+V\ast i\#$
8	$\# \;\lessdot\; U \;\doteq\; + \;\lessdot\; V \;\doteq\; \ast \;\doteq\; F \;\gtrdot\; \#$	$V \ast F$	$V \rightarrow V \ast F$	$\#U+V\# \Rightarrow \#U+V\ast F\#$
9	$\# \;\lessdot\; U \;\doteq\; + \;\lessdot\; V \;\gtrdot\; \#$	V	$T \rightarrow V$	$\#U+T\# \Rightarrow \#U+V\#$
10	$\# \;\lessdot\; U \;\doteq\; + \;\doteq\; T \;\gtrdot\; \#$	$U + T$	$U \rightarrow U + T$	$\#U\# \Rightarrow \#U+T\#$
11	$\# \;\lessdot\; U \;\gtrdot\; \#$	U	$E \rightarrow U$	$\#E\# \Rightarrow \#U\#$

relation over the vocabulary such that

$$U \ L \ X \qquad \text{iff there exists a production } U \rightarrow X \cdots$$

The transitive closure (Sec. 2-3.7) of this relation can be obtained by

$$U \ L^+ \ X \qquad \text{iff there exists some sequence of rules (at least one) such that}$$

$$U \rightarrow A_1 \cdots, \ A_1 \rightarrow A_2 \cdots, \ \cdots, \ A_n \rightarrow X \cdots$$

It is clear that $U \ L^+ \ X$ iff $U \overset{+}{\Rightarrow} X \cdots$. The reflexive transitive closure L^* can be defined as

$$U \ L^* \ X \qquad \text{iff} \qquad U \ L^+ \ X \quad \text{or} \quad U = X$$

In an analogous manner, the set of tail symbols $t(U)$ is defined by

$$t(U) = \{X \mid U \overset{+}{\Rightarrow} \beta X\}$$

Another relation R over the vocabulary is defined as

$$U \ R \ X \qquad \text{iff there exists a production } U \rightarrow \cdots X$$

Again R^+ and R^* are defined in an obvious manner. These relations are easily computed by using Warshall's algorithm (see Sec. 5-1.3). The two basic relations can now be used to define the precedence relations.

Definition 5-3.5 The *precedence relations* for a grammar G are defined over its vocabulary as follows:

(a) $S_1 \doteq S_2$ iff there exists a production $U \rightarrow \cdots S_1 \, S_2 \cdots$ in G.

(b) $S_1 <\cdot S_2$ iff there exists a production $U \rightarrow \cdots S_1 \, A \cdots$ in G such that $A \ L^+ \ S_2$ holds.

(c) $S_1 \cdot> S_2$ iff S_2 is a terminal symbol and there is production $U \rightarrow \cdots AB \cdots$ such that $A \ R^+ \ S_1$ and $B \ L^* \ S_2$ hold.

The relations L^+ and R^+ for G_5 in the previous subsection are given in Table 5-3.3.

The relation $\doteq$ is easily obtained from the productions of the grammar. The relation $<\cdot$ can be evaluated by first considering the symbol pairs $+ \ T$, $* \ F$, and $(E$. The pair $+ \ T$ will yield the relations $+ <\cdot V$, $+ <\cdot F$, $+ <\cdot i$, and $+ <\cdot ($. The relations $* <\cdot i$ and $* <\cdot ($ are obtained from the term $* \ F$. Finally, the pair $(E$ gives the relations $(<\cdot U$, $(<\cdot V$, $(<\cdot F$, $(<\cdot T$, $(<\cdot i$, and $(<\cdot ($. The relation $\cdot>$ is computed in a similar manner. Using this procedure, Table 5-3.1 can be easily verified.

Table 5-3.3

Nonterminal symbol	L^+	R^+
E	$U,T,V,F,i,($	$U,T,V,F,i,)$
U	$U,T,V,F,i,($	$T,V,F,i,)$
T	$V,F,i,($	$V,F,i,)$
V	$V,F,i,($	$F,i,)$
F	$i,($	$i,)$

These precedence relations are actually equivalent to those defined in terms of handles in the previous subsection.

Theorem 5-3.1 $S_1 \doteq S_2$ iff the substring $S_1 S_2$ appears in a handle of some sentential form.

PROOF Let us first assume that $S_1 \doteq S_2$. A syntax tree which has the substring $S_1 S_2$ in its handle must be constructed. By Definition 5-3.5a, there exists a production of the form $U \rightarrow \alpha S_1 S_2 \beta$. Since the grammar is assumed to be reduced, we have $S \overset{*}{\underset{R}{\Rightarrow}} \phi_1 U \phi_2$ for some ϕ_1 and ϕ_2, where S is the starting symbol of the grammar. The desired syntax tree can then be constructed as follows:

1 Construct the syntax tree for the sentential form $\phi_1 U \phi_2$.
2 Reduce the tree obtained in step 1 until U becomes part of the handle.
3 Modify the tree obtained in step 2 by extending the tree downward with the application of the production $U \rightarrow \alpha S_1 S_2 \beta$. Since U was in the handle of the previous tree, the handle of the presently constructed tree is $\alpha S_1 S_2 \beta$ and we therefore have the required tree.

Conversely, if $S_1 S_2$ is a substring of the handle, then by definition of a handle there must exist a production $U \rightarrow \alpha S_1 S_2 \beta$ and $S_1 \doteq S_2$. ////

The next two theorems can be proved using an approach similar to that taken in the previous theorem.

Theorem 5-3.2 $S_1 \lessdot S_2$ iff there exists a canonical sentential form $\alpha S_1 S_2 \beta$ in which S_2 is the head of the handle.

Theorem 5-3.3 $S_1 \gtrdot S_2$ iff there exists a canonical sentential form $\alpha S_1 S_2 \beta$ in which S_1 is the tail of the handle.

The formal definitions of the three precedence relations given here are equivalent to those given informally in terms of syntax trees in Sec. 5-3.3. Some insight into these definitions can be obtained by looking at their interpretation from a syntax tree point of view. A simple precedence grammar is defined as follows.

Definition 5-3.6 A grammar G is called a *simple precedence grammar* if the following conditions are satisfied:

(*a*) For any pair of symbols in the vocabulary, at most one of the relations $\doteq$, $\lessdot$, and $\gtrdot$ must hold.
(*b*) No two productions can have the same right-hand side.

This class of grammars is called simple because only one symbol on each side of a possible handle is used to determine the presence of the handle. In other words, the handle is determined by scanning the sentential form from left to right examining successive pairs of adjacent symbols until $S_1 \gtrdot S_2$; in this case S_1 is the tail of the handle, and S_2 is the right context symbol used to find it. Similarly, the head of the handle is found by scanning from right to left until $S_1 \lessdot S_2$ where S_2 is now the head of the handle and S_1 is the left context symbol.

So the first condition of the theorem tells us how to find the handle, while the second condition tells us which production to use. The next theorem which is stated without proof is important.

> **Theorem 5-3.4** A simple precedence grammar is unambiguous. Furthermore, each sentential form $S_1S_2\cdots S_n$ has a unique handle which is the leftmost substring $S_i\cdots S_j$ that satisfies
>
> $$S_{i-1} <\cdot\ S_i \doteq S_{i+1} \doteq \cdots \doteq S_j \cdot> S_{j+1}$$
>
> Note that we are assuming the presence of a special symbol # such that $\# <\cdot\ x$ and $x \cdot> \#$ for any symbol in the original vocabulary. This modification will also permit the detection of a handle when it contains the leftmost and/or rightmost symbol in the sentential form.

Once the precedence relations for a simple precedence grammar have been determined, the parsing of a sentence is straightforward. This is one of the simplest class of grammars that can be used in a practical manner in compiler writing. The relations $<\cdot$ and $\cdot>$ are easily computed from the basic relations L, R, and $\doteq$. From the definition of the product of relations and the definition for $<\cdot$ we can easily obtain

$$<\cdot\ = (\doteq) \circ (L^+)$$

Similarly, the relation $\cdot>$ can be expressed as

$$\cdot> = (R^+)^T \circ (\doteq) \circ (L^*)$$

where $(R^+)^T$ is the transpose of R^+. These relations can obviously be expressed as bit (Boolean) matrices as shown in Sec. 5-1.3, and the logical capabilities of modern computers make their evaluation easy. We turn next to the formulation of a parsing algorithm for simple precedence grammars.

5-3.5 Parsing Algorithm for Simple Precedence Grammars

We wish to formulate a general parsing algorithm for any simple precedence grammar. The precedence matrix and the productions of the grammar are represented in some suitable form.

Basically, the algorithm works in the following manner. The symbols of the given input string are scanned from left to right and placed on a stack S. This scanning continues until the relation between the symbol at the top of the stack and the next input symbol is $\cdot>$. At this point, the top element of the stack denotes the tail of the handle. The head of the handle is determined by comparing successive pairs of adjacent symbols in the stack until a pair is encountered that is $<\cdot$-related. This handle can then be reduced (i.e., removed from the stack) to the left part of a production (which is placed on the stack) whose right part is that handle. The entire process is repeated until the stack contains S and the next input symbol is the special symbol #.

Algorithm *PARSE* Given the precedence matrix and the productions for a particular grammar and a certain sentence $x = x_1x_2\cdots x_n\,\#$ which is to be parsed, it is required either to parse the sentence if it is valid or to output an error message if it is not. Let S denote a stack, and let j be an index which is used to designate the top element of the stack. The index i is used to find the handle on the stack while k is an index which refers to the current input symbol being scanned.

1 [Initialize] Set $S[1] \leftarrow \#$, set $j \leftarrow k \leftarrow 1$.

2 [Scan the next input symbol] Set $N \leftarrow x_k$, $k \leftarrow k + 1$.

3 [Tail of handle?] If $S[j] \cdot > N$, then $i \leftarrow j$; otherwise $j \leftarrow j + 1$, $S[j] \leftarrow N$, go to step 2.

4 [Head of handle?] If $S[i - 1] \lessdot \cdot S[i]$, then set $i \leftarrow i - 1$ and repeat this step.

5 [Find production to be applied] Search the productions for one which has the right-hand side $S_i \cdots S_j$. If the search succeeds, then $j \leftarrow i$, $S[j] \leftarrow U$ where U is the left part of the production $U \rightarrow S_i \cdots S_j$, go to step 3.

6 [Valid sentence?] If $i = 2$ and $S[i] = S$ (the start symbol of the grammar) and $N = \#$, then output 'VALID'; otherwise output 'INVALID'

////

A trace of this algorithm for the example grammar using the sentence $i * i + i$ and Table 5-3.1 is given in Table 5-3.4.

The precedence relations can be represented by a precedence matrix P whose element p_{ij} can be represented as

$$
p_{ij} = \begin{cases} 0 & \text{if no relation exists between } S_i \text{ and } S_j \\ 1 & \text{if } S_i \doteq S_j \\ 2 & \text{if } S_i <\cdot S_j \\ 3 & \text{if } S_i \cdot > S_j \end{cases}
$$

Table 5-3.4

Step	Input string	Stack contents	Relation	N	Handle
0	$i * i + i \#$	$\#$			
1	$* i + i \#$	$\#$	$<\cdot$	i	
2	$i + i \#$	$\# \, i$	$\cdot >$	$*$	i
3	$i + i \#$	$\# \, F$	$\cdot >$	$*$	F
4	$+ i \#$	$\# \, V *$	$<\cdot$	i	
5	$i \#$	$\# \, V * i$	$\cdot >$	$+$	i
6	$i \#$	$\# \, V * F$	$\cdot >$	$+$	$V * F$
7	$i \#$	$\# \, V$	$\cdot >$	$+$	V
8	$i \#$	$\# \, T$	$\cdot >$	$+$	T
9	$\#$	$\# \, U +$	$<\cdot$	i	
10		$\# \, U + i$	$\cdot >$	$\#$	i
11		$\# \, U + F$	$\cdot >$	$\#$	F
12		$\# \, U + V$	$\cdot >$	$\#$	V
13		$\# \, U + T$	$\cdot >$	$\#$	$U + T$
14		$\# \, U$	$\cdot >$	$\#$	U
15		$\# \, E$		$\#$	

Each element in the matrix can be represented by a 2-bit entry. For a particular grammar, the size of the precedence matrix varies as the square of the number of symbols in the vocabulary. In many cases, however, a great reduction in this matrix can be realized by replacing the matrix by two precedence functions f and g. These functions, if they exist, satisfy the following relations for all symbols in the grammar:

$$S_1 \doteq S_2 \quad \text{implies} \quad f(S_1) = g(S_2)$$
$$S_1 <\cdot\ S_2 \quad \text{implies} \quad f(S_1) < g(S_2)$$
$$S_1 \cdot> S_2 \quad \text{implies} \quad f(S_1) > g(S_2)$$

Thus the storage requirements for a grammar with n symbols in its vocabulary has been reduced from n^2 elements to $2n$ elements. In our example grammar, the precedence functions f and g are

	E	U	T	F	V	$+$	$*$	i	$($	$)$
f	2	4	5	7	6	4	6	7	2	7
g	2	3	4	6	5	4	6	7	7	2

There are more general classes of grammars for which syntax analyzers exist. These analyzers use more than one left and right context symbols to detect the handle. We will not pursue this discussion here.

EXERCISES 5-3

1 Let the grammar G be defined by

$$S \rightarrow AB \qquad B \rightarrow a$$
$$A \rightarrow Aa \qquad B \rightarrow Sb$$
$$A \rightarrow bB$$

Give derivation trees for the following sentential forms:
(a) $baSb$
(b) $baabaab$
(c) $bBABb$

2 Obtain the phrases, simple phrases, and handle for the sentential forms given in the previous problem.

3 Consider the grammar which has the following productions:

$$S \rightarrow aSBC \qquad bB \rightarrow bb$$
$$S \rightarrow aBC \qquad bC \rightarrow bc$$
$$CB \rightarrow BC \qquad cC \rightarrow cc$$
$$aB \rightarrow ab$$

Give derivation trees for the strings abc and $a^2b^2c^2$.

4 Can you find an inherently ambiguous context-free language?

5 Let a grammar G be defined by

$$S \rightarrow yAy$$
$$A \rightarrow (B$$

$$A \to x$$

$$B \to Ax)$$

Using only syntax trees, obtain as many of the precedence relations as possible.

6   Using the formal definition of precedence relations, obtain the precedence matrix for Prob. 5.

7   Prove Theorem 5-3.2.

8   Prove Theorem 5-3.3.

9   Prove Theorem 5-3.4.

10 Prove that $\cdot > = (R^+)^T \circ (\doteq) \circ (L^*)$.

11 Using the parsing algorithm of the text and the grammar of Prob. 5, give a tree of the parse for the strings $y(xx)y$, $(((xx)x)x)y$, $y((xx)x)y$.

12 Formulate an algorithm and write a program that will obtain a precedence matrix.

13 Write a program to use the precedence matrix obtained in Prob. 12 and parse a string according to the parsing algorithm of the text.

14 Can you obtain the precedence functions for the grammar of Prob. 5?

15 Is the following grammar a simple precedence grammar? If not, why not?

$$E \to a \qquad\qquad B \to R$$

$$E \to b \qquad\qquad B \to (B)$$

$$E \to (E + E) \qquad R \to E = E$$

5-4 FAULT DETECTION IN COMBINATIONAL SWITCHING CIRCUITS

The synthesis and analysis of combinational switching circuits were discussed in the previous chapter. In this section, we discuss a different but equally important problem, fault detection and fault diagnosis. Fault detection is concerned with determining whether a fault exists in a circuit. In fault diagnosis, one tries to locate a specific fault in a system.

The diagnosis of faults in modern computing systems is becoming more important as the complexity of such systems increases. Rapid and effective diagnosis of faults in computer systems is desirable since once these diagnoses are in service, down time can be kept at a minimum.

The detection and diagnosis of faults in early computers were performed by technicians. Although these computers were physically very large, the number of components in them was rather small as compared to present computers, and a skillful engineer could locate a fault in a reasonable period of time. With the advent of transistors and integrated circuits, the number of components in a modern computer has greatly increased and fault detection and diagnosis have become increasingly difficult tasks.

The logical conclusion is that if a computer is at all operational, it should diagnose itself, or at worst another computer should be used to perform the diagnosis.

In this section we shall consider a combinational circuit diagram to be a directed graph whose nodes are the gates and whose edges are the connections between gates. From this representation an algorithm will be given to generate a fault table. The purpose of such a table is to be able to detect and more generally diagnose faults. The algorithm will use certain notions of relations such as their composition, symmetry, transitive closure, etc. The first part of the section gives a description of faults in combinational switching circuits. This discussion is followed by the description of certain possible circuit representations of combinational circuits. An algorithm which generates a fault matrix is formulated.

5-4.1 Faults in Combinational Circuits

At first glance, it might seem that because of the great speed of digital computers, all that is required in order to detect and diagnose faults is to write a program that ensures the computer can add all combinations of numbers properly, shift any bit pattern left or right, etc. If we consider how much time it would take to perform an add test, it becomes clear that such an approach is futile. Let us assume that the computer to be diagnosed has a 32-bit word and an add time of 1 microsecond (10^{-6} sec). The number of possible combinations of operands for an add instruction is approximately 10^{19}. The number of add instructions required to perform such an exhaustive test would take about 3×10^5 yr, an obviously ridiculous situation. Even if this approach did not take so long, it would only state whether the computer was adding properly. This test would be a functional verification test rather than a diagnostic test.

The above example illustrates the point that there are two major requirements of a diagnostic procedure:

1 The procedure should be as fast as possible, and therefore it should involve as few tests as possible.

2 The result of the procedure should be as specific as possible. For example, rather than stating that "the computer cannot add," it should state that this is because the carry from bit 7 to bit 8 is incorrect.

In order to test combinational circuits, we must first be aware of the types of faults which can occur and what their overall effects are. There are two main types of faults which can occur. The first type consists of transient or intermittent faults, and this type is not included in the following discussion. The second type of fault is a permanent fault which can originate from a component failure, an open circuit, a short circuit, etc. Such faults will be denoted as "stuck-at faults." They will be considered to exist at the input and output terminals of its components. Stuck-at faults have the effect of making an input or output of a gate appear to be stuck at the value 0 or 1. We will denote a stuck-at-one fault and stuck-at-zero fault by the terms s-a-1 and s-a-0 respectively. We will also restrict our discussion to circuits which consist of only *NAND* gates.

For example, consider the *NAND* gate shown in Fig. 5-4.1. If the application of the three input symbols produces the results shown in Table 5-4.1, an s-a-1 fault exists at terminal x, according to our definition. The effect of this fault is that the output is changed from $x \uparrow y \uparrow z$ to $1 \uparrow y \uparrow z = y \uparrow z$; similarly, an s-a-0 fault at terminal x results in an output $0 \uparrow y \uparrow z = 1$. This last

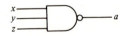

FIGURE 5-4.1   A *NAND* gate.

Table 5-4.1 ILLUSTRATION OF STUCK-AT FAULTS

x	y	z	s-a-1 fault at x a	s-a-0 fault at x a
0	0	0	1	1
0	0	1	1	1
0	1	0	1	1
0	1	1	0	1
1	0	0	1	1
1	0	1	1	1
1	1	0	1	1
1	1	1	0	1

output would be the same as an s-a-1 fault in the output. Table 5-4.1 shows the outputs due to s-a-1 and s-a-0 faults at the terminal x.

In the remainder of this section we also assume that only one fault exists in the circuit while the operation of fault detection is performed.

5-4.2 Notions of Fault Detection

Before we attempt a general formulation of the fault-detection problem, let us examine a specific example. A combinational circuit consisting of four inputs and three $NAND$ gates is given in Fig. 5-4.2.

Consider all possible cases in which any one terminal is stuck at 0 or 1. There are fourteen such possible cases which are shown in the second column of Table 5-4.2. Here $(x, 0)$ or $(x, 1)$ means that the terminal x is stuck at 0 or 1 respectively. The corresponding faults are designated by $f_1, f_2, \ldots, f_{14}$ in the first column of the table. Let the inputs at the terminals a, b, c, and d be $\overline{x_1}$, x_2, x_1, and x_3 respectively. For these inputs the output function corresponding to any of the faults is shown in the last column of the table. Because of our choice of inputs, we immediately notice that the output function is $x_1 x_3$ for each of the faults f_1, f_3, and f_{10}. A similar situation exists for other sets of faults. It would therefore not be possible to distinguish between the faults f_1, f_3, or f_{10} from the output. We shall return to this point later.

Instead of obtaining the output function for each individual fault, we may obtain the values of the output for all possible combinations of values for variables x_1, x_2, and x_3 for each single fault and enter them in a *table of faults*. Such a table of faults for the circuit of Fig. 5-4.2 is given in Table 5-4.3.

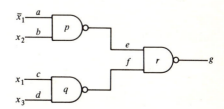

FIGURE 5-4.2 A switching circuit.

Table 5-4.2 SINGLE FAULTS FOR THE CIRCUIT OF FIG. 5-4.2

Fault designation	Description	Function at output (g)
f_1	$(a, 0)$	$x_1 x_3$
f_2	$(a, 1)$	$x_2 + x_1 x_3$
f_3	$(b, 0)$	$x_1 x_3$
f_4	$(b, 1)$	$\bar{x}_1 + x_3$
f_5	$(c, 0)$	$\bar{x}_1 x_2$
f_6	$(c, 1)$	$\bar{x}_1 x_2 + x_3$
f_7	$(d, 0)$	$\bar{x}_1 x_2$
f_8	$(d, 1)$	$x_1 + x_2$
f_9	$(e, 0)$	1
f_{10}	$(e, 1)$	$x_1 x_3$
f_{11}	$(f, 0)$	1
f_{12}	$(f, 1)$	$\bar{x}_1 x_2$
f_{13}	$(g, 0)$	0
f_{14}	$(g, 1)$	1

Table 5-4.3 RESULTS OF TESTS FOR THE CIRCUIT OF FIG. 5-4.2

Test	x_1	x_2	x_3	f_0	f_1	f_2	f_3	f_4	f_5	f_6	f_7	f_8	f_9	f_{10}	f_{11}	f_{12}	f_{13}	f_{14}
t_0	0	0	0	0	0	0	0	1	0	0	0	0	1	0	1	0	0	1
t_1	0	0	1	0	0	0	0	1	0	1	0	0	1	0	1	0	0	1
t_2	0	1	0	1	0	1	0	1	1	1	1	1	1	0	1	1	0	1
t_3	0	1	1	1	0	1	0	1	1	1	1	1	1	0	1	1	0	1
t_4	1	0	0	0	0	0	0	0	0	0	0	1	1	0	1	0	0	1
t_5	1	0	1	1	1	1	1	1	0	1	0	1	1	1	1	0	0	1
t_6	1	1	0	0	0	1	0	0	0	0	0	1	1	0	1	0	0	1
t_7	1	1	1	1	1	1	1	1	0	1	0	1	1	1	1	0	0	1

For a small circuit, the table of faults can easily be calculated or simulated. However, the computational effort required to obtain a table of faults for larger circuits may become very costly. We will therefore formulate an algorithm which generates, in an efficient manner, the table of faults.

Definition 5-4.1 A *test* in a combinational circuit is the application of a combination of input symbols to the circuit.

A test will be represented by t_i where the subscript i represents the decimal designation of its corresponding input combination. As an example, t_5 denotes the test in which $x_1 = 1$, $x_2 = 0$, and $x_3 = 1$ in Table 5-4.3.

Note that the columns f_1 and f_3 in Table 5-4.3 are identical for any test performed; i.e, the tests performed on the circuit cannot distinguish between faults f_1 and f_3. This phenomenon leads us to the next definition.

Definition 5-4.2 In a combinational circuit, two faults f_i and f_j are said to be *indistinguishable* if for any test the corresponding values in the presence of f_i alone and f_j alone are the same. Otherwise, the faults are *distinguishable*.

Table 5-4.4 FAULT MATRIX FOR THE CIRCUIT OF FIG. 5-4.2

Test	x_1	x_2	x_3	f_0	f_1	f_2	f_4	f_5	f_6	f_8	f_9	f_{13}
t_0	0	0	0	0	0	0	1	0	0	0	1	0
t_1	0	0	1	0	0	0	1	0	1	0	1	0
t_2	0	1	0	1	0	1	1	1	1	1	1	0
t_3	0	1	1	1	0	1	1	1	1	1	1	0
t_4	1	0	0	0	0	0	0	0	0	1	1	0
t_5	1	0	1	1	1	1	1	0	1	1	1	0
t_6	1	1	0	0	0	1	0	0	0	1	1	0
t_7	1	1	1	1	1	1	1	0	1	1	1	0

An interesting situation arises when a column f_i, for some i, is identical to f_0. This indicates that the presence of f_i in the circuit does not change the correct output. This situation occurs in a circuit which has *redundancies*.

Columns f_1, f_3, and f_{10} of Table 5-4.3 are indistinguishable; so are columns f_5, f_7, and f_{12}, and columns f_9, f_{11}, and f_{14}. Therefore Table 5-4.3 can be reduced to Table 5-4.4 in which only one fault from each set of indistinguishable faults has been retained. Such a table is called a *fault matrix*.

We now proceed to formulate an algorithm which can mechanically generate a fault matrix.

5-4.3 Algorithm for Generating a Fault Matrix

A combinational switching circuit can be represented as a directed graph whose nodes are the gates of the graph and whose edges are the connections between the gates in the circuit. In order to include the *primary inputs* in this representation, they are considered to be gates (nodes) which have an output but no inputs. The gates of a circuit are assigned successive integers, starting at 1, using the following procedure:

1 Initially assign successive integers, starting at 1, to each of the primary inputs.

2 Assign successive integers to those gates, all of whose inputs are derived from gates which have already been numbered. This step is repeated until all gates have been numbered.

The result of applying this procedure to the circuit of Fig. 5-4.2 is given in Fig. 5-4.3.

When the procedure is applied to an n-input circuit which has a total of m ($m > n$) gates (where m also includes the number of primary inputs), the integers 1 through n are assigned to the primary inputs. The numbers $n + 1$ to $m - 1$ are assigned to the intermediate gates, and, finally, the number m is assigned to the output gate. In Fig. 5-4.3 nodes 1, 2, 3, and 4 correspond to the primary inputs; nodes 5 and 6 correspond to the intermediate gates; and node 7 corresponds to the final output gate.

The adjacency matrix of the digraph representing a combinational circuit is also called a *connectivity matrix* and will be denoted by C. Naturally $c_{ij} = 1$ iff the output from gate i is connected to an input of gate j; otherwise $c_{ij} = 0$. Obviously, C is antisymmetric and irreflexive. Such a connectivity matrix will

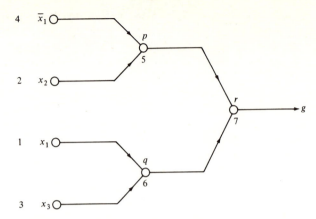

FIGURE 5-4.3   Directed graph representation of Fig. 5-4.2.

be useful in the algorithm because the entries in its jth column clearly show the inputs to the jth gate. $c_{ij} = 1$ will also be written as $i\, C\, j$, showing C as a relation on the set of gates.

A complete description of the circuit in Fig. 5-4.2 is given in Table 5-4.5 where the truth values for all intermediate gates are also included. Each row of the table shows the output of each gate for each combination of the input variables.

In general, the output of a gate in a circuit, with n primary inputs, can be expressed as a 2^n-tuple of bits; for example, the output of gate g in Table 5-4.5 is the 8-tuple $\langle 0, 0, 1, 1, 0, 1, 0, 1 \rangle$, or 00110101 for short.

This 8-tuple, or 2^n-tuple in general, also shows the minterms in the sum-of-products canonical form of any of the inputs or outputs. For example, $g = \sum (2, 3, 5, 7)$ and $x_2 = \sum (2, 3, 6, 7)$. The algorithm that we shall develop will require the product-of-sums canonical form; consequently, we shall use maxterms in place of minterms and express any input or output in terms of the products of maxterms. Accordingly, we write $g = \Pi\, (0, 1, 4, 6)$ and $x_2 = \Pi\, (0, 1, 4, 5)$. Since we will be using only maxterms in our discussion here, it would be convenient to drop the symbol Π and present the product-of-sums canonical form

Table 5-4.5

Inputs			Intermediate outputs		Final outputs
x_1	x_2	x_3	p	q	g
0	0	0	1	1	0
0	0	1	1	1	0
0	1	0	0	1	1
0	1	1	0	1	1
1	0	0	1	1	0
1	0	1	1	0	1
1	1	0	1	1	0
1	1	1	1	0	1

of a function simply by a set of maxterms that are present in the canonical form. Accordingly, we shall represent g and x_2 of our example simply as $\{0, 1, 4, 6\}$ and $\{0, 1, 4, 5\}$ respectively, and we call these sets the maxterm sets of g and x_2. If we do not need the maxterms of any function x explicitly, we shall simply denote it by (x). Recall that for the purposes of comparison or determination of equivalence of functions using a computer, it is necessary to assume that these sets are ordered.

It will now be useful to consider what operations a $NAND$ gate performs on maxterm sets at its inputs and, particularly, how s-a-0 and s-a-1 faults are represented.

The maxterm representation of a gate whose terminal is subject to an s-a-1 fault will always be the empty set. Similarly, an s-a-0 fault occurring at a terminal of a gate will cause the maxterm set to be the universal set consisting of all the maxterms.

To see what the output of a $NAND$ gate is in terms of the maxterm sets at the input, note from Table 5-4.5 that the output at gate q is 1 whenever x_1 or x_3 has a value of zero. More generally, if a maxterm is present at an input to a $NAND$ gate, then this maxterm will not appear at the output of that gate. This result holds for an arbitrary number of input terminals to a $NAND$ gate. We can represent the function of a $NAND$ gate with r inputs $x_1, x_2, \ldots, x_r$ and output y as

$$(y) = \overline{(x_1) \cup (x_2) \cup \cdots \cup (x_r)}$$

This is an important result which is used successively for every gate of the circuit to obtain the maxterm set of each gate, provided we first have the maxterm sets of the primary input gates. Such maxterm sets are easily generated by a computer. As a next step, we obtain the maxterm set of successive gates, taking advantage of the fact that their ordering was done in such a way that the maxterm set of the output of any gate is calculated only after the maxterm sets of all its inputs are known. The term "output maxterm set" is used to refer to the maxterm set produced at the output of a gate. Similarly, the term "input maxterm set" is used to denote those maxterms at the input of a gate. In our example of Fig. 5-4.2 as shown in Fig. 5-4.4, we first have the input maxterm set $\{4, 5, 6, 7\}$ and $\{0, 1, 4, 5\}$ for the inputs $\overline{x_1}$ and x_2, respectively, to gate 5, and the output maxterm set is $\{2, 3\}$. Other maxterm sets are shown in Fig. 5-4.4. These sets are also denoted by F_i for the gate i, so that for a circuit the maxterm sets are denoted by $F_1, F_2, \ldots, F_m$. These sets are represented on a computer as a bit string or a vector whose typical element is a maxterm.

The notation for stuck-at faults that will be used in the remainder of the section is as follows:

$p - q/1$ will denote that the input to gate q from gate p is s-a-1 and similarly $p - q/0$ for an s-a-0 fault.

$r/1$ will denote that the output at gate r is s-a-1 and similarly $r/0$ for an s-a-0 fault.

In developing the algorithm we will restrict the circuits being examined to those in which the output of any gate in the circuit is connected to a single

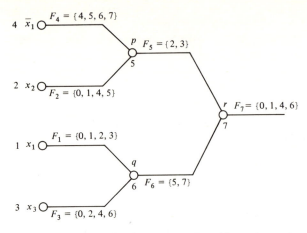

FIGURE 5-4.4   Circuit representation with maxterm sets.

gate at the next stage; i.e., each node in the graph of the circuit has an out-degree of 1. Such a circuit will be denote an f-o-1 (fan out of 1) circuit. Un-restricted circuits are referred to as f-o-n circuits

For f-o-1 circuits, $p\,C\,q$ implies that the faults $p - q/1$ or $p - q/0$ have the same effect as, and are indistinguishable from, the faults $p/1$ or $p/0$ respectively. However, this is not true in f-o-n circuits, because if we have $p\,C\,q$ and $p\,C\,r$, then fault $p/1$ does not necessarily have the same effect as either of the single faults $p - q/1$ or $p - r/1$. A similar remark holds for s-a-0 faults. The effects of stuck-at faults are easier to determine in an f-o-1 circuit. Therefore, the F vector will be sufficient to describe all maxterm sets in an f-o-1 circuit.

Consider the graph shown in Fig. 5-4.5 which represents some portion of an f-o-1 circuit. Let us determine the effect of a fault $x/1$ on the output maxterm sets of the successive gates z, p, and q. Let the output maxterm set of a gate g in the presence of a fault be denoted by $(g)'$.

Recall that a $NAND$ gate outputs those maxterms which do not appear at any of its inputs. Therefore for gate z

$$(z) \;=\; \overline{(w) \cup (x) \cup (y)}$$

It will now be shown that the effects of $x/1$ on (z) will depend on whether any of the maxterms in (x) are contained in (w) or (y). There are three possible cases which can occur:

1   All the maxterms in (x) are contained in $(w) \cup (y)$, that is, $(x) \subseteq [(w) \cup (y)]$. In this case $(z) = \overline{(w) \cup (x) \cup (y)} = \overline{(w) \cup (y)}$, and consequently the fault has no effect and $(z)' = (z)$.

2   None of the maxterms in (x) are contained in $(w) \cup (y)$. This will result in all the maxterms of (x) appearing at gate z, so that $(z)' = (z) \cup (x)$.

3   Some, but not all, of the maxterms in (x) are contained in $(w) \cup (y)$. In this final case, some of the maxterms of (x) will appear at the output of gate z. Let this subset of (x) be denoted by $(x)_z$. Then $(z)' = (z) \cup (x)_z$.

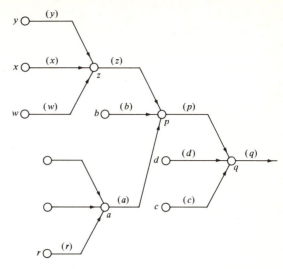

FIGURE 5-4.5 Graphic representation of a partial circuit.

The first case will arise when x is a redundant gate, and these redundancies can be determined by purely mechanical means.

The remaining two cases indicate that the fault $x/1$ has increased the maxterm set (z) by some nonempty subset of (x). These cases can obviously be combined so that $(x)_z \subseteq (x)$ and is nonempty. This fault propagates through to the input of gate p, and the original maxterm set for (z) has now become the set

$$(z)' = (z) \cup (x)_z \qquad (1)$$

The maxterm set at the input to gate p has consequently been increased by the fault (assuming no redundancies), and therefore the resulting output set at gate p will contain fewer elements. Again there are three possibilities:

4 If $(x)_z \subseteq [(a) \cup (b)]$, then $(p)' = (p)$.

5 If $(x)_z \cap [(a) \cup (b)]$ is empty, then $(p)' = (p) - (x)_z$.

6 Otherwise, if $(x)_z \cap [(a) \cup (b)]$ is not null, then $(p)' = (p) - (x)_p$ where $(x)_p \subseteq (x)_z$.

Since additional maxterms in cases 5 and 6 have been added to the z input of gate p which were not previously there, some of these same maxterms [depending on the sets (a) and (b)] will be removed from the output of that gate. In case 5, all of $(x)_z$ is removed while in case 6 a nonempty subset of the original $(x)_z$ subset [denoted by $(x)_p \subseteq (x)_z \subseteq (x)$] is lost. By combining both cases, the output maxterm set of gate p becomes

$$(p)' = (p) - (x)_p \qquad (2)$$

If we continue in this fashion, it is clear that the maxterm set at gate q is

$$(q)' = (q) \cup (x)_q$$

where $(x)_q \subseteq (x)_p \subseteq (x)_z \subseteq (x)$.

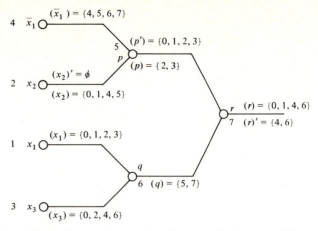

$(\overline{x}_1) = \{4, 5, 6, 7\}$

4   $\overline{x}_1$

5   $(p') = \{0, 1, 2, 3\}$

  p $(p) = \{2, 3\}$

$(x_2)' = \phi$

2   x_2

$(x_2) = \{0, 1, 4, 5\}$

r $(r) = \{0, 1, 4, 6\}$

7   $(r)' = \{4, 6\}$

$(x_1) = \{0, 1, 2, 3\}$

1   x_1

q

6   $(q) = \{5, 7\}$

3   x_3

$(x_3) = \{0, 2, 4, 6\}$

FIGURE 5-4.6   Propagation of an s-a-1 fault at terminal x_2.

In general, let x be an input to gate g_1, g_1 be an input to gate g_2, g_2 be an input to gate g_3, etc., until g_{j-1} is an input to gate g_j. Then the output maxterm set of each gate through which the fault at terminal x propagates is given as follows:

$$(g_1)' = (g_1) \cup (x)_{g_1} \qquad \text{where } (x)_{g_1} \subseteq (x)$$

$$(g_2)' = (g_2) - (x)_{g_2} \qquad \text{where } (x)_{g_2} \subseteq (x)_{g_1}$$

.

.

.

$$(g_j)' = (g_j) \cup (x)_{g_j} \qquad \text{where } (x)_{g_j} \subseteq (x)_{g_{j-1}} \text{ and } j \text{ odd}$$

or

$$(g_j)' = (g_j) - (x)_{g_j} \qquad \text{where } (x)_{g_j} \subseteq (x)_{g_{j-1}} \text{ and } j \text{ even}$$

Note that since $(x)_{g_j} \subseteq (x)_{g_{j-1}} \subseteq \cdots \subseteq (x)_{g_1} \subseteq (x)$, the only maxterms that can be picked up or lost at a particular gate affected by the fault must belong to (x). From this discussion, we can easily see that if the path length from where the fault $x/1$ is applied to gate g_j is odd, then the maxterm set at g_j will be $(g_j)' = (g_j) \cup (x)_{g_j}$; otherwise, $(g_j)' = (g_j) - (x)_{g_j}$. Furthermore, at gate g_j we obtain the identity

$$(g_j)' \oplus (g_j) = (x)_{g_j}$$

where $\oplus$ denotes the exclusive OR or symmetric-difference operation. We shall shortly make use of the equivalent equation:

$$(g_j)' = (g_j) \oplus (x)_{g_j} \qquad (3)$$

By generating $(x)_{g_j}$ for every gate in the circuit and by applying either Eq. (1) or Eq. (2), all the s-a-1 functions of a circuit can be produced. For example, an s-a-1 fault at terminal x_2 will cause the maxterm sets at gates p and r to change as shown in Fig. 5-4.6, where $(x_2)_p = (0, 1)$ and $(x_2)_r = (0, 1)$.

So far, we have shown that the ultimate effect of an s-a-1 fault at the output of a particular gate depends on the other maxterm sets which are inputs to the gates through which the fault propagates. If these maxterm sets contain maxterms which are also present at the faulty gate, then these common maxterms are not affected at the output function. For example, in Fig. 5-4.5 the condition under which gate x will affect the output is stated as

$$(x) - [(w) \cup (y) \cup (a) \cup (b) \cup (c) \cup (d)] \neq \varnothing$$

where the left part of the inequality is the set $(x)_q$. If q is the final output gate in a circuit, then $(x)_q$ is the *error maxterm* set for gate x, and this set contains the maxterms which will change at the output in the presence of the fault at x. If $(x)_q$ is null, then the output of gate x is redundant.

For an s-a-1 fault at gate x, the effect of (w) and (y) on (x) can be easily determined from the connectivity matrix for the circuit. The remaining maxterm sets, however, cannot directly be determined from the matrix.

So far we have discussed a relation C of connection between the gates of a circuit. The corresponding relation matrix is called the connectivity matrix. Let us now introduce another relation which shows the dominance of a gate over another gate in some sense. For this purpose, let x be any gate which is faulty and $(x)_g$ be the subset of (x) which appears at the output gate g. Let p be any other gate which is such that both p and x are not connected to the same terminal. If the maxterm set of p, (p), affects $(x)_g$, then the gate p is said to *dominate* the gate x, and we shall express it by writing $p\,D\,x$. We shall also use D to denote the corresponding relation matrix. It must be emphasized that p can dominate x only if both p and x are not connected to the same gate.

In our example of Fig. 5-4.5, a, b, c, and d all dominate x, but w and y do not, since x, y, and w are connected to the same gate.

In a given circuit, if a gate p dominates x, then we must have a gate q such that p is an input to this gate and the fault at x propagates through q. Of course, both p and x are not connected to the gate q, that is, $x \not\subset q$. If we denote a relation C^+ to mean a path from one gate to another, that is, $a\,C^+\,b$ if there exists a path from a to b, then we can say that for $p\,D\,x$ we must have a gate q such that $p\,C\,q$ and $x\,(C^+ - C)\,q$, where $C^+ - C$ shows that there is a path from x to q which is not of length 1, that is, $x \not\subset q$. These two conditions can be written down as

$$p\,[C \circ (C^+ - C)']\,x$$

where $(C^+ - C)'$ is the converse of $C^+ - C$ and $\circ$ denotes the composition of relations C and $(C^+ - C)'$. However, this condition is not sufficient, as can be seen from Fig. 5-4.5 by observing that $a\,C\,p$ and $r\,(C^+ - C)\,p$, implying $a\,[C \circ (C^+ - C)']\,r$. But the output $(r)_q$ is not affected by (a); in fact, (a) depends upon (r), hence a does not dominate r. In this case $r\,C^+\,a$ or $a\,(C^+)'\,r$, and we should eliminate such cases. We finally arrive at a criterion which is necessary and sufficient for the dominance relation, that is,

$$p\,D\,x \qquad \text{iff} \qquad p\,[C \circ (C^+ - C)' - (C^+)']\,x$$

From this result and using the matrix C, we can obtain the matrix D. As a next step, we shall calculate the error maxterm set for each gate, using the matrices C, D, and vector F. The error maxterm sets can be represented by vector E and can be obtained by the following procedure in which the vector V is used to store intermediate results.

1 [Initialize] Set $E_m \leftarrow F_m$. Repeat for $i = 1, 2, \ldots, m$: Set $V_i \leftarrow F_i$.

2 [Set up next row] Repeat step 3 for $i = m - 1, m - 2, \ldots, 1$.

3 [Perform dominance computation] Repeat for $j = m - 1, m - 2, \ldots, 1$: If $d_{ij} = 1$, then $V_j \leftarrow V_j - V_i$.

4 [Initialize common input computation] Repeat steps 5, 6, and 7 for $i = n + 1, n + 2, \ldots, m$.

5 [Set temporary maxterm sets to empty] $W \leftarrow Y \leftarrow \varnothing$.

6 [Obtain common maxterms] Repeat for $j = 1, 2, \ldots, i - 1$: If $c_{ji} = 1$, then set $W \leftarrow W \cup (Y \cap V_j)$, $Y \leftarrow Y \cup V_j$.

7 [Compute error maxterm set] Repeat for $k = 1, 2, \ldots, i - 1$: If $c_{ki} = 1$, then set $E_k \leftarrow V_k - W$.

For each maxterm set (gate) in a circuit, steps 2 and 3 remove those maxterms which also occur in the maxterm sets which it dominates, thus producing the intermediate vector V. Table 5-4.6 shows the dominance matrix for the circuit in Fig. 5-4.2. After the first three steps of the previous procedure have been performed on this circuit, the intermediate sets in the V vector will be obtained as shown in Fig. 5-4.7a.

Steps 4 to 7 remove those maxterms which occur in at least two of the sets which are common inputs to a gate. These steps produce the E vector containing the error maxterm set for each gate. Figure 5-4.7b shows the error maxterm sets obtained after steps 4, 5, 6, and 7 of the procedure have been performed on the circuit of Fig. 5-4.2.

The dominance computation must be performed before the common input computation. For example, in Fig. 5-4.5 gate c dominates gates a, b, w, x, y, and z. If we first remove common maxterms occurring in two or more of the sets (c), (d), and (p) which are common inputs to gate q, then some maxterms in (c) may be removed which dominate those in (a), (b), etc. The dominance computation must therefore be performed first.

From the E vector we can now generate all the functions produced by single s-a-1 faults in a circuit. Before doing this, let us briefly consider s-a-0 faults.

It was shown previously that an s-a-0 fault at the input to a gate caused the

Table 5-4.6 DOMINANCE MATRIX OF FIG. 5-4.2

		1 x_1	2 x_2	3 x_3	4 $\overline{x_1}$	5 p	6 q	7 r
1	x_1	0	0	0	0	0	0	0
2	x_2	0	0	0	0	0	0	0
3	x_3	0	0	0	0	0	0	0
4	$\overline{x_1}$	0	0	0	0	0	0	0
5	p	1	0	1	0	0	0	0
6	q	0	1	0	1	0	0	0
7	r	0	0	0	0	0	0	0

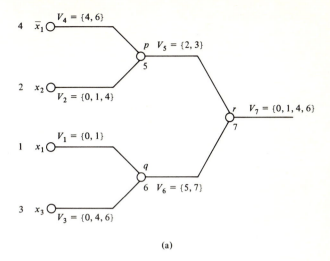

(a)

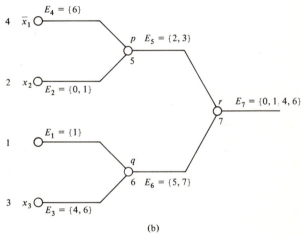

(b)

FIGURE 5-4.7 Generation of (a) a V vector and (b) an E vector for s-a-1 faults in Fig. 5-4.2.

output of that gate to become s-a-1. The fault functions produced for s-a-1 faults will include all the functions produced by s-a-0 faults at the input to any gate. The final output gate is the only gate which is not an input to any other, and so the zero function (universal maxterm set) must be included in the fault table separately. With this in mind, the fault matrix can now be produced.

Using Eq. (3), we can produce the fault function for each gate in the circuit and include it in the fault-table vector f. The following algorithm accomplishes this.

Table 5-4.7 FAULT MATRIX FOR FIG. 5-4.2

Test	x_1	x_2	x_3	f_0 {0, 1, 4, 6}	f_1 {0, 4, 6}	f_2 {4, 6}	f_3 {0, 1}	f_4 {0, 1, 4}	f_5 {0, 1, 2, 3, 4, 6}	f_6 {0, 1, 4, 5, 6, 7}	f_7 $\varnothing$	f_8 {0, 1, 2, 3, 4, 5, 6, 7}
t_0	0	0	0	0	0	1	0	0	0	0	1	0
t_1	0	0	1	0	1	1	0	0	0	0	1	0
t_2	0	1	0	1	1	1	1	1	0	1	1	0
t_3	0	1	1	1	1	0	1	1	0	1	1	0
t_4	1	0	0	0	0	0	1	0	0	0	1	0
t_5	1	0	1	1	1	0	1	1	1	0	1	0
t_6	1	1	0	0	0	0	1	1	1	0	1	0
t_7	1	1	1	1	1	1	1	1	1	0	1	0

1 [Include the circuit function] Set $f_0 \leftarrow E_m$.

2 [Initialize fault matrix index] Set $i \leftarrow 1$.

3 [Initialize fault function loop] Repeat step 4 for $j = 1, 2, \ldots, m$.

4 [Is it a new fault function?] If $(E_m \oplus E_j) \notin \{f_0, f_1, \ldots, f_{i-1}\}$, then $f_i \leftarrow (E_m \oplus E_j)$, and $i \leftarrow i + 1$.

5 [Include the zero function] If the zero function is not already in $\{f_0, f_1, \ldots, f_{i-1}\}$, then $f_i \leftarrow$ the universal maxterm set.

The fault matrix for the circuit in Fig. 5-4.2 is obtained by using the above procedure, as shown in Table 5-4.7. Observe that both the maxterm set and its equivalent bit string form for the fault function are given. It is interesting to compare Tables 5-4.4 and 5-4.7. Except for relabeling, these tables are identical. In fact, functions f_0, f_1, f_2, f_3, f_4, f_5, f_6, f_7, and f_8 correspond to the functions f_0, f_6, f_4, f_8, f_2, f_1, f_5, f_9, and f_{13}, respectively, in Table 5-4.4. Now that we have an algorithm for generating a fault matrix for a circuit, the question that naturally arises is: How do we detect faults? This is the topic of the next subsection.

5-4.4 Procedure for the Detection of Faults

The previous subsection was concerned with the development of an algorithm for generating the fault matrix of a circuit. We now wish to investigate how a particular fault can be detected by making use of this matrix. One obvious approach is to apply all possible tests to the circuit and observe their corresponding output values, but this is clearly inefficient. We shall therefore develop a strategy which will require the application of a minimum number of tests in order to detect a fault.

Let us first reexamine Table 5-4.4. The application of test t_1 to the fault-free circuit will result in an output of 0. If the same test is applied to the circuit under fault f_6, then the observed output is 1, which is different from its corresponding output for a fault-free circuit. The application of test t_1 can detect fault f_6. If the same test is applied to the circuit under fault f_1, however, then the observed output is the same as the output obtained from the fault-free circuit, and in this case the test fails to detect f_1. These ideas are formalized in the following definition.

Definition 5-4.3 A test t_j detects a fault f_i if the observed output under the application of fault f_i alone is different from its corresponding output when the circuit is fault-free. Otherwise, t_j *fails to detect* f_i.

A more useful form of the fault matrix will be defined. This revised matrix will be called the *fault-detection matrix* for the circuit. If for some test t_j the output of the circuit under fault f_i is different from the observed output for the fault-free circuit, then an entry of 1 is entered in the table; otherwise, a value of 0 is recorded. The fault-detection table which corresponds to Table 5-4.4 appears in Table 5-4.8. Note that the f_i's in Table 5-4.8 are obtained by exclusively ORing the f_i's in Table 5-4.4 with f_0.

The selection of a minimum number of tests for fault detection requires obtaining a cover for the set of fault functions (a similar approach was used

Table 5-4.8 THE FAULT-DETECTION TABLE OF FIG. 5-4.2

Test	x_1	x_2	x_3	f_1	f_2	f_4	f_5	f_6	f_8	f_9	f_{13}
t_0	0	0	0	0	0	1	0	0	0	1	0
t_1	0	0	1	0	0	1	0	1	0	1	0
t_2	0	1	0	1	0	0	0	0	0	0	1
t_3	0	1	1	1	0	0	0	0	0	0	1
t_4	1	0	0	0	0	0	0	0	1	1	0
t_5	1	0	1	0	0	0	1	0	0	0	1
t_6	1	1	0	0	1	0	0	0	1	1	0
t_7	1	1	1	0	0	0	1	0	0	0	1

in the Quine-McCluskey algorithm in Sec. 4-4). Observe that in column f_2 there exists only one non-zero element, namely that entry which corresponds to test t_6. Therefore t_6 is an essential test which must be performed if f_2 is to be detected. An analogous situation exists in column f_6 where t_1 is an essential test. The selection of tests t_1 and t_6 reduces the fault detection table to that shown in Table 5-4.9. Since rows t_0 and t_4 contain all 0s, these two tests can be dropped. Since rows t_2 and t_3 are the same, we arbitrarily choose test t_2. Test t_5 is chosen in the same manner.

The remaining fault-detection table consists of rows t_2 and t_5 which are both essential. The test cover thus obtained is the set $\{t_1, t_2, t_5, t_6\}$. So, only these four tests need be applied, instead of all eight, in order to detect a permanent fault. The reduced fault-detection table which is equivalent to Table 5-4.8 appears in Table 5-4.10. Observe, however, that we cannot precisely identify by applying t_1, t_2, t_5, and t_6 which fault has occurred, if one exists, since columns f_4 and f_6 are the same as are columns f_2 and f_8.

Table 5-4.9 REDUCED FAULT-
DETECTION TABLE
FOR FIG. 5-4.2

Test	f_1	f_5	f_{13}
t_0	0	0	0
t_2	1	0	1
t_3	1	0	1
t_4	0	0	0
t_5	0	1	1
t_7	0	1	1

Table 5-4.10 REDUCED FAULT-DETECTION TABLE FOR
FIG. 5-4.2

Test	f_1	f_2	f_4	f_5	f_6	f_8	f_9	f_{13}
t_1	0	0	1	0	1	0	1	0
t_2	1	0	0	0	0	0	0	1
t_5	0	0	0	1	0	0	0	1
t_6	0	1	0	0	0	1	1	0

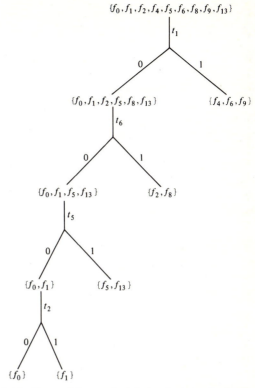

FIGURE 5-4.8 Sequential test schedule for the example circuit.

Let us now examine the order in which the four tests can be applied. Intermediate test results will be used to determine which additional tests should be applied. For the circuit in our example, a possible sequential test schedule is given in Fig. 5-4.8.

Initially, it is not known whether a fault has occurred. This uncertainty is denoted by the set $\{f_0, f_1, f_2, f_4, f_5, f_6, f_8, f_9, f_{13}\}$ at the root of the tree. On applying test t_1, more information is known about the state of the circuit. If the observed output of the circuit is 1, then, from Table 5-4.10, there is definitely a fault; otherwise the circuit either is fault-free or could have a fault in the set $\{f_0, f_1, f_2, f_5, f_8, f_{13}\}$. Consequently, the uncertainty sets $\{f_0, f_1, f_2, f_5, f_8, f_{13}\}$ and $\{f_4, f_6, f_9\}$ appear at the next level of the tree. If the result of t_1 is a 1, then we know that a fault f_4 or f_6 or f_9 has occurred, and the testing process terminates. If t_1 yields an observed output of 0, the procedure must be continued with the application of test t_6. By continuing this process, the test tree is easily constructed.

EXERCISES 5-4

1 Construct a table of single faults for the circuit shown in Fig. 5-4.9 similar to Table 5-4.2 in the text.

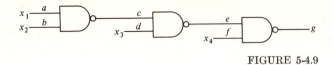

FIGURE 5-4.9

2   Prove Eq. (3) in Sec. 5-4.3.
3   Generate the error maxterm sets of Fig. 5-4.9 to permit single-fault detection.
4   For the circuit of Fig. 5-4.9 generate the fault-detection table as shown in Table 5-4.8.
5   Obtain a test cover for the circuit of Fig. 5-4.9 and construct a decision tree for it.

5-5   PERT AND RELATED TECHNIQUES

A directed graph is a natural way of describing, representing, and analyzing complex projects which consist of many interrelated activities. The project might be, for example, the design and construction of a power dam or the design and erection of an apartment building. In this section we are interested in determining the critical path of a digraph. Such a critical path is a very important management tool that can be applied to many situations. There are a number of management techniques such as PERT (Program Evaluation and Review Technique) and CPM (Critical Path Method) which employ a graph as the structure on which analysis is based. The problem of finding a minimal path between two nodes was discussed in Sec. 5-1.3. A critical path, however, involves finding the longest path between two nodes in a weighted digraph.

This section introduces certain basic terminology associated with finding the critical path of a graph. An informal algorithm is given for computing the critical path(s) of a weighted graph.

Formally, a PERT graph is a finite digraph with no parallel edges or cycles, in which there is exactly one source (i.e., a node whose indegree is 0) and one sink (i.e., a node whose outdegree is 0). Furthermore, each edge in the graph is assigned a weight (time) value. The directed edges are meant to represent activities, with the directed edge joining the nodes which represent the start time and finish time of the activity. The weight value of each edge is taken to be the time it takes to complete the activity.

Although there will be a number of independent activities in the graph, there will usually be certain essential dependencies, with respect to time, which have the form that activity a_i must be completed before activity a_j can begin. If all such time dependencies are available, then they can be conveniently displayed in a directed graph such as in Fig. 5-5.1. The project has ten activities, and the activities follow a particular order in the sense that certain activities must be completed before certain other activities can begin. Each node is called an *event* and represents a point in time. In particular, node v_1 denotes the start of the entire project (its source) and v_6 its completion (its sink). The numbers associated with the edges represent the number of days required to do that particular activity. From the graph, we see that before activities $\langle v_3, v_4 \rangle$ and $\langle v_3, v_6 \rangle$ can begin, activities $\langle v_1, v_3 \rangle$ and $\langle v_2, v_3 \rangle$ must both be completed. Similarly, before activities $\langle v_4, v_5 \rangle$ and $\langle v_4, v_6 \rangle$ can begin, activities $\langle v_1, v_4 \rangle$ and $\langle v_3, v_4 \rangle$ must both be

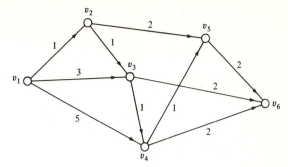

FIGURE 5-5.1 A PERT graph.

done, etc. Finally, in order to complete the project, activities $\langle v_5, v_6 \rangle$, $\langle v_3, v_6 \rangle$, and $\langle v_4, v_6 \rangle$ must all be completed.

We process the PERT graph by computing the earliest completion time for each activity under the restriction that before an activity can begin, every activity on which it depends must be completed. In terms of the graph, this computation corresponds to the assignment of time values to each node in such a manner that the value assigned to a node is the length of time to complete the activities along the longest path leading into that node. That is, we assign to a node the value which is the maximum, over all incoming edges, of the weight of an edge plus the time associated with that edge's source node. By definition, the value of 0 is assigned to the source node.

In summary, we can associate a time value with each event node in the following manner:

$$TE(v_1) = 0$$

$$TE(v_j) = \max \{t(P)\} \qquad j \neq 1$$

where $t(P)$ denotes the sum of all time durations for a path P and where the maximum is taken over all paths from v_1 to v_j. When we finally assign a value to the sink node, this value is the earliest completion time for the entire project.

Referring to Fig. 5-5.1, node v_2 has only one incoming edge, and consequently a value of 1 $[= 0 + 1]$ is assigned to that node. Node v_3 has two incoming edges, so we must take the longer path length (v_1, v_3) $[= 0 + 3]$ rather than the path (v_1, v_2, v_3) $[= 1 + 1]$ and assign 3 to node v_3. Node v_4 has two incoming paths (v_1, v_3, v_4) and (v_1, v_4). The value for the first path is 4 while that of the second is 5, and therefore a value of 5 is assigned to v_4. Continuing this process, v_6 is assigned a value of 8, which indicates that the project will require at least 8 days to complete. The network with the earliest completion time, TE, assigned to each node is given in Fig. 5-5.2.

Having progressed this far, we can next calculate the latest completion time associated with each node. This is the latest time an activity can be completed without causing a delay in the earliest completion date of the project (i.e., they are the latest completion times associated with the activities that do not cause the TE value of the sink node to be increased). These latest completion times TL are assigned to nodes in such a way that the assigned TL value is the

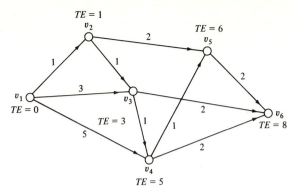

FIGURE 5-5.2   A PERT graph with earliest completion time.

largest value which will still allow every activity starting at that node to be completed without an overall time increase. In terms of the graph, we assign to a node the value which is the minimum, over all outgoing edges, of the edge's destination node TL value minus the edge weight. By definition, the TL value of the sink node equals its TE value.

In summary, we can associate a time value with each event node in the following manner:

$$TL(v_n) = TE(v_n)$$
$$TL(v_j) = TE(v_n) - \max \{t(P)\} \quad j \neq n$$

where $t(P)$ denotes the sum of time durations for a path P from v_j to v_n and where the maximum is taken over all such paths and subtracted from $TE(v_n)$.

Returning to Fig. 5-5.2, since v_5 has only one outgoing edge, we assign to v_5 a TL value of 6 [$= 8 - 2$]. Node v_4 has two outgoing edges, $\langle v_4, v_5 \rangle$ and $\langle v_4, v_6 \rangle$. The minimum of 5 is assigned to that node. Continuing this process yields a TL value of 0 for the source node. The PERT graph of our example with its TE and TL values is given in Fig. 5-5.3.

After having computed the TE and TL values for each node in a graph, we can determine its critical path(s). A *critical path* is a path from the source node to the sink node such that if any activity on the path is delayed by an amount t, then the entire project is delayed by t. Each node on the critical path has its TL value equal to its TE value. This means that if the project is to be completed by its earliest completion time, the nodes on the critical path must be reached at their earliest completion times. For the graph in our example, the nodes on the critical path are v_1, v_4, v_5, v_6, and the critical path is $\langle v_1, v_4, v_5, v_6 \rangle$. Nodes that are not on the critical path have a slack time associated with them. *Slack time* of a node is merely the difference between its TL and TE values, and it indicates the amount of spare time which is available in doing a particular activity. In our example, node v_3 has a slack time of 1 day. This means that the activities that must be completed at node v_3 can be delayed 1 day if necessary. In fact, although activity $\langle v_1, v_3 \rangle$ could be delayed only 1 day, activity $\langle v_2, v_3 \rangle$ could be delayed 2 days as long as $\langle v_1, v_3 \rangle$ was begun immediately and completed on time.

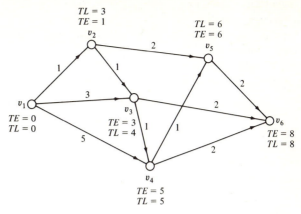

FIGURE 5-5.3 A PERT graph with earliest and latest completion times.

In order to reduce the earliest completion time for the project, only those activities on the critical path must be speeded up. Since in practice the number of activities which lie on the critical path in large graphs is a small percentage of the total number of activities, say 10 percent, only those 10 percent need to be improved.

We shall now consider a representation of a PERT graph similar to the structure suggested at the end of Sec. 5-2.2. A linked list of all event nodes in the graph will be kept. The structure of a typical event node in this simple linked list will have the form

OUT	NAME	IN	TE	TL	LINK

where OUT is a pointer to a list of its outgoing edges, $NAME$ is its label, IN is a pointer to a list of its incoming edges, TE is its earliest completion time, TL is its latest allowable completion time, and $LINK$ is a pointer to the next event node in the list. The assignment $P \leftarrow NODE$ creates an event node of this type and stores its address in P. We shall also need a list of edges whose typical node is of the form

OUTL	SOURCE	TIME	DEST	INL

where $OUTL$ is a pointer to the next edge in a list of outgoing edges from $SOURCE$, $SOURCE$ points to the event node which is the source node of this edge, $TIME$ is weight (time) of the edge, $DEST$ points to the event node that is the destination of the edge, and INL is a pointer to the next edge node in a list of incoming edges into $DEST$. The statement $P \leftarrow EDGE$ creates a node of this type and stores its address in P.

We further assume that there is an additional event node that serves as a list head for the list of event nodes. $HEAD$ points to this list head. The following algorithm will create the desired structure.

Algorithm *CREATE*   Given *HEAD*, the list head for a list of event nodes as previously described, along with *A* (the label of the source node for some edge), *B* (the edge's destination node label), and *LENGTH* (the edge length in time units), this algorithm inserts nodes *A* and *B* into the event node list, if they are not already present. It then creates an edge node which is subsequently inserted in the proper outgoing and incoming edge lists and updates all pointers.

1   [Initialize] Set $PA \leftarrow PB \leftarrow NULL$, $T \leftarrow HEAD$.

2   [Check node label] If $LINK(T) = NULL$, then go to step 3; otherwise set $T \leftarrow LINK(T)$. If $NAME(T) = A$, then set $PA \leftarrow T$. If $NAME(T) = B$, then set $PB \leftarrow T$. If $PA = NULL$ or $PB = NULL$, then repeat this step.

3   [Add required nodes] If $PA = NULL$, then set $PA \leftarrow NODE$, $TE(PA) \leftarrow TL(PA) \leftarrow -1$, $OUT(PA) \leftarrow IN(PA) \leftarrow LINK(PA) \leftarrow NULL$, $NAME(PA) \leftarrow A$, $LINK(T) \leftarrow PA$, $T \leftarrow PA$. If $PB = NULL$, then set $PB \leftarrow NODE$, $TE(PB) \leftarrow TL(PB) \leftarrow -1$, $OUT(PB) \leftarrow IN(PB) \leftarrow LINK(PB) \leftarrow NULL$, $NAME(PB) \leftarrow B$, $LINK(T) \leftarrow PB$.

4   [Create edge node] Set $E \leftarrow EDGE$, $SOURCE(E) \leftarrow PA$, $DEST(E) \leftarrow PB$, $TIME(E) \leftarrow LENGTH$, $OUTL(E) \leftarrow OUT(PA)$, $OUT(PA) \leftarrow E$, $INL(E) \leftarrow IN(PB)$, $IN(PB) \leftarrow E$. Exit.

Algorithm *PROCESS*   Given a linked list representation of a PERT network as formed by algorithm *CREATE*, with *HEAD* as the list head pointer, this routine first identifies *START* and *STOP*, the source and sink nodes, respectively. Then the *TE* and *TL* values are computed for each graph node. When this is completed, the node label, earliest completion time, and associated slack time are printed for each node.

[Find the source and sink nodes]:

1   [Initialize] Set $T \leftarrow HEAD$, $START \leftarrow STOP \leftarrow NULL$.

2   [Test indegrees and outdegrees] Set $T \leftarrow LINK(T)$. If $T = NULL$, then Exit. (There is a missing source or sink node.) If $OUT(T) = NULL$, then set $STOP \leftarrow T$. If $IN(T) = NULL$, then set $START \leftarrow T$, $TE(T) \leftarrow 0$. If $START = NULL$ or $STOP = NULL$, then repeat this step.

[Compute *TE* values]:

3   [Reinitialize] Set $T \leftarrow HEAD$.

4   [Unprocessed node?] Set $T \leftarrow LINK(T)$. If $T = NULL$, then go to step 3. If $TE(T) > 0$, then repeat this step; otherwise set $P \leftarrow IN(T)$.

5   [Compute *TE* value if all source *TE* values are computed] If $TE(SOURCE(P)) < 0$, then set $TE(T) \leftarrow -1$ and go to step 4; otherwise, set $TE(T) \leftarrow MAXIMUM[TE(T), TE(SOURCE(P)) + TIME(P)]$. Set $P \leftarrow INL(P)$. If $P \neq NULL$, then repeat this step. If $T = STOP$, then set $TL(T) \leftarrow TE(T)$; otherwise go to step 4.

[Compute *TL* values]:

6   [Reinitialize] Set $T \leftarrow HEAD$

7   [Unprocessed node?] Set $T \leftarrow LINK(T)$. If $T = NULL$, then go to step 6. If $TL(T) > 0$, then repeat this step; otherwise set $P \leftarrow OUT(T)$.

8   [Compute *TL* value if all destination *TL* values are computed] If

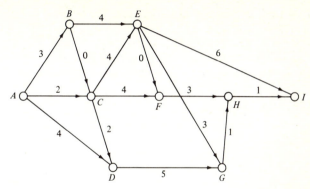

FIGURE 5-5.4

$TL(DEST(P)) < 0$, then set $TL(T) \leftarrow -1$ and go to step **7**; otherwise set $TL(T) \leftarrow MINIMUM\ NONNEGATIVE[TL(T),\ TL(DEST(P)) - TIME(P)]$. Set $P \leftarrow OUTL(P)$. If $P \neq NULL$, then repeat this step. If $T \neq START$, then go to step **7**.

[Printout results]:

9 [Output and Exit] Repeat for $T = LINK(HEAD)$, $LINK(T)$, $LINK(T)$, ... until $LINK(T) = NULL$. Output $NAME(T)$, $TE(T)$, and $TL(T) - TE(T)$. Exit.   ////

EXERCISES 5-5

1 Compute the earliest completion times and the latest allowable completion times for the nodes in the PERT network given in Fig. 5-5.4. What is the minimum length of time it will take to complete the project? What is the critical path(s)? What could be the interpretation of the edges that have a time of zero assigned to them (edges B-C and E-F)?

2 Design a data representation for processing a PERT graph based on the discussion of the representation of general graphs given at the end of Sec. 5-2.2 (i.e., list structures).

BIBLIOGRAPHY

AHO, A. V., and J. D. ULLMAN: "The Theory of Parsing, Translation, and Compiling," vol. 1, Parsing, Prentice-Hall, Inc., Englewood Cliffs, N. J., 1972.

BERZTISS, A. T.: "Data Structures: Theory and Practice," Academic Press, Inc., New York, 1971.

EVEN, SHIMON: "Algorithmic Combinatorics," The Macmillan Company, New York, 1973.

FOSTER, J. M.: "Automatic Syntactic Analysis," American Elsevier Publishing Company, Inc., New York, 1970.

GRIES, D. E.: "Compiler Construction for Digital Computers," John Wiley & Sons, Inc., New York, 1971.

HARARY, F., R. Z. NORMAN, and D. CARTWRIGHT: "Structural Models: An Introduction to the Theory of Directed Graphs," John Wiley & Sons, Inc., New York, 1965.

HOPGOOD, F. R. A.: "Compiling Techniques," American Elsevier Publishing Company, Inc., New York, 1969.

KNUTH, D. E.: "The Art of Computer Programming," vol. 1, Fundamental Algorithms, 2d ed., Addison-Wesley Publishing Company, Inc., Reading, Mass., 1973.

KORFHAGE, R. R.: "Discrete Computational Structures," Academic Press, Inc., New York, 1974.

LEVIN, RICHARD I., and CHARLES A. KIRKPATRICK: "Planning and Control with PERT/CPM," McGraw-Hill Book Company, New York, 1966.

ORE, O.: "Theory of Graphs," American Mathematical Society, Providence, R. I., 1962.

PREPARATA, F. P., and R. T. YEH: "Introduction to Discrete Structures," Addison-Wesley Publishing Company, Inc., Reading, Mass., 1973.

TORNG, H. C.: "Switching Circuits: Theory and Logic Design," Addison-Wesley Publishing Company, Inc., Reading, Mass., 1972.

TREMBLAY, J. P., and P. G. SORENSON: "An Introduction to Data Structures with Applications," Lecture notes, University of Saskatchewan, Saskatoon, 1974. (To be published by the McGraw-Hill Book Company, New York, 1976.)

WELLS, M. B.: "Elements of Combinatorial Computing," Pergamon Press, Oxford, 1971.

INTRODUCTION TO COMPUTABILITY THEORY

INTRODUCTION

In this chapter we shall briefly introduce a general model for performing computations—a Turing machine. This machine has an infinite memory, but the size of this memory for any terminating computation must be finite. The operation of a Turing machine is controlled by a finite device similar to the finite-state machine discussed in Sec. 4-6.2.

The Turing machine model is important because the set of computations that can be realized with such a model is believed to include all computations that any machine can perform. In the last section of the chapter, it will be shown that Turing machines can compute any partial recursive function.

Since the more complex models of computation are controlled by a finite-state machine, this class of machines is discussed in Sec. 6-1. Recall that in Sec. 3-3 we defined four classes of grammars for generating languages. Alternatively, one can define four classes of machines which can recognize languages. The finite-state acceptor is the simplest kind of recognizer that one can have. It is shown that the class of languages that can be recognized by a finite-state acceptor is precisely the set of those languages which are generated by T_3 (regular) grammars.

6-1 FINITE-STATE ACCEPTORS AND REGULAR GRAMMARS

In Sec. 3-3, a generating device called a grammar was introduced as a means of specifying infinite languages. The importance of a grammar is twofold: first, it is a finite device, and second, the rules of the grammar impose structure on the strings of the language. Another method of finitely specifying languages is by using an acceptor or recognizer. An *acceptor* is a machine which can identify strings of a language. It is possible to define four classes of acceptors which correspond, in terms of specifying languages, to the four types of grammars introduced in Sec. 3-3. In this section we are concerned with the simplest type of acceptor—the finite-state acceptor (automaton). This class of machine is computationally equivalent to the family of finite-state machines introduced in Sec. 4-6. Finite-state machines are important, since the more complex machines, such as the Turing machine which is discussed in Sec. 6-2, are controlled by a finite-state machine.

It will be shown that the family of languages that can be generated by T_3 (regular) grammars contains precisely those languages that can be accepted by finite automata. In order to accomplish this task, a distinction will have to be made between a deterministic and a nondeterministic finite automaton. They are, however, equivalent in that they accept the same family of languages.

In Secs. 3-3 and 5-3 the membership question, i.e., whether a given string was in the language defined by a grammar, was discussed. We will now look at this question and concern ourselves with the following problems throughout the remainder of the section:

1 Given a regular grammar which generates a language, obtain a finite automaton which will accept exactly that language.

2 Conversely, given a machine which accepts a particular language, obtain a grammar which generates exactly this language.

Before attempting to solve these problems, we proceed to give a definition of a finite-state acceptor.

Definition 6-1.1 A *finite-state acceptor* or *finite automaton* M is a 5-tuple $\langle I, Q, q_0, \delta, F \rangle$, where I is a finite set of input symbols called the *input alphabet*, Q is a finite set of *states*, $q_0 \in Q$ is the *initial state* of the machine, δ is a mapping of $Q \times I$ into Q, and $F \subseteq Q$ is a set of *final states*.

This machine is similar to the finite-state machine which was defined in Sec. 4-6.2 except that the finite automaton does not have an output alphabet; instead it has a set of acceptance states, F. The acceptor reads an input tape from left to right in a sequential manner. The finite automaton is, initially, in state q_0. The interpretation of $\delta(p, a) = q$, where $p, q \in Q$ and $a \in I$, is that M, in state p, scans the tape symbol a, moves its read head one position to the right, and enters state q.

As was done in Sec. 4-6.2, the domain of δ can be extended from $Q \times I$ to $Q \times I^*$ by defining a new mapping $\hat{\delta}$ as

$$\hat{\delta}(q, \Lambda) = q$$
$$\hat{\delta}(q, xa) = \delta(\hat{\delta}(q, x), a) \qquad \text{for every } x \in I^* \text{ and } a \in I$$

Since there is no chance of confusion, the function $\hat{\delta}$ will be simply written as δ in the remaining pages.

A string y is *accepted* by a finite automaton M if $\delta(q_0, y) = p$ for some $p \in F$. The set of all such y's accepted by M is called the *language accepted* by M and is denoted by $T(M)$, that is,

$$T(M) = \{y \mid \delta(q_0, y) \in F\}$$

The language accepted by a finite automaton is often called a *regular* language.

As an example, consider a finite-state acceptor that will accept the set of natural numbers x which are divisible by 3. A machine M to accomplish this recognition is $M = \langle I, Q, q_0, \delta, F \rangle$, where $I = \{0, 1, 2, 3, 4, 5, 6, 7, 8, 9\}$, $Q = \{q_0, q_1, q_2\}$, $F = \{q_0\}$, and δ is defined as

$$\delta(q_0, a) = q_0 \qquad \delta(q_1, a) = q_1 \qquad \delta(q_2, a) = q_2 \qquad \text{for } a \in \{0, 3, 6, 9\}$$
$$\delta(q_0, b) = q_1 \qquad \delta(q_1, b) = q_2 \qquad \delta(q_2, b) = q_0 \qquad \text{for } b \in \{1, 4, 7\}$$
$$\delta(q_0, c) = q_2 \qquad \delta(q_1, c) = q_0 \qquad \delta(q_2, c) = q_1 \qquad \text{for } c \in \{2, 5, 8\}$$

The transition diagram for this machine is given in Fig. 6-1.1 where the final state q_0 is denoted by a double circle. The initial state is marked by an arrow. Observe that the edges have multiple labels. For example, the edge labeled "1, 4, 7" which originates at state q_0 and terminates at state q_1 is interpreted to mean that if the acceptor is in state q_0, then on scanning 1, or 4, or 7, it will enter state q_1. The other labeled edges can be interpreted in a similar manner.

Assuming an input string of 150, the computation

$$\delta(q_0, 150) = \delta(\delta(\delta(q_0, 1), 5), 0) = \delta(\delta(q_1, 5), 0)$$
$$= \delta(q_0, 0) = q_0 \quad (\text{accept})$$

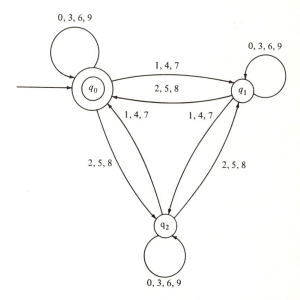

FIGURE 6-1.1 An example of a finite-state acceptor.

yields an acceptance state, while the string 136 is rejected since

$$\delta(q_0, 136) = \delta(\delta(\delta(q_0, 1), 3), 6) = \delta(\delta(q_1, 3), 6)$$

$$= \delta(q_1, 6) = q_1 \quad \text{(reject state)}$$

In this example let us define a relation R on the set I^* such that $x\,R\,y$ iff $\delta(q_0, x) = \delta(q_0, y)$. It is obvious that this relation is an equivalence relation. Therefore, R partitions the set I^* into three equivalence classes corresponding to the three states of the acceptor. The equivalence class associated with the final state is denoted by $[q_0]$ and consists of all natural numbers which are divisible by 3. A simple characterization can be given for the sets $[q_1]$ and $[q_2]$. Furthermore, if $x\,R\,y$, then we have for some $z \in I^*$ that $xz\,R\,yz$, since

$$\delta(q_0, xz) = \delta(\delta(q_0, x), z) = \delta(\delta(q_0, y), z) = \delta(q_0, yz)$$

It will be shown that the equivalence relation R will permit an association to be made between the states of an acceptor and the nonterminals of the grammar, providing that the grammar is derived in some way from the acceptor.

A precise form of the second recognition problem mentioned earlier will now be given. Assume that a finite automaton M, which accepts a language $T(M)$, is given. The input alphabet of this machine is the set V_T (the terminal alphabet of the language). We shall derive from this acceptor a grammar G such that $L(G) = T(M)$. That is, the sentences generated by the grammar are precisely those which cause M to reach an accepting state if it starts in its initial state.

The algorithm for finding the productions of a regular grammar which is equivalent to a given finite-state acceptor is as follows:
For an acceptor $M = \langle V_T, Q, q_0, \delta, F \rangle$,

1   If $\delta(q_i, a_{ij}) = q_j$, then construct the production $A_i \rightarrow a_{ij}A_j$.
2   If $q_j \in F$, then include the production $A_i \rightarrow a_{ij}$ for all i.

This simple procedure generates all rules of the required grammar. Observe that the rules thus obtained are indeed T_3 rules and also that the start symbol of the grammar is the initial state of the machine. We have essentially formed rewriting rules which are similar to the states of the machine.

The regular grammar obtained from Fig. 6-1.1 by using the algorithm is $G = \langle V_N, V_T, S, \Phi \rangle$, where $V_T = \{0, 1, 2, 3, 4, 5, 6, 7, 8, 9\}$, $V_N = \{A_0, A_1, A_2\}$, $S = A_0$, and Φ is the set

$$\{A_0 \rightarrow 1A_1, \quad A_1 \rightarrow 2A_0, \quad A_2 \rightarrow 1A_0,$$
$$A_0 \rightarrow 4A_1, \quad A_1 \rightarrow 5A_0, \quad A_2 \rightarrow 4A_0,$$
$$A_0 \rightarrow 7A_1, \quad A_1 \rightarrow 8A_0, \quad A_2 \rightarrow 7A_0,$$
$$A_0 \rightarrow 0A_0, \quad A_1 \rightarrow 0A_1, \quad A_2 \rightarrow 0A_2,$$
$$A_0 \rightarrow 3A_0, \quad A_1 \rightarrow 3A_1, \quad A_2 \rightarrow 3A_2,$$
$$A_0 \rightarrow 6A_0, \quad A_1 \rightarrow 6A_1, \quad A_2 \rightarrow 6A_2,$$
$$A_0 \rightarrow 9A_0, \quad A_1 \rightarrow 9A_1, \quad A_2 \rightarrow 9A_2,$$
$$A_0 \rightarrow 2A_2, \quad A_1 \rightarrow 1A_2, \quad A_2 \rightarrow 2A_1,$$

Table 6-1.1

Input symbol	Present state	Sentential form
		A_0
1	q_0	$1A_1$
5	q_1	$15A_0$
0	q_0	$150A_0$
3	q_0	$1503A_0$
6	q_0	$15036A_0$
3	q_0	150363
	q_0	

$$A_0 \rightarrow 5A_2, \quad A_1 \rightarrow 4A_2, \quad A_2 \rightarrow 5A_1,$$
$$A_0 \rightarrow 8A_2, \quad A_1 \rightarrow 7A_2, \quad A_3 \rightarrow 8A_1,$$
$$A_0 \rightarrow 0, \quad A_1 \rightarrow 2, \quad A_2 \rightarrow 1,$$
$$A_0 \rightarrow 3, \quad A_1 \rightarrow 5, \quad A_2 \rightarrow 4,$$
$$A_0 \rightarrow 6, \quad A_1 \rightarrow 8, \quad A_2 \rightarrow 7,$$
$$A_0 \rightarrow 9\}$$

The nonterminals A_0, A_1, and A_2 of G correspond to the state symbols q_0, q_1, and q_2 respectively. Also, the start state of the grammar A_0 corresponds to the initial state q_0 of the machine. Table 6-1.1 illustrates the relationship between the operation of the acceptor and the derivation for the string 150363, which is a sentence in the language.

Assume that we wish to formulate the converse recognition problem. That is, given a grammar G, we want to obtain a machine M which has an input alphabet V_T (the same terminal alphabet as the grammar). Whenever a sentence is in $L(G)$ and the machine is started in its initial state, the machine should accept this sentence; otherwise, the machine should reject it.

A natural approach to solving this problem is to try to reverse the procedure given earlier. For example, if the grammar contains the rule $A_i \rightarrow aA_j$, then we could define $\delta(q_i, a) = q_j$. However, assume that the grammar also contains a rule $A_i \rightarrow aA_i$. We should also have a transition $\delta(q_i, a) = q_i$ with input a. If the machine is in state q_i and the input symbol a is read, it can either stay in q_i or enter a new state q_j; consequently there are two possible moves. This machine is nondeterministic. The machine that was defined in Definition 6-1.1 was deterministic; i.e., at each step in the acceptor's operation the input symbol and the current state uniquely determined the next state by using the δ mapping. This property was preserved for all moves made by the finite automaton. We shall therefore define a nondeterministic finite automaton and show that the class of languages accepted by such machines is exactly the same as that accepted by deterministic finite-state acceptors.

Definition 6-1.2 A *nondeterministic finite automaton* (acceptor) M is a 5-tuple $\langle I, Q, q_0, \delta, F \rangle$, where Q is a finite set of states, I is a finite *input alphabet*, $q_0 \in Q$ is the *initial state*, δ is a mapping of $Q \times I$ into subsets of Q, and $F \subseteq Q$ is the set of *final states*.

An important distinction between a deterministic and a nondeterministic acceptor should be made. In the case of the latter, $\delta(q, a)$ is a (perhaps empty) set of states, while in the former it is a single state. The meaning of $\delta(q, a) = \{p_1, p_2, \ldots, p_n\}$ is that the nondeterministic machine, when in state q and scanning the symbol a, moves right and chooses any one of $p_1, p_2, \ldots, p_n$ as its next state.

The domain of the mapping δ can be extended to $Q \times I^*$, as done earlier, by defining

$$\hat{\delta}(q, \Lambda) = \{q\}$$

and

$$\hat{\delta}(q, xa) = \bigcup_{p \in \hat{\delta}(q,x)} \delta(p, a) \qquad \text{for each } x \in I^* \text{ and } a \in I$$

Furthermore, $\hat{\delta}$ can be extended to the domain $2^Q \times I^*$ by defining

$$\hat{\hat{\delta}}(\{p_1, p_2, \ldots, p_n\}, x) = \bigcup_{i=1}^{n} \hat{\delta}(p_i, x)$$

We will simply denote $\hat{\hat{\delta}}$ as δ in the remaining discussion. A sentence x is said to be *accepted* by the acceptor M if there exists some state in both F and $\delta(q_0, x)$. That is,

$$T(M) = \{x \mid \delta(q_0, x) \cap F \neq \varnothing\}$$

As an example of a nondeterministic finite automaton, we shall construct a machine that will accept the set of strings in $\{a, b, c\}^*$ such that the last symbol in the input string also appears earlier in the string. For example, *bab* is accepted, but *cbbca* is not. State q_0 will denote the initial state of the machine. States q_1, q_2, and q_3 are "guess" states, and the final state is q_4. A state diagram for the machine is given in Fig. 6-1.2. For δ defined by Table 6-1.2, the machine is given as

$$M = \langle \{a, b, c\}, \{q_0, q_1, q_2, q_3, q_4\}, q_0, \delta, \{q_4\} \rangle$$

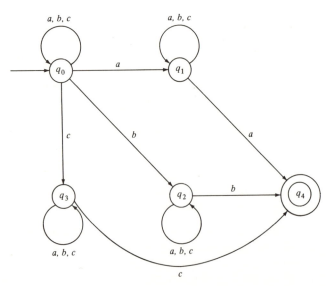

FIGURE 6-1.2   A transition diagram of a nondeterministic acceptor.

**Table 6-1.2   NEXT-STATE MAPPING FOR NONDETER-
MINISTIC ACCEPTOR**

Present state	Input symbol a	b	c
q_0	$\{q_0, q_1\}$	$\{q_0, q_2\}$	$\{q_0, q_3\}$
q_1	$\{q_1, q_4\}$	$\{q_1\}$	$\{q_1\}$
q_2	$\{q_2\}$	$\{q_2, q_4\}$	$\{q_2\}$
q_3	$\{q_3\}$	$\{q_3\}$	$\{q_3, q_4\}$
q_4	$\varnothing$	$\varnothing$	$\varnothing$

On input aca, the value of $\delta(q_0, aca)$ is obtained in the following manner:

$$\delta(q_0, aca) = \delta(\delta(q_0, a), ca) = \delta(\{q_0, q_1\}, ca)$$
$$= \delta(q_0, ca) \cup \delta(q_1, ca)$$
$$\delta(q_0, ca) = \delta(\delta(q_0, c), a) = \delta(\{q_0, q_3\}, a)$$
$$= \delta(q_0, a) \cup \delta(q_3, a)$$
$$\delta(q_0, a) = \{q_0, q_1\}$$
$$\delta(q_3, a) = \{q_3\}$$
$$\delta(q_1, ca) = \delta(\delta(q_1, c), a) = \delta(q_1, a)$$
$$\delta(q_1, a) = \{q_1, q_4\}$$

Therefore,

$$\delta(q_0, aca) = \delta(q_0, a) \cup \delta(q_3, a) \cup \delta(q_1, a)$$
$$= \{q_0, q_1\} \cup \{q_3\} \cup \{q_1, q_4\}$$
$$= \{q_0, q_1, q_3, q_4\}$$

and since $\delta(q_0, aca) \cap \{q_4\} \neq \varnothing$, the sentence aca is accepted.

We wish to emphasize that although a nondeterministic machine doesn't have unique moves, it does not contain a random device which chooses its moves. Rather than making some guess and possibly obtaining the wrong answer to the membership question for a given input string, the acceptor explores all possible move sequences that the input string could cause. If at least one of these sequences leads to an acceptance state, then the input string is in the language.

The question that naturally arises at this point is, Are nondeterministic finite-state acceptors more powerful than deterministic finite-state acceptors? The answer to this question is contained in the following theorem.

Theorem 6-1.1   Let a language L be accepted by a nondeterministic finite-state acceptor. Then there exists an equivalent deterministic finite-state acceptor that accepts L.

PROOF   We shall give a constructive proof. Let $M = \langle I, Q, q_0, \delta, F \rangle$ be a nondeterministic finite-state acceptor with n states that accepts L, that is, $T(M) = L$. Let us define a deterministic finite-state acceptor $M' = \langle I, Q', q_0', \delta', F' \rangle$ in the following way. The states of M' are all the possible nonempty subsets of the set of states for M. That is, M' has $2^n - 1$ states which will permit it to simulate all the states in which M could be at any particular point in time. The state symbols in Q' will be denoted by $[q_0]$, $[q_1]$, $\ldots,[q_{n-1}]$, $[q_0,\,q_1]$, $[q_0,\,q_2]$, $\ldots$, $[q_0,\,q_{n-1}]$, $[q_1,\,q_2]$, $\ldots$, $[q_1,\,q_{n-1}]$, $\ldots$, $[q_{n-2},\,q_{n-1}]$, $\ldots$, $[q_0,\,q_1,\,q_2]$, $\ldots$, $[q_{n-3},\,q_{n-2},\,q_{n-1}]$, $\ldots$, $[q_0,\,q_1,\,\ldots,\,q_{n-1}]$.

Both machines have the same alphabet and $q_0' = [q_0]$. We define the mapping δ' as follows:

$$\delta'([q_1,\,q_2,\,\ldots,\,q_j],\,a) = [p_1,\,p_2,\,\ldots,\,p_i]$$

if and only if

$$\delta(\{q_1,\,q_2,\,\ldots,\,q_j\},\,a) = \{p_1,\,p_2,\,\ldots,\,p_i\}$$

That is, δ', when applied to an element of Q', is evaluated by applying δ to each state q_1, q_2, $\ldots$, q_j in M and by then taking the union to yield a new set of states $\{p_1,\,p_2,\,\ldots,\,p_i\}$. This new set of states has a corresponding element $[p_1,\,p_2,\,\ldots,\,p_i]$ in Q', and this particular element is the value of $\delta'([q_1,\,q_2,\,\ldots,\,q_j],\,a)$. Also, $\delta'(q_0',\,x) \in F'$ exactly when $\delta(q_0,\,x) \cap F \neq \varnothing$, that is, $F' = \{[p_1,\,p_2,\,\ldots,\,p_k]\,|\,\{p_1,\,p_2,\,\ldots,\,p_k\} \cap F \neq \varnothing\}$. By construction it is clear that M' is deterministic.

We must now show that $T(M') = T(M)$. It will be done by showing first that $T(M') \supseteq T(M)$ and second that $T(M') \subseteq T(M)$.

1 $T(M') \supseteq T(M)$

The mapping δ' is constructed so that Q' contains all possible states of M at the next move. Therefore M' simulates all possibilities that M could explore. Also, M' will reach an acceptance state whenever there exists at least one sequence of state transitions in M which leads to a final state in that machine. Thus M' will accept any sentence accepted by M.

2 $T(M') \subseteq T(M)$

The proof is left as an exercise. ////

As an example, let $M = \langle\{a,\,b\},\,\{q_0,\,q_1,\,q_2\},\,q_0,\,\delta,\,\{q_2\}\rangle$ be a nondeterministic finite-state acceptor, where δ is given as follows:

$$\delta(q_0,\,a) = \{q_0,\,q_1\} \qquad \delta(q_0,\,b) = \{q_2\}$$
$$\delta(q_1,\,a) = \{q_1\} \qquad \delta(q_1,\,b) = \{q_0\}$$
$$\delta(q_2,\,a) = \{q_0\} \qquad \delta(q_2,\,b) = \{q_1,\,q_2\}$$

We shall construct an equivalent deterministic finite-state acceptor, $M' = \langle\{a,\,b\},\,Q',\,[q_0],\,\delta',\,F'\rangle$, which accepts $T(M)$ as follows: Q' contains all subsets of $\{q_0,\,q_1,\,q_2\}$ (except the empty set); that is, $Q' = \{[q_0],\,[q_1],\,[q_2],\,[q_0,\,q_1],\,[q_0,\,q_2],\,[q_1,\,q_2],\,[q_0,\,q_1,\,q_2]\}$. Since $\delta(q_0,\,a) = \{q_0,\,q_1\}$, then

$$\delta'([q_0],\,a) = [q_0,\,q_1]$$

Similarly,

$$\delta'([q_0],\,b) = [q_2] \qquad \delta'([q_1],\,a) = [q_1] \qquad \delta'([q_1],\,b) = [q_0]$$
$$\delta'([q_2],\,a) = [q_0] \qquad \delta'([q_2],\,b) = [q_1,\,q_2]$$

**Table 6-1.3 TRANSITION FUNCTION FOR AN
EQUIVALENT DETERMINISTIC
ACCEPTOR**

	Input symbol	
Present state	a	b
$[q_0]$	$[q_0, q_1]$	$[q_2]$
$[q_1]$	$[q_1]$	$[q_0]$
$[q_2]$	$[q_0]$	$[q_1, q_2]$
$[q_0, q_1]$	$[q_0, q_1]$	$[q_0, q_2]$
$[q_0, q_2]$	$[q_0, q_1]$	$[q_1, q_2]$
$[q_1, q_2]$	$[q_0, q_1]$	$[q_0, q_1, q_2]$
$[q_0, q_1, q_2]$	$[q_0, q_1]$	$[q_0, q_1, q_2]$

Let us now consider $\delta'([q_0, q_2], a)$. Since

$$\delta(\{q_0, q_1\}, a) = \delta(q_0, a) \cup \delta(q_1, a) = \{q_0, q_1\} \cup \{q_1\}$$
$$= \{q_0, q_1\}$$

then
$$\delta'([q_0, q_1], a) = [q_0, q_1]$$

Also, since

$$\delta(\{q_0, q_1\}, b) = \delta(q_0, b) \cup \delta(q_1, b) = \{q_0, q_2\}$$

then
$$\delta'([q_0, q_1], b) = [q_0, q_2]$$

The remainder of the mapping is easily obtained in a similar fashion and is summarized in Table 6-1.3. The set of final states for M' is given by

$$F' = \{[q_2], [q_0, q_2], [q_1, q_2], [q_0, q_1, q_2]\}$$

We are now able to obtain from a nondeterministic machine an equivalent deterministic one. We now return to the relationship between the class of languages generated by T_3 grammars and the class of languages accepted by finite automata.

Theorem 6-1.2 Let $G \langle V_N, V_T, S, \Phi \rangle$ be a T_3 grammar which generates the language $L(G)$. Then there exists a finite-state acceptor $M = \langle V_T, Q, S, \delta, F \rangle$ such that $T(M) = L(G)$.

PROOF The machine M that will be constructed is nondeterministic with $Q = V_N \cup \{X\}$, where $X \notin V_N$. The initial state of the acceptor is S (the start symbol of the grammar), and its final state is X. For each production of the grammar, construct the mapping δ in the following manner:

1 $A_j \in \delta(A_i, a)$ if there is a production $A_i \to aA_j$ in G.
2 $X \in \delta(A_i, a)$ if there is a production $A_i \to a$ in G.

The acceptor M, when processing a sentence x, simulates a derivation of x in the grammar G. We want to show that $T(M) = L(G)$. Let $x = a_1 a_2 \cdots a_m, m \geq 1$, be in the language $L(G)$. Then there exists some derivation in G such that

$$S \Rightarrow a_1 A_1 \Rightarrow \cdots \Rightarrow a_1 a_2 \cdots a_{m-1} A_{m-1} \Rightarrow a_1 a_2 \cdots a_m$$

Table 6-1.4

Present state	Input symbol	
	a	b
q_0	$\{q_0, q_1\}$	$\{q_2\}$
q_1	$\{q_0\}$	$\{q_1\}$
q_2	$\{q_1\}$	$\{q_0, q_1\}$

for a sequence of nonterminals $A_1, A_2, \ldots, A_{m-1}$. From the construction of δ, it is clear that $\delta(S, a_1)$ contains A_1, $\delta(A_1, a_2)$ contains A_2, $\ldots$, and that $\delta(A_{m-1}, a_m)$ contains X. Therefore, $x \in T(M)$ since $\delta(S, x)$ contains X and $X \in F$.

Conversely, if $x \in T(M)$, then we can easily obtain a derivation in G which simulates the acceptance of x in M, thereby concluding that $x \in L(G)$.

////

It can be shown that finite-state acceptors can be designed to accept the union, intersection, complementation, concatenation, etc., of sets. This property carries over to the regular grammar as well. That is, if L_1 and L_2 are regular languages, so are $L_1 \cup L_2$, $L_1 \cap L_2$, $\sim L_1$, $L_1 \circ L_2$, L_1^*, etc. In context-free languages, the intersection or complementation of two context-free languages is not necessarily context-free.

EXERCISES 6-1

1 Design a deterministic finite-state acceptor for sentences in $\{a, b\}$ such that every a has a b immediately to its right.
2 From the acceptor obtained in the previous problem, construct a type 3 grammar which generates that language.
3 Find a deterministic finite-state acceptor equivalent to the nondeterministic one given as

$$M = \langle \{a, b\}, \{q_0, q_1, q_2\}, q_0, \delta, \{q_2\} \rangle$$

where δ is given by Table 6-1.4.
4 Complete the proof of part 2 of Theorem 6-1.1.

6-2 TURING MACHINES AND PARTIAL RECURSIVE FUNCTIONS

In Sec. 4-6 we introduced a finite-state machine which was capable of reading an input tape from left to right and whose only memory was provided by its finite set of internal states. Such a machine could add, but other arithmetic operations such as multiplication were beyond its range. A finite-state machine turns out to be a member of one of the weakest classes of machines that can be defined.

This section deals with the most powerful type of machine, a Turing machine. Like a finite-state machine, a Turing machine has a finite set of internal states but can move left or right on a tape which contains a finite but arbitrarily large number of cells; each cell is capable of storing one character. It will be shown that a Turing machine is an extremely powerful device for carrying out an algorithm. Indeed, such a machine can compute any partial recursive function.

A modern large-scale digital computer is very close to being equivalent to a Turing machine. A computer can have several billion bits of memory, which, from a practical standpoint, approaches the memory capacity of a Turing machine.

The first part of this section is concerned with the definition of a Turing machine. This type of machine can mechanically evaluate numerical and non-numerical functions. It is shown, by construction, that such a machine can compute the zero, successor, and identity functions. Furthermore, machines are presented for performing the operations of composition, primitive recursion, and minimization, thus proving that Turing machines can compute any partial recursive function (see Sec. 2-6.1). An outline is also given of a proof which asserts that any function which can be computed by a Turing machine is partial recursive.

In Sec. 1-3 the notion of a decision problem was introduced in relation to the determination of certain properties of formulas in the statement calculus. Another very important question that is often asked, especially of certain attempted manipulations on data of almost any nature, is whether this manipulation can be performed in a purely mechanical manner.

To answer this very general question, we must first specify more precisely what is meant by performing a task in a purely mechanical manner. A more detailed characterization of manipulation of data is required. Since computing science is, at its most general level, the study of the manipulation of symbols and since computers operate in a purely mechanical way, it is fitting that we attempt to provide as our characterization a model of computation in this most general sense of symbol manipulation.

We will therefore say that some particular operation, function, etc., is *computable* if it can be represented as an object within the general model of computation.

In the mid-1930s and early 1940s Turing and Post investigated this question of computability. As models for computing devices, Turing suggested certain automata, which today are known as Turing machines. A brief description of these models will now be given. The notation used is essentially that of Post.

A Turing machine can be viewed as a simple control device together with a tape of arbitrary length. This tape is divided into cells, each of which can hold one symbol. At any instant, the machine can be in exactly one of a finite number of internal states; the control device is always aware of the present state of the machine. The control device can read one cell of the tape at a time and then take certain specified actions. It can erase the current tape symbol and print a new symbol, it can shift itself one cell to the left, or it can shift one cell to the right. The action taken by the machine is determined completely by the state of the machine and the symbol just scanned. After any one of these actions is taken, the control device then updates the current internal state. It may be the same state as the previous one, or it may be a new state. The machine repeats this cycle by scanning the cell over which it is now positioned. The process stops when the machine is in a particular state-symbol combination for which no action has been specified.

Some authors assume the tape to be infinite in length; however, all that needs to be assumed is that the tape can grow to any length required, simply by the addition of new cells to either end. Such an addition is considered to occur whenever the control unit attempts to read one cell beyond either end of the current tape.

Intuitively, a Turing machine can be represented as in Fig. 6-2.1. This machine is currently in a state q_j, and the control device is currently scanning a cell which contains the symbol s_l. The entire tape contains blanks except for the six contiguous cells containing the symbols s_i through s_n.

The actions of the machine are determined by the specification of actions for particular current state–scanned symbol pairs. Such specifications are expressed as quadruples of the form

$q_i s_j s_k q_m$ meaning that a machine in state q_i scanning symbol s_j is to replace s_j in the tape cell by the symbol s_k and enter state q_m

$q_i s_j \mathbf{R} q_m$ meaning that a machine in state q_i scanning symbol s_j is to move one cell to its right and enter state q_m

$q_i s_j \mathbf{L} q_m$ meaning the same as the previous quadruple except that the control unit moves one cell to its left

As an example, let us consider a Turing machine in which the contiguous cells contain $s_0 s_0 s_0 s_1 s_1 s_2 s_1 s_0 s_0 s_0$ and the machine is in state q_0 and scanning the leftmost s_1. This is shown by writing the tape configuration as shown in the first row of Table 6-2.1. Notice that we indicate the cell being scanned by writing the current state of the machine immediately to the left of the scanned cell. This notation is merely a convenience; the machine state does not actually occupy a cell of the tape. In the example, the machine starts in state q_0, and the quadruples of instructions are $q_0 s_1 s_2 q_0$, $q_0 s_2 \mathbf{R} q_0$, $q_0 s_0 s_3 q_1$. Table 6-2.1 shows the tape configuration and the states after each instruction. It is assumed that no action is specified when the machine is in state q_1, no matter what symbol it is scanning.

A more formal and rigorous specification of a Turing machine follows. A finite alphabet of tape symbols, $A = \{s_0, s_1, s_2, \ldots, s_n\}$, is assumed where the symbol s_0 is commonly taken to be a blank (represented by B). This symbol is assumed to be contained by all tape cells unless otherwise indicated, as well as

Table 6-2.1 TRACE OF A COMPUTATION

Apply quadruple	Instantaneous description
	s_0 s_0 s_0 q_0 s_1 s_1 s_2 s_1 s_0 s_0 s_0
$q_0 s_1 s_2 q_0$	s_0 s_0 s_0 q_0 s_2 s_1 s_2 s_1 s_0 s_0 s_0
$q_0 s_2 \mathbf{R} q_0$	s_0 s_0 s_0 s_2 q_0 s_1 s_2 s_1 s_0 s_0 s_0
$q_0 s_1 s_2 q_0$	s_0 s_0 s_0 s_2 q_0 s_2 s_2 s_1 s_0 s_0 s_0
$q_0 s_2 \mathbf{R} q_0$	s_0 s_0 s_0 s_2 s_2 q_0 s_2 s_1 s_0 s_0 s_0
$q_0 s_2 \mathbf{R} q_0$	s_0 s_0 s_0 s_2 s_2 s_2 q_0 s_1 s_0 s_0 s_0
$q_0 s_1 s_2 q_0$	s_0 s_0 s_0 s_2 s_2 s_2 q_0 s_2 s_0 s_0 s_0
$q_0 s_2 \mathbf{R} q_0$	s_0 s_0 s_0 s_2 s_2 s_2 s_2 q_0 s_0 s_0 s_0
$q_0 s_0 s_3 q_1$	s_0 s_0 s_0 s_2 s_2 s_2 s_2 q_1 s_3 s_0 s_0

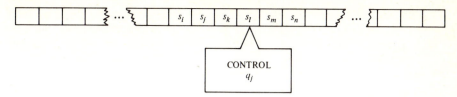

FIGURE 6-2.1 A Turing machine.

by new cells added to the end of the tape whenever the control device reaches the end of the tape. Furthermore, there is a finite set of *internal states*, $Q = \{q_0, q_1, q_2, \ldots, q_m\}$, where the state q_0 is usually taken to be the initial (start) state of the machine. An *expression* is a finite sequence of zero or more elements, each belonging to the set $A \cup Q \cup \{\mathbf{R}, \mathbf{L}\}$, and a *tape expression* is an expression containing only elements of A. The set of tape expressions will be denoted by A^*. A *quadruple* is an expression having one of the forms $q_i s_j s_k q_m$, $q_i s_j \mathbf{R} q_m$, or $q_i s_j \mathbf{L} q_m$ (i, j, k, m need not be distinct).

A *Turing machine* is defined to be the structure $T = \langle A, Q, X, P \rangle$, where A is the alphabet of symbols, Q is the set of states (with q_0 as the initial state), X is the initial tape configuration or axiom which is a tape expression such that $X \in A^*$, and P is a set of quadruples defined in such a manner that no two quadruples begin with the same state-symbol pair.

An *instantaneous description* is an expression of the form $\alpha q_i \beta$, where $\alpha \in A^*$, $\beta \in A^+$, and $q_i \in Q$. The second column of Table 6-2.1 contains a series of instantaneous descriptions. These are simply a sequence of "snapshots" of the tape contents with the machine's present state positioned just to the left of the symbol being scanned.

Each action taken by a Turing machine is considered to generate another instantaneous description (which need not differ from its immediate predecessor). The sequence of instantaneous descriptions produced provides a trace of the operation of the machine. Let us denote the elements of such a sequence of instantaneous descriptions by $w_1, w_2, w_3, \ldots$. We can now formally define on instantaneous descriptions a "yields" relation that indicates under what conditions one instantaneous description is generated from its predecessor in the sequence. This "yields" relation is somewhat analogous to the "is derivable from" relation that exists between steps in a proof in statement logic. Having available this formal definition of "yields," we are then able to define a computation—the notion we have been attempting to characterize in this discussion.

We shall say that the instantaneous description w_f yields the instantaneous description w_t for Turing machine T ($\omega_f \mapsto_T w_g$) if and only if one of the following cases hold; for tape expressions $a, b \in A^*$ and symbol B (the blank symbol),

(1)

$$w_f = a q_i s_j b \qquad w_g = a q_m s_k b \qquad \text{and} \qquad q_i s_j s_k q_m \in P$$

(2) (a)

$$w_f = a q_i s_j s_k b \qquad w_g = a s_j q_m s_k b \qquad \text{and} \qquad q_i s_j \mathbf{R} q_m \in P$$

or   (b)

$$w_f = aq_is_j \qquad w_g = as_jq_mB \qquad \text{and} \qquad q_is_j\mathbf{R}q_m \in P \text{ (a new cell containing } B \text{ is added to the right end of the tape)}$$

(3) (a)

$$w_f = as_kq_is_jb \qquad w_g = aq_ms_ks_jb \qquad \text{and} \qquad q_is_j\mathbf{L}q_m \in P$$

or   (b)

$$w_f = q_is_jb \qquad w_g = q_mBs_jb \qquad \text{and} \qquad q_is_j\mathbf{L}q_m \in P \text{ (a new cell containing } B \text{ is added to the left end of the tape)}$$

A *terminal instantaneous description* for machine T is an instantaneous description of the form aq_is_jb, where $a, b \in A^*$, and P contains no quadruples whose first two elements are q_is_j.

A *computation* (*terminal proof*) of machine T is a finite sequence of instantaneous descriptions $w_1, w_2, \ldots, w_n$ such that w_n is terminal, w_1 is q_0X (the instantaneous description formed by positioning the start state immediately to the left of the initial tape expression), and $w_i \mapsto_T w_{i+1}$ for $1 \le i < n$. Note that not all Turing machines stop on every initial tape expression. For example, a machine with the quadruple $q_is_ms_mq_i$ will go into an endless loop of instantaneous descriptions as soon as it generates for the first time the instantaneous description aq_is_mb, for $a, b \in A^*$.

There is a distinct difference between a finite-state machine and a Turing machine, with the former being basically a restriction of the latter. The tape associated with a finite-state machine is of fixed length, and it can be processed in only one direction, e.g., from left to right. Furthermore, the tape cannot be read again, and no writing on the tape is permitted. A Turing machine, on the other hand, can move either left or right on the tape, can write intermediate and final results on it, and can rescan any portion of the tape. The tape can grow to any length by creating new cells to the left or right of the ends of the existing tape. This difference essentially permits a Turing machine to have an arbitrarily large memory.

An an example, let us construct a Turing machine $T = \langle A, Q, X, P \rangle$ in which the alphabet $A = \{a, b, B\}$ with B showing a blank. The set of states is $Q = \{q_i \mid 0 \le i \le n\}$ in which n is to be determined. The initial tape configuration is $X \in A^*$. Let us assume that X is given in the form $\gamma\alpha B\beta\delta$ with $\gamma, \delta \in \{B\}^*$ and $\alpha, \beta \in (A - \{B\})^*$. In such a case, we want the machine to concatenate the strings α and β, that is, move string β across the only blank and position β adjacent to the end of string α.

Our task is to determine the set P of quadruples of the required machine which will accomplish the function. This is often done with the help of a state diagram. A state diagram is a digraph in which each node corresponds to a distinct state of the machine. A directed edge shows the present and the next state. The label on the edge shows the scanned symbol and the particular action taken. For our example, such a state diagram is given in Fig. 6-2.2.

In order to understand the development of the state diagram, it is best to consider it in steps. Our Turing machine begins in state q_0. At this stage there

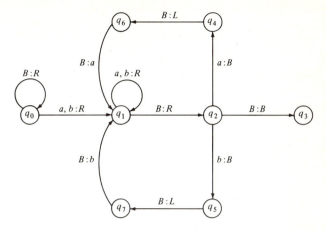

FIGURE 6-2.2   A Turing machine for concatenation.

may be some leading B's, and we want to be sure that the control gets past these blanks. This is shown by the edge B:R which returns the machine to stage q_0 and moves the control to the right as long as the blanks are encountered. As soon as any a or b is encountered, the action a,b:R is taken, and the machine enters into the state q_1. Here again, as long as the machine reads a or b, it stays in state q_1 and keeps moving right. However, if it encounters a blank, then the action taken is as shown by B:R, and the machine enters in state q_2. If another blank is encountered, then it enters state q_3 and halts, because no further action is specified. In state q_2 it may encounter the a. In this case a letter of β has been found, and it must be moved to the end of the current string α. This is done by erasing a and printing a blank in its place, thus forming a new B, and entering a state q_4. This action is shown by a:B. In state q_4, scanning a blank (the only symbol it can ever scan) causes the machine to move left and enter state q_6. The control is now positioned over the B that originally separated α and β. State q_6, on seeing a B (the only symbol it can ever see), causes an a to be printed to replace this blank, thus forming a new string α, and the machine then enters state q_1 to repeat the cycle. In a similar fashion, states q_2, q_5, and q_7 move a b from the front of β to the rear of α. The final-state diagram for the machine is given in Fig. 6-2.2.

Hence, the set of quadruples, P, is

$$\{q_0BRq_0, \quad q_1aRq_1, \quad q_2BBq_3, \quad q_4BLq_6,$$

$$q_0aRq_1, \quad q_1bRq_1, \quad q_2aBq_4, \quad q_6Baq_1,$$

$$q_0bRq_1, \quad q_1BRq_2, \quad q_2bBq_5, \quad q_5BLq_7,$$

$$q_7Bbq_1\}$$

The Turing machine that has been obtained computes the concatenation of α and β on each initial tape expression. The set of all such possible initial tape ex-

Table 6-2.2 TRACE OF A TURING MACHINE WHICH CONCATENATES

Apply quadruple	Instantaneous description	Comments
	$q_0BBabbBba$	initial instantaneous description
q_0BRq_0	$Bq_0BabbBba$	move over leading B's
q_0BRq_0	$BBq_0abbBba$	
q_0aRq_1	$BBaq_1bbBba$	found a string; move over it
q_1bRq_1	$BBabq_1bBba$	
q_1bRq_1	$BBabbq_1Bba$	
q_1BRq_2	$BBabbBq_2ba$	found the separating B
q_2bBq_5	$BBabbBq_5Ba$	found a b
q_5BLq_7	$BBabbq_7BBa$	move it left
q_7Bbq_1	$BBabbq_1bBa$	write the b
q_1bRq_1	$BBabbbq_1Ba$	pass over it
q_1BRq_2	$BBabbbBq_2a$	found the separating B
q_2aBq_4	$BBabbbBq_4B$	found an a
q_4BLq_6	$BBabbbq_6BB$	move it left
q_6Baq_1	$BBabbbq_1aB$	write the a
q_1aRq_1	$BBabbbaq_1B$	pass over it
q_1BRq_2	$BBabbbaBq_2B$	grow one extra cell after finding the separating B
q_2BBq_3	$BBabbbaBq_3B$	final configuration; machine halts

pressions is often called an *axiom schema*. A trace of the machine,

$$T = \langle \{a, b, B\}, \{q_i \mid 0 \le i \le 7\}, BBabbBba, P \rangle$$

is given in Table 6-2.2 for a particular instance of the axiom schema described.

In general, we say that some function, operation, etc., is Turing-computable if a Turing machine can be constructed which will perform the required manipulation. We therefore have given a more precise (though as yet unjustified) characterization of computability. A Turing-computable process is one for which a Turing machine exists. Observe that there is no restriction on the alphabet other than its being a finite set.

Having given this characterization, we now wish to indicate the extent of the class of operations which can be computed by Turing machines. In order to do this, however, certain additional terms must be defined.

A computation for a Turing machine has already been defined. The *resultant of X* [*Res* (X)] for a Turing machine $T = \langle A, Q, X, P \rangle$ is defined as the terminal instantaneous description of the computation. *Res* (X) is the "answer" formed by the machine with X as its input argument.

Since the extent of Turing machine applicability will be analyzed in terms of numerical functions, certain conventions regarding the representation of numerical quantities in a Turing machine are required. Because it is convenient, a tally notation is chosen to represent numbers. An inductive definition of *tally* is as follows:

1 The symbols B and 1 are tallies.
2 If α is a tally, then $B\alpha$ and $\alpha 1$ are tallies.
3 Clauses 1 and 2 generate all, and only, the tallies.

The number 0 is represented by a finite string of one or more B's. Any number $n > 0$ is represented by a string of finite length composed of zero or more B's followed by n 1s. Leading B's are therefore treated as insignificant zeros. The strings $B111$, 111, and $BBB111$ all represent the number 3. Abbreviations 1^0 and 1^n will sometimes be used to denote B and $111\cdots11$ (n times) respectively.

Further, the convention will be adopted of using marker symbols on the tape to indicate the location of each of the arguments of some function $f\langle x_1, x_2, \ldots, x_n \rangle$ whose value a Turing machine is to compute. Hence, the tape expression representing an argument n-tuple $\langle a_1, a_2, \ldots, a_n \rangle$ for the function $f\langle x_1, x_2, \ldots, x_n \rangle$ would be $1^{a_1}x_1 1^{a_2}x_2 \cdots 1^{a_n}x_n$, where $x_1, x_2, \ldots, x_n$ are marker symbols. Last, it is assumed that the value of the function, when it has been evaluated by the Turing machine computation, is to be represented by a number in tally notation placed adjacent to the marker symbol y. Consequently, *Res* (X), the terminal instantaneous description of the computation, has the location of the function value indicated by the marker y. For example, a Turing machine to compute $f\langle x_1, x_2 \rangle = x_1 + x_2$ would, for the argument $\langle 2, 3 \rangle$, begin with the axiom $X = 11x_1 111x_2 By$, and the initial instantaneous description would be $q_0 11x_1 111x_2 By$. When the computation is completed, the terminal instantaneous description would be $\gamma x_1 \delta x_2 11111 q_n y$, where q_n is a state such that no quadruple begins with $q_n y$, and where γ and δ are finite sequences of B's and 1s. (We make the latter proviso because the steps of the computation might result in the alteration of the original arguments and there is no way of knowing, in general, the nature of these possible alterations.) Observe that the placement of the state q_n is somewhat arbitrary. It is convenient to show it located as positioned over the y, but, as a matter of fact, the terminal instantaneous description could have state q_n in almost any location as long as the halting criterion is fulfilled. Finally, the relative order of the tally-x_i pairs and the tally-y pair among themselves does not really matter. A particular tally can always be identified by the x_i marker or y marker associated with it.

We shall denote the *value of a computation* of a Turing machine by $\langle Res(X) \rangle$. We define it as the number represented by the tally found immediately to the left of the marker y in the tape expression that is formed by deleting the state symbol from the terminal instantaneous description, $Res(X)$, produced by the operation of the machine on the axiom X. More simply, $\langle Res(X) \rangle$ is the number corresponding to the tally found on the tape to the left of y when the Turing machine finally halts. In the example for addition, given X as $11x_1 111x_2 By$ and the appropriate Turing machine, $\langle Res(X) \rangle$ is 5.

We can associate with machine T, for any n, an n-ary partial function of integers $\psi_T^n \langle x_1, x_2, \ldots, x_n \rangle$, such that if there exists a computation $w_1, w_2, \ldots, w_k$ where $w_1 = q_0 X$ for $X = 1^{a_1}x_1 1^{a_2}x_2 \cdots 1^{a_n}x_n By$ and $w_k = Res(X)$, then $\psi_T^n \langle a_1, a_2, \ldots, a_n \rangle = \langle Res(X) \rangle$. Otherwise there is no computation by machine T for X (because T never halts), and $\psi_T^n \langle a_1, a_2, \ldots, a_n \rangle$ is undefined. The function ψ_T^n is said to be computed by T.

In general, a partial function $f\langle x_1, x_2, \ldots, x_n \rangle$ is *partially computable* if and only if there exists a Turing machine T which computes it; that is, f is partially computable if and only if there exists some T such that $f = \psi_T^n$. If $\psi_T^n \langle x_1, x_2, \ldots, x_n \rangle$ is defined for all n-tuples, then it is a total function and f is *computable*.

Although the definition of a computable function has been based on numerically oriented notions, it should be made clear that such notions also apply to the processing of nonnumeric information by Turing machines. Actually, B, 1, and the markers are only symbols which are manipulated.

It is not obvious that nonnumeric processing can be performed by a numeric-type Turing machine. If a one-one correspondence between sequences of symbols over a nonnumeric alphabet and the tally strings can be obtained, then nonnumeric information can be manipulated by performing numeric operations on its numerical equivalent. A numeric machine can, in fact, be constructed which is equivalent to a machine that manipulates nonnumeric data.

For example, the alphabet $\{a, b, B\}$ in the concatenation example discussed earlier can be first converted to the alphabet $\{1, 2, B\}$. The strings α and β then become strings over the set $\{1, 2\}$. Such strings can be treated as numeric quantities expressed in dyadic notation (see Sec. 2-5.2) since there is a one-to-one correspondence between dyadic numbers and the natural numbers. Hence, each of α and β is associated with a particular natural number. This integer can in turn be expressed in the tally alphabet $\{1, B\}$ as described previously. The empty string has no dyadic representation, but it can be represented by zero. Leading B's on the tape were not considered to be significant in the example, but the number of separating B's was. However, they were significant only because two consecutive blanks were used to indicate the end of a string (or the nonexistence of a string). This function is now performed by the marker symbols following the arguments, and so the separating blanks can also be ignored.

Under this transformation, the axiom $X = BBabbBba$ in the example would first be written as $X = BB122B21$. From this, it is seen that $\alpha = 122$ and $\beta = 21$ in dyadic notation. Hence, α corresponds to the integer 10, and β to the integer 5. The axiom for a numerically oriented machine becomes $X = 1^{10}x_1 1^5 x_2 By$. The result, $\alpha\beta$, is 12221 in dyadic notation, corresponding to the integer 45. Hence, when the machine halts, the tally 1^{45} will be immediately to the left of the marker y.

Naturally, the quadruples of this machine will be different than those of the original machine; in addition, the workings of the new machine would be made more complex because of bookkeeping details. In general, for example, the arguments would have to be decoded with $1^{10}x_1$ giving rise to a decoded sequence $1B11B11Bx_1'$ and 1^5x_2 forming $11B1Bx_2'$. These decoded sequences have markers x_1' and x_2'; either these are new markers (if the original arguments are to be preserved intact) or else they are x_1 and x_2 (if the decoding is done "in place"). Also, the recognition of "symbols" would be more complex. Instead of recognizing an a or b, the machine would have to recognize a sequence $1B$ or $11B$. However, the important point is that all this additional bookkeeping can be done mechanically. Decoding and encoding can be done by what is essentially a counting-type operation; recognition can also be performed quite readily. However, an encoded sequence such as $1B$ or $11B$ will not be recognized until the second (or third) symbol is encountered, rather than the first.

In general, a symbolic-type Turing machine which manipulates an axiom formed of strings $\alpha_1, \alpha_2, \ldots, \alpha_k$, separated by B's on an alphabet $A = \{s_0, s_1, s_2, \ldots, s_n\}$, with $s_0 = B$, can be reformulated into an equivalent numeric-type machine. The alphabet for this new machine is $A' = \{1, B, x_1, x_2, \ldots, x_k, y,$

x_1', x_2', ..., x_k'} with axiom $X' = 1^{a_1}x_1 1^{a_2}x_2 \cdots 1^{a_k}x_k By$, where a_i is the natural number associated with α_i' and α_i' is an n-adic number which is formed from α_i by replacing s_j by the numeral j. If the separating B's between the α_i are significant, then the entire axiom can be rewritten as an $(n + 1)$-adic number by replacing B $[= s_0]$ by the numeral $n + 1$ and replacing s_j, for $j > 0$, by the numeral j. The new axiom would then be $X' = 1^{a_1}x_1 By$, for a_1 being the integer associated with this $(n + 1)$-adic number.

The previous discussion was not intended to be any sort of rigorous proof that symbolic manipulations can be simulated by Turing machines which accept arguments that are numeric. However, it was intended to argue this case, and thereby to provide justification for our claim that by restricting ourselves to numeric-type Turing machines, we are still, in effect, considering all Turing machines and all processes computable by such machines.

Our ultimate goal is to characterize what is intuitively meant by a computable process. To this end, having defined a computable process as one computed by some Turing machine, we wish to investigate the range of applications of such machines. This will be done by examining the class of numeric partial functions, ψ_{T^n}, which are associated with Turing machines and are therefore partially computable.

The result that we aim to establish is that the set of partial recursive functions is the same as the set of partially computable functions. Recall that in Sec. 2-6.1, the primitive recursive, recursive, and partial recursive functions were defined. It was shown that such functions were constructed by applying a finite number of times the operations of primitive recursion, composition, and minimization to the initial functions or to functions already constructed by these operations from the initial functions. To establish our result we must show that:

1 Every partial recursive function is a partially computable function (i.e., every partial recursive function is ψ_{T^n} for some T).

2 Every partially computable function is partial recursive (i.e., each ψ_{T^n} is partial recursive).

We will show (1) by constructing Turing machines (i.e., giving functions ψ_{T^n}) that will compute the three initial functions, and by showing that the composition, primitive recursion, and minimization operations can also be performed by Turing machines. For (2) we will only provide a sketch of the outline of a proof citing sources in the literature for the details. In the following discussion, it is assumed that these machines are used properly, i.e., that input arguments are of the form specified as the axiom for each machine.

(**a**)   The zero function Z, defined as $Z(a_1) = 0$ for all $a_1 \geq 0$.

Let $A_Z = \{B, 1, x_1, y\}$, $Q_Z = \{q_0, q_1\}$, $X_Z = 1^{a_1}x_1 By$, and P_Z be the set of quadruples $\{q_0\bar{x}_1 Rq_0, q_0 x_1 x_1 q_1\}$, where the notation $q_i \bar{s}_j Dq_m$ for $D \in \{R, L\} \cup A_Z$ stands for the collection of quadruples $\{q_i s_p Dq_m \mid s_p \in A_Z \text{ and } s_p \neq s_j\}$. Clearly, this machine $T_Z = \langle A_Z, Q_Z, X_Z, P_Z \rangle$ will always halt leaving its input unchanged, and the tally in the y area (namely, $B = 1^0$) is the tally form for 0. Hence, $Z(a_1) = \langle Res(X_Z) \rangle = \psi_{T_Z}^1(a_1)$. Z is a computable function because T_Z always halts.

(**b**) The successor function S, defined as $S(a_1) = a_1 + 1$ for all $a_1 \geq 0$.

Let $T_S = \langle A_S, Q_S, X_S, P_S \rangle$, where $A_S = \{B, 1, x_1, y\}$, $Q_S = \{q_i \mid 0 \leq i \leq 9\}$, $X_S = 1^{a_1}x_1By$, and P_S is the set

$$\{q_0BRq_0, \quad q_21Rq_2, \quad q_41Lq_4, \quad q_6yLq_7,$$
$$q_01Bq_1, \quad q_2Byq_3, \quad q_4B1q_5, \quad q_71Lq_7,$$
$$q_0x_1Rq_6, \quad q_3\bar{x}_1Lq_3, \quad q_51Rq_0, \quad q_7B1q_8,$$
$$q_1\bar{y}Rq_1, \quad q_3x_1Lq_4, \quad q_6\bar{y}Rq_6, \quad q_8\bar{x}_1Lq_8,$$
$$q_1y1q_2, \qquad\qquad\qquad\qquad\qquad q_8x_1x_1q_9\}$$

The tracing of machine T_S for a few examples should make it clear that T_S will always halt in the configuration $1^{a_1}q_9x_11^{a_1+1}y$. Hence $S(a_1) = \langle Res(X_S) \rangle = \psi_{T_S}^1(a_1)$ and S is computable since the machine always halts.

(**c**) The projection function $U_i{}^n$, defined as $U_i{}^n \langle a_1, a_2, \ldots, a_i, \ldots, a_n \rangle = a_i$ for all n-tuples over N^n.

Let $T_U = \langle A_U, Q_U, X_U, P_U \rangle$, where $A_U = \{B, 1, x_1, x_2, \ldots, x_n, y\}$, $Q_U = \{q_i \mid 0 \leq i \leq 8\}$, $X_U = 1^{a_1}x_11^{a_2}x_2 \cdots 1^{a_i}x_i \cdots 1^{a_n}x_nBy$, and P_U is the set

$$\{q_0\bar{x}_iRq_0, \quad q_11Bq_2, \quad q_31Rq_3, \quad q_4x_iLq_5, \quad q_61Lq_7,$$
$$q_0x_iLq_1, \quad q_2\bar{y}Rq_2, \quad q_3Byq_4, \quad q_51Lq_5, \quad q_71Bq_2,$$
$$q_1BBq_8, \quad q_2y1q_3, \quad q_4\bar{x}_iLq_4, \quad q_5B1q_6, \quad q_7\bar{1}Rq_8\}$$

Again, working through several examples should verify that T_U will always halt in one of the following configurations, with the input arguments unchanged in value:

$$q_81^{a_1}x_1 \cdots x_nBy \qquad\qquad \text{if } i = 1 \text{ and } a_i = 0$$
$$Bq_81^{a_1}x_1 \cdots x_nB1^{a_1}y \qquad \text{if } i = 1 \text{ and } a_i \neq 0$$
$$1^{a_1}x_1 \cdots x_{i-1}q_81^{a_i}x_i \cdots x_nB1^{a_i}y \qquad \text{if } i \neq 1 \text{ and } a_i \neq 0$$
$$1^{a_1}x_1 \cdots x_{i-1}q_81^{a_i}x_i \cdots x_nBy \qquad \text{if } i \neq 1 \text{ and } a_i = 0$$

In all cases, the tally in the y area is the correct value. Therefore,

$$U_i{}^n \langle a_1, a_2, \ldots, a_n \rangle = \langle Res(X_U) \rangle = \psi_{T_U}^n \langle a_1, a_2, \ldots, a_n \rangle.$$

$U_i{}^n$ is a computable function because T_U always halts.

We have now established that the three initial partial recursive functions are computable. Hence, they are partially computable. Recall that the set of partial recursive functions is generated by applying the operations of composition, primitive recursion, and minimization to partial recursive functions. In order to conclude the proof of (1), it must be shown that when applied to partially computable functions, these operations yield only partially computable functions. Consequently, by an inductive argument, every partial recursive function is partially computable.

It thus remains to show that the operations of composition, primitive recursion, and minimization yield partially computable functions when applied to partially computable functions as arguments. We will do this by indicating how to construct Turing machines that will perform (i.e., simulate) these operations. The task of construction will be simplified if we ensure that such simulating machines have certain features that are possessed by the machines that compute the initial functions. These features are:

1 The original input tape expression for the arguments is preserved intact when the machine halts (i.e., the input arguments are returned unchanged).

2 On termination, the scanned symbol is one of the original input symbols (i.e., the control is no further to the left than the first symbol of the first argument and no further to the right than the last argument marker, say x_n).

3 Though the axioms were presumed to be written in such a manner that the input tallies had no leading B's, the quadruple sets were formulated in a way that permits the function to be computed correctly even if the input tallies do have leading B's.

4 The quadruple sets are written in such a way that copying actions all work by searching for a specific marker symbol (and thus, extraneous markers can be present without affecting the computation).

5 Halting occurs when the machine enters the highest numbered state and no quadruple begins with this state.

The reason for proceeding in this manner is simple—we wish to impose a certain uniformity of effect on the computations of any machine. We know that the arguments of composition, primitive recursion, or minimization can themselves be compositions, primitive recursions, or minimizations. We wish to be able to proceed with the knowledge that when such arguments are presented to a function and the computation halts, then the control is in the highest numbered state and no action is defined for that state. Furthermore, the result is directly to the right of the unaltered input arguments, the control is located somewhere within this input tape expression, leading blanks on arguments (as is possible when they are intermediate computed values) have no effect, and extraneous markers (as can be present in intermediate computations) have no effect.

We now turn to the construction of the machines that simulate the operations of composition, primitive recursion, and minimization. For composition, we give both a general sketch of the machine's actions and a detailed construction of the machine. For the other two operations, only the general sketch will be given. The details of construction are very similar to that of composition. For convenience, we assume that the argument markers appear on the input tape in the order x_1, x_2, x_3, $\ldots$. This will simplify the bookkeeping details of the simulation.

(*d*) $f\langle a_1, a_2, \ldots, a_n \rangle$ is partially computable for $f\langle a_1, a_2, \ldots, a_n \rangle$ being defined by composition as

$$h[g_1\langle a_1, a_2, \ldots, a_n \rangle, g_2\langle a_1, a_2, \ldots, a_n \rangle, \ldots, g_m\langle a_1, a_2, \ldots, a_n \rangle]$$

Note that $g_i\langle a_1, a_2, \ldots, a_n \rangle$ (for $1 \leq i \leq m$), denoted by b_i, is partially computable and $h\langle b_1, b_2, \ldots, b_m \rangle$, denoted by c, is also partially computable.

Since $g_1, g_2, \ldots, g_m$ and h are all partially computable, there must exist Turing machines $T_1, T_2, \ldots, T_{m+1}$ which compute them as the functions $\psi_{T_1}^n$, $\psi_{T_2}^n, \ldots, \psi_{T_m}^n, \psi_{T_{m+1}}^m$. That is to say,

$$T_i = \langle \{1, B, x_1, x_2, \ldots, x_n, y\}, \{q_j \mid 0 \leq j \leq r_i\}, X, \text{and } P_i \text{ for } 1 \leq i \leq m \rangle$$

$X = 1^{a_1}x_1 1^{a_2}x_2 \cdots 1^{a_n}x_n By$. Note that machine T_i has $r_i + 1$ states. Since $b_i = g_i\langle a_1, a_2, \ldots, a_n \rangle = \langle Res(X) \rangle$ of $\psi_{T_i}^n$, we can now define machine T_{m+1} consisting of $r_{m+1} + 1$ states as

$$T_{m+1} = \langle \{1, B, x_1', x_2', \ldots, x_m', y\}, \{q_j \mid 0 \leq j \leq r_{m+1}\}, X', P_{m+1}\rangle$$

where $X' = 1^{b_1}x_1' 1^{b_2}x_2' \cdots 1^{b_m}x_m' By$ and $c = h\langle b_1, b_2, \ldots, b_m \rangle = \langle Res(X') \rangle$ of $\psi_{T_{m+1}}^m$. Seeing this, it should be clear that machine $T_{m+2}(= T_C)$, which will perform the composition operation, acts as follows:

(1) First, the actions of T_1 for input X are performed yielding 1^{b_1} in the y area. Then, instead of halting, machine T_{m+2} changes this y marker to x_1' and adds a new tape sequence By to the right of x_1'. Control is repositioned to the beginning of axiom X (which is unaltered).

(2) The actions of step 1 are then repeated for machines $T_2, T_3, \ldots, T_{m-1}$.

(3) The actions of machine T_m for input X are performed yielding 1^{b_m} in the y area. T_{m+2} then changes the y marker to x_m' and adds a new tape sequence By to the right of x_m'. Control is then positioned to the beginning of axiom X' (between the x_n and x_1' markers).

(4) The actions of machine T_{m+1} for input X' are performed to yield 1^c in the y area.

(5) T_{m+2} then erases all the b_i tallies and their associated x_i' markers, moves the c tally and its y marker adjacent to the x_n marker, repositions the control to x_n, and finally halts.

Various stages in the development of the final tape expression can be seen by tracing the tape contents through these steps as is done in Table 6-2.3. An arrow marks the position of the control. It should be noted that T_{m+2} does possess the features we were interested in preserving; namely, at termination, the scanned symbol is one of the original input symbols, the input arguments are returned unaltered, and leading blanks on arguments and extraneous markers have had no effect. It is merely a matter of proper quadruple design and numbering of states to ensure that T_{m+2} halts in its highest state with no action defined for it.

We now turn to the detailed construction of machine T_{m+2} to compute the composition of functions. We will first have to build into it all the machines

Table 6-2.3

Phase	Tape contents
Start	$BB1^{a_1}x_1 1^{a_2}x_2 \cdots 1^{a_n}x_n By$ $\uparrow$
after step (1) 1 time	$BB1^{a_1}x_1 1^{a_2}x_2 \cdots 1^{a_n}x_n 1^{b_1}x_1' By$ $\uparrow$
after step (2) [i.e. step (1) $m-1$ times]	$BB1^{a_1}x_1 1^{a_2}x_2 \cdots 1^{a_n}x_n 1^{b_1}x_1' 1^{b_2}x_2' \cdots 1^{b_{m-1}}x_{m-1}' By$ $\uparrow$
after step (3)	$BB1^{a_1}x_1 1^{a_2}x_2 \cdots 1^{a_n}x_n 1^{b_1}x_1' 1^{b_2}x_2' \cdots 1^{b_{m-1}}x_{m-1}' 1^{b_m}x_m' By$ $\uparrow$
after step (4)	$BB1^{a_1}x_1 1^{a_2}x_2 \cdots 1^{a_n}x_n 1^{b_1}x_1' 1^{b_2}x_2' \cdots 1^{b_{m-1}}x_{m-1}' 1^{b_m}x_m' 1^c y$ $\uparrow$
after step (5)	$BB1^{a_1}x_1 1^{a_2}x_2 \cdots 1^{a_n}x_n 1^c y$ $\uparrow$

$T_1, T_2, \ldots, T_m, T_{m+1}$, and then add the additional capability to do the required copying and bookkeeping actions. This first task can be done readily enough. The alphabet A_{m+2} simply becomes the union of the symbols in the two axioms X and X'. The axiom for T_{m+2} is simply X. A proper subset of the state set S_{m+2} is formed by taking the union of the state sets of $T_1, T_2, \ldots, T_{m+1}$, where each state q_j is rewritten as q_j^i if it came from the machine, T_i. The purpose of this superscript is to identify each state as belonging to a particular machine. The balance of S_{m+2} handles bookkeeping and will be given below. A proper subset of the quadruple set P_{m+2} is formed by taking the union of the quadruple sets for machines $T_1, T_2, \ldots, T_{m+1}$, with each quadruple being rewritten to reference states q_j^i rather than q_j for each machine T_i. Again, this modification is done to make possible the identification of quadruples as belonging to specific machines. The rest of P_{m+2} will be constructed below when we construct the actions that take care of the bookkeeping.

Tasks that are specific to T_{m+2} are adding new output areas, changing marker symbols, repositioning the control as required, and recopying the final result. These tasks will be performed by quadruples that reference states without superscripts (thus showing that they are specific to T_{m+2}), and we will simply ensure that these quadruples act in such a way as to preserve the general features of uniformity we are trying to maintain. These quadruples complete the set P_{m+2} and the states in them without superscripts complete the set S_{m+2}. The maintenance actions required are:

1 Ensure the control is properly positioned for T_1 to begin.

We define set $A = \{q_0BRq_0,$ Move right to skip leading B's.

$q_011q_0^1,$ Enter start state for T_1 at the tally start.

$q_0x_1Lq_0^1\}$ Enter start state for T_1 at a zero tally.

2 For $1 \leq i \leq m$, after machine T_i has completed its computation T_{m+2} does not halt; instead, it rewrites the marker y as x_i', it adds the tape sequence By to the right of x_i', and it repositions the control for the start of machine T_{i+1}. We define the sets B_i, for $1 \leq i \leq m$, as

$B_i = \{q_{r_i}^i \bar{y}Rq_{r_i}^i,$ Use the "halt" state of T_i to find the y marker.

$q_{r_i}^i yx_i'q_{i,1},$ Change y to x_i' and enter the first of the five states needed for this bookkeeping function. For notational simplification we write $q_{i,j}$ for $q_{5(i-1)+j}$.

$q_{i,1}x_i'Rq_{i,1},$ Move right to add a B.

$q_{i,1}BRq_{i,2},$ Move right to add a second B.

$q_{i,2}Byq_{i,3},$ Change the second B to the marker symbol y.

$q_{i,3}\bar{D}Lq_{i,3},$ Find marker x_1 or x_1'. If $i = m$, D is x_1'; otherwise D is x_1.

$q_{i,3}DLq_{i,4},$ Move past marker into the argument tally. $D \in \{x_1, x_1'\}$

$q_{i,4}BBq_0^{i+1},$ For input of zero, enter start state for T_{i+1}.

$q_{i,4}1Lq_{i,5},$ Argument is non-zero.

$q_{i,5}1Lq_{i,5},$ Move over 1's to find start of tally.

$q_{i,5}KRq_0^{i+1}\}$ Set control to leftmost 1 and enter start state for T_{i+1}. If $i < m$, K is B; but if $i = m$, then K is both B and x_n (i.e., if $i = m$, we have two quadruples rather than one).

3 When T_{m+1} finishes, T_{m+2} erases the b_i tallies and their x_i' markers, copies the c tally and the y marker to the right of x_n, positions the control to x_n, and finally halts.

We define set $C = \{ q_{r_{m+1}}^{m+1} \bar{x}_n \mathbf{L} q_{r_{m+1}}^{m+1}$,

Use the "halt" state to find x_n.

$q_{r_{m+1}}^{m+1} x_n \mathbf{R} q_{\bar{1}}$,

Go into erasing state. For notational simplification, we write q_j^- for

$$q_{m+1,j} = q_{5m+j}$$

$q_{\bar{1}} \bar{x}_m' B q_{\bar{2}}$,

Erase everything to the left of x_m'.

$q_{\bar{2}} B R q_{\bar{1}}$,

Return to erasing state and go right.

$q_{\bar{1}} x_m' B q_{\bar{3}}$,

Erase x_m' and prepare to copy.

$q_{\bar{3}} B R q_{\bar{3}}$,

Look for something to copy.

$q_{\bar{3}} y B q_{\bar{7}}$,

Found the y, the last thing to copy.

$q_{\bar{3}} 1 B q_{\bar{4}}$,

Erase a 1 and move it down.

$q_{\bar{4}} \bar{x}_n \mathbf{L} q_{\bar{4}}$,

Look for x_n.

$q_{\bar{4}} x_n R q_{\bar{5}}$,

Found it. Look now for a B.

$q_{\bar{5}} 1 R q_{\bar{5}}$,

Pass over 1's.

$q_{\bar{5}} B 1 q_{\bar{6}}$,

Write the 1.

$q_{\bar{6}} 1 R q_{\bar{3}}$,

Move right and go back.

$q_{\bar{7}} B \mathbf{L} q_{\bar{7}}$,

Move the y down.

$q_{\bar{7}} 1 R q_{\bar{8}}$,

Prepare to write the y; $c > 0$.

$q_{\bar{7}} x_n R q_{\bar{9}}$,

Prepare to write By; $c = 0$.

$q_{\bar{9}} B R q_{\bar{8}}$,

This writes the B; next is the y.

$q_{\bar{8}} B y q_{\overline{10}}$,

Write the y and prepare to move left.

$q_{\overline{10}} \bar{x}_n \mathbf{L} q_{\overline{10}}$,

Look for x_n.

$q_{\overline{10}} x_n x_n q_{\overline{11}} \}$

Halt, scanning x_n in state with no defined actions.

When we add all these quadruples and the new states to T_{m+2}, we have completed our construction. It should be noted that those general features we were attempting to maintain are, in fact, maintained by this construction. We can verify this by observing that the trace in Table 6-2.3 is produced by T_{m+2} and that state q_{5m+11} is the highest numbered state specific to T_{m+2} and that no quadruple begins with q_{5m+11}.

To sum up, then, we have constructed machine

$$T_{m+2} = \langle A_{m+2}, S_{m+2}, X, P_{m+2} \rangle$$

where $A_{m+2} = \{1, B, x_1, x_2, \ldots, x_n, x'_1, x'_2, \ldots, x'_m, y\}$

$$\overset{i}{S}_{m+2} = \{q_j \mid 0 \leq j \leq 5m + 11\} \cup \overset{m+1}{\underset{i=1}{\cup}} S_i \qquad \text{(where each state has } i \text{ as a superscript)}$$

$$X = 1^{a_1}x_1 1^{a_2}x_2 \cdots 1^{a_n}x_n By$$

$$P_{m+2} = A \cup \overset{m}{\underset{i=1}{\cup}} B_i \cup C \cup \overset{m+1}{\underset{i=1}{\cup}} P_i \qquad \text{(where each state has the appropriate value of } i \text{ as a superscript)}$$

Since T_{m+2} always halts with c in the output area whenever all machines T_1, $T_2, \ldots, T_m, T_{m+1}$ halt and fails to halt whenever at least one of $T_1, \ldots, T_{m+1}$ fails to halt, the function $\psi_{T_{m+2}}^n$ and the function $f\langle a_1, a_2, \ldots, a_n \rangle = c$ are both defined over identical domains and have the same value wherever they are defined. Hence, $f\langle a_1, a_2, \ldots, a_n \rangle = h[g_1\langle a_1, a_2, \ldots, a_n \rangle, g_2\langle a_1, a_2, \ldots, a_n \rangle, \ldots, g_m\langle a_1, a_2, \ldots, a_n \rangle]$ is partially computable.

(**e**) $f\langle a_1, a_2, \ldots, a_n, k \rangle$ is partially computable for $f\langle a_1, \ldots, a_n, k \rangle$ defined via primitive recursion as

$$f\langle a_1, \ldots, a_n, 0 \rangle = g\langle a_1, \ldots, a_n \rangle$$

$$f\langle a_1, \ldots, a_n, c+1 \rangle = h[a_1, \ldots, a_n, c, f\langle a_1, \ldots, a_n, c \rangle]$$

where $g\langle a_1, \ldots, a_n \rangle$ and $h\langle b_1, \ldots, b_n, b_{n+1}, b_{n+2} \rangle$ are total and (partially) computable.

The proof proceeds as in the case for composition. A machine, T_P, is constructed that will do the required computation. The detailed construction of the machine will be omitted [the flavor of the method can be sampled by actually constructing a machine similar to the machine given in (**d**)]. Instead, we shall merely indicate the general outlines of a machine that would do the required manipulation.

The axiom is assumed to be $X = 1^{a_1}x_1 1^{a_2}x_2 \cdots 1^{a_n}x_n 1^k x_{n+1} By$.

(*1*) Compute $g\langle a_1, \ldots, a_n \rangle$ and store the value in the y area. If the tally in the x_{n+1} area is a B, then halt the machine. The correct value is in the y area, the input is unaltered, and the scanner is positioned to the immediate right of x_n.

(*2*) If the x_{n+1} area has a tally greater than 0, then set the x_{n+1} area to $BB \cdots B$ (k times) by erasing all the 1s. It might be necessary first to copy the right portion of the tape leftwards so as to eliminate any leading B's on the tally for k ($k > 0$). Change the marker y to x_{n+2} and attach a new By sequence to the right of x_{n+2}. Reposition the scanner to the left of a_1.

(*3*) Compute $h[a_1, \ldots, a_n, c, f\langle a_1, \ldots, a_n, c \rangle]$ on the arguments in the x_1, $x_2, \ldots, x_n, x_{n+1}, x_{n+2}$ areas and store the value in the y area. Change the rightmost B in the x_{n+1} area to a 1, delete the tally in the x_{n+2} area and the x_{n+2} marker, and copy the tally in the y area (and the y marker) immediately to the right of the x_{n+1} marker, deleting the y marker and its tally as you do it.

(4)   If there are still leading B's in the x_{n+1} area, change the y marker to x_{n+2}, reestablish By to the right of x_{n+2}, position the scanner to the left of a_1, and go to step 3.

If the x_{n+1} area is now all 1s, the process terminates. The correct value of the function is in the y area. Simply position the scanner just to the right of x_n and halt. The input arguments are now in their original form except possibly for the removal of leading B's on the tally for k. The final configuration will be $B1^{a_1}x_1 1^{a_2}x_2 \cdots 1^{a_n}x_n q_t 1^k x_{n+1} 1^c y$, for some final state q_t where

$$c = f\langle a_1, \ldots, a_n, k \rangle = \begin{cases} g\langle a_1, \ldots, a_n \rangle & \text{for } k = 0 \\ h[a_1, \ldots, a_n, k - 1, f\langle a_1, \ldots, a_n, k - 1\rangle] & \text{for } k > 0 \end{cases}$$

Hence, $f\langle a_1, \ldots, a_n, k \rangle = \langle Res(X) \rangle = \psi_{T_P}^{n+1}\langle a_1, \ldots, a_n, k \rangle$; since g and h are total, they are defined everywhere. Hence T_P will always halt, and therefore f is computable.

(f) $f\langle a_1, a_2, \ldots, a_n \rangle$ is partially computable for $f\langle a_1, a_2, \ldots, a_n \rangle$ defined by minimization as

$$f\langle a_1, \ldots, a_n \rangle = \begin{cases} \mu_k[g\langle a_1, \ldots, a_n, k \rangle = 0] & \text{if such a } k \text{ exists} \\ \text{undefined} & \text{otherwise} \end{cases}$$

where $g\langle a_1, \ldots, a_n, k \rangle$ is total and (partially) computable.

Again, we shall omit the details and provide only a general outline of a machine, T_M, which will perform the required operation. The axiom is assumed to be $X = 1^{a_1}x_1 1^{a_2}x_2 \cdots 1^{a_n}x_n By$.

(1)   Change the marker y to x_{n+1}, and reposition the scanner to the left of a_1 after attaching By to the right of x_{n+1}.

(2)   Compute $g\langle a_1, \ldots, a_n, k \rangle$ on the arguments in the $x_1, x_2, \ldots, x_n, x_{n+1}$ areas and store the result in the y area. (Note that this computation can always be done since g is a total function.)

(3)   If the result in the y area is a single B, then the process terminates. Delete the y area and its tally, change the x_{n+1} marker to y, position the scanner to the left of x_n, and halt. If the y area tally is greater than 0, delete the y marker and its tally, change the x_{n+1} marker to a 1, attach the marker x_{n+1} to the right of this new 1, attach By to the right of x_{n+1}, reposition the scanner to the left of a_1, and go to step 2.

If the machine T_M halts, then the correct value is found in the y area, and the final configuration is

$$B1^{a_1}x_1 1^{a_2}x_2 \cdots 1^{a_n} q_t x_n 1^p y$$

for a final state q_t, where $p = \mu_k[g\langle a_1, \ldots, a_n, k \rangle = 0]$. Note, however, that machine T_M may never halt because this least k value may not exist as a zero for $g\langle a_1, \ldots, a_n, k \rangle$. In this case, the $\psi_{T_M}^n$ function remains undefined according to our definition.

Hence, $f\langle a_1, \ldots, a_n \rangle = \langle Res(X) \rangle = \psi_{T_M}^n\langle a_1, \ldots, a_n \rangle$. If T_M always halts, then f is a total function and is computable; otherwise f is only partially computable.

The proof of (1) is now complete. In summary, we have shown that the initial functions, which are partial recursive by definition, are also partially computable. Furthermore, since the set of partial recursive functions is generated by the application of composition, primitive recursion, and minimization, and since these three operations preserve the property of partial computability, it follows that every partial recursive function is partially computable.

To show case (2)—that every partially computable function is partial recursive—is more difficult. We will not give the details of the proof here, but simply refer to sources where such a proof is given. Davis, Kreider and Ritchie, Kleene, and Mendelson all give proofs of this theorem in more or less detail. Kleene's proof might well be the simplest, but it is dissimilar in form to the other three which proceed, roughly, along the following lines.

A Gödel numbering is introduced. It enables us to arithmeticize Turing machines, i.e., to convert them into numeric quantities. Statements about Turing machines then become number-theoretic predicates, which are characterized by number-theoretic functions. Hence, the statements that can be made about the existence of a particular machine, or a certain computation, or the value of a particular computation, etc., are all encoded in the set of partial recursive functions. In particular, by a series of complicated definitions, the predicate $T_n\langle z, x_1, x_2, \ldots, x_n, y \rangle$, meaning "$y$ is the Gödel-number (g-no.) of a computation of a Turing machine with g-no. z on the axiom $1^{x_1}x_11^{x_2}x_2\cdots 1^{x_n}x_nBy$", is shown to be a primitive recursive predicate of $n + 2$ natural numbers. Since $T_n\langle z, x_1, x_2, \ldots, x_n, y \rangle$ is primitive recursive, the function $\mu_y T_n\langle z, x_1, x_2, \ldots, x_n, y \rangle$ is a partial recursive function of $n + 1$ natural numbers, whose value (where defined) is the least g-no. of a computation of the machine with g-no. z on the given axiom. Again, by a series of definitions, the function $\mathbf{R}(y)$ is shown to be recursive, where $\mathbf{R}(y) = \langle Res(X) \rangle$ and y is the g-no. of the computation $X = w_1, w_2, \ldots, w_n = Res(X)$. By composition, then, $\mathbf{R}(\mu_y T_n\langle z, x_1, x_2, \ldots, x_n, y \rangle)$ is a partial recursive function whose value (where defined) is $\langle Res(X) \rangle$ as computed by the machine with g-no. z on the axiom $X = 1^{x_1}x_11^{x_2}x_2\cdots 1^{x_n}x_nBy$ by the computation (if any exist) with the g-no. y. Hence, $f\langle z, x_1, x_2, \ldots, x_n \rangle = \mathbf{R}(\mu_y T_n\langle z, x_1, x_2, \ldots, x_n, y \rangle)$ is an $n + 1$-ary partial recursive function. For a particular, fixed Turing machine, then, with g-no. z_0, $f\langle z_0, x_1, x_2, \ldots, x_n \rangle$ is an n-ary partial recursive function whose value is the same as that produced by the machine, where both values are defined, and which is undefined otherwise. That is, $f\langle z_0, x_1, x_2, \ldots, x_n \rangle = \psi^n_{T_{z_0}}\langle x_1, x_2, \ldots, x_n \rangle$, and hence $\psi^n_{T_{z_0}}$ is partial recursive. Since f has as its domain all $n + 1$ tuples—i.e., all Turing machines and all axioms of finite length—this result holds for all machines and all possible axioms. Hence, every partially computable function is partial recursive.

The essence, then, of the proof of (2) is establishing that $T_n\langle z, x_1, x_2, \ldots, y \rangle$ is a primitive recursive predicate and that $\mathbf{R}(y)$ is a recursive function.

At this point we have indicated the extent of the applicability of Turing machines and thereby have provided a characterization of what is meant by computability. Of course, this entire endeavor is based upon the adequacy of the Turing machine as a model which captures our intuitive notions of computability.

One cannot prove in any formal manner the adequacy because in order to do so, one would have to formalize our intuitive notions. One can only provide evidence which could lead a person to see the plausibility of the Turing machine model as an adequate formalization of our intuitive notions and to accept the model as adequate. The statement that this formalization does, in fact, express our intuitive notions is the essence of what is known as Church's thesis (or, to be fair, the Church-Turing thesis, since Turing quite explicitly set out to formalize our intuitive notions via the machines). A good presentation of the evidence in favor of accepting Church's thesis is found in Kleene.

EXERCISES 6-2

1 Construct a Turing machine, similar to the one in (**d**), that does the primitive recursion operation on (partially) computable functions.
2 Repeat Prob. 1 for the minimization operation.
3 Construct Turing machines that will compute $f\langle x, y \rangle$ where f is (a) multiplication (b) addition, (c) proper subtraction, and (d) $| x - y |$.

BIBLIOGRAPHY

AHO, A. V., and J. D. ULLMAN: "The Theory of Parsing, Translation, and Compiling," vol. 1, Parsing, Prentice-Hall, Inc., Englewood Cliffs, N. J., 1972.

DAVIS, M.: "Computability and Unsolvability," McGraw-Hill Book Company, New York, 1958.

HOPCROFT, J. E., and J. D. ULLMAN: "Formal Languages and Their Relation to Automata," Addison-Wesley Publishing Company, Inc., Reading, Mass., 1969.

KAIN, RICHARD Y.: "Automata Theory: Machines and Languages," McGraw-Hill Book Company, New York, 1972.

KLEENE, STEPHEN COLE: "Introduction to Metamathematics," D. Van Nostrand Company, Inc., Princeton, N. J., 1952.

KREIDER, DONALD L., and ROBERT W. RITCHIE: "Notes on Recursive Function Theory," Lecture notes, Dartmouth University, 1965.

MENDELSON, ELLIOT: "Introduction to Mathematical Logic," D. Van Nostrand Company, Inc., Princeton, N. J., 1964.

NELSON, RAYMOND J.: "Introduction to Automata," John Wiley & Sons, Inc., New York, 1968.

The notation for algorithms used is best described with the aid of examples. Consider the algorithm for determining the largest element of a vector:

Algorithm *GREATEST* Given a vector A consisting of n elements, find the largest element and store it in MAX.

    1   [Is the vector empty?] If $n < 1$, then print message and Exit.

    2   [Initialize] Set $MAX \leftarrow A[1]$, $i \leftarrow 2$. (We assume initially that $A[1]$ is the greatest element.)

    3   [All done?] If $i > n$, then Exit.

    4   [Exchange MAX if it is smaller than next element] If $MAX < A[i]$, then set $MAX \leftarrow A[i]$.

    5   [Get next subscript] Set $i \leftarrow i + 1$ and go to step 3.   ////

The algorithm is given an identifying name (*GREATEST*, in this example); this name is followed by a brief description of the tasks the algorithm performs, thus providing an identification for the variables used in the algorithm. This description is followed by the actual algorithm—a sequence of numbered steps.

Every algorithm step begins with a phrase enclosed in brackets which gives an abbreviated description of that step. Following this phrase is an ordered sequence of statements which describe actions to be executed or tests to be performed. Note that, in general, the statements in each step must be executed from left to right, in order. An algorithm step may terminate with a comment enclosed in parentheses which is intended to help the reader better understand the step. The comments specify no action and are included only for clarity.

Step 2 in the example algorithm contains the arrow symbol $\leftarrow$ which is used to denote the assignment operator. The statement $MAX \leftarrow A[1]$ is taken to mean that the value of $A[1]$ is to replace the contents of the variable MAX. In this algorithmic notation, the symbol $=$ is used as a relational operator (the ".EQ." of FORTRAN), never as an assignment operator. One assignment statement, or a group of several assignment statements separated by commas, is preceded by the word "set." The action of incrementing i by 1 in step 5 is indicated by $i \leftarrow i + 1$. Many variables can be set to the same value by using multiple assignments. The statements $i \leftarrow 0$, $j \leftarrow 0$, and $k \leftarrow 0$ could be rewritten as the single statement $i \leftarrow j \leftarrow k \leftarrow 0$. An exchange of the values of two variables (as accomplished by the sequence of statements $TEMP \leftarrow A1$, $A1 \leftarrow B$, $B \leftarrow TEMP$) will sometimes, for convenience, be written as $A1 \leftrightarrow B$. Observe that subscripts for arrays are enclosed in brackets. Thus, $A[4]$ is the fourth element of array A.

The execution of an algorithm begins at step 1 and continues from there in sequential order unless the result of a condition tested or an unconditional transfer (a "GO TO") specifies otherwise. In the sample algorithm, first step 1 is executed. If vector A is empty, the algorithm terminates; otherwise step 2 is performed, in which MAX is initialized to the value of $A[1]$ and the subscript variable i is set to 2. In step 3 the algorithm terminates if we have already tested the last element of A. Otherwise, step 4 is taken. In this step, the value of MAX is compared with the value of the next element of the vector. If MAX is less than the next element, then MAX is set to this new value. If the test fails, no reassignment takes place. The completion of step 4 is followed by step 5 where the next subscript value is set; control then returns to the testing step, step 3.

Throughout the text, an element of a vector may be denoted either by A_i or by $A[i]$; in an algorithm, such an array reference would appear as $A[i]$, while in actual FORTRAN or PL/I programs, such a reference would appear as A(I). Variables, in algorithms, are usually written in capital letters (for example, MAX and A), but single-letter variables used as loop counters, subscripts, or string position indices, etc., will often appear in lowercase letters.

Two of the more complicated instructions available for use as statements in algorithm steps are the IF statement and the REPEAT statement. These are now described in more detail.

The IF statement has one of the following forms:

1   If _____, then _____, _____, $\cdots$, _____.
2   If ____, then _____, _____, $\cdots$, _____; otherwise _____, _____,
$\cdots$, _____.

Following the "THEN" is an ordered sequence of statements which are all to be executed if the condition tested is true. Unless a "GO TO" must be followed, control then passes to the first statement after the IF statement. A semicolon (type 2) or the period (type 1) terminates the range of the THEN clause. If the tested condition is false, then either the next statement (type 1) is executed or the ordered sequence of statements following the OTHERWISE (type 2) is executed. In this latter case, when the OTHERWISE clause has been completed, control goes to the next statement (unless there was a GO TO in the OTHERWISE clause). IF statements can be nested within other IF statements, though to improve the reader's understanding of algorithms, we try to avoid the excessive nesting of IFs and the nesting of IFs within THEN clauses.

To provide for easy control of iteration, a REPEAT statement has been provided.

This statement has one of the following forms:

1 Repeat for index = sequence: _____, _____, ..., _____.
2 Repeat steps n and $n + 1$ for index = sequence.
3 Repeat steps n to p for index = sequence.

Type 1 is used to repeat the sequence of statements immediately following the colon in the same algorithm step. This sequence is terminated by a period. Type 2 is simply a special case of type 3. Type 3 is used to repeat, in order, all the steps in the indicated range of steps. 'Index' is simply some variable of the algorithm used as a loop counter, while 'sequence' is some representation of the sequence of values that 'index' will successively take. The starting value, the final value, and the increment size must be indicated in some way by the representation chosen. For example, 'Repeat for $i = 1, 2, ..., 25$: _____.', 'Repeat for $TOP = n + k, n + k - 1, ..., 0$: _____.', and 'Repeat steps 5 and 6 for $k = 9, 11, ..., 2 * MAX + 1$.' are various examples of valid REPEAT statements. As soon as all the statements in the range of a REPEAT statement have been executed, the index assumes the next value in the sequence of values, and the statements in the range are executed in order once again. We assume testing of an index for completion takes place prior to execution of any statement, so that a REPEAT statement may, in fact, cause a loop to be executed 0 times. For example, 'Repeat for $i = -1, -2, ..., 10$' and 'Repeat for $k = 5, 6, ..., -17$' would not cause any statements to be executed; instead, the REPEAT statements would be treated as having completed their execution. As soon as a REPEAT statement has finished its execution, control is transferred to the first statement outside the range of the REPEAT statement. If, however, a GO TO is encountered during the execution of a REPEAT statement and control is transferred out of its range, then the REPEAT statement is considered to have finished its execution, and the sequence of steps for execution of the algorithm continues normally from the point the GO TO transferred to.

Note however the following segment:

.
.
.

6 [Initialize counter] Set $COUNT \leftarrow 0$.
7 [Processing loop] Repeat steps 8 and 9 for $i = 1, 2, ..., n$.
8 [Get number] Read $A[i]$.
9 [Count if negative] If $A[i] < 0$, then $COUNT \leftarrow COUNT + 1$.
10 [Output results] Print $COUNT$.

.
.
.

If n has the value 5 and the first numbers in the data stream are 7, 4, -3, -2, 6, -17' 8, ..., then the number 2 will be printed in step 10 because steps 8 and 9 will execute 5 times. The IF statement in step 9 does *not* cause control to go to step 10 when it has finished execution. Instead, control is returned to the REPEAT statement where the index is incremented, and steps 8 and 9 are executed once again. (You may think of these steps 8 and 9 as including a CONTINUE-like statement immediately after the IF statement.)

Since many of the applications that will concern us in the areas of logic, set theory, algebraic structures, etc., involve nonnumeric processing (i.e., symbol manipulation rather than "number crunching"), it was felt advisable to incorporate into the algorithmic notation certain features that facilitate the processing of strings of symbols. These features are provided as an addition to those standard mathematical functions and operations which one would expect to find useful in most applications. The programs appearing throughout are all written either in FORTRAN or in PL/I. Since FORTRAN's string processing capabilities are minimal, these additional features are patterned after certain PL/I string processing functions. The features we add are the functions $LENGTH$, $INDEX$, and SUB (patterned after PL/I's LENGTH, INDEX, and SUBSTR functions respectively).

The definitions of the functions for their arguments follow:

1 $LENGTH(ITEM)$ returns as a value the number of symbols in $ITEM$, the argument string. The value 0 is returned if $ITEM$ is the null string. For example, $LENGTH('TOP')$ is 3, $LENGTH(STRING)$ where $STRING$ is 'ABAB' is 4. $LENGTH(' ')$ is 0.

2 $INDEX(SOURCE, SUBJECT)$ returns as a value the position index of the leftmost occurrence of the string $SUBJECT$ in the string $SOURCE$. If $SUBJECT$ does not occur in $SOURCE$, the value 0 is returned. For example, for $SOURCE = $ 'BACABABA', $INDEX(SOURCE, 'ABA')$ is 4, $INDEX(SOURCE, 'A')$ is 2, and $INDEX('ABC', SOURCE)$ is 0.

3 $SUB(STRING, i, j)$ or $SUB(STRING, i)$ returns as a value the substring of $STRING$ that is specified by the parameters i and j, or i and an assumed value for j. The parameter i indicates the starting position of the substring, while j specifies the length of the required substring. If j is not provided, j is assumed to be equal to $k - i + 1$, where k is equal to $LENGTH(STRING)$ (that is, j is set to a length value equal to that of the substring starting at position i and including the last symbol in the string). A full definition of this function, which handles cases where the specified substring does not exist (because it is not included within $STRING$), can be formulated as follows. For a string, $STRING$, of length k, $k \geq 1$, $SUB(STRING, i, j)$ or $SUB(STRING, i)$ has the value:

the null string	if $j \leq 0$ (regardless of i), or
	if $i \leq 0$ (regardless of j) or
	if $i > k$ (regardless of j)

the substring of length $k - i + 1$ starting at position i of $STRING$ (i.e., the balance of $STRING$),   if $0 < i \leq k$ and j is not specified or
        if $0 < i \leq k$ and $i + j > k + 1$

the substring of length j starting at position i of $STRING$ (i.e., the specified substring),   if $0 < i \leq k$ and $i + j \leq k + 1$

For example, letting $STRING$ be 'ABCDE', $SUB(STRING, 0, 3)$ and $SUB(STRING, 6)$ both return ' '. $SUB(STRING, 2)$ and $SUB(STRING, 2, 7)$ both return 'BCDE', while $SUB(STRING, 3, 2)$ returns 'CD'.

The following algorithm is intended to illustrate the use of these functions as well as the REPEAT statement.

Algorithm $PUNCTUATION$ Given $TEXT$, a string of text, this algorithm counts and records the number of occurrences of each punctuation symbol (in the array $COUNT$) and the total number of such occurrences ($TOTAL$). The string $PUNCT$ is formed out of the acceptable punctuation symbols. $TEMP$ is simply the current symbol of $TEXT$ being examined.

1 [Initialize symbols and total] Set $PUNCT \leftarrow ',.;:?!'$, $TOTAL \leftarrow 0$.

2 [Initialize counts] Repeat for $i = 1, 2, \ldots, LENGTH(PUNCT)$: Set $COUNT[i] \leftarrow 0$.

3 [Read the text] Read $TEXT$.

4 [Processing loop] Repeat steps 5 and 6 for $i = 1, 2, \ldots, LENGTH(TEXT)$.

5 [Get new symbol of text] Set $TEMP \leftarrow SUB(TEXT, i, 1)$.

6 [If symbol is punctuation, count it] Set $j \leftarrow INDEX(PUNCT, TEMP)$. If $j \neq 0$, then set $COUNT[j] \leftarrow COUNT[j] + 1$, $TOTAL \leftarrow TOTAL + 1$.

7 [Print results] Print $COUNT$ and $TOTAL$. Exit.

Step 2 uses the length of $PUNCT$ (that is, 6) to set an upper limit to the loop which zeroes the elements of $COUNT$. Step 4 uses the number of symbols in $TEXT$ (i.e., its length) to determine how many times steps 5 and 6 are to execute. Step 5 takes one symbol from $TEXT$ and holds it in $TEMP$. Successive symbols are taken on successive passes through the loop defined in step 4 because i is incremented by 1 each time. Step 6 determines if $TEMP$ is one of the punctuation symbols. The $INDEX$ function returns a non-zero value iff $TEMP$ is one of the symbols we are interested in counting. Once the loop consisting of steps 5 and 6 has executed $LENGTH(TEXT)$ times, the REPEAT statement in step 4 is finished, and step 7 is executed. This then terminates the algorithm. ////

It should be noted that we assume one algorithm can invoke another. Algorithm $PUNCTUATION$ could have included the statement (in step 7) 'Call $GREATEST$ $(COUNT, 6, TOTAL)$'. This would have provided a total for the most frequently occurring punctuation symbol. If step 3 in algorithm $GREATEST$ had been 'If $i > n$, then set $GREATEST \leftarrow MAX$ and Exit.', then a function-type invocation could have been used; e.g., 'Set $TOTAL \leftarrow GREATEST(COUNT, 6)$' would specify the same value for $TOTAL$—that of the most commonly used punctuation symbol.

INDEX